£1
14/1

CU00953347

Indonesia's
Eastern Islands

Peter Turner

991809034 0

WITHDRAWN

Indonesia's Eastern Islands

1st edition

Published by
Lonely Planet Publications
Head Office: PO Box 617, Hawthorn, Vic 3122, Australia
Branches: 150 Linden Street, Oakland, CA 94607, USA
               10a Spring Place, London NW5 3BH, UK
               71 bis rue du Cardinal Lemoine, 75005 Paris, France

Printed by
Colorcraft Ltd, Hong Kong

Photographs by
Sara-Jane Cleland
Richard I'Anson
Mark Strickland/Oceanic Impressions
Martin Tullemans
Peter Turner

Front cover: Buy my ikat! Umabara, Sumba (Peter Turner)

First Published
October 1998

Although the authors and publisher have tried to make the information as
accurate as possible, they accept no responsibility for any loss, injury or
inconvenience sustained by any person using this book.

**Gloucestershire
County Library**

991809034 O

| Askews | 14·12-98 |
| 915.986 | £11.99 |

National Library of Australia Cataloguing in Publication Data

Turner, Peter.
    Indonesia's eastern islands.

    Includes index.
    ISBN 0 86442 503 1.

    1. Indonesia – Guidebooks.

915.98

text & maps © Lonely Planet 1998
photos © photographers as indicated 1998
Mataram climate chart compiled from information supplied by Patrick J Tyson, © Patrick J Tyson, 1998

All rights reserved. No part of this publication may be reproduced, stored in a retrieval system or transmitted
in any form by any means, electronic, mechanical, photocopying, recording or otherwise, except brief extracts
for the purpose of review, without the written permission of the publisher and copyright owner.

Peter Turner

Peter Turner lives in Melbourne and has a long held interest in Indonesia and South-East Asia. Since his first extended trip through Indonesia in 1978, he has returned eight times, travelling throughout the archipelago. He joined Lonely Planet in 1986 as an editor, and worked as a fieldwriter on *Malaysia, Singapore & Brunei* and *Singapore city guide*. Now a full-time travel writer, he has also contributed to *South-East Asia on a shoestring* and *Indonesia,* and is the author of *Jakarta city guide* and *Java*.

From the Author

This book only became a reality with the help of many people who offered their time, knowledge and assistance. In Australia, thanks to Peter Pangaribuan and Gabrielle Davies of the ITPO, and thanks to the many regional tourist offices throughout Nusa Tenggara. In Lombok, particular thanks go to Pak Adianto, Hartati and Abdul Haris, and especially Agus Wirawan. Thanks to Hadji Radiah of Lendang Nangka for his help in preparing the Lombok language section. In Dompu, Suryadi H Ahmad and the gang were a great help.

On Flores, Paul Boleng shared his wealth of experience, as did Frans Mola, one of the most enlightened people working in tourism in Indonesia. Thanks also to Muhammad Fatta in Ende, Bode da Gama in Maumere and Marcel Litong in Larantuka.

On Sumba, thanks to Pak Sylvester of the East Sumba tourist office. To Charma, Teo and Stefanus – thanks for the fun as well as knowledgeable experiences.

On Timor, special thanks to Pae Nope of Soe, a prince among guides. Thanks also to the Hash and everyone in Kupang, and Paulo in East Timor.

From the Publisher

This 1st edition of *Indonesia's Eastern Islands* was produced in LP's Melbourne office. It was edited by Emma Miller and designed by Glenn Beanland. Anna Judd produced the maps, and Pete Cruttenden proofed the book and took it through layout. Paul Harding

Warning & Request

Things change – prices go up, schedules change, good places go bad and bad places go bankrupt – nothing stays the same. So, if you find things better or worse, recently opened or long since closed, please tell us and help make the next edition even more accurate and useful.

We value all of the feedback we receive from travellers. Julie Young coordinates a small team who read and acknowledge every letter, postcard and email, and ensure that every morsel of information finds its way to the appropriate authors, editors and publishers.

Everyone who writes to us will find their name in the next edition of the appropriate guide and will also receive a free subscription to our quarterly newsletter, *Planet Talk*. The very best contributions will be rewarded with a free Lonely Planet guide.

Excerpts from your correspondence may appear in new editions of this guide; in our newsletter, *Planet Talk*; or in updates on our Web site – so please let us know if you don't want your letter published or your name acknowledged. ■

chipped in with the proofing, Anna Judd and Jenny Bowman drew the illustrations, Quentin Frayne looked after the language sections and Simon Bracken designed the front cover.

Contents

Map Legend

BOUNDARIES

▄▬▄▬▄▬▄▬▄	.... International Boundary
─·─·─·─·─·─·	.... Provincial Boundary
─ ─ ─ ─ ─ ─	.... Disputed Boundary

ROUTES

═════ A25 ═══	..... Freeway, with Route Number
────────────	.... Major Road
────────────	.... Minor Road
─ ─ ─ ─ ─ ─ ─	.... Minor Road - Unsealed
════════════	.... City Road
════════════	.... City Street
════════════	.... City Lane
├─┼─┼─┼─●─┼─┤	............Train Route, with Station
══════●══════	.... Metro Route, with Station
╫─╫─╫─╫─╫─╫─╫─╫	.... Cable Car or Chairlift
─ ─ ─ ─ ─ ─ ─	.... Ferry Route
─ ─ ─ ─ ─ ─ ─	.... Walking Track

AREA FEATURES

	.... Building
	.... Cemetery
	.... Desert
	.... Market
	.... Park, Gardens
	.... Pedestrian Mall
	.... Reef
	.... Urban Area

HYDROGRAPHIC FEATURES

	.... Canal
	.... Coastline
	.... Creek, River
	.... Lake, Intermittent Lake
	.... Rapids, Waterfalls
	.... Salt Lake
	.... Swamp

SYMBOLS

✪	**CAPITAL**	.... National Capital	✈	.... Airport	✆	.... National Park
◉	**CAPITAL**	.... Provincial Capital		...Ancient or City Wall	←	.........One Way Street
●	**CITY**	.... City	∴	.... Archaeological Site	℗	.... Parking
●	Town	.... Town	❸	.... Bank	)(	.... Pass
●	Village	.... Village	➶	.... Beach	⛽	.... Petrol Station
			🏰	.... Castle or Fort	○	.... Point of Interest
■	.... Place to Stay		🛏 🕇	...Cathedral or Church	★	.... Police Station
⚁	.... Camping Ground		⌒	.... Cave	✉	.... Post Office
⌗	.... Caravan Park		⌒⌒⌒	.... Cliff or Escarpment	❖	.... Shopping Centre
⌂	.... Hut or Chalet		◣	.... Dive Site	◎	.... Spring
			◔	.... Embassy	⚲	.... Surf Beach
▼	.... Place to Eat		⊕	.... Hospital	▭	.... Swimming Pool
☗	.... Pub or Bar		🕎	.... Lighthouse	☎	.... Telephone
			❊	.... Lookout	▮	.... Temple
			⚱	.... Monument	❶	..... Tourist Information
			◪	.... Mosque	⊖	.... Transport
			▲	.... Mountain or Hill	🐗	.... Zoo

Note: not all symbols displayed above appear in this book

Introduction

Indonesia's eastern islands, stretching from Lombok to Timor, are collectively known as Nusa Tenggara (the name means 'South-East Islands'). The region is quite different from the rest of Indonesia – as you travel east, the climate becomes drier, so people raise corn and sago rather than rice; the flora and fauna are more evocative of parts of Australia than of tropical Bali; the people are poorer than those elsewhere in Indonesia; and there is an astonishing variety of cultures and religions.

Each island has its own peculiar sights, some of which rival anything seen in the rest of Indonesia. The great stone-slab tombs and traditional villages of Sumba, the intricate *ikat* weaving of Sumba and Flores, the brilliantly coloured lakes of Kelimutu in Flores and the huge monitor lizard 'dragons' of Komodo must rate as some of the finest attractions in South-East Asia. Throw in some superb beaches, coral atolls and the well equipped resorts of Lombok, and Nusa Tenggara is a tourist dream just waiting to happen.

Although Lombok is well trafficked, only a small number of travellers venture further east. Travel can be hard, but it is rewarded by the richness of seeing fascinating cultures, the true gem of this region. Transport connections have improved immeasurably over the years and there are now many more opportunities for explorations off-the-beaten-track. The lack of foreign travellers in these parts also means that your reception will be more natural than it usually is in Indonesia's tourist meccas.

Nusa Tenggara is divided into three provinces: West Nusa Tenggara (comprising Lombok and Sumbawa), with its capital at Mataram on Lombok; East Nusa Tenggara (comprising Flores, Sumba, Timor and a number of small islands), with the capital at Kupang in Timor; and East Timor, with its capital at Dili.

Only about 4% of the Indonesian population lives in Nusa Tenggara, but there are so many different languages and cultures that it's impossible to think of these people as one

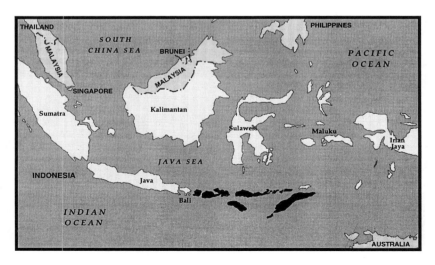

group. There are several languages on the tiny island of Alor alone, though you will get by with Bahasa Indonesia almost anywhere in Nusa Tenggara. Many of the region's people are now at least nominally Christian; Christians predominate on Flores, Roti and Timor. Muslims form a majority on Lombok and Sumbawa, while in isolated areas such as the western half of Sumba, a large section of the population still adheres to traditional animist beliefs. A layer of animism persists alongside Christianity in other areas, with customs, rituals and festivals from this older tradition still very much a part of life.

Everyone will want to lie on the beaches of Lombok, see Komodo dragons and the coloured lakes of Kelimutu, but beyond these popular activities the eastern islands of Indonesia offer the stuff of adventure. Explore and enjoy.

Facts About the Region

HISTORY
Pre-History

Until Dutch missionary and amateur archaeologist, Theodor Verhoeven, amassed evidence in the 1960s of Neolithic settlers on Flores, it was thought that humans migrated to Nusa Tenggara 60,000 years ago at the very earliest. Verhoeven's discoveries were dismissed by academia, but recent research supports his findings that these cave dwellers date back 800,000 years to *Homo erectus*, the early hominid predating modern humans. Possible *Homo erectus* artefacts have also been found on Lombok and Timor.

Java Man, the 'missing link' of popular science, inhabited Java at least one million years ago. Early humans migrated to Java via land bridges from the Asian landmass, but Lombok lies east of the Wallace Line (see the Flora & Fauna section later in this chapter) across deep straits from Bali and it is doubtful that the islands from Lombok to Timor were ever linked to Asia. This means that *Homo erectus* migrated by sea and was much more ad-vanced than previously thought.

What happened to the original *Homo erectus* settlers is a mystery, for today's inhabitants are descended from much later migrations. Definite evidence of modern human settlement on Timor dates back 13,000 years, though most migrations came later when the seafaring Austronesian peoples of Asia migrated throughout the eastern islands. These hunter-gatherers were joined by later migrants from Asia, introducing agriculture around 2000 BC.

Bronze drums, such as the *moko* from the island of Alor, are possible evidence of contact with the Dongson culture of China and Vietnam around this time. The origin of these drums is a mystery, but it does show that the region was not totally isolated from the great Asian civilisations. The Hindu-Buddhist cultures that arose in Java and Sumatra never penetrated Nusa Tenggara, but the region did lie close to this sphere of influence. By the 4th century AD, merchants from India were trading in the Indonesian archipelago and as trade increased, undoubtedly some contact was made with the eastern islands.

Migration also continued and some ethnic groups, such as the Tetum of Timor, arrived as late as the 14th century. These migratory waves came through the islands to the west, but the existence of Papuan languages in East Timor shows that some migration also came from the Melanesian people to the east.

Early Trade

Trade throughout the Indonesian archipelago increased dramatically from around the 7th century AD and, by the 14th century, Indonesia was well established on the European trade routes to India and China. Indian, Arab and Chinese merchants traded a variety of goods, much of it through the main port of the region, Melaka on the Malay Peninsula. The most sought after were spices such as cloves and nutmeg from the islands of the Moluccas (present-day Maluku), to the north of Timor.

The 14th century Javanese chronicle, the *Nagarakertagama*, places the islands from Lombok to Timor under the realm of the great Majapahit Empire of Java. It is unlikely that Majapahit exerted any influence or control, but Javanese exploratory voyages put the region on the map.

Traders sailed past Flores and Timor on their way to the spice islands, but the only reason to detour was for the sandalwood trade on Timor. Chinese chronicles identified Timor as an important source of this prized, perfumed wood from at least the 13th century, possibly much earlier. Apart from the sandalwood trade, contact with the outside world was limited, though Makassarese and Bugis seafarers from southern Sulawesi visited the north coasts of Flores, Sumbawa and Lombok.

The Portuguese Arrive

European technological advances in seafaring and warfare from the 15th century ushered in a new era of maritime exploration. Urged on by Prince Henry the Navigator, the Portuguese were the first Europeans to venture east in search of the riches of the spice trade. After conquering Goa in 1510, they took Melaka in 1511 and then set about controlling the spice islands.

As early as 1512, Flores was sighted by the Portuguese navigator Antonio de Abreu, and a decade later Portuguese ships were calling at Timor in search of sandalwood. The Portuguese were more concerned with their interests in the spice islands so colonisation was left to a handful of Dominican friars who in 1556 established the first Portuguese settlement at Lifau in Timor. Thousands were converted on Timor and then on Flores. Missionaries arrived on the island of Solor in eastern Flores in 1561 and after attacks by Muslims built a fort in 1566. They also went on to build a fort on the south coast at Ende, but this was already a Muslim port of some note and the settlement was regularly attacked and had to be abandoned.

Both Lifau and Solor were forgotten outposts with only a negligible Portuguese population. The Portuguese presence was largely accounted for by the Topasses – *mestizo* (mixed blood) descendants of intermarriages between the Portuguese, slaves from Melaka and India, and the local population. Known by the Dutch as the 'Black Portuguese', the Portuguese-speaking, Christian Topasses carried the flag for Portugal, but went on to become a law unto themselves forming their own kingdoms among the many chiefdoms in eastern Flores and Timor.

Dutch Era

The first Dutch expedition to the Indonesian archipelago left Holland in 1595 and when it returned with a boatload of spices that made its investors rich, more ships followed. The Dutch government, recognising the potential of the East Indies trade, amalgamated the competing merchant companies into the United East India Company or the Veerigde Oost-Indische Compagnie (VOC). This government monopoly soon challenged the Portuguese and took Maluku in 1605.

In 1613, a Dutch expedition under Apollonius Scotte attacked Solor, forcing the Topasses to flee to Larantuka on Flores, and then sailed to Kupang (Timor). Scotte forged an alliance with a local chief to build a Dutch fort before he sailed on, but the Dutch then promptly forgot about Timor. Apart from sporadic attempts to rid Flores of the Topasses, the VOC had little interest in Nusa Tenggara due to its few economic temptations.

The Portuguese presence on Timor was confined to the coastal colony in Lifau, but in 1642 the Topasses marched into the interior of Timor to defeat the local kingdoms. The Topasses went on to settle Timor and headed their own powerful kingdoms.

It was after this that the Dutch decided it needed a presence on Timor and returned to Kupang in 1653 to build Fort Concordia. Dutch forces tried to expand their control beyond the Kupang Bay area, but military expeditions into the interior were soundly defeated. For the next 200 years Kupang remained an isolated colonial outpost while the Dutch concentrated on more important areas such as Java.

Meanwhile, further west, the Dutch had to contend with the growing power of the Islamic Makassarese state of Gowa in southern Sulawesi. The VOC's aim was to establish a trade monopoly, but Gowa continued to trade and exert control over the sea lanes. Gowa had already invaded Sumbawa in 1619, converting the rulers to Islam and reducing them to vassals. Sumbawa comprised two main sultanates – Sumbawa in the west and Bima in the east. The western sultanate invaded the Sasak kingdom in east Lombok, while Bima expanded its territory and laid claim to Sumba, a source of slaves.

The VOC finally overcame the Makassarese in 1669, with the of help the competing Bugis kingdom in Sulawesi. The fragmentation of power saw southern Sulawesi wracked by war and many people fled south to settle on Sumbawa and Flores, the first of many migrations from Sulawesi. The VOC signed a treaty and built a fort in Bima, but the Bimanese were given a free hand and took over where the Makassarese left off, eventually claiming western Flores.

The western Sumbawans fared less well and their hold over eastern Lombok was weakened in the 1677-78 wars with the Sasaks. Then in 1750 the Balinese invaded Lombok and for 30 years the Sumbawans intermittently battled with the Balinese, who eventually captured western Sumbawa before the VOC intervened to counter the growing Balinese power.

The Dutch were not so much colonial masters as power brokers. They skilfully applied policies of divide and rule, forging alliances and using their superior military might only when needed to halt the rise of kingdoms that might pose a serious threat. In Nusa Tenggara, their presence was limited to a few trading posts and they had neither the manpower nor the desire to rule directly. Their aim was to make profits for the company and to monopolise trade, and in this they were successful.

The Portuguese never recovered to seriously threaten Dutch power. In 1701, the Portuguese Viceroy of Goa officially made Lifau a colony and appointed a governor, but he was driven out by the Topasses. The Portuguese maintained their interest in Timor, but abandoned Lifau and moved the colony east to Dili. Just as the Dutch had little control outside Kupang, so too the Portuguese rarely ventured into the interior from Dili.

As the spice trade declined and the VOC became increasingly enmeshed in expensive wars in Java, so profits flagged and in 1799 the VOC was declared bankrupt. The Dutch government stepped in to directly administer the East Indies, but while direct rule was established in Java, little changed in Nusa Tenggara. Local rulers and their conflicts, and traditional ways of life (including animist religions) were left largely to run their own course.

The government stopped Dutch involvement in the slave trade in Sumba, which the VOC had once sought to monopolise. However, traders from Ende (Flores) continued to plunder Sumba, dragging off whole villages,

and in 1838 the Dutch attacked Ende in an effort to stop slavery.

In 1851 the Dutch finally gained control of the nominally Portuguese region around Larantuka in Eastern Flores, forcing Portugal to relinquish all claims on Flores and negotiate a settlement on Timor. Timor was divided in half, with Portugal claiming the east and the north coast pocket of Oecussi (Lifau), while Holland got the rest of the west.

Dutch and Portuguese influence expanded in the interior, with the establishment of coffee plantations in Portuguese Timor and a more systematic exploitation of sandalwood in Dutch Timor, but Timor and the rest of the islands were still a long way from being under colonial control. The system of treaties with favoured *rajas* (kings) continued and though the Dutch appointed advisers in some areas, traditional rulers held sway.

20th Century
All was to change with the dawn of a new century and the introduction of the Dutch government's so-called Ethical Policy. The East Indies government would truly govern for the first time and provide social infrastructure such as roads, schools and hospitals. In return, the administration was to collect taxes to pay for it all. This applied mostly to Java, the only real Dutch colony, but in 1905 the order went out to the far flung territories for the Dutch administration to take control and bring the local rulers to heel.

Various small kingdoms were amalgamated under Dutch-preferred rajas who would collect taxes. A series of rebellions followed. They were easily crushed, but it took a decade or more before Dutch rule was effectively established. In Timor, the Niki Niki royal family self-immolated rather submit to Dutch rule, a mirror of the famous mass suicide in Bali at the same time.

The Dutch built roads, established plantations and founded provincial capitals to administer their territories, but even though many areas were opened to the outside world for the first time, most people had little direct contact with the Dutch. In Sumba, the interior was not controlled and considered safe for travel until 1933.

Rajas maintained their traditional authority and the new provincial boundaries reflected existing political and ethnic divisions. The greatest change was brought by missionaries. Lombok and Sumbawa had long been Muslim, so Christian missionaries concentrated on the islands further east. Dutch Catholic missionaries began wholesale conversion on Flores, as did Portuguese Catholics in East Timor. Sumba and West Timor became the domain of Protestant missionaries. Whole populations were converted in one generation, but animist traditions remain strong in many areas.

Effective Dutch rule in the eastern islands was to last little more than 30 years. In 1942, the Japanese stormed through Indonesia, meeting little resistance. Initially welcomed as liberators, they soon developed a reputation as cruel masters; as the war progressed, labour was conscripted and crops confiscated for the war effort. Many people in Nusa Tenggara died of starvation.

When the Japanese surrendered, the provisional Indonesian government in Jakarta, under the leadership of Soekarno, declared Indonesia's independence from the Netherlands on 17 August 1945. The Dutch refused to accept the proclamation and returned to claim their colony. An independence war broke out, but the fighting was mostly confined to Java and southern Sulawesi.

For four years the Dutch stubbornly refused to quit and Nusa Tenggara became incorporated into the State of East Indonesia (Negara Indonesia Timor or NIT) – part of the Dutch plan to divide Indonesia under a federal government and isolate the east from the nationalist movement in Java. NIT was jokingly referred to as Negara Ikut Tuan, the state that follows the master.

World pressure finally forced the Dutch to quit Indonesia in 1949 and the eastern islands became part of the independent Republic of Indonesia. The news was generally greeted with celebration in Nusa Tenggara, though on the Christian islands some viewed integration under Muslim Java with suspicion.

Independence

The road to independence was not a smooth one and uncertainty accompanied the early years. Unstable government and secessionist movements plagued the new republic and in 1957 Soekarno declared martial law with army backing, issuing in his new era of 'Guided Democracy'.

The other main political force, the Indonesian Communist Party, also grew in power, much to the chagrin of the army and the Muslim parties. Soekarno held the country together through force of rhetoric, but his charisma was not enough to stop the country disintegrating. In 1965 an attempted communist coup was followed by an army counter-coup under the leadership of Colonel Soeharto from Java. Civil war in the countryside turned to a bloodbath, with as many as 300,000 people slaughtered while the army looked on. Communists, or simply anyone of suspect political or religious affiliation, were butchered.

Most of the turmoil occurred on Java and Bali. Nusa Tenggara remained a remote and lonely outpost, administered by a handful of officials and soldiers, who considered themselves virtual exiles. The difficulty of the mountainous terrain, poor communications and, in particular, the islands' location on the path to nowhere, all helped to maintain this isolation.

The regional divisions created by the Dutch remained with slight variations, but in the late 50s the Indonesian government abolished the power of local rulers. Governors were appointed, often selected from the local royal families who still retained widespread respect.

After the massacres of 1965, Indonesia moved on under Soeharto, who was officially appointed president in 1967. Stability ensued and Indonesia allied itself to the west and the world economy. By the 70s, effective control and peace returned to the former Dutch areas, but the small enclave of Portuguese Timor remained a colony.

Then in 1975, the Portuguese government rapidly divested itself of its colonies and Timorese political parties formed. Left-wing

Fretilin became the major party in newly independent East Timor, but the opposition UDT staged a coup in Dili which led to a brief civil war. Indonesia, fearing a communist state on its doorstep, invaded while the USA and Australia turned a blind, if not complicit, eye. A bloody war ensued and it took nearly a decade before the Indonesian army pacified East Timor. Hundreds of thousands of East Timorese died through warfare or famine and the province remains a political flashpoint.

In the 80s, the rest of Indonesia began to see the benefits of stability and economic reform. Foreign investment flowed into the country, mostly to Java where industry flourished. Nusa Tenggara remained an outpost with little economic interest, but from 1988 the region was targeted by the central government for development programs to provide basic social amenities. New roads were pushed into the interior and it is only in the past decade that many communities have had a modicum of access to the modern world. Accordingly, Nusa Tenggara is still one of the most traditional parts of Indonesia, and still the poorest. The only island with a hint of wealth is Lombok, thanks to tourism.

The 90s witnessed a huge influx of foreign investment into Indonesia and the rise of a wealthy business class in Java. The bubble burst in August 1997 when the Asian currency crisis spilled over into Indonesia. The value of the rupiah crumbled and the country again found itself in social turmoil in the face of growing foreign debt and rising prices on the streets. Sporadic rioting, mostly in Java, followed and opposition groups called for Soeharto to resign. Ever the consummate power broker, President Soeharto brushed off dissent and was again re-elected for a five year term in March 1998.

The Fall of Soeharto

Although Soeharto's re-election seemed to at least promise stability, students continued to demonstrate, demanding his resignation and an end to the corruption and nepotism that characterised his administration. The demonstrations were largely peaceful and confined to the campuses, but then in late April 1998 violence spilled onto the streets in the Sumatran city of Medan as looters went on the rampage.

With unfortunate timing, the government then announced price rises for petrol and electricity, as demanded by the IMF as part of their multi-billion dollar bail-out package. These price rises, destined to hit the poor even harder, resulted in an increase in disturbances that culminated in the shooting of four university students at Trisakti university in Jakarta on 12 May. Two days later, Jakarta was burning as the urban poor went on the rampage, looting shops, banks and houses in the worst rioting the country had witnessed since 1965.

The political pressure on Soeharto mounted as some within the ruling party as well as the opposition forces called on him to resign. Facing huge demonstrations planned across the country, and with the country seemingly on the brink of chaos, Soeharto finally resigned on 21 May and Vice-President BJ Habibie was sworn in as the new president of the republic.

It remains to be seen how far down the road of reform the new government will travel, but certainly new political hope has returned to the country. The economy remains in crisis, however, and Indonesia has a long way to go before economic certainty returns.

GEOGRAPHY

The Republic of Indonesia is the world's most expansive archipelago, with more than 13,000 islands stretching almost 5000km from Sabang off the northern tip of Sumatra, to a little beyond Merauke in south-eastern Irian Jaya. It stretches north and south of the equator for a total of 1770km, from the border with Sabah in Borneo to the small island of Roti off the southern tip of Timor.

The islands of Nusa Tenggara are sited between eight and eleven degrees south of the equator. The principal islands in the archipelago are Lombok (4619 sq km), Sumbawa (15,255 sq km), Flores (13,540 sq km), Sumba (10,854 sq km) and Timor

(28,498 sq km), and a host of smaller islands of which Alor (2125 sq km), Lembata (1242 sq km) and Roti (1214 sq km) are the largest.

The region is geologically complex, lying between the Australian Plate and the Sunda Shelf on which the islands of Bali, Java, Sumatra and Kalimantan lie. It is surrounded by some of the world's deepest sea trenches. The islands are relatively young, geologically speaking, and were thrust up from the sea bed because of pressure from the meeting of the two main plates. The fault lines mean that minor earthquakes are common from Lombok to Sumba, and in 1992 an earthquake measuring 6.8 on the Richter scale demolished Maumere and killed thousands on Flores. Timor lies outside the earthquake zone and is stable.

The western chain of islands from Lombok through to Sumbawa and Flores to Alor are volcanic islands with some 24 active volcanoes and another dozen or so dormant. Minor eruptions are common and in 1815 Gunung Tambora exploded in one of the largest volcanic eruptions in recorded history. Not counting Irian Jaya, Gunung Rinjani (3726m) on the island of Lombok is the highest mountain in Indonesia; it last erupted in 1994.

Sumba and Timor are non-volcanic and geologically very different. The origin of Sumba is unknown, but it is believed that Timor was once part of the Australian continental shelf and rose from the ocean some 40 million years ago. Although the soils on both these islands are mostly limestone-based (and lack the fertility of volcanic soils found on the other islands), both Sumba and Timor have significant mountain ranges, with Timor home to a number of peaks over 2000m.

Low rainfall and the geography and size of the islands means that there are few significant rivers and agricultural basins. Away from the mountain areas in the dry season, landscapes are dry and craggy. The richest agricultural areas are mostly mountain valleys and a few irrigated basins such as the plains around Bima in Sumbawa, but in most areas wet-rice cultivation is nonexistent and corn is the main staple.

CLIMATE

The region's climate is the result of the monsoon and trade winds. The wet season begins around November or December, and peaks in January and February, when winds from the north-west bring rain. But the winds have already passed over western Indonesia and by the time they reach Nusa Tenggara have lost much of their moisture. The wet continues through March and then the winds switch direction and the drier south-east winds blow from April to October.

Nusa Tenggara is the driest part of Indonesia, but the wet season can still bring downpours and wreak havoc, flooding rivers and washing away roads. But the rains are fickle and can bring too little as easily as too much.

The islands are spread out in a line and all are roughly oriented west-east. The western parts of the islands receive the rains the first and are wetter than the east. Similarly, the further east you head from Lombok the drier it becomes.

Climate patterns are not uniform, however, and the topography also plays a major role. Most islands have a string of mountains running along them, creating rain shadows. The southern parts of the islands are wetter than the northern and receive some rain throughout the year. The northern side of the mountains are often bone dry from May to October. The mountains also create microclimates with areas of high rainfall around the peaks.

The dry season in this part of Indonesia is very dry, bringing drought conditions to many areas, particularly on Sumba and Timor, but the north and east region of Flores, Sumbawa and Lombok are also very dry. As the dry progresses, temperatures rise and the landscape browns off. This is the *musim lapar* (hungry season) when most agricultural activity ceases and villages survive on stores of food from the harvest at the end of the west season.

Maximum temperatures are uniformly around 30°C (86°F) to 33°C (91.4°F) in the coastal areas and drop to the low 20s overnight. The mountain areas are slightly cooler

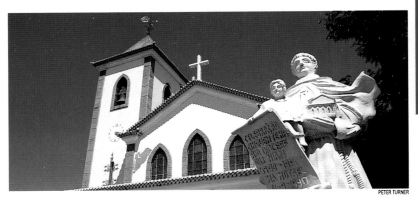

PETER TURNER

SARA-JANE CLELAND

PETER TURNER

PETER TURNER

Highlights of Indonesia's Eastern Islands
Top: The Igreja Motael church (Dili) is a fine example of Portuguese architecture in East Timor.
Middle Left: The famous Komodo dragon, which also can be seen on the neighbouring island of Rinca.
Middle Right: A Florinese *caci* whip fighter – just one outlet for the local passion of ritual combat.
Bottom: The coloured crater lakes of Kelimutu continue to be one of the region's biggest drawcards.

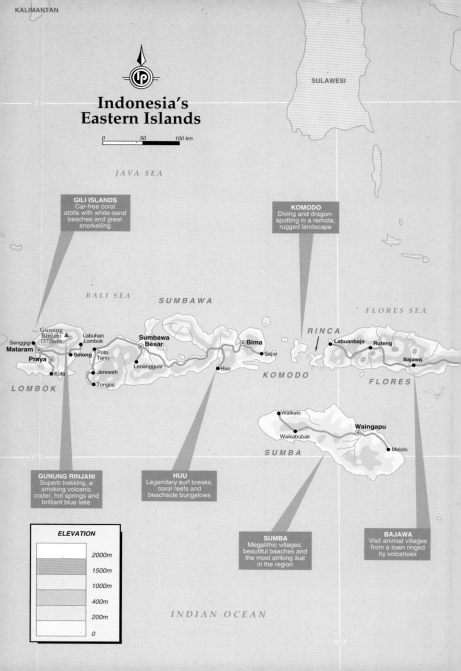

KALIMANTAN

SULAWESI

Indonesia's Eastern Islands

0   50   100 km

JAVA SEA

GILI ISLANDS
Car-free coral
atolls with white-sand
beaches and great
snorkelling

KOMODO
Diving and dragon-
spotting in a remote,
rugged landscape

BALI SEA

SUMBAWA

FLORES SEA

RINCA

Gunung
Rinjani
(3726m)
Senggigi   Labuhan
            Lombok   **Sumbawa**
Mataram   **Besar**   **Bima**   Labuanbajo   Ruteng
Praya Selong   Sape
        Poto
        Tano   Bajawa
    Kuta   Lenangguar   Huu
        Jereweh   *KOMODO*   *FLORES*
LOMBOK   Tongos   Huu

GUNUNG RINJANI
Superb trekking, a
smoking volcanic
crater, hot springs and
brilliant blue lake

HUU
Legendary surf breaks,
coral reefs and
beachside bungalows

Waikelo   **Waingapu**

Waikabubak   Melolo

SUMBA

SUMBA
Megalithic villages,
beautiful beaches and
the most striking ikat
in the region

BAJAWA
Visit animist villages
from a town ringed
by volcanoes

ELEVATION

2000m
1500m
1000m
400m
200m
0

INDIAN OCEAN

120° E

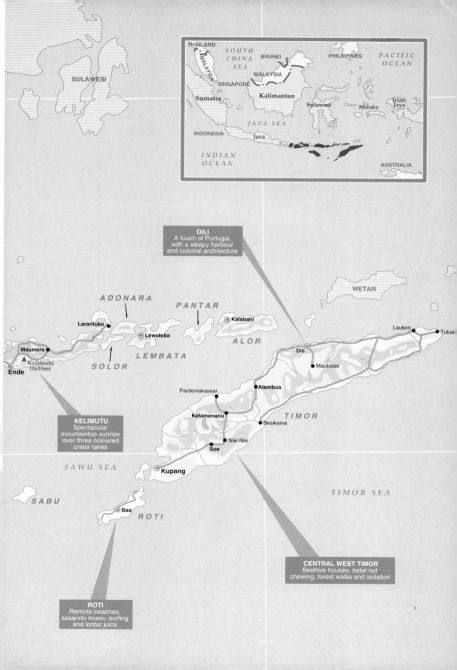

SULAWESI

THAILAND
SOUTH
CHINA
SEA
BRUNEI
PHILIPPINES
PACIFIC
OCEAN
MALAYSIA
MALAYSIA
SINGAPORE
Sumatra
Kalimantan
Sulawesi
Maluku
Irian
Jaya
JAVA SEA
INDONESIA
Java
INDIAN
OCEAN
AUSTRALIA

DILI
A touch of Portugal,
with a sleepy harbour
and colonial architecture

WETAR

ADONARA

PANTAR

Larantuka
● Kalabahi

● Lewoleba
ALOR

Maumere ●
Dili ●

▲ Kelimutu
(1635m)
LEMBATA
● Maubisse

Ende ●
SOLOR

Lautem ●
Tutua ●

Pantemakassar
● Atambua

KELIMUTU
Spectacular
mountaintop sunrise
over three coloured
crater lakes

Kefamenanu ●
TIMOR

● Besikama

● Niki Niki
● Soe

SAWU SEA
● **Kupang**

TIMOR SEA

SABU
● Baa
ROTI

CENTRAL WEST TIMOR
Beehive houses, betel nut
chewing, forest walks and isolation

ROTI
Remote beaches,
sasando music, surfing
and lontar juice

PETER TURNER

MARTIN TULLEMANS

PETER TURNER

MARK STRICKLAND

Activities in Indonesia's Eastern Islands
Top: Trekking opportunities abound – here a group of porters rest on the rim of Gunung Rinjani.
Middle Left: From Kuta in Lombok to Roti off Timor's coast, Nusa Tenggara is a surfer's paradise.
Middle Right: Traditional villages throughout the islands provide insights into many ancient cultures.
Bottom: Pristine beaches, clear water and beautiful reefs make for fabulous diving and snorkelling.

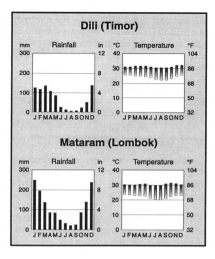

during the day and temperatures drop as low as 15°C (59°F) at night at altitudes of around 1000m. The only really cold areas are at very high altitude on mountain peaks. Temperatures on Gunung Rinjani (3726m) can drop to 5°C (41°F) at night.

ECOLOGY & ENVIRONMENT
Population pressures, rising consumption and persistent poverty all point to ecological degradation in a country that does not have the resources to give environmental issues high priority. Nevertheless there are environmental protection programs in place in Indonesia, but typically they are poorly funded and enforcement is difficult or ignored.

The problems are less severe in lightly populated Nusa Tenggara. By far the most crowded and quickly developing island is Lombok, where population pressures cause the most environmental concerns. Despite a growing economy due to tourism, which itself raises environmental issues, the problems of industrialisation, car emissions and overcrowding are nothing compared to those on Bali or Java.

Nonetheless the loss of natural habitat is a concern throughout the region. Biodiversity

is small, because of the islands' lack of contact with the Asian landmass, and the remaining species are threatened. Forest is mostly confined to remote mountain areas where access is difficult and agriculture is unsuitable. Sumbawa has the region's most significant forest areas, but logging is taking its toll as are *transmigrasi* migrants from overcrowded Lombok and other islands who clear new areas to raise crops.

Many species are protected, but enforcement is difficult and hunting is still a necessary supplement to the local economy in many areas. However, some societies do practice traditional forms of conservation. In parts of Timor, for example, when a forest becomes depleted in animals because of overhunting, then it is designated as a *kio*, similar to a traditional wildlife reserve and it is placed off limits for a couple of years.

Increasing numbers of national parks and reserves are being created in Nusa Tenggara, but often the management by the understaffed and poorly funded PHPA (the forest and wildlife department) is not particularly effective.

FLORA & FAUNA
The British naturalist Alfred Wallace in his classic study *The Malay Archipelago* first classified the Indonesian islands into two ecological zones – a western, Asian zone and an eastern, Australian zone. The 'Wallace Line' dividing these two zones ran at the edge of the Sunda Shelf through the straits between Bali and Lombok. West of this line, Indonesian flora and fauna shows great similarities to that of the rest of Asia, while to the east the islands gradually become drier and the flora and fauna resembles that of Australia's.

Nusa Tenggara is thus a transitional area, but it has relatively few endemic species of flora and fauna. Except for the famous Komodo dragon, these mostly dry islands are not home to the exotic flora and fauna found elsewhere in Indonesia,. The islands of the Sunda Shelf (Bali, Java, Sumatra and Kalimantan) were once linked by land bridges to the Asian mainland and have an astonishingly rich biodiversity that never reached Nusa Tenggara. Similarly Nusa Tenggara was never connected to the Australian landmass, except for Timor which possibly was a submerged island before it broke away.

Flora

Nusa Tenggara is the driest area of Indonesia and much of the landscape is composed of dry savannah, grasslands and dry monsoonal forest. The lontar palm is a marvel of adaptation to the dry conditions and is widely grown for its abundant juice, used in making alcoholic *tuak* and sugar, while the leaves are used for thatch.

The islands are not desert, however, and in the wet season the land turns green and many plants that have died off in the dry season bloom back to life. The substantial mountain ranges on all the main islands also produce a variety of ecosystems, and support year-round rainforest, ferns and tropical plant varieties. Although much forest has disappeared due to clearing for stock grazing and agriculture, some areas remain, from the truly tropical rainforest on Gunung Rinjani on Lombok, to large areas of mixed forest in south-west Sumbawa, right across to montane eucalyptus forest on Timor.

Evergreen rainforest only occurs at higher altitudes and in the hills along the southern coasts of the main islands where the southeast trade winds bring moisture during the long dry season. The mighty dipterocarp rainforest found throughout much of Indonesia occurs only on Lombok, around Gunung Rinjani, and in the south-west of Sumbawa and around Gunung Tambora. Dipterocarps do not exist further east.

Most of Nusa Tenggara's forests are monsoonal and consist of tree varieties than can withstand the long dry season, such as casuarinas, acacias and tamarinds, reflecting both Asian and Australian types. In very dry areas, such as Komodo and the north coasts of Sumba and Timor, only thorn forest grows.

Sandalwood, which first attracted traders to Timor, was almost harvested to extinction, but is now protected and replanted as a plantation crop. Teak and mahogany are introduced trees occurring in plantations and natural forest. Other native trees include bintangur, kesambi, bungur and fig, all of which are used widely for building houses and furniture.

Fauna

Although evidence of pygmy stegodonts (pre-historic animals related to the elephant) has been found in Nusa Tenggara, no large Asian mammals are present in Nusa Tenggara.

The Wallace Line

The 19th century naturalist Sir Alfred Wallace (1822-1913) observed great differences in fauna east of Bali when compared to fauna west of Bali – as great as the differences between Africa and South America. In particular, there were no large mammals (elephants, rhinos, tigers etc) east of Bali and very few carnivores. He postulated that during the ice ages when sea levels were lower, animals could have moved by land from what is now mainland Asia all the way to Bali, but the deep Lombok Strait would always have been a barrier. Thus he drew a line between Bali and Lombok, which he believed marked the biological division between Asia and Australia.

Plant life, on the other hand, does not reveal such a sharp division, but rather a gradual transition from predominantly Asian rainforest species to mostly Australian plants like eucalypts and acacias, which are better suited to long dry periods. This is associated with the lower rainfall as one moves east of Java. Environmental differences, including those in the natural vegetation, are now thought to provide a better explanation of the distribution of animal species than Wallace's theory about limits to their original migrations.

Modern biogeographers do recognise a distinction between Asian and Australian fauna, but the boundary between the regions is regarded as much fuzzier than Wallace's line. This transitional zone between Asia and Australia is nevertheless referred to as 'Walacea'. ■

All endemic mammals are of the shrew, mouse, rat or bat species.

Other mammals are introduced. Monkeys (mostly long-tailed macaques and black apes), civets, deer, wild pigs, feral cattle, water buffalo, dogs and cats are found on all the main islands. Other introduced species on Lombok include squirrels (a favourite pet of the Balinese), pangolin (or scaly anteater) and the leopard cat (a small, spotted wild cat). Javan porcupine are found from Lombok to Flores, and Timor has one rare species of possum or cuscus *(Phalanger orientalis timorensis)* that was probably introduced from nearby Wetar in Maluku.

Birdlife is prolific and Nusa Tenggara has 28 endemic species and around 400 resident and migratory species. Birds are of Asian and Australian origin, and Timor is the most diverse island for birdlife with around half the birds of Australian origin.

Marine mammals are widely distributed and include various species of whale, including the orca or killer whale, dophins and dugong.

Nusa Tenggara has one astonishing and famous animal, the Komodo dragon, the world's largest lizard, found only on the island of Komodo and a few neighbouring islands. Many other varieties of somewhat smaller lizards are found, including the gecko, which is a common motif in ikat weaving in some areas, notably Timor. Saltwater crocodiles inhabit the region, but have been hunted almost to extinction. Frogs and snakes are also common. The small island of Komodo alone has about 10 species of snake. The green viper is common. Of the insects, most memorable are the birdwing butterflies, among the world's largest.

National Parks

Indonesia's national park service, Perlindungan Hutan dan Pelestarian Alam (PHPA), maintains information offices at various points around the country, including posts in the national parks and in some reserves. Nusa Tenggara does not have an extensive system of national parks, but it is growing.

Gunung Rinjani, at 3726m, is the highest mountain in Indonesia outside Irian Jaya,

and dominates the island of Lombok. It is a very popular three to five day trek to the top and the huge crater contains a large green crescent-shaped lake, Segara Anak, which is 6km across at its widest point. Some 40,000 hectares of Rinjani's slopes are protected by a national park and a further 66,000 hectares are protected by the surrounding Gunung Rinjani Protection Forest.

Two-thirds (22,250 hectares) of Pulau Moyo, off the northern coast of Sumbawa Besar, is a nature reserve with savanna and some forest, though hunting is permitted. Good coral reefs are found around the island, especially to the south and west, and are protected by a 6000 hectare marine park.

The mostly dry savanna of Komodo National Park (75,000 hectares) encompasses Komodo and Rinca islands, and numerous smaller islands. It is home to Indonesia's most famous beastie, the Komodo dragon, and is the most visited park outside Gunung Rinjani. The park also has coral reefs and hiking.

In Flores, the tri-coloured lakes of Kelimutu, one of Indonesia's most impressive sights, is now protected by the Kelimutu National Park (5000 hectares). Other reserves on Flores include the Seventeen Islands Marine Park, covering the islands off the coast of Riung, and the Teluk Maumere Marine Recreation Park (59,450 hectares) in eastern Flores, which covers Pulau Besar and the other islands near Wairterang.

Timor has no national parks, but the Cagar Alam Gunung Mutis is a 12,000 hectare forestry reserve near Fatumenasi, which is co-managed by the World Wide Fund for Nature (WWF). It has montane eucalyptus forests, and Gunung Mutis (2427m) can be climbed. The Taman Wisata Camplong (Camplong Recreation Park), 47km from Kupang, is a small (400 hectare) reserve noted for its birdlife. The islands of Pulau Semau and Pulau Kera in Kupang Bay are also protected within a marine park.

Sumba has some isolated forest reserves. Gunung Langgaliru Nature Reserve (15,600 hectares) in south-central Sumba, halfway between Waingapu and Waikabubak, is a large area of lowland monsoon forest rich in avifauna. Proposals have been made to turn it into a national park, as is the case with the superb forest areas surrounding Gunung Wanggameti (1255m), Sumba's highest mountain in the south-east.

GOVERNMENT & POLITICS
National Government
Indonesia is often called a military dictatorship by some western commentators, but this is not strictly accurate. Certainly ABRI (the acronym for the armed forces) is a major political player, but Indonesia has a civilian administration.

The ruling party is Golkar, which officially is not a political party, but is designed to be an all-things-to-all-people 'group' representing wide interests inside and outside of government. One of the major groups within it is the army, even though President Soeharto (who rose to power through the army) is keen to have a civilian cabinet and keep a lid on ABRI's political aspirations.

The opposition, what there is of it, was created from the forced amalgamation of opposition parties in the 1970s to form the Partai Persatuan Pembangunan (PPP), representing Islamic groups, and Partai Demokrasi Indonesia (PDI), Soekarno's old party which has become an amalgam of nationalists, Christians and 'the rest'.

Opposition parties must accept the national ideology of Pancasila (see the boxed text on the following page for details). The government has the power to decide the opposition parties' policies, leaders and election candidates. The opposition is not allowed to destabilise the government by criticising it, the media is tightly controlled and Golkar, as the government party, has enormous resources to put into its election campaigns. Not surprisingly, the government wins elections by handsome majorities, typically capturing around 70% of the vote.

Elections are held every five years to elect 400 of the 500 members of the House of Representatives. The other 100 members are appointed by the armed forces. Executive power rests with the president, who is head of state and holds office for a period of five years. The president is elected indirectly through the People's Consultative Congress (MPR), which is composed of the House of Representatives and 500 appointees representing various groups and regions – the armed forces and Golkar are again well represented. The president appoints cabinet ministers, and this inner sanctum is the core of government power in Indonesia.

Regional Government
Although national policy, international wranglings and multimillion dollar deals are the preserve of the central government, for most Indonesians Jakarta is far removed and real government is at the district or village level.

Indonesia is made up of 27 provinces, and the region covered by this book comprises three of these provinces:

Nusa Tenggara Barat or NTB – West Nusa Tenggara covers Lombok and Sumbawa and the capital is Mataram.
Nusa Tenggara Timur or NTT – East Nusa Tenggara encompasses Komodo, Flores, Sumba and West Timor with Kupang as the capital.
Timor Timur or Tim-Tim – East Timor is Indonesia's newest province, but Indonesia's claim has never been officially recognised by the United Nations. The capital is Dili and as well as the eastern half of Timor it includes the coastal enclave of Oecussi (Ambenu) in western Timor.

Collectively the region is referred to as Nusa Tenggara.

Each province has its own political legislature with extensive powers with which to administer the area. Provinces are further broken down into various regional divisions. Although this extended hierarchy of government is sometimes confusing, it is well worth trying to understand, as the administrative divisions in Nusa Tenggara reflect ethnic and cultural boundaries. Addresses also quote this hierarchy and it is important to know the difference between a *desa* and a *kampung* (both mean village) if you are hunting out a destination in the countryside.

From top to bottom, areas in Indonesia are divided as follows:

Propinsi (Province) – headed by a *gubernur* (governor), the most powerful administrative level reporting directly to the central government in Jakarta.

Kabupaten (Regency) – each province is broken down into numerous kabupaten, headed by a *bupati* (regent or district head). In Nusa Tenggara, kabupaten boundaries usually define ethnic/linguistic areas.

Kecamatan (District) – each district is headed by a *camat*, and a kecamatan also often reflects ethnic loyalties, dialect groups or the boundaries of former kingdoms.

Desa (Village) – a desa can take in an area of up to 5000 people. It may be concentrated area or it can extend for quite a few kilometres and comprise a number of small villages. The desa is the most basic and functional political/social unit, and for villagers the most important. It is headed by the *kepala desa* (village head), who handles the day-to-day running of the village, neighbourhood disputes and local affairs. The kepala desa is the government representative at the most fundamental level, and the person to see if you want to visit a traditional village or spend the night. In very traditional villages, the spiritual head is the *kepala suku*, the chief of the clans, and you may have to contact the kepala suku to visit sacred sites.

Kampung (Village or Hamlet) – this is a small village, a collection of houses and family groupings. Large desas (villages) and towns comprise a number of kampungs. The distinction between a desa and a kampung can be a hazy one. Indonesians often think of desas not kampungs when describing points of interest or giving directions, when the name of the kampung is more important.

Indonesian education, access to national media and the use of Bahasa Indonesia as the main language linking the various ethnic groups means that national Indonesian identity is strong in Nusa Tenggara. Nevertheless, the government in Jakarta is seen as very remote. There is no hint of a secessionist movement and the people stand proudly in the Indonesian realm, but many do feel the region has been neglected by the central government and resent the dominance of Java – a common feeling in most of the outlying regions of Indonesia.

Feelings run highest within Christian communities, which are suspicious of Muslim aspirations for power and Islamic dominance in Java. The national government has always promoted tolerance and religious diversity within the country and is keen to keep a lid on Muslim power groups, simply because it

---

Pancasila

Since it was first expounded by Soekarno in 1945, the Pancasila (Five Principles) have remained the philosophical backbone of the Indonesian state. It was meant by Soekarno to provide a broad philosophical base on which a united Indonesian state could be formed. All over Indonesia you'll see the Indonesian coat of arms with its symbolic incorporation of the Pancasila hung on the walls of government offices and the homes of village heads, on the covers of student textbooks or immortalised on great stone tablets. These principles are:

Faith in God – symbolised by the star. This is perhaps the most important and contentious principle. As interpreted by Soekarno and the Javanese syncretists who have ruled Indonesia since independence, this can mean any god – Allah, Vishnu, Buddha, Christ etc. For many Muslims, it means belief in the only true God, Allah, but the government goes to great lengths to suppress both Islamic extremism and calls for an Islamic state in multi-ethnic and multi-religious Indonesia.

Humanity – symbolised by the chain. This represents the unbroken unity of humankind, and Indonesia takes its place among this family of nations.

Nationalism – symbolised by the head of the buffalo. All ethnic groups in Indonesia must unite.

Representative government – symbolised by the banyan tree. As distinct from the western brand of parliamentary democracy, Soekarno envisaged a form of Indonesian democracy based on the village system of deliberation *(permusyawaratan)* among representatives to achieve consensus *(mufakat)*. The western system of 'majority rules' is considered a means by which 51% potentially oppresses the other 49%.

Social justice – symbolised by the sprays of rice and cotton. A just and prosperous society gives adequate supplies of food and clothing for all – these are the basic requirements of social justice. ■

would create a damaging split in the country. The government in Nusa Tenggara Timur, however, is not dominated by Javanese or Muslims, but indigenous Christians.

ECONOMY

Nusa Tenggara is the poorest region of Indonesia. The majority of the population is engaged in subsistence agriculture, but poor soil and lack of rain mean Nusa Tenggara is much less productive than other parts of Indonesia. East Nusa Tenggara is poorer than West Nusa Tenggara.

Wet-rice grown in paddy fields is the staple in many parts of Indonesia, but most of Nusa Tenggara is too dry to grow it. Wet-rice is grown on Lombok in the west of the island and on the southern slopes of Gunung Rinjani, in parts of Sumbawa and in the fertile basins around Ruteng on Flores. Elsewhere it is grown only in small pockets and instead dry rice or corn is the staple. Dry rice only produces one crop per year while paddy fields can produce two or even three crops a year. Rice is considered a luxury in some areas.

Export crops are grown, mostly for other parts of Indonesia. Lightly populated Sumbawa has cattle ranching and plantation areas

in the west producing coffee, cashews and other export crops, and the fertile plains around Bima produce onions, buffalo, cattle and salt for export. Cattle and horses are exported from Sumba, and buffalo from Flores, but most livestock rearing is for domestic consumption. Buffalo, cattle, horses, chickens and pigs (in the non-Muslim areas) play an important role in the village economy. As well as a source of food, animals often form part of the bride price or are ritually slaughtered to appease the ancestors.

The barter economy is still strong in the villages, and goods and services are often tallied in terms of livestock. For example, for help in building a house the price may be paid in pigs or chickens. Other traditional items may be as important as money in the dowry for a bride. In eastern Flores, elephant tusks are still given as part of the bride price.

Large coffee, cotton, coconut and other plantations exist and many villagers also grow cash crops to earn a little extra money. Cloves, vanilla, pepper, pineapples, tobacco, tapioca and other vegetables are all grown in small plots. The lontar palm is grown everywhere in the drier regions, and its by-products have many uses. Fishing is widespread along

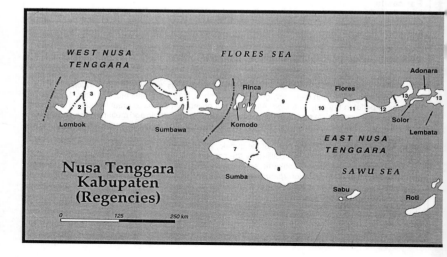

the coastlines which, edged by coral, have many good spawning areas.

Industry is virtually nonexistent in Nusa Tenggara. The biggest foreign income earner is undoubtedly tourism, but it is mostly confined to Lombok, visited by around 150,000 people annually. Mining promises to bring some wealth to the region. A new gold mine is opening on Sumbawa and oil from the Timor Gap, between Timor and Australia, promises jobs and an influx of capital.

Compounding widespread poverty is Indonesia's currency crisis of 1998. Although there are few businesses in Nusa Tenggara big enough to worry about foreign loans, rising prices will make life that much harder for the poor. Tourism has also slumped because of rioting in the wake of rising prices, though Nusa Tenggara is one of the quieter areas. For information on the impact of the economic crisis, see the Money entry in the Facts for the Visitor chapter.

POPULATION & PEOPLE
Of Indonesia's 200 million people, only about eight million live in Nusa Tenggara. The provincial breakdown, according to 1995 census figures, is:

Province	Population	People/sq km
Nusa Tenggara Barat	3.64 million	181
Nusa Tenggara Timur	3.58 million	75
East Timor	840,000	56

By far the most crowded island is Lombok. Although one of the smallest main islands, it contains a third of the region's entire population, while the other islands are lightly populated.

Nusa Tenggara has an astonishingly rich ethnic mix. On the basis of language, there a some 64 different ethnic groups, and considerable variation within those groups. The peoples of Nusa Tenggara are primarily of the 'Malay' race, having migrated from Asia, but further east the people have mixed Melanesian features, showing the influence of migration.

Lombok is relatively homogenous and is settled by the majority Sasaks and a Balinese minority, while Sumbawa has two main groups – the Sumbawans and the Bimanese. Flores on the other hand has five main ethnic groups, but 16 different language groups, all with their own customs and cultures. Timor

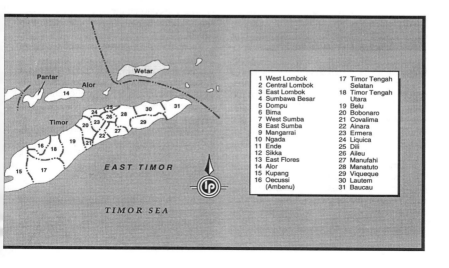

has two main ethnic groups – the Dawan and Tetum – but a host of other groups live in pockets all over the island. Sumba has a common culture, but is divided into seven language groups. Then there are the smaller islands such as ethnically distinct Roti, Sabu, Alor and Lembata and isolated pockets like Pulau Palue off the north coast of Flores or the Dou Donggo area of Sumbawa, each with its own language and customs. See the island destination chapters for more details.

As well as the indigenous populations, many migrants from other regions have settled in Nusa Tenggara. The Muslim sea-faring peoples of Sulawesi – the Makassarese, Bugis and sea gypsy Bajau (or Bajo) people – live in coastal pockets on many of the islands, particularly Lombok, Sumbawa and Flores. The Balinese colonised Lombok in the 17th century and now form a large minority in West Lombok. Balinese can also be found in smaller numbers throughout the islands, as can migrants from Java and Sumatra.

Indonesia has also a Chinese minority, comprising less than 3% of the population. The Chinese are the major force in the economy and can be found in all the cities and towns of Nusa Tenggara, operating shops, hotels, restaurants and other businesses. The Chinese are by far the wealthiest ethnic group in the country and there is much anti-Chinese resentment in Indonesia that sometimes threatens to boil over into violence.

There are also small pockets of Arabs, descendants of merchants who followed the trade routes and settled in Nusa Tenggara, most notably in Ampenan (Lombok), Ende (Flores), Waingapu (Sumba) and Kupang (Timor).

Transmigration
Overcrowded Lombok is targeted by government *transmigrasi* programs that take the pressure off heavily populated areas by moving people out to less populated islands.

Many Lombok residents have been resettled on Sumbawa, where they are joined by settlers from Java and Bali, the two most crowded islands in Indonesia. The rest of Nusa Tenggara is not a large transmigrant area because the islands are not particularly fertile. The transmigrasi programs have caused a lot of conflict in East Timor, where the local population sees it as an attempt to 'Indonesianise' the province. Some islands such as Flores have internal transmigration programs, called *translok*, aiming to resettle people from the poorest districts to more fertile areas or plantation districts within the island.

EDUCATION
In Indonesia, education begins with six years of primary school (Sekolah Dasar or SD), then three years of junior high school (Sekolah Menengah Pertama or SMP) and three years of senior high school (Sekolah Menengah Atas or SMA), which leads on to university.

While primary school enrolments have risen nationally to 90%, the figure would be slightly lower in Nusa Tenggara and fewer than 25% would complete secondary school. Schools fees are nominal, but still a burden for the very poor and some prefer their children to help with work in the fields or the village. Also, some areas are still very isolated. The national literacy rate is around 77%.

There are plenty of private schools, many operated by mosques and churches. Private schools generally have higher standards, and this is where the upper crust educate their children. On Flores, the Catholic seminaries are prestigious centres of learning and educate many of the island's elite.

Going to university is expensive and only a few can afford it. Universities are found in the provincial capitals of Mataram, Kupang and Dili.

ARTS
For a detailed discussion of traditional arts and crafts, see the Things to Buy section in the following Facts for the Visitor chapter, as well as introductory sections in the destination chapters.

Ikat

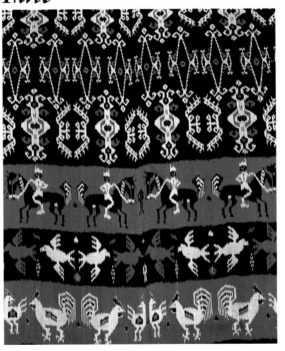

Title Page: Traditional ikat design from Kaliuda in Sumba's famed ikat-producing district of Mangili (Photograph by Peter Turner).

Top: Traditional dyes and their constituents used to colour the threads prior to the weaving process.

Middle Left: Once the warp (lengthwise) threads are positioned on the loom, the weaver matches the pattern with the weft thread.

PETER TURNER

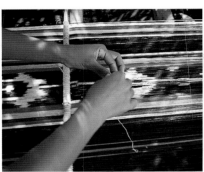

SARA-JANE CLELAND

SARA-JANE CLELAND

Middle Right: Detail of a typically intricate Florinese ikat design. Ikat made from natural dyes and thread is the most highly prized in Flores. Check out examples originating from the Ende region and the Lembata and Solor islands.

Bottom: A Florinese ikat weaver in action, with an extensive range of other styles and designs on display and awaiting a buyer.

PETER TURNER

Ikat

 The Indonesian word *ikat*, which means to tie or bind, is used as the name for intricately patterned cloth whose threads are tie-dyed by a very painstaking and skillful process before they are woven together. Ikat cloth is made in many regions of the archipelago, from Sumatra to Maluku, but it's in Nusa Tenggara that this ancient art form thrives.

Ikat garments are still in daily use in many areas, and there's an incredible diversity of colours and patterns. The spectacular ikat of Sumba and the intricate patterned work of Flores are the best known, but Timor, Lombok and small islands like Roti, Sawu, Ndao and Lembata all have their own varied and high quality traditions.

Making Ikat

Ikat cloth is nearly always made of cotton, and is still often hand spun, though factory-made threads have come into use. Dyes are traditionally handmade from local plants and minerals, and these give ikat its characteristically earthy brown, red, yellow and orange tones, as well as the blue of indigo.

Ikat comes in a variety of shapes and sizes, including *selendang* (shawls); sarongs; 2m long tubes which can be used as a cloak or rolled down to the waist to resemble a sarong; *selimut* (blankets); and 4m long pieces (known as *kapita* in Flores) used as winding cloths for burial of the dead.

Some aspects of ikat production are changing with the use of manufactured dyes and thread. A description of the traditional method follows.

All the work belongs to the women – they produce the dyes and plant, harvest, spin, dye and weave the cotton. Spinning is done with a spindle or sometimes a simple spinning wheel. The thread is strengthened by immersion in stiffening baths of grated cassava, finely stamped rice or a meal made of roasted maize, and then threaded onto a winder. The product is usually thicker and rougher than machine-spun cotton.

Traditional dyes are made from natural sources. The most complex processes are those concerned with the bright rust colour, known on Sumba as *kombu*, which is produced from the bark and roots of the kombu tree. Blue dyes come from the indigo plant, and purple or brown can be produced by dyeing the cloth deep blue and then overdyeing it with kombu.

Each time the threads are dipped in dye, the sections that are not due to receive colour are bound together ('ikatted') beforehand with dye-resistant fibre. A separate tying-and-dyeing process is carried out for each colour that will appear in the finished cloth – and the sequence of dyeing has to consider the effect of over-dyeing. This tying-and-dyeing stage is what makes ikat and it requires great skill, since the dyer has to work out – before the threads are woven into cloth – exactly which parts of the thread are to receive each colour in order to give the usually complicated pattern of the final cloth. After dyeing, the cloth is woven on a simple hand loom.

There is a defined schedule of work for the traditional production of ikat. On Sumba the thread is spun between July and October, and the patterns bound between September and December. After the rain ends in April, the blue and kombu dyeing is carried out. In August the weaving starts – more than a year after work on the thread began.

Origins & Meaning of Ikat

The ikat technique probably came to Indonesia more than 2000 years ago with migrants bringing the Dongson culture from southern China and Vietnam. It has survived in more isolated areas that were bypassed by later cultural influences.

Ikat styles vary according to the village and sex of the wearer, and some types of cloth are reserved for special purposes. In parts of Nusa Tenggara high quality ikat is part of the 'dowry' that a bride's family must give to the bridegroom's family. On Sumba, less than 90 years ago only members of the highest clans could make and wear ikat textiles. Certain motifs were traditionally reserved for noble families (as on Sumba and Roti) or members of a particular tribe or clan (Sawu or among the Dawan of Timor).

In the 20th century, traditional motifs have become mixed up with some of European origin, and ikat's function in indicating its wearer's role or rank has declined.

Motifs & Patterns

An incredible range of ikat designs is employed. Some experts believe that motifs found on Sumba, such as face-on people, animals and birds, stem from an artistic tradition even older than Dongson. The main Dongson influence was in geometric motifs like diamond and key shapes (which often go together), meanders and spirals.

A particularly strong influence was cloth known as *patola*, from Gujarat in India. In the 16th and 17th centuries these became highly prized in Indonesia and one characteristic motif was copied by local ikat weavers. It's still a favourite today – a hexagon framing a sort of four pronged star. On the best patola and geometric ikat, repeated small patterns combine to form larger patterns and the longer you look at it the more patterns you see – rather like a mandala.

Judging Ikat

It's not so easy! Books on the subject aren't much use when you're confronted with a market trader telling you that yes, this cloth is definitely hand spun and yes, of course the dyes are natural. Taking a look at the process is informative: you can see women weaving in many places, and at the right time of year you may see dye-making, thread-spinning or tie-dyeing. Cloths made in villages will nearly always be hand spun and hand woven. Here are some tips on distinguishing the traditional product:

Thread Hand spun cotton has a less perfect 'twist' to it than factory thread.

Weave Handwoven cloth, whether made from hand spun or factory thread, feels rougher and, when new, stiffer than machine-woven cloth. It will probably have imperfections (perhaps minor) in the weave.

Dyes Until you've seen enough ikat to get a feel for whether colours are natural or chemical, you often have to rely on your instincts as to whether they are 'earthy' enough. Some cloths contain both natural and artificial dyes.

Dyeing Method The patterns on cloths which have been individually tie-dyed by the authentic method will rarely be perfectly defined, but they're unlikely to have the detached specks of colour that often appear on mass-dyed cloth.

Age No matter what anybody tells you, there are very few antique cloths around. Most of what you'll be offered for sale will be new or newly second-hand. There are several processes to make cloth look old.

IKAT

Left: This traditional motif is a common feature of the ikat produced in Sumba. Like many Sumbanese motifs, it echoes the island's turbulent past of internicine war, raids and head-taking.

Music & Dance

Music and dance styles vary from district to district, but have much in common. Dances are primarily performed by women and accompany the ritual cycles and main village events – planting, the harvest, marriage, courtship, the building of a house, religious ceremonies etc. Many are based on war dances, as tribal warfare was once common everywhere in Nusa Tenggara, and these dances were performed to welcome warriors back from battle and celebrate their victories.

Drums are the most important instrument, and the order and way they are beaten may have spiritual significance. Bronze gongs are also common and often imbued with magical powers, but they are not native to the region. Unlike the gamelan orchestras of Bali and Java, where large ensembles play complex sets of gongs, usually only one or two gongs are beaten, much like percussion instruments.

Bamboo flutes and stringed lutes are also common. Lutes have many regional variations and names, such as *rebab*, *gambus* and *bijola*, while the *fiol* (violin) is common on Timor and shows Portuguese influence. The island of Roti has its own unique, multi-stringed instrument called the *sasando*, which is fashioned from lontar leaves to form a resonating bowl.

Singing is important and is often based on the *pantun*, an ancient Malay verse form of rhyming couplets or quatrains. A lead singer sings verses telling the story of the settling of the village or great battles of the past, and they are then repeated by the group. The verses may also be spontaneous, with each individual making it up as they go along, accompanied by much laughter and amusement.

Dances are most commonly based on the 'circle dance', where groups of dancers link arms. Dances may tell the stories of village history, but are not based on the great epics and theatrical performances of Hindu-Buddhist literature common in other parts of Indonesia. An exception is the Panji stories introduced to Lombok by the Balinese and based on a much-loved legendary prince of East Java. Some Sasak dances are based on Panji's exploits.

Dances in Muslim areas may be influenced by Islam. In Bima (Sumbawa), the *hadrath* is commonly performed for weddings, circumcisions and religious events. A group of men kneel on the floor and play tambourines while swaying to the chants of a Muslim leader who sings verses from the Koran or other religious texts.

Ritual Combat While dances are mostly performed by women, the men engage in ritualised forms of combat that hark back to tribal warfare. Although not dancing as such, these combats are usually accompanied by music and singing, and are performed for many ritual and social occasions. These sometimes dangerous events improve fighting abilities and, just as women perform courtship dances, men are given the chance to show off their courage and skills to admiring women. Big crowds come to watch and injury (usually minor) is not uncommon.

These contests take many forms. On Lombok, the Sasaks have stick fights called *peresehan*, while on Sumbawa, head-butting contests are held. In Flores, the Manggarai have *caci* whip fights, while in the Ngada area around Boawae, men box with lumps of wood in their hands or have gloves studded with broken glass! The most famous of all these events is the great Pasola festival of Sumba, when men on horseback hurl blunted spears at each other. Deaths have been recorded.

Architecture

Nusa Tenggara has very rich architectural traditions and each ethnic group has it own distinctive style of *rumah adat* (traditional house). The rumah adat is more than just a house and specific laws govern its construction, unlike a modern building. Construction must commence on a propitious day, and it is a communal event involving most of the village. Payment is often made by slaughtering animals and the food is then distributed, again according to traditional laws. The completion is a cause for celebration and usually accompanied by feasting, music and dance.

A rumah adat may be a traditional house for a family to live in, but often the term

A typical example of a Ngada village with the male totem, the *ngadhu*, in the foreground.

applies specifically to a communal building constructed to honour the ancestors and provide a central meeting house for the village. It may also be a clan house, built for the leading family of one of the village's clans, to which more spiritual significance is attached. Within the structures of traditional society, one's clan is extremely important and the position within the clan is as important as the overall village hierarchy.

The layout of the house follows a set design imbued with symbolism, eg the pillars of the house may represent ancestors or spirits. The house may be male or female, or incorporate both elements into one house, and it is often compared to the human body, with the supporting pillars the legs and the roof the head.

Traditional houses are multifunctional with two, three or four levels, each used for different purposes. They are often raised off the ground because of flooding, and the open lower level may be a holding area for animals or an informal sitting area with a bamboo platform. The next level is the main living room, which may be partitioned or is often one large room that includes the kitchen and sleeping area. The attic in the roof may be a sleeping area, but it is usually a storage area where corn and other food is kept. Smoke from the kitchen fires rises up and keeps the bugs away, for the stores have to last through the long dry season. The communal house may also use the roof area for storing the sacred heirlooms of the village – drums, gongs, elephant tusks, ikat cloths etc.

Many people now live in more modern rectangular houses with a corrugated iron roof. They are easier and cheaper to build and iron roofs do not require the constant maintenance of lontar or coconut palm thatch. In some areas, such as the mountains of Central Timor, the government discourages traditional houses because they are considered unhealthy as smoke from the kitchen fires causes lung and eye infections.

In Lombok, most houses are modern, except for a few traditional villages. The much-celebrated *lumbung* can still be found in many areas and inspires the architecture of luxury hotels, but they are mostly used for grain storage now and are no longer lived in. The large, high-peaked communal houses in Sumba are still the main house form in villages and the small conical houses of the Dawan in Timor dot the countryside. Traditional houses in Flores are mostly meeting houses, but many villagers around Bajawa still live in their traditional houses.

SOCIETY & CONDUCT

Most of the region is very traditional, particularly the islands of Flores, Sumba and Timor. Modern ways and outside influences are hardly noticeable in the villages, where life goes on as it has for generations.

Traditional values of the family, the clan and the village are strong. The head of the family is accorded great respect and children acquiesce to their parents and elders. The notion of clan is very important, and these related family units have their own heads who combine under a central kepala suku, chief of the clans, who oversees ritual. The head of the village, the kepala desa, is often a separate, almost secular leader who oversees the organisation of the village and is the government representative at the most basic level. Within these traditional structures, the concerns of the individual are less important than in western society, and western notions of individualism are seen as odd or selfish.

Although modernity is still remote in many areas, that doesn't mean it isn't welcome. New roads and electricity have now reached most areas, but the peoples of Nusa Tenggara are poor and modern conveniences are lacking. Economic conditions are slowly improving, and with that will come change and the loss of tradition, but many villages are keen to maintain traditional ceremonies and practices, even though the trappings of tradition will disappear. Plastic buckets will inevitably replace hand-crafted water pots and jeans will replace sarongs, but even in the wealthier areas, traditional houses are still built as a focus for the community and the age-old rituals of the harvest and marriage are followed.

Tourism also plays a role in the breakdown of traditional societies, mostly because it brings money. Most villages are delighted at the prospect of receiving tourists and the income it can bring, as long as visitors respect the culture and traditions. Villagers are usually keen to discuss their traditions – show some interest, rather than simply taking photos, and it will be amply rewarded.

Avoiding Offence

Indonesians will accept any lack of clothing on the part of poor people who cannot afford them; but for westerners, thongs, bathing costumes, shorts or strapless tops are considered impolite except perhaps at beach resorts like Senggigi on Lombok. Nude or topless bathing is offensive everywhere. Elsewhere you should look respectable; revealing clothes are not appropriate. Women should dress modestly – Indonesia is a male-oriented society and scant clothing may invite unwanted attention or advances. For men, shorts are considered low class and only worn by boys.

At places of worship, permission should be requested to enter, particularly when ceremonies or prayer are in progress, and you should ensure that you're decently dressed. Always remove footwear before entering a mosque. Always ask permission before visiting sacred areas in traditional villages, and also ask permission to take photographs. Remember that entering a village is like entering someone's home (see the boxed text on Visiting Villages).

When transacting, and especially when dealing with officialdom, hand over or receive things with the right hand, as the left hand is considered unclean. Hospitality is highly regarded, and when food or drink is placed in front of you, don't start until you are asked to by your host, who will usually say *silahkan* (please). It is impolite to refuse a drink, but not necessary to drink it all.

Many people on Lombok fast during Ramadan. During this time it is insensitive and offensive for foreign visitors to eat, drink

Visiting Villages

The islands from Lombok to Timor are among the most traditional and fascinating in Indonesia. To appreciate the many cultures and the lives of the majority of people it is necessary to get away from the resorts and towns and into the villages. That said, wandering into a village is like wandering into someone's home, and a few rules of etiquette apply.

Many villages are now used to tourists and some villages on Lombok are almost tourist theme parks. Others, even though they receive a steady trickle of visitors, are still puzzled by foreigners who front up just to observe 'exotic' cultures. Take the time to introduce yourself, chat to your hosts and don't just wander through and start snapping photos or they may be offended.

Most villages welcome tourists because they can see the advantage – the very tangible benefit of much-needed income. The better organised villages will have a visitors' book, where you sign in and make a donation. The amount may be fixed, but often it is *tersera* (up to you). A couple of thousand rupiah per visitor is usually sufficient (with perhaps an adjustment for inflation), though you can always give more. In traditional villages that are not used to tourism, it is customary to bring betel nut *(sirih pinang)*, particularly on Sumba, Timor and Flores.

Always seek out the kepala desa first and ask permission before wandering around. If the kepala desa is not there you will be taken to another senior person. Chances are you will be led into the front room of the kepala desa's house, offered a drink or perhaps betel nut. It is impolite to refuse, but betel nut is definitely an acquired taste and allowances are usually made for foreigners. Take some betel nut and put it in your pocket if you don't want to chew.

If you want to visit an ancestral village or other sacred site it may also be necessary to consult the *kepala suku*, the chief of the clans or adat priest. You should also take a guide from the village. Ancestral villages are often not inhabited and may be some distance from the main village, but the guide is not so much to show you the way as to keep an eye on you. Otherwise you may inadvertently step on a sacrificial altar or otherwise offend the ancestors. These areas may also be a repository of sacred heirlooms and villagers are worried about thieves. Don't just head off alone, and ask permission before taking photos.

All in all, the best advice is to bring a guide with you, at least to remote villages, especially if there is likely to be language difficulties. Villagers find it very frustrating to be confronted by a stranger who cannot communicate with them. A guide can make the introductions, teach you protocol and greatly enhance your visit by explaining points of interest, even if you speak Indonesian well. The guide should be local and preferably known to the village, or at least be able to speak the dialect. Indonesian is not always spoken and in some isolated areas of Timor and Sumba, strangers are viewed with great suspicion – Indonesian strangers perhaps more so than foreign tourists.

It is also possible to stay with the kepala desa in villages. Indonesians are renowned for their hospitality and will go out their way to accommodate guests. Unusually elaborate meals may be prepared and it is important not to be a burden. The kepala desa's home is not a hotel – you are a guest – but pay around the same as you would in a losmen and extra for meals (see the Accommodation section in the Facts for the Visitor chapter for more on staying in villages). ∎

---

or smoke in public during the day. Islamic law forbids drinking alcohol and, although booze is widely available on Lombok, public drunkenness is frowned on. It's particularly offensive near a mosque.

RELIGION

Nusa Tenggara's religious divide runs between Sumbawa and Flores – to the west Islam prevails, and to the east Christianity.

The province of Nusa Tenggara Barat, comprising the islands of Lombok and Sumbawa, is overwhelmingly Muslim except for a minority of Balinese Hindus in West Lombok.

Nusa Tenggara Timur is predominantly Christian, though animist beliefs still prevail alongside Christianity in most areas. Parts of Sumba have never converted to Christianity, and isolated animist communities can be found on most islands. Muslim communities are found in the east – usually coastal villages of Bugis, Bajau or other immigrants – but they comprise only a small minority. East Timor is almost 100% Catholic.

Freedom of worship is guaranteed by the first principle of the state philosophy of Pancasila, but the only recognised religions are Hinduism, Buddhism, Islam and Christianity.

Animism is officially classed as 'no religion', but age-old practices generally come under the heading of *adat* (customary law or tradition) that exists across Indonesia in different regional forms, despite sometimes contradictory practices to the established religions.

Islam

The great majority of the people of Lombok and Sumbawa are Muslims. Islam reached Indonesia in the 13th century via the trade routes and though initially adopted peacefully, it was carried further by sword. The Muslim Makassarese state of Gowa in Sulawesi invaded Sumbawa in the early 17th century and converted the local rulers to Islam. Sumbawa then invaded eastern Lombok and spread Islam further, but Lombok had earlier been visited by Muslim missionaries from Java who are generally accredited as the founders of Islam on Lombok.

Today Islam is the professed religion of 90% of the Indonesian people, and its traditions and rituals affect all aspects of their daily life. Friday afternoon is the officially decreed time for believers to worship, and all government offices and many businesses are closed. Scrupulous attention is given to cleanliness, including ritualistic washing of hands and face. The pig is considered unclean and is not kept or eaten in strict Muslim regions.

Indonesian Muslims may have more than one wife, though this is not common, partly because few men can afford to keep a second wife. Those who make the pilgrimage to Mecca are known as *haji* if they are men, *haja* if they're women, and are deeply respected.

Islam not only influences daily routines and personal politics, but also affects the politics of government. Orthodox Muslims demand that the government protects and encourages Islam. Power brokers around Soeharto view the idea of a strong Islamic bloc in the People's Representative Council (Indonesia's most influential policy-making body) to be a security risk and a situation to be avoided at all costs.

The founder of Islam, Mohammed, was born in 571 AD and began his teachings in 612. He forged an early Hebraic kind of monotheism and a latent Arab nationalism, and by 622 was beginning to gain adherents. Mohammed did not demonstrate supernatural powers, but he did claim he was God's only teacher and prophet, charged with the divine mission of interpreting the word of God. Mohammed's teachings are collated and collected in the scripture of Islam, the Koran, which was compiled from his oral and written records shortly after his death. It is divided into 14 chapters, and every word in it is said to have emanated from Mohammed and been inspired by God himself, in the will of Allah.

The fundamental tenet of Islam is 'there is no god but Allah and Mohammed is his prophet'. The word 'Islam' means submission, and the faith demands unconditional surrender to the wisdom of Allah, not just adherence to a set of beliefs and rules. It involves total commitment to a way of life, philosophy and law. Aspects of Islam have been touched by animist, Hindu and Buddhist precepts, influencing both peripheral details like mosque architecture and fundamental beliefs like the attitudes to women.

Muslim women in Indonesia are allowed more freedom and shown more respect than women in some other Islamic countries. They do not have to wear veils, nor are they segregated or considered to be 2nd class citizens. There are a number of matrilineal and matriarchal societies and sometimes special mosques are built for women. Muslim men in Indonesia are only allowed to marry two women and must have the consent of their first wife to do so. Throughout Indonesia it is the women who initiate divorce proceedings where necessary, under the terms of their marriage agreement.

Christianity

Christianity first came to the eastern islands with the Portuguese in the 16th century. Dominican friars arrived on Timor in 1556 and started converting the population around the enclave of Oecussi, and soon ventured to eastern Flores, to Larantuka, Solor and along the south coast as far as Ende. They carried the flag for Portugal, building forts to resist attacks from Muslims and to provide a harbour for Portuguese trading ships.

Catholicism became the main religion of East Timor and Flores, but the majority of conversions on Flores were conducted by Dutch Catholics in the late 19th and early 20th centuries.

West Timor and Sumba are primarily Protestant. The Calvanists on Sumba and the Lutherans in West Timor set about converting with great zeal only in the 20th century and many parts of Sumba remain animist. Timor is overwhelmingly Christian, but a strong layer of animism survives.

In fact, animism survives in one form or another in most Christian areas. Although villagers may attend mass and defer to the local priest or pastor, ceremonies and animal sacrifices to honour the ancestors and ensure a good harvest continue.

Muslims and Christians, where they exist in the same communities, generally live side-by-side in harmony, but the relationship is not without its problems. This is particularly true in the east, which has a significant Muslim minority in some areas. Communal disturbances are rare, but not unheard of, though the problem is often in areas with large numbers of newly arrived Muslim immigrants from Java and other islands.

Christians are very aware of their minority status in overwhelmingly Muslim Indonesia. There is often resentment of the central government and many Christians feel excluded from mainstream power. Regional governments in Nusa Tenggara Timur are dominated by Christians, however, and the elite are often seminary educated. Muslims tend to be looked down upon as poorly educated and lazy, and are often excluded from positions of power, in much the same fashion as Christians are excluded nationally.

Hinduism

Lombok has a significant minority of Balinese Hindus and Balinese temples are scattered around West Lombok. The Balinese are nominally Hindus, but Balinese Hinduism is

a world away from that of India. When the Majapahits evacuated from Java to Bali they took with them their religion and its rituals as well as their art, literature, music and culture. The Balinese already had strong religious beliefs and an active cultural life, and the new influences were simply overlaid on existing practices – hence the peculiar Balinese interpretation of Hinduism.

The Balinese worship the same gods as the Hindus of India – the trinity of Brahma, Shiva and Vishnu – but they also have a supreme god, Sanghyang Widi. Unlike in India, the trinity is never seen – a vacant shrine or empty throne tells all. Nor is Sanghyang Widi often worshipped, though villagers may pray to him when they have settled new land and are about to build a new village. Other Hindu gods such as Ganesh, Shiva's elephant-headed son, may occasionally appear, but a great many purely Balinese gods, spirits and entities have far more relevance in everyday life.

The Balinese believe that spirits are everywhere, an indication that animism is the basis of much of their religion. Good spirits dwell in the mountains and bring prosperity to the people, while giants and demons lurk beneath the sea and bad spirits haunt the woods and desolate beaches. The people live between these two opposites and their rituals strive to maintain the middle ground. Offerings are carefully put out every morning to pay homage to the good spirits and nonchalantly placed on the ground to placate the bad ones. Although it enforces a high degree of conformity it is not a fatalistic religion – there are rules and rituals to placate or drive out the bad spirits, and ensure the favour of the gods and the good spirits.

Traditional Religion

Animist beliefs and customs survive in many islands, particularly in the east from Flores to Timor.

Ancestor worship is the basis of traditional religion. The region's history is one of migration and each society has legends telling of the arrival of the first people, but more important are the ancestors who first settled the village. Other ancestors also play a prominent role, and the spirits of the dead look after the welfare of the village, ensure good harvest and require ritual appeasement.

Villages may have statues representing the ancestors, though more often graves are a central spiritual focus and are placed in a prominent position in the village compound. Graves may be a source of spiritual power and grave cleaning ceremonies – when the bones are taken out, cleaned and sometimes wrapped in ikat cloth – are an important ritual in many societies.

The ancestral spirits mediate on behalf of the community and are the link between the living and the spirit world. Nature spirits of the sun, earth, rain etc also feature prominently and are very important in a region where subsistence agriculture can be a precarious existence. Low soil fertility and low rainfall means that many ceremonies are held to celebrate the harvest and ensure a good crop for the next season.

Animal sacrifice plays a important role and blood must be spilt for many ceremonies. Returning blood to the earth ensures fertility, and the sacrifice itself is an offering to the spirits. Sacrifices also perform a social role, for feasting follows a sacrifice and often the wealthy give more animals so that the poor can also feast. Such ceremonies can be a burden, however, and scores of animals may be killed to celebrate the harvest, crop planting, a funeral, the building of a traditional house, the naming of a child, etc. In some areas, sacrifices are made to volcanoes to ensure the arrival of the rains. In past times human sacrifices were also made, for war and head-hunting were widespread.

Although most people are now Christian or Muslim, many trappings of the old religion survive and animist ceremonies are still important. Magic is widely believed in, and adat priests divine the future from chicken entrails or eggs. Black magic also exists and spells are cast against enemies.

The old beliefs are strongest in Christian areas – head east if you are interested in traditional beliefs and customs. Islam has always followed a tolerant path in Indonesia, and while older traditions and the belief in magic still exist in Muslim areas, they are less important. This is particularly true in the past couple of decades as more and more Indonesians make the pilgrimage to Mecca and come into contact with orthodox Islam.

Many of the adat beliefs are also dying out in Christian areas, especially where missionary activity has been around the longest, such as the former Portuguese Catholic areas of Flores and East Timor. However, Catholicism has generally been more tolerant of existing traditions than Protestantism. Protestant missionaries in West Timor and Sumba have been the most keen to denounce older traditions as the work of the devil and stamp them out.

Ultimately though, modern education, urbanisation, migration and national culture are the greatest threats to traditional beliefs. Tradition has survived because the majority of the people have been isolated from the modern world. Roads have only been built in many areas in the past few years, and with them comes development, modernity, increased education and the loss of adat.

LANGUAGE

Of the more than 300 languages spoken throughout Indonesia, some 64 are spoken in Nusa Tenggara, with dozens more dialects. Barriers created by islands, mountains and warfare have meant that many groups, even those which are related, have developed their own languages in virtual isolation. For example, the small island of Alor has eight languages and at least 25 dialects, while the even smaller island of Roti has 18 dialects which are mutually unintelligible – each is sufficiently different that they could well class as languages in their own right.

The bulk of the region's languages are Malayo-Polynesian and belong to the Austronesian family of languages used throughout most of Indonesia. In East Timor and Alor many of the languages belong to the Trans-New Guinea family, and are related to the languages of Irian Jaya further to the east. The languages with the most native speakers are: Sasak, spoken on Lombok by well over two million people, Bimanese on Sumbawa (500,000 speakers), Manggarai on Flores (500,000 speakers) and Dawan on Timor (700,000 speakers). Some of the more obscure languages may have less than 1000 speakers. The destination chapters later in the book list a few words and phrases in some of the local languages.

The vast number of individual tongues has meant that the national language, Bahasa Indonesia, has become a necessity for communication in the modern world. It is now spoken almost everywhere, though there are still a few remote areas where it isn't understood. It's taught in schools, so if you have problems communicating with adults, ask children for help.

English is spoken in the tourist areas and by educated people in the cities and towns. High school students learn English and may know more than just 'Hello'. In Lombok, some tourist guides also speak Italian, French, German, Dutch or Japanese. Older people educated in colonial times may speak Dutch, but they are becoming harder to find. Portuguese is quite widely spoken by the middle classes in East Timor, and they appreciate you using it.

In the villages some understanding of Indonesian is essential for independent travel. It can be very frustrating, if not rude, to arrive at a traditional village and not be able to communicate at all with your hosts. It pays to take the time to learn at least the basics – it's an easy language to learn and will greatly enhance travel in Nusa Tenggara. Otherwise take a guide, preferably one who also speaks the local dialect, which may be necessary in some villages.

Bahasa Indonesia

Today, the national language of Indonesia is Bahasa Indonesia (bahasa means 'language'), which is almost identical to Malay. Most Indonesians speak Bahasa Indonesia as well as their own regional language.

Like any language, Indonesian has its simplified colloquial form and its more classical literary form. For the visitor who wants to pick up enough to get by, Indonesian is one of the easiest languages to learn. There are no tenses or genders and often one word can convey the meaning of a whole sentence. Furthermore, it's easy to pronounce, with none of the complex rules and tone systems which make some Asian languages so difficult to learn. It can also be a delightfully poetic language: *hari* is 'day' and *mata* 'eye' – therefore *matahari* is 'the eye of the day', ie 'the sun'.

A few essentials are listed here. For a more comprehensive overview, try Lonely Planet's *Indonesian phrasebook* or the *Indonesian audio pack*. They're set out with a view to helping you communicate easily, rather than just listing endless phrases.

An English-Indonesian dictionary is also very useful and they're sold quite cheaply in Indonesia. You can also get bilingual dictionaries in French, German, Dutch and Japanese. Good dictionaries are hard to find in Nusa Tenggara – try the bookshops in Bali or Java, or bring one with you.

Pronunciation

Most sounds are the same as in English. Nearly all syllables have equal emphasis, but a good general rule is to stress the second to last syllable. The main exception to the rule is the unstressed 'e' in words such as *besar* (big), pronounced 'be-SARRR'.

a	as in 'father'
e	as in 'bet' when unstressed; when stressed, as the 'a' in 'may'
i	as the 'ee' in 'meet'
o	as in 'go'
u	as in 'flute'
ai	as in 'Thai'
au	as the 'ow' in 'cow'
ua	at the start of a word, as a 'w', eg *uang*, 'money' (pronounced 'wong')

The pronunciation of consonants is very straightforward. Some which may cause problems are listed here:

c	as the 'ch' in 'chair'
g	as in 'get'
ng	as in 'sing'

ngg	as the 'ng' in 'anger'
j	as in 'John'
r	trilled, as in Spanish 'r'
h	a little stronger than the 'h' in 'her'; almost silent at the end of a word
k	like the English 'k', except at the end of a word, when it's more like a closing of the throat with no sound, eg *tidak* (pronounced 'tee-dah')
ny	as the 'ny' in 'canyon'

Basics

Yes.	*Ya.*
No. (also 'not')	*Tidak.*
Thank you (very much).	*Terima kasih (banyak).*
You're welcome.	*Kembali.*
Please. (asking for help)	*Tolong.*
Please open the door.	*Tolong buka pinta.*
Please. (giving permission)	*Silakan.*
Please come in.	*Silakan masuk.*
Welcome.	*Selamat datang.*
Sorry.	*Ma'af.*
Excuse me.	*Permisi.*

Greetings

Good morning. (before 11 am)	*Selamat pagi.*
Good day. (11 am to 3 pm)	*Selamat siang.*
Good afternoon. (3 to 7 pm)	*Selamat sore.*
Good night.	*Selamat malam.*
Goodbye. (by the person leaving)	*Selamat tinggal.*
Goodbye. (by the person staying)	*Selamat jalan.*

Small Talk

How are you?	*Apa kabar?*
I'm fine.	*Kabar baik.*
What is your name?	*Siapa nama anda?*
My name is ...	*Nama saya ...*
I'm from ...	*Saya dari ...*
Are you married?	*Sudah kawin?*
I'm married.	*Saya sudah kawin.*
I'm not married yet.	*Saya belum kawin.*

Language Difficulties

Do you speak English?	*Bisa berbicara bahasa Inggris?*
I (don't) understand.	*Saya (tidak) mengerti.*
Please write that word down.	*Tolong tuliskan kata itu untuk saya.*

Getting Around

I want to go to ...	*Saya mau pergi ke ...*
Where is ...?	*Dimana ada ...?*
Which way?	*Ke mana?*
How many kilometres?	*Berapa kilometer?*
What time does the ... leave/arrive?	*Jam berapa ... berangkat?*
bus	*bis*
train	*kereta api*
ship	*kapal*
aeroplane	*kapal terbang*
Where can I hire a ...?	*Dimana saya bisa sewa ...?*
bicycle	*sepeda*
motorcycle	*sepeda motor*
Stop here.	*Berhenti disini.*
Go straight on.	*Jalan terus.*
Turn right.	*Belok kanan.*
Turn left.	*Belok kiri.*
Please slow down.	*Pelan-pelan saya.*
station	*stasiun*
ticket	*karcis/tiket*
first class	*kelas satu*
economy class	*kelas ekonomi*

Accommodation

Is there a room available?	*Ada kamar yang kosong?*
What's the daily rate?	*Berapa tarip hariannya?*
Can I see the room?	*Boleh saya lihat kamarnya?*
I'd like to pay now.	*Saya mau bayar sekarang.*
air-conditioning	*ac* ('ah-say')
bathroom	*kamar mandi*

bed	*ranjang/tempat tidur*
hotel	*hotel*
price list	*daftar harga*
(quiet) room ...	*kamar (tenang) ...*
with private bath	*mandi di dalam*
with shared bath	*mandi diluar*

Around Town

bank	*bank*
market	*pasar*
police station	*kantor polisi*
post office	*kantor pos*
postage stamp	*perangko*
telephone	*telepon*
telephone number	*nombor telepon*
toilet	*kamar kecil/ WC ('way say')*
town square	*alun-alun*
What time does it open/close?	*Jam berapa buka/tutup?*
What is the exchange rate?	*Berapa kursnya?*

Shopping

How much is it?	*Berapa harga?*
Can you lower the price?	*Boleh kurang?*
cigarettes	*rokok*
film	*filem*
matches	*korek api*
mosquito coil	*obat nyamuk*
mosquito net	*kelambu*
soap	*sabun*
toilet paper	*kertas WC*
towel	*handuk*

Numbers

1	*satu*	6	*enam*
2	*dua*	7	*tujuh*
3	*tiga*	8	*delapan*
4	*empat*	9	*sembilan*
5	*lima*	10	*sepuluh*

After the numbers one to 10, the 'teens' are *belas*, the 'tens' are *puluh*, the 'hundreds' are *ratus* and the 'thousands' *ribu*. Thus:

11	*sebelas*
12	*duabelas*
13	*tigabelas*
20	*duapuluh*
21	*duapuluh satu*
25	*duapuluh lima*
30	*tigapuluh*
90	*sembilanpuluh*
99	*sembilanpuluh sembilan*
100	*seratus*
200	*duaratus*
250	*duaratus limapuluh*
254	*duaratus limapuluh empat*
888	*delapanratus delapanpuluh delapan*
1000	*seribu*
1050	*seribu limapuluh*

'A half' is *setengah (pronounced 'stengah')*, so *stengah kilo* is 'half a kilo. 'Approximately' is *kira-kira*.

Time

What is the time?	*Jam berapa?*
7 o'clock	*jam tujuh*
5 o'clock	*jam lima*
How many hours?	*Berapa jam?*
five hours	*lima jam*
When?	*Kapan?*
tomorrow/yesterday	*besok/kemarin*
rubber time	*jam karet*
hour	*jam*
week	*minggu*
month	*bulan*
year	*tahun*

Days of the Week

Monday	*Hari Senin*
Tuesday	*Hari Selasa*
Wednesday	*Hari Rabu*
Thursday	*Hari Kamis*
Friday	*Hari Jumat*
Saturday	*Hari Sabtu*
Sunday	*Hari Minggu*

Health & Emergencies

I'm sick.	*Saya sakit.*
Call a doctor!	*Panggil dokter!*
Call an ambulance!	*Panggil ambulan!*

Call the police!	*Panggil polisi!*	I'm lost.	*Saya kesasar.*
It's an emergency!	*Keadaan darurat!*	Where are the toilets?	*Dimana ada WC?*
Help!	*Tolong!*	doctor	*dokter*
Thief!	*Pencuri!*	hospital	*rumah sakit*
Fire!	*Kebakaran!*	chemist/pharmacy	*apotik*

Facts for the Visitor

PLANNING
When to Go
The dry season, from June to October, is better for trekking and travel to remote areas. The wet season is considerably more humid, but quite OK for travelling; in some ways it's more pleasant than dry, dusty conditions, and the landscape is greener and more attractive. Many of the region's most interesting events occur at the start or the end of the wet season to accompany planting and harvest, such as the ancient horse-jousting festival of Pasola in Sumba.

Many of the roads are now sealed, so travel in the wet is not the arduous and often impossible task that it used to be, but wash-outs can occur and travel off the main roads can still be difficult.

The Muslim fast of Ramadan applies to Lombok and Sumbawa and it's not the best time to visit, particularly if you want to travel to traditional rural areas (see Public Holidays & Special Events later in this chapter for more information).

Maps
The best commercial maps to Indonesia are produced by Periplus publications. They can be bought overseas and in Indonesia, but can be hard to find east of Lombok. Their *Lombok and Sumbawa* map shows the topography well, although the roads aren't always accurate. It includes a good street map of Mataram. As yet, their series of maps does not cover the rest of the eastern islands in detail. *Indonesia III Lombok* published by Travel Treasure Maps (Knaus Publications, distributed in Indonesia by Periplus) is not super detailed, but has interesting notes and useful maps of the main tourist areas on the back.

The best available commercial map to the whole region is the Nelles *Java & Nusa Tenggara* map, but because Nusa Tenggara is included with Java, detail is severely lacking. Local tourist maps are available in some areas, but they usually have limited detail and are often unreliable.

For Nusa Tenggara Timur (Flores, Sumba and West Timor), the maps in this book are probably the best you'll find. Although many of the roads on these maps have been personally travelled, many more have not. When venturing off the main highways, always ask about the condition of the road. An increasing number of roads are sealed and in good condition, but many are unsealed and may only be just better than goat tracks. The quickest route between two points is often not the shortest.

Detailed maps of East Timor are classified and the only decent maps available were produced by the Portuguese before 1975.

What to Bring
Bring as little as possible. It is better to buy something you've left behind than to have to throw things away because you have too much to carry. You can buy almost anything you need in the main cities such as Mataram and Kupang, but not in the very remote areas.

Before deciding what to bring, decide what you're going to carry it in. The backpack is still the best single piece of luggage for the job. Make sure that it can be locked. A small day pack is also very useful. Whatever you bring, try and make it small; bemos are packed to the hilt with passengers and there's next to no space left over to stow baggage.

Temperatures are uniformly tropical year-round in Indonesia so short-sleeved shirts and T-shirts are the order of the day. Bring at least one long-sleeved shirt for the cool evenings. The mountain areas get chilly at night; in Bajawa and Ruteng in Flores and Soe in Timor temperatures drop to around 15°C (59°F). You don't need Antarctic survival gear, but long jeans, shoes and possibly a jacket are necessary. At very high altitudes, night temperatures can be as low as 5°C (41°F), but these will only be experienced if trekking on mountain peaks such as Rinjani on Lombok and Tambora on Sumbawa. Clothing is quite cheap in Indonesia and you can always buy more, though it can be hard to find clothes and shoes in sizes to fit western frames.

Modesty should prevail. If you must wear shorts, they should be the loose-fitting type which come down almost to the knees, but shorts are considered very low class in Indonesia and only for the beach. Higher dress standards apply particularly whenever you're visiting a government office; have something suitable for more formal occasions.

Dark-coloured clothes hide the dirt better, but are hotter. Artificial fibres like rayon and nylon are too hot and sticky in this climate; drip-dry cotton or silk are best. You need clothes which will dry fairly quickly in the humidity – thicker jeans are a problem in this regard, although you'll need some heavy clothing if you plan to travel by motorcycle.

A hat and sunglasses are essential, and don't forget sunscreen (UV) lotion. A water bottle is a good idea, but you can easily buy water in plastic bottles.

A sarong is an all-purpose marvel. Besides wearing it, a sarong can serve as an impromptu blanket during cold evenings; you can lie on it on a white-sand beach; wrap it round your head to counter the pounding sun; use it as a top sheet or, alternatively, as a barrier between yourself and an unhealthy-looking mattress in an unhealthy-looking hotel; pin it up over the window of your hotel room to block the outside lights that burn fiercely all night long; and even use it as a towel.

A sleeping bag is really only useful if you intend doing a lot of high-altitude camping. Toiletries like soap, shampoo, conditioner, toothpaste and toilet paper are all readily available in Indonesia. Dental floss and shaving cream are hard to find, however. Tampons can be found in major cities and tourist areas, such as in Java and Bali, but pads are all you are likely to find from Lombok to Timor so bring your own supplies.

The following is a checklist of other things you might consider packing, but don't feel obliged to bring everything on this list:

Address book, name cards, visa and passport photos, Swiss army knife, cup, padlock, camera and accessories, sunglasses, alarm clock, torch (flashlight) and batteries, comb, compass, nylon jacket, sweater, raincover for backpack, rainsuit or poncho, sewing kit, spoon, sunhat, sunscreen, toilet paper, tampons, nail clippers, tweezers, mosquito repellent, vitamins, Panadol (Tylenol), laxative, Lomotil, birth control (including condoms) and any special medications you use.

A final thought: airlines do lose bags from time to time and you have a much better chance of not losing your bag if it is tagged with your name and address *inside* as well as outside. Other tags can always fall off or be removed.

SUGGESTED ITINERARIES

It is easy to spend all of a 60 day tourist pass exploring the region in depth, but a good cross-section of highlights can be sampled in three weeks. Allow one week for each major island, or more if you want to travel off the beaten track.

The most common tour of the region takes in Lombok, Sumbawa, Komodo and Flores, which easily can be done in a month or less. Most visitors start in Bali, island hop all the way to Flores and then fly back from Maumere to Bali. Given the fickleness of domestic flights in Indonesia, if time is limited and you have to catch an international flight at the end of the journey, it is best to fly first to Maumere and travel overland back to Bali.

Sumba and Timor don't have the big attractions, such as Komodo dragons, the coloured lakes of Kelimutu or the beach resorts of Lombok, but they do have the most fascinating traditional cultures. Timor has good flight and ferry connections to the other islands and its highlights can be sampled in a week. Sumba can also be 'done' in a week, but allow two to three days getting to and from Sumba by ferry or by air as flights are subject to cancellation.

Lombok

The highlights of Lombok are the unspoilt villages in the centre of the island, the local handcrafts, beach areas like Senggigi and the Gili Islands, the superb trekking possibilities on Gunung Rinjani, and the more remote parts of the coast. You'll need at least five days to appreciate Lombok, plus another day or two if you're taking the slow ferry from Padangbai. The island is relatively small and has an extensive transport network. Self-drive cars and motorbikes are readily available for hire, making Lombok the easiest island to explore. It also has the best tourist facilities and more tourists than all the rest of the eastern islands put together.

Coming from Lembar harbour, spend your first night in Ampenan, Cakranegara or Senggigi, and make an early start for Senaru the next day if you want to climb Rinjani. Allow two, three or more days for trekking, and then head back to the beaches for relaxing. The Gili Islands are easily reached from Senaru. You can spend two days or two weeks on the Gilis, depending on your taste for island life. From the Gilis you can reach the villages of central Lombok in a single day, and you may even have time to look at the Art Market in Cakranegara and Narmada water palace on the way. It's worth spending two or three days in central Lombok, exploring the local markets and craft villages, and walking in the rice fields to forests and waterfalls. Tetebatu is the main base. If you want some more beach time, make your way to Kuta on the south coast. If you want to explore the back blocks or the less accessible parts of the coast, rent or charter your own transport for a few days; this is most easily done in Senggigi or Mataram.

Sumbawa

Sumbawa's main attractions are the south coast beaches. Huu, only a couple of hours from Bima, is primarily a destination for surfers, but the superb beach also attracts non-surfers and it has good budget to mid-range facilities. Maluk in the south-west also has surf and superb beaches, but facilities are limited and it's isolated. Three days or more

could be spent at each, but allow more travelling time to reach Maluk.

The main towns, Sumbawa Besar and Bima, have old sultan's palaces which are worth a look, but otherwise they are merely transit towns. Day trips can be made to craft and semi-traditional villages, but they are often difficult to reach.

Pulau Moyo has good beaches and snorkelling, but only one ultra-expensive hotel which can only be reached by boat charter. The southern tip of the island can be visited from Sumbawa Besar on a day trip or you can camp overnight. Gunung Tambora has good trekking, and the Tambora Peninsula has other points of interest, but there are no hotels and it is an excruciating bus journey to get there. Five days should be allowed for the climb to Gunung Tambora, including travelling time from Dompu.

The main highway running right across the island is serviced by air-con coaches, but travel off the highway is on slow and crowded local buses. Car and motorbike hire is possible, but difficult to arrange. Chartered taxis and bemos can be hired in Bima, but are relatively expensive.

If you have time and a spirit of adventure you can get right away from other tourists, but most travellers take the easy option and pass straight through Sumbawa in two days on the buses between Lombok and Sape, where ferries go to Komodo. Sumbawa Besar is the best place to break the long journey, being halfway between Sape and Lombok, though Huu, reached via Dompu, is by far the biggest tourist destination and some interesting day trips can be done from Bima.

Komodo & Rinca

Many visitors venture east from Lombok just to see the famed Komodo dragons, a big drawcard of the region. Komodo can be visited on day trips from Labuanbajo in western Flores or as an overnight stop on the ferry between Sumbawa and Flores. It only takes one day to see the dragons, but it is easy to spend two or more days on Komodo, which has walking, snorkelling and diving possibilities.

Rinca, Komodo's smaller sister island, is

not on the ferry route, but is easier to visit on a day trip from Komodo. A new, daily shuttle runs from Labuanbajo or cheaper charter boats also do the trip. Rinca has plenty of dragons, accommodation and fewer visitors.

Flores

The most visited main island outside Lombok, Flores has lush mountain scenery, a string of volcanoes, good beaches and traditional cultures. However, visitor numbers are still only a trickle compared to Lombok, facilities are limited and travel harder. The main roads are now sealed and travel has improved immeasurably, but the buses are still crowded and slow, and the roads forever winding. When planning an itinerary don't overestimate your endurance abilities. A full day's travel on the buses will leave you *setengah mati* (half dead), a common phrase used by Indonesian bus travellers. Shorter hops are quite tolerable.

Flores' most famous attraction is the coloured lakes of Kelimutu. They are spectacular, but many travellers, in their desire to knock over all the big attractions, catch buses straight through from Labuanbajo to Moni, the gateway village to Kelimutu. After 16 hours or more of gruelling bus travel, they are, not surprisingly, disappointed.

A more manageable itinerary is Labuanbajo (two or three days), Ruteng (one day), Bajawa (two days), Ende (one day), and then Moni and Kelimutu (two or three days). Labuanbajo is a good place to relax and take boat trips to Komodo and Rinca or other nearby islands with fine beaches and snorkelling. Bajawa has many interesting and accessible traditional villages to visit. Moni is a cool mountain village and another good spot to relax for a few days. Ruteng and Ende have a few attractions around town, but they are more difficult to reach. These two towns can be skipped if time is limited. From Bajawa a side trip can be made to the Seventeen Islands Marine Park off Riung.

From Kelimutu you can return to Ende for the ferry to Sumba or go right back across Flores by bus, but most prefer to head on to Maumere where there are regular flights to

Bali, via Bima, or to Kupang (Timor). Maumere also has some pleasant, low-key beach resorts nearby.

The eastern tip of Flores is less visited. Larantuka has ferries to Timor, but the main reason to venture this far is to visit the Solor and Alor archipelagos. The ferry trip past rugged, dry islands dominated by volcanoes is one of the finest in Indonesia. The main point of interest is the traditional whaling village of Lamakera on Solor island, but travel is hard in these parts. Ferries go from Larantuka right through to Alor and then on to Atapupu on Timor, but you need a week or more for this route.

Timor

Kupang is a major travel hub for the region and for flights to Australia. Kupang has a few decent beaches and points of interest around the town, or it is four hours on the ferry to Roti, an isolated but interesting island with a good beach at Nemberala.

The most interesting part of Timor is in the central mountains of West Timor. Although tourism is almost nonexistent, the area has many scenic spots and very traditional villages to explore. Soe is the best base, from where you can head north into the mountains around Fatumenasi or south-east to visit traditional markets and villages such as Boti. Other villages can be visited from Kefamenanu or an interesting side trip can be taken to Oecussi, a small, former Portuguese, enclave. Further east around Atambua and Betun, the traditional matriarchal villages of the Belu people can be visited. You'll need from three days to a week to sample the area.

East Timor has been open to tourists since 1989, but you'll be hard-pressed to meet any other travellers. For a taste of Portugal in the tropics, Dili is easily visited and makes a worthwhile two or three day trip from Atambua in West Timor or by plane from Kupang. Travel is possible right throughout East Timor, but it pays to know what is happening before venturing outside Dili (see Travelling in East Timor in the Timor chapter for more information). The cool hill town of Maubisse is a pleasant overnight trip from

Dili and from there you can head south to other hill towns and climb Gunung Tatamailau, the highest mountain in Timor. Baucau has fine Portuguese architecture and you can travel right through to Tutuala at the eastern tip in three days from Dili. Suai, on the south coast near the West Timor border, is one of the easiest areas to visit for a taste of East Timor.

Sumba

Sumba is one of the 'in' destinations of the region. Its isolation has left a fascinating megalithic culture largely intact, but it lies well off the main travel routes and tourist numbers are still very low. The island is neatly split into two regions: East and West Sumba.

West Sumba is the more traditional region and if you use Waikabubak as a base many interesting villages can be visited, some within the town itself. To the south lie some superb beaches with good surf, but accommodation is very limited and basic. To the west, Pero has one homestay that is a popular base for visiting villages in the area. The best way to see West Sumba is by motorbike, easily hired in Waikabubak, or buses and bemos run to the towns and main villages. Buses are crowded, but travel on the main highway is relatively quick. It is harder going off the highway.

Waingapu in East Sumba is the gateway to the island and from there a number of weaving villages can be visited. Sumba's famous ikat blankets are only produced in East Sumba, where villages are often very traditional, but have been open to outside influences longer.

After landing in Waingapu, visitors with limited time usually head straight across the island to Waikabubak. From Waikabubak, Sumbanese culture can be sampled in only a few days, but it pays to allow a week to explore the area more fully.

HIGHLIGHTS

See the earlier Suggested Itineraries section for an overview of each island; there's also a detailed highlights box at the start of each chapter.

Listed below are the main attractions of the whole region. My top ten list is just that – *my* top ten. Remember, it's highly personal, but useful nevertheless as a guide. Here goes (from west to east):

- Gili Islands (Lombok) – wonderful beaches, good snorkelling and diving, and cheap living.
- Senggigi (Lombok) – a developed, more expensive resort, but with the region's best tourist facilities and it's much more relaxed than Bali's big resorts.
- Gunung Rinjani (Lombok) – Indonesia's largest mountain outside Irian Jaya, with a stunning crater lake and smoking volcanic cone. The two to five day trek is one of Indonesia's best.
- Huu (Sumbawa) – surf city, but the wonderful beach is not just for surfers.
- Komodo – home to the Komodo dragons, huge monitor lizards like something from the age of the dinosaurs and one of Indonesia's natural marvels.
- Labuanbajo (Flores) – just a village, but the gateway to Komodo and nearby islands, fine beaches, snorkelling and diving.
- Bajawa (Flores) – ringed by volcanoes, this town is the base for visiting some of the region's most accessible and interesting traditional villages.
- Kelimutu (Flores) – these spectacularly coloured volcanic lakes have been famed since Dutch times.
- West Sumba – home to fascinating megalithic villages hardly touched by modernity, the Pasola festival in February and remote, beautiful beaches.
- Central West Timor – the scenic mountains around Soe have some of the region's most traditional villages, rarely visited by tourists. It's one of Indonesia's best kept secrets.

TOURIST OFFICES
Local Tourist Offices

Each provincial government has a tourist office called Departemen Pariwisata Daerah (DIPARDA), located in the capital or major cities. The tourist office in Mataram is the region's best, but only covers Nusa Tenggara Barat (Lombok and Sumbawa). In addition, every kabupaten (regency) has its own tourist office. The sign on the building is usually written only in Indonesian. Look for *dinas pariwisata* (tourist office).

The usefulness of the regional tourist offices varies greatly from place to place. Their budgets are limited and they often have little or no literature or maps. They will always try to help and can advise of any special events in the area, but English is not always spoken. They can be good contact points for guides or hiring transport, but local travel agents or hotels may be just as good. Some tourist offices are inconveniently located on the outskirts of town and simply not worth the effort of visiting.

For specific details about local offices, see the Information sections listed under the main cities and towns in the destination chapters.

Tourist Offices Abroad

Indonesian Tourist Promotion Offices (ITPO) abroad can supply brochures and information about Indonesia. Useful publications include the *Travel Planner*, *Tourist Map of Indonesia* and the *Calendar of Events* for the whole country. ITPO offices are listed below. Garuda Airlines offices overseas are also worth trying for information. The seven ITPO overseas offices are:

Australia
    (☎ (02) 9233 3630) Level 10, 5 Elizabeth St, Sydney, NSW 2000
Germany
    (☎ (069) 233677) Wiessenhuttenstrasse 17 D.6000, Frankfurt am Main 1
Japan
    (☎ (03) 3585 3588) 2nd Floor, Sankaido Building, 1-9-13 Akasaka, Minatoku, Tokyo 107
Singapore
    (☎ 534 2837) 10 Collyer Quay, Ocean Building, Singapore 0104
Taiwan
    (☎ (02) 537 7620) 5th Floor, 66 Sung Chiang Rd, Taipei
UK
    (☎ (0171) 493 0030) 3-4 Hanover St, London W1R 9HH
USA
    (☎ (213) 387 2078) 3457 Wilshire Blvd, Los Angeles, CA 90010

VISAS & DOCUMENTS
Passport

A valid passport is required to enter Indonesia. Check your expiry date. Indonesia requires that your passport is valid for six months from your date of arrival.

Visas

For many nationalities, a visa is not necessary for entry and you can stay in Indonesia visa-free for up to 60 days. These are: Argentina, Australia, Austria, Belgium, Brazil, Brunei Darussalam, Canada, Chile, Denmark, Egypt, Finland, France, Germany, Greece, Hungary, Iceland, Ireland, Italy, Japan, Kuwait, Liechtenstein, Luxembourg, Malaysia, Maldives, Malta, Mexico, Monaco, Morocco, Netherlands, New Zealand, Norway, Philippines, Saudi Arabia, Singapore, South Korea, Spain, Sweden, Switzerland, Taiwan, Thailand, Turkey, United Arab Emirates, UK, USA and Venezuela.

If you're from one of these countries, a 60 day tourist pass (which is a stamp in your passport) is issued on arrival, as long as you enter and exit through recognised entry ports (see the Recognised Entry/Exit Points list below). Officially (but not always in practice), you must have a ticket out of the country when you arrive and you may be asked to show sufficient funds for your stay. Officially (and almost certainly), you cannot extend your pass beyond 60 days. If you're intent on exploring Indonesia beyond 60 days, you will have to exit the country and re-enter.

For citizens of countries not on the visa-free list, a visitor visa can be obtained from any Indonesian embassy or consulate.

Recognised Entry/Exit Points The Indonesian government has a list of recognised 'no visa' entry and exit points.

Airport entry/exit points are:

Ambon	(Maluku)
Balikpapan	(Kalimantan)
Bandung	(Java)
Batam	(Sumatra)
Biak	(Irian Jaya)
Denpasar	(Bali)
Jakarta	(Java)
Kupang	(Timor)
Manado	(Sulawesi)
Mataram	(Lombok)
Medan	(Sumatra)
Padang	(Sumatra)
Pekanbaru	(Sumatra)
Pontianak	(Kalimantan)
Surabaya	(Java)

Seaports with 'no visa' entry and exit points are:

Ambon	(Maluku)
Batam	(Sumatra)
Belawan	(Sumatra)
Benoa	(Bali)
Dumai	(Sumatra)
Jakarta	(Java)
Manado	(Sulawesi)
Padangbai	(Bali)
Semarang	(Java)
Surabaya	(Java)
Tanjung Pinang	(Sumatra)

The only designated 'no visa' land crossing is at Entikong in West Kalimantan, between Pontianak and Kuching. The official list is rarely updated, but does change, so if you're planning an odd entry or exit, find out the latest story. Entering by air on a regular flight is usually not a problem, and the airline will often be better informed than an Indonesian embassy. Entering or leaving Indonesia overland or by unusual sea routes usually requires a visa.

If you plan to arrive or depart through an unrecognised 'gateway' eg entering Jayapura from Papua New Guinea then you have to get an Indonesian visitor visa (as opposed to a tourist pass) before you cross. A visitor visa is also required to *leave* Indonesia via a non-designated port, even if you used a designated port to enter.

Visitor visas are only valid for one month, not 60 days as for visa-free entry, and can only be extended for two weeks. Indonesian embassies are usually not keen to issue visitor visas.

Visa Extensions Tourist passes cannot be extended beyond 60 days. You may get a few extra days in special circumstances, like missed flight connections or illness, but don't count on it. Whatever you do, do not simply show up at the airport with an expired visa or tourist pass and expect to be able to board your flight. You may be sent back to the local immigration office to clear up the matter.

Overstaying attracts very steep fines, up to 500,000 rp per day, or a stint in jail if you can't pay.

If you arrived in Indonesia on a one month visitor visa, it is usually extendable only for two weeks. An extension costs around 50,000 rp, and can be obtained through any immigration office.

Onward Ticket The best answer to the 'ticket out' requirement is to buy a return ticket to Indonesia, or include Indonesia as a leg on a through ticket. The main problem is for people with open-ended travel plans, for whom an onward ticket may not be an attractive option. Medan-Penang and Singapore-Jakarta tickets are cheap, popular options for satisfying the requirement.

However, the 'ticket out' requirement is not always strictly enforced, and evidence of sufficient funds is sometimes acceptable in lieu. US$1000 is the magic number. If you fly to Kupang (in Timor) from Darwin, or take the ferry to Batam (in Sumatra's Riau Archipelago) from Singapore, it's unlikely that any great fuss will be made. Entry into Kupang can be problematic, and Kupang immigration have a reputation as the most corrupt in Indonesia. Not only may they ask to see your money, but insist that you hand some of it over. Show them your travellers cheques, but not cash.

Expect to flash your cash if arriving in Medan (Sumatra) on the ferry from Penang (Malaysia). In Bali they may still ask to see a ticket, but most Bali visitors are on short-stay package trips, so you're unlikely to be troubled. Jakarta can be a hassle. Some visitors have been forced to buy an onward ticket on the spot.

The main problem is likely to be with airlines overseas, who may strictly enforce official requirements and not let you on flights to Indonesia without an onward ticket.

Study & Work Visas Temporary-stay visas for work or study purposes can be arranged if you have a sponsor, such as an educational institution or employer, in Indonesia. They are valid up to one year.

Work visas are an almighty hassle to get and should be arranged by your employer.

The 60 day tourist pass supposedly also covers business travel where the holder is not employed in Indonesia. However, if you arrive without a visa and put 'business' as a reason for travel on your embarkation card you may run into trouble.

Visits for conventions or exhibitions are not a problem, but business visits usually require a visa.

Travel Insurance
A travel insurance policy to cover theft, loss and medical problems is a wise idea. There are a wide variety of policies and your travel agent will have recommendations. Some policies offer lower and higher medical expenses options, and a mid-range one is usually recommended for Asia where high medical costs are not so high. Check the small print:

- Some policies specifically exclude 'dangerous activities' which can include scuba diving, and even trekking and motorcycling (no doubt because of the legendary accident rate of tourists in Bali). A motorcycle licence acquired in Bali may not be valid under your policy. If such activities are on your agenda you don't want that sort of policy.
- You may prefer a policy which pays doctors or hospitals direct, rather than you having to pay on the spot and claim later. If you have to claim later make sure you keep all documentation. Some policies ask you to call back (reverse charges) to a centre in your home country where an immediate assessment of your problem is made.
- Check whether the policy covers ambulances or an emergency flight home. If you have to stretch out you will need two seats and somebody has to pay for them!

Other Documents
Keep a separate record of your passport number, issue date, and a photocopy of your old passport or birth certificate. While you're compiling that info add the serial numbers of your travellers cheques, details of health insurance and US$200 or so as emergency cash and keep all that material totally separately from your passport, cheques and other cash.

If you plan to drive in Indonesia you'll need

to get an International Driving Permit from your local automobile association. It is often not required to rent a vehicle, but police may request it if they stop you.

A Hostelling International (HI) card is of very limited use in Indonesia; no hostels in the eastern islands recognise it.

The International Student Identity Card (ISIC) can be useful, such as for getting a discount on domestic flights, however, maximum age limits (usually 26) often apply.

Remember that a student is a very respectable thing to be, and if your passport has a blank space for occupation you are much better off having 'student' printed there than something nasty like 'journalist' or 'photographer'. The same applies to the embarkation card you fill out when you enter the country.

EMBASSIES
Indonesian Embassies
Indonesian embassies abroad include:

Australia
    Embassy: (☎ (02) 6250 8600) 8 Darwin Ave, Yarralumla, ACT 2600
    Consulates: Adelaide, Darwin, Melbourne, Perth and Sydney
Cambodia
    (☎ (23) 216148) 179, 51 St, Phnom Penh
Canada
    Embassy: (☎ (613) 724 1100) 55 Parkdale Ave, Ottawa, Ontario K1Y 1E5
    Consulates: Vancouver and Toronto
France
    Embassy: (☎ 01 45 03 07 60) 47-49 Rue Cortambert, Paris
    Consulate: Marseilles
Germany
    Embassies: (☎ (228) 382990) 2 Bernkasteler Strasse, Bonn
    Consulates: Berlin, Bremen, Dusseldorf, Hamburg, Hannover, Kiel, Munich and Stuttgart
India
    (☎ 611 8642) 50-A Chanakyapuri, New Delhi
Malaysia
    Embassy: (☎ (03) 242 1151) 233 Jalan Tun Razak, Kuala Lumpur
    Consulates: Kota Kinabalu, Kuching, Penang, and Tawau
Netherlands
    (☎ (070) 310 8100) 8 Tobias Asserlaan, KC Den Haag

New Zealand
  (☎ (04) 475 8697) 70 Glen Rd, Kelburn, Wellington
Papua New Guinea
  (☎ 325 3116) 1 & 2/410, Kiroki St, Sir John Guise Drive, Waigani, Port Moresby
Singapore
  (☎ 737 7422) 7 Chatsworth Rd
Thailand
  (☎ 252 3135) 600-602 Phetburi Rd, Bangkok
UK
  (☎ (0171) 499 7661) 38 Grosvenor Square, London W1X 9AD
USA
  Embassy: (☎ (202) 775 5200) 2020 Massachussetts Ave NW, Washington DC
  Consulates: Chicago, Honolulu, Houston, Los Angeles, New York and San Francisco

Foreign Embassies in Indonesia

Countries that have diplomatic relations with Indonesia have their embassies in Jakarta, the national capital. Australia, Denmark, France, Finland, Germany, Italy, Japan, Netherlands, Norway, Sweden, Switzerland and the USA all have consulates in Bali, but they perform more limited functions. The eastern islands from Lombok to Timor have no consulates.

Embassies in Jakarta (area code ☎ 021) include:

Australia
  (☎ 522 7111) Jalan Rasuna Said, Kav 15-16
Cambodia
  (☎ 548 3716) 4th floor, Panin Bank Plaza, Jalan 52, Palmer Utara
Canada
  (☎ 525 0709) 5th Floor, Wisma Metropolitan I, Jalan Jenderal Sudirman, Kav 29
France
  (☎ 314 2807) Jalan Thamrin 20
Germany
  (☎ 384 9547) Jalan Raden Saleh 54-56
India
  (☎ 520 4150) Jalan Rasuna Said, Kav S-1, Kuningan
Malaysia
  (☎ 522 4947) Jalan Rasuna Said, Kav X/6 No 1
Netherlands
  (☎ 525 1515) Jalan Rasuna Said, S-3, Kuningan
New Zealand
  (☎ 330680) Jalan Diponegoro 41
Papua New Guinea
  (☎ 725 1218) 6th floor, Panin Bank Centre, Jalan Jenderal Sudirman No 1

Singapore
  (☎ 520 1489) Jalan Rasuna Said, Block X, Kav 2 No 4
Thailand
  (☎ 390 4055) Jalan Imam Bonjol 74
UK
  (☎ 330904) Jalan Thamrin 75
USA
  (☎ 360360) Jalan Merdeka Selatan 5

CUSTOMS

Customs allow you to bring in a maximum of 2L of alcoholic beverages, 200 cigarettes or 50 cigars or 100g of tobacco, and a 'reasonable' amount of perfume per adult.

In addition to the usual restricted items such as drugs and arms, it is also prohibited to bring TV sets, radio receivers, pornography, fresh fruit, printed matter in Chinese characters and Chinese medicines into the country. The rules state that 'film, pre-recorded video tape, video laser disc, records, computer software must be screened by the Censor Board', presumably to control pornography.

Photographic equipment, computers, typewriters and tape recorders should be declared to customs on entry and taken out on departure. Customs officials rarely worry about how much gear tourists bring into the country – at least if you have a western face. Personal effects are not a problem. There is no restriction on the import or export of foreign currency, but import or export of rupiah is limited to 50,000 rp.

MONEY
Costs

With the fall in the rupiah, Indonesia is cheaper than ever. It remains to be seen where rising prices and the value of the rupiah will stabilise, but you can be certain that Indonesia will be a cheap destination.

In the eastern islands, rock-bottom budget travel works out to around US$10 to 15 per day. Count on more like US$50 a day if you need such luxuries as air-conditioning, but even if you want a luxury hotel or a meal at a flash restaurant you'll be hard pressed to spend your money outside Lombok. Lombok has range of luxury hotels and tourist services, but elsewhere it is very low key.

Warning on Prices

After the run on the Indonesian currency in 1997/98, prices are constantly rising. However, the rupiah's devaluation against the US dollar means that travel is very cheap if you have foreign currency.

This book was researched when the rupiah's plunge began and you can expect prices quoted in rupiah to have risen, substantially in some cases. Inflation is currently running at 40% and hyperinflation may result unless the economy stabilises soon.

Use prices for hotels, transport, food etc quoted in this book as a guide. Within a few days of arrival in Indonesia, you should be able to gauge how much prices have risen. If you find hotels have risen 30% higher than the prices quoted here, then you can expect similar rises across the region. If bus prices have risen 50%, then use that as a guide to working out what the correct fare should be. The same applies to all goods and services.

Price rises in Indonesia have not been consistent with the fall of the rupiah against the US dollar. In the main tourist areas, such as Bali and parts of Lombok, US dollars have always been quoted for upper range hotels and services, but the quoting of prices in US dollars in the tourist industry is now more common. Although the prices may be quoted in US dollars, you pay with rupiah. The exchange rate used by hotels may be extremely disadvantageous. However, most prices quoted in US dollars have always been subject to discounts and you can now expect even greater discounts. Outside Lombok, the other islands covered in this book are not major tourist areas. Most hotels, restaurants and transport services rely more on local business than tourism, and US dollar prices have much less relevance. ■

Transport is cheap, even if you include a couple of airfares, but distances are longer so costs are slightly more than travel in Java or Bali. Car hire is cheap in Lombok at around US$20 a day for a self-drive car, but elsewhere you will pay around US$40 or more for a car and driver, if you can find one.

Carrying Money

Preferably your money should be in relatively safe travellers cheques issued by a major bank. Also bring at least a few hundred US dollars in cash as there are a handful of towns where banks do not accept travellers cheques.

US dollars are the most widely accepted foreign currency. If you intend travelling extensively around Indonesia then bring US dollars either in cash or travellers cheques from a major company such as American Express (the most widely accepted), Citicorp or Bank of America or you'll be sorry. In the main tourist areas of Lombok and the provincial capitals such as Kupang, it is also easy to change Australian dollars and major European currencies such as German marks, Netherlands guilders, pounds sterling, and French or Swiss francs. Slightly more obscure currencies such as Canadian dollars

can be difficult to change outside of the main tourist areas. The Bank BNI now has many branches throughout Nusa Tenggara and will accept most major currencies, but rates are better for US dollars and you'll find yourself in some towns where only US dollars can be changed.

Credit Cards & ATMs

Credit cards are not widely accepted in Nusa Tenggara, but bring your cards anyway. Luxury hotels and a few tourist shops on Lombok accept them, but elsewhere they are of limited use. You can use them to buy airline tickets in the main provincial cities of Mataram, Kupang and Dili, but not in the smaller towns.

Cash advances can be obtained over the counter from major banks in Mataram and Kupang, but in between it is difficult. A few banks in these two main cities also have ATMs that accept Visa and MasterCard, but this facility is still very limited. Bank Danamon has branches in many provincial towns and some, but not all, of their branches give cash advances over the counter on Visa and MasterCard.

Unlike Java and Bali where numerous banks now give cash advances and have

ATMs that accept credit cards, high-tech banking hasn't really hit the eastern islands. Bring a credit card for backup, but don't rely on it as the main way to carry money. Bring travellers cheques.

Giro
Dutch travellers with a Dutch post office account can conveniently obtain cash from Indonesian post offices. These girobetaalkaarten are useful in the many Indonesian towns where there is no bank.

Currency
The unit of currency in Indonesia is the rupiah (rp). Coins of 25, 50, 100 and 500 rp are in circulation, both the old silver coloured coins and the new bronze coloured coins. The 25 rp coin has almost vanished. Notes come in 100, 500, 1000, 5000, 10,000, 20,000 and 50,000 rp denominations.

There is no restriction on the import or export of foreign currencies in cash, travellers cheques or any other form, but you're not allowed to take in or take out more than 50,000 rp.

For many years the Indonesian rupiah was a relatively stable currency based primarily on the US dollar, and traded at around 2000 to 2400 rp to the dollar. Then in late 1997 the currency crises of Thailand and then Malaysia spilled over into Indonesia. The central bank was unable to defend the rupiah and abandoned the currency to the market. Within weeks the rupiah plunged to over 10,000 rp to the US dollar. The currency continues to fluctuate wildly based on the latest political developments or International Monetary Fund (IMF) pronouncements. At 10,000 rp to the US dollar, the rupiah is probably undervalued and your foreign currency will go a long way, despite rampant inflation.

Exchange Rates

Australia	A$1	=	9643 rp
Canada	C$1	=	10,536 rp
France	FF1	=	2581 rp
Germany	DM1	=	8650 rp
Japan	¥100	=	11,291 rp
Malaysia	M$1	=	3926 rp
Netherlands	G1	=	7674 rp
New Zealand	NZ$1	=	8203 rp
Singapore	S$1	=	9311 rp
UK	UK£1	=	26,420 rp
USA	US$1	=	15,800 rp

The rupiah has a floating rate, and in recent years it has tended to fall by about 4% a year against the US dollar.

Changing Money
As you travel eastwards, banks are few and far between, and the exchange rate falls below that in Bali or Java. The best rates are in Mataram, Kupang and the tourist areas of Lombok, which are as good as you'll find anywhere. Elsewhere, expect rates of five to 10% less. Undoubtedly the safest currency to bring is US dollars; travellers cheques should be from the larger companies (such as Amex, Thomas Cook or Bank of America).

Bank Rakyat Indonesia has branches in the main towns and traditionally provided atrocious rates and very limited exchange facilities, but competition has forced it to improve. Bank BNI has now opened many branches in the main towns, and it provides better service and cashes most major currencies at reasonable rates, though US dollars still have the edge. Bank Danamon is starting to open branches and promises to provide cash advances on credit cards in the future, but bring travellers cheques or cash.

If venturing away from the major towns, it pays to change larger amounts to tide you over. Banks are usually open Monday to Friday from 8 am to 4 pm, and some are open until noon on Saturday, but for foreign currency transactions they may close at 1 pm. Do your banking in the morning.

Tipping & Bargaining
Tipping is not a normal practice in Indonesia, but is often expected for special service. Someone who carries your bag, guides you around a tourist attraction etc will naturally expect a tip. The tip varies depending on the level of service, but is rarely more than a couple of thousand rupiah.

Many everyday purchases in Indonesia require bargaining. This applies particularly to handcrafts, clothes and artwork, but can also apply to almost anything you buy in a shop. Restaurant meals, transport and accommodation are generally fixed in price; restaurants usually have their menus and prices posted up on the wall and hotels usually have a price list. Sometimes when room supply exceeds tourist demand hotels may be willing to bend their prices rather than see you go next door. Although transport prices are fixed, bemos throughout Indonesia have a well earned reputation for charging westerners more, particularly in the main tourist areas.

Your first step should be to establish a starting price. It's usually easiest to ask them their price rather than make an initial offer, unless you know very clearly what you're willing to pay. As a rule of thumb your starting price could be anything from a third to two-thirds of the asking price, assuming that the asking price is not completely crazy. Then with offer and counter-offer you move closer to an acceptable price. Don't show too much interest when bargaining, and if you can't get an acceptable price walk away. You will often be called back and offered a lower price.

A few rules apply to good bargaining:

- First of all it's not a question of life or death, where every rupiah you chisel away makes a difference. Don't pass up something you really want that's expensive or unobtainable at home because the seller won't come down a few hundred rupiah – it is nothing compared with the hundreds of dollars you spent on the airfare!
- Secondly, when your offer is accepted you have to buy – don't then decide that you don't want it after all.
- Thirdly, while bargaining may seem to have a competitive element in it, it's a mean victory knocking a poor becak driver down from 1000rp to 800 rp for a ride.

Bargaining is sometimes fun and often not. A lot depends on whether you and the vendor are smiling or yelling at each other. Sometimes it seems as if people don't want your money if they can't overcharge you. Sometimes they will ask ludicrous prices and get very upset if you offer a ridiculously low price back, even if you mean it as a joke. This also works in the other direction; there is a nauseating type of tourist on the Asian trail who will launch into a lengthy whinge session about being overcharged five cents for an orange.

Ask Indonesian friends or hotel staff for information about correct prices. If you do not know the right price for transport, you might try asking another passenger what the regular price *(harga biasa)* is. Then you can offer the correct fare. There's not much point doing this when you're buying something in a shop or at a market as the onlookers will naturally side with their own people.

Don't get hassled by bargaining and don't go around feeling that you're being ripped off all the time – too many people do. It is too easy to become obsessed with always getting the 'local' price. Even locals don't always get the local price, and Indonesian visitors to Bali will get overcharged on the bemos just like westerners.

In Indonesia, if you are wealthy it is expected that you pay more, and *all* westerners are rich when compared with the grinding poverty of most Indonesians. Above all, keep things in perspective. The 500 rp you may overpay for a becak ride wouldn't buy a newspaper at home, but it is a meal for a poor becak driver.

POST & COMMUNICATIONS

The postal service is fairly reliable, but slow. Letters and small packets bound for overseas or domestic delivery may be registered *(tercatat)* for an extra fee at any post office branch. There are also two forms of express service available for mail within Indonesia: *kilat* for regular air mail and *kilat khusus* for air mail express.

Overseas parcels can be posted, insured and registered from a main post office, but staff may want to look at the contents first so there's not much point sealing it up before you get there.

If you're heading to Singapore you'll find

Telephone Codes

Telephone codes are usually quite logical, even if the sporadic changes to telephone numbers and codes are not. The area code for the main town of a district will usually cover all the surrounding towns (not that you are likely to find many telephones outside the main towns).

On Lombok, ☎ 0370 covers Mataram, west and south Lombok, while ☎ 0376 covers the east. For Sumbawa, ☎ 0371 covers the west of the island except for the south-west around Taliwang, which is ☎ 0372. The centre of the island around Dompu is ☎ 0373 and the east is ☎ 0374. Sumba is easy – ☎ 0387 for the whole island. Flores and Timor are more complicated, but telephones are rare outside the main towns (see the full list below).

Atambua (Timor)	☎ 0389	Labuanbajo (Flores)	☎ 0385
		Larantuka (Flores)	☎ 0383
Bajawa (Flores)	☎ 0384		
Bima (Sumbawa)	☎ 0374	Mataram (Lombok)	☎ 0370
		Maumere (Flores)	☎ 0382
Camplong (Timor)	☎ 0380		
		Pantemakassar	
Denpasar (Bali)	☎ 0361	(Timor)	☎ 0378
Dili (Timor)	☎ 0390		
Dompu (Sumbawa)	☎ 0373	Ruteng (Flores)	☎ 0385
Ende (Flores)	☎ 0381	Sembalun (Lombok)	☎ 0376
		Senggigi (Lombok)	☎ 0370
Gili Islands (Lombok)	☎ 0370	Soe (Timor)	☎ 0388
		Sumbawa Besar	
Jakarta (Java)	☎ 021	(Sumbawa)	☎ 0371
Kalabahi (Alor)	☎ 0397	Taliwang (Sumbawa)	☎ 0372
Kefamenanu (Timor)	☎ 0388	Tetebatu (Lombok)	☎ 0376
Kupang (Timor)	☎ 0380		
Kuta (Bali)	☎ 0361	Waikabubak (Sumba)	☎ 0387
Kuta (Lombok)	☎ 0370	Waingapu (Sumba)	☎ 0387

it considerably cheaper to post packages and parcels from there.

Post office hours vary. In small towns they may be open only standard office hours, but often they have extended hours for basic postal services until 6 or 8 pm during the week, and on Saturdays and Sundays from 8 am to noon or later. Go during normal business hours for poste restante. *Warpostels* and *warparpostels* are private post and telephone agencies that are open extended hours and provide an efficient postal service for slightly higher rates.

Receiving Mail

The postal service in Indonesia is generally pretty good, and the poste restante services at Indonesian post offices *(kantor pos)* are reasonably efficient. Expected mail always

seems to arrive eventually. In Nusa Tenggara you are better off having mail sent to the main centres such as Mataram and Kupang. Have your letters addressed to you with your surname in capitals and underlined, the poste restante, Kantor Pos, and city in question. 'Lost' letters may have been misfiled under Christian names so always check under both your names.

Telephone

Telkom, the government-run telecommunications company, has offices *(kantor Telkom)* in most cities and towns. They are invariably open 24 hours and often offer fax services as well as telephone and telex. These are the cheapest places to make international and long-distance *(inter-lokal)* phone calls, and the place to make collect calls.

Telecommunications agencies, both Telkom and those privately run, are called *wartel*, *warpostal* or *warparpostel* and offer much the same services. They may be marginally more expensive, but are often more convenient. They are usually open from around 7 am until midnight, but sometimes 24 hours. As a rule, wartels don't offer a collect-call service, or in the rare cases that they do, a first minute charge may apply.

Rates are rising in Indonesia with the fall of the rupiah, but are still cheap. The premium rates are current from 9 am to 3 pm Monday to Saturday, while after 6 pm calls cost 50% less and after 11 pm calls are only 25% of the normal rate. Sundays from 6 am to 11 pm are 50% off, and from 11 pm to 6 am rates are 25% of the normal rate.

Public Phones Public coin phones are blue and take 50 rp and 100 rp coins. When the phone begins to beep, feed in more coins or you'll be cut off. Card telephones *(telepon kartu)* are also common. You can buy Telkom telephone cards *(kartu telepon)* with a face value of 60, 100, 140, 280, 400 or 680 units. They are sold at Telkom offices, as well as in many wartels, bookshops and moneychangers.

International calls rarely can be made from public phones, either coin or card, though some card phones at big hotels and outside Telkom offices have this facility.

There are also some Home Country Direct phones, where one button gets you through to your home country operator and you reverse the charges. These telephones are found at some Telkom offices, airports, luxury hotels etc.

International Calls For International Direct Dialling (IDD), dial ☎ 001 or 008, then the country code, area code (minus the initial zero if it has one) and then the number you want to reach. Two companies provide international connections: ☎ 001 is for Indosat and ☎ 008 is for Satelindo. Public phones rarely support this facility and you'll have to go to a Telkom office or wartel. Many of the more expensive hotels allow IDD calls, but add a hefty surcharge.

Collect international calls can be made through the operator, from Telkom offices, or from Home Country Direct phones (see Public Phones in this section). The Home Country Direct facility also can be used from any private phone where exchanges support the service by dialling ☎ 00 801 and then the country code (but this varies depending on the number of telephone suppliers in the home country).

Useful Numbers Some useful numbers include:

Directory assistance, local	☎ 108
Directory assistance, long-distance	☎ 106
Directory assistance, international	☎ 102
Operator assisted domestic calls	☎ 100
Operator assisted international calls	☎ 101
Police	☎ 110
Fire Brigade	☎ 113
Ambulance	☎ 118
International Direct Dial	☎ 001 or 008
	+ country code
Indonesia country code	☎ 62

Fax, Telegraph & Email
You can send messages by fax and telegraph from Telkom offices and wartels in most cities and towns. Upper end hotels also have fax facilities.

Email facilities are few and far between in Nusa Tenggara. Upper end hotels in the towns of Mataram (Lombok) and Kupang and Dili (Timor) are your best bet.

BOOKS
Very few books cover the Indonesian islands from Lombok to Timor. Most are specialised ethnographic works, and perhaps the largest body of literature covering the region dates from colonial times and is in Dutch. A number of titles cover East Timor after the Indonesian takeover, but little is available on East Timorese cultures and for anything on the history of East Timor before 1975, you'll have to venture to Lisbon.

Most books are published in different

editions by different publishers in different countries. As a result, a book might be a hardcover rarity in one country while it's readily available in paperback in another. The following are some of the more accessible books, but many are available only in academic libraries – don't expect to find them in your local bookshop.

Lonely Planet

Lonely Planet's *Indonesia* guide covers all Indonesia, and Lombok is also covered in *Bali & Lombok*. Lonely Planet also produces the *Indonesia phrasebook* and the *Indonesian audio pack*. Nusa Tenggara is also covered in the *Diving & Snorkeling Guide to Bali and The Komodo Region* in Lonely Planet's Pisces series.

Guidebooks

Periplus Editions produces a number of beautifully illustrated, detailed books about Indonesia, including a regional guide called *East of Bali: Lombok to Timor*. *Diving Indonesia* and *Surfing Indonesia* cover the best dive spots and waves in Nusa Tenggara, as well as the rest of Indonesia.

Indo Surf & Lingo by Peter Neely is an informative booklet for finding good waves on Bali and the rest of Indonesia. Buy it in Kuta surf shops in Bali or order from the publisher at PO Box 950 Noosa Heads 4567, Queensland, Australia (fax 074 475937).

Paul Ryan's *Timor: A Travellers Guide* is an inspiring travel guide and essential reading for exploring Timor in depth. It is packed with relevant travel detail and explanations of Timorese culture. It is a little dated and hard to find on Timor, but might be available in Darwin, Australia.

Travel

If you think travel through the outer islands of Indonesia is time-consuming now, then read Helen & Frank Schreider's *Drums of Tonkin* (published 1965), in which they overcame the lack of transport by island hopping all the way from Java to Timor in a tiny amphibious jeep, defying landslides, oncoming monsoons, hostile (or just over-enthused?)

indigenous inhabitants and the strange propensity Jakarta soldiers once had to shoot at vehicles making illegal turns.

While the Schreiders took only their pet dog with them, zoologist-cum-TV personality David Attenborough left the UK with practically nothing and returned from the archipelago with an orang-utan, a couple of pythons, civets, parrots and assorted other birds and reptiles. The whole saga of the enterprise, eventually to be dignified by the title 'expedition', is recounted in his book *Zoo Quest for a Dragon*, published in 1957.

The Malay Archipelago by Alfred Russel Wallace is an 1869 classic of this famous naturalist's wanderings throughout the Indonesian islands.

General

Books that provide an overall view of the region are very rare. The only one that comes close is *The Ecology of Nusa Tenggara and Maluku* by Kathryn A Monk, Yance de Fretes and Gayatri Reksodiharjo-Lilley. This almost 1000 page volume is part of an ecology series on Indonesia, and though it is primarily concerned with the region's ecosystems, biodiversity and land use, it has interesting sections on the peoples of the region.

Two good illustrated books on Indonesian wildlife are *The Wildlife of Indonesia* by Kathy MacKinnon and *Wild Indonesia* by Tony & Jane Whitten.

There are no books that cover the specific history of the region, but for an overall look at Indonesian history with passing reference to the eastern islands, *A History of Modern Indonesia* by MC Ricklefs is the best. It covers Indonesian history from the rise of Islam around 1300 to the present.

Ethnic Groups of Insular Southeast Asia, Volume 1, edited and compiled by Frank LeBar, is an amazing collection of summaries on numerous South-East Asian ethnic groups, including some 50 pages on the peoples of the eastern islands, from the Sasak to the Tetum. Slightly dated, it is still a very impressive reference.

Kinship and Religion in Eastern Indonesia

by David Hicks is a study of political, social and religious structures in the region with reference to the Tetum and other groups on East Timor, and the Manggarai in Flores.

The Flow of Life: Essays on Eastern Indonesia edited by James J Fox is an interesting collection of ethnographic articles on the Manggarai of Flores, Makassai of East Timor, the Sumbanese, Sabunese and others.

Lombok *Lombok: Conquest, Colonization & Underdevelopment, 1870-1940* by Alfons van der Kraan is a history of the colonial period. *The Spell of the Ancestors and the Power of Mekkah: A Sasak Community on Lombok* by Sven Cederroth is the best study of Sasak society.

Sumbawa *Islam and Identity in Eastern Indonesia* by Michael Hitchcock is a detailed study of Bimanese courts and culture, one of the few ethnographic works about Sumbawa. *Bima en Sumbawa* by J Noorduyn is the most detailed study of Sumbawa's history, but is only available in Dutch.

Flores *Gift of the Cotton Maiden: Textiles of Flores and the Solor Islands* edited by Roy W Hamilton is a coffee table format book with numerous colour photos of Flores ikat styles and interesting historical photos. Not only a good source on weaving, it is also a good introduction to the history and cultures of Flores.

Kedang: a Study of the Collective Thought of an Indonesian People by Robert H Barnes is a study of the Kedang people who inhabit the far eastern tip of Pulau Solor.

Sumba *Sumba: a Unique Culture* by John Carrier & Tracey Kissoon is a good introduction to Sumbanese culture, available in art shops in Waikabubak (Sumba).

Rindi: An Ethnographic Study of a Traditional Domain In Eastern Indonesia by Gregory L Forth is a weighty, classic study based on the author's extensive research in East Sumba.

Sumba and the Slave Trade by Rodney Needham (the Centre of South-East Asian Studies, Monash University, Melbourne) is a fascinating insight into the slave trade on Sumba and involvement of the Makassarese, Endenese and Dutch.

Timor *The Political System of the Atoni of Timor* by HG Schult Nordholt is a detailed study of the Atoni (Dawan) of West Timor. *Traditional Textiles of West Timor: Regional Variations in Historical Perspective* by Mark Ivan Jacobson & Ruth Marie Yeager is primarily concerned with Timorese textiles, but is also an excellent reference on West Timorese kingdoms and culture.

Probably the best account of events surrounding the Indonesian invasion of East Timor is John Dunn's *Timor: A People Betrayed*. Dunn was the Australian consul in East Timor from 1962 to 1964; he was also part of an Australian government fact-finding mission to East Timor from June to July 1974, and returned in 1975, just after the Fretilin-UDT war. *Timor, The Stillborn Nation*, by Bill Nicol, tends to criticise Fretilin's leaders and places much more blame on the Portuguese. For the inside story from the Fretilin point of view, read *Funu: The Unfinished Saga of East Timor*, by Jose Ramos-Horta.

Bookshops
Lombok has the best bookshops in the region, but it's hard to pick up new books in English. Stock up on books in Bali or Jakarta.

In Lombok, there are a couple of bookshops on Jalan Pabean in Ampenan and others in Cakranegara. Senggigi has a small selection at the supermarket and a second-hand bookshop stocks titles in French, German, Dutch etc. The best bookshop for titles in English is at the Sheraton Hotel in Senggigi and most other luxury hotels also have a small selection. A few of the popular *losmen* (small hotels) have selections of second-hand paperbacks.

Kupang has a few general bookshops on Jalan Ahmad Yani, but titles in English are very limited. Elsewhere you'll have to swap books with other travellers.

NEWSPAPERS & MAGAZINES

The news media is expected to (and does) practise self-censorship. 'Politeness' is the key word, and in typically indirect Indonesian style, stories of corruption, wastage of funds and government ineptitude are frequently run, but care is always taken not to point the finger too closely.

Whenever you buy newspapers and magazines in Indonesia, take a close look at the publication date. It is not uncommon for vendors to try to sell papers from two or three weeks ago.

Local

The English-language press is limited mostly to the *Jakarta Post* which is published daily and available around the country, although difficult to get outside Jakarta and the major tourist areas. It is available in Lombok and Kupang, but not elsewhere. While subject to the same 'self-censorship' as other Indonesian publications, it manages to tell you quite a lot about Indonesia and the rest of the world in a roundabout way.

The other main English-language newspaper is the *Indonesian Observer*, but its coverage and independence are a long way behind that of the *Jakarta Post*.

Of course, Indonesian-language newspapers are on sale throughout the country. Two of the leading newspapers are the Jakarta daily *Sinar Harapan* and the Catholic newspaper *Kompas*. *Suara Karya* is the mouthpiece of Golkar, the government political party.

Foreign

The *International Herald-Tribune*, *Asian Wall Street Journal* and major Asian dailies are sold in Indonesia. Western magazines like *Time*, *Newsweek*, *The Economist* and the excellent Hong Kong-published *Far Eastern Economic Review* are available in Indonesia. They are available from newsstands in luxury hotels, eg in Lombok.

For information on what's happening in Indonesia today (including Indonesian politics, history and culture) take out a subscription to *Inside Indonesia*, published in Australia at PO Box 190, Northcote, Vic 3070, Australia. Excellent articles cover everything from power plays within the army, to the environment, and it discusses issues not raised in the Indonesian media and rarely covered overseas.

RADIO & TV

The national radio station, Radio Republik Indonesia (RRI), broadcasts 24 hours a day in Bahasa Indonesia from every provincial capital. Indonesia also has plenty of privately run stations.

Thanks to satellite broadcasting, TV can be received everywhere in Indonesia. You'll see plenty of satellite dish antennas around the country, aimed almost straight up, as broadcast satellites are put in geostationary orbit so they travel around the equator at the same speed as the earth. You'll also see plenty of Indonesians in geostationary orbit around the TV set in many hotels as they are among the world's foremost TV addicts.

Televisi Republik Indonesia (TVRI) is the government-owned Indonesian-language TV station, which is broadcast in every province. It broadcasts on two channels, but the second channel is not available in the more remote areas. Some English-language programs are transmitted with Indonesian subtitles. Televisi Pendidikan Indonesia (TPI) is a government-owned educational station.

Private stations include Rajawali Citra Televisi Indonesia (RCTI), Andalas Televisi (AN-TV), Indosair and Surya Citra Televisi (SCTV).

Satellite dishes also pick up overseas stations transmitting in the region, including CNN, BBC, Television Australia, Malaysian TV and French TV.

PHOTOGRAPHY & VIDEO

Colour print film is readily available in the major towns throughout the region and prints can be developed at processing shops in the main towns. Bring your own video tapes.

Colour transparency film is not easy to find, and the range of camera accessories is limited. Shops in Bali have a much better range and cheaper prices – stock up there for slide film, specialist batteries, lenses or anything else you need.

In Lombok, Ampenan and Cakranegara have a few specialist film and camera shops with a limited range, while general stores in Senggigi may have slide film and batteries. In Timor, Kupang has a few good shops that stock slide film and a reasonable range of accessories. In between, the only other city with a half-decent range of film and accessories is Ende on Flores.

Technical Tips

Shoot early or late as from 10 am to 1 or 2 pm the sun is uncomfortably hot and high overhead, and you're likely to get a bluish washed-out look to your pictures. A polarising filter helps reduce glare and darkens an otherwise washed-out sunlit sky. A lens hood will reduce your problems with reflections and direct sunlight on the lens. Beware of the sharp differences between sun and shade – if you can't get reasonably balanced overall light you may have to opt for exposing only one area or the other correctly. Alternatively, use a fill-in flash.

Those lush, green rice fields come up best if backlit by the sun. For sunset shots set your exposure on the sky without the sun making an appearance, then shoot at the sun. Photography from fast-moving trains and buses doesn't work well unless you use a fast shutter speed. Dust can also be a problem – hazy days will make it difficult to get sharp shots.

Photographing People

There are fantastic opportunities for portrait photography in Indonesia – not only are there 200 million or so people from which to choose, but the number and variation of ethnic groups is staggering.

Few people expect payment for their photos, but what Indonesians *do* go for is a copy of the photo. If you hang around Indonesia long enough you'll wind up with a pocketful of bits of paper with addresses of people to send photos to.

Indonesians are usually quite happy to have their photo taken. Whatever you do, photograph with discretion and manners. Obviously, many people don't like having a camera lens shoved down their throat – it's always polite to ask first and if they say no, then don't. A gesture, a smile and a nod are all that is usually necessary. In traditional villages you should also ask before photographing sacred sites, graves, sacred houses etc. It is usually not a problem, but we have come across a few villages in eastern Indonesia where people don't like it.

Don't take photographs at public bathing places – intruding with your camera is no different to sneaking up to someone's bathroom window and pointing your camera through. Remember, wherever you are in Indonesia, the people are *not* exotic birds of paradise and the village priest is *not* a photographic model. Finally, don't be surprised if Indonesians turn the tables on you – they have become fond of sneaking up on westerners and shooting a few exotic photos to show their friends!

Video

Properly used, a video camera can give a fascinating record of your holiday. As well as videoing the obvious things – sunsets, spectacular views – remember to record some of the everyday details of life in the country. Often the most interesting things occur when you're intent on filming something else. Remember too that, unlike still photography, video 'flows' – so, for example, you can shoot scenes of countryside rolling past the train window, to give an overall impression that isn't possible with ordinary photos.

Video cameras these days have amazingly sensitive microphones, and you might be surprised how much sound will be picked up. This can be a problem if there is a lot of ambient noise – filming by the side of a busy road might seem OK when you do it, but viewing it back home might simply give you a deafening cacophony of traffic noise. One good rule to follow for beginners is to try to film in long takes, and don't move the camera around too much. Otherwise, your

Traditional Architecture

PETER TURNER

Top: A sacrificial altar in the village of Wolondopo in Flores. The village is also notable for the inexplicably mummified body which can be seen near the rumah adat above the village.

Middle Left: Interior detail of a Sumbawanese traditional house, or uma lengge in Sambori. The A-frame design has three levels – a sitting area, the main house, and an attic for storing rice.

PETER TURNER

PETER TURNER

Middle Right: This traditional house, or lopo, in the Timorese village of Fatuoni, shows the skilful use of grass thatch in its roof construction.

Bottom: One of the oldest villages in Sumba, Prainatang has a host of traditional houses and ceremonial buildings. Its isolation has allowed the villagers to retain many aspects of their traditional culture.

PETER TURNER

Arts & Crafts

Top: After dyeing, the weft threads of ikat weaving are carefully positioned on the loom to produce the outline of the pattern.

Middle Left: A basketweaver in Kualeu (Timor) prepares the materials for a new piece.

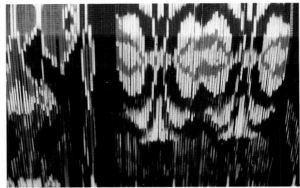

RICHARD I'ANSON

PETER TURNER

SARA-JANE CLELAND

Middle Right: Long-bladed knives in ornamented wooden sheaths are still a common fashion accessory for Sumbanese men and are tucked into the waistband of a sarong.

Bottom: The fine, grey soil around the village of Webriamata (Timor) provides excellent clay for potting. Villagers use local designs and motifs, particularly the akidiran or gecko.

PETER TURNER

video could well make your viewers seasick! If your camera has a stabiliser, you can use it to obtain good footage while travelling on various means of transport, even on bumpy roads.

Finally, remember that you are on holiday – don't let the video take over your life and transform your trip into a Cecil B de Mille production.

Make sure you keep the batteries charged and have the necessary charger, plugs and transformer for the country you are visiting. In most countries, it is possible to obtain video cartridges easily in large towns and cities, but make sure you buy the correct format. It is usually worth buying at least a few cartridges duty-free to start off your trip.

Finally, remember to follow the same rules regarding people's sensitivities as for a still photography – having a video camera shoved in their face is probably even more annoying and offensive for locals than a still camera. Always ask permission first.

TIME

There are three time zones in Indonesia. Nusa Tenggara, Bali, South and East Kalimantan, and Sulawesi are on Central Indonesian Time, which is eight hours ahead of GMT. Sumatra, Java, and West and Central Kalimantan are on Western Indonesian Time, which is seven hours ahead of GMT, and one hour ahead of Singapore. Irian Jaya and Maluku are on East Indonesian Time, which is nine hours ahead of GMT. In a country straddling the equator, there is of course no daylight saving time.

International daylight saving variations aside, when it is noon in Jakarta it's 9 pm the previous day in Los Angeles, midnight in New York, 5 am in London, 1 pm in Bali and Nusa Tenggara, and 3 pm in Sydney.

Strung out along the equator, Indonesian days and nights are approximately equal in length, and sunrises and sunsets occur very rapidly with almost no twilight. Sunrise is around 5.30 to 6 am and sunset is around 5.30 to 6 pm, varying slightly depending on distance from the equator.

ELECTRICITY

Electricity is almost always 220V, 50 cycles AC. Sockets are designed to accommodate two round prongs of the European variety. Recessed sockets are designed to take earth (ground) facilities, but wiring in many hotels and most appliances aren't earthed, so take care. Electricity is usually reliable in cities, but occasional blackouts occur in rural areas. It's wise to keep a torch (flashlight) or candles handy for such occasions. Safe adaptors for foreign plugs are hard to find, so bring your own.

WEIGHTS & MEASURES

Indonesia has fully adopted the international metric system.

LAUNDRY

Virtually every hotel has a laundry service, and in most places this is very inexpensive. About the only thing you need to be concerned about is the weather – clothes are dried on the line, so a hot, sunny day is essential. Give staff your laundry in the morning as they like to wash clothes before 9 am so it has sufficient time to dry before sunset.

HEALTH

Being a tropical country with a low level of sanitation and a high level of ignorance, Indonesia is a fairly easy place to get ill. The climate provides a good breeding ground for malarial mosquitoes, but the biggest hazards come from contaminated food and water. You should not worry excessively about all this. With some basic precautions and adequate information few travellers experience more than upset stomachs.

Predeparture Planning

Immunisations Indonesia requires no vaccinations to enter the country, apart from yellow fever if you are arriving from a yellow fever infected area within six days. While not compulsory, other vaccinations are highly recommended. Record vaccinations on an

International Health Certificate, which is available from your doctor or government health department. While you may not ever be required to show it, a record of your vaccinations is useful for future travels and getting boosters.

Plan ahead for getting your vaccinations: some require an initial shot followed by a booster, while some vaccinations should not be given together. It is recommended you seek medical advice at least six weeks prior to travel. Be aware that there is often a greater risk of disease with children and in pregnancy.

Discuss your requirements with your doctor, but vaccinations you should consider for Indonesia include:

- **Hepatitis A** The most common travel-acquired illness after diarrhoea which can put you out of action for weeks. Havrix 1440 and VAQTA are vaccinations which provide long term immunity (possibly more than 10 years) after an initial injection and a booster at six to 12 months.

    Gamma globulin is ready-made antibody collected from blood donations. It should be given close to departure because, depending on the dose, it only protects for two to six months.

    A combined hepatitis A and hepatitis B vaccination, Twinrix, is also available. This combined vaccination is recommended for people wanting protection against both types of viral hepatitis. Three injections over a six month period are required.
- **Typhoid** This is an important vaccination to have where hygiene is a problem. It's available either as an injection or oral capsules.
- **Diphtheria & Tetanus** Diphtheria can be a fatal throat infection and tetanus can be a fatal wound infection. Everyone should have these vaccinations. After an initial course of three injections, boosters are necessary every 10 years.
- **Hepatitis B** This disease is spread by blood or by sexual activity. Travellers who should consider a hepatitis B vaccination include those visiting countries: where there are known to be many carriers; where blood transfusions may not be adequately screened; or where sexual contact is a possibility. It involves three injections – the quickest course takes three weeks with a booster at 12 months.
- **Polio** Polio is a serious, easily transmitted disease, still prevalent in many developing countries. All travellers should keep up to date with this vaccination. A booster every 10 years maintains immunity.
- **Rabies** Vaccination should be considered by those who will spend a month or longer in Indonesia, especially if they are cycling, handling animals, caving, travelling to remote areas, or for children (who may not report a bite). A pre-travel rabies vaccination involves having three injections over 21 to 28 days. If someone who has been vaccinated is bitten or scratched by an animal they will require two booster injections of vaccine; those not vaccinated require more.
- **Japanese B Encephalitis** This mosquito-borne disease is not common in travellers, but occurs in Indonesia. Consider the vaccination if spending a month or longer in a high risk area, making repeated trips to a risk area or visiting during an epidemic. It involves three injections over 30 days. The vaccine is expensive and has been associated with serious allergic reactions so the decision to have it should be balanced against the risk of contracting the illness.
- **Tuberculosis** TB risk to travellers is usually very low. For those who will be living with or closely associated with local people in high risk areas such as Asia, Africa and some parts of the Americas and Pacific, there may be some risk. As most healthy adults do not develop symptoms, a skin test before and after travel to determine whether exposure has occurred may be considered. A vaccination is recommended for children living in these areas for three months or more.

Malaria Medication Antimalarial drugs do not prevent you from being infected, but kill the malaria parasites during a stage in their development and significantly reduce the risk of becoming very ill or dying.

Expert advice on medication should be sought, as there are many factors to consider including the area to be visited, the risk of exposure to malaria-carrying mosquitoes, the side effects of medication, your medical history and whether you are a child or adult or pregnant. Travellers to isolated areas in high risk countries may like to carry a treatment dose of medication for use if symptoms occur. For more details, see Malaria under Insect-Borne Diseases later in this section.

Health Insurance Make sure that you have adequate health insurance. See Travel Insurance under Documents earlier in this chapter for details.

Travel Health Guides

If you are planning to be away or travelling

Medical Kit Check List
Consider taking a basic medical kit including:

☐ **Aspirin** or paracetamol (acetaminophen in the USA) – for pain or fever.
☐ **Antihistamine** (such as Benadryl) – useful as a decongestant for colds and allergies, to ease the itch from insect bites or stings, and to help prevent motion sickness. Antihistamines may cause sedation and interact with alcohol so care should be taken when using them; take one you know and have used before, if possible.
☐ **Antibiotics** – useful if you're travelling well off the beaten track, but they must be prescribed; carry the prescription with you.
☐ **Loperamide** (eg Imodium) or Lomotil for diarrhoea; prochlorperazine (eg Stemetil) or metaclopramide (eg Maxalon) for nausea and vomiting.
☐ **Rehydration mixture** – for treatment of severe diarrhoea; particularly important for travelling with children.
☐ **Antiseptic** such as povidone-iodine (eg Betadine) – for cuts and grazes.
☐ **Multivitamins** – especially for long trips when dietary vitamin intake may be inadequate.
☐ **Calamine lotion** or aluminium sulphate spray (eg Stingose) – to ease irritation from bites or stings.
☐ **Bandages** and **Band-aids**
☐ **Scissors, tweezers** and a **thermometer** (note that mercury thermometers are prohibited by airlines).
☐ **Cold and flu tablets** and **throat lozenges**. Pseudoephedrine hydrochloride (Sudafed) may be useful if flying with a cold to avoid ear damage.
☐ **General:** Insect repellent, sunscreen, chap stick and water purification tablets.
☐ **A couple of syringes**, in case you need injections in a country with medical hygiene problems. Ask your doctor for a note explaining why they have been prescribed. ■

in remote areas for a long period of time, you may like to consider taking a more detailed health guide.

Staying Healthy in Asia, Africa & Latin America, Dirk Schroeder, Moon Publications. Probably the best all-round guide to carry; it's compact, detailed and well organised.
Travellers' Health, Dr Richard Dawood, Oxford University Press, 1995. Comprehensive, easy to read, authoritative and highly recommended, although it's rather large to lug around.
Where There is No Doctor, David Werner, Macmillan, 1994. A very detailed guide intended for someone, such as a Peace Corps worker, going to work in an underdeveloped country.
Travel with Children, Maureen Wheeler, Lonely Planet Publications, 1995. Includes advice on travel health for younger children.

There are also a number of excellent travel health sites on the Internet. From the Lonely Planet home page there are links at www.lonelyplanet.com/weblinks/wlprep.htm to the World Health Organisation and the US Center for Diseases Control & Prevention.

Other Preparations Ensure you're healthy before you start travelling. If you are going on a long trip make sure your teeth are OK. If you wear glasses take a spare pair and your prescription.

If you require a particular medication take an adequate supply, as it may not be available locally. Take part of the packaging showing the generic name, rather than the brand, which will make getting replacements easier. It's a good idea to have a legible prescription or letter from your doctor to demonstrate that you legally use the medication to avoid any problems.

Basic Rules
Food When it comes to food, use your best judgement. Have a good look at that restaurant or warung - if it looks dirty, think twice. Street food generally runs a higher risk, but may be better than restaurants if it is cooked on the spot before your eyes. To be absolutely safe, everything should be thoroughly cooked - you can get dysentery from salads

Nutrition

If your food is poor or limited in availability, if you're travelling hard and fast and therefore missing meals, or if you simply lose your appetite, you can soon start to lose weight and place your health at risk.

Make sure your diet is well balanced. Cooked eggs, tofu, beans, lentils (dhal in India) and nuts are all safe ways to get protein. Fruit you can peel (bananas, oranges or mandarins for example) is usually safe (melons can harbour bacteria in their flesh and are best avoided) and a good source of vitamins. Try to eat plenty of grains (including rice) and bread. Remember that although food is generally safer if it is cooked well, overcooked food loses much of its nutritional value. If your diet isn't well balanced or if your food intake is insufficient, it's a good idea to take vitamin and iron pills.

In hot climates make sure you drink enough – don't rely on feeling thirsty to indicate when you should drink. Not needing to urinate or small amounts of very dark yellow urine is a danger sign. Always carry a water bottle with you on long trips. Excessive sweating can lead to loss of salt and therefore muscle cramping. Salt tablets are not a good idea as a preventative, but in places where salt is not used much, adding salt (perhaps in the form of the salty soy sauce *kecap asin*) to food can help. ■

and unpeeled fruit. Fish, meat and dairy products are generally OK provided they are fresh; if they spoil, you could become violently ill. Fish can also be a problem if they lived in contaminated water, and shellfish is a much higher risk. Fish from the 'black rivers' of Indonesia are the fastest ticket to the hepatitis clinic.

Water Much of the water that comes out of the tap in Indonesia is little better than sewage water. Depending on how dirty it is and how sensitive you are, it might not even be safe to brush your teeth with tap water; use bottled or boiled water instead.

Bottled water is widely available in Indonesia. It's expensive at hotels and restaurants, but is reasonably priced in grocery stores or supermarkets. You can boil your own water if you carry an electric immersion coil and a large metal cup (plastic will melt), both of which are available in department stores and supermarkets in Indonesia.

Fruit juices, soft drinks, tea and coffee will not quench your thirst when it's really hot, you need water - *clean* water. The No 1 rule is *be careful of the water* and especially ice. If you don't know for certain that the water is safe, assume the worst. Reputable brands of bottled water or soft drinks are generally fine, although in some places bottles may be refilled with tap water. Only use water from containers with a serrated seal – not tops or

corks. Take care with fruit juice, particularly if water may have been added. Milk should be treated with suspicion as it is often unpasteurised, though boiled milk is fine if it is kept hygienically. Tea or coffee should also be OK, since the water should have been boiled.

Water Purification The simplest way of purifying water is to boil it thoroughly. Vigorously boiling should be satisfactory; however, at high altitude water boils at a lower temperature, so germs are less likely to be killed. Boil it for longer in these environments.

Consider purchasing a water filter for a long trip. There are two main kinds of filter. Total filters take out all parasites, bacteria and viruses, and make water safe to drink. They are often expensive, but they can be more cost effective than buying bottled water. Simple filters (which can even be a nylon mesh bag) take out dirt and larger foreign bodies from the water so that chemical solutions work much more effectively; if water is dirty, chemical solutions may not work at all. It's very important when buying a filter to read the specifications, so that you know exactly what it removes from the water and what it doesn't. Simple filtering will not remove all dangerous organisms, so if you cannot boil water it should be treated chemically.

Chlorine tablets (Puritabs, Steritabs or other brand names) will kill many pathogens, but not some parasites like giardia and amoebic cysts. Iodine is more effective in purifying water and is available in tablet form (such as Potable Aqua). Follow the directions carefully and remember that too much iodine can be harmful.

Medical Problems & Treatment

Self-diagnosis and treatment can be risky, so you should always seek medical help. Although we do give drug dosages in this section, they are for emergency use only. Correct diagnosis is vital.

Antibiotics should ideally be administered only under medical supervision. Take only the recommended dose at the prescribed intervals and use the whole course, even if the illness seems to be cured earlier. Stop immediately if there are any serious reactions and don't use the antibiotic at all if you are unsure that you have the correct one. Some people are allergic to commonly prescribed antibiotics such as penicillin or sulpha drugs; carry this information when travelling eg on a bracelet.

In most cases you can buy virtually any medicine across the counter in Indonesia without a prescription. If you need some special medication, take it with you. However, you shouldn't have any trouble finding common western medicines in Indonesia, at least in the main big cities like Mataram and Kupang where there are well stocked pharmacies (apotik). In rural areas, pharmacies are scarce, but grocery stores will gladly sell you all sorts of dangerous drugs, which are often long beyond their expiry dates (check it). Some of the big tourist hotels on Lombok also have pharmacies.

In each apotik there is an English-language copy of the Indonesian Index of Medical Specialities (IIMS), a guide to pharmaceutical preparations available to doctors in Indonesia. It lists drugs by brand name, generic name, manufacturer's name and therapeutic action. Drugs may not be of the same strength as in other countries or may have deteriorated due to age or poor storage conditions.

Hospitals and private doctors can be found in main towns throughout Nusa Tenggara, but facilities are not always good. The best hospitals are in the provincial capitals Kupang and Mataram (and some of the mission hospitals on Flores have high standards), but for serious ailments requiring hospitalisation, have good health insurance that will fly you out. For well equipped hospitals comparable to the west, Jakarta has the country's best hospitals, while Singapore and Darwin (Australia) have the closest outside Indonesia.

The general hospital (☎ 21354), Jalan Pejanggik 6, Mataram, is the biggest available on Lombok. Let staff know you can pay cash for a private doctor and any drugs you need. The Catholic hospital (☎ 21397) on Jalan Koperasi in Ampenan might be better for visitors.

Environmental Hazards

Fungal Infections Fungal infections occur more commonly in hot weather and are usually found on the scalp, between the toes (athlete's foot) or fingers, in the groin (jock itch or crotch rot) and on the body (ringworm).

Everyday Health

Normal body temperature is up to 37°C or 98.6°F; more than 2°C (4°F) higher indicates a high fever. The normal adult pulse rate is 60 to 100 per minute (children 80 to 100, babies 100 to 140). As a general rule the pulse increases about 20 beats per minute for each 1°C (2°F) rise in fever.

Respiration (breathing) rate is also an indicator of illness. Count the number of breaths per minute: between 12 and 20 is normal for adults and older children (up to 30 for younger children, 40 for babies). People with a high fever or serious respiratory illness breathe more quickly than normal. More than 40 shallow breaths a minute may indicate pneumonia. ■

You get ringworm (which is a fungal infection, not a worm) from infected animals or other people. Moisture encourages these infections.

To prevent fungal infections wear loose, comfortable clothes, avoid artificial fibres, wash frequently and dry carefully. If you do get an infection, wash the infected area at least daily with a disinfectant or medicated soap and water, and rinse and dry well. Apply an antifungal cream or powder like tolnaftate (Tinaderm). Try to expose the infected area to air or sunlight as much as possible and wash all towels and underwear in hot water, change them often and let dry in the sun.

Heat Exhaustion Dehydration and salt deficiency can cause heat exhaustion. Take time to acclimatise to high temperatures, drink sufficient liquids and do not do anything too physically demanding. It's a good idea to carry a water bottle with you. You are dehydrating if you find you are urinating infrequently or if your urine turns a deep yellow or orange; you may also find yourself getting headaches. Dehydration is a real problem if you go hiking in Indonesia.

Salt deficiency is characterised by fatigue, lethargy, headaches, giddiness and muscle cramps; salt tablets may help, but adding extra salt to your food is better.

Anhydrotic heat exhaustion, caused by an inability to sweat, is quite rare. It is likely to strike people who have been in a hot climate for some time, rather than newcomers.

Heatstroke This serious, occasionally fatal, condition can occur if the body's heat-regulating mechanism breaks down and the body temperature rises to dangerous levels. Long, continuous periods of exposure to high temperatures and insufficient fluids can leave you vulnerable to heatstroke.

The symptoms are feeling unwell, not sweating very much (or at all) and a high body temperature (39°C to 41°C or 102°F to 106°F). Where sweating has ceased the skin becomes flushed and red. Severe, throbbing headaches and lack of coordination will also occur, and the sufferer may be confused or aggressive. Eventually the victim will become delirious or convulse. Hospitalisation is essential, but in the interim get victims out of the sun, remove their clothing, cover them with a wet sheet or towel and then fan continually. Give fluids if they are conscious.

Hypothermia The climate may be tropical, but you *can* catch a cold in Indonesia. One of the easiest ways is leaving a fan on at night when you go to sleep, and air conditioners are even worse. You can also freeze your hide by sleeping out on the decks of ships at night, or going up to mountainous areas without warm clothes.

Hypothermia occurs when the body loses heat faster than it can produce it and the core temperature of the body falls. It is surprisingly easy to progress from very cold to dangerously cold due to a combination of wind, wet clothing, fatigue and hunger, even if the air temperature is above freezing. It is best to dress in layers; silk, wool and some of the new artificial fibres are all good insulating materials. A hat is important, as a lot of heat is lost through the head. A strong, waterproof outer layer (and a 'space' blanket for emergencies) are essential. Carry basic supplies, including food containing simple sugars to generate heat quickly and fluid to drink.

The symptoms of hypothermia are exhaustion, numb skin (particularly toes and fingers), shivering, slurred speech, irrational or violent behaviour, lethargy, stumbling, dizzy spells, muscle cramps and violent bursts of energy. Irrationality may take the form of sufferers claiming they are warm and trying to take off their clothes.

To treat mild hypothermia, first get the person out of the wind and/or rain, remove their clothing if it's wet and replace it with dry, warm clothing. Give them hot liquids – not alcohol – and some high-kilojoule, easily digestible food. Do not rub victims, instead allow them to slowly warm themselves. This should be enough to treat the early stages of hypothermia. The early recognition and treatment of mild hypothermia is the only way to prevent severe hypothermia, which is a critical condition.

Jet Lag Jet lag is experienced when a person travels by air across more than three time zones (each time zone usually represents a one hour time difference). It occurs because many of the functions of the human body (such as temperature, pulse rate and emptying of the bladder and bowels) are regulated by internal 24 hour cycles. When we travel long distances rapidly, our bodies take time to adjust to the 'new time' of our destination, and we may experience fatigue, disorientation, insomnia, anxiety, impaired concentration and loss of appetite. These effects will usually be gone within three days of arrival, but to minimise the impact of jet lag:

- Rest for a couple of days prior to departure.
- Try to select flight schedules that minimise sleep deprivation; arriving late in the day means you can go to sleep soon after you arrive. For very long flights, try to organise a stopover.
- Avoid excessive eating (which bloats the stomach) and alcohol (which causes dehydration) during the flight. Instead, drink plenty of non-carbonated, non-alcoholic drinks such as fruit juice or water.
- Avoid smoking.
- Make yourself comfortable by wearing loose-fitting clothes and perhaps bringing an eye mask and ear plugs to help you sleep.
- Try to sleep at the appropriate time for the time zone you are travelling to.

Motion Sickness Eating lightly before and during a trip will reduce the chances of motion sickness. If you are prone to motion sickness, try to find a place that minimises movement – near the wing on aircraft, close to midships on boats, near the centre on buses. Fresh air helps; reading and cigarette smoke don't. Commercial motion-sickness preparations, which can cause drowsiness, have to be taken before the trip begins. Ginger (available in capsule form) and peppermint (including mint-flavoured sweets) are natural preventatives.

Prickly Heat Prickly heat is an itchy rash caused by excessive perspiration trapped under the skin. It usually strikes people who have just arrived in a hot climate. Keeping cool, bathing often, drying the skin and using a mild talcum or prickly heat powder or resorting to air-conditioning may help.

Sunburn Bring sunscreen (UV) lotion and something to cover your head. You can also buy sunscreen in better Indonesian pharmacies – two popular brands are Pabanox and Parasol. In the tropics, the desert or at high altitude you can get sunburnt surprisingly quickly, even through cloud. Sunglasses will protect your eyes from the scorching Indonesian sun. Amber and grey are said to be the two most effective colours for filtering out harmful ultraviolet rays.

Infectious Diseases

Diarrhoea Simple things like a change of water, food or climate can all cause a mild bout of diarrhoea, but a few rushed toilet trips with no other symptoms is not indicative of a major problem.

Dehydration is the main danger with any diarrhoea, particularly in children or the elderly as dehydration can occur quite quickly. Under all circumstances *fluid replacement* (at least equal to the volume being lost) is the most important thing to remember. Weak black tea with a little sugar, soda water, or soft drinks allowed to go flat and diluted 50% with clean water are all good. With severe diarrhoea a rehydrating solution is preferable to replace minerals and salts lost. Commercially available oral rehydration salts (ORS) are very useful; add them to boiled or bottled water. In an emergency you can make up a solution of six teaspoons of sugar and a half teaspoon of salt to a litre of boiled or bottled water. You need to drink at least the same volume of fluid that you are losing in bowel movements and vomiting. Urine is the best guide to the adequacy of replacement – if you have small amounts of concentrated urine, you need to drink more. Keep drinking small amounts often. Stick to a bland diet as you recover.

Lomotil or Imodium can be used to bring relief from the symptoms, although they do not actually cure the problem. Only use these drugs if you do not have access to toilets eg if you *must* travel. For children under 12 years Lomotil and Imodium are not recommended. Do not use these drugs if the person has a high fever or is severely dehydrated.

In certain situations antibiotics may be required: diarrhoea with blood or mucus (dysentery), any fever, watery diarrhoea with fever and lethargy, persistent diarrhoea not improving after 48 hours and severe diarrhoea. In these situations gut-paralysing drugs like Imodium or Lomotil should be avoided.

A stool test is necessary to diagnose which kind of dysentery you have, so you should seek medical help urgently. Where this is not possible the recommended drugs for dysentery are norfloxacin 400mg twice daily for three days or ciprofloxacin 500mg twice daily for five days. These are not recommended for children or pregnant women. The drug of choice for children would be co-trimoxazole (Bactrim, Septrin, Resprim) with the dosage dependent on weight. A five day course is given. Ampicillin or amoxy-cillin may be given during pregnancy, but medical care is necessary.

Amoebic dysentery is gradual in onset; cramping abdominal pain and vomiting are less likely than with other types of dysentery, and fever may not be present. It will persist until treated and can recur and cause other health problems.

Giardiasis is another type of diarrhoea. The parasite causing this intestinal disorder is present in contaminated water. The symptoms are stomach cramps; nausea; a bloated stomach; watery, foul-smelling diarrhoea; and frequent gas. Giardiasis can appear several weeks after you have been exposed to the parasite. The symptoms may disappear for a few days and then return; this can go on for several weeks. Tinidazole, known as Fasigyn, or metronidazole (Flagyl) are the recommended drugs. Treatment is a 2g single dose of Fasigyn or 250mg of Flagyl three times daily for five to 10 days.

Hepatitis Hepatitis is a general term for inflammation of the liver. It is a common disease worldwide. The symptoms are fever, chills, headache, fatigue, feelings of weakness and aches and pains, followed by loss of appetite, nausea, vomiting, abdominal pain, dark urine, light-coloured faeces, jaundiced (yellow) skin and the whites of the eyes may turn yellow. **Hepatitis A** is transmitted by contaminated food and drinking water. The disease poses a real threat to the western traveller. You should seek medical advice, but there is not much you can do apart from resting, drinking lots of fluids, eating lightly and avoiding fatty foods. People who have had hepatitis should avoid alcohol for some time after the illness, as the liver needs time to recover.

Hepatitis E is transmitted in the same way, and it can be very serious in pregnant women.

There are almost 300 million chronic carriers of **Hepatitis B** in the world. It is spread through contact with infected blood, blood products or body fluids, for example through sexual contact, unsterilised needles and blood transfusions, or contact with blood via small breaks in the skin. Other risk situations include having a shave, tattoo, or having your body pierced with contaminated equipment. The symptoms of type B may be more severe and may lead to long term problems. **Hepatitis D** is spread in the same way, but the risk is mainly in shared needles.

Hepatitis C can lead to chronic liver disease. The virus is spread by contact with blood - usually via contaminated transfusions or shared needles. Avoiding these is the only means of prevention.

HIV & AIDS HIV, the Human Immunodeficiency Virus, develops into AIDS, Acquired Immune Deficiency Syndrome, which is a fatal disease. HIV is a major problem in many countries. Any exposure to blood, blood products or body fluids may put the individual at risk. The disease is often transmitted through sexual contact or dirty needles – vaccinations, acupuncture, tattooing and body piercing can be potentially as dangerous as intravenous drug use. HIV/AIDS can also be spread through infected blood transfusions; some developing countries cannot afford to screen blood used for transfusions.

Official HIV figures in Indonesia are pathetically low, though it is widely believed that the real figures are much higher and set to increase significantly unless the promotion of safe sex and hospital practices are improved. The primary risk for most travellers is contact with workers in the sex industry, and in Indonesia the spread of HIV is primarily through heterosexual activity. Apart from abstinence, the most effective prevention is always to practise safe sex using condoms.

If you do need an injection, ask to see the syringe unwrapped in front of you, or take a needle and syringe pack with you.

Fear of HIV infection should never preclude treatment for serious medical conditions.

Intestinal Worms These parasites are most common in rural, tropical areas. The different worms have different ways of infecting people. Some may be ingested on food including undercooked meat and some enter through your skin. Infestations may not show up for some time, and although they are generally not serious, if left untreated some can cause severe health problems later. Considering having a stool test when you return home to check for these and determine the appropriate treatment.

Sexually Transmitted Diseases Gonorrhoea, herpes and syphilis are among these diseases; sores, blisters or rashes around the genitals, discharges or pain when urinating are common symptoms. In some STDs, such as wart virus or chlamydia, symptoms may be less marked or not observed at all, especially in women. Syphilis symptoms eventually disappear completely, but the disease continues and can cause severe problems in later years. While abstinence from sexual contact is the only 100% effective prevention, using condoms is also effective. The treatment of gonorrhoea and syphilis is with antibiotics. The different sexually transmitted diseases each require specific antibiotics. There is no cure for herpes or AIDS.

Eye Infections Trachoma is a common eye infection; it's easily spread by contaminated towels which are handed out by restaurants and even airlines. The best advice about wiping your face is to use disposable tissue paper. If you think you have trachoma, you need to see a doctor the disease can damage your vision if untreated. Trachoma is normally treated with antibiotic eye ointments for about four to six weeks.

Typhoid Typhoid fever is a dangerous gut infection caused by contaminated water and food. Medical help must be sought.

In its early stages sufferers may feel they have a bad cold or flu on the way, as early symptoms are a headache, body aches and a fever which rises a little each day until it is around 40°C (104°F) or more. The victim's pulse is often slow relative to the degree of fever present – unlike a normal fever where the pulse increases. There may also be vomiting, abdominal pain, diarrhoea or constipation.

In the second week the high fever and slow pulse continue and a few pink spots may appear on the body; trembling, delirium, weakness, weight loss and dehydration may occur. Complications such as pneumonia, perforated bowel or meningitis may occur.

The fever should be treated by keeping the victim cool and giving fluids as dehydration should be watched for. Ciprofloxacin 750mg twice a day for 10 days is good for adults.

Chloramphenicol is recommended in many countries. The adult dosage is two 250mg capsules, four times a day. Children aged between eight and 12 years should have half the adult dose; and younger children one-third the adult dose.

Insect-Borne Diseases
Filariasis and typhus are insect-borne diseases, but they do not pose a great risk to travellers. For more information on them see Less Common Diseases towards the end of the health section.

Malaria This serious and potentially fatal disease is spread by mosquito bites. Malaria is found throughout the region, from Lombok right through to Timor, and is more prevalent than in more developed areas of Indonesia, such as Java and Bali. Malaria is not everywhere and it comes and goes, but an outbreak can occur anywhere at any time. As a general rule, the more isolated and undeveloped the region, the higher the malarial risk. The towns and tourist areas are low risk, but not guaranteed to be malaria free. Outbreaks do occasionally occur in towns, and though tourist operators claim that Lombok is malaria free, it can occur on all the islands, and in mountain regions.

It is extremely important to avoid mosquito bites and to take tablets to prevent this disease. Symptoms range from fever, chills and sweating, headache, diarrhoea and abdominal pains to a vague feeling of ill-health. Seek medical help immediately if malaria is suspected. Without treatment malaria can rapidly become more serious and can be fatal.

If medical care is not available, malaria tablets can be used for treatment. You need to use a malaria tablet which is different from the one you were taking when you contracted malaria. The treatment dosages are mefloquine (three 250mg tablets and a further two six hours later), fansidar (single dose of three tablets). If you were previously taking mefloquine and cannot obtain fansidar then alternatives are halofantrine (three doses of two 250mg tablets every six hours) or quinine sulphate (600mg every six hours). There is a greater risk of side effects with these dosages than in normal use if used with mefloquine, so medical advice is preferable.

Travellers are advised to prevent mosquito bites at all times. The main messages are:

- wear light coloured clothing.
- wear long trousers and long sleeved shirts.
- use mosquito repellents containing the compound DEET on exposed areas (prolonged overuse of DEET may be harmful, especially to children, but its use is preferable to being bitten by disease-transmitting mosquitoes).
- avoid wearing perfume or aftershave.
- use a mosquito net impregnated with mosquito repellent (permethrin) – it may be worth taking your own.
- impregnating clothes with permethrin effectively deters mosquitoes and other insects.

Dengue Fever There is no preventative drug available for this mosquito-spread disease

which can be fatal in children. A sudden onset of fever, headaches and severe joint and muscle pains are the first signs before a rash develops. Recovery may be prolonged. Indonesia experienced a major outbreak of dengue during the wet season of 1998, mostly in Kalimantan, Sumatra and Java.

Japanese B Encephalitis This viral infection of the brain is transmitted by mosquitoes. Most cases occur in rural areas as the virus exists in pigs and wading birds. Symptoms include fever, headache and alteration in consciousness. Hospitalisation is needed for correct diagnosis and treatment. There is a high mortality rate among those who have symptoms; of those that survive many are intellectually disabled.

Cuts, Bites & Stings
Rabies is passed through animal bites. See Less Common Diseases for details.

Bedbugs & Lice Bedbugs live in various places, but particularly in dirty mattresses and bedding, evidenced by spots of blood on bedclothes or on the wall. Bedbugs leave itchy bites in neat rows. Calamine lotion or Stingose spray may help.

All lice cause itching and discomfort. They make themselves at home in your hair (head lice), your clothing (body lice) or in your pubic hair (crabs). You catch lice through direct contact with infected people or by sharing combs, clothing and the like. Powder or shampoo treatment will kill the lice and infected clothing should then be washed in very hot, soapy water and left in the sun to dry.

Insect Bites & Stings Bee and wasp stings are usually painful rather than dangerous. However in people who are allergic to them severe breathing difficulties may occur and require urgent medical care. Calamine lotion or Stingose spray will give relief and ice packs will reduce the pain and swelling. There are some spiders with dangerous bites, but antivenenes are usually available. Scorpion stings are notoriously painful and in some parts of Indonesia can actually be fatal. Scorpions often shelter in shoes or clothing.

Cuts & Scratches Take good care of all cuts and scratches. In this climate they take longer to heal and easily can get infected. Treat any cut with care; wash it out with sterilised water, preferably with an antiseptic (Betadine), keep it dry and keep an eye on it they can turn into tropical ulcers! It would be worth bringing an antibiotic cream with you, or you can buy one in Indonesia ('NB' ointment). Cuts on your feet and ankles are particularly troublesome – a new pair of sandals can quickly give you a nasty abrasion which can be difficult to heal. For the same reason, try not to scratch mosquito bites.

Coral cuts are notoriously slow to heal and if not adequately cleaned, small pieces of coral can become embedded in the wound.

Jellyfish Heeding local advice is the best way of avoiding contact with these sea creatures with their stinging tentacles. The box jellyfish found in inshore waters in some parts of Indonesia is potentially fatal, but stings from most jellyfish are simply rather painful. Dousing in vinegar will deactivate any stingers which have not 'fired'. Calamine lotion, antihistamines and analgesics may reduce the reaction and relieve the pain.

Leeches & Ticks Leeches may be present in damp rainforest conditions; they attach themselves to your skin to suck your blood. Trekkers often get them on their legs or in their boots. Salt or a lighted cigarette end will make them fall off. Do not pull them off, as the bite is then more likely to become infected. Clean and apply pressure if the point of attachment is bleeding. An insect repellent may keep them away.

You should always check all over your body if you have been walking through a potentially tick-infested area as ticks can cause skin infections and other more serious diseases. If a tick is found attached, press down around the tick's head with tweezers, grab the head and gently pull upwards. Avoid pulling the rear of the body as this may squeeze the tick's gut contents through the attached mouth parts into the skin, increasing the risk of infection and disease. Smearing chemicals on the tick will not make it let go and is not recommended.

Snakes Indonesia has several poisonous snakes (*ular* is the Indonesian word for snake), the most famous being the cobra *(ular sendok)*. There are many other poisonous species. *All* sea snakes are poisonous and are readily identified by their flat tails. Although not poisonous, giant-sized pythons lurk in the jungle. They do not generally consume humans, but have been known to do so. They do frequently eat pigs, and are thus an enemy of non-Muslim farmers.

To minimise your chances of being bitten always wear boots, socks and long trousers when walking through undergrowth where snakes may be present. Don't put your hands into holes and crevices, and be careful when collecting firewood.

Snake bites do not cause instantaneous death and antivenenes are usually available. Keep the victim calm and still, wrap the bitten limb tightly, as you would for a sprained ankle, and then attach a splint to immobilise it. Then seek medical help, if possible with the dead snake for identification. Don't attempt to catch the snake if there is even a remote possibility of being bitten again. Tourniquets and sucking out the poison are now comprehensively discredited.

Less Common Diseases

The following diseases pose a small risk to travellers, and so are only mentioned in passing. Seek medical advice if you think you may have any of these diseases.

Cholera This is the worst of the watery diarrhoeas and medical help should be sought. Outbreaks of cholera are generally widely reported, so you can avoid such problem areas. *Fluid replacement is the most vital treatment* – the risk of dehydration is severe as you may lose up to 20L a day. If there is a delay in getting to hospital then begin taking tetracycline. The adult dose is

250mg four times daily. It is not recommended for children under nine years nor for pregnant women. Tetracycline may help shorten the illness, but adequate fluids are required to save lives.

Filariasis This is a mosquito-transmitted parasitic infection found in many parts of Africa, Asia, Central and South America and the Pacific. Possible symptoms include fever, pain and swelling of the lymph glands; inflammation of lymph drainage areas; swelling of a limb or the scrotum; skin rashes and blindness. Treatment is available to eliminate the parasites from the body, but some of the damage already caused may not be reversible. Medical advice should be obtained promptly if the infection is suspected.

Rabies Rabies is rare in Indonesia, but can be caused by a bite or scratch by an infected animal. Dogs are carriers, as are monkeys and cats, but any bite, scratch or even lick from a warm-blooded, furry animal should be cleaned immediately and thoroughly. Scrub with soap and running water, and then apply alcohol or iodine solution. Medical help should be sought promptly to receive a course of injections to prevent the onset of symptoms and death.

Tetanus Tetanus occurs when a wound becomes infected by a germ which lives in soil and in the faeces of horses and other animals. It enters the body via breaks in the skin. All wounds should be cleaned promptly and adequately and an antiseptic cream or solution applied. Use antibiotics if the wound becomes hot, throbs or pus is seen. The first symptom may be discomfort in swallowing, or stiffening of the jaw and neck; this is followed by painful convulsions of the jaw and whole body. The disease can be fatal.

Tuberculosis (TB) TB is a bacterial infection usually transmitted from person to person by coughing, but may be transmitted through consumption of unpasteurised milk. Milk that has been boiled is safe to drink, and the souring of milk to make yoghurt or cheese also kills the bacilli. Travellers are usually not at great risk as close household contact with the infected person is usually required before the disease is passed on.

Typhus Typhus is spread by ticks, mites or lice. It begins with fever, chills, headache and muscle pains followed a few days later by a body rash. There is often a large painful sore at the site of the bite and nearby lymph nodes are swollen and painful. Typhus can be treated under medical supervision.

Seek local advice on areas where ticks pose a danger and always check your skin (including hair) carefully for ticks after walking in a danger area such as a tropical forest. A strong insect repellent can help, and serious walkers in tick areas should consider having their boots and trousers impregnated with benzyl benzoate and dibutylphthalate.

Women's Health
Gynaecological Problems STDs are a major cause of vaginal problems. Symptoms include a smelly discharge, painful intercourse and sometimes a burning sensation when urinating. Male sexual partners also must be treated. Medical attention should be sought and remember in addition to these diseases HIV or hepatitis B may also be acquired during exposure. Besides abstinence, the best thing is to practise safe sex using condoms.

Antibiotic use, synthetic underwear, sweating and contraceptive pills can lead to fungal vaginal infections when travelling in hot climates. Maintaining good personal hygiene, and loose-fitting clothes and cotton underwear will help to prevent these infections.

Fungal infections, characterised by a rash, itch and discharge, can be treated with a vinegar or lemon-juice douche, or with yog-hurt. Nystatin, miconazole or clotrimazole pessaries or vaginal cream are the usual treatment.

Pregnancy It is not advisable to travel to some places while pregnant, as some vaccinations which are normally used to prevent serious diseases are not advisable during pregnancy (eg yellow fever). In addition, some diseases are much more serious for the mother (and may increase the risk of a still-born child) in pregnancy (eg malaria).

Most miscarriages occur during the first three months of pregnancy. Miscarriage is not uncommon, and can occasionally lead to severe bleeding. The last three months should also be spent within reasonable distance of good medical care. A baby born as early as 24 weeks stands a chance of survival, but only in a good modern hospital. Pregnant women should avoid all unnecessary medication, vaccinations and malarial prophylactics should still be taken where needed. Additional care should be taken to prevent illness and particular attention should be paid to diet and nutrition. Alcohol and nicotine should be avoided.

WOMEN TRAVELLERS

Indonesia is a Muslim society and very much male-oriented. However, women are not cloistered or forced to wear purdah and generally enjoy more freedom than in many more orthodox Middle Eastern societies.

Plenty of western women travel in Indonesia either alone or in pairs. Most seem to enjoy the country and its people, and get through the place without any problems, or else suffer only a few minor hassles with the men. Your genetic make-up plays a part – blonde-haired, blue-eyed women seem to have more hassles than dark women. There are some things you can do to avoid being harassed; dressing modestly helps a lot.

Indonesians, both men and women, are generally not comfortable being alone and even on a simple errand they are happier having a friend along. Travelling alone is considered an oddity and women travelling alone even more of an oddity. It is certainly tougher going for a woman travelling alone in isolated regions. Nevertheless, for women travelling alone or with a female companion, Indonesia can be easier going than some other Asian countries.

GAY & LESBIAN TRAVELLERS

Gay travellers in Indonesia will experience few problems. Physical contact between same-sex couples is quite acceptable, even though a man and a woman holding hands may be seen as improper. Homosexual behaviour is not illegal, and the age of consent for sexual activity is 16 years. Immigration officials may restrict entry to people who reveal HIV positive status. Gay men in Indonesia are referred to as *homo* or *gay*.

Indonesia's transvestite/transexual *banci* community has always had a very public profile. Also known as *waria* (from *wanita*, meaning woman and *pria*, meaning man), they are often extrovert performers, as entertainers on stage and as street-walkers, mostly in Java.

Perhaps because of the high profile of the banci, community attitudes to the wider gay community are surprisingly tolerant in a traditional, conservative family-oriented society. Although orthodox Islamic groups are against homosexuality, their views in general are not dominant and there appears to be no queer bashing or campaigns against gays.

There are a few gay organisations, mostly in Java. Gaya Nusantara (☎ 593 4924, fax 593 9070), Jalan Mulyosari Timur 46, Surabaya, coordinates many activities and publishes a monthly magazine also called *Gaya Nusantara*.

TRAVEL WITH CHILDREN

Indonesians love children and travel with children can be very rewarding, both for the children and for the parents. However, travel with young children is not as much of an option in Nusa Tenggara. It is no problem to scoot across to the resorts of Lombok from Bali, but elsewhere travel can be very tough.

Travel with children is not out of the question if you keep it to a minimum, but adults find it hard to endure gruelling bus trips, let alone children. For example, you could fly into Maumere and spend some time at the nearby beaches or rent a car and driver for trips further afield. Australian families also fly to Kupang and head to the beach at Nemberala on Roti for a few weeks, but most destinations require some hard travel and facilities are often very basic when you get there.

The main reservation about bringing kids is

the risk of malaria. Discuss malaria prevention with your doctor. Weekly tablets are probably easier for kids than daily ones. You can also get antimalarials for children in syrup form. Protection against mosquitoes is the most important preventive measure, for malaria and other illnesses. Dehydration is also a major concern, especially for young children (see the previous Health section in this chapter).

DANGERS & ANNOYANCES
Theft
While violent crime is very rare in Indonesia, theft can be a problem. If you are mindful of your valuables and take precautions, the chances of being ripped off are small. Most thefts are the result of carelessness or naivety. The chance of theft is highest in crowded places and when you are travelling, especially on public bemos and buses.

The eastern islands are generally lower risk than other parts of Indonesia. Although this is one of the poorest regions of Indonesia, it is also one of the most traditional and theft is very rare in the villages. Lombok is the most high risk, simply because tourists attract thieves. A number of incidents of theft from hotel rooms and pickocketing on bemos have been reported on Lombok. If you take the following precautions throughout the region, the chances of a mishap are very low.

A money belt worn under your clothes is the safest way to carry your passport, cash and travellers cheques, particularly when travelling on the crowded buses. Keep a separate stash of money (say US$200) hidden in your luggage, with a record of the travellers cheque serial numbers and your passport number; you'll need the cash if you have a long trip to replace stolen cheques. If you get stuck, try ringing your embassy or consulate.

Crowded buses and bus stations are favourite haunts of pickpockets, as are major tourist areas. The thieves are very skilful and often work in gangs – if you find yourself being hassled and jostled, check your wallet, watch and bag. 'Pencuri' is the Indonesian word for thief.

Don't leave valuables unattended, and in crowded places, hold your handbag or day pack closely. Don't carry your passport, travellers cheques or wallet in a bag that can be pickpocketed. Keep an eye on your luggage if it is put on the roof of a bus, but it is usually safe and looked after by the bus jockey. It is good insurance to have luggage that can be locked, as other passengers sometimes ride on the top of buses. It is worth sewing on tabs to hiking packs to make them lockable.

Always lock your hotel room door and windows at night and whenever you go out, even if momentarily. If you leave small items like sunglasses and books lying around, expect them to disappear. It's a depressing reality that your fellow travellers can be the ones who rip you off. Bring your own locks for those hotel rooms that are locked with a padlock.

Drugs
In most of eastern Indonesia, marijuana and chemical drugs are utterly unheard of. Being caught with drugs will result in jail or, if you are lucky, a large bribe. Marijuana is rare and the only place you are likely to come across it is in Lombok. Ecstasy has become quite prevalent in nightclubs, but mainly in Bali and Jakarta.

Hotel owners are required by law to turn in offenders. Bali used to be the place to float sky high, but the scene has all but disappeared. You'll still get plenty of offers, but nine times out of ten those 'buddha sticks' are banana leaves, and remember that there are still westerners soaking up the sunshine in Bali's prison.

Noise
If you're deaf, you won't have any problem with noise in Indonesia. If you're not, you might well be after a few months there. The major source of noise are radios and TVs – Indonesians always set the volume knob to maximum. You can easily escape the racket at remote beaches and other rural settings by walking away, but there isn't much you can do on a bus with a reverberating stereo system. In hotels, the lobby often contains a booming TV set, but if you choose your

room carefully, you might be able to avoid the full impact. If you complain about the noise, it's likely the TV or radio will be turned down, but then turned back up again five minutes later.

Another major source of noise is the mosques, which start broadcasting the calls to prayer at 4 am, repeating the procedure four more times during the day. Again, choose your hotel room carefully.

'Hello Mister' Fatigue
This is the universal greeting given to foreigners, regardless of whether you are male or female. The less advanced English students know only 'Mister', which they will enthusiastically *scream* in your ear every five seconds 'Mister Mister Mister!' especially if you ignore them. Just smile and say hello. Most have no idea what 'mister' means, but they have been told by their parents and school teachers that this is the proper way to greet foreigners. After two months of listening to this, some foreigners go over the edge – try to remember that they think it's polite. Nusa Tenggara is probably the home of the hello mister cult in Indonesia, and though it is receding, outside the cities it is still prevalent.

Other Hassles
You tend to get stared at in Indonesia, particularly in places where few foreigners go. But on the whole Indonesians stand back and look, rather than gather around you. Those who do come right up to you are usually kids, though some teenagers also do this. Getting stared at is nothing new; almost 500 years ago when the first Portuguese arrived in Melaka the *Malay Annals* recorded that:

... the people of Melaka ... came crowding to see what the Franks (Portuguese) looked like; and they were all astonished and said, 'These are white Bengalis!' Around each Frank there would be a crowd of Malays, some of them twisting his beard, some of them fingering his head, some taking off his hat, some grasping his hand.

The insatiable curiosity of Indonesians manifests itself in some peculiar ways. Many

Indonesians take their holidays in Bali not for the beach, but just so they can stare at foreigners. Sometimes people follow you on the street just to look at you – such people are called *buntut* (tails). If you read a book or write something down, it's not unusual for people to poke their nose right into your book or writing pad, or take it from your hands so that they can have a better look.

Another habit which is altogether ordinary to Indonesians is touching. The Indonesians are an extraordinarily physical people; they'll balance themselves on your knee as they get into a bemo, or reach out and touch your arm while making a point in conversation, or simply touch you every time they mean to speak to you or when they want to lead you in a new direction when they're showing you around a house or museum. This is considered friendly behaviour – some Indonesians just have to be friendly regardless of the time or situation, even if it means waking you from your peaceful slumber!

While casual touching among members of the same sex is regarded as OK, body contact between people of different sexes is not. Walking down the street holding hands with a member of the opposite sex will provoke stares, pointing, loud comments and shouting. Public displays of affection (like kissing) may incur the wrath of moral vigilantes.

Sometimes you'll come across young guys who hang around bus stations, cinemas and ferry docks with not much else to do except stir foreigners. They'll crack jokes, laugh, and sometimes make obscene gestures. Don't give them their entertainment by having a fit, just ignore their puerile antics.

On the whole you'll find the Indonesians (including the army and the police, despite the reputation they have with the locals) *extraordinarily* hospitable and very easy to get along with.

BUSINESS HOURS
Government office hours are variable (sometimes very variable), but offices are generally open Monday to Friday from 7 am to 3 pm or 8 am to 4 pm, and Saturday until noon. Go

in the morning if you want to get anything done. Most close for lunch around noon to 1 pm and in Muslim areas (Lombok and Sumbawa) offices close from around noon to 2.30 pm for Friday prayers.

Most post offices have similar opening hours, but many central post offices in the cities have extended hours until 6 pm or later and are also open on weekends for basic postal services.

The main Telkom offices are open 24 hours for phone calls, while private telephone agencies are usually open until midnight. Private business offices are open Monday to Friday from 8 am to 4 pm, or 9 am to 5 pm, with a break in the middle of the day. Some offices also are open on Saturday morning until noon.

Banks usually are open Monday to Friday from 8 am to 3 or 4 pm. Some banks in the cities also open on Saturday mornings, while others may have limited hours for foreign currency transactions, eg 8 am to 1 pm. Moneychangers in tourist areas stay open until the evening.

Shops tend to open about 9 am and stay open until around 9 pm. Sunday is a public holiday, but some shops and many airline offices open for at least part of the day.

PUBLIC HOLIDAYS & SPECIAL EVENTS
Public Holidays

Indonesia has many faiths and many festivals, celebrated on different days throughout the country. Islam, as the country's major religion, provides many of the holidays. The most important time for Muslims is Ramadan (Bulan Puasa), the traditional Muslim month of daily fasting from sunrise to sunset.

The following list describes national public holidays, but remember that Muslim holidays are celebrated with great gusto only in Lombok and Sumbawa, and a few Muslim pockets elsewhere, such as Ende on Flores. The predominantly Christian islands of Flores, Sumba and Timor go all out for Easter and Christmas instead.

Muslim events are affected by the lunar calendar and dates move back 10 or 11 days each year. Buddhists and Hindus have their own lunar calendars. Many of the projected dates are decided only the year before and may vary by one day or so.

January
New Year's Day (1 January)
Idul Fitri (19 and 20 January 1999, 8 and 9 January 2000) – also known as Lebaran, this marks the end of Ramadan and is a noisy celebration at the end of a month of gastronomic austerity. It is a national public holiday lasting two days.
March
Idul Adha (28 March 1999, 16 March 2000) – this Muslim festival commemorates Abraham's willingness to sacrifice his son, Isaac, and is celebrated with prayers and feasts. Animals (usually goats) are sacrificed at mosques and the meat is distributed.
April
Nyepi – Balinese New Year, marking the end of the Hindu saka calendar. For the Balinese community in Lombok, on the day before Nyepi evil spirits are chased away with gongs, drums and flaming torches, but on Nyepi itself Balinese stay at home and all Balinese businesses close down so that bad spirits will see the deserted streets and leave. It's a quiet time to be in Bali as everything closes, but Nyepi is only a minority celebration in Lombok. The date is only announced at the start of the year; usually it is held in April, sometimes in March.
Muharram (17 April 1999, 6 April 2000) – Islamic New Year, the start of the Muslim calendar. *Good Friday* (2 April 1999, 21 April 2000) – Easter is a major event in Nusa Tenggara Timur, and Larantuka in Flores is noted for its Easter procession.
May-June
Waicak Day (1 May 1999, 18 June 2000) – marks the Buddha's birth, enlightenment and death.
Ascension of Christ (13 May 1999, 1 June 2000)
Maulud Nabi Mohammed (26 June 1999, 15 June 2000) – the birthday of the Prophet Mohammed, also known as Hari Natal.
August
Independence Day (Hari Proklamasi Kemerdekaan) – on 17 August 1945, Soekarno proclaimed Indonesian independence in Jakarta. It is a national public holiday, and the parades and special events are at their grandest in Jakarta.
October-November
Isra Miraj Nabi Mohammed (6 November 1999, 26 October 2000) – celebrates the ascension of the Prophet Mohammed.
December
Christmas Day (25 December)

Public Holidays & Special Events
continued on page 80

Activities

Trekking

The region has some good trekking possibilities, mostly climbs to the top of volcanoes.

Gunung Rinjani (3726m) on Lombok is a superb area for trekking. This is one of the finest hikes in Indonesia, and is easy to arrange in Batu Koq/Senaru, or Sembalun Lawang at the other end of the trek. Equipment, guides and porters can be hired at both ends, or most of it can be done independently if started in Senaru. It's possible to get up to the crater rim and back in a single day, but it's much more rewarding to do a longer trip, which will involve at least two nights camping out. There are several routes up, and a world of possibilities for those who want to spend some days hiking in a relatively remote area.

Gunung Tambora (2851m) on Sumbawa is potentially another fine hike, but the trail head is difficult to reach. Little English is spoken in the area, guides are essential and bring your own equipment (sleeping bag and tent) with you. It is usually done as a three day hike from Pancasila, near Calabai on the Tambora Peninsula.

Other treks are one day hikes to various mountain tops. No special equipment is required and many can be done from the main towns, though sometimes it is better to stay in a nearby village so that the climb can be started in the early morning to avoid the heat of the day. Make sure you bring food and plenty of water. Many treks can be done without a guide, but they are not regularly travelled by hikers so trails are not always easy to follow. Guides can be found in nearby villages.

On Flores good day hikes can be made to the top of the volcanic peaks of Gunung Inerie from Bajawa, Gunung Ebulobo from Boawae and Gunung Egon outside Maumere. Just outside Ende, Gunung Meja is an easy climb or Gunung Iya can also be climbed.

The Solor archipelago also has a couple of volcanoes to climb: Ili Api on Lembata and Ili Boleng on Adonara.

On Timor, the peaks of Gunung Mutis (West Timor) and Gunung Tatamailau and Gunung Matabai (East Timor) are also day hikes. See the island chapters for details on these peaks.

Otherwise, hiking possibilities are limited. Hiking is not a recreational sport in these parts, but it can be a necessity to reach the more remote villages. Many regional areas are best explored on foot, such as the villages around Pero in West Sumba, while others have no public transport, such as the village of Boti in West Timor.

Diving & Snorkelling

Nusa Tenggara has some fine diving possibilities, with a myriad of islands and reefs to explore and rich marine life. Diving is best outside the wet season (from October to April), when waters can be murky and visibility reduced. Two good diving guidebooks with good coverage of Nusa Tenggara, are *Diving Indonesia* by Kal Muller and *The Dive Sites of Indonesia* by Guy Buckles.

Snorkellers are also well catered for, mostly on small islands just off the main islands. Good snorkelling can be found on the Gili Islands in Lombok, and access is easy. Other good snorkelling spots require boat charter or are reached on inexpensive tours from the tourist centres. Flores has the most accessible snorkelling outside Lombok, including the islands off Labuanbajo in Flores, such as Sabola Besar and Sabola Kecil; the Seventeen Islands Marine Park off Riung; and the islands off Wairterang in eastern Flores. Komodo also has a couple of good snorkelling spots.

Dive Operators The biggest number of dive operators can be found at Senggigi and the Gili Islands in Lombok. Dive tours also can be arranged at Komodo and Labuanbajo in Flores, and at Waiara, just outside Maumere in Flores. Further east, Kupang is the best place to arrange dives.

It pays to check out dive services and guides carefully. Some are good, very experienced and well equipped, but others are lackadaisical. Dives are often from small, local boats without hi-tech equipment, let alone medical kits and oxygen equipment. All diving equipment needs to be checked thoroughly as maintenance can be lacking. If you plan to do a lot of diving it pays to bring your own gear, or at least mask, fins, snorkel and regulator. The general rule is that you have to be responsible for your own safety – this is not a problem for experienced divers perhaps, but novices should exercise more caution and are well advised to stick with well known and reputable operators, and make sure that all guides and instructors are properly qualified.

Dive costs vary depending on the location, but typically are around US$75 per person for two dives, including all gear, tanks, guide and boat charter. Some resorts also offer accommodation and dive packages.

Dive Courses No responsible dive operation will take you on a dive unless you have certification from PADI, CMAS, ISSA or another recognised body. If you are not certified, most operators offer a complete open-water course, including theo-

Considerations for Responsible Diving

The popularity of diving is placing immense pressure on many sites. Please consider the following tips when diving and help preserve the ecology and beauty of reefs:

- Do not use anchors on the reef, and take care not to ground boats on coral. Encourage dive operators and regulatory bodies to establish permanent moorings at popular dive sites.
- Avoid touching living marine organisms with your body or dragging computer equipment across the reef. Polyps can be damaged by even the gentlest contact. Never stand on corals, even if they look solid and robust. If you must secure yourself to the reef, only hold fast to exposed rock or dead coral.
- Be conscious of your fins. Even without contact the surge from heavy fin strokes near the reef can damage delicate organisms. When treading water in shallow reef areas, take care not to kick up clouds of sand. Settling sand can easily smother the delicate organisms of the reef.
- Practise and maintain proper buoyancy control. Major damage can be done by divers descending too fast and colliding with the reef. Make sure you are correctly weighted and that your weight belt is positioned so that you stay horizontal. If you have not dived for a while, have a practice dive in a pool before taking to the reef. Be aware that buoyancy can change over the period of an extended trip: initially you may breathe harder and need more weighting; a few days later you may breathe more easily and need less weight.
- Take great care in underwater caves. Spend as little time within them as possible as your air bubbles may be caught within the roof and thereby leave previously submerged organisms high and dry. Taking turns to inspect the interior of a small cave will lessen the chances of damaging contact.
- Resist the temptation to collect or buy corals or shells. Aside from the ecological damage, taking home marine souvenirs depletes the beauty of a site and spoils the enjoyment of others.
- The same goes for marine archaeological sites (mainly shipwrecks). Respect their integrity; they may even be protected from looting by law.
- Ensure that you take home all your rubbish, and any litter you may find as well. Plastics in particular are a serious threat to marine life. Turtles will mistake plastic for jellyfish and eat it.
- Resist the temptation to feed fish. You may disturb their normal eating habits, encourage aggressive behaviour or feed them food that is detrimental to their health.
- Minimise your disturbance of marine animals. In particular, do not ride on the backs of turtles as this causes them great anxiety.

ry, training and four dives. It will take about four or five days and cost around US$300. Most dive trips and courses will need a minimum of about four people. Lombok has the widest range of courses. Once you have your open-water certificate, you are permitted to hire equipment and go diving anywhere in the world. It may still take some time to get your certificate, which is usually issued out of Singapore.

Some operators also do an 'introduction to scuba' course, with some classroom and pool training, and a shallow dive on Lombok – this will cost from US$50 to US$85. This can give you a taste of diving, but will not give you any qualification. Some of the less professional outfits in Indonesia conduct these courses with inexperienced, even unqualified dive masters and minimal back-up, so beware.

Lombok There is quite good snorkelling off the Gili Islands, and some excellent scuba diving. A few dive operations are located on these islands and the Senggigi tourist strip; some are better than others. A day trip on a boat with two dives and all equipment will cost from US$55. New diving areas are still being explored on Lombok, such as Gili Petangan off the east coast, but you'll need the help of a good operator and guide. Reputable diving operations on Lombok include:

Albatross Diving
(Senggigi – ☎ 93399; Gili Trawangan – ☎ 30134) This is one of the longest established operators, and offers trips all around the Gili Islands and a full range of courses.
Baruna Water Sports
(☎ 93210) This big Bali-based operation has an office at the Senggigi Beach Hotel.
Blue Cora
(Senggigi – ☎ 93441; Gili Trawangan – ☎ 34496) These operators have PADI certified instructors, and a full range of courses and dive trips.
Blue Marlin Dive Centre
(☎ 32424) A well run operation based on Gili Trawangan, this company also has information counters on Gili Air and Senggigi (at Nazareth Tours ☎ 93033). PADI-qualified instructors offer a full open-water course and dive guides with good local knowledge.
Reefseekers Pro Dive
(☎ 34387) Based on Gili Air, this is a new and very enthusiastic operation, with PADI-qualified instructors and a commendable commitment to marine conservation.

Komodo A number of good dive sites are found in and around Komodo and Rinca, particularly off the southern ends of those islands, but currents are very strong. Dive trips can be arranged at Loh Liang (the park headquarters on Komodo) to sites around Komodo, to Gili Banta west of Komodo and islands closer to Labuanbajo. Pantai Merah is easily reached from Loh Liang, but it is more a snorkelling than a diving site.

Flores Labuanbajo is the main base for dives around Komodo, and other offshore islands. The islands of Sebayur and especially Tatawa are the most noted dive sites, while Bidadari, Sabola Besar and Sabola Kecil have good snorkelling and diving opportunities. Labuanbajo dive operators tend to come and go, but there is at least one reliable operator. Some of the dive guides attached to the travel agents lack experience.

Seventeen Islands Marine Park, off the north coast near Riung, has good snorkelling on reefs off the small islands. No dive operators cover this area, but boat tours to the islands are cheap and easily arranged in Riung.

Waiara is the most famous dive spot in Flores, but reef damage from the 1992 earthquake also damaged its diving credentials. Nonetheless good diving can be found at the offshore islands, particularly Pulau Besar, and there is a WWII Japanese cargo ship wreck just off the beach at Wairterang. Two dive resorts at Waiara offer accommodation and dive packages, and snorkelling trips can be arranged from the homestays at Wairterang, 15km further east.

One of the most famed dive sites in Nusa Tenggara is on the island of Alor, lying at the end of the string of islands east of Flores and in sight of East Timor. Alor has prolific reefs, walls and large populations of pelagic and reef species. Although Alor is covered in the Flores chapter, dive trips on Alor are arranged in Kupang (see the following dive entry on Timor for a list of operators). Flores dive operators include:

Flores Sao Resort
   (☎ 21555; fax 21666) Alt Waiara, this fancy resort has packages from US$140/215 a single/double for three nights and two days' diving.
Puri Bagus Komodo
   (☎/fax 41030) A well equipped dive operator based at the Puri Bagus Komodo resort north of Labuanbajo; it also has an office in town.
Sea World Club
   (☎ 21570; fax 21102) Also at Waiara, this resort is popular for its cheap dive packages with accommodation from US$70 per day.

Timor On West Timor, reasonable diving can be found just off Kupang around Pulau Semau and off Roti further south-west. Diving at Pulau Alor, near Flores's Solor Archipelago, is operated out of Kupang, but it is covered in the Flores chapter of this book. Operators in Timor include:

Dive Trek East
   (☎ 21154; fax 24833) Graeme and Donavan Whitford, two Australian dive masters based in Kupang, specialise in diving trips to Alor, and can also arrange dives around Timor and further afield.
Flobamor Diving
   (☎ 32560; fax 33476) Based at the Hotel Flobamor II in Kupang, diving is organised through the hotel's small resort on Pulau Semau.

Surfing

Indonesia is a top surfing destination, and with a string of islands facing the strong southern swells, Nusa Tenggara has it's fair share of great waves from May to September. The only problem is reaching them. Trade, and its accompanying outside influences, came via the main sea routes to the north of the islands, so the southern coasts have always been undeveloped. With a few exceptions, such as Kuta on Lombok and Huu on Sumbawa, the surfing spots are in isolated, lightly populated and difficult to reach areas where facilities are minimal.

Expensive yacht surf tours operate from Bali to the more remote destinations on Lombok and Sumbawa, but for most other waves you'll have to lug your board on local buses. The surf operators in Bali are concentrated in Kuta – try the surf shops on Jl Legian, or Tubes Bar and Indo Dreams on Poppies Gang II. Surf companies overseas include the Surf Travel Company (☎ (02) 9527 4722) in Sydney and Waterways Travel (☎ (818) 376 0341) in California.

Surfing guidebooks include *Surfing Indonesia* by Leonard & Lorca Lueras, which covers Nusa Tenggara (mostly Lombok and Sumbawa), and *Indo Surf & Lingo* by Peter Neely. The easiest place to buy them is in surf shops in Kuta, Bali.

Lombok The southern and eastern coasts of Lombok get the same swells that generate the big breaks on Bali's Bukit Peninsula. The main problem is getting to them. Lombok's Kuta Beach is the most accessible beach by road. There are places to stay and eat there, and boat owners will take you out to the reef breaks. Other south-coast places which you can get to by land, with a little difficulty, include Selong Blanak, Mawun and Ekas – there are lots of reef breaks accessible by boat from these areas. Desert Point, near Bangko Bangko, on the south-western peninsula, is Lombok's most famous break – a classic, fast, tubular left. You can reach it by land, but there is no regular transport and no visitor facilities. The easiest way is with a surf tour on a chartered yacht, usually from Bali, though boats can be chartered from Lembar. Desert Point does not work regularly and needs a good size swell.

Sumbawa Sumbawa is one of the biggest surf destinations, because of the relatively easy access to Huu on the south coast. You can fly into Bima and then charter a taxi to Huu, or good buses run right across Lombok and Sumbawa to Dompu, where it is only a 30 minute taxi ride to Huu. The great attraction of Huu is its variety of surf breaks and the availability of decent accommodation. Right in front of the accommodation strip is Lakey Peak, breaking left and right, while just along is Lakey Pipe, a left hander. Nangas, another left, is further along the bay in front of the small Tunangas River. Periscopes, a right hander, is 1km north.

The Maluk region of south-west Sumba is also a good place to head, but facilities are limited and access more difficult. The well known Supersuck left-hand break is the best at Maluk. Yo Yo's is a right hander in the next bay along and is usually working if Supersuck is flat. Jelengah, 20km from Maluk, is home to Scar Reef, famous for its tubing left hander. Maluk and Jelenga have losmen accommodation, or yacht tours are arranged out of Bali.

Sumba Sumba's surf destinations are for the adventurous – they're difficult to get to, but you'll probably have the waves to yourself. Sumba has extreme conditions – big waves or flat and not much in between.

The easiest spot to reach is on the eastern tip at Kallala, near Baing, but it's still a 3½ hour bus trip from Waingapu, the main entry point to Sumba. Tarimbang is Sumba's most noted surf destination – when it's working it has good barrels and the waves are all but deserted. Tarimbang is on a beautiful horseshoe bay, and accommodation is available in two homestays 1km from the beach. It is a four hour bus trip from Waingapu.

South of Waikabubak in West Sumba, the beaches at Ngihiwatu and west along the coast to Pantai Morosi have some good breaks, but are often wind affected later in the day. Primitive accommodation is available at Watukarere village, on a hill above the beach at Ngihiwatu, or the long-suffering, upmarket Sumba Reef Lodge nearby may one day reopen. You might be able to stay with villagers at Pantai Morosi.

On the western tip of Sumba, Pero has good left and right breaks that can be huge. You can stay ar Pero's losmen.

Timor Timor is a little explored surf destination with a lot of potential along the south coast, but surf tourism is confined to Nemberala on the island of Roti, a ferry ride away from Kupang. Nemberala's big left hander, known as T-land, is attracting fame and an increasing, but still small, number of surfers. Nemberala has homestays and a mid-range resort right near the beach and, although it involves a ferry trip and then a bus ride right across the island, it is the easiest surf spot to reach east of Huu.

Public Holidays & Special Events
continued from page 72

Ramadan

Ramadan is the ninth month of the Muslim calendar, the month of fasting *(puasa)*. During Ramadan people rise early for a big breakfast, then abstain from eating, drinking and smoking until sunset. Many visit family graves and royal cemeteries, recite extracts from the Koran, sprinkle the graves with holy water and strew them with flowers. Special prayers are said at mosques and at home. During this time many restaurants are closed, and it is considered rude for non-Muslims to eat or smoke in public. It's a good time to avoid fervent Muslim areas of Indonesia – you get woken up in your losmen at 3 am to have a meal before the fasting period begins. Many restaurants shut down during the day in Lombok and Sumbawa, but Chinese and Balinese establishments stay open.

Idul Fitri (Lebaran) marks the end of Ramadan, and it is a noisy two day public holiday when half the country seems to be on the move and hotels fill up and prices skyrocket. Don't plan on travelling anywhere – stay put. This climax to a month of austerity is characterised by wild beating of drums all night, fireworks and no sleep. At 7 am everyone turns out for an open-air service. Women dress in white and mass prayers are held followed by two days of feasting. Extracts from the Koran are read and religious processions take place. Gifts are exchanged and pardon is asked for past wrongdoings. Everyone dresses in their finest and newest clothes, and neighbours and relatives are visited with gifts of specially prepared food.

It is traditional to return to one's home village, so many Indonesians travel at this time. At each house visited, tea and sweet cakes are served, and visiting continues until all the relatives have been seen.

Dates for Ramadan, including Idul Fitri, are:

20 Dec 1998 - 20 Jan 1999
9 Dec 1999 - 9 Jan 2000
28 Nov 2000 - 28 Dec 2000

Special Events

Various regular events are held throughout the region from triathlons to surfing championships, and Easter processions to cultural festivals. The most interesting, however, are the traditional celebrations held mostly at planting time at the beginning of the rainy season around October to December, or at harvest time around April to May. Special one-off ceremonies also may be held for the building of a *rumah adat* (traditional house), the naming ceremony for a child, for tombstone dragging in Sumba, weddings, funerals, you name it.

Feasting, dancing, singing or ritual combat often accompanies these ceremonies in villages throughout the region. Animal slaughter is common, particularly in Nusa Tenggara Timur (Flores, Sumba and West Timor), and are often made as offerings to the ancestors or animist spirits and gods. The bigger the celebration, the greater the number of animals sacrificed – it's not for the squeamish.

Such events are often large communal celebrations and visitors are welcome, but ask around before you just front up. They may be held anywhere at any time. Tourist offices and hotel staff are good sources of information, and if you spend any time in the region you may well find yourself invited to a traditional shindig.

The provinces also hold regular cultural festivals to showcase the music and dance from the various ethnic groups, and these are well worth attending. Nusa Tenggara Barat (Lombok and Sumbawa) has one every year, usually in Mataram. Nusa Tenggara Timur has one in Timor; it's held in different cities, but dates are not fixed. Most dates for festivals and ceremonies vary each year. Harvest and planting ceremonies may depend on the moon or the rains, and even dates for regular annual events vary markedly (an extension of Indonesian 'rubber time' perhaps).

The Indonesian Tourist Promotion Office (ITPO) produces an all-Indonesia *Calendar of Events*, available from their offices overseas, and the tourist offices in Mataram and Kupang produce events calendars for their provinces.

Following are some of the more regular and interesting events held throughout the region and the approximate month in which they may fall. The most famous of all events is undoubtedly the Pasola, held in Sumba around February/March.

January

Reba (Flores) – this major festival of the Bajawa people is held during the rainy season, to celebrate the new year and to honour the ancestors. Many animals, mostly pigs, are slaughtered, and a great feast follows with performances of traditional dance and music. The Reba season kicks off on 15 December in Bena village, but most villages celebrate in January (Nage on the 1st, Wogo on the 6th and Langa on the 15th) while others celebrate in February. Dates are fixed and the tourist office in Bajawa has a list.

Hari Raya Ketupat (Lombok) – this is a Wektu Telu (indigenous) celebration held at Batulayar, near Senggigi, seven days after the end of Ramadan.

February-March

Nyale Ceremony (Lombok) – the arrival of nyale seaworms on the south coast of Lombok, a few days after the full moon in February or March, is accompanied by all-night festivities and impromptu boat races. In Sumba, the arrival of the nyale marks the start of the Pasola season.

Pasola (Sumba) – in this most spectacular of Nusa Tenggara's events, warriors on horseback charge and hurl spears at each other. This ancient contest, harking back to the days of internecine warfare, ensures a good harvest. It is held in February near Kodi in West Sumba and in the Lamboya district. It is held a month later in the Wanokaka district.

March-April

Good Friday Procession (Flores) – in Larantuka, an image of the Virgin Mary is carried around the town from church to church, accompanied by shrouded figures, chants and singing. This colourful event owes much to Portuguese influence.

Harvest Ceremony (Lombok) – held at Gunung Pengsong some time around March or April, this ceremony is a thanksgiving for a good harvest. Of Balinese Hindu origins, the ceremony involves a buffalo being dragged up a steep hill and then sacrificed.

May-June

Whale Hunting (Flores) – in Lamakera on the island of Solor in eastern Flores, whales are hunted by hand-held harpoons and the whale season begins around 1 May with a whale-calling ceremony.

Etu/Sagi (Flores) – these traditional boxing matches are held to celebrate the harvest in the Ngada regency around Bajawa. There are various regional differences – boxers use everything from lumps of wood to glass-studded gloves! – but the object is the same, to draw blood that will ensure the fertility of the soil for next year's crop. Around the town of Boawae the matches are usually called *etu* and are held in May and June, sometimes earlier. The most famous contest that attracts spectators from all over the district is held in June in the village of Loa, where it is called *sagi*.

August

Independence Day (National) – on 17 August Indonesia celebrates its independence and parades are held everywhere. In the preceding month many towns have fairs with sideshow attractions, and cultural events and sporting contests are held. Horse racing is a big event in Nusa Tenggara, especially on Sumbawa and Sumba, and finals are often held on 17 August.

October-December

Pura Meru (Lombok) – this is a special Bali Hindu temple ceremony held around October (variable) at full moon in the Balinese temple in Cakranegara.

Perang Ketupat (Lombok) – this annual rain festival is held at Lingsar, between October and December. Adherents of the Wektu Telu religion and Balinese Hindus give offerings and pray at the temple complex, then come out and pelt each other with *ketupat*, sticky rice wrapped in banana leaves (see Lingsar in the Lombok chapter for more information).

ACCOMMODATION
Hotels

Lombok is the main repository of luxury hotels, mostly at Senggigi, but elsewhere in Nusa Tenggara hotels are simple and cheap. The bigger towns and tourist areas also have a few comfortable mid-range hotels, but there is little above one star standard. Outside Lombok, Sumbawa has one luxury hotel and Kupang has a few three star business hotels, and that's about it for top end accommodation.

If you insist on hot water and air-con you'll be out of luck in many places, but hotels are usually clean, well run and are often friendly, family businesses that are much more interesting places to stay than the big hotels.

Most hotels have a *mandi* rather than a

shower – water is scarce in these parts and towards the end of the dry season it can even be hard to get a full mandi in some places. Like most of Indonesia, hotels are putting in western toilets in preference to squat toilets, but flushing cisterns are a rarity, so the squat toilets are often more hygienic.

Hotels usually start at around US$5 a double for a simple room, or slightly more for a one with a bathroom attached. Prices are slightly higher than Bali or Java for the same facilities, but cheap by any standards. In some places – like the popular village of Moni in Flores – hotels are very basic but can be ridiculously cheap; often as little as US$1.50 per person in the off season.

The cheaper hotels are also called *losmen* – a term which is still widely used despite the government's desire for all registered accommodation providers to take the title of hotel. Rooms in mid-range hotels start at around US$10, and in many places you'll be hard-pressed to spend much more – even if you wanted to.

Lombok has a wide selection of tourist hotels in all ranges, but elsewhere tourism is limited and hotels often cater for local business as much as tourism. In out-of-the-way places there are also a few homestays, which are usually simple rooms in a family house or out the back. Meals are usually provided.

Staying in Villages

Hotels are limited outside the main towns, and if you are travelling out in the countryside, then it is usually possible to stay with the *kepala desa* (village head), or someone will always put you up if you are stuck. Protocol when entering a village is that the kepala desa should be the first contact point.

In the larger administrative villages, the house of the kepala desa operates almost as an unofficial guesthouse and government officials on overnight business will stay there. In the more important desas, and if the kepala desa is wealthy (at least in village terms), he might also have an office and a few rooms specifically set aside for visitors. In small district towns, at the centre of a kecamatan, you can also try the camat (head of the district) or other government officials such as the police.

Usually, however, it's simply a case of dossing down at the kepala desa's house and you share facilities with the family. Remember that you are a guest in the house and it is not a hotel. The same rules apply if you meet someone who invites you to stay at their house.

It can be an inconvenience to put someone up and all that may be available is a mat on the floor. More often than not, as an exotic foreign visitor you will be treated as an honoured guest and afforded great hospitality. Your hosts may vacate their bedroom for you and prepare elaborate meals. People are poor in Nusa Tenggara and often feel embarrassed that their simple houses are not up to the standard they think foreigners expect. They may go to considerable expense to accommodate you and kill an animal such as an expensive chicken just for your meal, so try not to be a financial burden.

When staying with the kepala desa, you are expected to make a contribution. The kepala desa may suggest a price if you ask, but usually the cost is by donation and how much you pay is *tersera* (up to you). Politely offer to compensate the kepala desa for putting you up and pay around the same as at a losmen, say 10,000 rp, and for meals (5000 rp or so), more if they really feed you up. It is generally more polite to place money on a table rather than hand it directly to your host. In very traditional villages there may be a betel nut container where you should place your contribution.

If you meet someone who invites you to stay in their house, they may not want payment, but you should always offer. If they say no, offer again, pointing out that you would very much like to contribute to the cost of your stay. Small gifts, especially something typical of your country or something for the children of the family, are also an appreciated gesture.

FOOD

In this poor region restaurants cater to the masses and are mostly cheap and straightforward. In tourist areas you can always find something more than the usual rice and noodle dishes, but even in the most unlikely looking roadside food stall you can come across some real treats. In particular, fish is plentiful, cheap and cooked with style. Restaurants may be simple, but classic Indonesian dishes can be found, and some of the homestays offer excellent home-cooked meals.

Lombok's tourist resorts, such as Senggigi, have restaurants offering a broad selection of Indonesian, Chinese and western meals. Lombok even has some authentic Italian restaurants. Kupang has the most varied selection of restaurants further east, but nowhere will you find the huge range of choice as in Bali.

Most restaurants are run by migrants from other parts of Indonesia. Javanese or Padang restaurants abound, and every decent-sized town has a selection of Chinese restaurants. The Minangkabau from the Padang region of Sumatra are the greatest exporters of their cuisine and in many towns Padang food is all you will find. Dishes in Javanese restaurants are sometimes a poor reflection of the rich culinary traditions of Java, but in some restaurants they really do know how to cook.

Each district has a few specialities, but local food is often simple country fare, such as *jagung titi* (fried corn) from East Flores, and *jagung bose* (boiled corn) and *se'i* (smoked beef) from Timor. One regional dish that deserves a place alongside the great dishes of Indonesian cuisine is *ayam Taliwang*, fried or grilled chicken from the Taliwang region of Sumbawa. Cooked with coconut and spices and served with a piquant chilli sauce, it can be found all over Sumbawa and Lombok.

Restaurants

At the bottom of the barrel in terms of price is the *warung*. This is the poor person's restaurant, found everywhere in Indonesia. It is usually just a rough table and bench seats, surrounded by canvas strung up to act as walls. Often the food is as drab as the warung looks, but occasionally you find something outstanding. One thing you can be sure about is that warungs are cheap. A night market *(pasar malam)* is often a congregation point for warungs.

One step up from the warung, sometimes in name only, is the *rumah makan* (literally, the house to eat). Often distinguished from the warung only by its fixed position and the addition of solid walls, many rumah makan call themselves warungs, so it's a fairly hazy distinction.

A *restoran* is a restaurant, but once again often little more than the name distinguishes it from a rumah makan. But in many cases a restoran will be an up-market place, often Chinese-run and with a Chinese menu. Chinese food is nearly always more expensive than Indonesian food, but there is usually a more varied menu.

Many travellers lose weight in Indonesia, and some say a trip through Indonesia is the best crash diet they know of. This has more to do with illness than the lack of tasty food, so take care in some places. 'Hygiene' is often just a slogan. As a general guide, the cleanliness of a warung or restaurant is a good indicator of how sanitary its kitchen is likely to be. A bad meal at the local Rumah Makan Dysentery can spoil your trip so be wary of uncooked vegetables and fruits and rubbery seafood. Food that is cooked and handled properly before your eyes is rarely a problem.

Snacks

Indonesians are keen snackers and everywhere you'll find lots of street stall snacks, such as peanuts in palm sugar, shredded coconut cookies or fried bananas. Potatoes and other starchy roots are eaten as a snack either steamed, with salt and grated coconut, or thinly sliced and fried.

Food section continued on page 90

Indonesian Food

Some of the dishes you're likely to encounter in eastern Indonesia are listed here:

abon – spiced and shredded dried meat often sprinkled over *nasi rames* or *nasi rawon*

acar – pickle; cucumber or other vegetables in a mixture of vinegar, salt, sugar and water

ayam – chicken; *ayam goreng* is fried chicken; *ayam Taliwang* from the Taliwang region of Sumbawa is a particularly delicious chicken dish

babi – pork; not found in Muslim restaurants but is widely available in restaurants run by Chinese, and is eaten in all the Christian areas

bakmi – rice-flour noodles, either fried *(bakmi goreng)* or in soup

bakso or ba'so – meatball soup

bawang – onion

bubur ayam – Indonesian porridge with chicken. The porridge is generally sweetened and made from rice, black sticky rice or mung beans.

bubur kacang – mung bean porridge cooked in coconut milk

buncis – beans

cap cai – usually pronounced 'chop chai'. This is a mix of fried vegetables, although it sometimes comes with meat as well.

cassava – known as tapioca to westerners, this is a long, thin, dark brown root which looks something like a shrivelled turnip

cumi cumi – squid

daging babi – pork

daging kambing – goat or mutton

daging sapi – beef

emping – powdered and dried *melinjo* nuts, fried as a snack to accompany a main meal

es krim – ice cream; in Indonesia you can get western brands like Flipper's and Peters, and also locally manufactured varieties.

fu yung hai – a sort of sweet and sour omelette

gado gado – another very popular Indonesian dish of steamed bean sprouts, various vegetables and a spicy peanut sauce

garam – salt

gula – sugar

gula gula – lollies (sweets, candy)

gulai/gule – thick curried-meat broth with coconut milk

ikan – fish; understandably there's a wide variety to choose from: *ikan laut* is saltwater fish, *ikan danau* is freshwater fish. *Ikan asam manis* is sweet and sour fish and *ikan bakar* is barbecued fish. If you're buying fresh fish (you can often buy it at a market and get your hotel to cook it up), the gills should be a deep red colour, not brown, and the flesh should be firm to the touch.

jahe – ginger

kacang – peanuts or beans
kacang hijau – mung bean sprouts; these can be made into a sweet filling for cakes and buns
kare – curry; as in *kare udang* (prawn curry)
kecap asin – salty soy sauce
kecap manis – sweet soy sauce
keju – cheese
kentang – potatoes; usually the size found in the west and used in various ways, including dishes of Dutch origin and as a salad ingredient
kepiting – crab; features in quite a few dishes, mostly of Chinese origin
kodok – frog
kroket – mashed potato cake with minced meat filling
krupuk – is made of shrimp and cassava flour or of fish flakes and rice dough, cut in slices and fried to a crisp
krupuk melinjo (emping) – made of the seeds of the melinjo fruit *(gnetum-gnemon)*, it is pounded flat, dried and fried to make a crisp chip and served as a snack with a main course
kueh – cake

lemper – sticky rice with a small amount of meat inside, wrapped up and boiled in a banana leaf; a common snack found throughout the country
lombok – chilli; there are various types: *lombok merah* (large, red); *lombok hijau* (large, green); and *lombok rawit* (rather small but deadliest of them all, often packaged with *tahu* etc).
lontong – rice steamed in a banana leaf
lumpia – spring rolls; small pancake filled with shrimp and bean sprouts and fried

madu – honey
martabak – found on food trolleys all over the archipelago. A martabak is basically a pancake but there are two varieties: savoury, or more usually, sickly sweet.
mentega – butter
mentimun – cucumber
merica – pepper
mie goreng – fried wheat-flour noodles, served sometimes with vegetables, sometimes with meat

mie kuah – noodle soup

nasi campur – steamed rice topped with a little bit of every-thing – some vegetables, some meat, a bit of fish, a krupuk or two – a good, usually tasty and filling meal

nasi goreng – this is the most common of Indonesian dishes; almost like hamburgers are to Americans, meat pies to Australians, fish and chips to the British – popular at any time of the day, including breakfast time. Nasi goreng simply means fried (*goreng*) rice (*nasi*) – a basic nasi goreng may be little more than fried rice with a few scraps of vegetable to give it some flavour, but sometimes it includes some meat. *Nasi goreng istimewa* (special) usually means nasi goreng with a fried egg on top. The dish can range from dull and dreary to very good.

nasi gudeg – unripe jackfruit cooked in *santan* (squeezed grated coconut) and served up with rice, pieces of chicken and spices

nasi padang – Padang food, from the Padang region of Sumatra, is popular all over Indonesia and is often all you will find to eat in the small towns of Nusa Tenggara. It's usually served cold and consists of the inevitable rice, with a whole variety of side dishes, including beef, fish, fried chicken, cur-ried chicken, boiled cabbage, sometimes fish and prawns. The dishes are laid out before you and your final bill is calculated by the number of empty dishes when you've finished eating. Nasi padang is traditionally eaten with the fingers and it's also traditionally very hot (*pedas* not *panas*) – sometimes hot enough to burn your fingers, let alone your tongue! It's some-times wonderful, and sometimes very dull. It's also one of the more expensive ways to eat in Indonesia, although it can be well worth it.

nasi pecel – similar to gado gado, with boiled papaya leaves, tapioca, bean sprouts, string beans, fried soybean cake, fresh cucumber, coconut shavings and peanut sauce

nasi putih – white (*putih*) rice, usually steamed; glutinous rice is mostly used in snacks and cakes

nasi rames – rice with a combination of egg, vegetables, fish or meat

nasi rawon – rice with spicy hot beef soup, fried onions and spicy sauce

nasi uduk – rice boiled in coconut milk or cream

opor ayam – chicken cooked in coconut milk

pete – a huge broad bean, quite spicy, which is often served in the pod

pisang goreng – fried banana fritters; a popular street-side snack

rijsttafel – Dutch for 'rice table'; Indonesian food with a Dutch interpretation, it consists of lots of individual dishes with rice. Rather like a glorified *nasi campur* or a hot *nasi padang*. Bring a big appetite.
roti – bread; the stuff you get in Indonesia is nearly always snow white and sweet

sago – a starchy, low protein food extracted from a variety of palm tree. Sago is the staple diet of the Maluku islands.
sambal – a hot, spicy chilli sauce served as an accompaniment with most meals
sate – one of the best known of Indonesian dishes, sate (satay) are small pieces of various types of meat on a skewer served with a spicy peanut sauce. Street sate-sellers carry their charcoal grills around with them and cook the sate on the spot.
saus tomat – tomato sauce; ketchup
sayur – vegetables
sayur-sayuran – vegetable soup with coconut milk
sembal pedis – hot sauce
sop – clear soup with mixed vegetables and meat or chicken
soto – meat and vegetable broth, often a main meal eaten with rice and a side dish of sambal

tahu – tofu, or soybean curd; soft bean cake made from soybean milk. It varies from white and yellow to thin and orange-skinned. It's found as a snack in the food stalls and is sometimes sold with a couple of hot chillies or with a filling of vegetables.
telur – egg
tempe – made of whole soybeans fermented into cake, wrapped in plastic or a banana leaf; rich in vegetable protein, iron and vitamin B. Tempe goreng is pieces of tempe (*tempeh*) fried with palm sugar and chillies.

ubi – sweet potato; spindle-shaped to spherical with a pulpy yellow or brown skin and white to orange flesh
udang – prawns or shrimps
udang karang – lobster

Fruit

It's almost worth making a trip to Indonesia just to sample the tropical fruit – apples and bananas curl and die before the onslaught of *nangkas*, *rambutans*, *mangosteens*, *salaks* and *sirsaks*.

apel – apple; most are imported from Australia, New Zealand and the USA, and are expensive. Local apples grown in mountain areas, such as Malang in Java, are much cheaper and fresher.

apokat – avocado; they are plentiful and cheap, try an avocado and ice-cream combo

belimbing – the 'starfruit' is a cool, crispy, watery tasting fruit – if you cut a slice you'll immediately see where the name comes from

durian – the most infamous tropical fruit, the durian is a large green fruit with a hard, spiky exterior. Inside are pockets of creamy white fruit. Stories are told of a horrific stench emanating from an opened durian – hotels and airlines often ban them because of their foul odour. Some don't smell so bad – unpleasant yes, but certainly not like holding your nose over an overflowing sewer. The durian season is in the later part of the year.

jambu air – water apple or *wax jambu*. These glossy white or pink bell-shaped fruits come from a popular street and garden tree found throughout Indonesia. Children can often be seen selling the fruit skewered on a sliver of bamboo. The jambu air is crisp and refreshing when eaten chilled, but fairly tasteless. The single seed should not be eaten.

jambu batu – guava; also known as *jambu klutuk*, the guava comes from Central America and was bought to Asia by the Spanish. The fruit comes in many colours, shapes and sizes; the most common is light green and pear-shaped, turning yellow when fully ripe. The pinkish flesh is full of seeds. Ripe guava have a strong smell that some find overpowering. In Asia, the unripe fruit are also popular sliced and dipped in thick soy sauce with sliced chilli; mango also can be served this way.

jeruk – the all-purpose term for citrus fruit. There are several kinds available. The main ones include the huge *jeruk muntis* or *jerunga*, known in the west as the pomelo. It's larger than a grapefruit but has a very thick skin, tastes sweeter (more like an orange) and has segments that break apart very easily. Regular oranges are known as *jeruk manis* – sweet jeruk. The small tangerine-like oranges which are often quite green are *jeruk baras*. Lemons are *jeruk nipis*.

kelapa – coconut; as plentiful as you would expect! *Kelapa muda* means young coconut and you'll often get them straight from the tree. Drink the milk and then scoop out the flesh.

mangga – mango; in season in during the second half of the year

manggis – mangosteen; one of the most famous of tropical fruits, this is a small purple-brown fruit. The outer covering cracks open to reveal pure-white segments with an indescribably fine flavour. Queen Victoria once offered a reward to any-one able to transport a mangosteen back to England while still edible. The mangosteen season is from November to February. Beware of stains from the fruit's casing, which can be permanent.

nanas – pineapple

nangka – also known as jackfruit, this is an enormous yellow-green fruit that can weigh more than 20kg. Inside are individual segments of yellow fruit, each containing a roughly egg-shaped seed. The segments are held together by strong white fibres. The fruit is moist and fairly sweet, with a slightly rubbery texture. It is used mostly in cooking. As nangkas ripen on a tree they may be individually protected in a bag. The skin of a nangka is green when young, and yellow when ripe. The *cempadak* is a close relative of the nangka, but smaller, sweeter and more strongly flavoured.

papaya – or paw paw are not unusual in the west. It's actually a native of South America and was brought to the Philippines by the Spanish, and from there spread to other parts of South-East Asia.

pisang – banana. The range in Indonesia is astonishing – from midgets to specimens well over a foot long. A bunch of bananas, by the way, is *satu sisir pisang*.

rambutan – a bright red fruit covered in soft, hairy spines – the name means hairy. Break it open to reveal a delicious white fruit closely related to the lychee. November to February is the rambutan season.

salak – found chiefly in Indonesia, the salak is immediately recognisable by its perfect brown 'snakeskin' covering. Peel it off to reveal segments that, in texture, are like a cross between an apple and a walnut, but in taste are unique. Each segment contains a large, brown oval-shaped seed. Bali salaks are much nicer than any others.

sawo – brown-skinned, looks like a potato and has honey-flavoured flesh

sirsak – the sirsak is known in the west as soursop or zurzak. Originally a native of tropical America, the Indonesian variety is one of the best. The warty green skin covers a thirst-quenching, soft, white, pulpy interior with a slightly lemonish, tart taste. You can peel it off or slice it into segments. Sirsaks are ripe when the skin has begun to lose its fresh green colouring and become darker and spotty. It should then feel slightly squishy rather than firm.

Food section continued from page 83

Main Dishes

Food in Indonesia is related to other Asian cuisines, but local ingredients such as lemon grass *(sereh)*, shrimp paste *(terasi)*, coconut milk and a variety of spices are combined to create purely Indonesian dishes. Pork is not widely used since it is regarded by Muslims as unclean, but it appears in Chinese dishes and is eaten in Christian areas. Javanese cooking uses fresh spices and a mixture of ingredients, the chilli mellowed by the use of sugar in many dishes. Sumatran cooking, on the other hand, blends fresh and dry spices to flavour the main ingredient. The types of fresh spices that Indonesians use are known to most westerners only as dried ground powders. There is also some Dutch influence in the use of vegetables from temperate zones in some recipes.

Rice is the basis of the meal, with an assortment of side dishes, some hot (with chilli) and spicy, and some just spicy. Many dishes are much like soup, the water being used to moisten and flavour the large quantity of rice eaten. Salad is usually served, along with *sambal* (a spicy side dish) and *acar* (pickles). Many dishes are cooked in *santan*, the liquid obtained when grated coconut is squeezed. Indonesians use every part of a plant, including the leaves of cassavas, papayas, mangoes and beans.

A few basic words and phrases will help make ordering a meal easier.

asam manis	sweet and sour
bakar	barbecued
bon	the bill
daftar makanan	the menu
dingin	cold
enak	delicious
garpu	fork
goreng	fried
makan	to eat
makanan	food
makan malam	dinner
makan pagi/ makan siang	lunch
manis	sweet
minum	to drink
minuman	a drink
nasi bungkus	take-away food
panas	hot (temperature)
pedas	spicy hot
pisau	knife
rebus	boiled
sarapan pagi	breakfast
(Saya) mau makan.	I want to eat.
(Saya) mau bayar.	I want to pay.
sendok	spoon

Self-Catering

Unlike Java and Bali, supermarkets are a rarity in Nusa Tenggara, so to explore the local snacks and ingredients venture into the hustle and bustle of the markets. There you'll find fresh fruits, vegetables, eggs, chickens (both living and recently deceased), freshly ground coffee and just about anything else. There are no price tags, so bargaining is often necessary. Chinese shops in the towns sell a wide variety of foodstuffs, and small roadside stalls (often called *kios)* have bottled water, biscuits, fruit and some uniquely Indonesian snacks to try.

DRINKS

A general rule when travelling in developing countries is to avoid drinking tap water or iced drinks, and in Indonesia health campaigns have taught locals, too, not to drink the water unless it has been boiled. So in restaurants and hotels boiled water is almost invariably offered. Bottled water is widely available. Ice is prepared commercially under relatively hygienic conditions, but it is not uncommon at grotty warungs to see it chopped up on the side of the road.

Tea *(teh)* is commonly served with meals. Alcohol is not overly common on Lombok and Sumbawa because the population is predominantly Muslim, though beer is available everywhere and the bars and restaurants in Senggigi and the Gili Islands are well stocked. *Tuak* (palm wine) and further distilled *arak* are very much a part of the culture in the Christian areas. Some other popular Indonesian drinks, both alcoholic and nonalcoholic, include:

air – water. You may get a glass of it with a restaurant meal. It should have been boiled (and may not have cooled down since). Ask for *air putih* (literally, white water) or drink tea. Hygienic bottled water is available everywhere.

air jeruk – citrus fruit juice; *jeruk manis* is orange juice and *jeruk nipis* is lime juice.

air minum – drinking water

arak – a stage on from *tuak*; it's usually home produced, although even the locally bottled brands look home-produced. Taken in copious quantities it has a similar effect to being hit on the head with an elephant.

Aqua – the most common brand of mineral water; it is highly recommended if you're dubious about drinking other water, although it's not cheap.

brem – Balinese rice wine; either home produced or there's the commercially bottled 'Bali Brem'. A bit of an acquired taste, but not bad after a few bottles!

es buah – more a dessert than a drink; a curious combination of crushed ice, condensed milk, shaved coconut, syrup, jelly and fruit. Sickening say some, wonderful say others.

es juice – iced fruit drinks; although you should be a little careful about ice and water, these delicious drinks are irresistible. Just take one or two varieties of tropical fruit, add crushed ice and pass it through a blender. You can make mind-blowing combinations of orange, banana, pineapple, mango, jackfruit, soursop or whatever else is available.

Green Sands – a pleasant soft drink, made not from sand, but from malt, apple and lime juice.

kopi – coffee; excellent coffee is grown in Indonesia. The best comes from Sulawesi, though Sumatra, Bali and Java also produce some mean brews. Like Turkish coffee, it is made from powdered coffee beans, but it is spooned straight into a glass with lots of sugar and boiling water added. Served sweet and black with the coffee granules floating on top, it is a real kick start in the mornings. Travellers' restaurants have adopted the odd habit of serving kopi without sugar. *Kopi susu* is white coffee, usually made with sweetened, condensed milk.

stroop – cordial

susu – milk; fresh milk is found in supermarkets in large cities, although long-life milk in cartons is more common. Cans of condensed milk are also sold in Indonesia and are very sweet.

teh – tea; some people are not enthusiastic about teh, but if you don't need strong, bend-the-teaspoon-style tea you'll probably find it's quite OK. *Teh tawar* or *teh pahit* is tea without sugar and *teh manis* is tea with sugar.

tuak – an alcoholic drink fermented from the sap tapped from a type of palm tree.

ENTERTAINMENT

The local population is not big on nightlife – cinemas *(bioskop)* in the larger towns are about as exciting as it gets. The tourist office might be able to tell you where to find a traditional dance performance at which you will probably be welcome, but dances are not usually performed for tourists.

On Lombok there is some action at Senggigi, with local bands doing some good rock, reggae and dance music. When hundreds of young Europeans descend upon Gili Trawangan, there's lots of dancing, drinking and late-night loitering in the beachside bars and restaurants. The full moon parties on the Gilis don't quite match their famous counterparts in Thailand, but can get lively in the main tourist season.

Outside Lombok, nightlife is limited to a few karaoke bars in the bigger towns; Kupang has a few bars and seedy nightclubs.

SPECTATOR SPORT

You'll come across soccer matches everywhere, but the most interesting 'sports' are the ritual combats held for festivals and ceremonies. Most regions have their own specialities – stick fighting in Lombok, whip fights in western Flores, spear throwing from horseback in Sumba and even head-butting contests in Sumbawa. Based on warrior contests common in a region once wracked by tribal war, these are now festive events accompanying the harvest or special events.

Horse racing is also big and held on all the islands. The best places to see them are in the main towns on Sumbawa and Sumba. A series of practice races in the dry season leads up to finals held around Independence Day on 17 August.

THINGS TO BUY

Lombok has the best range of crafts, and certainly the biggest range of outlets. The island is noted mostly for its pottery and basketware handmade from natural materials such as palm leaf, bamboo, grass fibres and rattan. The Pasar Seni (Art Market) in Cakranegara has the best selection of Lombok crafts. You can buy 'direct from the manufacturer' and see the process in craft villages, but prices depend on your bargaining skills.

Lombok's basketware is the best in Indonesia, and decorative boxes of woven palm leaves are a speciality. Lombok pottery is also well known and widely exported. Lombok produces horn, bone and wood carvings and some weaving, but weaving enthusiasts will head further east. See the Arts section in the Lombok chapter for a further discussion of Lombok's many fine crafts and the location of craft villages.

Nusa Tenggara Timur is famed for its fine ikat weaving. Ikat is the process where threads are tie-dyed together and then woven to produce complex patterns. Ikat blankets and sarongs are still widely worn in Sumba, Flores and Timor, and weaving plays an important part in the culture. In most areas, women have to learn to weave before they can marry; cloths form part of the bride price and are important for ceremonial occasions or are used at funerals to wrap the body. Traditionally, hand-spun cotton and natural dyes were used; although they can still be found, machine-spun cotton and chemical dyes are becoming more common. This greatly reduces the time to produce a cloth, but the actual weaving is still labour intensive and fine work is produced. Chemical dyes can produce striking colours, but may run when washed.

In Flores, Ende has a weaving market with a wide variety of cloth for sale or almost every village produces weaving. The most famous weaving village of central Flores is on the south coast at Nggela, where a huge amount of cloth is produced. Further east, near Maumere, Sikka is also an important weaving centre.

Ikat from the remote Solor Archipelago still uses mostly hand-spun cotton and natural dies. Timor also produces some fine weaving, though bright chemical dyes are now mostly used. The cloths, however, are striking and produced in many villages.

The most famous cloths are the large ikat blankets of Sumba. Traditionally they were only worn and produced for the royal families and are still only woven in the royal villages of East Sumba around Waingapu. Kaliuda on the east coast is famed for its fine weaving, but good pieces can also be found in Praiyawang, Umabara, Pau, Prailiu and other villages, and in art shops in Waingapu itself. For more information on ikat, see the special section in the previous Facts about the Country chapter.

Sumba is also a good place to pick up woodcarvings, most of which come from the village of Pero on the west coast. Although based on traditional ancestor statues, they are often far removed from the original, but are cheap and make fine souvenirs. Larger horses and primitive statues are particularly striking if you can work out a way to ship them. Art shops in Waikabubak also have a good selection and sell a wide variety of *mamuli* earrings.

In Timor, art shops in Kupang and Soe also have some stunning artefacts. Timor doesn't have a big tourist industry, so many of the carvings, jewellery and weavings are either produced for local consumption or are antiques. Intricately carved bamboo lime containers, used in betel nut chewing, and fine beaded pouches are inexpensive souvenirs. These items and weavings, which sell for up to 50 times the price in Balinese art shops, can be bought in many local markets.

Lontar palm hats and *sasando*, a type of lute, come from the island of Roti and make unusual souvenirs. Of the woodcarvings, the most prized are the small but chunky carved doors from traditional houses, engraved with crocodiles, lizards and other motifs. Many are antiques, but Balinese art shops have a regular production line coming out of Timor, so those pieces offered in Timor also may be new.

Any time you are offered an antique, assume that it is not. Most are newly aged. Leave antiques to the collectors who know their stuff or be prepared to get your fingers badly burned. New artefacts are often just as good, sometimes better, and real antiques have spiritual value that are best left in the place of origin.

Getting There & Away

AIR

The only direct international connections to the region covered by this book are the Silk Air flights from Singapore to Mataram (Lombok) and Merpati flights between Darwin (Australia) and Kupang (Timor). The principal gateways for entry to Indonesia are Jakarta and Bali, and Bali is the usual first stop for a trip through Nusa Tenggara.

For bargain fares, it is usually better to go to a travel agent than to an airline, as the latter can only sell fares by the book. Budget tickets may come with lots of restrictions. Check how long the ticket is valid, the minimum period of stay, stopover options, cancellation fees and any amendment fees if you change your date of travel. Plenty of discount tickets are valid for six or 12 months, allowing multiple stopovers with open dates. Make sure you get details in writing of the flights you've requested (before you pay for the ticket). 'Round-the-world' tickets may also be worth looking into.

Fares quoted below are an approximate guide only. Fares vary depending on the season (high, shoulder or low) and special deals are often available. Fares can vary from week to week, and it pays to shop around by ringing a variety of travel agents for the best fare and ticket to suit your needs.

Australia

Bali is the major gateway to Australia, with almost all flights to/from Indonesia routed via Denpasar. Direct flights connect Denpasar with Sydney, Melbourne, Brisbane, Perth and Darwin. Garuda, Qantas and Ansett Australia are the main carriers and compete on most of these runs. From Denpasar you can take a domestic flight to Lombok, Flores, Sumba or Timor or take the ferry to Lombok and island hop.

A few flights also go directly to Jakarta from Melbourne, Perth and Sydney, but the other flight of most interest is Merpati's Darwin-Kupang connection, flying in both directions on Wednesdays and Saturdays. From Australia the published fare is A$396 return or A$244 one way, rising to A$536 return and A$319 one way in the high season. (If going to Australia, you won't be allowed on the plane without an Australian visa – obtainable in Denpasar or Jakarta, but not Kupang.) Tickets can be bought from Merpati in Darwin (☎ (08) 8941 1606) or through travel agents, but there is not much discounting. If bought in Kupang, the one way fare to Darwin is US$180. Merpati has also been offering very cheap Darwin-Kupang-Denpasar flights for A$330 one way or A$550 return. From Denpasar direct to Darwin costs around US$250.

Warning
The information in this chapter is particularly vulnerable to change: prices for international travel are volatile, routes are introduced and cancelled, schedules change, special deals come and go, and rules and visa requirements are amended. Airlines and governments seem to take a perverse pleasure in making price structures and regulations as complicated as possible. You should check directly with the airline or a travel agent to make sure you understand how a fare (and ticket you may buy) works. In addition, the travel industry is highly competitive and there are many lurks and perks.

The upshot of this is that you should get opinions, quotes and advice from as many airlines and travel agents as possible before you part with your hard-earned cash. The details given in this chapter should be regarded as pointers and are not a substitute for your own careful, up-to-date research. ■

Sample Airfares (in Australian dollars)

From	To	One Way (low/high season)	Return (low/high season)
Melbourne, Sydney, Brisbane	Denpasar	$650/850	$1000/1150
Darwin, Perth	Denpasar	$450/500	$650/850
Darwin	Kupang	$244/319	$396/536

Listed above are sample fares in Australian dollars, ranging from the low season to the high season (December and January).

Flights to Jakarta usually cost slightly more than to Denpasar, but special deals have been offered because of the recent drop-off in business travel.

Travel agents are the best place to shop for cheap tickets, but because Bali is such a popular destination flight discounting is not large and most agents prefer to sell Bali packages. The cheapest tickets are usually for 35 days and have penalties if you change dates. Sixty day tickets are a little more expensive, but more flexible.

Travel agents to try include the big networks like STA Travel or Flight Centres International, which have offices in the main cities, or check the travel pages of the main newspapers. The highest demand for flights is during school holidays and especially the Christmas break – book well in advance.

New Zealand

Garuda and Air New Zealand have direct flights between Auckland and Denpasar. Air New Zealand's fares are generally a little lower than Garuda's. The return economy airfare from Auckland to Denpasar or Jakarta is about NZ$1150 to NZ$1300, depending on the season.

Check the latest fare developments and discounts with the airlines, or shop around a few travel agents for possible deals. As in Australia, STA Travel and Flight Centres International are popular discount travel agents.

The UK

Ticket discounting is a long-established business in the UK and it's wide open – the various agencies advertise their fares and there's nothing under the counter about it at all. To find out what is available and where to get it, pick up a copy of the free newspapers *TNT, Southern Cross* or *Trailfinder,* or the weekly 'what's on' guide *Time Out.* These days discounted tickets are available all over the UK; they're not just a London exclusive. The magazine *Business Traveller* also covers cheap fare possibilities.

A couple of excellent places to look are Trailfinders and STA Travel. Trailfinders is at 194 Kensington High St, London W8 (☎ (0171) 938 3939) and at 46 Earls Court Rd (☎ (0171) 938 3366). Trailfinders also has offices in Manchester (☎ (061) 839 6969) and Glasgow (☎ (041) 353 2224). STA Travel is at 74 Old Brompton Rd, London W7 (☎ (0171) 581 1022) and at Clifton House, 117 Euston Rd (☎ (0171) 388 2261).

Garuda is one of the main discounters to Indonesia. Rock-bottom one way/return fares (low season) from London to Indonesia are around £290/£420 to Denpasar or Jakarta. A host of other airlines fly to Indonesia, including Lauda and Gulf Air, which regularly have cheap fares but more stopovers, while Qantas, Thai and Singapore Airlines are usually more expensive. Most tickets are valid for six months.

Continental Europe

Amsterdam, Brussels and Antwerp are good places for buying discount air tickets. In Antwerp, WATS has been recommended, while in Amsterdam, NBBS is a reputable agency. Many flights go to Denpasar, but it is usually cheaper to fly to Jakarta. The cheapest flights often go via Singapore, with another stop en route.

From Amsterdam, 60 day return tickets with KLM to Denpasar cost around NLG 1850 in the low season, and NLG2000 in the high season (June to September). Tickets to Jakarta are up to NLG300 cheaper. Garuda flies to Denpasar via Jakarta for around the same price. Other airlines such as Royal Brunei, Kuwait Airlines, Air India and Malaysian Airlines often have cheaper fares, but go via more inconvenient routes or have more stopovers.

From Frankfurt, Garuda flies to Jakarta and Denpasar for around DM1450, but flights with Lauda, Malaysian Airlines and Royal Brunei are often cheaper, while Lufthansa tends to be more expensive.

Garuda has flight connections between Jakarta and several other European cities, including Paris, Zurich and Rome. From Paris, Garuda flights to Denpasar are around FF5500 to 6000 or you can fly with Cathay Pacific via Hong Kong for around the same price. Lauda is also a regular discounter on Paris-Denpasar flights. In Zurich try SOF Travel and Sindbad. In Geneva try Stohl Travel.

The USA

There are some very good open tickets which remain valid for six months or one year, but don't lock you into any fixed dates of departure. Flights to Indonesia, either Jakarta or Denpasar, go via Taiwan, Hong Kong, Singapore, Malaysia or another Asian destination and will include that country as a stopover (sometimes you have to stopover). Garuda used to have a direct Los Angeles-Denpasar flight, but suspended it in the wake of the currency crisis – it may start up again.

Return fares to Jakarta or Denpasar start from around US$1050 return in the low season (outside summer and Christmas) from the west coast, and around US$1250 from New York. Recently there have been even lower prices and some real bargains. China Airlines via Taipei is often one of the cheapest, while Singapore Airlines is one of the most direct.

If you are visiting other parts of Asia, some good deals can be found. For example,

there are cheap tickets between the US west coast and Singapore with stopovers in Bangkok for very little extra money. However, plan ahead for the peak season (summer and Chinese New Year) because seats will be hard to come by unless they are reserved months in advance.

The *New York Times*, the *LA Times*, the *Chicago Tribune* and the *San Francisco Examiner* all produce weekly travel sections in which you'll find any number of travel agent ads. Council Travel and STA Travel have offices in major cities nationwide.

Canada

Getting discount tickets in Canada is much the same as in the USA – go to the travel agents and shop around until you find a good deal. Again, you'll probably have to fly into Hong Kong or Singapore and carry on from there to Indonesia.

CUTS is Canada's national student bureau and has offices in a number of Canadian cities including Vancouver, Edmonton, Toronto and Ottawa – you don't necessarily have to be a student. There are a number of good agents in Vancouver for cheap tickets. The *Toronto Globe & Mail* and the *Vancouver Sun* carry travel agent ads.

Asia

Jakarta and Denpasar are connected to all the main centres in Asia. Silk Air's flight from Singapore to Lombok goes every day except Monday and Wednesday and a ticket will cost around US$200 one way. The cheapest flights to Indonesia are the US$70 flights from Singapore to Jakarta.

Other Regions of Indonesia

Bali is the gateway for air services to Nusa Tenggara, with direct Merpati flights from Denpasar to Mataram (Lombok), Maumere (Flores), Bima (Sumbawa), Waingapu (Sumba) and Kupang (Timor). For more details on domestic flights, see the following Getting Around chapter.

Apart from flights to Bali, there are also direct flights between Mataram and Surabaya (East Java), and one flight from Ujung

Air Travel Glossary

Apex Apex, or 'advance purchase excursion', is a discounted ticket which must be paid for in advance. There are penalties if you wish to change it.

Baggage Allowance This will be written on your ticket and usually includes one 20kg item to go in the hold, plus one item of hand luggage.

Bucket Shops These are unbonded travel agencies specialising in discounted airline tickets.

Budget Fares These can be booked at least three weeks in advance, but the travel date is not confirmed until seven days prior to travel.

Bumped Just because you have a confirmed seat doesn't mean you're going to get on the plane – see Overbooking.

Cancellation Penalties If you have to cancel or change an Apex or other discounted ticket, there are often heavy penalties involved; insurance can sometimes be taken out against these penalties. Some airlines impose penalties on regular tickets as well, particularly against 'no-show' passengers.

Check-in Airlines ask you to check in a certain time ahead of the flight departure (usually one to two hours on international flights). If you fail to check in on time and the flight is overbooked, the airline can cancel your booking and give your seat to somebody else.

Confirmation Having a ticket written out with the flight and date you want doesn't mean you have a seat until the agent has checked with the airline that your status is 'OK' or confirmed. Meanwhile you could just be 'on request'.

Courier Fares Businesses often need to send urgent documents or freight securely and quickly. Courier companies hire people to accompany the package through customs and, in return, offer a discount ticket which is sometimes a phenomenal bargain. In effect, what the companies do is ship their freight as your luggage on the regular commercial flights. This is a legitimate operation, but there are two shortcomings – the short turnaround time of the ticket (usually not longer than a month) and the limitation on your luggage allowance. You may have to surrender all your allowance and take only carry-on luggage.

Discounted Tickets There are two types of discounted fares – officially discounted (such as promotional fares) and unofficially discounted. The lowest prices often impose drawbacks like flying with unpopular airlines, inconvenient schedules or unpleasant routes and connections. Discounted tickets only exist where there is fierce competition.

Economy-Class Tickets Economy-class tickets are usually not the cheapest way to go, though they do give you maximum flexibility and they are valid for 12 months. If you don't use them, most are fully refundable, as are unused sectors of a multiple ticket.

Full Fares Airlines traditionally offer 1st class (coded F), business class (coded J) and economy class (coded Y) tickets. These days there are so many promotional and discounted fares available that few passengers pay full economy fare.

ITX An ITX, or 'independent inclusive tour excursion', is often available on tickets to popular holiday destinations. Officially it's a package deal combined with hotel accommodation, but many agents will sell you one of these for the flight only and give you phoney hotel vouchers in the unlikely event that you're challenged at the airport.

Lost Tickets If you lose your airline ticket, an airline will usually treat it like a travellers cheque and, after inquiries, issue you with another one. Legally, however, an airline is entitled to treat it like cash and if you lose it then it's gone forever. Take good care of your tickets.

MCO An MCO, or 'miscellaneous charge order', is a voucher that looks like an airline ticket, but carries no destination or date. Any International Association of Travel Agents (IATA) airline will exchange it

Pandang (Sulawesi) to Maumere (Flores), but it doesn't go in the other direction. No flights go from Nusa Tenggara to Maluku or Irian Jaya, despite their proximity to Timor – you'll have to take a Pelni boat or fly via Bali.

Air Passes Garuda issues a Visit Indonesia Decade Pass, but because Garuda does not fly in Nusa Tenggara it is only worth consid-

ering for travel in other regions of the country. Each sector costs around US$100 and restrictions apply. Enquire at Garuda offices.

SEA

Rumours of imminent ferry services between Kupang (Timor) and Darwin (Australia) are forever circulating, but don't hold your breath.

for a ticket on a specific flight. It's a useful alternative to an onward ticket in those countries that demand one, and is more flexible than an ordinary ticket if you're unsure of your route.

No-Shows No-shows are passengers who fail to show up for their flight. Full-fare passengers who fail to turn up are sometimes entitled to travel on a later flight. The rest are penalised – see Cancellation Penalties.

On Request This is an unconfirmed booking for a flight.

Open Jaw Tickets These are return tickets where you fly out to one place, but return from another. If available, this can save you backtracking to your arrival point.

Overbooking Airlines hate to fly empty seats and since every flight has some passengers who fail to show up, airlines often book more passengers than they have seats. Usually excess passengers make up for the no-shows, but occasionally somebody gets bumped. Guess who it is most likely to be? The passengers who check in late.

Point-to-Point Tickets These are discount tickets that can be bought on some routes in return for passengers waiving their rights to a stopover.

Promotional Fares These are officially discounted fares like Apex fares, available from travel agents or direct from the airline.

Reconfirmation At least 72 hours prior to departure time of an onward or return flight, you must contact the airline and 'reconfirm' that you intend to be on the flight. If you don't do this the airline can delete your name from the passenger list and you could lose your seat.

Restrictions Discounted tickets often have various restrictions on them – Apex is the most usual one. Others are restrictions on the minimum and maximum period you must be away, such as a minimum of 14 days or a maximum of one year.

Round-the-World Tickets RTW tickets are just that. You have a limited period in which to circumnavigate the globe and you can go anywhere the carrying airlines go, as long as you don't backtrack. These tickets are usually valid for one year, the number of stopovers or total number of separate flights is worked out before you set off and they often don't cost much more than a basic return flight.

Stand-by This is a discounted ticket where you only fly if there is a seat free at the last moment. Stand-by fares are usually only available on domestic routes.

Tickets Out An entry requirement for many countries is that you have a ticket out of the country. If you're unsure of your next move, the easiest solution is to buy the cheapest onward ticket to a neighbouring country or a ticket from a reliable airline which can later be refunded if you do not use it.

Transferred Tickets Airline tickets cannot be transferred from one person to another. Travellers sometimes try to sell the return half of their ticket, but officials can ask you to prove that you are the person named on the ticket. This is unlikely to happen on domestic flights, but on an international flight tickets may be compared with passports.

Travel Agencies Travel agencies vary widely and you should choose one that suits your needs. Some simply handle tours, while full-service agencies handle everything from tours and tickets to car rental and hotel bookings. If all you want is a ticket at the lowest possible price, then go to an agency specialising in discounted tickets.

Travel Periods Some officially discounted fares, Apex fares in particular, vary with the time of year. There is often a low (off-peak) season and a high (peak) season. Sometimes there's an intermediate or shoulder season as well. Usually the fare depends on your outward flight – if you depart in the high season and return in the low season, you pay the high-season fare. ■

There are no international passenger ships to any islands in Nusa Tenggara. Pelni, the domestic passenger line, has ships from other regions in Indonesia to Nusa Tenggara, but the only ones of real interest are those to/from Sulawesi, Maluku and Irian Jaya, which are not serviced by direct flights. (See the following Getting Around chapter for details of Pelni services.)

While regular ferries run throughout the islands of Nusa Tenggara, the only ferry connection to other regions of Indonesia is the ferry between Bali and Lombok.

Bali

Regular ferries run throughout the day between Padangbai in east Bali to Lembar in Lombok and take around five hours or more.

A luxury jet-powered ferry also runs daily from Benoa in Bali to Lembar in about 2½ hours. See the Lombok Getting There & Away section for full details. Tickets can be bought from travel agents in the main tourist centres in Bali – tickets include bus transport to and from both ends of the ferry.

DEPARTURE TAX

Airport tax on international flights from Jakarta and Denpasar is 25,000 rp. From Lombok and Kupang it's 20,000 rp. On domestic flights, airport tax is between 5500 and 11,000 rp, depending on the airport. This is no longer included in the ticket price and has to be paid at the airport at check-in.

ORGANISED TOURS

While package tours to Bali are big business, very few overseas companies have tours to Nusa Tenggara. Some have a Lombok supplement that can be added to Bali packages, but otherwise you'll be hard pressed to find overseas travel agents that offer tours to the region. A few regular tours are organised out of the Netherlands, by companies such as Djoser, that go as far as Flores and sometimes Sumba. Italian travel agents sell a variety of Lombok tours and a couple of companies organise overland tours beyond Lombok.

Overland tours are limited and don't expect luxury – it simply isn't available in many areas. The only luxury options are on the cruises operated out of Bali on ships such as the *Bali Sea Dancer*. They go to Komodo with stops in Flores and Sumbawa with onshore visits to traditional villages. Most bookings are via travel agents in the USA.

Of course you can make your own way to Indonesia and take day tours to surrounding attractions. Hotels and guides in a number of areas arrange tours and travel agents in the main towns can arrange tailor-made tours, though they won't be cheap.

Getting Around

The good news is that transport in Nusa Tenggara has improved immensely in the past decade. There are now more surfaced roads, more regular ferries and buses, and a reasonable network of flights. Previously, a lot of travel in Nusa Tenggara was just plain awful – you'd spend days in dreary ports waiting for boats, or hour upon hour shaking your bones loose in trucks, attempting to travel on roads which resembled minefields. Travel can still be arduous but, on the whole, if you stick to the main routes you shouldn't have much trouble. Nevertheless, most people who travel right through Nusa Tenggara by surface transport are quite happy not to repeat the experience and, unless travelling to/from Australia, fly back to their starting point.

AIR

The main airlines in Indonesia are Garuda, Merpati, Sempati and Bouraq, but only the latter three service Nusa Tenggara and almost all flights are with Merpati.

On top of the basic fares, a 10% tax is charged, along with a small insurance fee and domestic departure tax which varies from 5500 to 11,000 rp, depending on the airport.

Tax and insurance is paid when you buy the ticket, but the departure tax is paid at the airport. Baggage allowance is usually 20kg, or only 10kg on the smaller planes. You may incur a fee for excess baggage.

Most airlines offer student discounts of up to 25%. You need a valid International Student Identity Card (ISIC) to take advantage of this. The age limit for claiming the student discount is usually 26. The only airline offices in Nusa Tenggara that accept credit cards are in Mataram, Kupang and Dili.

Merpati has a good network of flights in Nusa Tenggara, but poor quality service. The main transport hubs are Kupang (Timor), Maumere (Flores) and Mataram (Lombok). These are the easiest places from which to get flights. Other airports tend to be serviced by small aircraft, seats can be harder to get and cancellations are more common. The less used and less profitable the run, the more chance of a cancellation, which Merpati usually blames on 'technical problems'.

Merpati has two networks of flights – commercial flights and its Perintis (Pioneer) flights. The commercial flights run between the main airports, such as Denpasar and Kupang, and are reasonably efficient. On Perintis flights, small planes fly between small towns that are not on the computer booking system – consequently overbooking and cancellation are common. Most flights in Nusa Tenggara are Perintis flights.

The booking system is very haphazard.

Warning
In the wake of Indonesia's currency crisis, some airlines in Indonesia were on the verge of bankruptcy. Prices had risen more than 100% by mid-1998, but air travel will still be very cheap while the rupiah remains depressed.

Domestic air tickets bought overseas are quoted on a US dollar rate, which is much higher than the cost of tickets bought in the country. Unless you can get a huge discount overseas, it is cheaper to wait until you arrive in Indonesia to buy tickets.

Air services have also been cut back substantially to save costs. Sempati and Bouraq were severely affected, and many of their routes are no longer operating. Merpati has cut back on the frequency of flights, but the main runs were still operating at the time of research. Shorter hops in Nusa Tenggara have always been subject to cancellation – expect more of the same. ■

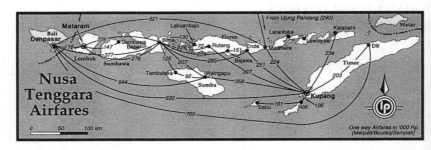

Nusa Tenggara Airfares

Kupang and Mataram have computerised booking systems and you can make confirmed bookings for flights originating in those cities from the main centres, such as Bali, and from overseas – at least in theory.

Other Merpati offices in Nusa Tenggara have to make and confirm bookings by telephone or on their primitive short-wave radio system and it is often impossible to make a booking originating in another town. For example, if you front up in Bima and want to make a booking from Waingapu to Kupang, you may well be told to make it in Waingapu. Tickets are often only issued in the city of departure. *Always* reconfirm bookings in the city of departure.

Problems are worst in the main tourist season around August, when demand is at its highest, and during domestic holiday periods, such as Christmas and at the end of Ramadan. Merpati offices are overrun and airports can fill up with stranded passengers. At these times you should book well in advance – at least one week, or two if possible. At other times it is often possible to get on a flight with minimal notice, even up to the day of departure. If you can't get onto a flight, but are desperate to leave, it may be worth fronting up at the airport before the flight leaves. Multiple bookings are common and there are usually a few no-shows on every flight.

If a flight is cancelled, Merpati may put on another one, but you may have to wait a day or two. If you are relying on a domestic flight from Nusa Tenggara to meet an international flight, it is wise to allow at least a couple of days in case something goes wrong.

Nusa Tenggara is not well connected to the other island groups. Most flights to/from Nusa Tenggara are via Bali. There are direct flights from Ujung Pandang (Sulawesi) to Maumere (Flores), but it doesn't go in the reverse direction. There are no direct flights at all from Nusa Tenggara to Maluku and Irian Jaya.

BOAT
Ferries
Most of the islands are connected by regular ferry services. There are several trips daily between Bali and Lombok, and Lombok and Sumbawa. Between Sumbawa and Flores one ferry goes daily (except Friday), stopping at Komodo along the way.

Ferry services in Nusa Tenggara Timur (Flores, Sumba and West Timor) are subject to change. The routes vary only slightly, but schedules are constantly changing. Those listed in this book should be used as a guide only. Ferries go twice a week between Kupang on Timor and Larantuka on Flores, and another ferry connects Kupang with Ende (Flores), Waingapu (Sumba) and Sabu once a week. Two ferries a week go from Kupang to Alor and on to Atapupu (Timor) then return. Ferries also service the Solor and Alor archipelagos from Larantuka (Flores), and regular ferries run to Roti from Kupang. All of these ferries take cars as well as passengers and, in addition, there are smaller boats from Flores to the islands of Adonara, Solor and Lembata. Details are provided in the relevant sections later in the book.

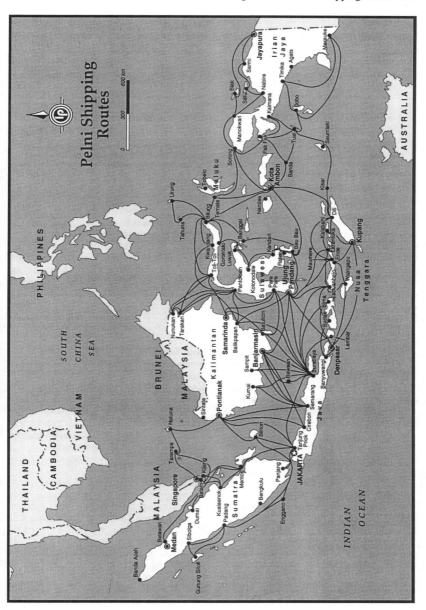

Pelni Shipping Routes

Pelni Ships

Pelni is the national shipping line, offering passenger services almost everywhere. They have modern, air-con ships and operate regular fortnightly or monthly routes around the islands. Comfort depends on the class – Ekonomi is very basic, but OK for one leg. The ships usually stop for four hours in each port, so there's time for a quick look around.

In Nusa Tenggara, ferries are more regular and more convenient, but Pelni services a few ports not covered by ferry. Where ferries are less regular, such as between Flores, Sumba and Timor, Pelni ships can also save you time. If travelling on to Sulawesi, Maluku or Irian Jaya, Pelni ships are the only option, apart from flying to Bali and then out again.

The big problem with Pelni is that routes and schedules change every six months, so it is all but impossible to find out sailing times before you arrive in Indonesia. Pelni produces a six monthly schedule for the whole country, available at Pelni offices, but current schedules can be hard to find. Each office will at least have the latest schedules for the boats that call in at their port.

The main ships servicing Nusa Tenggara are the *Pangrango*, *Sirimau*, *Dobonsolo* and *Awu*. The Pelni Shipping Routes map will give you an idea of the routes throughout Indonesia, but expect some changes.

Travel on Pelni ships is made up of four cabin classes, followed by Kelas Ekonomi which is the modern version of the old deck class. There you are packed into a large room with a space to sleep, but even in Ekonomi it's air-con and can get pretty cool at night, so bring warm clothes or a sleeping bag. It is possible to book a sleeping place in Ekonomi – sometimes – otherwise you have to find your own empty space. Mattresses can be rented and many boats have a 'tourist deck' upstairs. There are no locker facilities in Ekonomi, so keep an eye on your gear.

Class I *(Kelas I)* is luxury plus with only two beds per cabin and a price approaching air travel. Class II is a notch down in style, with four to a cabin, but still very comfortable. Class III has six beds and Class IV has eight beds to a cabin. Class I, II and III have

a restaurant with good food, while in Ekonomi you queue up to collect an unappetising meal on a tray and then sit down wherever you can to eat it. It pays to bring some other food with you.

Ekonomi is fine for short trips and is cheap. Class IV is the better for longer hauls, but some ships only offer Class I and II in addition to Ekonomi. As a rough approximation, Class IV costs 50% more than Ekonomi, Class III is 100% more, Class II is 200% more and Class I is 400% more.

You can book tickets up to a week ahead; it's best to book at least a few days in advance. Pelni is not a tourist operation, so don't expect any special service, although there is usually somebody hidden away in the ticket offices who can help foreigners.

As well as their luxury liners, Pelni have Perintis (Pioneer) ships that visit many of the other ports not covered by the passenger liners. They can get you to just about any of the remote outer islands, as well as the major ports. The ships are often beaten up old crates that also carry cargo. They offer deck class only, but you may be able to negotiate a cabin with one of the crew.

Boat Tours

A popular way of travelling between Flores and Lombok is on a five day boat tour, stopping at Komodo and other islands along the way. See Labuanbajo in the Flores chapter or Getting There & Around in the Lombok chapter for details.

For shorter hops, you can often charter sailing boats or small motorboats.

BUS

Although the roads have improved enormously over the past few years, bus travel is still uncomfortable. Air-con express coaches run right across Lombok and Sumbawa, but elsewhere small buses with limited leg room are crammed with passengers and all manner of produce. They constantly stop to drop off and pick up passengers and, if buses are not full, they will endlessly loop around town searching for passengers until they are full. This constant search for more paying customers can last an hour or more before you even leave town.

Many of the roads are now paved, but even if the road is paved, it is usually narrow and winding, and there are always sections under repair that will rattle your fillings. It varies with the islands. The main highways on Timor and Sumbawa are the best and fastest. The Sumba highway is also good, as is the main highway across Lombok, but it is crowded with traffic. The main Flores highway is sealed, but forever winding and slow. Secondary roads are sometimes excellent, but are usually rough, while some are downright atrocious.

Don't underestimate journey times – a trip of only 100km, even on the highways, may take three hours or more – and don't overestimate your endurance abilities. The road's condition is just as important as the distance. Sealed roads come in two varieties – *'asfal'* (asphalt) and 'hot mix'. Asphalt is a tar road, but laid with primitive methods, and is often very bumpy and may be little better than an unsealed road except that it is passable in the wet season. Hot mix refers to the method of preparing the tar using machinery that sprays it on the road. These roads are smooth and more like roads in western countries. Travel is a lot quicker on a hot mix road. Unfortunately road engineering is not always of a high standard, and even the best surfaces get washed away because of inadequate base preparation.

Most buses leave in the morning around 7 or 8 am, so be prepared for early starts. Where buses leave later in the day, they are limited and less patronised so they often spend longer looking for passengers. Some night buses, leaving around 5 pm, are available between major towns, but you miss out on the scenery. Long-distance buses usually meet the main ferries if you want to travel straight on to other destinations.

Bus terminals are often on the outskirts of town, and it can be a hassle lugging your gear in a bemo to get to them. Fortunately, it is rare that you actually have to go the terminal to catch a long-distance bus. In most towns, hotels can book buses and arrange for them

to pick you up. At the other end, give the bus jockey the name of your hotel and you will be dropped off at the front. In larger cities like Kupang and Mataram this may not apply, and a few other places ban buses from entering the town, but they are exceptions rather than the rule.

On long-distance buses you can buy your ticket in advance through your hotel, at bus station ticket offices or through agents in shops around town. You can also book a seat – remember, the closer to the front the more comfortable. The prime seats with the most leg room are next to the driver, if you can stand the bird's eye view of the crazy driving. The next best are in the row behind the driver. Seats up front may cost 1000 rp or so more, but are often worth it to avoid the crush behind.

If you buy your ticket on the bus, you will usually be charged the correct amount, but the ticket price may be jacked up for foreigners. Ask other passengers the correct fare or watch what they pay and tender the correct amount.

MINIBUS (BEMO)

Public minibuses are used both as local transport around cities and towns and on short intercity runs, but their speciality is delivering people out into the hills and villages. They service the furthest reaches of the transport network.

The general term for a minibus is 'bemo' (a contraction of *becak*, a three wheeled bicycle-rickshaw, and *motor)* but minibuses go by a mind-boggling array of other names such as *opelet*, *mikrolet*, *angkot* or *colt* (after the *Mitsubishi Colt*, a favoured make).

Most minibuses operate a standard route, picking up and dropping off people and goods anywhere along the way. They can be very cramped and often have even less room for luggage than the buses. So, if you have a choice, the buses are usually more comfortable.

Within cities, there is usually a standard fare no matter how long or short the distance. On longer routes between cities, you may have to bargain a bit. Minibus drivers often try to overcharge foreigners – it's more prevalent in some places than in others.

Chartering a bemo can be a good way to reach remote villages or attractions from a town. As a general rule, bemos take 12 passengers, so work out what the fare would be to get there, multiply it by 12, double it for the return journey and add extra for waiting time. You can charter a bemo for a whole day for around 70,000 rp.

TRUCK

One of the great ironies of Indonesia is that farm animals ride in buses and people ride in the backs of farm trucks! Trucks come in many varieties. The luxurious ones operate with rows of bench seats in the tray at the back to sit on. More likely, you will have to sit on the floor or stand. It's imperative to try and get a seat in front of the rear axle, otherwise every time the truck hits a pothole you find out what it's like to be a ping-pong ball. Trucks service the roads that are so rough they are impassable for other vehicles.

CAR & MOTORCYCLE

Undoubtedly the best way to see the region is with your own wheels. The public transport network is fairly extensive, and it presents a never ending parade of Indonesian life, but buses are crowded, hard to see out of, and travel to remote areas involves a great deal of waiting for connections. Buses whiz by scenic areas and make it harder to experience rural life. Many interesting villages are very difficult to reach unless you charter transport.

It's fine to take the buses between the main towns, but once there consider hiring a motorcycle or car or chartering a bemo.

Self-drive cars can be found at reasonable rates on Lombok. Elsewhere it is much more difficult and expensive to rent a car. A self-drive vehicle is almost impossible to find in some parts and you'll have to rent a car and driver. Hotels are good contact points, but they charge commission, as do travel agents. It is cheaper to negotiate directly with the driver. Expect to pay around US$40 a day, including petrol.

If you are an experienced rider, a motorbike is ideal and gives you enormous flexibility to get out into the countryside and daytrip to points of interest. You can transport a bike on all the ferries, but if that's your plan it's best to bring your own. Almost anywhere someone will rent you their motorbike to make a few extra rupiah, but it's difficult to convince anyone to let you take their bike to other islands. Motorbikes are almost all between 90cc and 125cc, with 100cc as the usual size. You really don't need anything bigger – the distances are short and the roads are rarely suitable for going very fast.

Indonesia is not the place to learn how to ride – inexperienced riders are asking for trouble. Although you can rent a bike without a licence, get one before you come to Indonesia. Without one, travel insurance won't cover you and you might run into problems with the police, especially if there is an accident.

Bring an International Driving Permit as well as your home licence if you intend to drive a car or motorcycle. It is usually not required to rent a vehicle, but police may ask to see it.

Driving in Indonesia

People in Indonesia drive on the lefthand side of the road (usually!). Defensive driving is the name of the game and the horn is used liberally, to warn drivers that you are overtaking and to alert pedestrians. The good thing about Nusa Tenggara is that traffic is light. Lombok is a very crowded island, but even there traffic is minimal away from the cities and the main east-west highway.

Combined with all the normal driving hazards there are narrow roads, unexpected potholes, crazy drivers, buses and trucks which (because of their size) reckon they own the road, children who dart onto the road, bullocks that lumber in, dogs and chickens that run around in circles, and unlit traffic at night. Take it slowly and cautiously around curves to avoid hitting oncoming traffic and take extreme care in populated areas.

The legal implications of an accident can be a nightmare, that is if you survive the angry mob should someone be hurt. In the case of a serious accident involving injury or death in the villages, Indonesian drivers don't hang around and drive straight to the nearest police station.

Always ask about the condition of a road before you venture down it. A tar road can quickly become a nightmare of pot holes and gravel further along.

Punctures are easily repaired at roadside stands known as *tambal ban*. Petrol is cheap. There are petrol stations in the larger towns, but out in the villages small wayside garages and shops scoop it out of barrels – look for signs that read *press ban*, or crates of bottles with a sign saying *bensin*. Some of the stuff off the roadside stands can be of dubious quality, so it's best to refill whenever you see a proper petrol station *(pompa bensin)*.

BICYCLE

Bicycles can be rented around the main centres of Lombok and a few other areas. Long-distance cycling is a possibility on Sumba, where there's a lot of flat terrain, but cycling on hilly Flores or Timor requires legs of iron and a state-of-the-art mountain bike. Lombok, with its light traffic, is good for cycling.

HITCHING

Hitching is not really part of the culture in Indonesia, but if you put out your thumb someone may give you a lift. Confusion may arise as to whether payment is required or not. On the back roads where no public transport exists, hitching may be the only alternative to walking, and passing motorists or trucks are often willing to help.

Bear in mind, however, that hitching is never entirely safe in any country in the world, and we do not recommend it. Travellers who decide to hitch should understand that they are taking a small but potentially serious risk. People who do choose to hitch will be safer if they travel in pairs and always let someone know where they are planning to go.

LOCAL TRANSPORT
To/From the Airport

Taxis are usually waiting outside the airports. They don't have meters, but fares into town are usually fixed and tickets for the journey can be bought from the taxi desk in the airport terminal. From the town to the airport, bargain a fare with the driver. Local buses or bemos may pass within walking distance of the airport and are considerably cheaper. In some areas, the airports are a long way from the town and not serviced by regular road transport, but the airlines usually have minibuses to take passengers to these airports.

Bemo

Most towns have a bemo service where fares are a fixed rate for any distance, usually 400 or 500 rp. Be careful of pickpockets on bemos in the main cities.

Taxi

The bigger cities, like Mataram, Kupang and Dili have taxi fleets, but meters are not used and you'll have to bargain the fare in advance. Private unlicensed taxis are more common and can also be chartered by the hour for sightseeing around town.

Other Transport

In Lombok and Sumbawa, *cidomo* are jingling, horse-drawn carts that run around town, often on fixed routes, and sometimes to nearby villages. They cost around 300 rp per person, but you may have to charter a whole cart.

Ojek are motorcycle riders that take pillion passengers for a bargainable price. They are found at bus stations and markets, mostly in Lombok and Sumbawa. They will take you around town and can go where no other public transport exists.

ORGANISED TOURS

Lombok is the tour capital of the region with dozens of travel agents offering city, countryside, craft, diving, boat and trekking tours. Senggigi is the easiest place to arrange tours. In Timor, Kupang has the next highest number of travel agents and tour operators offering city and countryside tours, but opportunities are more limited. In Flores, Maumere and Labuanbajo are the best places to arrange tours.

In the smaller tourist areas guides will offer their services and put together some interesting trips. They can take you to traditional villages and scenic areas by public transport or they can arrange car or motorbike hire. Guides are recommended for visiting traditional villages. They can smooth over language difficulties, teach you correct protocol and greatly enhance your understanding. Guides registered with the Indonesian Guiding Association (ask to see their ticket) have received training and are usually better than non-registered guides.

Lombok

Locator & Map Index

REGIONAL MAP LIST
West Lombok   p 128
North Lombok   p 155
Central Lombok   p 168
South Lombok   p 173
East Lombok   p 177

Gili Islands p 149
Senggigi p 139
Labuhan Lombok p 178
Lendang Nangka p 170
Ampenan, Mataram, Cakranegara & Sweta p 130

Highlights

- **Senggigi** – the main beach resort area has the biggest range of accommodation and services, and the beachfront restaurants are delightful in the evening.

- **Gili Islands** – Gili Air, Gili Meno and Gili Trawangan are small coral atolls with superb beaches and good snorkelling. They all have super-peaceful cottages under coconut palms and no cars, motorcycles or hawkers. Trawangan is the 'party island' with the best diving and snorkelling, while Air and Meno are the places for complete relaxation.

- **Gunung Rinjani** – an active volcano of great spiritual significance, this spectacular mountain offers superb trekking and stunning scenery. Trek into the crater to the hot springs and the brilliant blue-green Lake Segara Anak.

- **Handcrafts** – many villages specialise in particular crafts – sarongs in Sukarara, baskets in Beleka, pottery in Penujak. You can watch the women working and buy some beautiful pieces.

- **Hill Villages** – relax in small, friendly rural villages on the flanks of Gunung Rinjani. Tetebatu is the main base to walk through rice fields and rainforest or stay in nearby Lendang Nangka. Senaru and Sembalun, at the approaches to the Rinjani trek, also have fine scenery.

- **Traditional villages** – both Segenter and Senaru have rectangular bamboo and thatch houses, laid out in traditional Sasak style.

- **Kuta** – Lombok's Kuta Beach has budget accommodation in a lovely location targeted for luxury tourist resorts. Venture further along the undeveloped south coast for superb scenery and beaches, and 'secret' surf spots.

- **Ampenan/Mataram/Cakranegara** – Lombok's port in colonial times, Ampenan retains a quaint down-at-heel charm, picturesque streetscapes and interesting antique shops. Cakranegara has Balinese temples and the not-to-be-missed Pasar Seni (Art Market).

Lombok is the first stepping stone on the journey through the eastern islands. Lombok is by far the most touristed island east of Bali, lying just across the Lombok Strait. It has received the flowover from Bali for years, but even though it now has luxury resort hotels and a full range of tourist services, it is much more relaxed and the hustle for the dollar is much less frenetic than in Bali. Lombok has fine beaches, a mixed culture and Gunung Rinjani is one of the finest treks in Indonesia. It is a good first stop to appreciate the eastern islands, or an excellent place for some R&R if coming from the other direction after more rigorous travel.

Lombok has both the lushness of Bali and the starkness of outback Australia. Parts of the island drip with water, while pockets are chronically dry and droughts can last for months, causing crop failure and famine. Recent improvements in agriculture and water management have made life on Lombok less precarious.

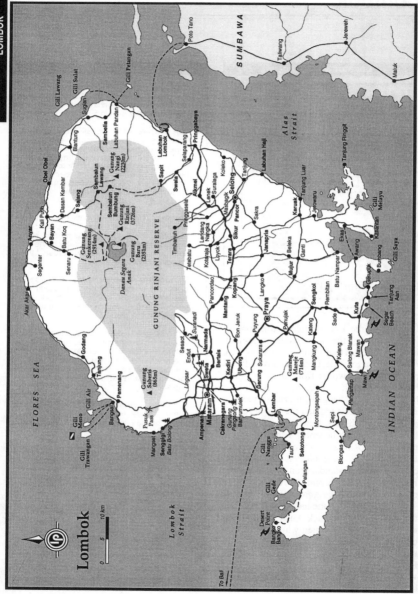

The indigenous Sasak population make up about 80% of the population. Religiously, the Sasaks adhere to the Islamic faith, but they have a culture and language unique to Lombok. There is also a significant minority who have Balinese culture, language and religion – a legacy of the time when Bali controlled Lombok. Balinese-style processions and ceremonies are conducted and there are several Balinese Hindu temples.

Facts About Lombok

HISTORY

The earliest recorded society on Lombok was the relatively small kingdom of the Sasaks. The Sasaks were agriculturalists and animists who practised ancestor and spirit worship. The original Sasaks are believed to have come overland from north-west India or Burma in waves of migration that predated most other Indonesian ethnic groups. Few relics remain from the old animist kingdoms and the majority of Sasaks today are Muslim, although animism has left its mark on the culture. Not much is known about Lombok before the 17th century, at which time it was split into numerous, frequently squabbling states each presided over by a Sasak 'prince' – a disunity which the neighbouring Balinese exploited.

Balinese Rule

In the early 17th century the Balinese from the eastern state of Karangasem established colonies and took control of western Lombok. At the same time, the roving Makassarese crossed the strait from their colonies in western Sumbawa and established settlements in eastern Lombok. This conflict of interests ended with the war of 1677-78, in which the Makassarese were booted off the island and eastern Lombok temporarily reverted to the rule of the Sasak princes.

Balinese control soon extended east and by 1740 or 1750 the whole island was in their hands. Squabbles over the royal succession soon had the Balinese fighting

among themselves on both Bali and Lombok, and Lombok split into four separate kingdoms.

It was not until 1838 that the Matarams subdued the other three kingdoms, reconquered east Lombok (where Balinese rule had weakened during the years of disunity) and then crossed the Lombok Strait to Bali and overran Karangasem, thus reuniting the 18th century state of Karangasem-Lombok.

While the Balinese were now the masters of Lombok, the basis of their control in western and eastern Lombok was quite different and this would eventually lead to a Dutch takeover. In western Lombok, where Balinese rule dated from the early 17th century, relations between the Balinese and the Sasaks were relatively harmonious. The Sasak peasants, who adhered to the mystical Wektu Telu version of Islam, easily assimilated Balinese Hinduism, participated in Balinese religious festivities and worshipped at the same shrines. Intermarriage between Balinese and Sasaks was common.

The western Sasaks were organised into similar irrigation associations *(subak)* that the Balinese used for wet-rice agriculture. The traditional Sasak village government – which was presided over by a chief who was a member of the Sasak aristocracy – was done away with, and the peasants were ruled directly by the raja or a land-owning Balinese aristocrat.

Things were very different in the east, where the recently defeated Sasak aristocracy hung in limbo. Here the Balinese had to maintain control from garrisoned forts and, although the traditional village government remained intact, the village chief was reduced to little more than a tax collector for the local Balinese district head *(punggawa)*.

The Balinese ruled like feudal kings, taking control of the land from the Sasak peasants and reducing them to the level of serfs. With their power and land-holdings slashed, the Sasak aristocracy of eastern Lombok was hostile to the Balinese. The peasants remained loyal to their former Sasak rulers, and supported rebellions in 1855, 1871 and 1891.

Dutch Involvement

The Balinese succeeded in suppressing the first two revolts, but the 1891 uprising was a different story. Towards the end of 1892 the third uprising had almost been defeated, but the Sasak chiefs sent envoys to the Dutch resident in Buleleng (Singaraja) asking for help and inviting the Dutch to rule Lombok. Although the Dutch planned to take advantage of the turmoil on Lombok, they backed off from military action – partly because they were still fighting a war in Aceh (Sumatra) and partly because of the apparent military strength of the Balinese in Lombok.

Dutch reluctance to use force began to dissipate when the ruthless Van der Wijck succeeded to the post of Governor General of the Dutch East Indies in 1892. He made a treaty with the rebels in eastern Lombok in 1894 and then, with the excuse that he was setting out to free the Sasaks from tyrannical Balinese rule, sent a fleet carrying a large army to Lombok. Although the Balinese raja quickly capitulated to Dutch demands, the younger Balinese princes of Lombok overruled him and attacked and routed the Dutch. It was a short-lived victory; the Dutch army dug its heels in at Ampenan and in September reinforcements began arriving from Java. The Dutch counterattack began, Mataram was overrun and the Balinese stronghold of Cakranegara was bombarded with artillery. The raja eventually surrendered to the Dutch and the last resistance collapsed when a large group of Balinese, including members of the aristocracy and royal family, were killed in a traditional, suicidal *puputan*, deliberately marching en masse into the fire from Dutch guns.

Dutch Rule

The Dutch rule of Lombok is a case study in callous colonial rule. New taxes resulted in the impoverishment of the majority of peasants and the creation of a new stratum of Chinese middlemen. The peasants were forced to sell more of their rice crop in order to pay the taxes; the amount of rice available for consumption declined by about a quarter between 1900 and the 1930s. Famines occurred from 1938 to 1940 and in 1949.

For nearly half a century, by maintaining the goodwill of the Balinese and Sasak aristocracy and using a police force that never numbered more than 250, the Dutch were able to maintain their hold on more than 500,000 people. The peasants wouldn't act against them for fear of being evicted from their land and losing what little security they had. There were several failed peasant uprisings, but they were never more than localised rebellions; the aristocracy never supported them and the peasants themselves were ill-equipped to lead a widespread revolt. Even after Indonesia attained its independence, Lombok continued to be dominated by its Balinese and Sasak aristocracy.

Post-Colonial Lombok

Under Dutch rule the eastern islands of Indonesia, from Bali on, were grouped together as the Lesser Sunda Islands. When Soekarno proclaimed Indonesian independence on 17 August 1945, the Lesser Sunda Islands were formed into a single province called Nusa Tenggara, which means 'islands of the south-east'. This proved far too unwieldy to govern and it was subsequently divided into three separate regions – Bali, West Nusa Tenggara and East Nusa Tenggara. Thus Lombok became part of West Nusa Tenggara in 1958, and Mataram became the administrative capital of the region.

Lombok & the New Order

Following the attempted coup of 1965 which led to Soekarno's downfall, Lombok experienced mass killings of communists, sympathisers and ethnic Chinese, as did Bali and other parts of Indonesia. Details of the circumstances, and the numbers killed, are still obscure. Under President Soeharto's 'New Order', Lombok has had stability and some growth, but nothing like the booming wealth of Java or Bali, and it remains a poor island with uneven development. Crop failures led to famine in 1966 and to severe food shortages in 1973. People have moved away from Lombok under the *transmigrasi* (transmigration) program, and several foreign aid projects have attempted to improve water supply, agricultural output and health.

Tourist development did not really start until around 1980, when Lombok first gained attention as an alternative to Bali. The beaches have always been seen as the prime attraction, and while low-budget bungalows proliferated at places like Senggigi and the Gili Islands, big businesses from outside Lombok became interested and speculation on beachfront land became epidemic. Some problems have already surfaced – dispossession of traditional land-holders, dominance of outside business interests, pressure on water resources, and conflict between tourist behaviour and traditional Muslim values.

Lombok is small and somewhat remote, in a large country which has a very centralised power structure. Small scale agriculture is still the main activity in a mostly undeveloped economy. In this context, the emerging tourist industry is the big game on Lombok, and will be the major economic, social and political influence for the next few years.

GEOGRAPHY

Lombok is eight degrees south of the equator and stretches some 80km east to west and about the same distance north to south. It is dominated by one of the highest mountains in Indonesia, Gunung Rinjani, which soars to 3726m. A not-so-dormant volcano, it has a large caldera with a crater lake, Segara Anak, 600m below the rim, and a new volcanic cone which has formed in the centre. Rinjani last erupted in 1994, and evidence of this can be seen in the fresh lava and yellow sulphur around the inner cone.

Central Lombok, south of Rinjani, is similar to Bali, with rich alluvial plains and fields irrigated by water flowing from the mountains. In the far south and east it is drier, with scrubby, barren hills. This area gets little rain and often has droughts which can last for months. In recent years a number of dams have been built, so the abundant rainfall of the wet season can be retained for year-round irrigation. The majority of the population is concentrated in the fertile but narrow east-west corridor sandwiched between the dry southern region and the slopes of Rinjani to the north.

CLIMATE

In Lombok's dry season – from June to September – the heat can be scorching. At night, particularly at higher elevations, the temperature can drop so much that a sweater and light jacket are necessary. The wet season extends from October to May, with December and January the wettest months.

GOVERNMENT

Lombok and Sumbawa are the two main islands of the province of West Nusa Tenggara (Nusa Tenggara Barat, or NTB), which has its capital in Mataram, a civilian governor and a military commander. Lombok itself is divided into three *kabupaten* (districts): Lombok Barat (West Lombok; capital Mataram); Lombok Tengah (Central Lombok; capital Praya); and Lombok Timur (East Lombok; capital Selong).

ECONOMY

Lombok's economy is based on agriculture and the rice grown here is noted for its excellent quality. However, the climate on Lombok is drier than Bali's and, in many areas, only one crop can be produced each year. In some years water shortages caused by poor rains can limit rice production, or even cause a complete crop failure, leading to rising prices and unstable markets. The last major crop failure was caused by drought in 1966, and many people perished for want of food. In 1973 there was another bad crop and, although the outcome was not as disastrous, rice on Lombok rose to double the price it was on Bali.

Dam building and the improvement of agricultural techniques, in part supported by foreign-aid projects, will hopefully ensure better and more reliable crops in the future. Although rice is the staple crop, there are small and large plantations of coconut palms, coffee, kapok and cotton. Tobacco is a common cash crop, and square brick drying towers are often seen. In the fertile areas the land is intensively cultivated, often with a variety of crops planted together. Look for the vegetables and fodder trees planted on the levees between the paddy fields. Crops such as cloves, vanilla, pepper and pineapples are being introduced. Where possible, two rice crops are grown each year, with a third crop, perhaps of pineapples, grown for cash.

Fishing is widespread along the coastline which, edged by coral, has many good spawning areas. Stock-breeding on Lombok is done only on a small scale. Pumice stone is a profitable export, especially when stone-washed denim is in fashion.

Tourism

Lombok is keen to develop its tourist industry, perhaps inspired by Bali's obvious success. The first step in this direction has been the development of Senggigi Beach and, particularly, the upmarket Senggigi Beach Hotel, owned by Garuda, the national airline. Both the Indonesian and the West Nusa Tenggara governments want to attract 'quality' tourists, and are promoting the establishment of expensive resort hotels. Most of the initial development is at Senggigi, but large tracts of beachfront land all around the island have been acquired for 'co-developments' with Javanese and foreign interests. Some local people who sold their land used the money for a pilgrimage to Mecca and now live in poverty.

Regulations make it increasingly difficult to establish budget accommodation on the many beautiful but undeveloped beaches. There is some conflict of interest between big development interests and the operators of small, low-budget tourist facilities, for example, on the Gili Islands. On the bright side, stringent environmental standards are being imposed on new developments.

After a rash of speculation, development slowed somewhat in the face of hard economic reality. With more and more deluxe hotels on Bali, and a depressed international economy, there were second thoughts about how many fancy hotel rooms could be filled. Lombok's airport does not have the capacity for large numbers of arrivals, and though there is talk of a new international airport in southern Lombok, investors are unlikely to put up the large sums necessary for luxury

hotels until there is something concrete. Other improvements in infrastructure, like reliable electricity and water supplies, are also necessary.

There is one new luxury hotel near Sira, on the north-west coast, but the main development area is on the south coast, where all the land has been bought up, new roads completed and a grandiose master plan prepared. The plan envisages 17 luxury hotels, two golf courses, a marina, museum, shopping centre and so on. It's difficult to imagine that local people will be big participants in this development.

POPULATION & PEOPLE

Lombok has a population of around 2.7 million people, with the majority living in and around the main centres of Praya, Ampenan, Cakranegara, Mataram and Selong. More than 80% of the people are Sasak, about 10% are Balinese, and there are minority populations of Chinese, Javanese and Arabs.

Sasaks

The Sasaks are assumed to have originally come from north-western India or Myanmar (Burma), and the clothing they wear even today – particularly the women – is very similar to that worn in those areas. Sasak women traditionally dress in long black sarongs called *lambung* and short-sleeved blouses with a V-neck. The sarong is held in place by a 4m-long scarf known as a *sabuk*, trimmed with brightly coloured stripes. They wear very little jewellery and never any gold ornaments. Officially, most Sasaks are Muslims, but, unofficially, many of the traditional beliefs have become interwoven with Muslim ideology.

Balinese

The Balinese originally settled in the west, and the majority of Lombok's Balinese still live there today and retain their Hindu customs and traditions. Historically, as one-time feudal overlords of Lombok, the Balinese earned the ill will of the Sasaks. Even today, the Sasaks regard the Dutch as liber-

Lombok Food

There are few tourist restaurants on Lombok, which means you'll be eating Indonesian or Chinese dishes in most places, though simple Sasak and Padang food is also available. In Bahasa Indonesia, the word *lombok* means chilli pepper and it's used liberally in the local cooking. Unless you like having your mouth on fire beware of adding more before you really taste a dish.

By and large the Chinese restaurants on Lombok are cleaner and have more variety and tastier food than the Indonesian *rumah makan* (eating places). As on Bali, there is no question that you will eat well and cheaply.

Sasak food uses white rice as a staple, served with vegetables and hot chilli. A little chicken is used, some fish, very little meat and no pork. The meat component is frequently offal, such as liver, brains or intestine. Some specialities include:

ares – a dish made from the pith of a banana tree stem, with coconut juice, garlic and spices, and is sometimes mixed with chicken or meat

ayam Taliwang – this delicious dish of fried or grilled chicken with chilli sauce is originally from Taliwang on Sumbawa, but it has almost become a Lombok speciality

kàngkung – water convolvulus, the leaves are used as a green vegetable like spinach; you can see it growing in the river at Ampenan and it is widely used in Chinese cooking

kelor – hot soup with kangkung and/or other vegetables

pelecing – a sauce made with chilli, fish paste *(trassi)*, tomato, salt and bumbu

pelecing manuk – fried chicken with pelecing

sate pusut – a snack with a sausage-shaped mixture of grated coconut, meat, spices and brown sugar wrapped onto a sate stick; try it at the market

serebuk – a dish of grated coconut, sliced vegetable and kangkung

timun urap – sliced cucumber with grated coconut, onion and garlic

Sweets Sweet sticky things are popular in Sasak cooking. They are typically combinations of sticky rice or rice flour, palm sugar, coconut and coconut milk, wrapped in a banana leaf or pressed into a small cake. They are commonly offered to visitors with coffee or tea. ■

---

ating them from an oppressive power, but by and large the Balinese and Sasaks co-exist amicably. The Balinese contributed to the emergence of Lombok's Wektu Telu religion, and Balinese temples, ceremonies and processions are a colourful part of west Lombok's cultural life.

The Balinese are also involved in commercial activities, particularly within the tourist industry. Many of the cheap and mid-range hotels are run by Balinese, with the same friendliness and efficiency you find on Bali.

Chinese

The Chinese first came to Lombok with the Dutch as a cheap labour force and worked as coolies in the rice paddies. Later they were given some privileges and allowed to set up and develop their own businesses, primarily restaurants and shops. Most of the Chinese living on Lombok today are based in Ampenan and Cakranegara. Almost every shop and

every second restaurant in Cakra is run or owned by Chinese.

Arabs

In Ampenan there is a small Arab quarter known as Kampung Arab. The Arabs living here are devout Muslims who follow the Koran to the letter, and marry amongst themselves. They are well educated and relatively affluent; many follow professions such as teaching and medicine, while others are insurance agents or office workers.

Buginese

In the late 19th century seafaring immigrants from southern Sulawesi started to settle on the coastal areas of Lombok. Their descendants still operate much of the fishing industry. In Labuhan Lombok, Labuhan Haji and Tanjung Luar, Bugis-style houses are a common sight, constructed on stilts with low-pitched roofs and sometimes carved decorations on the verandahs and gables.

LOMBOK

ARTS
Weaving
Lombok is renowned for its traditional weaving, and the techniques are handed down from mother to daughter. Each piece of cloth is woven on a hand loom in established patterns and colours. Some fabrics are woven in as many as four directions and interwoven with gold thread, and many take at least a month to complete. Flower and animal motifs of buffalos, dragons, lizards, crocodiles and snakes are sometimes used to decorate this exquisite cloth. Several villages specialise in weaving, particularly Sukarara, near Praya, and Pringgasela in Central Lombok.

Basketware & Pottery
Lombok is noted for its woven basketware, bags and mats. The quality of Lombok's fine, spiral baskets is the best in Indonesia, and this traditional craft has been adapted to produce a variety of goods for the tourist market, such as placemats. Decorative boxes of woven palm leaves studded with small cowrie shells are a Lombok speciality. Beleka, Suradadi, Kotaraja and Loyok are noted for fine basketware, while Rungkang,

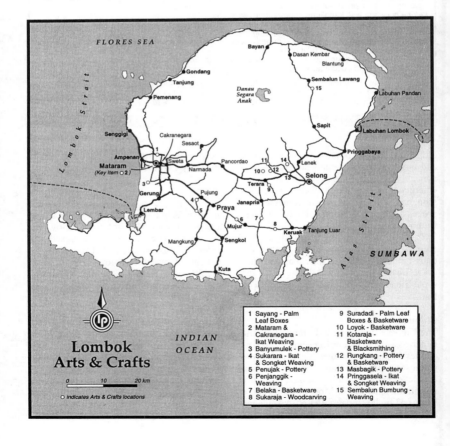

FLORES SEA

Lombok Strait

Alas Strait

INDIAN OCEAN

Lombok
Arts & Crafts

0   10   20 km

○ indicates Arts & Crafts locations

1 Sayang - Palm Leaf Boxes
2 Mataram & Cakranegara - Ikat Weaving
3 Banyumulek - Pottery
4 Sukarara - Ikat & Songket Weaving
5 Penujak - Pottery
6 Penjanggik - Weaving
7 Belaka - Basketware
8 Sukaraja - Woodcarving
9 Suradadi - Palm Leaf Boxes & Basketware
10 Loyok - Basketware
11 Kotaraja - Basketware & Blacksmithing
12 Rungkang - Pottery & Basketware
13 Masbagik - Pottery
14 Pringgasela - Ikat & Songket Weaving
15 Sembalun Bumbung - Weaving

A typical example of Lombok's exquisite arts and crafts – a handcarved betel nut wood container.

a few kilometres east of Loyok, combines pottery and basketware in their pots, which are finished with a covering of woven cane for decoration and extra strength. Sayang is known for palm-leaf boxes.

Lombok pottery is well known and widely exported. Large and small earthenware pots are popular, and large decorative plates with subtle colours and 'primitif' motifs are particularly in vogue. Penujak, Banyumalik and Masbagik are noted pottery centres.

Music & Dance

Lombok has some brilliant dances found nowhere else in Indonesia. But unlike Bali which encourages – in fact hustles – westerners to go along to its dances, getting to see any on Lombok has, until recently, always depended on word of mouth or pure luck. For good or ill, performances are now being staged for tourists in some of the luxury hotels and in the village of Lenek, which is known for its dance traditions.

Cupak Gerantang This is a dance based on one of the Panji stories, an extensive cycle of written and oral stories originating on Java in the 15th century. Panji is a romantic hero and this dance is popular all over Lombok. It is usually performed at traditional celebrations, such as birth and marriage ceremonies, and at other festivities.

Kayak Sando This is another version of a Panji story, but here the dancers wear masks. This dance is only found in central and east Lombok.

Gandrung This dance is about love and courtship – *gandrung* means being in love or longing. It is a social dance, usually performed outdoors by the young men and women of the village. Everyone stands around in a circle and then, accompanied by a full gamelan orchestra, a young girl dances dreamily by herself for a time, before choosing a male partner from the audience to join her. The Gandrung is common to Narmada, Suangi, Lenek and Praya.

Oncer This is a war dance performed by men and young boys. It is a highly skilled and dramatic performance which involves the participants playing a variety of unusual musical instruments in time to their movements. The severe black of the costumes is slashed with crimson and gold waistbands, shoulder sashes, socks and caps. The dance is performed with great vigour at traditional *adat* festivals, in central and eastern Lombok.

Rudat Also a traditional Sasak dance, the Rudat is performed by pairs of men dressed in black caps and jackets and black-and-white checked sarongs. The dancers are backed by singers, tambourines and cylindrical drums called *jidur*. The music, lyrics and costume used in this dance reflect a mixture of Islamic and Sasak cultures.

Tandak Gerok Traditionally a performance from eastern Lombok, the Tandak Gerok combines dance, theatre and singing to music played on bamboo flutes and the bowed lute called a *rebab*. Its unique and most attractive feature is that the vocalists imitate the sound of the gamelan instruments. It is usually performed after harvesting or other hard physical labour, but is also put on at adat ceremonies.

Genggong Seven musicians are involved in this performance. Using a simple set of instruments which includes a bamboo flute, a rebab and knockers, they accompany their music with dance movements and stylised hand gestures.

Barong Tengkok This is the name given to the procession of musicians who play at weddings or circumcision ceremonies.

Contemporary Music The Sasak enjoyment of music and dance extends to rock, and you're most likely to encounter it blaring from the cassette player in a taxi, bus or bemo. Indonesian performers, mostly from Java, do some pretty good cover versions of western hits, as well as original rock songs, mostly in Indonesian and often with a strong reggae influence. Shops in Mataram have thousands of cassettes in stock, so if you hear something you like you can usually buy a copy to take home. Lombok bands can be heard at Senggigi, and young locals are enthusiastic on the dance floor.

Architecture

Traditional laws and practices govern Lombok's architecture, as they do any other aspect of daily life. Construction must begin on a propitious day, always with an odd-numbered date, and the frame of the building must be completed on that same day. It would be bad luck to leave any of the important structural work to the following day.

In a traditional Sasak village there are three types of buildings: the communal meeting hall *(beruga)*, family houses *(bale tani)*, and rice barns *(lumbung)*. The beruga and the bale tani are both rectangular, with low walls and a steeply pitched thatched roof, though of course the beruga is larger. The arrangement of rooms in a family house

is also very standardised – there is an open verandah *(serambi)* at the front and two rooms on two different levels inside: one for cooking and entertaining guests, the other for sleeping and storage.

Lumbung The lumbung, with its characteristic horseshoe shape, has become something of an architectural symbol on Lombok. You'll see rice-barn shapes in the design of hotel foyers, entrances, gateways and even phone booths. A lumbung design is often used for tourist bungalows. On an island that has been regularly afflicted with famine, a rice barn must be a powerful image of prosperity. Ironically, the new strains of high-yield rice, which have done so much to increase the food supply in Indonesia, cannot be stored in a traditional rice barn. It is said that the only lumbung built these days are for storing tourists.

TRADITIONAL CULTURE

Traditional law (adat) is still fundamental to the way of life on Lombok, particularly customs relating to courting and marriage rituals and circumcision ceremonies. In western Lombok you can see Balinese dances and temple ceremonies, and colourful processions with decorative offerings of flowers, fruit and food. Sasak ceremonies are often less visible, though you may see colourful processions. Ask around and you will probably find out when and where festivals and celebrations are being held.

Birth

One of the Balinese rituals adopted by the Wektu Telu religion is a ceremony which takes place soon after birth and involves offerings to, and the burial of, the placenta. This ceremony is called *adi kaka* and it is based on the belief that during the process of each birth, four siblings escape from the womb, symbolised by the blood, the fertilised egg, the placenta and the amniotic fluid that protects the foetus during pregnancy. If the afterbirth is treated with deference and respect, these four siblings will not cause harm to the newborn child or its mother. The

LOMBOK

priest then names the newborn child with a ritualistic scattering of ashes known as *buang au*. When the child is 105 days old it has its first haircut in another ceremony called the *ngurisang*.

Circumcision

The laws of Islam require that all boys be circumcised *(nyunatang)*, and in Indonesia this is usually done somewhere between the ages of six and 11. Much pomp and circumstance mark this occasion on Lombok. The boys are carried through the village streets on painted wooden horses and lions with tails of palm fronds. The circumcision is performed without anaesthetic as each boy must be prepared to suffer pain for Allah, and as soon as it is over they all have to enact a ritual known as the *makka* – a kind of obeisance involving a drawn kris dagger which is held unsheathed.

Courting

There's much pageantry in Sasak courting mores. Traditionally, teenage girls and boys are kept strictly apart except on certain festival occasions – weddings, circumcision feasts and the annual celebration of the first catch of the strange *nyale* fish at Kuta. On these occasions they are allowed to mingle with each other freely. However, if at one of these occasions a girl publicly accepts a gift from a boy – food for example – she is committed to marrying him.

Harvest time is another opportunity for courting. Traditionally, the harvesting of rice was women's work and the men carried the sheaves away on shoulder-poles. Under the watchful eyes of the older men and women, a group of girls would approach the rice paddy from one side, a group of boys from the other. Each group would sing a song, each would applaud the other and do some circumspect flirting. This courtship ritual is still carried on in the more isolated, traditional villages.

Marriage Rituals

Young couples have a choice of three rituals: the first is an arranged marriage; the second a union between cousins; and the third elope-

ment. The first two are uncomplicated: the parents of the prospective bridal couple meet to discuss the bride's dowry and sort out any religious differences. Having handled the business arrangements, the ceremony, *sorong serah*, is performed.

The third method is far more complicated and dramatic. Theoretically, a young girl is forbidden to marry a man of lower caste, but this rule can be broken through kidnapping and elopement. As a result, eloping is still a widespread practice on Lombok, despite the fact that in most instances the parents of the couple know what's afoot. Originally it was used as a means of eluding other competitors for the girl's hand or in order to avoid family friction, but it also minimised the heavy expenses of a wedding ceremony!

The rules of this ritual are laid down and must be followed step by step. After the girl is spirited away by the boy, he is required to report to the *kepala desa* (head of the village) where he has taken refuge. He receives 44 lashes for such a 'disrespectful' action and has a piece of black cotton string wound around his right wrist to indicate to all that he has kidnapped his future bride. The kepala desa then notifies the girl's family through the head of their village. A delegation from the boy's family visits the girl's parents, and between them they settle on a price for the bride, which is distributed among members of the bride's family in recompense for losing her.

Traditional dowries are worked out according to caste differences; the lower his caste and the higher hers, the more he has to pay. Payment is in old Chinese coins *(bolong)* and other ceremonial items, rather than in cash. Once this has been settled the wedding begins. Generally the bride and groom, dressed in ceremonial clothes, are carried through the streets on a sedan chair on long bamboo poles. The sounds of the gamelan (known as the *barong tengkok*) mingle with the shouts and laughter of the guests as the couple are swooped up and down and around on their way to the wedding place. Throughout the whole ceremony the bride must look downcast and unhappy at the prospect of leaving her family.

LOMBOK

Death

The Balinese inhabitants of Lombok hold cremation ceremonies identical to those on Bali. A Balinese funeral is amazing, colourful, noisy and exciting and represents the destruction of the body and the release of the soul so that it can be united with the supreme god.

The body is carried to the cremation ground in a high, multi-tiered tower made of bamboo, paper, string, tinsel, silk, cloth, mirrors, flowers and anything else bright and colourful. Carried on the shoulders of a group of men, the tower represents the cosmos, while the base, in the shape of a turtle entwined by two snakes, symbolises the foundation of the world. On the base is an open platform where the body is placed – in the space between heaven and earth.

At the cremation ground the body is transferred to a funeral sarcophagus and the whole lot – funeral tower, sarcophagus and body – goes up in flames. Finally, the colourful procession heads to the sea (or a nearby river if the sea is too far away) to scatter the ashes.

Members of the Wektu Telu religion have their own rituals. The body is washed and prepared for burial by relations in the presence of a holy man, and then wrapped in white sheets and sackcloth. The corpse is placed on a raised bamboo platform, while certain sections of the Koran are read out and relations pray to Allah and call upon the spirits of their ancestors. The body is then taken to the cemetery and interred with the head facing towards Mecca. During the burial, passages of the Koran are read aloud in Sanskrit and afterwards more quotations from the Koran are recited in Arabic.

Relatives and friends of the dead place offerings on the grave – pieces of hand-carved wood if it's a man or decorative combs if it's a woman. Various offerings which include combs and cloth are also made in the village. Several ceremonies, involving readings from the Koran, are performed on the third, seventh, 40th and 100th day after the death. A special ceremony, known as *nyiu*, is carried out after 1000 days have elapsed –

the grave is sprinkled with holy water and the woodcarvings or combs removed and stones put in their place.

A Muslim cemetery is typically a low hill covered with gnarled and twisted frangipani trees. Small 'headstones', about 40 cm high, stand under the trees. You'll see these cemetery mounds all over Lombok, and you might find them spooky places even if you're not superstitious.

There's also an interesting Chinese cemetery just north of Ampenan. Some of the graves are quite large and elaborately decorated. Wealthy Chinese are buried with many of the material possessions they enjoyed during their life. Clothes, cooking equipment, radios, TV sets and even motorcycles are said to be interred with their owners in this cemetery.

Contests

The Sasaks are fascinated by physical prowess and heroic trials of strength, fought on a one-to-one level. As a result they have developed a unique contest of their own and adapted others from nearby Sumbawa. These contests are most frequently seen in July, August and September – August is the best month.

Peresehan This peculiar man-to-man combat is a great favourite all over Lombok. Usually held in the late afternoon in the open air, a huge crowd – all men apart from the occasional curious female traveller – gather together to watch two men battle it out with long rattan staves, protected only by small rectangular shields made from cow or buffalo hide. The staves are ceremoniously handed around the crowd. With great drama the gamelan starts and two men, dressed in exquisite finery featuring turbans or headscarves and wide waist sashes, feign the movements of the contest about to be fought.

Having shown everyone how it is supposed to be done, the two men look around the crowd for contestants, who are carefully chosen to match each other as closely as possible in height and strength. Anyone can be chosen; some perform several times during the afternoon, while others refuse to take part at all. While it is quite permissible to refuse, it is clearly of great status to win. Those who agree to participate must quickly find scarves to wrap around their heads and waists if they aren't already wearing them (the head gear and waist sash are supposed to have magical protective powers). They next take off their shirts and shoes, roll up their trousers, pick up their staves and shields, and begin laying into each other.

If either of the fighters loses his headscarf or waist sash the contest is stopped immediately until he puts it back on. It goes for three rounds – often five with more experienced fighters – or until one of the two is bleeding or surrenders. The *pekembar* (umpire of the contest) can also declare the contest over if he thinks things are getting too rough. This often happens, for though the movements are very stylised, there is absolutely nothing carefully choreographed or rigged about the peresehan. Both contestants generally finish with great welts all over them, the crowd gets wildly excited and each fighter has his own groupies cheering him on. At the end of each contest the winner is given a T-shirt or sarong, and the loser also gets some small token.

Before the event, as part of the spectacle and atmosphere, a greasy pole contest is often held. Two tall poles are erected, topped by a gaily decorated, large wooden wheel with goodies dangling from it, such as cloth, bags and shorts. Amid much mirth and merriment two small boys attempt to clamber up the slippery pole and untie the loot.

Lanca This trial of strength originated in Sumbawa, but the Sasaks have adopted the lanca and perform it on numerous occasions, particularly when the first rice seedlings are planted. Like the peresehan it is a contest between two well matched men, who use their knees to strike each other. It involves a lot of skill and strength.

Sport
Sasaks (males anyway) are keen on competitive sports. There's quite a large football

(soccer) stadium near Cakranegara, and every town has a football field. Volleyball, badminton and table tennis are also popular. Late afternoon in almost any village you will find young men enjoying an enthusiastic game of volleyball or soccer, often with an enthusiastic audience as well. Just north of Mataram is a horse-racing track, where young bareback riders compete furiously.

RELIGION
The majority of Lombok's population is Muslim, but there's a significant minority of Balinese Hindus, who live mostly in West Lombok. Lombok has its own indigenous religion, Wektu Telu, unique to the island. Although most adherents have now converted to Islam, pockets of Wektu Telu survive.

Wektu Telu
This unique religion originated in the village of Bayan, in northern Lombok. Officially only a very small proportion of the population belongs to this faith, which is not one of Indonesia's 'official' religions. More and more young people turn to Islam.

The word *wektu* means 'result' in the Sasak language, while *telu* means 'three' and signifies the complex mixture of the three religions which comprise Wektu Telu: Balinese Hinduism, Islam and animism. Members of the Wektu Telu religion regard themselves as Muslims, although they are not officially accepted as such by mainstream Muslims.

The fundamental tenet of Wektu Telu is that all important aspects of life are underpinned by a trinity. One example of this principle is the trinity of Allah, Mohammed and Adam. Allah symbolises the one true God, Mohammed is the link between God and human beings, and Adam represents a being in search of a soul. The sun, the moon and the stars are believed to represent heaven, earth and water. The head, body and limbs represent creativity, sensitivity and control.

On a communal basis the Wektu Telu hold that there are three main duties which they must fulfil: belief in Allah; avoiding the temptations of the devil; and co-operating with, helping and loving other people. The faithful must also pray to Allah every Friday, meditate and undertake to carry out good deeds.

The Wektu Telu do not observe Ramadan, the month-long period of abstinence so important in the Islamic faith. Their concession to it is a mere three days of fasting and prayer. They also do not follow the pattern of praying five times a day in a holy place, one of the basic laws of Islam. While prayer and meditation are of supreme importance in their daily rituals, the Wektu Telu believe in praying from the heart when and where they feel the need, not at appointed times in places specifically built for worship. According to them, all public buildings serve this purpose and all are designed with a prayer corner or a small room which faces Mecca. Wektu Telu do not make a pilgrimage to Mecca, but their dead are buried with their heads facing in that direction.

As for not eating pork, the Wektu Telu consider everything which comes from Allah to be good. Unlike the Muslims, the Wektu Telu have a caste system. There are four castes, the highest being Datoe, the second Raden, the third Buling and the fourth Jajar Karang.

LANGUAGE

Most people on Lombok are bilingual, speaking their own ethnic language, Sasak, and the national language, Bahasa Indonesia. Indonesian is taught in schools and used as the formal and official mode of communication.

Apart from those working in the tourist industry, few people on Lombok speak English (police and other officials included). Nevertheless, English is becoming more widely spoken. Travellers with no grasp of Bahasa Indonesia can get by, but some knowledge of it will enrich your understanding of the people and their island, and could also be invaluable in an emergency. Outside the main centres, finding anyone with more than a few phrases of English is extremely rare. If you can't speak Indonesian, arm yourself with a phrasebook and a dictionary.

Sasak

Sasak is not derived from Malay, so don't expect to be able to understand Sasak if you can speak Bahasa Indonesia. Nevertheless, some words are similar, and Sasak speakers use Indonesian words when there are no Sasak equivalents. Sasak only expresses what is important in traditional contexts, but in these instances it can be precise and subtle.

For example, where English has one word for rice, Indonesian has three – *padi* for the growing rice plant, *beras* for uncooked grain, and *nasi* for cooked rice. Sasak not only has equivalents for those (*pare, menik* and *me*), but also has *gabah*, for rice grains with their husks ready for planting, *binek* for a rice seedling up to three days old, *ampar* for small rice plants up to 20 days old and *lowong* for rice plants which are ready to be transplanted from the seed beds into the flooded paddy field.

Sasak would be a difficult language to learn – it has no written form so its usages are not well documented. There are also substantial variations from one part of Lombok to another. Learning Bahasa Indonesia would be a much more practical option for a visitor to Lombok, but some of the following expressions may be useful. Pronounce the words as if they were written in Bahasa Indonesia.

Greetings & Civilities Sasak does not have greetings such as 'Good morning'. A Sasak person approaching a friend might ask, in the local language, 'What are you doing?' or 'Where are you going?' simply as a form of greeting. Local people will frequently ask foreigners questions like this in English as a greeting – it may be their only English! Don't be put out – they are just trying to be polite. A smile and a 'Hello', or a greeting in Indonesian, is a polite and adequate response.

Some Useful Phrases

How are you?	*Berem be khabar?*
Where are you going?	*Wah me aning be?*
I'm going to Senggigi.	*Senggigi wah mo ojak ombe.*
Which way is Senggigi?	*Embe langan te ojok Senggigi?*

How far is it from here to Senggigi?	*Berembe kejab ne olek te ojok Senggigi?*
Where is Radiah's place?	*Embe tao' balem Radiah?*
I want to go to the toilet.	*Tiang melet ojok aik.*
Leave me alone!	*Endotang aku mesak!*
	Endotang aku mesak mesak! (stronger)
Go away!	*Nyeri to!* (say it forcefully, emphasising the 'to')

Some Useful Words

good	*solah*
big	*belek*
small	*kodek*
hot	*beneng*
cold	*enyet*
north	*daya*
south	*lauk*
east	*timuk*
west	*bat*
day	*jelo*
Monday	*senen*
Tuesday	*selasa*
Wednesday	*rebo*
Thursday	*kmis*
Friday	*jumat*
Saturday	*saptu*
Sunday	*ahat*

People & Families

person	*dengan*
woman	*dengan nine*
man	*dengan mama*
baby	*bebeak*
child	*kanak*
girl	*kanak mine*
boy	*kanak mama*
young unmarried woman	*dedare*
widow	*bebalu mine*
widower	*bebalu mama*
mother	*inak*
father	*amak*
wife	*senine*
husband	*semama*

Numbers

1	*skek*	6	*enam*
2	*dua*	7	*pituk*
3	*telu*	8	*baluk*
4	*empat*	9	*siwak*
5	*lima*	10	*sepulu*

11	*solas*
12	*dua olas*
13	*telu olas*
14	*empat olas*
20	*dua pulu*
30	*telung dasa*
40	*petang dasa*
50	*seket*
60	*enam pulu*
70	*pituk pulu*
100	*satus*
200	*satak*
300	*telungatus*
400	*samas*
500	*limangatus*
600	*enamgatus*
700	*pitungatus*
800	*bali ratus*
900	*siwak ratus*
1000	*sia*

Getting There & Away

Lombok is easily accessible by air and sea from the neighbouring islands. The vast majority of travellers arrive from Bali, less than 100km away, while those island-hopping from the east will reach Lombok from Sumbawa. It's also possible to fly directly to Lombok from Java, Sulawesi and even Singapore.

AIR

Lombok's Selaparang airport is at Rembiga, just north of Mataram. Silk Air, a Singapore Airlines subsidiary, has a daily direct flight to/from Singapore, which connects with flights from London. A one way ticket bought on Lombok costs around US$200. All other international connections go via Denpasar.

Domestic airlines serving Lombok are:

Bouraq
(☎ 27333) Selaparang Hotel, Jl Pejanggik 40-42, Mataram
Garuda
(☎ 23235) Nitour agency, Jl Yos Sudarso 6, Ampenan
Merpati (main office)
(☎ 36745) Jl Selaparang, Cakranegara
Sempati
(☎ 21612) Cilinaya shopping centre, Mataram

A number of agents in Mataram and Senggigi sell tickets and reconfirm flights, and you can also buy tickets at the airport. It's important to reconfirm, as the flights are on quite small planes and it's easy to get bumped. Flights are often cancelled at short notice.

Merpati has at least half a dozen flights per day in each direction between Denpasar and Mataram. Sempati and Bouraq also have daily flights. It's a very short flight, about 25 minutes, with fine views of Nusa Penida, the south-eastern coast of Bali and the Gili Islands. Although the ferry is much cheaper, many low-budget travellers still fly to save the long ferry trip and the time and expense of getting to and from the ports of Padangbai (Bali) and Lembar (Lombok).

Merpati also has daily flights to Bima on Sumbawa and two flights a week to Sumbawa Besar, but the seats on the latter are very limited. Daily direct flights also go to Surabaya on Java.

SEA
Bali
Lombok is connected by sea to most major islands in Nusa Tenggara, as well as Bali.

Ferry Scheduled ferries between Padangbai (Bali) and Lembar (Lombok) depart every two hours between 2 am and 10 pm. Sometimes they leave later, or even earlier, than the scheduled times. Economy costs around 5500 rp (2900 rp for children), and 1st class is 9000 rp (5000 rp for children). You can take a bicycle (2000 rp), motorcycle (7000 rp) or car (price depends on size – more than 70,000 rp for a Suzuki Jimny) on the ferry.

For 1st class passengers, there's an air-con cabin with aircraft-type seats, a snack bar and video entertainment. Economy passengers sit on bench seats or wherever they can find a spot. Food and drinks are available on board or from the numerous hawkers who hang around the wharf until the ferry leaves. The trip takes at least four hours, and sometimes up to seven.

Mabua Express The luxury jet-powered *Mabua Express* provides a fast boat service between Lembar on Lombok and Benoa Port on Bali. The more expensive 'Diamond' and 'Emerald' class tickets include pick-up and drop-off service from/to Denpasar, Kuta, Nusa Dua, Sanur and Ubud on Bali, or Bangsal, Mataram or Senggigi on Lombok. The cheaper economy class tickets include pick-up only, but no agents in the tourist areas will sell these tickets – you have to book directly with Mabua in Benoa or Lembar.

The *Mabua Express* leaves Bali's Benoa Port at 8 am and takes about 2½ hours to reach Lembar. A second service leaves at 2.30 pm in peak seasons around Christmas and July/August. In the other direction, it leaves Lembar at 10.30 am (also 5.30 pm in peak times). The fare is US$20 in economy, US$25 in 'Emerald Class' and US$30 for 'Diamond Class'; the latter two classes include a snack and soft drink on the boat. Children aged between two and 12 are charged half price. Mabua charges extra for a surfboard or a bicycle. For the latest details, call Mabua's office on Bali (☎ (0361) 721212) or Lombok (☎ 81195).

Tourist Shuttle The shuttle bus services save the hassle of the bemo connections to the ports at each end. Perama has services running to/from Lembar, Mataram, Senggigi, Bangsal and Kuta Beach on Lombok, various tourist centres on Bali, and also connections to Java and Sumbawa. Other companies have similar services at similar prices. For example, a ticket from Ubud to Kuta on Lombok costs 27,500 rp, including the bus to Padangbai, the ferry to Lombok and the Lembar-Kuta bus. On public transport you could probably do this trip for about 10,000 rp (if you weren't overcharged), but it would involve at least five bemo connections and would certainly take longer. From Kuta in Bali, travel agents sell tickets to Senggigi for around 20,000 rp.

Sumbawa

Passenger ferries from Labuhan Lombok (eastern Lombok) to Poto Tano (Sumbawa) take 1½ hours. Ferries run hourly from around 6 am to 8 pm. The fare is 3600 rp, bicycles costs 3300 rp, motorbikes 6000 rp and a small car 36,600 rp.

Direct public buses run from the Bertais terminal near Mataram to destinations on Sumbawa, including Taliwang, Sumbawa Besar, Dompu and Bima. Fares include the ferry trip.

Other Islands

The national shipping line, Pelni, has passenger ships doing regular loops through the islands of Indonesia, with the *Sirimau* and *Awu* calling at Lembar once a fortnight. The only service of note for visiting the eastern islands is the *Awu*, which runs from Lembar direct to Waingapu on Sumba. The Pelni office (☎ 37212) on Lombok is at Jl Industri 1 in Ampenan.

Organised Tours

Boat trips from Lombok to islands further east are widely promoted, especially in Senggigi. The main destination is usually Komodo, near Flores, to see the Komodo dragons. The trips also make stops at other islands for snorkelling, trekking and beach parties. The cheaper, quicker ones include land and sea transport, crossing Lombok and/or Sumbawa by bus. Some of the longer ones go all the way by boat, starting at Bangsal, on Lombok's north-east coast, but most start from Labuhan Lombok on the

west coast. The trips finish at Labuanbajo on Flores, where most of the operators are based. See Labuanbajo in the Flores chapter for more details.

Some of these trips are pretty rough – try to get a recent personal recommendation and check the operation as carefully as you can. Perama is one of the bigger, but not necessarily better, operators that advertises widely on Lombok with a variety of trips from four to seven days. Natural Island Adventures (☎ 34861) has trips from Bangsal and Labuhan Lombok to Flores, lasting six days and five nights, for US$110.

Getting Around

Lombok has an extensive network of roads, although there are many outlying villages that are difficult to get to by public transport. There is a good main road across the middle of the island between Mataram and Labuhan Lombok, and quite good roads to the south of this route. The road around the north coast is rough but useable, while roads to the extreme south-west and south-east are very rough or nonexistent.

Public buses and bemos are generally restricted to main routes. Away from these routes, you have to hire a *cidomo* (pony cart), get a lift on a motorcycle or walk. In the north-east and the south there is usually some public transport between the bigger towns, but it might mean waiting a long time and riding in the back of a truck. Most public transport becomes scarce in the afternoon and ceases after dark, often earlier in more remote areas. If you find yourself out in the sticks without your own wheels you can try to charter a bemo or just make yourself as comfortable as you can until sunrise.

You can get around the whole island and to most of the remote locations if you have your own transport. A motorcycle is the cheapest and most versatile option. A rental car with good ground clearance will get you to most places where there's a road. A bicycle, especially a mountain bike, would be ideal as you could put it on boats to visit small islands. If you are exploring remote regions, remember that food and drinking water are often scarce so it's a good idea to carry your own.

During the wet season many unsealed roads are flooded or washed away, and others are impassable because of fallen rocks and rubble, making it impossible to get to many out-of-the-way places. The damage may not be repaired until the dry season.

Lombok has the usual Indonesian methods of transport – bemos, buses, minibuses, cidomos, outrigger canoes *(prahus)* or small boats for short sea voyages. A few taxis are available, and charge either by the hour or a fixed sum for a particular distance, such as from the airport to Senggigi. They're not common and they don't have meters.

BEMO & BUS

The cheapest and most common way of getting around is by bemo or minibus (both of these terms, and sometimes *colt* and *mikrolet*, are used) for shorter distances, or bus for longer stretches. On rough roads in remote areas trucks may be used as public transport vehicles. There are several bus/bemo terminals on Lombok. The main one is at Bertais, about 4km east of Cakranegara. Other terminals are at Praya, Kopang and Selong, and you may have to go via one or more of these transport hubs to get from one part of Lombok to another.

Public transport fares are set by the provincial government, and at Bertais there is a prominently displayed list of fares to most places on the island. However, prices are rising rapidly in the wake of the currency crisis. Overcharging is also common, especially for tourists. Children on a parent's knee are free, and kids up to the age of 11 cost around half price. You may have to pay more if you have a large bag.

As with all public transport in Indonesia, drivers wait until their vehicles are filled to capacity before they contemplate moving. The maximum permitted number of passengers is usually written somewhere in or on the vehicle. The limit is enforced, but still

permits pretty cramped conditions, especially if there is all sorts of other stuff being carried. More often than not you won't be able to see the countryside. On the other hand, people are very friendly, many offer to share their food with you and most ask where you come from *(Dari mana?)*, and generally want to find out all they can.

Chartering a Bemo

Many trips involve several changes and a lot of waiting around. If you're pressed for time, and you can get a few people together, hiring a bemo (or a taxi) by the day or even from one village to the next can be affordable and convenient. One limitation is that drivers may be reluctant to venture off sealed roads. They don't want to damage their vehicles and, if the truth be known, some of them are not very skilled drivers.

Some bemos are restricted to certain routes or areas, for example, the yellow ones which shuttle around the main town cannot be chartered for a trip to Lembar. The white minibus bemos can go anywhere and can be chartered for 60,000 to 80,000 rp per day (from 8 am to 5 pm), including petrol and an English-speaking driver. Work out where you want to go and be prepared for some hard bargaining. If you detour on the way, be prepared to pay extra.

You can probably arrange to charter a bemo through your *losmen* or hotel. Alternatively, you can simply go to a bemo stop and ask the drivers. Check that the vehicle is roadworthy. A straightforward trip can quickly turn into a nightmare if you find yourself out after dark, in the rain, with a wiperless and unlit bemo!

Tourist Shuttle Buses

As happens on Bali, the minibuses that shuttle between the main tourist destinations on Lombok are usually comfortable and reliable. They're considerably more expensive than public transport, but very convenient. You usually have to book them the day before you want to travel. Perama is the most established operator, but there are some smaller outfits.

OJEK

An *ojek* is a motorcycle which you ride as a paying pillion passenger. The cost is around 1000 rp for up to 5km, and you can't take much luggage.

CAR & MOTORCYCLE

Lombok is by far the best place in the eastern islands to rent a car or motorcycle. Driving yourself around has some advantages, but also some obvious disadvantages. Traffic is lighter here than on Bali or Java, but many of the back roads are in poor shape. Ironically, road improvements can be a hazard, particularly at night when you round a corner and come slap up against a grader, rocks piled into the middle of the road and 44 gallon drums of tar. Warning signs are rarely, if ever, put up when road work is in progress. In the mountains there are unprotected drops down sheer cliff faces.

There are petrol stations around the larger towns; out in the villages, petrol is often available from plastic containers at small wayside shops – look out for signs that read *premium* or *press ban* (literally, tyre repair). If you intend going to out-of-the-way places it may be advisable to take some petrol with you, if you can carry it safely. Petrol is cheap. Tyre repair should cost around 1000 rp for each hole, but you won't be in a good bargaining position.

Rental

There are a few car and motorcycle rental companies in Ampenan, Mataram and Senggigi, but it can be more convenient to arrange something through your hotel. Travel agents also arrange car hire, but are often more expensive.

Car Car rental is becoming more organised on Lombok, though in some cases you are still just borrowing a car from a private owner. The owners may insist on an International Driving Permit and sometimes want you to leave a passport for security. There is sometimes an insurance cover for theft or damage of the car, but not for injury to other people or property. It costs about 45,000 to 50,000 rp per day for a small vehicle, such as a Suzuki Jimny, with 'half insurance' (you pay the first US$250 of any claim). For the lowest price, shop around, haggle, and take the vehicle for a few days or a week. Large 4WD vehicles can actually be cheaper (around 45,000 rp), while a large Toyota Kijang will be around 65,000 rp, but you will pay more for petrol. Between four people it can be quite a cheap way to get around. If you don't feel up to driving yourself, a car with driver can be easily arranged through hotels and travel agents from as little as 70,000 rp a day, or more if long distances are involved.

It is possible, but difficult, to hire a car to take to the other islands. Most operators don't have the insurance or the confidence to let you take a car off the island, but you can probably arrange something through the larger travel agents in Mataram. It will be more expensive, perhaps 70,000 rp a day, but self-drive cars are all but impossible to hire in the eastern islands and a car with driver will cost at least 100,000 rp a day on Sumbawa, Flores, Timor or Sumba. It is easier to arrange to take a car to Sumbawa, which is part of the same province as Lombok, than to the other islands. Make sure you have all the necessary paperwork and a letter from the hirer giving you permission to take the car off the island, otherwise the ferry officials may stop you. In general, we would advise against taking a car beyond Sumbawa. Ferry connections between the other islands are less frequent and you may get stranded for a few days if they are full, and it is a long way from Lombok if something goes wrong with the vehicle.

Motorcycle There's a place in Mataram where motorcycle renters congregate (see the West Lombok section later in this chapter), and also a few losmen that rent motorbikes. The bikes are similar to those on Bali, but the rental charges are more expensive – for a 100cc Honda Astrea with automatic clutch, you'll pay about 12,500 to 15,000 rp for one day, with a 10% discount if you take it for a week. Yamaha trail bikes

(110cc) are also available for slightly more. The owners want to see an International Driving Permit (one for cars only is OK by them, if not strictly legal). They usually want you to leave a passport for security (they give you a receipt for it, but remember to change plenty of cash first because it may be difficult to get cash later without a passport). Check the condition of the motorcycle. Some are not well maintained and you can quickly get into areas where there's no spare parts or mechanical help.

In remote areas a motorcycle can get by on tiny, rough roads which would be difficult or impassable by car. Once you get out of the main centres there's not much traffic on the roads, apart from people, dogs and water buffalos, but you do have to contend with numerous potholes and people at work upgrading the roads.

You can bring a rented motorcycle on the ferry from Bali, if the owner arranges the right paperwork. If you've found a really good machine on Bali, and negotiated a low, long-term price, this can be a good idea and you may be able to take it on to the other eastern islands. As with a car, most hirers are not keen for you to take a bike to the far reaches of Indonesia, but it may be possible and you won't have any problems getting a motorbike on the ferries.

BICYCLE
Bicycles are available for rent in and around the main tourist centres of Lombok. There are very good bikes for around 5000 rp per day near the Cirebon Restaurant in Ampenan.

CIDOMO
The type of pony cart used on Lombok is called a cidomo, and it has car tyres instead of the spoked wooden wheels of the Balinese *dokar*. 'Cidomo' is a contraction of *cika* (a traditional handcart), *dokar* (the usual Indonesian word for a pony cart) and *mobil* (because motorcar wheels and tyres are used). They are usually brightly coloured with decorative motifs, and are fitted out with bells that chime when they're in motion. The small ponies that pull them often have

long colourful tassels attached to their gear. A typical cidomo has bench seating on either side which can comfortably fit three people, or four if they're all slim. It's not unusual, however, to see half a dozen or more passengers, plus several bags of rice and other paraphernalia piled up in a cart.

Some visitors get upset that the ponies seem to be heavily laden and harshly treated, but they're usually looked after reasonably well as the owners depend on them for their livelihood. Cidomos are a very popular form of transport in many parts of Lombok, and often go to places that bemos don't, won't or can't go.

Count on paying around 250 rp per person for up to two or 3km, or maybe 750 rp for the whole cidomo. If you're alone, you'll have to wait for others or pay for the whole thing yourself.

BOAT
Prahu are the elegant, brilliantly painted outrigger boats, commonly used for fishing, but also chartered for short trips to snorkelling spots or surf breaks. They mostly use a small outboard motor, though sail-powered ones are still very common.

A *jukung* is a slightly larger version of a prahu, used for inter-island hops, like travelling from Bangsal to the Gili Islands.

ORGANISED TOURS
A number of agents on Bali offer tours of Lombok, which may be worthwhile if your time is limited. They tend to be expensive, using air transport and upmarket accommodation. A tour of three days and two nights would be around US$150 per person, twin share.

Lombok is also crawling with travel agents. The largest are based in Mataram (see the West Lombok section of this chapter) though Senggigi has the biggest concentration. As well as arranging tours, the large agents also sell hotel packages that offer substantial discounts at luxury hotels.

Specialised tours, such as a 'nature tour' or a 'handcraft tour', will give a quick introduction to a specific aspect of the island, and you can revisit your favourite places independently. They cost from US$10 for a half-day tour, or US$20 to US$35 for a full-day tour. Standard tours include a half-day tour of Mataram, and full-day tours to Kuta and the south coast, to the central craft villages, or to the Gili Islands and the north coast.

The tourist office in Mataram can give you some suggestions, and most hotels have an arrangement with a tour operator. If you want to arrange a tour yourself, Senggigi is the best place to look and has the biggest collection of budget and mid-range operators. Generally, however, the real attractions of Lombok are the landscapes, the people and the relaxed pace of life, which you won't appreciate on a whirlwind tour of the main 'sights'.

See the North Lombok section for details on trekking up Gungung Rinjani.

West Lombok

AMPENAN, MATARAM, CAKRANEGARA & SWETA

Although officially four separate towns, Ampenan, Mataram, Cakranegara and Sweta actually run together, so it's virtually impossible to tell where one stops and the next starts. Collectively, they make up the main 'city' on Lombok, but often they are simply called Mataram, the capital of Lombok. Travellers often use it as a base to organise trips elsewhere on the island, but it really is just another city and many visitors head straight to Senggigi or the Gili Islands and don't stay in the town at all. There are banks, travel agents, some interesting shops and markets, and a few things to see, but these towns are not among Lombok's major attractions. The main bus station for Lombok is in the suburb of Bertais, 2km east of Sweta.

Ampenan
Once the main port of Lombok, Ampenan is now not much more than a small fishing harbour. It's a bit run down and dirty, but it has character compared to the more ordered but less interesting sprawl of adjoining Mataram. The main road does not quite reach the coast at Ampenan, it simply fades out just before it gets to the port's grubby beach.

Ampenan has a curious mixture of people. Apart from the Sasaks and Balinese, there are also some Chinese and a small Arab quarter known as Kampung Arab (*kampung* means district or quarter). The Arabs living here are devout Muslims, usually well educated and friendly towards foreigners.

Mataram
Mataram is the administrative capital of the province of Nusa Tenggara Barat (West Nusa Tenggara). Some of the public buildings, such as the banks, the post office and the governor's office and residence, are substantial. The large houses around the outskirts of town are the homes of Lombok's elite.

Cakranegara
Now the main commercial centre of Lombok, bustling Cakranegara is usually referred to as Cakra (pronounced Chakra). Formerly the capital of Lombok under the Balinese rajas, Cakra has reminders of the Balinese presence and today has a thriving Chinese community, as well as many Balinese residents. Most of the shops and restaurants are run or owned by Chinese, and there are friendly *losmen* run by Balinese. The Pasar Seni (Art Market) is not to be missed; it has the best selection of crafts on Lombok, but hard bargaining is usually required.

Sweta
Seven kilometres east of Ampenan and only about 2.5km beyond Cakra is Sweta, an old market area. However, the main market and Lombok's huge central bus terminal have now moved 2km east to Bertais.

Orientation
West Lombok's main 'city' is effectively divided into four functional areas: Ampenan, the port; Mataram, the administrative centre; Cakranegara, the trading centre; and Sweta. The towns are spread along one main road which starts as Jl Pabean in Ampenan,

LOMBOK

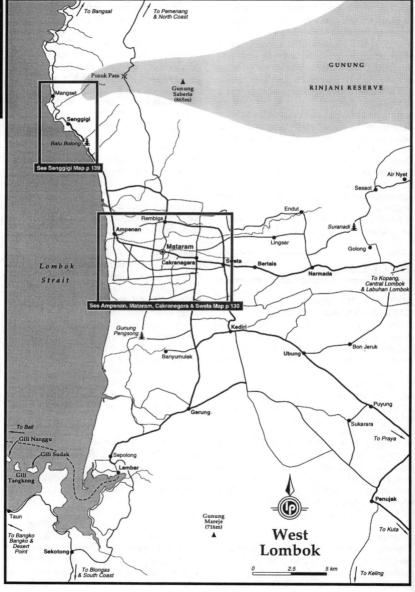

To Bangsal
To Pemenang & North Coast
GUNUNG
Pusuk Pass
RINJANI RESERVE
Mangset
Gunung
Saberis
(865m)
Senggigi
Batu Bolong
Air Nyet
See Senggigi Map p 139
Sesaot
Endut
Rembiga
Suranadi
Ampenan
Lingsar
Mataram
Golong
Cakranegara
Sweta
Bertais
Lombok
Strait
Narmada
To Kopang,
Central Lombok
& Labuhan Lombok
See Ampenan, Mataram, Cakranegara & Sweta Map p 130
Kediri
Gunung
Pengsong
Bon Jeruk
Banyumulek
Ubung
Gerung
Puyung
To Bali
Sukarara
Gili Nanggu
To Praya
Gili Sudak
Sepolong
Gili
Tangkong
Lembar
Penujak
Taun
Gunung
Mareje
(716m)
To Kuta
To Bangko
Bangko &
Desert
Point
West
Lombok
Sekotong
To Blongas
& South Coast
0   2.5   5 km
To Keling

quickly becomes Jl Yos Sudarso, changes to Jl Langko, then Jl Pejanggik, and finishes up in Sweta as Jl Selaparang. It's a one way street, running west to east. It's difficult to tell where the road changes names. Indeed, it seems that they overlap, since some places appear to have more than one address.

A second one way street, Jl Sriwijaya/Jl Majapahit, brings traffic back in the other direction. Bemos shuttle between the smaller terminal in Ampenan and the main terminal in Bertais, about 9km east. Getting back and forth is therefore dead easy. You can stay in Ampenan, Mataram or Cakra since there are hotels and restaurants in all three places.

Mataram has a small commercial 'centre' near the river, and there is a larger shopping area past the Jl Selaparang/Jl Hasanuddin intersection. You'll find the Cakra market just east of here, south of the main road. The Mataram government buildings are chiefly found along Jl Pejanggik. The main square, Lapangan Mataram, is on the south side of Jl Pejanggik, and is a venue for occasional public performances and exhibitions.

Information
Tourist Offices The main government tourist office (Kantor Dinas Pariwisata Daerah or DIPARDA; ☎ 31730) is at the Ampenan end of Mataram at Jl Langko 70, on the north side, almost diagonally opposite the wartel. The people at the tourist office are friendly, helpful and well informed. It opens Monday to Thursday from 8 am to 3 pm, Friday and Saturday until noon.

The Perama office (☎ 35936) is at Jl Pejanggik 66. The staff are very helpful and provide good information, organise shuttle bus connections, change money (unless they are out of cash), arrange day tours around Lombok and treks on Rinjani, and try to sell Land-Sea Adventure tours to Komodo and Flores. It's open daily from around 6 am to 10 pm.

Immigration The island's *kantor imigrasi* (immigration office) is on Jl Udayana, the road out to the airport.

Money There are a number of banks along the main drag, mostly in Cakranegara. The Bank Ekspor-Impor in Cakra and the BCA on the other side of the road will change travellers cheques and give cash advances on credit cards. Standard banking hours are weekdays from 8 am to 3 pm and Saturday until 11 am.

There are also moneychangers in Ampenan and in Mataram's Cilinaya shopping centre on the south side of Jl Pejanggik. They're efficient, open for longer hours and have rates similar to the banks. You can also change travellers cheques at the airport and, sometimes, at the Perama office.

Post Mataram's main post office, on Jl Sriwijaya, has the only poste restante service. It's open 8 am to 8 pm Monday to Friday, and Saturday from 8 am to 6 pm, and until noon on Sunday. For other postal business, there's a more convenient post office opposite the tourist office.

Telephone The Telkom *wartel* at the Ampenan end of Mataram on Jl Langko has telegram and fax services; it's open 24 hours daily. The international telephone service from here is very efficient. There's another wartel in the Cilinaya shopping centre in Cakra, and a few others around town. All of Lombok is in the 0370 telephone district.

Travel Agencies The bulk of Lombok's travel agents are based in Mataram/Ampenan. For short tours in the countryside, the smaller agents in Senggigi are usually cheaper, but many are merely branches of those in Mataram. To arrange something from overseas, the main agents are more reliable and can provide tours and services for any sized group. Most also sell discounted packages at Lombok's luxury hotels and arrange international and domestic air ticketing.

Lombok's biggest agent with an excellent reputation is Biddy Tours (☎ 32127), at Jl Ragi Genep 17 in Ampenan. It has a wide variety of tours and services. They are also one of the best for air ticketing. Satriavi (☎ 31788), at Jl Pejanggik 17 in Mataram, is another large agent. Sasak Lombok (☎ 22321),

LOMBOK

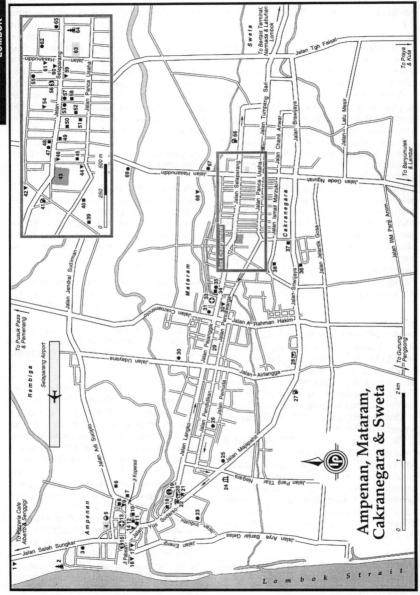

Ampenan, Mataram, Cakranegara & Sweta

PLACES TO STAY
6   Wisma Triguna
7   Losmen Horas
8   Losmen Angin
    Mammiri
10 Wisata Hotel &
    Restaurant
12 Hotel Zahir
18 Nitour Hotel &
    Restaurant
34 Hotel Kertajoga
36 Hotel Sahid Legi
    Mataram
37 Puri Indah Hotel
38 Graha Ayu
39 Hotel Granada
40 Hotel Lombok Raya
45 Oka Homestay
48 Selaparang Hotel
49 Mataram Hotel
50 Hotel & Restaurant
    Shanti Puri
51 Losmen Ayu
52 Adiguna Homestay
58 Astiti Guest House

PLACES TO EAT
1   Flamboyan
    Restaurant
9   Poppy Nice Cafe

14 Restoran Betawi
16 Rainbow Cafe
17 Pabean & Cirebon
    Restaurants
32 Taman Griya
42 Denny Bersaudra
44 Friendship Cafe
46 Aroma
54 Cafe Candung
59 Sekawan Depot Es
60 KFC
61 Rumah Makan
    Madya
68 Dua Em

OTHER
2   Pura Segara
3   Antique Shops
4   Ampenan Market
5   Ampenan Terminal
    (Local Bemos)
11 Antique Shops
13 Catholic Hospital
15 Moneychangers
19 Main Tourist Office
20 Post Office
21 Police
22 Telkom Wartel
23 Pelni Office
24 Museum Negeri

25 Lombok Pottery
    Centre
26 Mataram University
27 Petrol Station
28 Main Post Office
    (Poste Restante)
29 Main Square
    (Lapangan
    Mataram)
30 Immigration Office
31 Governor's Office
33 Hospital
35 Perama Office
41 Petrol Station
43 Cilinaya Shopping
    Centre
47 Rinjani Hand Woven
53 Mataram Plaza
55 Motorcycle Rental
56 Bank Ekspor-Impor
57 Merpati Office
62 Selamat Riady
63 Cakra Market
64 Pura Meru
65 Mayura Water
    Palace
66 Petrol Station
67 Pasar Seni
    (Art Market)
69 Rungkang Jangkuk

at Jl Subak 1/9 in Cakranegara, is mostly a wholesaler, but can arrange tours from one person up. Discover Lombok (☎ 36781) at the Pizzeria Cafe Alberto near Ampenan, is an Italian-run agency that offers a few unique tours. The city has around 40 other travel agents – the tourist office in Mataram can help with advice.

Bookshops There are a few bookshops along Jl Pendidikan near Mataram University, mainly stocking text books, with very little in English. The bookshop in the Cilinaya shopping centre has the odd magazine in English – the daily *Jakarta Post* usually arrives at 2 pm the day after publication. Senggigi has a much better selection.

Pura Segara
This Balinese sea temple is on the beach 1km north of Ampenan. Nearby are the remnants of a Muslim cemetery and an old Chinese cemetery – worth a wander through if you're visiting the temple.

Museum Negeri
The Museum Negeri Nusa Tenggara Barat is on Jl Panji Tilar Negara in Ampenan. It has exhibits on the geology, history and culture of Lombok and Sumbawa, and is well worth browsing around if you have a couple of free hours. If you intend buying any antiques or handcrafts have a look at the krises, *songket* (silver or gold-threaded cloth), basketware and masks to give you a starting point for comparison. It's open Tuesday to Sunday from 8 am to 4 pm. Admission is 200 rp (100 rp for children).

Mayura Water Palace
On the main road through Cakra, this 'palace' was built in 1744 and was once part of the Balinese kingdom's royal court on Lombok. The main feature is a large artificial lake with an open-sided pavilion in the centre, connected to the shoreline by a raised footpath. This *bale kambang* (floating pavilion) was used as both a court of justice and a meeting place for the Hindu lords. There

Battleground of Yesteryear

The grounds of the Mayura Water Palace are used today as a place to unleash fighting cocks and make offerings to the gods. However, less than a century ago it was the site of bloody battles with the Dutch:

In 1894 the Dutch sent an army to back the Sasaks in a rebellion against their Balinese rajah. The rajah quickly capitulated, but the crown prince decided to fight on while the Dutch-backed forces were split between various camps.

The Dutch camp at the Mayura Water Palace was attacked late at night by a combined force of Balinese and western Sasaks. The camp was surrounded by high walls, and the Balinese and Sasaks took cover behind them as they fired on the exposed army, forcing the Dutch to take shelter in a nearby temple compound. The Balinese also attacked the Dutch camp at Mataram, and soon after the entire Dutch army on Lombok was routed and withdrew to Ampenan where, according to one eyewitness, the soldiers 'were so nervous that they fired madly if so much as a leaf fell off a tree'. The first battles resulted in enormous losses of men and arms for the Dutch.

Although the Balinese had won the battle, they had just begun to lose the war. Now they would not only have to continue to fight the eastern Sasaks, but also the Dutch, who were quickly supplied with reinforcements from Java. The Dutch attacked Mataram a month after their initial defeat, fighting street to street against Balinese and west Sasak soldiers, and also the local population. The Balinese crown prince was killed in the battle for the palace and the Balinese retreated to Cakranegara, where they were well armed and the complex of walls provided good defence against infantry. Cakra was attacked by a combined force of Dutch and eastern Sasaks, and, as happened in Mataram, Balinese men, women and children staged repeated suicidal lance attacks, to be cut down by rifle and artillery fire. The rajah and a small group of *punggawas* (commanders) fled to the village of Sasari near the pleasure gardens at Lingsar. A day or two later the rajah surrendered to the Dutch, but even his capture did not lead the Balinese to surrender.

In late November the Dutch attacked Sasari and a large number of Balinese chose the suicidal *puputan* (fight to the death) rather than surrender. With the downfall of the dynasty, the local population abandoned its struggle against the Dutch. The conquest of Lombok, thought about for decades, had taken the Dutch barely three months. The old rajah died in exile in Batavia in 1895. ■

are other shrines and fountains dotted around the surrounding park. The entrance to the walled enclosure of the palace is on the western side (entry 500 rp).

Pura Meru

Directly opposite the water palace on the main road is Pura Meru, the largest temple on Lombok. It's open every day, and a donation is expected (about 500 rp or 'up to you'). It was built in 1720 under the patronage of the Balinese prince Anak Agung Made Karang of the Singosari kingdom as an attempt to unite all the small kingdoms on Lombok, and as a symbol of the universe, dedicated to the Hindu trinity of Brahma, Vishnu and Shiva.

The outer courtyard has a hall housing the wooden drums that are beaten to call believers to festivals and special ceremonies. In the middle courtyard are two buildings with large raised platforms for offerings. The inner court has one large and 33 small shrines, as well as three *meru* (multi-roofed shrines), which are in a line: the central one, with 11 tiers, is Shiva's house; the one to the north, with nine tiers, is Vishnu's; and the seven tiered one to the south is Brahma's. The meru are also said to represent the three great mountains, Rinjani, Agung and Bromo. A festival is held here each June.

Places to Stay – budget

The most popular cheap places to stay are in Ampenan and Cakranegara. Jl Koperasi branches off Jl Yos Sudarso in the centre of Ampenan. Only a short stroll from the centre is the *Hotel Zahir* (☎ 34248) at Jl Koperasi 9. It's a basic place with singles/doubles for 8000/10,000 rp, including breakfast and tea or coffee throughout the day. The rooms each have a small verandah facing a central courtyard. The owners are friendly and helpful, and can arrange cheap motorcycle rental.

Continue along the road to Jl Koperasi 19, where the newer *Wisata Hotel & Restaurant* (☎ 26971) is the best of the hotels in the range. Clean and comfortable rooms straddle the budget and middle price ranges, from 12,000/15,000 to 35,000/40,000 rp, and the better ones have air-con. The good restaurant is also a drawcard.

Another few metres along brings you to the basic *Losmen Horas* (☎ 31695), where rooms with Indonesian-style bathrooms go for 9000/12,500 rp. Continuing along this road you come to the better *Wisma Triguna* (☎ 31705), operated by the same people as the Horas. It's a little over a kilometre from central Ampenan and is a quiet, relaxed place. Spacious rooms, opening on to a wide verandah or the garden, start from 9,500/ 12,000 rp, including breakfast. The people at Horas and Wisma Triguna have good information and can arrange treks to Gunung Rinjani. The nearby *Losmen Angin Mammiri* (☎ 31713) is a dump, but it's one of the cheapest around at 6000/12,000 rp for singles/doubles.

Back in the centre of Ampenan is *Losmen Pabean* (☎ 21758) at Jl Pabean 146, the eastern end of Jl Yos Sudarso opposite the Pabean Restaurant. It's basic, but a bit better inside than it looks from the outside. Rooms are 6000/9000 rp with shared mandi.

At Jl Pejanggik 64 in Mataram, just west of the Perama office, the *Hotel Kertajoga* (☎ 21775) is nothing special, but it is good value with fan-cooled rooms going for 15,000/18,500 rp and air-con rooms at 22,000/27,500 rp.

In Cakranegara, south of the main drag and just north of Jl Panca Usaha, are a number of Balinese-style losmen which are quite good places to stay, though there seem to be an inordinate number of mosques within earshot. The *Oka Homestay* (☎ 22406), on Jl Repatmaja, has a quiet garden and singles/doubles for 9000/12,000 rp with breakfast. *Astiti Guest House* (☎ 23670), further east on Jl Subak, has rooms from 10,000/12,000 rp (less with shared bathroom) up to 35,000 rp with air-con, including breakfast, and tea anytime. It's popular with

surfers, and the staff can help with transport information, rental cars etc.

Adiguna Homestay (☎ 25946), on Jl Nursiwan, is another good budget place with singles/doubles from 9000/12,500 rp. The very friendly *Losmen Ayu* (☎ 21761), on the same street, has cheap rooms at about 9000 rp a double, and a range of better rooms up to 40,000 rp with air-con. The price includes breakfast, and there's a kitchen for guests to use. The bemos from Lembar come close to here; get off on Jl Gede Ngurah and walk west on Jl Panca Usaha, looking for sign boards at the ends of the streets.

In the same area, the *Hotel & Restaurant Shanti Puri* (☎ 32649) at Jl Maktal 15 is almost mid-range quality, with singles/ doubles from 15,000/20,000 rp; more expensive rooms are available with air-con and hot water. The management is helpful, and they can arrange motorcycle and car hire.

Places to Stay – middle

In Ampenan, the *Nitour Hotel & Restaurant* (☎ 23780; fax 36579) at Jl Yos Sudarso 4 is quiet and comfortable, with carpets, air-con, telephone etc. 'Superior' rooms are US$30/ 35 and 'deluxe' rooms US$35/40, but it discounts up to 30% at quiet times.

The heavily advertised and fading *Hotel Granada* (☎ 36015) is on Jl Bung Karno, south of the shopping centre in Mataram. All rooms are air-conditioned and there's a swimming pool. It has vaguely Iberian architecture and a depressing caged menagerie. The prices include breakfast and start at 64,500/69,500 rp plus 10% tax; ask for a low-season discount.

If you want this kind of comfort, the *Puri Indah Hotel* (☎ 37633), on Jl Sriwijaya in Cakranegara, also has a restaurant and a pool, and is much better value at 25,000 rp, or 38,000 rp with air-con – it's very clean and well run. The nearby *Graha Ayu* has rooms from 50,000 rp with all the mod cons, but doesn't look appealing.

There are quite a few good-value, mid-range places in Cakra. The *Selaparang Hotel* (☎ 32670) at Jl Pejanggik 40-42 has reasonably sized air-con rooms at 42,500/47,500 rp for singles/doubles, and fan-cooled rooms for about of half that. Across the road at No 105 is the *Mataram Hotel* (☎ 23411) with a small pool and standard double rooms at 25,000 rp; air-conditioned rooms with TV and hot water cost up to 50,000 rp. Both of these mid-range hotels have pleasant little restaurants.

Places to Stay – top end

The new *Hotel Lombok Raya* (☎ 32305; fax 36478), at Jl Panca Usaha 11, Mataram, has attractively furnished, fully equipped rooms, conference facilities and a big swimming pool. From US$50/55 for singles/doubles, plus 21% tax, it's a pretty good value three star hotel.

The new *Hotel Sahid Legi Mataram* (☎ 36282; fax 36281), Jl Sriwijaya 81, is the best hotel in town. Although only a three star hotel it has a full range of facilities and a big pool. Well appointed rooms cost US$90/110 plus 21% tax and service, but expect large discounts.

Places to Eat

Ampenan has a number of Indonesian and Chinese restaurants, including the popular *Cirebon*, at Jl Yos Sudarso 113, with a standard Indonesian/Chinese menu and most dishes from around 3000 rp. Next door is the *Pabean*, with similar food and prices. A little further west is *Rainbow Cafe*, a cheap, friendly little place with reggae-inspired decor, a few books, cold beer and OK food.

The *Restoran Betawi* on the corner of Jl Koperasi and Jl Yos Sudarso is housed upstairs in an impressive Dutch building. This more mid-range restaurant is a good place for a beer overlooking the street and has a wide variety of Indonesian and western dishes from around 5000 to 10,000 rp.

There are a couple of interesting restaurants in Mataram. *Taman Griya* (formerly the Garden House Restaurant) is a pleasant open-air place in a small shopping area by Jl Pejanggik, opposite the hospital. It has very tasty nasi campur, nasi goreng and other standard meals from 4000 to 6000 rp, but it's popular mainly for its home-made ice cream.

Denny Bersaudra, on Jl Pelikan, just north of the main road, is famous for Sasak-style food. It's a good place to try ayam taliwang (chicken with hot chilli sauce – grilled is usually better than fried).

In Cakra, handy to the cheap losmen, there's a choice of good budget eateries. Two cheap Chinese places are the *Friendship Cafe*, on Jl Panca Usaha, and *Aroma*, which is inconspicuously located on the same street as the Oka Homestay. It serves stir-fried meat and/or vegetable dishes for around 4000 rp. On Jl Selaparang, near the intersection with Jl Hasanuddin, is a modern shopping strip with a conspicuous *KFC* which is popular with affluent locals. Opposite is the more traditional *Sekawan Depot Es*, with cold drinks downstairs and a seafood and Chinese restaurant upstairs. Around the corner on Jl Hasanuddin is the *Rumah Makan Madya*, which serves very good and inexpensive authentic Sasak style food. Tucked away down a quiet residential street at Jl Cendrawasih 18, *Cafe Candung* is the city's most delightful restaurant. Bamboo huts are scattered around a Balinese-style garden and a wide variety of food, including Lombok dishes, is served.

On the backroad north of the shopping area in Cakranegara, *Dua Em* on Jl Transmigrasi is a large restaurant and one of the best for Sasak specialities. North of Ampenan, on the road to Senggigi, the *Flamboyan Restaurant* is a more up-market place with excellent Indonesian cuisine and seafood. Further up, *Pizzeria Cafe Alberto* (☎ 36781) has authentic cucina Italiania, which is a little more expensive than many places, but well worth it. It's not conveniently located, but it has a pick-up service.

Things to Buy

The best buys on Lombok are beautifully crafted functional artefacts, such as baskets, bird traps, palm boxes, pottery and hand-woven textiles. If you don't have time to visit the villages where these items are made, you'll find a good selection at shops and markets in town. Shops also sell 'primitive' decorative objects like masks and carvings,

LOMBOK

imported from other parts of Indonesia, or locally made imitations.

Items which are used or dirty are often described as antiques, though very few pieces are more than a few years old. Objects like wooden cowbells show some patina if they are genuinely old, but the best advice is to buy things for what they are, not because they purport to be from a certain period or a certain place.

Handcrafts & Antiques There's two areas in Ampenan which have a good selection of handcraft shops and are interesting to browse around. Look on and around the west side of Jl Saleh Sungkar (the road north to Senggigi) for shops like Hery Antiques, Sudirman Antiques, Fancy Art and Musdah.

Gang Sunda is a small street east off Jl Yos Sudarso just north of the bridge and it has several art/craft/antique shops, including Rora Antiques (with some excellent inlaid wooden boxes, carvings, baskets and traditional Lombok weavings), Renza Antiques and Preti.

The best place to start looking is the Pasar Seni (Art Market) on Jl Hasanuddin in Cakranegara. This market has a large collection of stalls with a representative range of Lombok crafts. Hard bargaining is essential. Rungkang Jangkuk, the Lombok Handicraft Centre, at Sayang north of Cakra, has a number of shops with a good selection of crafts from Lombok and elsewhere.

Pottery The Lombok Pottery Centre at Jl Majapahit 7, in Ampenan, displays and sells some of the city's best products. It's more interesting to go to the villages and see the pots being made, but this centre has an excellent selection from all of the main pottery places, and the prices are competitive.

Textiles There's a couple of weaving factories in Cakranegara, where you can view dyeing and weaving, and buy ikat or hand-woven songket sarongs. In fixed-price shops they charge from 16,000 to 22,000 rp per metre (1200mm width) for ikat woven with mercerised cotton, depending on the quality.

Silk fabric is 45,000 to 60,000 rp per metre. The hand-and-foot powered looms are amazing contraptions, but the most interesting feature is the complex process of resist dyeing the unwoven thread.

Selamat Riady is on Jl Tanun, a back street east of Jl Hasanuddin. It's open most mornings, and has a shop with textiles and a few other crafts. Rinjani Hand Woven at Jl Pejanggik 44-46, beside the Selaparang Hotel, has an interesting range of hand woven fabrics, and can make them up into shirts, dresses or cushion covers.

Getting There & Away

Air Flights from Mataram go direct to Denpasar, Sumbawa Besar and Bima on Sumbawa, Surabaya (Java) and Singapore. See the Getting There & Away section earlier in this chapter for details.

There's a Garuda/Merpati office (☎ 23762) next to the Nitour Hotel where you can book and reconfirm flights. It's at Jl Yos Sudarso 6 in Ampenan (open Monday to Saturday from 8 am to 5 pm, Sunday until noon). The main Merpati office (☎ 36745) is on Jl Selaparang in Cakra.

The Sempati office (☎ 21612) is in the Cilinaya shopping centre in Mataram. Bouraq (☎ 27333) has an office at the Selaparang Hotel, Jl Pejanggik 40-42, Mataram, and is open daily from 8 am to 6 pm.

Bus The main bus and bemo terminal for the entire island is the Terminal Mandaluka in Bertais, 2km south-east of Sweta. It's also the eastern terminus for the local bemos that shuttle back and forth to Ampenan. Bus fares are in an upward spiral, but the government approved fares are posted on a notice board at the front of the terminal. Check this before you're hustled on board one of the vehicles.

Long-distance, air-con coach services run through to Bali and Java. To Denpasar costs around 22,500 rp and to Surabaya 42,500 rp; prices include the ferry. Air-con/non-air-con buses to Sumbawa include: Sumbawa Besar (10,000/15,000 rp), Bima (22,500/27,500 rp), Sape (27,500/31,000 rp) and Taliwang (7000 rp non-air-con).

Bemos and smaller buses run to towns all over Lombok. Some distances and approximate fares (in rp) from Bertais to other parts of Lombok include:

Destination	Price (rp)
East (Jurusan Timur)	
Narmada (6km)	400
Mantang (17km)	800
Kopang (25km)	1000
Terara (29km)	1200
Sikur (33km)	1100
Paomotong (34km)	1300
Masbagik (36km)	1200
Selong (47km)	2000
Labuhan Haji (57km)	2200
Labuhan Lombok (69km)	2500
South & Central	
(Jurusan Selatan & Tenggara)	
Kediri (5km)	500
Lembar (22km)	700
Praya (27km)	700
Mujur (36km)	1000
Kuta (54km)	1500
North (Jurusan Utara)	
Senggigi (12km)	600
Pemenang (31km)	900
Tanjung (45km)	1100
Bayan (79km)	2000

The terminal at Ampenan is for local bemos. From this terminal, a trip up the coast to Senggigi costs 500 rp.

Boat The ferry docks at Lembar, 22km south of Ampenan (see the Lembar section later in this chapter for details). The *Mabua Express* office (☎ 81195) is in Lembar. The office of Pelni (☎ 21604), the national shipping line, is at Jl Industri 1 in Ampenan. See the Getting There & Away section earlier in this chapter for more information.

Getting Around

To/From the Airport Lombok's Selaparang airport is only a couple of kilometres from Ampenan. Taxis from there cost about 7000 rp to Ampenan, Mataram, Cakra and Sweta, 10,000 rp to Senggigi and 22,000 rp to Bangsal. Air-con taxis are 7500 rp, 12,000 rp and 26,000 rp, respectively. Alternatively, you can walk out of the airport carpark to the main road and take one of the frequent No 7

bemos which run to the Ampenan terminal for 300 rp.

Bemo Ampenan-Mataram-Cakra-Sweta is very spread out, so don't plan to walk from place to place. Yellow bemos shuttle back and forth along the main route between the Ampenan terminal at one end and the Bertais terminal at the other – from Bertais, routes D, E and F all go to Ampenan. The fare is a standard 300 rp regardless of the distance. The Ampenan terminal is a good place to charter a bemo.

Car & Motorcycle Hotels in town can help arrange car rental. Metro Rent Car (☎ 32146) at Jl Yos Sudarso, Ampenan, rents Suzuki Jimnys for 50,000 rp per day, including insurance, with a US$250 excess. Longer rentals are generally cheaper. Rinjani Rent Car (☎ 32259), opposite the Hotel Granada on Jl Bung Karno in Mataram, is slightly more expensive.

Hotels might also be able to help you rent a motorcycle, which can be a pretty informal arrangement. Lots of motorcycle owners hang around on Jl Gelantik, off Jl Selaparang near the junction with Jl Hasanuddin at the Cakranegara end of Mataram. They rent motorcycles privately for around 15,000 rp for one day, or maybe 12,500 rp per day for a week. There's no insurance, and they'll want your passport for security. Check any motorcycle carefully before taking it.

Bicycle You can rent good bicycles from the Cirebon Restaurant in Ampenan for about 5000 rp per day.

GUNUNG PENGSONG

This Balinese temple is built – as the name suggests – on top of a hill. It's 9km south of Mataram and has great views of rice fields, volcanoes and the sea. Try to get there early in the morning before the clouds envelop Gunung Rinjani. Once a year, generally in March or April, a buffalo is taken up the steep 100m slope and sacrificed to give thanks for a good harvest. The Bersih Desa Festival also occurs here at harvest time – houses and gardens are cleaned, fences whitewashed, and roads and paths repaired. Once part of a ritual to rid the village of evil spirits, it is now held in honour of the rice goddess Dewi Sri. There's no set admission charge, but you will have to pay the caretaker 300 rp or so, especially if you use the carpark.

BANYUMULEK
This is one of the main pottery centres of Lombok, specialising in decorated pots and pots with a woven fibre covering, as well as more traditional urns and water flasks. It's close to the city, a couple of kilometres from the Cakra-Lembar road, which has frequent bemos. It's easy to combine Banyumulek with a visit to Gunung Pengsong.

LEMBAR
Lembar, 22km south of Ampenan, is the main port on Lombok. The ferries to and from Bali dock here, as does the *Mabua Express*. There's a canteen at the harbour where you can buy snacks and drinks while waiting to catch the ferry. The only place to stay, the *Serumbung Indah* (☎ 37153) has rooms from 15,000 rp and a restaurant, but it's not very convenient, being about 2km north of the harbour on the main road.

Getting There & Away
You can buy your tickets to Bali at the wharf on the day of departure. Ferries leave every two hours from 2 am until 10 pm. The *Mabua Express* leaves at 10.30 am, with an extra service in peak times at 5.30 pm.

In theory, you should be able to get a bemo from Lembar to Bertais for about 700 rp; in practice they will try to get you on a special charter bemo, or otherwise manage to charge you more – maybe 3000 rp. If you come on the *Mabua Express* and want a public bemo to town, leave the port area and walk 200m to the left, then turn right to find the bemos waiting at the roadside. The *Mabua Express* also has air-con coaches which run to Mataram and Senggigi – the price is included in the more expensive tickets, or economy passengers can buy a ticket on arrival. There are set fares for 'taxis'; the price per person

depends on the number of passengers. To Mataram it's about 8000 rp each with two people, or 15,000 rp by yourself. Minibuses from the hotels in town sometimes meet the ferry.

SOUTH-WESTERN PENINSULA
If you approach Lembar by ferry you'll see a hilly and little-developed peninsula on your right. A road from Lembar goes round the eastern side of the harbour, some distance inland, and after almost 20km reaches a T-junction at **Sekotong**. From here the road left goes to the south coast, while the other road follows the coast, more or less, around Lombok's south-west peninsula. The further you go along this road, the rougher it gets and it may become impassable for ordinary cars.

Sekotong Indah Beach Cottages, near **Taun**, provides comfortable accommodation near a beach and is miles from any other tourist development. It has a restaurant, basic rooms with shared bathroom for 10,000/15,000 rp, better rooms with bathroom for 15,000/20,000 rp and individual cottages for 25,000/30,000 rp. There's no phone here, but you can get information and make bookings on a Senggigi number (☎ 93040) which would be a good idea as it's a long way to come if there are no rooms available.

If you keep following this track, you'll eventually reach **Bangko Bangko**, and from there it's two or 3km to **Desert Point**, the famous surf break, though there are no places there to stay or eat.

Islands
There are two groups of picturesque islands off the north coast of the peninsula, all visible from the boats coming in to Lembar. You can reach them by chartered *prahu* (outrigger) from Lembar for around 25,000 rp, and also from Taun for a little less. Only a few of these islands are inhabited, but most have unspoilt white beaches and lots of palm trees. The only tourist accommodation is on **Gili Nanggu**, where *Istana Cempaka* charges around 30,000 rp per person, including all

meals. Enquiries and bookings can be made by phoning a Cakra number (☎ 22898).

Further west, **Gili Gede** is in the second group of islands and is the largest of all of them. It has several villages, and some of the Bugis settlers here make a living from boat building.

SENGGIGI

On a series of sweeping bays, between three and 12km north of Ampenan, Senggigi is the most developed tourist area on Lombok. It has all the tourist facilities: restaurants, bars, travel agents, photo processors, money-changers, souvenir shops, and a range of budget, mid-range and top-end accommodation. Senggigi has experienced a lot of development in the past few years, and much of it is still pretty raw, unsoftened by landscaping. The nicest places are the isolated groups of bungalows north of the central area. There are ambitious plans for more luxury developments, though some projects seem to be stalled pending growth in tourist numbers and a new influx of investment.

Senggigi has fine beaches, although they slope very steeply into the water, and there are signs that erosion is starting to eat away the sand and foreshore. There's some snorkelling off the point and in the sheltered bay around the headland. There are beautiful sunsets over the Lombok Strait and you can enjoy them from the beach or one of the beachfront restaurants. As it gets dark, the fishing fleet lines up offshore, each boat with its bright lanterns (new arrivals often wonder which Balinese city is across the water). Senggigi has the only nightlife on Lombok – it's mostly low key, but it can be good fun.

Orientation

The area known as Senggigi is spread out along nearly 10km of coastal road. Most of the shops, travel agents and other facilities, and a fair concentration of the accommodation, are on the main road about 6km north of Ampenan. This road continues north to Bangsal, the port for the Gili Islands – it follows the coast with lots of turns and hills, and fantastic scenery.

Information

There's a private wartel and a postal agent on the main street, along with several money-changers. Banks have good rates and the BCA bank has an ATM for cash advances on Visa cards, while the ATM at the BNI bank accepts MasterCard. Moneychangers are easier and the rates are often as good as the banks, but it pays to shop around. The PT Muara Lintu Artha Moneychanger near the Graha Beach Hotel has the best rates and is open in the evenings. You can also change money and travellers cheques at most of the big hotels, but rates are poorer.

You can make bookings and reconfirm flights for Garuda and Merpati at numerous travel agents, such as Nazareth Tours & Travel (☎ 93033). Almost every hotel has a travel agent and can arrange tours. There's a Perama office (☎ 93007/8/9) which runs tourist transport. Other facilities include a supermarket, a Telkom wartel and some photo-processing places.

Batu Bolong Temple

This temple is on a rocky point which juts into the sea about a kilometre south of Senggigi Beach (or 5km north of Ampenan). The rock it sits on has a natural hole in it which gives the temple its name – *batu bolong* (literally, rock with hole). Being a Balinese temple, it's oriented towards Gunung Agung, Bali's holiest mountain, across the Lombok Strait. There's a fantastic view and it's a good place to watch the sunsets. Legend has it that beautiful virgins were once thrown into the sea from the top of the rock. Locals like to claim that this is why there are so many sharks in the water here.

Diving

Dive trips from Senggigi go to sites around the Gili Islands, so if you're a qualified diver, it may be better to base yourself there, unless you prefer Senggigi's swankier hotels. Also, some of the beginners dive courses do initial training in hotel swimming pools in Senggigi. Reliable dive operators, offering PADI standard open-water courses and more

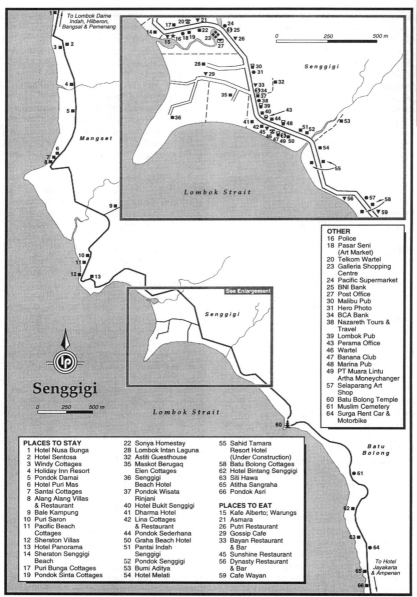

OTHER
16 Police
18 Pasar Seni (Art Market)
20 Telkom Wartel
23 Galleria Shopping Centre
24 Pacific Supermarket
25 BNI Bank
27 Post Office
30 Malibu Pub
31 Hero Photo
34 BCA Bank
38 Nazareth Tours & Travel
39 Lombok Pub
43 Perama Office
46 Wartel
47 Banana Club
48 Marina Pub
49 PT Muara Lintu Artha Moneychanger
57 Selaparang Art Shop
60 Batu Bolong Temple
61 Muslim Cemetery
64 Surga Rent Car & Motorbike

PLACES TO STAY
1 Hotel Nusa Bunga
2 Hotel Sentosa
3 Windy Cottages
4 Holiday Inn Resort
5 Pondok Damai
6 Hotel Puri Mas
7 Santai Cottages
8 Alang Alang Villas & Restaurant
9 Bale Kampung
10 Puri Saron
11 Pacific Beach Cottages
12 Sheraton Villas
13 Hotel Panorama
14 Sheraton Senggigi Beach
17 Puri Bunga Cottages
19 Pondok Sinta Cottages
22 Sonya Homestay
28 Lombok Intan Laguna
32 Astiti Guesthouse
35 Maskot Berugaq Elen Cottages
36 Senggigi Beach Hotel
37 Pondok Wisata Rinjani
40 Hotel Bukit Senggigi
41 Dharma Hotel
42 Lina Cottages & Restaurant
44 Pondok Sederhana
50 Graha Beach Hotel
51 Pantai Indah Senggigi
52 Pondok Senggigi
53 Bumi Aditya
54 Hotel Melati
55 Sahid Tamara Resort Hotel (Under Construction)
58 Batu Bolong Cottages
62 Hotel Bintang Senggigi
63 Siti Hawa
65 Atitha Sangraha
66 Pondok Asri

PLACES TO EAT
15 Kafe Alberto; Warungs
21 Asmara
26 Putri Restaurant
29 Gossip Cafe
33 Bayan Restaurant & Bar
45 Sunshine Restaurant
56 Dynasty Restaurant & Bar
59 Cafe Wayan

advanced training, are Albatross (☎ 93399), next to the Hotel Bukit Senggigi, and Blue Coral (☎ 93441, 93002), a few doors north on the main street. Baruna (☎ 93444) at the Holiday Inn Resort also has dives and PADI courses. Waterworld (☎ 93126) at the Pasar Seni has dive trips and courses, and rents out jet skis, windsurfers and kayaks. It also has expensive yacht tours.

A day trip to the Gilis, with two dives, will cost around US$50 to US$65, depending on demand and the amount of equipment provided. A PADI open-water course costs around US$300. Snorkelling trips to the Gilis also can be arranged (see also the following Gili Islands section).

Organised Tours

Day tours are available, taking in most of the usual attractions in western Lombok or some of the craft villages in Central Lombok. Costs run from US$20 to US$35, depending on the company, the destination and the number of passengers. Senggigi is crawling with travel agents and every second hotel has an agent or sells tours. Nazareth Tours & Travel (☎ 93033), on the main street, arranges treks on Gunung Rinjani, but it's much cheaper, and not much more difficult, to go to Batu Koq or Senaru (just to the north of the mountain) and make your own arrangements.

Boat trips to Gili Trawangan with CCT (☎ 993669) cost around US$40, including lunch and snorkelling gear. Sunshine Tours (☎ 93029) does similar trips as well as fishing outings and day trips to Kuta, Tetebatu, Mataram etc. Discover Lombok (☎ 36781, 93390), with offices at Pasar Seni and at Pizzeria Cafe Alberto, near Ampenan, does boat trips to the Gilis that include a BBQ lunch. They also offer horse treks and more conventional tours.

Places to Stay – budget

Senggigi is moving upmarket, and many of the shoestring places have increased their standards and prices. Basic rooms are still available for around 10,000 rp in the low season, but expect steep price hikes in the high season. *Pondok Senggigi* (☎ 93273), at

the southern end of the main tourist strip, used to be the main budget travellers' choice, and it still advertises rooms at 20,000 rp. In fact, it only has a few 'class B' rooms at this price, and most of the rooms are 'class A' and only a little better at US$15/20 for singles/doubles, plus 15.5% tax and service. The rooms run off a long verandah and face a pleasant garden, and there's a swimming pool. The restaurant is very popular and sometimes has live music, which can be fearfully noisy. Almost next door, *Pantai Indah Senggigi* asks 10,000/15,000 rp for horrid little rooms.

Pondok Sederhana (☎ 93040), north-west of Pondok Senggigi, has been rebuilt and has quite good rooms, some with great views, for 20,000/25,000 rp. On the beach side of the road, *Lina Cottages* (☎ 93237) is central, friendly and good value at 25,000/35,000 rp, and its restaurant is good. Next door, *Dharma Hotel* has rooms and spacious cottages in an open field by the beach for 25,000/30,000 to 50,000 rp – this must be a potential development site, but in the meantime it's good value for this location. A little further to the north, *Pondok Wisata Rinjani* (☎ 93274) has cottages with private bathrooms at 22,000/28,000 rp plus tax.

There are some small places off the main road and away from the beach, which are quiet and less expensive. *Bumi Aditya*, on a grassy slope up behind Pondok Melati Dua, has bamboo bungalows which are small but clean, and somehow appealing, from 15,000 rp. The *Astiti Guesthouse*, behind Pondok Wisata Rinjani, is less spacious, with ordinary rooms around a small courtyard for 25,000 rp. A few local guys hang around here, playing guitars and being friendly, so it could be a fun place to stay.

Further up the main road, on the left, *Sonya Homestay* (☎ 63447) is a family-run losmen that has been recommended by readers; the atmosphere is friendly and the small rooms are only 10,000 and 15,000 rp. Close by, *Pondok Sinta Cottages* asks the same price in slightly more spacious surroundings, but it lacks atmosphere and the rooms are run down.

A couple of kilometres further (100 rp on a bemo), and off to the east in Kampung Krandangan, *Bale Kampung* is billed as a backpackers' place and has dorm beds at 6000 rp, and rooms at 10,000 and 12,000 rp. It serves cheap food and gives good info about local attractions – it's not too far away from the sea, but seems like light years from the Senggigi scene.

Way to the north, in the area known as Mangset, *Pondok Damai* (☎ 93019) is a quiet seaside retreat, and has comfortable, moderately cheap cottages starting at around 30,000 rp.

Well south of the Senggigi strip, *Siti Hawa* (☎ 93414) is a very basic homestay, but it fronts a good stretch of beach. It serves home-cooked meals, and has a dinghy and bicycles for rent. The few, very small, very basic bamboo cottages cost 9000/10,000 rp.

Places to Stay – middle

Coming in from Ampenan, before you get to the main Senggigi strip, are some mid-range places like *Pondok Asri* (☎ 93075) and *Atitha Sangraha* (☎ 93070). They both have cottages that are clean, comfortable and near the beach, but they're nothing special and you'll need transport to Senggigi's facilities and restaurants. Prices start at around 25,000 rp in the low season, and considerably more around August.

Much closer to the action, *Batu Bolong Cottages* (☎ 93065) has spacious, well finished bungalows on both sides of the road. On the beach side they cost from 40,000 rp, and on the other side from 35,000 rp, including tax, which is pretty good value compared with some of the soulless new, mid-range concrete places.

On the right as you enter Senggigi central, *Hotel Melati* (☎ 93288) has standard cottages at 30,000 rp and better bungalows from 40,000 to 60,000 rp, including tax and breakfast. It's a short walk to the beach and generally an OK place. The *Graha Beach Hotel* (☎ 93101; fax 93400) has a good central beachside location, but most rooms are across the road in a new wing that lacks character. New rooms cost from US$40/45

with air-con, phone and TV, while beach side bungalows are US$65/70.

On the side road to the Senggigi Beach Hotel, the *Maskot Berugaq Elen Cottages* (☎ 93365; fax 22314) offers pleasant individual bungalows from US$35 to US$40, plus 21% service and tax. It has air-con, hot water and phone, but the best feature is the quiet garden setting which extends to the beach.

Bukit Senggigi (☎ 93173) is on the inland side of the road in central Senggigi. Motel-like rooms are staggered up the side of a small hill and some have views over the sea. Prices are from US$75/80, but discounts up to 40% are available in quiet times. There's also a swimming pool, a disco and karaoke lounge – none of them crowded.

A similar place is *Puri Bunga Cottages* (☎ 93013; fax 93286), also built up the hillside on the inland side of the road, with even better views and a lot more character. It's a bit of a trek to the higher rooms and to the beach, but the attractive individual bungalows have air-con, telephone, TV and hot water, and the pool is good. The published rate is US$60/65, but it discounts to US$30/35 which makes it good value.

At the northern end of Senggigi, *Pacific Beach Cottages* (☎ 93006; fax 93027) has all the standard luxuries – air-con, TV, hot water, swimming pool – but the old rooms are slightly tatty and it has no character at all. Standard rooms cost US$45, bungalows are US$55 and US$65, plus 21% tax and service. Expect a big discount. Nearby is the newer *Puri Saron* (☎ 93424), which has similar facilities, including a pool, but it also lacks character. Rooms are better, but a little sterile, and cost from US$55/60 plus 21% tax (or less with discount).

Further north, *Santai Cottages* (☎ 93038) has a homely, travellers' atmosphere and a lush garden. There's a good library and book exchange, and it serves traditional meals in a pleasant pavilion. Rooms with bathroom start at 15,000/20,000 rp (but most are 24,000/32,000 rp), or bungalows with hot water are 48,000 rp. It is a long way out and not a place to party, but is a very peaceful retreat. Next door, the small *Hotel Puri Mas* (☎ 93023) has Balinese-style bungalows surrounded by trees and shrubs. Bungalow rooms are a little tired and cost US$20 and $30, plus 15.5% tax. More luxurious villas are US$35 to US$125.

The *Alang Alang Villas* (☎ 93518) is the most stylish of the northern places. Boutique bungalows with Indonesian antique-style furniture are set in delightful grounds next to a private beach. It has a bar/restaurant and bungalows cost US$60 plus 15.5%. Part of its charm is its size – it has only eight bungalows – but a new block of rooms is being built.

Another good place to get away is *Windy Cottages* (☎ 93191), out by itself in spacious grounds 5km north of Senggigi. It charges 40,000 rp for standard rooms, or 50,000 rp for bigger bungalows with hot water. The restaurant has excellent food, and Perama will pick up and drop off here on request.

Places to Stay – top end

Senggigi is Lombok's centre for luxury hotels, though they are still low in number and none of them is well patronised outside the high season. They all add 21% tax and service to the prices given here. The first hotel you pass when you head north from Ampenan is the *Hotel Jayakarta* (formerly the Senggigi Palace Hotel; ☎ 93045; fax 93043) and you'll certainly see it – the central lobby building is massive. The hotel is of a good standard, but is looking tired. Sterile rooms with fridge, phone, TV and video cost US$60/70 for singles/doubles, or US$80/90 with an ocean view. It has a big garden, a vast swimming pool and is on a wide stretch of beach.

The first big 'international standard' hotel built at Senggigi is right on the headland. Although showing its age a little, *Senggigi Beach Hotel* (☎ 93210; fax 93200) has beautiful gardens, tennis courts, a swimming pool and other mod cons, and charges US$110 for an air-con room, US$180 for a deluxe bungalow, or US$550 for the presidential suite. Officially it's now called the Hotel Senggigi Aerowisata, but it's usually known by the

original name. At least as classy is the *Lombok Intan Laguna* (☎ 93090; fax 93185), a large and handsome luxury hotel, with a big pool and rooms from US$100/110 and suites from US$250.

Further to the north, the *Sheraton Senggigi Beach* (☎ 93333; fax 93140) is the best hotel in Senggigi and also the most expensive, with rooms from US$150 to US$170 and suites from US$350 to US$1000. Local handcrafts decorate the rooms and public areas. It's all very tasteful, the pool and gardens are lovely, and there's a children's playground and pool. The Sheraton promotes local crafts and culture, and is one of the few places to recycle waste water for the gardens.

Another new international hotel hot on the heels of the Sheraton is the *Holiday Inn Resort* (☎ 93444; fax 93092), which offers all the creature comforts from US$140 to US$450, and was giving 50% discounts in the low season.

Continuing north along the coast, some small, upmarket options offer more character and a more personal style. A good one is the well run *Hotel Nusa Bunga* (formerly Bunga Beach Cottages; ☎ 93035), with a splendid beachfront position, a pool and 28 comfortable, air-con bungalows in a pretty garden from US$45/50 to US$55/60. Further north, *Lombok Dame Indah* (☎ 93246; fax 93248) has a secluded location and good views, and is heavily decorated with fine examples of Indonesian arts and artefacts. Rooms cost US$140. The new *Hilberon* (☎ 93898; fax 93252) is very much in the style of Balinese beach bungalows. It is efficiently managed, and has a big pool and spacious, spotless rooms from US$120.

Places to Eat

You can eat well in Senggigi for a reasonable price, though there is not quite the range or the quality you find in Bali's tourist areas. Most of the places to stay have their own restaurants, and the main road in the centre of the strip has other eateries.

Local warungs have been priced out of the real estate market, but there is a good selection of open-air warungs at the Pasar Seni market – popular with locals and tourists. Mostly Indonesian food is served, although a few have western-oriented menus. Prices are as cheap as you'll find in Senggigi and you can dine overlooking the boats and the water. The most upmarket here is the *Kafe Alberto*, which does pasta, pizza and barbecued seafood – it's a bit better, and a bit pricier, than the standard tourist fare. It is a branch of the pizzeria and cafe of the same name further south, almost to Ampenan.

The restaurant at *Pondok Senggigi* hotel is the old favourite Senggigi stand-by. It's not the cheapest, but is still popular from breakfast time until late at night. The big open dining area is comfortable and convivial, and there's a wide selection of well prepared western and Indonesian food, with some interesting Sasak specialities as well.

The restaurant at *Lina Cottages* is also popular, with a big menu of very tasty dishes. It's a little cheaper and has a great location by the beach. Nearby, the popular *Sunshine Restaurant* is perched above the beach – it serves slightly westernised Chinese food, but it tastes great.

On the main road in the centre, the *Bayan Restaurant & Bar* is a new breed of restaurant – very chic with nouveau 'primitif' decor. Mains on the Chinese-influenced menu cost around 5000 to 10,000 rp and there is music in the evenings. The *Asmara* a few hundred metres north is also very stylish, but expensive.

Also near the centre, *Putri Restaurant* has a bar downstairs and a pleasant open dining area upstairs. It does a good line in Mexican food, which makes a change, but it's a tad expensive and the servings aren't huge.

South of the town centre, the slightly upmarket *Cafe Wayan* (☎ 93098) is related to the excellent Cafe Wayan in Ubud, which should be recommendation enough. The famous, fantastic chicken curry costs 7500 rp, while the homemade bread and yummy desserts are also highlights. It will pick you up in the Senggigi area if you call first.

Beachside dining is a Senggigi highlight; it's especially delightful in the evening, with cool sea breezes and blazing sunsets. In the centre, the *Graha Beach Hotel* has a well located outdoor restaurant. Further north is *Alang Alang* at the villas of the same name, which has average food, but everyone loves the location. The restaurant at *Windy Cottages* is even further up the coast, in an open-sided pavilion facing the sea. It's a scenic area and the beach is nice – a trip up here for lunch makes a good outing.

Entertainment
Pondok Senggigi, *Banana Club* and the *Marina Pub* have live music on occasions, with local bands doing good rock and reggae music with an Indonesian flavour, as well as covers of popular western numbers. In the busy season, these places can all get crowded with tourists and young locals, but at other times only one of them, if any, will have much action. A couple of the pubs can be quite sociable – try the *Lombok Pub* or the *Down Under Pub* at the Putri Restaurant. The *Moonlight Disco* at the Bukit Senggigi hotel is open until 3 am on Friday and Saturday nights if you're desperate for something to do.

The *Holiday Inn* puts on buffet dinner and cultural shows on Saturday nights for 30,000 rp. The *Sheraton* has similar dinner shows for 51,500 rp on Wednesday and Saturday.

Things to Buy
The Pasar Seni (Art Market) has a large variety of craft stalls and shops, including a Lombok pottery outlet and an antique shop. Hard bargaining is required. A couple of the craft/souvenir shops in the new Galleria shopping centre have interesting items, but prices are very high. If you have the time and interest, it's worth making trips to Ampenan for the craft and antique shops, to Cakranegara for the weaving workshops and to the small villages which specialise in various handcrafts.

Opposite the Galleria, the Pacific Supermarket is just an overgrown Chinese shop, but has most of the basics you'll need, and a small selection of books in English. The big hotels, such as the Sheraton, have the best bookshops and a couple of second-hand bookshops are on the main street. Film and photo processing are inexpensive at Hero Photo.

Getting There & Away

A public bemo to Senggigi is about 500 rp from Ampenan terminal, or 600 rp from Bertais. Note that most transport to Bangsal and the Gilis will go via Ampenan and the Pusuk Pass (and take 1½ hours or so), rather than going straight up the coast road to reach Bangsal in less than 30 minutes.

The Perama tourist shuttle has good connections from Senggigi to tourist centres on Bali and Lombok, including Bangsal (for the Gili Islands; 5000 rp), Tetebatu (7500 rp) and Kuta (that's Kuta on Lombok; 10,000 rp), and also sells tickets to Sumbawa.

Boat Sunshine Tours (☎ 930329) at the Sunshine Restaurant has a daily outrigger boat in the main season to Gili Trawangan (10,000/ 20,000 rp one way/return) and Gili Meno (12,500/25,000 rp). This is a very pleasant alternative to taking the road to Bangsal. Several travel agents also offer boat tours to the Gilis that include lunch and snorkelling.

Getting Around

To/From the Airport To get to Senggigi from the airport, first get a bemo to the Ampenan terminal (300 rp), then another to Senggigi. A taxi from the airport to Senggigi is 10,000 rp, or 12,000 rp for a taxi with air-con.

NARMADA

Laid out as a miniature replica of the summit of Gunung Rinjani and its crater lake, Narmada is a hill about 10km east of Cakra, on the main east-west road across Lombok. It takes its name from a sacred river in India. The temple, Pura Kalasa, is still used, and the Balinese Pujawali celebration is held here every year in honour of the god Batara, who dwells on Gunung Rinjani.

Narmada was constructed by the king of Mataram in 1805, when he was no longer able to climb Rinjani to make his offerings

to the gods. Having set his conscience at rest by placing offerings in the temple, he spent at least some of his time in his pavilion on the hill, lusting after the young girls bathing in the artificial lake.

Along one side of the pool is the remains of an aqueduct built by the Dutch and still in use. Land tax was tied to the productivity of the land so the Dutch were keenly interested in maximising agricultural output. They managed this by extending their irrigation systems to increase the area under cultivation. The Balinese had already built extensive irrigation networks, particularly in the west of Lombok.

It's a beautiful place to spend a few hours, although the gardens are neglected. Don't go there on the weekend, if you can help it, as it tends to be very crowded. Apart from the lake there are two other pools in the grounds. Admission is 500 rp, and there's an additional charge to swim in the pool.

Places to Eat

Right at the Narmada bemo stop is the local market, which sells mainly food and clothing and is well worth a look. There are a number of *warungs* scattered around offering soto ayam (chicken soup) and other dishes.

Getting There & Away

There are frequent bemos from Bertais to Narmada, costing 400 rp. When you get off at the bemo stop at Narmada, you'll see the gardens directly opposite. If you cross the road and walk 100m or so south along the side road you'll come to the entrance. There are parking fees for bicycles, motorcycles and cars.

LINGSAR

This large temple complex, just a few kilometres north of Narmada, is said to have been built in 1714. The temple combines the Bali Hindu and Wektu Telu religions in one complex. Designed in two separate sections and built on two different levels, the Hindu temple in the northern section is higher than the Wektu Telu temple in the southern section.

The Hindu temple has four shrines. On one side is Hyang Tunggal, which looks towards Gunung Agung, the seat of the gods on Bali. The shrine faces north-west rather than north-east as it would on Bali. On the other side is a shrine devoted to Gunung Rinjani, the seat of the gods on Lombok. Between these two shrines is a double shrine symbolising the union between the two islands. One side of this double shrine is named in honour of the might of Lombok, while the other side is dedicated to a king's daughter named Ayu Nyoman Winton who, according to legend, gave birth to a god.

The Wektu Telu temple is noted for its small enclosed pond devoted to Lord Vishnu. It has a number of holy eels that look like huge swimming slugs and can be enticed from their hiding places by the use of hard-boiled eggs as bait. The stalls outside the temple complex sell boiled eggs. Get there early to see the eels, because they've had their fill of eggs after the first few tour groups. Next to the eel pond is another enclosure with a large altar or offering place, bedecked in white and yellow cloth and mirrors. The mirrors are offerings from Chinese business people asking for good luck and success. Many local farmers also come here with offerings.

At the annual rain festival at the start of the wet season – somewhere between October and December – the Hindus and the Wektu Telu make offerings and pray in their own temples, then come out into the communal compound and pelt each other with *ketupat* – rice wrapped in banana leaves. The ceremony is to bring the rain, or to give thanks for the rain. Be prepared to get attacked with ketupat from both sides if you visit Lingsar at this time!

Getting There & Away
Lingsar is off the main east-west road across the island. After taking a bemo from Bertais to Narmada (400 rp), catch another one to Lingsar village (300 rp) and walk the short distance from there to the temple complex. It's easy to miss the temple, which is set back off the road behind the school.

SURANADI
A few kilometres east of Lingsar, Suranadi has one of the holiest temples on Lombok. This small temple, set in pleasant gardens, is noted for its bubbling, icy cold spring water and restored baths with ornate Balinese carvings. The eels here are also sacred and seldom underfed – how many hard-boiled eggs can an eel eat?

You can stop for a swim in the refreshingly cool pool at the hotel.

Hutan Wisata Suranadi
Not far from Suranadi on the road towards Sesaot, there's a small forest sanctuary, the Hutan Wisata Suranadi *(hutan* means forest or jungle), but it's sadly neglected and entry costs 1000 rp. There's a rumour of plans to make this place more interesting by introducing some 'wildlife', like an elephant.

Places to Stay & Eat
The *Suranadi Hotel* (☎ 33686) has rooms and cottages which are overpriced at US$25 to US$50, plus 21% tax and service, but it may give you a special deal – US$17, including tax and breakfast. This old Dutch building was originally an administrative centre, although it's no great example of colonial architecture. There are two swimming pools, tennis courts, a restaurant and a bar.

There's a cheaper homestay nearby, *Pondok Surya*, which has basic rooms, a nice outlook and excellent food. It's a casual, friendly place and costs 15,000 rp per person, with three meals – to find it, ask at the warungs on the main street.

Opposite the forest is a parking area, surrounded by souvenir shops and *warungs*, and obviously designed to be a place where tourists will have their lunch.

GOLONG
About halfway between Suranadi and the main road, on a quiet back road, Golong is the site of Lombok's main golf course, the *Rinjani Country Club* (☎ 33839). A game will cost around US$50, including caddy, clubs, shoes and tax, or Mataram travel agents do tours for around US$70, including

transport and a guide. It's usually deserted, and it makes you wonder why golf courses are part of the plans at all the luxury resorts the speculators are dreaming about. Accommodation here costs US$60 in a comfortable motel-style room, or US$240 for a villa. There's a great swimming pool, which you can use for 10,000 rp.

SESAOT

About 5km from Suranadi, and also worth a visit, is Sesaot, a small quiet market town on the edge of a forest where wood-felling is the main industry. There's regular transport from Suranadi to Sesaot, and you can eat at the *warung* on the main street, which has simple but tasty food.

Along the main street and left over the bridge are some nice places for picnics that are popular with locals on holidays, and you can swim in the river. The water is very cool and is considered holy as it comes straight from Gunung Rinjani. You can climb Gunung Rinjani from here, but a guide is essential.

Continue up the road about 3km to **Air Nyet**, a small village with more places for swimming and picnics.

Gili Islands

Off the north-west coast of Lombok are three small, coral-fringed islands – Gili Air, Gili Meno and Gili Trawangan – each with superb, white sandy beaches, clear water, coral reefs, brilliantly coloured fish and the best snorkelling on Lombok. Although known to travellers as the 'Gili Islands', *gili* actually means 'island', so this is not a local name. There are lots of other gilis around the coast of Lombok.

A few years ago, descendants of Bugis immigrants were granted leases to establish coconut plantations on the islands. The economic activities expanded to include fishing, raising livestock, and growing corn, tapioca and peanuts. As travellers started to visit Lombok, some came to the Gilis on day trips

and then began to stay for longer periods in local homes. Soon, many people on the islands found that the most profitable activity was 'picking white coconuts' – a local expression for providing services to tourists.

The islands have become enormously popular with visitors, especially young Europeans, who come for the very simple pleasures of sun, snorkelling and socialising. It's cheap, and the absence of cars, motorcycles and hawkers adds greatly to the pleasure of staying on the Gilis.

Their very popularity may be a problem, as numbers sometimes exceed the available rooms and put pressure on the island environment, especially the supply of fresh water and the capacity of septic systems to cope with waste. The local population is aware of environmental issues, but there is always pressure to build more and better facilities. Gili Meno and Gili Air have retained much of their unspoilt quality, but Gili Trawangan has become a little less attractive over the past few years.

Big business interests are trying to cash in on the popularity of the Gili Islands, and the government is keen to promote upmarket tourist development. A luxury resort has been built on the mainland at Sira and a golf course is planned for Gili Trawangan. Already ill-conceived plans have created two costly white elephants at Bangsal, the access point for the islands.

You have to get your feet wet when you board the small boats for the Gili Islands, which pull up on the beach at Bangsal. This doesn't worry most of the visitors, who arrive in shorts and sandals, but it was decided that a proper port was needed. A large stone and concrete structure was built, at considerable expense, right at the end of the main road. But the boats which ferry people to the islands all have a big bamboo outrigger on each side and they can't come alongside a jetty, so they pull up on the beach as they always have. The new jetty is a popular place for fishing.

Another aspect of access to the Gilis also seemed to need attention – there was a good deal of congestion and disorder when passengers transferred from buses, cars and horsecarts to the boats. The solution seemed to be a new bus terminal, which has now been completed, halfway between Bangsal and Pemenang, and not convenient for either place. It is as big as any bus terminal on Bali or Lombok, with lots of neat buildings for ticket sellers and administrative offices, and a vast paved area which is now growing weeds. If it is actually in use when you arrive, you will have to walk or find local transport for the last 300m to the boats at Bangsal, where you will certainly find a good deal of congestion and disorder.

Information

You can change money and make international phone calls on any of the islands. Trawangan has an electricity supply, but on the other islands most places have their own generators, which usually stop at about 10 pm. There are small shops selling basic supplies, second-hand books, some handcrafts, clothing and souvenirs.

Security

There is the occasional spate of thefts on the islands, and they are not always dealt with effectively. No police are stationed on the islands, and in such small communities, the perpetrators might be closely related to the local authority. None of the islands want any adverse publicity, so there can be a tendency to overlook any problems. Make sure your room, including the bathroom, is well secured, even when you're in the room at night. Keep your things locked in a bag and well away from windows, doors or other openings. Report any theft to the island *kepala* (headman), and if there is no response, make a report to the police yourself. The closest police station is in Tanjung (on the north coast), but the one in Ampenan might be easier to deal with.

Avoiding Offence

The islanders are Muslims, and visitors should respect their sensibilities. In particular, topless (for women) or nude sunbathing is offensive to them, although they won't say

so directly. Away from the beach, it is polite for both men and women to cover their shoulders and thighs. Many visitors are appallingly insensitive to local standards, and so many of them walk around in skimpy clothing that it's easy to get the impression that the local people don't mind any more. They do.

Dangers

Although not common, stonefish are found on coral reefs where they are camouflaged and almost invisible. If you stand on one, the venomous spines can cause excruciating pain and sometimes death. Don't walk on coral reefs.

Activities

You don't have to be totally inactive. A few places rent paddle boards (called canoes) – some boards even have a window so you can see the coral – or you can rent a boat to go fishing. There are two surf breaks off Gili Air, but they're very fickle.

Diving The coral around the islands is good for snorkelling. Ask locally to find the best spots, many of which you can reach from the shore. For scuba divers, the visibility is fair to good (best in the dry season), and there is some very good coral reef accessible by boat. Marine life includes turtles, rays, sharks (harmless) and giant clams. A particularly interesting attraction is the blue coral, with its almost luminous colouring. There are quality scuba diving operations on Gili Trawangan and Gili Air (see those entries later in this section for details).

Accommodation

The quality of accommodation is improving and a greater variety is available now, but there are still lots of basic places. The Gili Islands standard is a plain little bamboo bungalow on stilts, with a thatched roof, a small verandah out the front and a concrete bathroom block out the back. Inside, there will be one or two beds with mosquito nets. Prices are around 8000/10,000 rp for singles/doubles in the low season. In the busy

LOMBOK

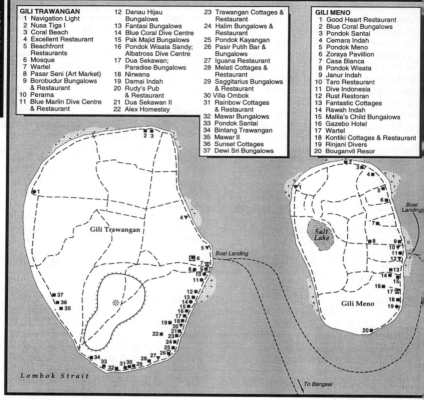

GILI TRAWANGAN	
1 Navigation Light	12 Danau Hijau Bungalows
2 Nusa Tiga I	13 Fantasi Bungalows
3 Coral Beach	14 Blue Coral Dive Centre
4 Excellent Restaurant	15 Pak Majid Bungalows
5 Beachfront Restaurants	16 Pondok Wisata Sandy; Albatross Dive Centre
6 Mosque	17 Dua Sekawan; Paradise Bungalows
7 Wartel	18 Nirwana
8 Pasar Seni (Art Market)	19 Damai Indah
9 Borobudur Bungalows & Restaurant	20 Rudy's Pub & Restaurant
10 Perama	21 Dua Sekawan II
11 Blue Marlin Dive Centre & Restaurant	22 Alex Homestay

23 Trawangan Cottages & Restaurant	
24 Halim Bungalows & Restaurant	
25 Pondok Kayangan	
26 Pasir Putih Bar & Bungalows	
27 Iguana Restaurant	
28 Melati Cottages & Restaurant	
29 Saggitarius Bungalows & Restaurant	
30 Villa Ombok	
31 Rainbow Cottages & Restaurant	
32 Mawar Bungalows	
33 Pondok Santai	
34 Bintang Trawangan	
35 Mawar II	
36 Sunset Cottages	
37 Dewi Sri Bungalows	

GILI MENO	
1 Good Heart Restaurant	
2 Blue Coral Bungalows	
3 Pondok Santai	
4 Cemara Indah	
5 Pondok Meno	
6 Zoraya Pavillion	
7 Casa Blanca	
8 Pondok Wisata	
9 Janur Indah	
10 Taro Restaurant	
11 Dive Indonesia	
12 Rust Restoran	
13 Fantastic Cottages	
14 Rawah Indah	
15 Mallia's Child Bungalows	
16 Gazebo Hotel	
17 Wartel	
18 Kontiki Cottages & Restaurant	
19 Rinjani Divers	
20 Bouganvil Resor	

seasons (July, August and around Christmas) the owners ask a lot more – maybe double the prices given here. Most places include a light breakfast.

Touts meet the boats as they land and can be quite helpful. But if you have decided to stay in a particular place, don't let a tout convince you that it's full, closed or doesn't exist.

Getting There & Away

From Ampenan or the airport, you can get to one of the islands and be horizontal on the beach within a couple of hours if you start early. Begin with a short bemo ride to Rembiga (about 300 rp), then a scenic trip to Pemenang (700 rp). Alternatively, you may be able to get a bus from Bertais direct to Pemenang for about 900 rp. From there it's a kilometre or so off the main road to the harbour at Bangsal (200 rp per person by cidomo). Tourist shuttle buses go from Mataram or Senggigi to Bangsal for 5000 rp, and make direct connections from Lembar. A taxi from the airport to Bangsal costs 22,000 rp (26,000 rp with air-con) and you can expect to pay the same from Mataram, or around 20,000 rp from Senggigi.

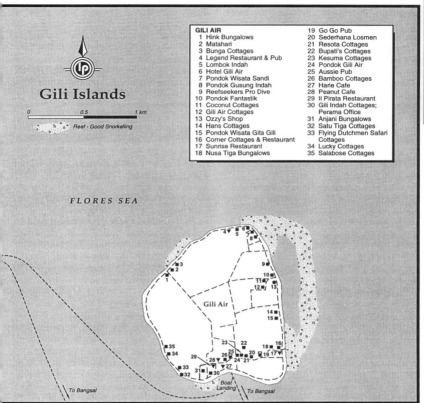

Gili Islands

0   0.5   1 km

Reef - Good Snorkelling

FLORES SEA

Gili Air

35
34
33
32
29
28
30
31
27
26
25
24
21
20
23
22
19 17
18
16
Boat Landing
To Bangsal
To Bangsal

1
2
3
4
5
6
7
8
9
10
11
12
13
14
15

GILI AIR
1 Hink Bungalows
2 Matahari
3 Bunga Cottages
4 Legend Restaurant & Pub
5 Lombok Indah
6 Hotel Gili Air
7 Pondok Wisata Sandi
8 Pondok Gusung Indah
9 Reefseekers Pro Dive
10 Pondok Fantastik
11 Coconut Cottages
12 Gili Air Cottages
13 Ozzy's Shop
14 Hans Cottages
15 Pondok Wisata Gita Gili
16 Corner Cottages & Restaurant
17 Sunrise Restaurant
18 Nusa Tiga Bungalows
19 Go Go Pub
20 Sederhana Losmen
21 Resota Cottages
22 Bupati's Cottages
23 Kesuma Cottages
24 Pondok Gili Air
25 Aussie Pub
26 Bamboo Cottages
27 Harie Cafe
28 Peanut Cafe
29 Il Pirata Restaurant
30 Gili Indah Cottages;
   Perama Office
31 Anjani Bungalows
32 Satu Tiga Cottages
33 Flying Dutchmen Safari
   Cottages
34 Lucky Cottages
35 Salabose Cottages

The Koperasi Angkutan Laut (Sea Transport Co-operative) is the boat owners' cartel which monopolises transport to the islands. Its office at Bangsal sells tickets to the islands – 1200 rp to Gili Air, 1500 rp to Gili Meno and 1600 rp to Gili Trawangan. It's a matter of sitting and waiting until there's a full boat load, about 15 people. If you have almost that number waiting, the boat will leave if you can pay the extra fares between you. As soon as you do this, you'll be amazed at how many local people appear from nowhere to fill the boat. Try to get to Bangsal by 9.30 or 10 am, as most boats go in the morning.

The system is inconvenient and perplexing for many visitors, but it suits the boat owners. Traditionally, their objective has been to make trips to and from the islands with a full boat, and the convenience of passengers is a much lower priority. There are two concessions to western desires for boats which depart on schedule or on demand. A shuttle service leaves at 10 am and 4 pm, and costs 3000 rp to Gili Air, 3500 rp to Gili Meno and 4000 rp to Gili Trawangan. Alternatively, you can charter a whole boat to the islands for 15,000 rp, 18,000 rp and 21,000 rp, respectively, with a maximum of 10 passengers. All the boats pull up on the beaches, so be prepared to wade ashore with your luggage.

Bangsal is not an unpleasant place to hang around while you're waiting for a boat, and the shaded *warungs* have good food and coffee. Moneychangers, shops and travel agents have cropped up to take advantage of the fact that most visitors will have to spend some time waiting here. If you get stuck, the new *Taman Sari* guesthouse, about 250m east, has neat, clean singles/doubles for 15,000/20,000 rp.

Getting Around

There is now a boat shuttle service between the islands, so you can stay on one and have a look, or a snorkel, around the others. The boat fares for 'island hopping' are 4000 rp between Gili Air and Gili Trawangan; and 3000 rp between Gili Meno and either of the other two islands. They do two runs a day: one between 8.30 and 10 am; and the other between 2.30 and 4 pm.

On the islands themselves there are cidomos trotting round the tracks (500 rp is the usual charge). If you're in a hurry (almost inconceivable on the Gilis) you can rent a bicycle, but the main mode of transport is walking.

GILI AIR

Gili Air is the closest island to the mainland and has the largest population, about 1000 people. There are beaches around most of the island, but some are not suitable for swimming because they're quite shallow with a sharp coral bottom. Homes are dotted amongst the palm trees, along with a few *losmen* and a couple of 'pubs'. More losmen are spread around the coast. Because the buildings are so scattered, the island has a pleasant, rural character and is delightful to wander around. There are plenty of other people to meet, but if you stay in one of the more isolated places, socialising is optional.

Orientation & Information

Boats beach at the south end of the island, and nearby are the boat ticket office and Gili Indah Cottages, with a small shop, *wartel* and moneychanger. There's a network of tiny tracks across the island, on which it's surprisingly easy to become disoriented. The simplest option is to follow the coast.

The best time to get a public boat back to Bangsal is around 7 to 8.30 am, otherwise you'll probably have to charter. The boat to Senggigi (15,000 rp) goes at 3 pm, and the shuttles to Meno and Trawangan go at 8.30 am and 3 pm.

Diving & Snorkelling

There's quite good snorkelling off the east and north side of the island, and excellent scuba diving within a short boat ride, with lots of whitetip sharks and underwater canyons. Reefseekers Pro Dive (☎ 34387), based on the east side of the island, is a very professional operation and does a range of trips for qualified divers, starting at US$50 for a day trip with two dives. It also offers night dives and longer trips to little-visited sites. For beginners, it does introductory

---

Coral Conservation

In the past there was much damage done to coral reefs by fish bombing and careless use of anchors. There is much greater awareness of this now and rehabilitation of damaged reefs is possible. Unfortunately, many visitors are unwittingly causing more damage by standing and walking on the reefs, often while snorkelling, boating or windsurfing. Perfectly formed corals are easily broken and take years to recover; the reef ecology is very sensitive.

If you're not into conservation, then think about the stonefish. These fish, with their venomous spines, are well camouflaged on the coral reefs of the Gilis – at times they are virtually invisible. Standing on a stonefish can cause excruciating pain and sometimes death. So keep off the reefs! ■

dives and conducts full PADI open-water certification courses from US$310 to US$350, depending on the number of people. Reef-seekers has a good knowledge of diving possibilities around Lombok, and a strong commitment to conserving the marine environment.

Places to Stay & Eat

Most of the accommodation is scattered around the southern end of the island, and near the east and north coasts. Many places are basic bungalows charging about the standard rates (10,000/15,000 rp for singles/doubles with breakfast) and are so similar that it seems hardly fair to mention any in particular. Pick one that appeals to you in a location you like, or one that's been recommended by other travellers.

The cheapest places tend to be those set back from the beach such as *Kesuma Cottages*, *Resota Cottages* and *Bupati's Cottages*, all with decent bungalows though they tend to be squashed together. In this area, *Pondok Gili Air* has some standard rooms at 10,000/15,000 rp, plus better bungalows at 20,000/25,000 rp. Its restaurant has a varied menu, with vegetarian dishes and homemade yoghurt.

Corner Cottages on the east coast is a touch better than most and is on a good stretch of beach. It costs 12,000/15,000 rp.

Coconut Cottages (☎ 35365) is also a bit better than average at 15,000/18,000 rp for standard bamboo bungalows, and 31,000 rp for very nice new ones. It serves great food, and does a Sasak buffet on Tuesdays. *Flying Dutchmen Safari Cottages* is secluded and well run, with good food, but the beach around here is not good for swimming.

Gili Indah Cottages (☎ 36341) is the biggest place on Gili Air, with a variety of good bungalows from 25,000 rp to 45,000 rp for a spacious, private pavilion. At the north end of the island, *Hotel Gili Air* (☎ 34435) is another upmarket option, with beautifully finished bungalows facing the beach from 55,000/66,000 to 77,000/88,000 rp, plus 15% tax and service. Its restaurant is a delight and not too expensive, and it does

BBQs next to the beach. Under the same management, *Hans Cottages* has a couple of very attractive Balinese-style bungalows, which are also pretty pricey.

Apart from eating at the losmens, the island has a few reasonable rumah makan such as the *Peanut Cafe* and *Sunrise Restaurant*. *Il Pirata* is a reasonably priced Italian restaurant styled after a pirate ship, and open for lunch and dinner. The *Legend*, *Go Go* and *Aussie* pubs all serve meals, and are also the venues for the island's limited nightlife.

GILI MENO

Gili Meno, the middle island, has the smallest population – about 500. It is also the quietest of the islands, with the fewest tourists. It has a salt lake which produces salt in the dry season and mosquitoes in the wet season. The mozzies are probably no worse than in other places at that time of year, but the usual precautions are called for, especially at dusk. You can make phone calls at the wartel by the Gazebo Hotel, and change money at the Gazebo and at Mallia's Child Bungalows.

The beach on the eastern side of the island is very nice, and there's good snorkelling just offshore and further north (you can rent mask, snorkel and fins for 5000 rp). Dive Indonesia and Rinjani Divers operate diving trips. The Rawah Indah organises interesting, five hour dolphin-spotting trips for 80,000 rp per boat. You can spend a couple of hours walking round the whole island, feeling like Robinson Crusoe for most of the way.

Places to Stay & Eat

The accommodation here is mostly on the eastern beach, and there's quite a wide range with several places that are pretty upmarket by Gili standards. Good bottom-end places include *Pondok Meno* and *Mallia's Child Bungalows*, both at around 10,000/15,000 rp for singles/doubles, but considerably more in high season. The similarly priced *Rawah Indah* is back from the beach, but very friendly and has spotless rooms with attached bathroom.

Janur Indah has a decidedly better class of bungalows for 30,000/40,000 rp. The overpriced *Zoraya Pavilion* (☎ 33801) has fairly basic rooms for US$12 and a variety of interesting bungalows from US$22.50 to US$35 a double, and offers various water sports and a tennis court. *Casa Blanca* (☎ 33847) is back from the beach, and has rooms from US$10/12 to US$45, but it's not particularly appealing, even with its tiny swimming pool.

The *Gazebo Hotel* (☎ 35795) has tastefully decorated Bali-style bungalows with private bathrooms and air-con, comfortably spaced amongst the coconut trees. It costs US$50/60 for bed and breakfast. Anyone can eat in its fancy balcony restaurant. *Kontiki Cottages* (☎ 32824) has standard as well as more expensive rooms – those at 15,000/18,000 rp are good value.

At the south end of the island, the new *Bouganvil Resor* (☎ 27435) has a swimming pool and large rooms with air-con for US$45 and US$60. The big problem with this place is the lack of water – in the rooms as well as the pool – and the beach down here is not attractive or swimmable.

Brenda Restaurant, the beachfront restaurant at Mallia's Child Bungalows, is one of the best places to eat and does a tasty pizza. *Kontiki* has pretty good food, in a big breezy pavilion, while *Good Heart*, on the other side of the island, is a pleasant place to pause on a round-island trek and has a great view at sunset. Don't expect snappy service or wild nightlife anywhere on Gili Meno.

GILI TRAWANGAN

The largest island, with a local population of around 800 people, Trawangan also has the most visitors and facilities, and a reputation as the 'party island' of the group. There's an idyllic beach for sunbathing and swimming, coral reefs for snorkelling and reliable dive operators for the more adventurous.

The island is about 3km long and 2km wide – you can walk right around it in a few easy hours. Look for the remains of the old Japanese gun behind the Dewi Sri Bungalows. The hill in the south-west corner is a

good place to enjoy the view across the straits to Bali's Gunung Agung, especially at sunset. The sunrise over Gunung Rinjani is also impressive; one islander described Trawangan's three main attractions as 'sunrise, sunset and sunburn'!

Orientation & Information

Most of the cheap places to stay and eat, and most of the tourist facilities, are on the east side of the island, south of where the boats pull in. There's a wartel here, and a group of shops around the Pasar Seni (Art Market), which sell basic supplies, souvenirs and second-hand books. Several places will change money or travellers cheques, but you'll get a better rate on the mainland. The Blue Marlin Dive Centre will give a cash advance on Visa or MasterCard, deducting a 3% commission.

There are also a few places to stay at other points around the coast, in more tranquil surroundings, but they're somewhat remote from the best beaches and the entertainment.

Diving & Snorkelling

The best area for snorkelling is off the north-eastern corner of the island. There is coral around most of the island, but much of the reef on the eastern side has been damaged. Beware of strong currents on the east side, between Gili Trawangan and Gili Meno. Masks, snorkels and fins can be rented for around 4000 rp per day.

Some excellent scuba diving sites are within a short boat ride, especially off Trawangan's west coast. There are several dive operations based in the main tourist area. It's worth checking them carefully, as the standards can vary and well qualified staff come and go. Reliable ones will not mind you looking around and asking to see the certification of instructors and dive masters. Most trips and courses have minimum and maximum number limits, so the bigger, more popular outfits will have more options on a given day.

Typically, a day trip for a certified diver, with two dives and all equipment, is about US$45 to US$50. PADI 'discover scuba'

The Wisdom of Government
In recent years, the island of Gili Trawangan has attracted an incredible number of visitors, and has also attracted the attention of the Lombok government and outside business interests.

The islanders only lease the land on which they developed their plantations, and later their tourist businesses. In the early 1990s the government decided that all the small bungalows should be located away from the north-east part of the island, and rumours began to circulate about a proposed luxury hotel and golf course on Gili Trawangan. There was some negotiation and compensation, and alternative leases were offered further south. But some of the people refused to move, and in 1992, after repeated requests, the authorities ordered in the army, and closed down the bungalows by the simple but effective means of cutting the posts off with chainsaws.

It's not clear whether this was to make way for a grandiose development project, or because the bungalows contravened the lease conditions, or because they did not meet environmental and health standards. A new power station has been established at the northern end of the island, but four years after relocating the bungalows there were still no signs of a big new hotel, and this whole area, which fronts the best beach on the island, was looking very desolate indeed.

Meanwhile, the south end of Gili Trawangan has been neatly subdivided into narrow allotments, where most of the accommodation and facilities for low-budget travellers are now concentrated. In 1993 a fire destroyed 15 or 20 bungalows, and the authorities encouraged new buildings in brick, concrete and tile. The result is reminiscent of Kuta Beach on Bali – charmless concrete boxes are cramped together as closely as possible, with no sense of local architectural style and no sensitivity at all to the natural environment. ■

introductory dives include some theory and a video, a training dive in sheltered water and a sea dive which should not go below 12m (around US$80). A four day PADI open water course, which gives an internationally recognised scuba certification, will cost about US$300, but some places charge a bit extra for a log book, dive tables and course materials.

Blue Marlin Dive Centre (☎ 32424) is a well established and well run operation, which does a full range of PADI courses, as well as night dives and trips to more remote sites. Albatross (☎ 30134) in the Pasar Seni was the first dive operation on Trawangan, and usually has a PADI instructor and/or dive master here, though it seems to be based more at Senggigi. Blue Coral (☎ 34497) started at Senggigi, but now has pretty comprehensive facilities on Trawangan, with PADI certified instructors, and a full range of courses and dive trips.

Places to Stay

The accommodation here is mostly basic, with budget prices from 8000/10,000 rp to 12,000/15,000 rp for singles/doubles in the low season, but increasing to as much as 25,000/30,000 rp in the high season. New places in the main tourist area tend to be uninspiring concrete boxes, but they are a bit more secure and have better bathrooms, and they cost more. Elsewhere, there are simple bamboo cottages on stilts, often attractively located among coconut palms, sometimes with a front balcony facing the sea.

Old-style bamboo places are in the southern part of the tourist area, including *Halim Bungalows* and *Sagittarius*. Some newer places include *Danau Hijau Bungalows* and *Fantasi* at about 12,000/15,000 rp. *Pak Majid* and *Melati* are better quality new places from 20,000 to 35,000 rp, but without much character. *Borobudur Restaurant & Bungalows* is similar and good bungalows cost 25,000/30,000 rp. It's very central and the restaurant is good. *Trawangan Cottages* have average rooms for 15,000/20,000 rp and good cottages for 35,000 rp (50,000 rp in the peak season). There are some really basic options inland from the main drag, like *Damai Indah* and *Alex Homestay*, where a room will cost as little as 7000 rp with a shared bathroom.

At the northern end of the island, *Nusa Tiga I* and *Coral Beach* are wonderfully isolated, dirt cheap and right by the beach, but a bit run down. The south-western coast doesn't have nice beaches, but there's secluded, cheap and adequate accommodation at places like *Mawar Bungalows* and *Bintang Trawangan*. *Pondok Santai* is a nice one for 17,500/20,000 rp. Right around on the west side, *Dewi Sri Bungalows* is a tidy place, well away from everything and pretty good value at 12,000 rp a double.

By far the best place on Trawangan, or any of the Gilis, is the stylish *Villa Ombok*. Cute, two storey, lumbung-styled villas cost US$50, or more luxurious air-con villas are US$60. The architecture is as much Mediterranean as Asian, fittings and furnishings are very tasteful and it has a large restaurant.

Places to Eat

Most of the places to stay also serve food, but a few of the bigger restaurants on the tourist strip are sociable places, and are more like bars in the evening. A few show video movies, which do nothing for conviviality. None of them stand out as gourmet treats, but most have a tasty selection of inexpensive western and Asian dishes, and the fresh seafood can be excellent.

Borobudur is a popular restaurant, with a typical menu and prices – a great tuna steak costs 5000 rp, plus 2000 rp for a crisp salad. Your standard mie or nasi goreng will cost under 2000 rp. *Pondok Trawangan* or *Blue Marlin Dive Centre & Restaurant* and *Rainbow Cottages & Restaurant* are other popular restaurants. *Iguana* is another good place to eat, with some Sasak-style food, seafood specials like squid with garlic butter and the best beef burgers on the island. They also have laser disc videos. During the day, there's a bunch of simple eateries by the beach just north of the boat landing.

Entertainment

Party nights – with music, dancing, much drinking and the odd mushroom – alternate between *Trawangan*, *Rainbow Cottages & Restaurant*, *Iguana Restaurant*, *Rudy's Pub* and the *Excellent Restaurant*, which is further north up near the beach. There are sometimes impromptu beach parties here as well. The highlight of Trawangan's social calendar is the full moon party, where a fixed price of about 10,000 rp gets you your first drink, good food and music. Although not quite Thailand, the full moon parties can get pretty lively in the main tourist season.

North Lombok

THE NORTH COAST

The road around the north coast is sealed all the way, and though there are some winding hilly sections, it's an easy drive. It's very scenic, with a variety of landscapes and seascapes, few tourists and even fewer facilities. You can do it on public transport, but you may have to change bemos several times and they can be infrequent in the afternoon. It's much better with your own transport, so you can stop more easily on the way and make side trips to the coast, waterfalls and inland villages. Organised tours from Senggigi will cover most of the attractions.

From Ampenan a road goes north to Senggigi and Mangset, and now continues to near Bangsal. It's a winding and wonderfully scenic coastal route, but it does not yet have a regular bemo service. The inland route going north from Mataram is a good road and travels through the Pusuk Pass (Baun Pusuk) to Pemenang. This is also a scenic route, and it's worth stopping on the pass for the view and the monkeys. A bemo for the 31km trip is 1000 rp. Pemenang is where you turn off for Bangsal and the Gili Islands, but you can keep going to Sira and the north coast. The Gili Islands and Bangsal are covered in the previous Gili Islands section of this chapter.

Sira

Just a few kilometres north of Pemenang, on the coast facing Gili Air, Sira has a white-sand beach and good snorkelling on the nearby coral reef. The whole tip of the peninsula is now taken up by the *Oberoi Lombok* (☎ (361) 730361). This new and very tasteful luxury hotel has villas of quasi-traditional

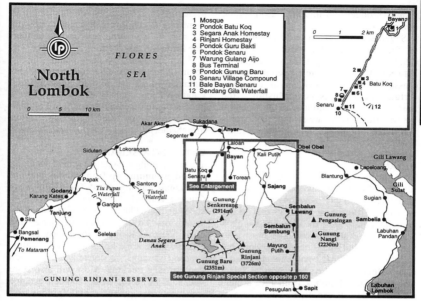

design, with thatch roofs, lumbung influences and Asian antique furnishings. Rooms are US$204 and US$256. The villas are walled compounds with outside living areas and cost US$320 and US$388, or US$472 to US$680 with a private pool.

Tanjung
This town is quite large and attractive, and has a big cattle market on Sunday. Just before Tanjung, *Manopo Homestay* has eccentric management, a lovely seaside location and four rooms from 15,000 to 25,000 rp. It offers French-Indonesian cuisine and is definitely not your average Indonesian homestay. Tanjung is 45km from Bertais and a bemo costs about 1100 rp.

Karang Kates
A little further north is Karang Kates (Krakas for short), where fresh water bubbles from the sea bed 400m offshore – the locals collect their drinking water from here. The sign on

the road announcing 'Water in the Sea' is not quite as daft as it appears.

Waterfalls
Further on, from Godang, you can go to the Tiu Pupas waterfall, around 4km inland by a rough track, mostly passable by motorcycle, but not by car. There are other waterfalls on the northern slopes of Rinjani, but they're only worth seeing up until the beginning of the dry season.

Segenter
This traditional Sasak village is a bit hard to find, but well worth the effort. If coming from the west, the turn-off is on your right immediately after you cross over the bridge, 1km before Sukadana. The rough road, little more than a track in places, heads inland through grassy fields for 2.2km, until you see the thatched roofs and the woven wooden fence of the village compound. The north coast is very dry and only one rice crop per

year is produced in this area. Corn is the other main staple.

Segenter is very neatly laid out, with rows of identical rectangular houses facing each other, and communal pavilions *(berugak)* in between. The houses are topped by *bungus* crosses to ward off evil spirits and misfortune. Segenter is now Muslim – the mosque is near the entrance to the village – but traditional ways are strong. Afterwards you make a donation and sign the visitors' book.

BAYAN

This northernmost part of Lombok is a stronghold of the Wektu Telu religion, and also the birthplace of Islam on Lombok. The mosque at Bayan, on the road east of the junction, is said to be the oldest on Lombok – more than 300 years old. The stone platform on which it stands may be very old, but the mosque itself has been renovated. It is a classic three-tiered Javanese mosque. Islam was brought to Lombok from Java around the end of the 16th century by Sunan Prapen, a religious leader and missionary from Giri, near present-day Surabaya.

There are a couple of *warungs* here, and accommodation a few kilometres away in Batu Koq (see the following Batu Koq & Senaru section).

Several buses a day go from the Bertais terminal in Mataram to **Anyar** on the coast, and some go on to Bayan, but you'll probably have to change at Anyar. Anyar is the main bus terminal for the north coast. It's a 79km, three hour trip, costing about 2000 rp, and you should try to get on an early bus. Otherwise, there are more frequent buses to Pemenang and you can change there for Bayan. Frequent bemos go from Anyar to Bayan, Batu Koq and Senaru, from where you can start a climb up Gunung Rinjani.

East of Bayan

From Bayan, the north-coast road continues for about 9km east to a junction called **Kali Putih**, where there are a couple of warungs, but not much else. The road south, which is pretty rough and steep in places, goes 18km

to Sembalun Lawang and another 2.5km to Sembalun Bumbung. These traditional villages are an alternative approach to Rinjani (see further in this section).

If you continue east from Kali Putih, it's 35km of winding road through landscapes alternately lush and arid to Sambelia and Labuhan Pandan on the east coast. There's good accommodation just south of Labuhan Pandan (see the East Lombok section later in this chapter).

BATU KOQ & SENARU

These adjoining villages are spread out along the ridge running up from Bayan, and are the usual starting point for a climb up Gunung Rinjani. There are several homestays in the village, some of which have superb views over the valley to the east and up to the rim of Rinjani. Most have places to eat, and there are a few which sell biscuits, canned fish, eggs, chocolate and other food you can take trekking. Most will also store your stuff while you climb, and help arrange transport, equipment rental, guides and porters.

Sendang Gila Waterfall

Make sure you go to this magnificent waterfall. It's a very pleasant half-hour walk, partly through forest and partly alongside an irrigation canal which follows the contour of the hill, occasionally disappearing into tunnels where the cliffs are too steep. Another half-hour walk takes you to some even better falls further up the hill.

Senaru Village

The traditional village compound of Senaru is opposite the Bale Bayan Senaru hotel and has an air of untainted antiquity. As late as the 1960s this village was completely isolated from the rest of the world, and it still seems remote, though trekkers pass by all the time. As you enter there is a visitors' book and a donation tin, and a notice indicating how proceeds are used to benefit the village. For all its quaintness, it is obviously a poor village and you should give something, though no-one hassles you at all.

Places to Stay

Pondok Batu Koq is the furthest from the mountain, but staff will organise transport to the roadhead at the start of your trek. They are very helpful with other trekking arrangements, and it costs only 5000/10,000 rp for singles/doubles. Further up the hill, *Segara Anak Homestay* has good views from some rooms, and is also helpful and inexpensive at 7500/10,000 rp. *Rinjani Homestay* is basic but cheap, as is *Pondok Guru Bakti* – 'Guru' Bakti is the school teacher who first helped visitors to discover this area. *Pondok Senaru* is the most salubrious, and has slightly better rooms for 10,000/15,000 rp, and its restaurant has a wonderful outlook. Closest to the trailhead is *Bale Bayan Senaru*, with helpful management, good food and adequate rooms for 7500/10,000 rp.

Getting There & Away

Bemos run right through to Senaru from Anyar (1000 rp), the main bus terminal for the north coast.

SEMBALUN

On the eastern side of Gunung Rinjani is the beautiful Sembalun valley. The inhabitants of the valley claim descent from the Hindu Javanese, and a relative of one of the Majapahit rulers is said to be buried here. While it seems unlikely that Java ever controlled Lombok directly, similarities in music, dance and language suggest that Lombok may have come under some Javanese influence several hundred years ago.

In the valley is the main Sasak village of **Sembalun Bumbung**, surrounded by fields of onion and garlic. Sembalun Bumbung is a sprawling and relatively wealthy village just off the main road. It has one losmen.

Sembalun Bumbung is often referred to simply as Sembalun; the 'Bumbung' is used to differentiate it from **Sembalun Lawang**, 2.5km north along the main road. This small satellite village has a 'big onion' monument and not a lot else, but it's at the start of the trek to Rinjani and is therefore the best place to stay. The two losmen in Sembalun Lawang can arrange guides and porters.

The main reason to visit Sembalun is to do the trek to Rinjani, but it is easy to spend a few days in this scenic and, as yet, untouristed area. Other points of interest include the steep 1½ to 2 hour climb to the saddle of **Gunung Pegasingan**, overlooking the valley to the east. This is best done at dawn when there are stunning views across to Sumbawa. **Mayung Putih**, 8km from Sembalun, is a sliver of a waterfall said to originate from the lake/hot springs in Rinjani's crater. The water is hot, but the source is dubious. It is 2km from the main road – walk from Sajang village.

Places to Stay

Right near the 'big onion' in Sembalun Lawang is the turn-off to Rinjani. This road, Jl Pelawangan, leads for about 2km to the start of the trail and along the road are two places to stay. Both can arrange guides, porters and hiking gear. A few hundred metres along the road, *Pondok Sembalun* is an attractive place with small bungalows for 10,000/12,500 rp a single/double. About 1km further is the *Wisma Cemara Siu* (☎ 21213) in a spacious, spotless house with views of the mountain. Good rooms cost 10,000/ 15,000 rp.

In Sembalun Bumbung, the *Puri Rinjani* has basic rooms in a house for 10,000 rp or new bungalows out the back for 15,000 rp. Although not as convenient for Rinjani, it makes a good base for exploring the valley.

Getting There & Away

From Kali Putih, on the north-coast road 9km east of Bayan, a road heads south, climbing to Sembalun Lawang and Sembalun Bumbung. A few bemos run along this route, usually in the morning, or you can charter a bemo or kijang to Bayan or Senaru for around 30,000 rp.

From the south, a new sealed road twists over the mountains to Sembalun Bumbung. Ten bemos a day run along this route to/from Aikmel (2500 rp) between 9 am and 4 pm. From Aikmel regular bemos and buses west run to Mataram (1500 rp) and east to Labuhan Lombok.

GUNUNG RINJANI

Gunung Rinjani

 Rinjani is the highest mountain on Lombok and, outside Irian Jaya, the highest in Indonesia. At 3726m it soars above the island and dominates the landscape, but by mid-morning on most days the summit is shrouded in cloud. There's a huge crater containing a large green crescent-shaped lake, Segara Anak (Child of the Sea), which is about 6km across at its widest point. There's a series of natural hot springs known as Kokok Putih, on the north-eastern side of this crater, said to have remarkable healing powers, particularly for skin diseases. The lake is 600 vertical metres below the crater rim, and in the middle of its curve there's a new cone, Gunung Baru (also known as Batujai), which is only a couple of hundred years old. Rinjani is an active volcano and erupted as recently as 1994, changing the shape of this inner cone and sprinkling ash over much of Lombok.

Both the Balinese and Sasaks revere Rinjani. To the Balinese it is equal to Gunung Agung, a seat of the gods, and many Balinese make a pilgrimage here each year. In a ceremony called Pekelem, held on the full moon around October/November, worshippers throw jewellery into the lake and make offerings to the spirit of the mountain. Some Sasaks make several pilgrimages a year – full moon is their favourite time for paying respects to the mountain and curing ailments by bathing in its hot springs.

The main approaches to Rinjani are from Batu Koq and Senaru, on a northern ridge, or from Sembalun Lawang to the east.

Climbing Rinjani

Many people climb up to Rinjani's crater lake every year. They are mostly local people making a pilgrimage or seeking the curative powers of the hot springs, especially during the full moon, when it can be very crowded. Many foreign visitors make the climb too, though only a few go the extra 1700m or so to the very summit of Rinjani. Even the climb to the crater lake is not to be taken lightly. Don't try it during the wet season as the tracks will be slippery and dangerous; in any case you would be lucky to see any more than mist and cloud.

The walk to the crater lake is demanding, but anyone of reasonable fitness can do it. The climb to the summit of Rinjani is much tougher, however. A number of climbers make it each year, but you need to be fit and have a good deal of stamina. Of those that do make it, most are left hobbling with sore leg muscles for days after.

Hikers have a few possibilities, from a strenuous dash to the rim and back, to a three, four or five day trek around the summit. Most visitors stay in Batu Koq or Senaru, climb from there to the crater lake and return the same way. The other main route is from Sembalun Lawang on the eastern side. The northern route has good services for trekkers, and if you are going halfway and then back, Senaru is the best starting point. The trail on the Senaru side goes through brilliant, dense forest and the view from the rim is better than that on the Sembalun side. However, if your main aim is to scale Rinjani, then it is shorter and easier from Sembalun. Undoubtedly the best option is to go right through from one side to the other, in which case it doesn't matter where you start from.

The northern slopes of Rinjani are covered in dense forest up to 2000m, but at around this height the vegetation changes from thick stands of mahogany and teak trees to the odd stand of pine. As you get closer to the rim the trees become sparser and the ground becomes rockier – it's almost an alpine landscape. There has been some logging on the slopes of Rinjani, but officially the area is now protected. Monkeys, wild pigs, deer and the occasional snake inhabit the forest.

Organised Tours A number of agencies, mostly in Mataram or Senggigi, organise guided all-inclusive treks. They seem expensive, but save time and trouble. A good operator should arrange all the equipment, food, guides and transport from Senggigi and back. They usually require a minimum of two people, and it's cheaper per person if you have a larger group. Satisfy yourself, before you hand over your cash and take the plunge, that the guides/leaders are reliable and knowledgeable – the quality and safety of your trip will depend on them.

Discover Lombok
(☎ 36781, 93390) With offices in the Pasar Seni at Senggigi and at Pizzeria Cafe Alberto near Ampenan, it will organise a trip to your requirements for about US$150 per person.
Lombok Wisata Indah
(☎ 32815, 24988) This company arranges a three day, two night trek from Senaru to the hot springs and back from US$150 per person.
Nazareth Tours & Travel
(☎ 31705) An established agency with offices in Senggigi and Ampenan, it offers a variety of treks from a two day, one night trip to the crater rim, to a four day trek from Sembalun to the summit and down to Senaru. With two people these trips cost US$150 and US$220 per person respectively; with seven people it's US$105 and US$155.
Perama
(☎ 93007, 35936) Treks are best arranged at the Mataram or Senggigi offices. Four day, three night treks, with a minimum of two people, cost US$120 per person from Senaru or US$150 per person from Sembalun.

GUNUNG RINJANI

Sahir Generations
(☎ 21688, 24464) Based at Masbagik in central Lombok, this operation may be well placed to do a trip from the south side, via Pesugulan/Sapit. It offers a variety of trips from a two day, one night trek to the hot springs for US$75 per person, to a six day, five night expedition, including the summit of Rinjani, for US$225 per person for two people, or US$150 per person with a group of four.

Guides & Porters You can trek from Senaru to the hot springs and back without a guide as the trail is well defined. However, as well as providing much needed local employment, guides and porters make the trip more enjoyable and they will carry all food and water, an important consideration. As water sources on the mountain are limited, always carry at least one day's water with you.

From Sembalun Lawang, the trail is often indistinct and overgrown, and a guide is essential. If descending from the Pelawangan II to Sembalun Lawang, it is possible but difficult without a guide. Climbing to the summit of Rinjani, you start in the dark, so it's good to have someone who knows the way.

A good guide will be informative, manage all the arrangements and add greatly to the enjoyment of the trek, but won't carry much, so you'll have to get at least one porter as well. Guides cost around 20,000 to 25,000 rp per day. Most of the porters know the trails, and will also carry your equipment and cook even if they don't speak much English. They cost about 15,000 rp per day and you have to provide food, water and transport for them, and probably cigarettes as well.

Equipment There are some very crude, open-sided shelters on the way, but don't rely on them – a sleeping bag and tent are essential. It is preferable to take a stove so you don't need to deplete the limited supply of firewood, but stoves are not easy to find. You'll also need solid footwear and some layers of warm clothing.

In Batu Koq you can rent a two or three person tent (15,000 rp for up to five days), cooking gear (3000 rp), and a sleeping bag and mat (10,000 rp). You could probably get the whole lot for about 25,000 rp for three days. Check the equipment before you take it. Equipment in Sembalun is more limited, but can be hired for around the same rates.

Tents are needed for the cold as much as the rain in the dry season. Most equipment for hire is adequate, but hardly hi-tech. Sleeping bags are usually Indonesian made, ie very thin. The standard tent is a two or three person dome tent of fibre-glass pole construction – quite good, but on the heavy side and unlikely to withstand a downpour. Rain is always possible, even in the dry season, but is rarely more than a shower in the

PETER TURNER

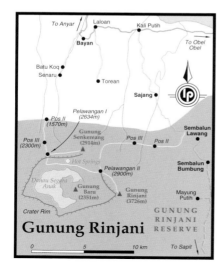

Danau Segara Anak (Child of the Sea), the stunning, crescent-shaped crater lake of Gunung Rinjani. The 'new' cone in the centre, Gunung Baru (2351m), may look appealing, but it's a dangerous climb.

Top: The view from Pelawangan II, the last staging post before the long and difficult climb to the summit of Gunung Rinjani.

Middle: The vista from the rim of Gunung Rinjani takes in the peaks of Gunung Agung and Gunung Batur on neighbouring Bali.

PETER TURNER

PETER TURNER

Bottom: The view from the summit of Gunung Rinjani, with Gunung Baru and Danau Segara Anak nestling within the crater walls.

PETER TURNER

dry. Few hikers bother when it is wet and hard going, but tents can be pitched under the shelters if they are empty.

If you are coming to Indonesia specifically to do Rinjani or other treks, it is worth bringing all your own gear – a good sleeping bag, light-weight waterproof tent, solid hiking boots, rain poncho, pack cover, Gore Tex jacket – the works. That said, most people can't be bothered lugging all this gear throughout Indonesia and make do with what they have. Light-weight hiking boots or even sand shoes are adequate for the walk to the lake, but you'll be glad of solid, ankle-high hiking boots if tackling the summit. A rain jacket and warm clothes are essential – temperatures drop to 5°C (41°F) at night, and even lower on the summit of Rinjani.

Food & Supplies Take rice, instant noodles, sugar, coffee, eggs, tea, biscuits or bread, some tins of fish or meat (and a can opener!), onions, fruit and anything else that keeps your engine running. Make sure you bring enough for the entire trip – it's a sad sight to see hikers begging for food at the lake camp.

Supplies are cheaper and more plentiful in Mataram or the supermarket in Senggigi, but you can get a fair range in Batu Koq. Take matches, a torch (flashlight) and plenty of water (the bottles you buy it in are adequate containers). Water is available in a few spots on the way, but occasionally it dries up. Water may be stagnant and contain parasites, so it should be boiled or at least treated (bring iodine, Puritabs or other water treatment chemicals). Bring at least 3L of water per person to get you to the lake from Senaru.

Environmental Care A lot of rubbish is dropped along the route. The only reason it doesn't look worse is that student groups from the university come and clean it up every few months. Remove all rubbish. Don't try to burn it or bury it. The other problem is fire-wood – supplies are depleted in some sections. Bring a stove and fuel for cooking if possible.

Rinjani Circuit

There are a number of options for this excellent walk. The walk is usually done from Senaru in the north, where equipment is readily available for hire and the trail is well defined. Independent walkers usually go halfway and back to Senaru, to return hiking equipment and pick up their luggage. If you take a guide and porter(s) from Senaru, they can carry your luggage right through to Sembalun in the east, but an extra porter may be necessary if your gear is heavy. Negotiate a price before you start, which will include transport back to Senaru for the guide and porter.

GUNUNG RINJANI

Independent walkers can make it right across from Senaru to Sembalun, and then take public transport or charter a bemo back to Senaru, but the trail from Pelawangan II to Sembalun Lawang is lightly travelled and indistinct. A guide is strongly recommended for this section.

Masochists in a hurry could walk from Senaru to Sembalun in two full days with one night at the hot springs, but that makes for a difficult first day and doesn't include the climb to Rinjani. Such a schedule is slightly easier if tackled from Sembalun to Senaru. More usual is a walk just to the hot springs and return from Senaru in three days, or a four or five day full-circuit including the ascent of Rinjani. The minimum time for the full circuit is three days/two nights.

Senaru to Hot Springs
Day 1 Senaru to Pos III – five to six hours
Day 2 Pos III to Hot Springs – three to four hours
Day 3 Hot Springs to Senaru – eight to nine hours

Full Circuit
Day 1 Senaru to Pos III – five to six hours
Day 2 Pos III to Hot Springs – three to four hours
Day 3 Hot Springs to Pelawangan II – three to four hours
Day 4 Pelawangan II to Rinjani summit and further on to
        Sembalun – 10 to 11 hours

The last day of the full circuit is a long slog, but is downhill all the way after the hard climb to Rinjani. Many walkers return to Senaru after climbing the summit; for a five day trip that includes another night at the hot springs.

Only a few hikers start in Sembalun, but the full circuit is just as easily started there, especially now that the road south to Aikmel is completed and Sembalun is serviced by regular public transport. Guides and porters can easily be found in Sembalun; the latter is essential for the first leg of the hike.

If starting from Sembalun, the usual breakdown is:

Day 1 Sembalun to Pelawangan II
Day 2 Pelawangan II to Rinjani summit and on to Hot Springs
Day 3 Hot Springs to Pos III
Day 4 Pos III to Senaru. You can also spend all of Day 3 at
        the hot springs and walk back to Senaru on Day 4.

The Route
Senaru to Pos III (5-6 hours) At the end of Senaru village is the PHPA post (Pos I on some maps; 860m). Sign in here and pay the entrance fee. Do sign in – they may not come looking for you if you get lost, but at least your relatives will have an idea of where to find your body!

Just beyond the post is a small warung and then the trail forks – continue straight ahead on the right fork. The trail steadily ascends through scrubby farmland for about half an hour to the sign at the entrance to Gunung Rinjani National Park. The forest, and one of the finest parts of the walk, begins here. It is cool at this altitude and shady, but very humid. Although *loris*, *babi hutan* (wild pig) and other animals inhabit the forest, all you are likely to see are brown *kera* monkeys. Birdlife is quite prolific.

The wide trail climbs for another 2½ hours until you reach Pos II (1570m), where there are two *pondok* (huts or shelters). The shelters have a raised floor and a corrugated iron roof, but no walls. Despite sporadic repairs, the floors have often been ripped up for firewood. Water can be found 100m down the slopes from the trail and this is the most reliable source on the ascent. Water should be treated or boiled.

Another 1½ hours' steady walk uphill brings you to Pos III (2300m), where there's another two shelters in disrepair. The trail levels off slightly and the forest is thinner as you approach Pos III. Water is 100m off the trail to the right, but sometimes dries up in the height of the dry season. Pos III is the usual place to camp at the end of the first day. Nights are very cold, but you'll be warmer in a tent.

Pos III to the Pelawangan I (1½-2 hours) From Pos III the forest gives way to grassy slopes, and as you approach the rim of the volcano it comes drier, rockier and steeper. It takes about 1½ hours to reach the rim, Pelawangan I, at an altitude of 2634m. (Pelawangan means gateway – this is one of the few places where you can enter the crater.) Set off very early to arrive at the crater rim for sunrise.

The view from the rim is stunning – it takes in the amazing crater, with Lake Segara Anak arcing around the smoking cone of Gunung Baru, while Gunung Rinjani towers over the whole landscape. In the other direction you can see the whole north coast of Lombok and Gunung Agung on Bali.

It is possible to camp at Pelawangan I. You can extend yourself to walk here at the end of the first day for a spectacular sunset and an equally spectacular sunrise the next morning. The drawbacks are that level camp sites are limited, there is no water, it is colder than Pos III and can be very blustery on this exposed rim if the winds are up.

Pelawangan I to Lake & Hot Springs (2-3 hours) After you've snapped your share of the view from the rim – one of the most impressive sights in Indonesia – it is time to descend to Segara Anak and around to the hot springs. It takes about two hours. The first hour is a very steep descent and involves

GUNUNG RINJANI

low-grade rock climbing in parts. The path clings to the side of the cliffs and is narrow, meandering and precarious. Watch out for rubble – in certain spots it's very hard to keep your footing, especially with a heavy pack. Some people take much longer to do this section – there's no hurry. At the bottom of the crater wall, it is then an easy one hour walk across undulating terrain around the lake edge.

The lake surface is about 2000m above sea level, with trees right down to the shore. There are several places to camp, but most prefer to be near the hot springs, where you can soak your weary body and recuperate. The hot springs are more like a hot river that flows away from the lake in a series of waterfalls, pools and springs, including the Milk Cave (Gua Susu) which discharges hot, white water. If you find the water too hot near the lake, follow the river further downstream to a pool of your choosing where the water is slightly cooler. Although the sulphur scum may look off-putting, this is a natural occurrence, and the water is superb to soak in. On the night of the full moon, many pilgrims take in the curative powers of the hot water and some immerse themselves to the neck and meditate on the moon.

Two dilapidated shelters are beside the lake, but the nicest camp sites are at the lake's edge. It's not as cold here as it is at Pos III, but it can be damp and misty from the steaming springs. Fresh water can be gathered from a spring near the hot springs. You can boil the lake water, but no amount of boiling will take away the acrid taste.

Some hikers spend two nights, or even more, at the lake, but most head back to Senaru the next day. The climb back up the rim is certainly taxing – allow at least three hours and start early to make it back to Senaru in one day. Allow five hours from the rim down to Senaru. The last bemo down the mountain from Senaru leaves around 4 pm.

Rather than retrace your steps, the best option is to press on to Sembalun if you can work out what to do with your gear.

Hot Springs to Pelawangan II (3-4 hours) The trail starts beside the last shelter at the hot springs and heads away from the lake for 100m or so before veering right. The trail traverses the northern slope of the crater, away from the lake, and it is an easy walk for one hour along the grassy slopes. Then you reach a ramshackle system of metal handrails secured in concrete and the hard slog begins. It is a steep and constant climb, not quite as clambering as the rim ascent on the other side, but the ascent is higher. Nearer the top the lake is finally seen again for great views, but there is still some more hard work to be done. From the lake it takes three to 3½ hours, all up until you finally reach the crater rim.

At the rim a sign points the way back to Segara Anak. Water can be found down the slope near the sign. The trail forks here – straight on to Sembalun, or continue along the rim to the campsite of Pelawangan II (2900m). It is only about 10 minutes more to the campsite on a bare ridge. The views from this side of the rim are not quite as good as from Pelawangan II because the volcanic cone of Gunung Baru is obscured, but Segara Anak is stretched out below and the views are stunning by any account. When clear, you can watch the sun set behind the rim on the other side. Bali's Gunung Batur and Gunung Agung are visible.

The campsite here is very cold at night. Try to find a sheltered spot in case the wind springs up.

Pelawangan II to Rinjani Summit (5-6 hours return)
Gunung Rinjani stretches in an arc above the campsite at Pelawangan II and looks deceptively close. The usual time to start the climb is at 3 am to reach the summit in time for the sunrise before the clouds roll in.

It takes about 45 minutes up to the ridge that leads to Rinjani. The steep trail goes through slippery, powdery scree. This is a foretaste – but only a taste – of things to come. The trail is hard to find in the dark unless you have a guide or have sussed it out the evening before. As everyone heads up at 3 am, you can always tag onto a group with a guide.

It is very cold on the mountain at this time and even colder if the winds are up. Having climbed the mountain when strong winds are blowing, we would advise against it. Not only is it another obstacle to battle against, the winds are icy and dust swirls in your eyes. It can upset your balance and the trail along the ridge is narrow and close to the precipice at times. The trail has deteriorated since the 1994 eruption. Although quite manageable in good conditions, at least one tourist lost their life recently and care must be taken.

Once on the ridge it is a relatively easy walk gradually uphill for an hour or so. There are fine views down into the crater of Gunung Baru and Segara Anak, but you won't be able to appreciate them until it gets light. After about an hour heading up towards what looks like the peak, the real summit of Rinjani looms behind and towers above you.

The trail gets steeper and steeper. About 500m before the summit with the steepest climb ahead, you hit the real killer. The scree here is composed of loose, fist-sized rocks and with each step you sink up to your ankle. For every two steps forward you slide one step back until it becomes easier to negotiate the slope on all fours. It's a slow grind to the top and more frequent rest stops have to be taken in the thin air. The last stretch – so close but yet so far – can take an hour of scrambling. Finally you make it onto solid rock and then the summit.

The views from the top are magnificent on a clear day. To the west lies Bali and in the east the sun rises behind Gunung Tambora on Sumbawa. But even on a clear day don't expect to be able to see forever. Low level cloud can obscure the land mass and it is often hazy. But even if the views are not clear it is certainly an achievement to have climbed one of Indonesia's highest peaks.

The descent is much easier, but take it easy on the scree. All up it takes three hours or more to reach the summit, two to get back down.

Pelawangan II to Sembalun Lawang (5-6 hours) After having negotiated the peak it is possible to reach Sembalun Lawang the same day. After a two hour descent, it is a long and hot, but easy, three hour walk. Head off early to avoid as much of the heat of the day as possible and make sure you have plenty of water to reach Sembalun Lawang.

From the camp site head back to the main trail and follow it for only a couple of hundred metres. The trail almost becomes a road, but don't keep following it – the trail to Sembalun is a small side trail branching off. It's not signposted. Keep looking over the edge until you find it – it follows the next ridge along from Rinjani, not the valley. Once on the trail, it is easy to follow and takes around two hours to the bottom (it will take longer if over taxed muscles are aching after Rinjani). The ridge is grassed and only has a few trees on it – this side of the mountain is much drier than the Senaru side.

On the way down there are fine views across the pretty Sembalun Valley sandwiched between Rinjani and another range of mountains. Sembalun Bumbung is the largest settlement in the valley, off to the right as you head down the mountain. At the bottom of the ridge the trail levels out and crosses undulating to flat grassland all the way to Sembalun Lawang. An hour's walk will bring you to Pos III, a relatively new shelter, and then it is another half hour to Pos II. Stagnant, slimy water can usually be found near Pos II – only if you're desperate.

Long grass obscures the trail, once a road, and in places you cannot see it more than a couple of metres ahead. A half hour beyond Pos II the trail crosses a bridge and then fords a small rise to a lone shade tree. The trail seems to fork here. The left forks leads down towards the valley, while the right one leads slightly uphill away from the valley. Take the right fork.

Having oriented Sembalun firmly in your mind, experienced hikers with plenty of water should be able to reach Sembalun without too much difficulty – as a general rule the trail follows the flank of Rinjani before swinging around to Sembalun Lawang at the end. However, the area is not populated and unless you come across other hikers there is no one to ask directions. A guide is strongly recommended for this part of the trip.

Starting from Sembalun Lawang it is six or seven hours to Pelawangan II and a guide is essential. It is much harder to get your bearings walking up the mountain and the trail is all but impossible to find on your own. This is an easier walk to the rim than from the Senaru side, with only a three hour walk up the ridge to tax you. Before starting off, sign in at the Departemen Kehutanan office on the main road in Sembalun Lawang, where the road to Rinjani starts, and pay the 1500 rp fee. Horses can be hired to take you to Pos III for 30,000 rp.

A Night Climb If you travel lightly and climb quickly, you can reach the crater rim from Senaru in about six hours – it's a 1770m altitude gain in 10km, approximately. With a torch and some moonlight, and/or a guide, set off at midnight and you'll be there for sunrise. Coming back takes about five hours, so you can be down in time for lunch. Take lots of snack food and a litre of water.

Around the Rim If you reach Pelawangan I early in the day, you can follow the crater rim around to the east for about 3km to Gunung Senkereang (2914m) at the end of the ridge. This point overlooks the gap in the rim where the stream from the hot springs flows out of the crater and north-east towards the sea. From here you can see east to Sumbawa and west to Bali, while Gunung Rinjani looms to the south. It's not an easy walk though, and the track is narrow and very exposed in places.

Other Routes on Rinjani You can climb up to the crater from Torean, a small village just south-east of Bayan. The trail follows Sungai Kokok Putih, the stream that flows from Lake Segara Anak and the hot springs, but it's hard to find; you'll need a guide. You can also climb the south side of Rinjani from either Sesaot (see the earlier West Lombok section) or Tetebatu (see the following Central Lombok Section). Either route will involve at least one night camping in the jungle, and you may not see any views at all until you get above the tree line. Again, a guide is essential. A better option from the south is from Pesugulan (near Sapit) towards Sembalun Bumbung, then to Pelawangan II.

Gunung Baru (2351m), the 'new' cone in the middle of Danau Segara Anak, may look tempting, but it's a very dangerous climb. The track around the lake to the base of Baru is narrow and people have drowned after slipping off it. The climb itself is over a very loose surface, and if you start sliding or falling there is nothing to stop you and nothing to hang on to. Also, many of the tracks around here were wiped out in the 1994 eruption.

LOMBOK

Central Lombok

The area on the southern slopes of Gunung Rinjani is well watered and lush, and offers opportunities for scenic walks through the rice fields and the jungle. Towards the south coast the country is drier, and dams have been built to provide irrigation during the dry season. Most of the places in central Lombok are more or less traditional Sasak settlements, and several of them are known for particular types of local handcrafts.

KOTARAJA

Kotaraja means 'city of kings', although no kings ruled from here and it's hardly a city. Apparently, when the Sasak kingdom of Langko (at Kopang in central Lombok) fell to the Balinese invaders, the rulers of Langko fled to Loyok, the village south of Kotaraja. After the royal compound in that village was also destroyed, two of the ruler's sons went to live in Kotaraja. The aristocracy of Kotaraja can trace their ancestry back to these brothers, although the highest caste title of *raden* has now petered out through intermarriage.

Kotaraja sits at a road junction and it's the central village of the area, though there's no accommodation here. Various villages around it are noted for blacksmithing and basketware. Traditional blacksmiths still use an open hearth and human-powered bellows, but old car springs are the favoured 'raw material' for knives, farm implements and other tools.

Getting There & Away

With your own transport you can easily make a day trip from the capital – it's only 30km from Bertais to Kotaraja – but it's better to stay nearby for a few days to appreciate the area.

There is a direct bus from the Bertais terminal in Mataram to Paomotong on the

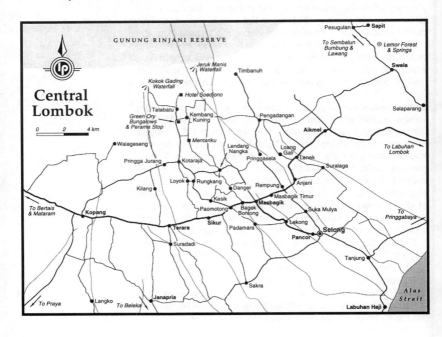

main road, but it may actually be quicker to take a bemo to Narmada then another to Paomotong. From Paomotong take a bemo or cidomo to Kotaraja (400 rp). If you're staying in Tetebatu or Lendang Nangka, you can take a cidomo or walk to Kotaraja.

TETEBATU

A mountain retreat at the foot of Gunung Rinjani, Tetebatu is 50km from Mataram and about 10km north of the main east-west road. It's quite a bit cooler here, and it can be misty and rainy, particularly between November and April.

There are magnificent views over southern Lombok, east to the sea and north to Gunung Rinjani. You can climb part of the way up the southern flank of Rinjani from here (a guide is essential), but the formerly magnificent stands of mahogany trees have virtually disappeared. Other destinations for walks include Jeruk Manis waterfall, 6km to the north-east, and the *hutan* (forest), 4km north-west, where lots of jet-black monkeys will shriek at you.

With its monkey forest, paddy fields and lushness, Tetebatu is the Lombok equivalent of Ubud in Bali, but without the culture or the crowds. It has a growing range of facilities and makes a great base for exploring the scenic surrounding countryside on foot, or by bicycle or by motorbike, which can be easily hired in Tetebatu.

Places to Stay & Eat

The original accommodation here is the *Hotel Soedjono* (formerly Wisma Soedjono; ☎ 22159), an old colonial house that was once a country retreat for a Dr Soedjono. A number of rooms and bungalows have been added, as well as a restaurant and a swimming pool. The simplest rooms are funky rice-barn-style bungalows for 15,000 rp; the best rooms down by the river and paddy fields are 45,000 rp and have hot water. All prices include continental breakfast, and the staff provide good information about walks in the area. The restaurant has tasty, inexpensive food, and you can even get a packed lunch if you want to spend a day out walking.

A crop of inexpensive accommodation has sprouted in the lovely rice fields around Tetebatu. One such place is *Diwi Enjeni*, on the southern side of town with a nice outlook. Bungalows cost 6000/10,000 rp for singles/doubles, including breakfast, and there's a small restaurant. *Pondok Tetebatu* is nearby, with cheap rooms at a similar price and much better ones for 10,000/15,000rp. *Mekar Sari* is next door, in a nice location set back from the road. Nearby is the *Shashak Restaurant* and a motorbike rental outlet.

To the south of Tetebatu a winding road leads east to Kembang Kuning, an increasingly popular area to stay with several simple but attractive accommodation options. Near the turnoff the *Green Ory* bungalows cost 12,000/15,000 rp in the low season, and there's one bungalow that could sleep several people. Further east is *Pondok Bulan*, with small, cute bungalows for 10,000 rp. Opposite, *Cendrawasi Cottages* are very classy for this area, with a wonderful, open, upstairs eating area and pleasant rooms for only 25,000 rp, or less in the off season.

A few more bends bring you to *Hakiki Inn*, with a fine rice-field view, a spacious restaurant and doubles from 15,000 rp. Next along, in the village of Kembang Kuning itself, the popular *Pondok Jeruk Manis* is a switched-on place with rooms for 10,000 rp. A few metres further is the left turn to Jeruk Manis waterfall. If you turn right down the dirt road instead, you'll come to *Wisma Rambutan*, where small cottages are nicely spaced in a garden of rambutan trees. The cottages cost 8000/12,000 rp, and the *Restoran Kelapa Muda* nearby has good, inexpensive fare.

The road from Tetebatu through Kembang Kuning swings south and leads to Lendang Nangka. Around 2km down this road from Kembang Kuning, and 5km before Lendang Nangka, *Mentariku* (☎ 22298) is a more substantial place sited in the paddy fields with bungalows for 15,000 and 20,000 rp, but it is a long way from anywhere.

Getting There & Away

From Kotaraja, it's just a couple of kilometres up the road to Tetebatu by infrequent bemo, cidomo, ojek or on foot. Direct bemos run between Tetebatu and Paomotong, and between Paomotong and the Bertais terminal outside Mataram. Perama runs one shuttle bus a day to Tetebatu (7500 rp) from Mataram.

LOYOK

Loyok, a tiny village just a few kilometres south of Kotaraja, is noted for its fine handcrafts, particularly basketware and weaving with natural fibres. Most of the craftspeople work from their homes, but there's a place on the main street where you can buy some of the excellent basketware, and also a Handcraft Centre with some work on display.

To get to Loyok, go first to Paomotong, on the main road, then get a bemo as far as Rungkang, the turn-off to the village, and walk the last kilometre or get a cidomo.

RUNGKANG

This small village, less than a kilometre east of Loyok, is known for its pottery, which is made from a local black clay. The pots are often finished with attractive cane work, which is woven all over the outside for decoration and greater strength. Similar pottery is made in a number of other villages in the area south of the main road.

MASBAGIK

Quite a large town on the main road at the turn-off to Selong, Masbagik has a big market on Monday morning. There's also a post office and a Telkom *wartel*. Masbagik Timur, a kilometre or so to the east, is one of the centres for pottery and ceramic production. A bemo from Bertais to Masbagik (42km) costs around 1200 rp.

LENDANG NANGKA

Seven kilometres south-east of Tetebatu, and lower down the mountain, this Sasak village is surrounded by picturesque countryside, with small roads and friendly people. In and around the village you can see blacksmiths who still make knives, hoes and other tools using traditional techniques. Silversmiths are also starting to work here. **Jojang**, the

biggest freshwater spring in Lombok, is a few kilometres north and Lendang Nangka can be used as base to visit Loyok and other points of interest.

In August you should be able to see traditional Sasak stick fighting at Lendang Nangka. It's a violent affair with leather-covered shields and bamboo poles. Traditional dances are sometimes performed in the area, but they're not scheduled events – ask at your *losmen* and you might strike it lucky.

Lendang Nangka is just another village, but it is on the tourist map because of Hadji Radiah, a local primary school teacher whose family homestay has become popular among travellers who want to experience typical Lombok village life. Hadji speaks English very well, and he will often take visitors on a guided walk through the fields, describing and explaining the local crops, agriculture and customs. His family is very hospitable and they have a map showing interesting features in the area, and can suggest various walks and day trips.

Places to Stay

Radiah's Homestay costs about 10,000/15,000 rp for a basic single/double, 15,000/20,000 rp for better rooms or 20,000/25,000 rp in the separate block out in the paddy fields. The price includes customary Sasak cake and fruit for breakfast, a good lunch and a communal dinner of authentic Sasak food. Note that this is a Muslim household, and alcohol is not available. It's not luxury standard, but it's good value and comes highly

Lendang Nangka

recommended. Radiah's house is fairly easy to find (and everyone knows him anyway).

Other places to stay on the outskirts of Lendang Nangka have a more rural setting, but aren't quite as culturally rewarding as Radiah's. The *Sasak Homestay* is a small, friendly place with a Sasak restaurant, but the rooms are cramped and uninspiring for 15,000 rp a double. About 200m west of town, *Pondok Wira* has some rice barn style rooms, some with views, in a nice garden. This could be a good place, but it is run down, overpriced and all but deserted. It costs 20,000 rp for rooms or 25,000 rp for bungalows, including three meals. About 400m north of the crossroads, on a small side track, *Pondok Bambu* is beautifully situated out in the countryside. It has a helpful owner, and a few simple bamboo bungalows for 12,500/25,000 rp, including three home-cooked Sasak meals.

Getting There & Away
Take a bemo from Bertais to Masbagik (42km; 1200 rp) and then a cidomo to Lendang Nangka (about 4km), which should cost 400 rp per person, but the driver will want at least three passengers or 1200 rp for the whole cart.

Alternatively, the most direct route is to take a bemo to Bagek Bontong, on the highway west of Masbagik, and then an ojek to Lendang Nangka. Lendang Nangka is about 5km from Paomotong and connected by a surfaced road – take a cidomo for about 500 rp.

PRINGGASELA
This village is a centre for traditional weaving done on simple backstrap looms. The cloths made here feature beautifully coloured stripes running the length of the material, with decorative details woven into the weft. You can see the weavers in action and buy some of their beautiful work, such as sarongs, blankets etc. You'll have to bargain, but don't bargain too hard – most of the work here is superb quality and takes the women a long time to make.

There are a couple of small homestays in Pringgasela offering simple accommodation, usually including local food. *Akmal Homestay* is run by a family of weavers, and they can arrange car and motorcycle rental, as well as treks to Rinjani. *Rainbow Cottages* is another good place, with similar services. They both cost around 15,000/20,000 rp for singles/doubles.

LENEK
Lenek has a traditional music and dance troupe that performs for tourists on a more or less regular basis. Ask at the tourist office in Mataram for the times. A little north and east of Lenek is the village of **Loang Gali**, where there's a spring and swimming pool in the forest. You can stay here at *Loang Gali Cottages* for 12,500 rp per person.

SAPIT
At Aikmel, a side road heads north up the shoulder of Gunung Rinjani past Swela to Pesugulan, the south-eastern entrance to the Gunung Rinjani Reserve. A new, paved road continues from here to Sembalun, the start of the eastern trail up Rinjani.

Sapit is a short distance to the east of Pesugulan, with cool air and stunning views across to Sumbawa, and Rinjani forming a spectacular backdrop. *Pondok Wisata Hati Suci* has bungalows in this splendid location for 10,000/15,000 to 20,000/35,000 rp for singles/doubles, including breakfast. There's a restaurant, and plenty of information on visiting villages and attractions in the immediate area. The staff can help with information about climbing Rinjani. About 1km further along the road is the *Hati Suci Indah*, with just four small bungalows for 10,000/20,000 rp a single/double. The views are great, but there is not a lot else here.

Between Swela and Sapit, a side road goes down into the **Lemor forest**, where there's a refreshing, spring-fed pool. Further down the road towards Pringgabaya, a side road goes to **Selaparang**, where you can see the burial place of the ancient Selaparang kings. It's nothing exciting, but a good excuse to wander around the back blocks.

LOMBOK

Getting There & Away
From Bertais take a bus to Pringgabaya (2000 rp), and then a bemo to Sapit (16km; 1000 rp).

South Lombok

PRAYA
This is the main town in the south. It's quite attractive, with spacious gardens, tree-lined streets, a few old Dutch buildings, and no tourists. Its bemo terminal, on the north-western side of town, is the transport hub for the area. If you want to stay here, *Dienda Hayu Hotel* (☎ 54319), at Jl Untung Surapati 28, is new, clean and not a bad place. It's pitched mainly at Indonesian visitors, but tourists are welcome; rooms cost 20,000 rp, or 35,000 rp with air-con, and the restaurant is good.

AROUND PRAYA
Several of the villages around Praya are noted for different handcrafts, though most people visit them on a day trip from Mataram or Senggigi, or on the way to Kuta. Most of the craft villages are close to main roads from Praya so you can reach them by public transport, but if you want to explore several of them, and buy lots of things, it's useful to have your own transport. Several small back roads wind through the hills to join the main east-west road, enabling a very pretty tour through central Lombok.

Sukarara
A little north-west of Praya, or 25km from Mataram, the small village of Sukarara is a traditional weaving centre, though it doesn't look very traditional. Much of the main street is given over to commercial craft shops so it's pretty touristy, but still well worth a visit to see the various styles of weaving. The surrounding villages are more typical, with thatched-roof houses, and some built from local stone.

There are looms set up outside workshops along the main street and displays of sarongs hanging in bright bands. Typically they have attractive young women working out the front, wearing the traditional black costume with brightly coloured edging. More women work inside, often wearing jeans and watching TV as they work, but most of the material is actually made in homes in surrounding villages. There are also bigger showrooms, with professional salespeople who can be informative, but very persuasive. These places are geared to tour groups and have a good range, but higher prices.

Before you go to Sukarara it may be a good idea to check prices in the Selamat Riady weaving factory in Cakranegara, and get some idea of how much to pay and when to start bargaining. There's such a range in quality and size that it's impossible to give a guide to prices, but the best pieces are magnificent and well worth paying for. If you're accompanied by a guide to Sukarara it will inevitably cost you more due to the addition of commissions.

Getting There & Away Get a bemo from Bertais towards Praya and get off at Puyung (about 700 rp). From Puyung you can hire a cidomo for about 250 rp to take you the 2km to Sukarara.

Penujak
This small village, 6km south of Praya, is well known for its traditional *gerabah* pottery made from a local clay with the simplest of techniques. The elegantly shaped pots range in size up to 1m high, and there are also kitchen vessels of various types and decorative figurines, usually in the shape of animals. The traditional pottery is a rich terracotta colour, unglazed, but hand burnished to a lovely soft sheen. Some new designs are brightly coloured.

It's one of several villages where the Lombok Craft Project, supported by a New Zealand development agency, has done a lot to promote the pottery industry and to develop export markets. The distinctive pottery is now available at fashionable shops in Australia, Europe and North America, and you can also see it at Lombok Pottery Centres

LOMBOK

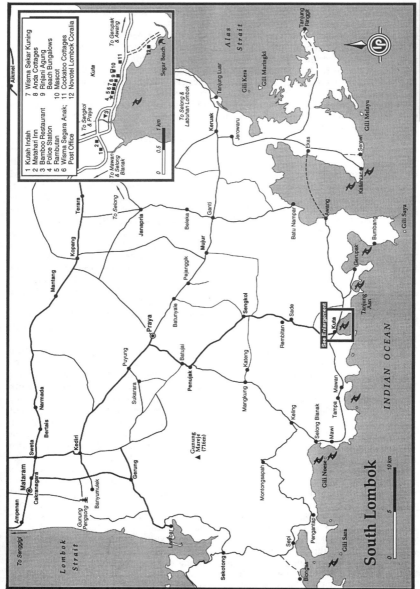

South Lombok

Map legend (enlargement):

1 Kutah Indah
2 Matahari Inn
3 Bamboo Restaurant
4 Police Station
5 Rambutan
6 Wisma Segara Anak; Post Office
7 Wisma Sekar Kuning
8 Anda Cottages
9 Rinjani Agung Beach Bungalows
10 Mascot
11 Cockatoo Cottages
12 Novotel Lombok Coralia

in Mataram, Senggigi and Nusa Dua, Bali. Production has increased, styles have diversified and the project has improved the living standards of the potters. Unfortunately, it has also made the village of Penujak much more commercial – its main street is lined with showrooms, and cute but persistent kids sell clay whistles. That's progress.

Penujak is on the main road from Praya to the south coast, and any bemo to Sengkol or Kuta will be able to drop you there.

Pejanggik

This is another village known for traditional weaving, but it's much more low key than Sukarara. There are a few workshops near the main road and just off to the south, but to find them you'll have to stop and look, and listen for the clack-clack of the looms.

Beleka

The main products here are baskets, mats and boxes made from natural fibres, such as rattan, grass, palm leaf and bamboo. Showrooms along the main road sell some fine examples of this quality work – strong, simple and beautifully made.

Rembitan & Sade

The area from Sengkol down to Kuta Beach is a centre of traditional Sasak culture. There are many relatively unchanged Sasak villages, as well as more touristed ones such as Rembitan and Sade. There are regular bemos on this route, especially in the morning, so you can get off at the villages and flag down another one when you're ready to move on. More traditional villages lie off the main road.

The village of Rembitan is about 4km south of Sengkol, on a hill just west of the main road. It's more a Sasak theme park than a traditional village, but it has an impressive row of traditional lumbung. The villagers now live elsewhere and the lumbung are used for storage, not living, but the village can be lively during the day when tour buses arrive, guides reel off their patter and craft demonstrations are held. On top of the hill is **Masjid Kuno**, an old thatched-roof mosque.

Guides will show you around for a small donation.

A little further south is Sade, which has concrete footpaths and some fine lumbung displaying stuff for sale. Sade is also a slightly sanitised Sasak village, but has a cluster of thatched houses and lumbung, surrounded by a wooden fence. It used to be the main tourist village, but now everyone goes to Rembitan and Sade is quieter.

KUTA BEACH

The best known place on the south coast is Lombok's Kuta Beach (sometimes spelt Kute Beach), a fine stretch of white sand and blue sea with rugged hills rising around it, but not much else. It is a very small development with far fewer tourists than the infamous Kuta Beach on Bali, but there are big plans to develop a whole stretch of the superb south coast with luxury hotels. Until then Kuta is a neglected little settlement and the nearby villages in this arid landscape are very poor. It may not have the crowds and hassles of Bali's Kuta, but neither does it have the facilities. It does have a few hawkers – ragged children selling coconuts who are as aggressive as any fake-watch seller in Bali.

A whole new resort city is planned for the area and the development includes condominiums, luxury hotels, golf courses, marinas and anything else that the wealthy Jakarta elite could want to invest in, but Indonesia's financial meltdown will undoubtedly stall these plans. The luxury Novotel hotel is finished, the road from Praya has been completely remade and big new roads run to as-yet-undeveloped beaches. The site for the island's new international airport lies north of Kuta on the Praya road, begging the question of why the airport would be relocated to this remote area. Well now, guess who's family had a big interest in the development ...

Meanwhile, the low-budget losmen at Kuta are all on limited leases, and seem to be trying to get maximum income from minimum investment – some of them are looking decidedly squalid.

Nyale Fishing Festival

A few days after the full moon in February or March, on the 19th day of the 10th month in the Sasak lunar calendar, nyale sea worms breed along the south coasts of Lombok and Sumba. They reproduce en masse by releasing their rear segments which swim to the surface releasing eggs and sperm. The water is alive with millions of worms, considered a delicacy, and a good turnout of these fertility symbols is also a favourable sign for the coming harvest.

In Lombok, a legend explains this unique phenomena. The legend takes many forms, but is based on a princess named Putri Mandalika, who was famed for her beauty. Many men came from kingdoms near and far to seek her hand, but she refused them all. For her insolence she was sacrificed and thrown into the sea. Her sacrifice ensured the fertility of the soil and the swarming nyale represent her body.

In Kuta on Lombok, hundreds of people camp on the beach for the nyale fishing festival. They sit around campfires all night and engage in spontaneous poetry competitions based on rhyming couplets or quatrains called *pantun*. The pantun is an ancient Malay verse, spoken by sparring warriors before battle or by courting couples.

The next day the worms are caught and impromptu boat races are held. The nyale are eaten raw or grilled, and are believed to have aphrodisiac properties.

In Sumba, priests of the Marapu religion scan the reefs for the arrival of the nyale, which traditionally signifies the start of the Pasola festival. ■

People flock to Kuta for the annual nyale fishing celebration, usually falling in February or March. It attracts thousands of people, many of whom sleep on the beach, plus visiting celebrities and TV crews. The main tourist season is August and for the rest of the year it's very quiet.

Information

You can change money at Anda Cottages, but the rates are not very good. Wisma Segara Anak is a postal agent and the booking desk for Perama. It also offers a telephone service (Kuta has no wartel) but calls are 10,000 rp minimum and a charge applies on reverse charge calls. There's a market on Sunday and Wednesday.

Surfing

Plenty of good waves break on the reefs around here – many are supposedly 'secret'. There are lefts and rights in the bay in front of Kuta, and some more on reefs east of Tanjung Aan. Local boatmen will take you out for a few thousand rupiah. Go about 7km east of Kuta to the fishing village of **Gerupak** where there are several potential breaks on the reefs at the entrance of Gerupak Bay. Again access is by local fishing boat. There's

more breaks further east and west, all the way from Blongas to Serewi, but nearly all require a charter boat. Bigger yachts from Bali do surf charters along the whole of Lombok's south coast and are better able to get to the right place at the right time. There aren't many secrets.

Places to Stay & Eat

Most of Kuta's accommodation is along the beachfront road to the east of the village, and all are of a similar price and quality. The following are the low-season prices; expect to pay up to 5000 rp more if there are other tourists around. After the police station you pass *Rambutan*, with rooms at 10,000 rp, including breakfast. The *Wisma Segara Anak* (☎ 54834), next door, has rough rooms at 6000/7000 rp for singles/doubles, better rooms at 8000/10,000 rp and bungalows at 12,000/15,000 rp, including breakfast. The hotel's restaurant is very popular, as much for the good service as anything else. Cheap warungs can be found nearby, such as the *Warung Melati*.

Next along, *Wisma Sekar Kuning* (Yellow Flower Cottage) has double rooms downstairs for 8000 rp, and upstairs, with a nice view, for 10,000 rp; it's not a bad place. *Anda*

Cottages (☎ 54836), next door, is the original losmen at Kuta. It has some pleasant trees and shrubs, a good restaurant with Chinese, Indonesian and western dishes, and singles/doubles from 7000/10,000 rp up to 15,000 rp a double, including breakfast.

A bit further along is *Rinjani Agung Beach Bungalows* (☎ 54849), with standard rooms from 12,000/15,000 rp. The restaurant has videos in the evening. Continue along to *Cockatoo Cottages & Restaurant* (☎ 54831), the last place along the beach, with a nice restaurant area and rooms for 5000/7000 rp, including breakfast.

In the village, *Matahari Inn* (☎ 54832), near the market on the road to Mawan, is of a somewhat higher standard, with rooms at 15,000/20,000 rp or 30,000/40,000 rp with air-con, as well as a pleasant restaurant. A little further west is Kuta's best mid-range hotel, the *Kuta Indah* (☎ 53781), which is a large modern edifice where the rooms have air-con, hot and cold water and TV for 50,000/60,000 rp, plus 15% tax and service. It may be comfortable, but it's not close to the beach or any of the beachfront restaurants/bars.

The architecturally impressive *Novotel Lombok Coralia* (☎ 53333; fax 53555) is about 1.5km east of the budget accommodation strip. Designed by a Thai architect, it employs traditional Lombok architecture with Sumbanese motifs and African style to give it an amazing cultural theme park look. Rooms are furnished in Asian style and cost US$130 and $140. Luxury-plus bungalow villas are US$250 to US$450.

Apart from the restaurants in the places above, there's the *Bamboo Restaurant* at the western end of the beach, which is worth a try, and *Mascot*, which is a place for a beer and music – it's almost a pub.

Getting There & Away

There is some direct public transport from Bertais to Kuta for 1500 rp, or get a bemo to Praya (700 rp) and another from there to Kuta (you may have to change again at Sengkol). Travel early or you may get stuck and have to charter a vehicle.

Perama has connections to Kuta from Mataram and Senggigi (10,000 rp) and other tourist areas. For Bali, change in Mataram. Perama's office (☎ 54846) is at Wisma Segara Anak. If you have your own transport it's easy – there's a wide road, sealed all the way.

EAST OF KUTA

Quite good roads go around the coast to the east, passing a series of beautiful bays punctuated by headlands. There's some public transport, but you will see more with your own transport – a bicycle would be good. All the beachfront land has been bought by speculators for planned tourist resorts. **Segar Beach** is about 2km east around the first headland and you can easily walk there. An enormous rock about 4km east of the village offers superb views across the countryside if you climb it early in the morning. The road goes 5km east to **Tanjung Aan** (Cape Aan), where there are two classic beaches with very fine, powdery white sand. This is an area slated for upmarket resort hotels.

The road continues another 3km to the fishing village of **Gerupak**, where there's a market on Tuesday. From there you can get a boat across the bay to **Bumbang**.

Alternatively, turn north just before Tanjung Aan and go to **Awang**, a fishing village which is getting into the seaweed business. You could get a boat from here across to **Ekas** and some of the other not-so-secret surf spots in this bay (see the following East Lombok section).

WEST OF KUTA

The road west of Kuta has been recently sealed as far as **Selong Blanak**, a lovely sandy bay. It doesn't follow the coast closely, but there are regular and spectacular ocean vistas. In between are more fine beaches like **Mawan**, **Tampa**, **Rowok** and **Mawi**, but you have to detour to find them. They all have surfing possibilities in the right conditions.

For accommodation, *Selong Blanak Cottages* are isolated, 1.5km north of Selong Blanak Beach, but the management provide transport to the beach and back free of charge, and to more isolated spots for a small price. It's a very nice place to stay, with a variety of rooms from 20,000 rp (5000 rp more in the high season) and a restaurant. The road north between Selong Blanak and Penujak is mostly sealed and passable.

To go further west, turn off this road at Keling, two or 3km from Selong Blanak (you almost double back at the junction). The road goes through pleasantly forested hills to Montongsapah, where it swings back to the coast, with a brilliant ocean vista as you descend to **Pengantap**.

From Pengantap, you climb across a head-land to descend to another superb bay, which you follow around for a kilometre or so. Look carefully for the turn-off west to **Blongas**, which is a very steep, rough and winding road with breathtaking scenery. There are good places for surfing and diving in Blongas Bay, but no facilities for either. You'll really need a boat to find the surfing and diving spots. There's some sandy beach, the usual local *warung* and you might even find a homestay, but don't count on it. This is as far west as you can go on this road – return to the junction and turn north to Sekotong (see the previous West Lombok section), by another scenic road, and on to Lembar.

This is an excellent trip, from Kuta around to Lembar, but it's pretty rugged, especially the detour to Blongas, and there are no phones or facilities en route. It's best done by motor-cycle if you're a competent rider – in places it may be too steep, narrow and rutted for even a little Jimny. The distance isn't huge (less than 100km), but allow plenty of time and don't try it in the wet season.

East Lombok

For most travellers, the only east coast town they visit is Labuhan Lombok, the port for ferries to Sumbawa. But improvements to the road around the north coast now make a round-the-island trip quite feasible. Similarly, the once-remote south-eastern penin-sula is becoming more accessible, particularly for those with their own transport.

LABUHAN LOMBOK
There are fantastic views of mighty Gunung Rinjani from the east coast port of Labuhan Lombok. From Khayangan Hill on the south side of the harbour you can look across the Alas Strait to Sumbawa. The town was once the main Dutch port on Lombok and a centre for the sandalwood trade from the islands further east. Today it is a sleepy little place with a large population of Bugis, the Sul-awesi seafarers who have been on this coast for generations. You can wander past some old Dutch warehouses to the Bugis stilt village around the mosque.

LOMBOK

1 Ticket Office;
   Ferry Take-off Point
2 Warungs
3 Carpark
4 Mosque
5 Dahlia Cafe
6 Warungs
7 Bemo Terminal
8 Post Office
9 Losmen Dian
   Dutaku
10 Hotel Lima Tiga
11 Hidayat
   Restaurant
12 Warung Kelayu
13 Losmen
   Munawar
14 Cinema

To Sumbawa

Alas
Strait

Gate

Labuhan
Lombok

0   250   500 m

To
Labuhan
Pandan

Jalan Khayangan

To Pringgabaya
& Mataram

If you're just passing through Labuhan Lombok on your way to Sumbawa there's no need to stay overnight. A bus from Bertais terminal only takes a couple of hours, and there are regular ferries to Sumbawa leaving from the jetty on the east side of the bay.

Places to Stay & Eat

In the village of Labuhan Lombok you can stay at the depressingly basic *Losmen Dian Dutaku*, on the main road coming into town, with singles/doubles for 4000/6000 rp. On Jl Khayangan, the road that runs around to the ferry port, *Hotel Lima Tiga* is by far the pick of the places to stay. It has a good upstairs restaurant and, though service has declined, it is the only place geared towards travellers, and has information available on the area. Rooms cost 10,000/15,000 rp and though fairly spartan they are the best in town. Each pair of rooms has a shared sitting area. The next best option is the *Losmen Munawar*, though it's fairly seedy. Rooms cost 4000/8000 rp. For food, there are a few warungs around the bemo terminal or the *Dahlia Cafe* opposite is the pick of the town's eateries.

Getting There & Away

Bus & Bemo Frequent buses and bemos run between Labuhan Lombok and Bertais and they cost 2200 rp for the 69km trip. The journey should take a bit less than two hours. If you're zipping west across Lombok and bound for Bali, you can take a bus from Labuhan Lombok via Bertais to Lembar. Other road connections go to Masbagik (1000 rp), Kopang (1500 rp), Aikmel (800 rp) and Pringgabaya (400 rp).

Boat Regular passenger ferries leave Labuhan Lombok for Poto Tano (Sumbawa) hourly from 6 am to 8 pm. If you get a through bus from Bertais to Sumbawa Besar you won't have to worry about it; if you're travelling independently, try to get to the port before noon to make the 1½ hour crossing and the two hour bus trip to Sumbawa Besar before dark.

The ferry costs 3600 rp, 3300 rp for a bicycle, 6000 rp for a motorcycle and a car costs around 37,000 rp. The ferries can get very crowded, especially at times such as Ramadan when local people travel.

The boats depart from the port on the east side of the harbour. It's about 2km from the port to the town of Labuhan Lombok – take a bemo, cidomo or ojek, all costing 500 rp. The ferry ticket office, with a wartel, warung and waiting room, is beside the carpark. There are a few more food stalls nearby and food vendors come on board the boat.

NORTH OF LABUHAN LOMBOK

Foreigners are still a curiosity along the coastline north of the port.

Check out the giant mahogany trees about 5km north of the harbour. **Pulu Lampur**, 14km north, has a black-sand beach and is popular with locals on Sunday and holidays. You can stay at *Gili Lampu Cottages*, simple bamboo bungalows back from the beach, for 10,000 rp.

Another few kilometres to the north you can stay at the pleasant and secluded *Siola Cottages*, just before the village of **Labuhan Pandan**. Siola sits by itself in a coconut grove on the seashore, with singles/doubles for 15,000/25,000 rp and three meals; or stop for a meal or a snack. Further north are the *Matahari Cottages*, charging the same price.

From here you can charter a boat to the uninhabited islands of **Gili Sulat** and the **Gili Petangan** group, with lovely white-sand beaches and good coral for snorkelling, although there are no facilities. A boat costs about 30,000 rp for up to five passengers for a day trip out and back, with a few hours on an island. Take drinking water and a picnic lunch. Perama has a camp on one of the Gili Petangan islands, which is a stopover on its expensive Land-Sea Adventure tours.

The road continues through **Sambelia** and **Sugian** to the north coast (see the previous North Lombok section in this chapter). The road is sealed and has good bridges. By public transport, you can get a bemo to Anyar (near Bayan) from Labuhan Lombok.

SOUTH OF LABUHAN LOMBOK

The capital of the East Lombok administrative district is **Selong**, which has some old buildings from the Dutch period. The Selong area has grown a lot in recent years, and there is an almost continuous urban strip from Pancor to the town of Tanjung. There's a tourist office in Selong now, but probably no tourists. Pancor is the bus and bemo terminal for the region, and you can change money at the BPD Bank. *Wisma Erina* (☎ 21247), on the north-east side of the main road, is not a bad place to stay, but there's no reason to.

On the coast is **Labuhan Haji**, accessible from Selong and Tanjung by bemo. Formerly a port for those departing on a *hajj* (pilgrimage to Mecca), the port buildings are abandoned and in ruins. The black-sand beach here is a bit grubby, but OK for swimming. Regular ferries run to Maluk in Sumbawa, transporting workers to the gold mine there. Although a private ferry, there is talk of opening it to the public. There's accommodation at *Melewi's Beach Cottages*, on the beach just north of where the road from Selong comes in. Doubles are 20,000 rp, including breakfast – other meals can be arranged. It doesn't appear to be very well run, but it's isolated and has great views across to Sumbawa. It is a prime place to feed mosquitoes, so take precautions.

Further south you come to **Tanjung Luar**, one of Lombok's main fishing ports, with a strong smell of fish and lots of Bugis-style houses on stilts. From there the road swings west to **Keruak**, where wooden boats are made, and continues past the turn to **Sukaraja**, a traditional Sasak village which tourists are welcome to visit, especially if they want to buy the local woodcarvings.

Just west of Keruak there's a road heading south to **Jerowaru** (3.6km) and the southeastern peninsula, which was inaccessible until recently. This peninsula is sparsely populated, has a harsh climate and scrubby vegetation, but the coastline has some interesting features.

A sealed road branches west 6.4km past Jerowaru – it gets pretty rough, but eventually reaches **Ekas**. There's no accommodation in Ekas itself, but *Laut Surga Cottages* is on the coast a few kilometres south. The cottages had become very run down when we last visited and it may even have closed by the time you read this. If you hear it's habitable, you can get there by boat from Ekas or from Awang across the bay (Awang is covered in the South Lombok section earlier in this chapter). In the dry season you can get there by road, turning left off the Ekas road and following the small blue signs. Laut Surga was mainly a place for surfers and it has a lovely little beach, but it's a long way to come if you can't stay here.

Kaliantan and **Serewi**, about 16km past Jerowaru on the far south coast, have brilliant ocean views, but no accommodation. You may be able to charter a bemo from Keruak to Ekas (maybe 30,000 rp) or Kaliantan (40,000 rp). If you want to explore you'll need your own transport, but it's easy to lose your way and the roads go from bad to worse. This area is really remote.

On the eastern coast of the peninsula, **Tanjung Ringgit** has some large caves which, according to local legend, are home to a demonic giant. There's a road to Tanjung Ringgit, but it may not be passable. It might be easier to charter a boat from Tanjung Luar. There's a cultivated pearl operation at **Sunut**, on the north coast of the peninsula.

Sumbawa

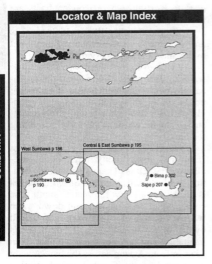

Locator & Map Index

West Sumbawa p 186

Central & East Sumbawa p 195

Sumbawa Besar ⊙
p 190

● Bima p 202
Sape p 207 ●

Highlights

- **Huu** – a superb beach with turquoise waters and excellent surf breaks. It is Sumbawa's biggest attraction, mostly for surfers, and has a good selection of budget to mid-range bungalows.

- **Sumbawa Besar** – a relaxed town with an old wooden sultan's palace. Day trips can be made to nearby villages.

- **Bima** – in this bustling small port city with a hint of Arabia, the sultan's palace has an impressive collection of artefacts. Traditional villages can be visited from Bima, but are hard to reach.

- **Maluk** – another great beach with good surf, but more difficult to reach than Huu and facilities are limited.

- **Pulau Moyo** – an island nature reserve with good beaches and coral reefs. It has one ultra-expensive hotel or it can be visited on a day trip by chartered boat.

- **Tambora Peninsula** – this remote region is dominated by towering Gunung Tambora, which can be climbed, and just offshore is Pulau Satonda, a tiny island with a crater lake. Definitely not for the air-conditioned bus set – travel is tough and time consuming.

Between Lombok and Flores, and separated from them by narrow straits, is the rugged land mass of Sumbawa. Larger than Bali and Lombok combined, Sumbawa is a sprawling island of twisted and jutting peninsulas, with a coast fringed by precipitous hills and angular bights, and a mountain line of weathered volcanic stumps stretching along its length.

Sumbawa is lightly populated, particularly the western half of the island which is still largely forested. As such, the west is a transmigrasi area, attracting sponsored migrants from overpopulated Lombok, as well as Java and Bali. The eastern half of the island is more extensively cultivated and populated, particularly the plains around Bima.

Sumbawa is a scenic island, with scope for exploring off the beaten track. Few visitors venture beyond Sumbawa Besar, Bima or Huu, mainly because once off the highway, transport is infrequent and uncomfortable.

To get out into the countryside you really need to charter transport or rent a motorcycle.

The mountain and coastal regions in the south – which were not converted to Islam until around the turn of the century – and the Tambora Peninsula in the north are rarely visited by travellers. Sumbawa's main tourist attraction is the wonderful surf beach at Huu.

If you're in the right place at the right time (on holidays and festivals), you might see traditional Sumbawan fighting, a sort of bare-fisted boxing called *berempah*. Horse and water buffalo races are held before the rice is planted. Horse racing is a big local event in the dry season and culminates on 17 August, Independence Day.

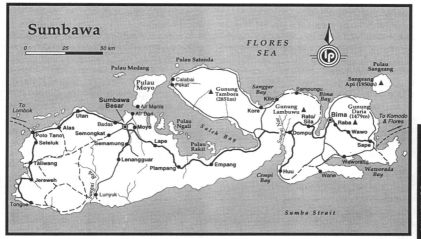

Facts About Sumbawa

HISTORY

For centuries Sumbawa has been divided between two linguistically and, to some extent, ethnically distinct peoples: the Sumbawanese speakers, who probably reached the west of the island from Lombok; and the Bimanese speakers, who independently occupied the east and Tambora Peninsula. The squatter, darker-skinned Bimanese are more closely related to the people of Flores, while the western Sumbawans are closer to the Sasaks of Lombok. Both their languages have considerable variation in dialect, but the spread of Bahasa Indonesia has made communication easier in the past couple of decades.

Sumbawa, with its rich timber resources in the west, was probably an early trading call for Javanese merchants on the way to or from the Spice Islands in Maluku. Bima, Sape, Dompu and Taliwang are claimed as part of the Majapahit Empire in the *Nagarakertagama*, the Javanese chronicle of 1365. Although Majapahit ships called at these ports, it is unlikely that effective Javanese control was established on Sumbawa.

Javanese influence was more than just an occasional visit, however, and inscribed boulders found near Bima have Old Javanese inscriptions and point to early Hindu influence.

Along the western coastal lowlands, the local population expanded and petty kingdoms developed along the entire length of the island. In eastern Sumbawa, the areas around the fertile Bima Bay and the Dompu plains became the leading centres for the Bimanese-speaking population. The name Bima comes from the Hindu epic, the *Mahabharata*, and Bimanese kings claimed Javanese descent. Sumbawa is thought to originate from the Sanskrit *sambhawa*. Although the kings embraced Javanese court ritual and probably Hinduism, before 1600 the population was primarily animist.

By that time, the domestic horse was being used, and irrigated rice agriculture – possibly introduced by Javanese traders – was well established. There appears to have been some intermarriage between the Balinese aristocracy and western Sumbawanese aristocracy, which may have linked the islands from the 15th or 16th centuries.

SUMBAWA

Rise of the Sultanates

In the early 17th century, the Islamic Makassarese state of Gowa in southern Sulawesi undertook a military expansion, invading Sumbawa in 1619. By 1625, the rulers of Sumbawa had been reduced to Makassarese vassals and had converted to Islam. Tribute was paid to Gowa in the form of sappanwood, horses and slaves. With Makassarese military backing the Sumbawan kingdoms expanded their influence, especially the western Sumbawans who invaded and controlled eastern Lombok.

Makassar's rise was halted by the United East India Company (Vereenigde Oost-Indische Compagnie; VOC). They invaded Gowa in 1660, but it was not until 1669 that they finally prevailed. To prevent Bimanese allies reaching Makassar, the Dutch blockaded Bima's harbour.

Soon afterwards treaties were made between the Dutch and the rulers of Sumbawa, and the Dutch built a trading fort at Bima. For their part, the Dutch maintained only a distant interest in what they considered to be a politically unstable island with poor commercial possibilities. The western Sumbawans, meanwhile, held nominal control over eastern Lombok. Their grip was weakened after attacks by the Sasaks in 1677-78, but they still claimed suzerainty until 1750, when the Balinese took over. Then followed 30 years of sporadic warfare between the Sumbawans and the Balinese, including at least one large-scale Balinese invasion of western Sumbawa. It was only through the intervention of the VOC, which was interested in maintaining the status quo, that the Balinese were turned back.

The Makassarese and the Bimanese maintained their alliance, and Bima's prestige grew as western Sumbawa declined. In 1727, a Makassarese princess married into the Bimanese court and Manggarai, the western regency of Flores, was given to Bima as part of the dowry. Manggarai chiefs paid tribute to Bima and on the northern coast of Flores, Reo became a Bimanese port. Bima also traded with and claimed control over Sumba, but apart from establishing trading settlements it is doubtful that Bima exerted any direct control.

Sumbawa's fortunes fell when Gunung Tambora erupted in 1815, killing 10,000 people in a shower of choking ash and molten debris. Agricultural land was wrecked and livestock and crops wiped out throughout the island. It is estimated that at least another 40,000 people either died of starvation or disease, or fled their lands.

By the middle of the 19th century, immigrants from other islands were brought in to help repopulate the blighted coastal regions. The people of Sumbawa are therefore a diverse lot. In the coastal regions there are traces of the Javanese, Makassarese, Bugis, Sasak and other groups who migrated to the island.

Dutch Control

The Dutch interest in Sumbawa was confined to trade and contracts were signed with the sultans to ensure most exports flowed through the Dutch fort in Bima. Apart from an occasional military skirmish to keep the balance of power in check, VOC involvement was minimal.

After the VOC went bankrupt, the Dutch government assumed direct control in 1799. The Dutch were keen to renew contracts, but little changed on Sumba until 1905 when it became Dutch policy to institute direct rule throughout Indonesia. The sultans remained in charge of local affairs under the eye of the Dutch administration, but lost all rights to independent trade and had to collect taxes for the government. Rebellions broke out and Ambonese troops were dispatched to crush resistance.

In 1908 the Dutch government sent administrators and soldiers to Sumbawa Besar and Taliwang to head off the prospect of war between the three separate states that comprised West Sumbawa. Effective Dutch control dates from this time. Minor incidents continued – against the Dutch and between various contenders to the courts – but colonial rule was established.

Sumbawa was reorganised, with control of Manggarai and Komodo transferred to

Timor, and smaller states were combined. The administrative boundaries devised by the Dutch remain largely unchanged today. Steamship services were set up to link Sumbawa and Surabaya in Java, and the main highway across the island began construction. However, the Dutch presence was short-lived. The Japanese took over in 1942, but while the Dutch returned to claim Sumbawa in 1945, they remained for only four more years before independence was granted to Indonesia.

Today, little evidence remains of the Dutch presence, and the only traces of the old sultanates are the palaces in the towns of Sumbawa Besar and Bima. The sultans held some sway until 1960 when governors were appointed, officially ending their rule.

GEOGRAPHY
Sumbawa is an elongated island, part of the volcanic chain stretching from Sumatra through Flores. Gunung Tambora (2851m) is Sumbawa's highest and most well known volcano, which erupted catastrophically in 1815. Olet Sanggenges (1923m) in West Sumbawa is dormant, while Sangeang Api on Pulau Sangeang, off Sumbawa's northeastern coast, is currently very active.

Sumbawa has extensive forest areas in the mountainous south-west while the northern and eastern coastal plains are much drier. Towards the east of the island, the narrow Teluk Bima (Bima Bay) cuts deep into the north coast, forming one of Indonesia's best natural harbours. It's surrounded by fertile lowlands which reach west into the rich interior Dompu plains.

CLIMATE
The main rains come from December to March, with some significant rainfall also in November and April. The average annual rainfall for Sumbawa Besar is around 1300 mm, which is typical for much of the island, though the eastern tip is noticeably drier.

The dry season is very dry and can bring great hardship. For visitors, Sumbawa is at its best at the end of the wet season around April/May. As the dry season progresses, the greenery dies off and much of the island becomes brown and dusty under the increasingly sweltering heat. The north coast is very dry, while parts of the south-west coast sandwiched between the mountains and the sea remain relatively lush.

ECONOMY
Wet and dry rice is extensively grown and garden plots support a variety of crops. Onions, buffalo, cattle and salt are agricultural exports, especially from the Bima region, and coffee and tobacco are important in the highland areas of West and Central Sumbawa. The government has sponsored large-scale cattle and buffalo ranches and cashew plantations on the depopulated slopes of Gunung Tambora, all produced with transmigrasi labour. The forest areas of Gunung Tambora and the dipterocarpaceous forests of West Sumbawa are extensively logged.

The biggest thing to hit Sumbawa in years is the massive goldmine being developed near Maluk in south-west Sumbawa, promising to be the biggest mining operation in the region.

Tourism is very low-key compared to Lombok, and most visitors pass through Sumbawa in a hurry between Lombok and Flores. Huu, home to surf tourism, is far and away the No 1 tourist destination and officially gets around 30,000 visitors a year, but that seems exaggerated.

POPULATION & PEOPLE
Sumbawa's population is around 900,000. Population density is very low compared to neighbouring Lombok, and Sumbawa has many transmigrants settled under government schemes from the overpopulated islands of Java, Bali and particularly eastern Lombok.

Bimanese & Sumbawanese
The two main peoples of Sumbawa are the Bimanese of East and Central Sumbawa (or Dou Mbojo as they refer to themselves in the local language) and the Sumbawanese (or Tau Semawa) of West Sumbawa. The

184 Facts about Sumbawa – Population & People

Bimanese people inhabit the region of Dompu and spread east through to Bima. The Bimanese are darker skinned and are believed to have settled the island from the east, probably Flores, while the Sumbawans came from the west. Sumbawa is the ethnographic dividing line in Nusa Tenggara.

The people of Dompu speak Bimanese and the Sanggar people of the Tambora Peninsula speak a different Bimanese dialect. Both formed kingdoms separate to the sultanate of Bima. In the west the people of Taliwang are a subgroup of the dominant Sumbawanese.

Dou Donggo

The Dou Donggo (literally, Mountain People) who inhabit the slopes of Gunung Lambuwu west of Bima, were long isolated from the main societies on Sumbawa. The Dou Donggo speak Bimanese and have attracted much interest from anthropologists because of their patrilineal, exogamous clans that are common in Flores and other eastern islands, but otherwise nonexistent in Sumbawa. Traditional religion is headed by hereditary priests or *ncuhi*; various gods, including the supreme creator Dewa Langi Lantu, are worshipped. However, Islam has now made inroads and modernisation has also contributed to the breakdown of traditional beliefs.

The origins of the Dou Donggo are uncertain, but they are thought to be the original inhabitants of Sumbawa pushed into the hills by later migrations. Another interesting but unlikely theory prevalent in Bima is that the Dou Donggo settled their highland villages only a few hundred years ago and were originally slaves from Flores granted freedom and land by the Sultan of Bima.

The term 'Donggo' is used by the Bimanese to refer to other highland groups, such as the Dou Wawo who inhabit the hills east of Bima. They speak a very different language from the Dou Donggo and the Bimanese, though their language has some words in common with Bimanese. Traditional ways are not much in evidence. The related Sambori people in the mountains of the south-east have also adopted Islam, but the

main village is still very traditional. Yet another distinct people, the Dou Kolo, live north of Bima on the eastern shores of Teluk Bima (Bima Bay).

Other Groups

Sumbawa has long history of influence from Sulawesi, and settlement by the Makassarese dates back to the 17th century. Later migrations from Sulawesi brought the Bugis and sea-gypsy Bajau people, and their stilt villages dot the north coast.

A significant number of Chinese live in the towns and Balinese are also active in commerce. Bima also has a long-established Arab community.

RELIGION

Sumbawa is the most predominantly Muslim island anywhere east of Java or south of Sulawesi and Islam overshadows Sumbawa's indigenous traditions. *Sanro*, spiritual healers or diviners, mediate with the spirit world and can appease the ancestral spirits, but they are becoming less important. Various other rituals, such as *doa* ceremonial feasts that accompany important events of life (much like the Javanese *slametan*) survive, but are subordinate to Islam and are often accompanied by chanting from the Koran.

Until very recently, pockets of animism existed in the mountain regions, particularly around Donggo, but most people have now converted to Islam. Balinese Hindus and Christians can be found, particularly in West Sumbawa, but most are migrants from other areas of Indonesia. Bima is considered to be the stronghold of Islam and sends many pilgrims to Mecca every year.

LANGUAGE

Bimanese is spoken throughout Central and East Sumbawa and has two main dialects: Bima and Sanggar. Kolo and Toloweri (Wawo) are minor and very different dialects. Bimanese is related to Sabunese and shows some similarity with Manggarai. Sumbawanese is spoken in the west of the island. It is very different to Bimanese and related to Sasak.

Indonesian is spoken everywhere and is

important as the linking language between the various ethnic and migrant groups.

Getting There & Around

AIR

Bima is the main airport on Sumbawa, and Merpati has scheduled direct flights between Bima and Denpasar (Bali), Mataram (Lombok), Ruteng (Timor), Ende (Flores), Labuanbajo (Flores), and Tambolaka (Sumba). The most popular links are to Labuanbajo (four times a week) and Denpasar (daily), but it is not always easy to get a seat.

In the main tourist season around August, Bima airport is notorious for stranding passengers. Apart from the usual overbooking problems, it only takes one flight cancellation to throw all schedules into turmoil. At other times it is usually not a problem, but always allow one extra day up your sleeve in case something goes wrong.

Merpati also flies between Sumbawa Besar and Mataram four days a week, but seats are limited.

BUS

Sumbawa's single main road runs all the way from Taliwang (near the west coast) through Sumbawa Besar, Dompu and Bima to Sape (on the east coast). It's surfaced all the way. Fleets of buses, some of them luxurious by Nusa Tenggara standards, link all the towns on this road.

Large, comfortable, air-con coaches ply the main highway from Poto Tano to Sape (the two ferry departure points) and run right through to Lombok and Bali. They are only for long-distance passengers, but you can usually get a seat on these buses between Sumbawa Besar and Bima or Sape.

Otherwise buses on Sumbawa are small, hot, crowded and stop everywhere. Travel is relatively quick between the main towns, but off the highway roads are rougher and travel slower.

Bemos go to the villages around the main centres.

CAR & MOTORCYCLE

Unlike Lombok, Sumbawa is not a major tourist destination and so vehicle hire is not easily arranged. A couple of hotels in Huu rent motorbikes (see the Huu/Lakey section later in this chapter), otherwise it is a case of asking around to see if someone wants to earn a few extra rupiah.

Self-drive cars are not available, but you can rent a car with driver. This is most easily done in Bima, where gung-ho taxi drivers abound, particularly at the airport. Rates are high, especially the official rates fixed at the airport taxi desk, but are slightly cheaper if negotiated directly with the driver. For day trips it is cheaper to hire a bemo, but the drivers are as crazed as the city's taxi drivers. Bima also has a few travel agents that can arrange vehicle hire at high rates.

Most car and motorbike hirers on Lombok will not allow you to take vehicles off the island, but if you shop around it may be possible. Rates will be higher, and make sure you have all the correct paperwork allowing you to drive on Sumbawa. A letter from the hirer giving permission to leave Lombok will satisfy ferry officials who otherwise turn back foreigners with wheels. It is much easier to rent a car with driver in Lombok, and much cheaper than in Sumbawa.

BOAT

Ferries run hourly between Lombok and Poto Tano from around 6 am to 8 pm and the crossing takes $1\frac{1}{2}$ hours. Some buses meet the ferry at Poto Tano, but it is much easier to catch a through bus from Lombok to your destination on Sumbawa. From Mataram, buses run directly to Taliwang, Sumbawa Besar, Bima and Sape. See the Poto Tano entry in the West Sumbawa section for more details.

From Sumbawa to Flores, a ferry goes every day except Friday between Sape and Labuanbajo (around nine hours), stopping at Komodo (six hours) on the way. Ferries are occasionally cancelled, but this is generally a very reliable service.

West Sumbawa

POTO TANO

The port for ferries to and from Lombok, Poto Tano is a hodgepodge of stilt houses beside a mangrove-lined bay. It's 10km off the main highway. There's no reason to stop in Poto Tano as through buses run between Lombok and all the main towns on Sumbawa.

Getting There & Away

Ferries run hourly between Poto Tano and Labuhan Lombok (1½ hours) from around 6 am to 8 pm. The fare is 3600 rp, bicycles cost 3300 rp, motorbikes 6000 rp and a small car 36,600 rp. The through buses from Mataram (Lombok) to Sumbawa Besar or Bima include the ferry fare.

Buses also meet the ferry and go to Taliwang (1500 rp; one hour), Sumbawa Besar (3000 rp; two hours) and Bima (8500 rp; nine hours). These same buses return to Poto Tano from all these towns.

ALAS

Alas is the largest town on the highway before reaching Sumbawa Besar, 70km

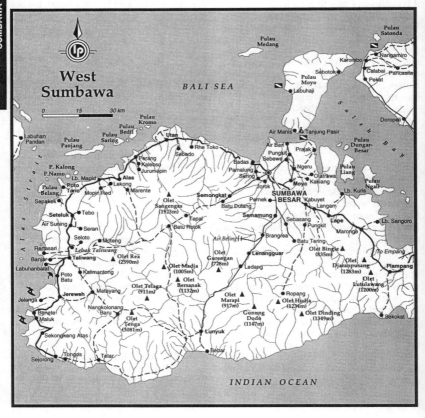

away. Founded on a good natural harbour, it used to be the main ferry port before Poto Tano took over that role, but this small town is still busy despite the loss of the ferry trade. The bus terminal is central, and the town's three hotels and a wartel are within walking distance.

The only points of interest are the small islands of **Pulau Bungin** and **Pulau Kaung**, straddling the entrance to the harbour. Established some 180 years ago by Bajau fishermen from Sulawesi, stilt-house villages take up every available scrap of space on the islands, which are low-lying coral atolls only 1.5m above sea level. Bungin is the easier to reach. It will cost around 30,000 rp to charter a boat, or at low tide you can wade across to the island from the western shore of the harbour. You can wander between the houses crammed together on this heavily populated island of 2500 people. Bungin has its own land reclamation programs, a la Singapore, using coral to create more space to construct yet more houses. Tourists rarely visit, people are friendly and you might see nets being repaired or the fishing haul being processed.

Places to Stay
Losmen Selamat (☎ 91026) is on the main street, 100m from the bus terminal towards Sumbawa Besar. Basic singles/doubles cost 6000/8000 rp. A little further along, *Hotel Telaga* (☎ 91182), at Jl Pahlawan 32, is the best choice. Simple but habitable rooms cost 10,000 rp a double. Further past the Telaga, the *Losmen Anda* (☎ 91169) is another basic choice.

TALIWANG
During the 19th century, Taliwang was one of the 'vassal states' of the kingdom of Sumbawa based in Sumbawa Besar. This region has its own dialect and, through migration, is closely linked to Lombok.

Today Taliwang is a sleepy, oversized village, with friendly people and no tourists. It lies close to the west coast of Sumbawa, 30km south of Poto Tano along a narrow road winding through the hills. **Lebok (Lake) Taliwang**, close to the Poto Tano road 8km

before Taliwang, is popular with local anglers, but is slowly being choked by lotus flowers – they're quite picturesque when in bloom, but otherwise an ecological disaster.

The coast south of Taliwang is quite spectacular and is first sighted 6km from Taliwang at **Poto Batu**, a popular beach for picnickers. The rocky outcrop just off the beach has a cave/blow hole spattered with the usual graffiti. Give a small donation to the odd but harmless caretaker. **Labuhan-balat**, a small Bugis stilt fishing community 7km from Taliwang, is on a very pretty bay and is reached by bus or bemo.

Places to Stay & Eat
Taliwang's market is next to the bus terminal. Behind the market and directly opposite the mosque, the friendly but spartan *Losmen Al Azhar* on Jl Pasar Baru has rooms for 7500 rp per person. *Hotel Taliwang Indah* (☎ 81079), at Jl Jenderal Sudirman 79, has a first floor porch overlooking the hills and a friendly manager who speaks good English. Good rooms cost from 12,500 rp. The attached restaurant has a long menu and excellent food. On the same street, opposite the cinema, *Losmen Tubalong* (☎ 81018), Jl Sudirman 111, is another hospitable place with a variety of rooms. Dingy rooms cost 6000 rp, or much better rooms at the back around a courtyard cost 15,000 rp and 20,000 rp with mandi.

Taliwang is famous for its delicious ayam Taliwang – spicy chicken cooked in coconut milk. Ayam Taliwang restaurants are found throughout Lombok and Sumbawa, but try it in its place of origin. Most of the rumah makan around town serve it.

Getting There & Away
Buses from Taliwang to Poto Tano cost 1500 rp or buses run right through to Mataram for 7000 rp. Most buses leave in the morning between 6 and 9 am. Direct buses also go from Taliwang to Sumbawa Besar (3200 rp; three hours).

SOUTH-WEST SUMBAWA
Many of the small trickle of visitors who make it to the Taliwang area are surfers in

search of the good waves along this coast. The area has many beautiful, but isolated, white-sand beaches.

Jelenga

From Taliwang, buses run 11km south over a good, paved road to Jereweh. Opposite the police station in Jereweh, a dirt road leads 6km to the beach at Jelenga. Home to the famous 'Scar Reef' surf break, this is one of the main surf destinations in south-west Sumbawa, famous for its large left-hander. The *Pondok Wisata Jelenga* has reasonable bungalows for 15,000 rp and food is available. No public transport runs to Jelenga – charter a bemo in Taliwang for around 20,000 rp.

Maluk

A popular surfing destination, Maluk is 30km south of Taliwang. The superb beach has white sand framing turquoise and deep blue waters. The reef, lying a few hundred metres off shore, shelters the bay and has some good coral, but the swells don't make for ideal snorkelling conditions. They do make for excellent surfing though and around the southern headland is the well known 'Supersuck' left-hand break, the best in the area. Yo Yo's is a right hander in the next bay along and is usually working if Supersuck is flat.

Apart from a few surfing tours out of Bali, Maluk has only ever received a trickle of surfers because of its isolation and has always been the poor cousin of Huu in Central Sumbawa. But Maluk is undergoing huge development, and in this case development isn't being driven by tourism. A couple of kilometres before Maluk, Newmont, an American company, has set up its 'base camp' to develop what promises to be one of Indonesia's biggest gold mines.

Within weeks of getting the go ahead, Newmont, in conjunction with local companies, cleared the landscape and started moving in equipment with military precision. With a harbour still under construction, ships started beach landings while helicopters buzzed overhead ferrying equipment to the mine site, some 30km inland in the mountains. The huge base camp is only the forerunner of a whole new city that will be built half way between Maluk and the mine. The city will house some 10,000 workers, dropping to a permanent population of 4000 when the mine is completed and in full operation. The open-cut mine is expected to process an astonishing 176,000 tonnes of ore a day.

The mine is the biggest thing to hit Sumbawa since Islam and will change the face of south-west Sumbawa in only a couple of years. Apart from a new road into the mine, the road past Maluk, which now finishes at Sejorong, will be pushed right through to Lunyuk. Tourism is also expected to boom. Access will be much improved and a large number of workers, including hundreds of highly paid expats who have flocked here from other mining projects in Indonesia, will use Maluk's wonderful beach for R&R. Maluk is still sleepy and the beach untouched, but local developers, in a smaller-scale mirror of the frantic activity around them, are building small restaurants and new bungalows. A big chunk of beachfront land is earmarked for a luxury hotel.

Ten kilometres further south, **Sekongkang** also has a fine surfing beach and the kepala desa offers accommodation. The beach is at Sekongkang Bawah, 2km downhill from Sekongkang Atas where some buses stop.

Places to Stay & Eat *Surya Beach Bungalows* on Jalan Pasir Putih is 400m from the beach at the southern end of Maluk village. For a long time the only place to stay, it has slightly worn bungalows with shared mandi for 15,000 rp and a restaurant. The *Maluk Beach Bungalows* is 200m closer to the beach and has new, more substantial singles/doubles with shared mandi for 10,000/15,000 rp. *Iwan's* is another new place further north and has similar accommodation for the same price.

Kafe & Rumah Makan Bisma has the best food around, a convivial owner and plenty of cold beer in the evenings. Expatriate mine workers flock here after work – for some jaw-dropping conversation, ask them how much they earn. *Rumah Makan Rasate* further south is another new addition with standard fare and a few open-sided bungalows for lesahan (traditional style, on straw mats) dining.

Getting There & Away At least five buses a day (more all the time) leave Taliwang for Maluk (2000 rp; 1½ hours) between 5 am and 7 pm. Some continue on to Sekongkang (1500 rp) and further to Tongos.

The mine operates a ferry to Lombok. The ferry is only for its workers, but the port is proposed to become a public utility and private ferries may start running.

SUMBAWA BESAR

At one time the name 'Sumbawa' only applied to the western half of the island, which fell under the sway of the sultan of the state of Sumbawa; the eastern half of the island was known as Bima. Almost all that remains of the old western sultanate is the wooden palace in Sumbawa Besar, the showpiece of the town.

Sumbawa Besar is the chief town of the western half of the island, a laid-back, friendly place where *cidomos* (horse-drawn carts) still outnumber bemos and where Muslims flood out of the mosques after midday prayer. There are some lovely tree-lined boulevards around the new palace, but the town has no remarkable attractions except for the old palace. A trip out to Pulau Moyo or to nearby villages can be rewarding, but they are difficult to reach and for most travellers Sumbawa Besar is just a rest stop on the journey across the island.

Apart from the steady stream of travellers who pass through Sumbawa Besar on their way to or from Komodo and Flores, the area is also popular with luxury cruises from Bali that dock at the small port of Badas, west of the town.

Orientation

Sumbawa Besar is small; you can easily walk to most parts of it, except maybe to the main

post office, which is only a bemo or cidomo ride away.

Information
Tourist Offices The tourist office (Dinas Pariwisata Daerah; ☎ 23714), at Jl Bungur 1, is 3km from town. It has little in the way of reliable information. Don't bother.

PHPA (national parks) office (☎ 21358) is at the Direktorat Jenderal Kehutanan, Jl Garuda 12, and has information on Pulau Moyo. The office is open Monday to Friday from 8 am to 2 pm, and on Saturday until noon.

Money Bank Negara Indonesia (BNI) at Jl Kartini 10 is open Monday to Friday from 7.30 am to 2.30 pm, and until noon on Saturday. Bank Danamon does credit card cash advances, but does not change travellers cheques or cash.

Post & Communications There is poste restante at the main post office, which is about 1.5km from the Hotel Tambora, down Jl Garuda. For stamps, there's a sub-post office near the town centre on Jl Yos Sudarso. Both are open from 8 am daily, closing at 2 pm Monday to Thursday, 11 am on Friday and at 12.30 pm on Saturday.

The Telkom office on Jl Setiabudi is open 24 hours, and there is a Telkom wartel at Jl Hasanuddin 105.

Travel Agencies The only real travel agent in town is at the Hotel Tambora, but they are only interested in handling tour groups from Bali. Perama has an agent on Jl Hasanuddinn next to the Losmen Saudara. It basically sells Perama boat tours, but is very informative and can arrange individual trips around Sumbawa.

Dalam Loka (Sultan's Palace)
Back in the early 1960s, Helen and Frank Schreider passed through Sumbawa Besar in their amphibious jeep.

They later described the remnants of the

SUMBAWA

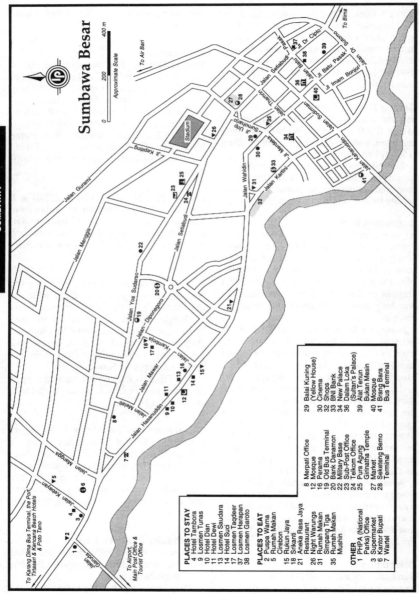

Sumbawa Besar

Approximate Scale

0   200   400 m

PLACES TO STAY
4   Hotel Tambora
9   Losmen Tunas
10 Hotel Dian
11 Hotel Dewi
13 Losmen Saudara
14 Hotel Suci
17 Losmen Taqdeer
37 Losmen Harapan
38 Losmen Garoto

PLACES TO EAT
2   Puspa Warna
5   Rumah Makan
    Cirebon
15 Rukun Jaya
18 Srikanti
21 Aneka Rasa Jaya
    Restaurant
26 Night Warungs
31 Rumah Makan
    Simpang Tiga
35 Rumah Makan
    Mushin

OTHER
1   PHPA (National
    Parks) Office
3   Supermarket
6   Kantor Bupati
7   Wartel

8   Merpati Office
12 Mosque
16 Perama
19 Old Bus Terminal
20 Bank Danamon
22 Military Base
23 Sub-Post Office
24 Telkom Office
25 Pura Agung
    Girinatha Temple
27 Market
28 Seketeng Bemo
    Terminal

29 Balai Kuning
    (Yellow House)
30 Cinema
32 Shops
33 BNI Bank
34 New Palace
36 Dalam Loka
    (Sultan's Palace)
39 Alat Tenun
    Bukan Mesin
40 Mosque
41 Brang Bara
    Bus Terminal

sultan's palace in their book *The Drums of Tonkin*:

Sumbawa Besar ... had a sultan. A small man with tortoise-shell glasses and a quiet, friendly dignity ... his old palace, now deserted except for a few distant relatives, was a long barn-like structure of unpainted wood that seemed on the point of collapsing. Beneath the ramshackle entrance, a rusted cannon from the days of the Dutch East India Company lay half-buried in the ground ... Mothers and fathers and naked little children made the palace shake as they followed us up the ramp into a great empty room that was once the audience chamber ... Only when the few remaining court costumes, the faded silver brocade kains, the gold-handled krises and the long gold fingernails that were a sign of royalty's exemption from labour were modelled for us did we have any idea of the extravagance of this past era. By government decree, the sultans are no longer in power.

Built in 1885, the palace was restored in the early 1980s, but only a few of the original pillars and carved beams remain. It is usually locked – ask around for the caretaker, who speaks English and can show you around. Inside are a few illustrations, explanations in Indonesian and an old palanquin, but otherwise it is empty. The main interest lies in the building itself, built without nails. A small donation towards the upkeep is customary, but not obligatory. Dance practice is often held here on Sunday mornings.

The descendants of the sultans now live at the **Balai Kuning** (Yellow House) on Jl Wahidin and they have numerous artefacts from the days of the sultanate. With advance notice, visits can be arranged for groups (contact the tourist office).

New Palace
The imposing building with the bell tower at its gate on Jl Merdeka is the headquarters of the *bupati* (governor) of West Sumbawa. It's built in imitation of the style of the old sultan's palace; a reminder that the national government now holds the power that was once the sultans'.

Other Attractions
The **Alat Tenun Bukan Mesin** is a small weaving factory near the Dalam Loka, down a small laneway, Gang Nuri 4. Balinese style material with Sumbanese motifs are handwoven, and can be bought by the metre at reasonable prices. Opposite is a traditional palace, home to members of the royal family.

The **Pura Agung Girinatha** is a Balinese Hindu temple on Jl Yos Sudarso, near the corner of Jl Setiabudi. Next door is a *banjar*, a Balinese community hall.

Places to Stay
The *Losmen Taqdeer* (☎ 21987), down a residential lane off Jl Kamboja near the old bus terminal on Jl Diponegoro, is a clean little establishment with rooms from 6000 rp. Another cheap option, right on the doorstep of the sultan's palace, is the small *Losmen Garoto* (☎ 22062) at Jl Batu Pasak 48. Clean, but tiny, rooms upstairs cost 4000/7000 rp or larger rooms with mandi cost 8000/12,000 rp. Next door is a small restaurant.

A group of cheap hotels is clustered along Jl Hasanuddin close to the mosque. The pick of them is the *Hotel Dian* (☎ 21708) at No 69. This friendly hotel has well kept rooms with mandi around a small courtyard at the back for 15,000/22,000 rp, including a decent breakfast. *Hotel Suci* (☎ 21589) has large double rooms with private mandi around a neat courtyard for 15,000 rp. *Losmen Saudara* (☎ 21528) has small rooms from 7500/10,000 rp. The *Losmen Tunas* (☎ 21212), at Jl Hasanuddin 71, and *Losmen Harapan* (☎ 21629), at Jl Dr Cipto 5, are other less appealing options.

Hotel Dewi (☎ 21170), Jl Hasanuddin 60, is a bright, mid-range hotel with stark tilework. Rooms are spotless and good value at 12,500/16,500 rp, 27,500/33,000 rp with aircon, and up to 55,000 rp for deluxe rooms. There's a restaurant here too.

Hotel Tambora (☎ 21555), on Jl Kebayan, is arguably the best hotel in town, but is overpriced. There's a wide range of rooms, all with attached bath, starting at 12,600/21,000 rp for singles/doubles. Air-con rooms are only average and cost 39,000/48,000 rp up to 93,000/120,000 rp. The hotel has a restaurant and a small supermarket next door.

A 10 minute bemo ride from town, *Tirtasari Hotel* (☎ 21987) is a reasonable option right on the beach opposite the new bus terminal. The beach is not great, but the water is clean. The hotel has spacious grounds, but is a little run down and a long way from town. Economy doubles cost 12,500 rp, larger bungalows are 25,000 rp with fan or 35,000 rp with air-con, and VIP bungalows with hot water are 40,000 rp and 45,000 rp.

The most luxurious hotel is the *Kencana Beach Hotel* (☎ 22555) on the highway, 11km west of town. Under the same management as the Hotel Tambora, and charging similarly greedy rates, it has a swimming pool, restaurant and poolside bar. Attractive bungalows fronting the beach cost US$30/35 with fan, US$45/55 with air-con, or deluxe bungalows cost US$65/75. The beach has black sand, but is wide, clean and very pleasant. The clear water is good for snorkelling.

Places to Eat

The cheapest food can be found at the streetside warungs that set up in front of the stadium in the evenings. Soto ayam, sate and other Javanese fare are on offer. The *Rukun Jaya*, on Jl Hasanuddin close to many of the hotels, is a small restaurant with cheap food. The *Rumah Makan Cirebon* on Jl Kebayan is a notch better and serves good Javanese food.

Rumah Makan Mushin, at Jl Wahidin 31, is a spotless little cafe with Lombok/Taliwang dishes. Meals are simple, but very tasty, and the ayam bakar (grilled chicken) is excellent. The more adventurous can try the jeroan ayam (chicken intestines).

Sumbawa Besar has three good Chinese restaurants: the *Aneka Rasa Jaya* at Jl Hasanuddin 14, the spotless *Puspa Warna* at Jl Cendrawasih 1 and the new *Srikanti* on Jl Diponegoro. All have extensive menus and specialise in seafood. The Puspa Warna has a few oddities like sea cucumber and 'sup adam', a herbal soup said to aid potency. The Srikanti has seductive air-con.

The *Tambora, Dewi* and *Tirtasari* hotels also have good restaurants.

Getting There & Away

Air Merpati (☎ 21416) on Jl Diponegoro has four flights a week to/from Mataram (Lombok) and on to Denpasar (Bali).

Bus Sumbawa Besar's main long-distance bus terminal is the new Karang Dima terminal, 5.5km north-west of town on the highway, although some morning buses to Bima leave from the Brang Bara terminal on Jl Kaharuddin. The old bus terminal (Terminal Bugis) in the centre of town still handles buses to the west and east, but this is likely to close in the near future. Fares and approximate journey times from Sumbawa Besar for local buses include: Sape (8500 rp; 7½ hours); Bima (7200 rp; seven hours); Dompu (5500 rp; 4½ hours); Taliwang (3200 rp; three hours); and Poto Tano (3000 rp; two hours).

Air-con buses to Bima leave between 7 and 9 am and at 8 pm, but between these times you have to hope for a seat on a bus coming through from Lombok. You can buy combined bus and ferry tickets from Sumbawa Besar through to Mataram (10,000 rp) or Bali. Buses to Lombok leave at 6, 8 and 9 am and 3 pm. Some hotels sell tickets and can arrange pick-up for a slight premium.

It's a beautiful ride from Sumbawa Besar to Bima. After Empang you start moving up into the hills through rolling green country, thickly forested, with occasional sprays of palm trees along the dramatic shoreline.

Boat Pelni's KM *Pangrango* stops every two weeks at the small port of Badas, 7km west of Sumbawa Besar, on its loop through the eastern islands. The Pelni office is at Labuhan Sumbawa, the town's fishing port, 3km west of town on the Poto Tano road.

Getting Around

To/From the Airport The airport is only 500m from the Hotel Tambora and you can easily walk into town. Turn right as you exit the airport terminal and cross the bridge. Alternatively, take a bemo (300 rp).

Bemo The streets here, apart from the bemo speedway along Jl Hasanuddin, are relatively

RICHARD I'ANSON

RICHARD I'ANSON

SARA-JANE CLELAND

SARA-JANE CLELAND

Lombok
Top: The fertile soils on the slopes of Gunung Rinjani produce up to three rice crops per year.
Middle Left: Elderly woman from Lombok.
Middle Right: Fresh produce on offer in a Lombok village market.
Bottom: Villagers at a Muslim circumcision festival in Lombok.

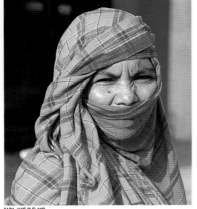

PETER TURNER

PETER TURNER

PETER TURNER

Sumbawa
Top Left: A Muslim woman in traditional garb.
Top Right: The salt-water crater lake at Pulau Satonda.
Bottom Left: The beach at Maluk, a well-known surfing destination in Sumbawa.
Bottom Right: View of the traditional village of Sambori in East Sumbawa.

stress free. Bemos and cidomos cost 300 rp for trips anywhere around town. Otherwise, ojek (motorcycle) riders hang around the bus stations and will transport you around town for 500 rp.

The local Seketeng bemo terminal is on Jl Setiabudi, in front of the market; cidomos congregate along Jl Urip Sumoharjo near where it meets Jl Setiabudi. For trips to villages around Sumbawa Besar, there should be public bemos. Get to the terminal early in the morning, as sometimes there's only one bemo daily; after that you'll have to charter (prices are negotiable).

AROUND SUMBAWA BESAR

A number of attractions can be visited around Sumbawa Besar if you have time to kill. All are difficult to reach by public transport – hire a motorcycle and preferably a guide in Sumbawa Besar.

Pulau Moyo

Two-thirds (about 22,250 hectares) of Pulau Moyo, an island off the coast just north of Sumbawa Besar, is a nature reserve with good coral reefs teeming with fish. Moyo rises to 648m; its centre is composed mainly of savanna with stands of forest. The reserve is inhabited by wild domestic cattle, deer, wild pigs and several varieties of birds, though its main attractions are diving and snorkelling.

Moyo has a few villages – Sebotok facing Calabai on the east coast and Labuhaji on the west coast are the largest – but accommodation is limited to one ultra-expensive resort. The west coast has good beaches, snorkelling and an impressive wall for diving, but the Amanwana resort all but controls the area. The south coast also has good snorkelling and fine beaches. It is possible, but difficult, to visit Moyo independently on a day trip. For travel to the island, the PHPA office in Sumbawa Besar has information and a good map of Pulau Moyo.

Normal access is from Air Bari on the coast north of Sumbawa Besar. Public bemos (1500 rp; one hour) run from Sumbawa Besar to Air Bari three or four times daily to no fixed schedule, starting at around 7 am. They leave from the turn-off to Air Bari at the far end of Jl Sudirman behind the market. Otherwise, you'll have to charter a bemo (around 7500 rp if you bargain hard).

From Air Bari, you can hire a motorised outrigger or fishing boat for the half hour, 3km crossing to the south coast of the island. You must bargain – 10,000 rp each way is a good price, petrol included. The boats can take you to Air Manis, which has reasonable snorkelling. Tanjung Pasir, just to the east, has better snorkelling and the PHPA has built huts for campers here.

It is difficult to arrange a trip through a travel agent. The only agent in Sumbawa Besar is the Hotel Tambora, which primarily handles boat tours from Bali, or the Hotel Tambora's sister hotel, Kencana Beach Hotel, has a good speedboat taking up to 15 people for 350,000 rp per day.

The cheap boat tours between Lombok and Flores stop at Moyo, but since they are not welcome on the west coast and the PHPA levies an entry charge on boats visiting the south, most now go by the less interesting north coast.

Places to Stay The only accommodation is at the *Amanwana Resort* (☎ 22233) on the western side of the island. This ultra-exclusive resort is part of the Aman chain and most guests come on package tours from the Aman hotels on Bali. Princess Di stayed here and could no doubt afford the rates: US$400/450 and US$450/625 per day. The price is incredible when you consider that accommodation is in tents, though admittedly they're luxurious tents on platforms and creature comforts are well catered for. Activities include diving, snorkelling, trekking, windsurfing and fishing. Resort boats run from Badas, but other boats are chased away.

Air Manis has a small, basic resort, but after damage by tidal waves it lies deserted and is unlikely to be rebuilt. You could camp in the ramshackle bungalows if you brought your own food and water, but camping at Tanjung Pasir is a better option – check with the PHPA in Sumbawa Besar.

SUMBAWA

There are four PHPA guard posts on Moyo; one at Tanjung Pasir, the others in villages. Take your own food and water.

Other Attractions

Some of the best *songket* (silver or gold threaded) sarongs are made in the village of **Poto**, 12km east of Sumbawa Besar (600 rp by bus or bemo) and 2km from the small town of Moyo. Traditional designs include the *prahu* (outrigger boat) and ancestor head motif. Modern Balinese-style ikat is also woven on handlooms and is more common than songket; head into the village across from the football field and ask around to see it being made.

Semongkat, 17km south-west of Sumbawa Besar in the hills, is an old swimming pool fed by a mountain river. Once the bathing spot of the sultan, it's now just a slimy, tiled pool. However, the road to Semongkat and beyond has impressive scenery and the area is thickly forested.

The paved road continues past Semongkat to Batu Dulang, a cool mountain village with fine views down the mountain. The mosque dominates the town and Javanese dominate commerce. At the end of the village the asphalt ends and the dirt road continues up into the hills to **Tepal**, an isolated village of 300 people that has remained more traditional because of its lack of contact with the outside world. The buildings at least are more traditional, though Islam and modernity have penetrated. The drawback to visiting Tepal is that it is six hours on foot from Batu Dulang. Horses can be hired for 20,000 rp to do the trek, but are no quicker and more painful on tender behinds. Traders, mostly from Lombok, regularly make the trip, trading eggs, cigarettes, plastic buckets and other luxuries for coffee, the main crop of the village. It is possible to stay with the kepala desa.

Near **Batu Tering** are megalithic sarcophagi believed to be the 2000 year old tombs of ancient chiefs. Footprints in the stones are said to be those of the gods. Batu Tering is about 30km by bemo from Sumbawa Besar, via Semamung – take a bemo from the Brang Bara terminal. The sarcophagi are 4km on foot from the village, and then it is another 2km to **Liang Petang** (Dark Cave) with stalactites and bats.

Air Beling is a pretty waterfall in the southern mountains. Take the road south through Semamung a further 8km to Brangrea, then the turn-off to the falls, from where it is 6km along a rough road with many forks. You'll need a guide.

Buffalo races, wedding ceremonies and *karaci* (traditional stick fighting) are staged regularly at **Pamalung** village, 7km west of Sumbawa Besar, and **Perung**, 12km south. They are put on for the cruise ships from Bali, usually on Tuesday and Saturday.

Central Sumbawa

Apart from Huu, Sumbawa's main tourist destination, this part of Sumbawa is little explored by travellers. Bimanese is spoken throughout this area and it encompasses the former kingdoms of Dompu and Sanggar. There aren't many traditional areas left, but the coastline to the south is quite beautiful and developers are eyeing-off several sites along it. The Tambora Peninsula, home to Gunung Tambora, has some interesting attractions, but travel is tough.

TAMBORA PENINSULA

The Tambora Peninsula, also known as the Sanggar Peninsula, is a large, isolated region in north-central Sumbawa dominated by the 2851m volcano, Gunung Tambora. Tambora's peak was obliterated in the explosion of April 1815, but the volcano has been quiet since. The eruption wiped out the entire population of Tambora and Papekat (two small states at the base of the mountain), as well as devastating much of the rest of Sumbawa.

Tambora can be climbed from the western side. It is a hard three day return walk to the huge crater and when clear there are views as far as Gunung Rinjani (on Lombok), but Tambora gets few climbers because of difficult access and the lack of facilities.

The whole peninsula is still very lightly

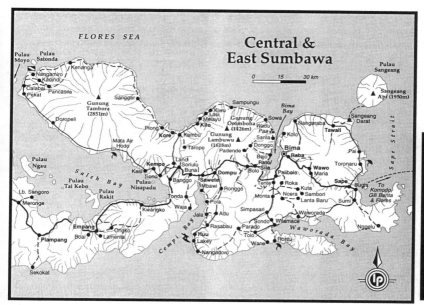

populated despite transmigrasi projects that have seen an influx of settlers from Lombok, Java and Bali. The government is developing agriculture in the area, primarily cattle rearing, plantations and logging on the southern slopes of Tambora. Although parts of Tambora's slopes are thickly forested, the peninsula is otherwise dry and barren.

The main town on the peninsula is the small logging settlement of Calabai. The usual access is by bus from Dompu, or Calabai is only a one hour speedboat trip from Sumbawa Besar, but you'll have to charter at high rates.

Calabai is only a stone's throw from the north-eastern tip of Pulau Moyo, and is a staging post for visiting the beautiful island of Pulau Satonda. Gunung Tambora, also approached from Calabai, is the principal attraction, but though the area has tourism potential, it is a gruelling bus trip to get there and the area has no hotels. The road is being upgraded, which will improve access, but

until then don't expect to meet any other tourists. You'll be hard pressed to find someone who speaks English, so a working knowledge of Indonesian is needed.

Dompu to Calabai

The road from Dompu to Calabai runs along the southern coast of the peninsula and crosses dry volcanic plains, almost deserted except for a few dusty, poor transmigrasi settlements. A few points of interest are passed on the way if you have transport, but if travelling by bus keep heading straight through to Calabai. Buses are infrequent on this route and so crowded that if you're caught mid-way the only space left is usually on the roof.

The road to Calabai branches off the main highway around 20km west of Dompu. It runs along wide Saleh Bay and the first third is paved but bumpy. The road hits the coast near the small village of Sono and offshore is **Pulau Nisapudu**, a small island with white-sand beaches in contrast to the volcanic sands of the coast. Nisapudu is a popular local destination, particularly on and around the Independence Day holiday (17 August) when campers inundate the island and bands play. The island is reputed to have decent snorkelling.

Mata Air Hodo is a fresh-water spring right next to a black-sand beach and the main road, 40km from Dompu. Water, originating from the slopes of Tambora, bubbles into bathing pools and the sea is dead calm and ideal for swimming. This is a popular picnic spot for Dompu residents.

The road then runs through flat, desolate plains extending all the way to the base of Tambora. Large cattle and water buffalo stations have been set up on the savannah, reminiscent of parts of Australia or Africa, and there are even local cowboys to herd them. The road across the plains is being upgraded and the newly sealed sections are almost an autobahn by Indonesian standards.

At the 90km mark is the PT Bali Anakardia **cashew plantation**. Known as *jambu mente* or *jambu monyet* (monkey jambu) in Indonesian, cashews are widely grown in Lombok and Sumbawa because of their drought-resistant qualities. Cashew fruit resembles the jambu, or water apple, grown throughout Indonesia, but is unrelated and smaller. The nut forms like a misshapen growth on top of the fruit. Cashews are grown and part-processed with transmigrasi labour and then shipped to Surabaya in Java. Staff are happy to show you around and the plantation has a guesthouse with eight rooms where you can stay for around 20,000 rp a night.

The last 30km to Calabai is unpaved and bone rattling.

Calabai

On the western tip of the peninsula, Calabai is the main administrative centre with a few small shops, district offices and a lumber yard at the port, but not much else. The large Sunday market attracts traders from as far away as Lombok.

Pulau Moyo lies just across the water. Boats can be chartered to Moyo, but the island's main attractions are on the south and west coasts and access is easier from Sumbawa Besar.

Places to Stay & Eat The timber company has a *guesthouse* overlooking the water – a nice spot to stay if it's not full with company workers. There are no fixed rates, but expect to pay around 15,000 to 20,000 rp a night. Otherwise ask at the office of the *camat* (district government official) in the centre of town. He is a gruff but helpful man.

The *Warung Makan Saung Kuning* on the main road near the timber yard has decent food.

Getting There & Away The Dompu-Calabai road is two-thirds sealed so it is not quite the horror trip it used to be – but the remaining unsealed sections are still very rough. Buses leave Dompu around 8 am, noon and 4 pm for Calabai (4500 rp; five hours) and continue on to the surrounding villages, including Pancasila, if there are enough passengers. These are the most crowded buses in Sum-bawa, if not all Indonesia, and stop everywhere. As well as the usual crush of people inside the bus, a dozen or more passengers ride on the roof. Beg, steal or pay extra to get a more comfortable front seat in Dompu. Going to Dompu from Calabai, three morning buses leave when full and the last bus goes around 3 pm.

Bemos also run from Calabai to the surrounding villages.

The asking rate for a speedboat from Sumbawa Besar is a hefty 200,000 rp, but this is a viable option for a group. Otherwise a lumber ship, the KM *Duta Karya* departs Labuhan Lombok on Saturday evenings, reaching Calabai eight hours later in the middle of the night. It takes passengers, mostly traders coming for the Sunday market. It returns to Lombok on Monday around 10 or 11 am.

Pulau Satonda

This small island, only 4km in circumference, is 12km north of Calabai. Some 4000 years ago it was a volcano that exploded, leaving behind a crater with a fresh water lake. After Tambora's eruption in 1815, the island was swamped and the lake is now a mixture of fresh and salt water with traces of sulphur.

This beautiful island is ringed by beaches, and forest surrounds the 200 hectare lake in the middle, which is 70m deep. Only small fish survive in the lake, but wild deer, pigs, fruitbat, salamander and python inhabit the island, as well as a large variety of birdlife. The coral reef along the southern tip is pleasant for diving.

Pulau Satonda features in Bimanese mythology and the first king of Bima, Sang Bima, is said to have been shipwrecked here after setting sail from Java. He took as his wife the naga (serpent) of the lake and their two sons flew to Bima where they established the Bimanese dynasty.

Pulau Satonda's unique ecosystem has attracted scientists, but most visitors come on cruise ships from Bali or the cheap boat tours that run between Lombok and Flores. Sprightly Pak Pujadir acts as caretaker and spends most of his time alone on the island, taking groups to the lake and looking after the environment. He speaks English, Dutch and a little German and is an informative guide to the island and its lake. Small shelters

for campers have been built on the beach facing the coast from where it is only a five minute walk up the crater to the lake.

Getting There & Away Boats can be hired from Calabai to visit Satonda, but the island is closer to the villages of Nangamiro, 8km north, or Kenanga, 5km further north. Bemos run along the rough road to both villages from Calabai. Pak Pujadir has a house in Kenanga and can arrange transport to the island, or if he is on the island ask at the beach in Kenanga. A small motorboat costs around 30,000 rp for the return trip, and takes 30 minutes one way. In the dry season, strong winds spring up mid-morning and the boats bob around uncomfortably in the swells, so leave as early as possible.

Gunung Tambora

Tambora dominates the landscape of the peninsula and is visible from all points around. It is one of Nusa Tenggara's most important geological sites because of its historic eruption in 1815; for some travellers, it is also one of the main climbing destinations in the eastern islands, but it is only for well prepared, experienced hikers. Compared to Rinjani, it is difficult to get to, a more difficult

---

Eruption of Tambora

Tambora's catastrophic eruption, the largest volcanic eruption in recorded history, began on 5 April 1815 and reached its zenith one week later. Once 4000m high, over 1000m was ripped off Tambora's summit, sending 180 cubic km of ash and rock into the air, some 20 times more than the infamous volcano of Krakatau off the west coast of Java.

Swirling wind tore trees out by the roots and carried away people and animals. Lava streams issued down the flanks of the mountain destroying all in their path and a 30m tsunami followed. At least 10,000 people were killed on Sumbawa and up to 40,000 died later from famine and disease, amounting to 35% of the island's entire population.

The path of destruction didn't stop on Sumbawa. The tsunami swept away villages on Lombok and Balinese villages were also lashed. By far the greatest damage was caused by the huge quantity of ash which blackened the sky for a 500km radius and fell in large quantities as far away as Brunei, 1500km to the north. The effects on world climate were such that it is said Napoleon's attack on Brussels was hampered.

Crop failure on Lombok resulted in over 20% of the population dying of starvation, and similar problems in Bali were accompanied by resultant mudslides that killed 10,000 people.

Today Tambora is still active though no longer threatening. The huge crater left behind by the explosion, 12km in diameter and 600m deep, is calm, but a new volcanic fissure has opened on the south side of the mountain. ■

climb, difficult to organise and guides are essential. The summit is often covered in cloud, so don't count on panoramic views from the top.

Tambora gets few climbers – the majority are 'expeditions' by Javanese university students who come in groups of 20 to 30 in the June/July holiday period. There are no huts on the three day walk so camping equipment is more or less essential, but it cannot be hired on the peninsula.

You can start the climb from a couple of destinations. Pancasila, 15km from Calabai in Desa Tambora, is the main starting point. Surrounded by coffee plantations, Pancasila lies on the slopes of the mountain and is a pretty village in which to spend the night. The kepala desa, Pak Hasanuddin, provides accommodation for around 15,000 rp per night. Guides in Pancasila ask 25,000 rp per day, but will take less with a little negotiation. Porters cost around 15,000 rp per day. A couple of guides claim proficiency in English, but you really need to speak some Indonesian.

Pancasila is a former Dutch coffee plantation and two old factories survive, one in Pancasila and the other in nearby Garuda. The area produces 400 tonnes of robusta coffee annually and you can wander around the village and see the process.

It is also possible to stay in Kadindi with the kepala desa, Pak Mustafa Amat, who is a congenial host and provides bunk accommodation for visitors. Many walkers have stayed here, and his sons act as guides, but Kadindi is 6km down the mountain from Pancasila and not as convenient a place to spend the night.

The mountain is criss-crossed with trails and climbers have become lost. The camat in Calabai insists that climbers register with his office beforehand; it's a good idea, but inconvenient if you don't stay in Calabai. If you take a guide and sign in with the kepala desa in Pancasila or Kadindi there should be no problem.

Climbing Tambora Tambora is usually done as a three day walk. A sleeping bag is essential and a tent is highly recommended. Guides can string up a makeshift shelter of plastic sheeting in case of rain, which can occur at higher altitudes in the dry season, but this will only keep out the lightest of showers. It's not worth contemplating climbing Tambora in the wet season, when the rain is heavy, trails are slippery and leeches are out in force.

Pancasila has a kiosk selling bottled water, biscuits and basic food supplies or the shops in Calabai are better equipped. Bring enough food and water with you – a porter can arrange it all and will cook basic rice and noodle meals; a guide can provide the same service if you go alone. At Pos III is a spring for water – the only water on the mountain.

The walk takes in five posts – Pos I to Pos V – but apart from an open-sided hut at Pos I the other posts are merely clearings for tents.

From Pancasila it's a four hour walk to Pos I. Initially you follow a dirt road through the coffee plantations and a trail branches off the road further up the mountain. The trail runs through light forest before reaching dense forest at Pos I. Wild pig, deer and monkeys inhabit the forest and the lower reaches are home to the rare *Troides haliphron* butterfly, a black and yellow species of birdwing. Unfortunately the butterfly is still hunted by collectors, despite it being a protected species.

It is a hard four hour walk from Pos I to Pos III. You cross gullies and the trail can be slippery after rain. Pos III is the usual camping point. At around 1200m it gets cold at night.

The forest thins out after Pos III and it is a steady climb to Pos IV and then a steeper climb to Pos V; this stretch will take four to five hours in all. Camp the night at Pos V to reach the top for the sunrise, when you have a better, but no means guaranteed, chance of clear views. However, it is barren and very cold and even if you have a good tent and sleeping bag, guides and porters don't, so they are not keen to spend the night at this freezing altitude. It is more usual to camp two nights at Pos III and spend the second day going to the crater and back.

From Pos V it is a 3km, one hour climb to the top along barren scree. The huge crater is some 4km across and 600m deep. A slightly murky turquoise lake is at the bottom and in the wet season it fills up and turns a muddy brown. When clear there are spectacular views across western Sumbawa to Lombok. It is a steep and hazardous climb down to the crater and few people attempt it, with good reason. Steam issues from the sides of the crater, but the main volcanic activity is on the southern slopes of the mountain, well away from the crater.

It is possible to walk from the top back to Pancasila in a long day; it's four hours to Pos III if you camped the night there.

Getting There & Away Buses to Calabai continue on to the surrounding villages and will usually drop you in Pancasila or Kadindi if you ask. Otherwise bemos run from Calabai to Kadindi and Pancasila (1000 rp). Morning buses to Dompu stop in Pancasila in their search for passengers.

DOMPU

The seat of one of Sumbawa's former independent states, Dompu is the third biggest town on the island and capital of the kabupaten of the same name. Dompu is ethnically and linguistically related to Bima.

Unkindly dubbed 'Dump-u', the town is not such a bad place if you have to spend a night. Dompu has a big, colourful market snaking around narrow back streets, but otherwise it boasts no attractions and is merely a stopover on the way to Huu or to Gunung Tambora.

Horse races are held at the Lepadi stadium to the south of town on Independence Day (17 August) and Heroes Day (5 October). Head-butting fights, known as *ntumbututa*, are a traditional attraction in the Dompu area.

Information

The tourist office (☎ 21446) is on Jalan Soekarno Hatta opposite the Wisma Samada, and produces a brochure on the region and will try to help, but English is not spoken.

Change money at the Bank BNI, which is open Monday to Friday from 7.30 am to 3 pm and Saturday from 8.30 am to noon.

Places to Stay & Eat

The *Hotel Manuru Kupang* (☎ 21387), Jalan Jendral Sudirman 1, is opposite the town's oversized mosque. Gloomy rooms cost 11,000 rp or better rooms are 16,000 rp; all come with mandi.

Closer to the market on Jalan Soekarno Hatta, *Hotel Pusaka* (☎ 21577) has bright and presentable but overpriced singles/doubles for 15,000/20,000 rp with mandi. Directly opposite, the *Wisma Kartika* (☎ 21429) has similar but older rooms for the same price.

If you continue along Jalan Soekarno Hatta one block to the traffic lights, on the corner you'll find the best hotel in town, the *Wisma Samada* (☎ 21417) at Jl Gajah Mada 18. This spick-and-span place has rooms around small garden areas for 20,000 rp with mandi or 35,000 rp with air-con.

Restaurants are very limited. Apart from some cheap *warungs* around the market, a couple of mediocre Javanese restaurants are near the Hotel Pusaka on Jalan Soekarno Hatta. Nearby, the *Rumah Makan Meriah* is at least a bright and presentable place for Padang food.

Getting There & Away

If you're travelling between Sumbawa Besar and Bima, you don't get to see Dompu: buses detour via the lonely Ginte bus terminal (on a hill 2km out of Dompu). From there, bemos run into town (300 rp).

Buses run from Ginte bus terminal to Bima (1800 rp; two hours), Sape (3100 rp; 3½ hours) and Sumbawa Besar (5500 rp; 4½ hours). A combined air-con bus/ferry ticket through to Mataram costs 13,000 rp (17,000 rp with air-con).

HUU/LAKEY

Huu is best known as a stronghold of one of the most traditional cultures in the world – surf culture. Several hotels have sprung up along Lakey Beach, 3km from Huu village,

SUMBAWA

to cater to surfers who have been coming here since the mid 1980s. Lately an attempt has been made to woo the average garden-variety tourist to Lakey's long stretch of tree-lined, white-sand beach. It is certainly a superb beach, and the surf breaks out on the reef, which makes for sheltered swimming closer to shore. Huu is far and away Sumbawa's major tourist destination, and although Australian and American surfers like to think of it as their domain, increasing numbers of non-surfers are visiting.

The great attraction of Huu is its variety of surf breaks and the availability of decent accommodation. Right in front of the accommodation strip is Lakey Peak, breaking left and right, while just along is Lakey Pipe, a left hander. Nangas, another left hander, is further along the bay in front of the small Tunangas river. Periscopes, a right hander, is off by itself, 1km north. Local lore has it that Periscopes was 'discovered' in 1985 an by Australian surfing tour operator, starting the boom at Lakey, which is one of most popular surf destinations outside Bali.

Lakey (pronounced 'luck-ay' but 'lucky' will do) is now on the international surfing championship circuit. The ugly judge's box out on the water near the reef was built for the 1997 competition, won by a Balinese surfer, Rizal Tanjung. His win was a real fillip for the local surfing scene.

Information

A few of the hotels will change US and Australian dollars at poor rates. Bring enough rupiah with you. The nearest bank is in Dompu.

Lakey now has a wartel on the main road opposite the entrance to Lakey Peak Bungalows. It is the only telephone at Lakey. They can book and reconfirm flights with Merpati in Bima (best of luck) or hotels can do it for you.

Places to Stay & Eat

Mona Lisa Bungalows is one of the largest hotels and a good place to start looking. It has a good restaurant and comfortable bungalows with bathroom for 15,000/20,000 rp

or well appointed air-con bungalows for 30,000/40,000 rp. Like all the places here, prices drop outside the May to August peak season.

Heading south from Mona Lisa, *Hotel Aman Gati* is another popular place and has the best bungalows in Lakey. The good restaurant has a huge TV screen showing non-stop surfing videos. Bungalows with fan and bathroom cost 25,000/35,000 rp for singles/doubles. Quite luxurious bungalows with air-con cost 60,000/80,000 rp.

Next along, *Lakey Peak Bungalows* has a dowdy restaurant, but good bungalows for 20,000 rp and more are being built. *Balumba* is cheaper and has bungalows starting from 15,000 rp.

Intan Lestari is the one of the original surf camps, with a rustic little restaurant, and rooms for 12,000 rp without mandi and 15,000 rp with mandi. The position is hard to beat – right in front of Lakey Peak and Lakey Pipe. Motorbikes are available for rent.

South of Intan Lestari, *Anton* has a few dilapidated bungalows for 5000 rp per person (the cheapest on the beach), but most popular are the comfortable bungalows for 25,000 rp a double with bathtub, shower and mosquito net – good value.

Anton's restaurant is nothing to speak of, but right next door is the French-managed *Fatmah Restoran* which is the best on the beach. The only drawback is that service can be slow when the crowds pile in.

At the very southern end of the beach is *Anton II*, promising to be the most luxurious hotel of all, but building has stalled due to lack of money.

A couple of hundred metres north of Mona Lisa, *Primadona Lakey Cottages* has a huge restaurant, the de rigeur pool table and table tennis. Rooms back from the beach have shared mandi and cost 15,000 rp, but those with bath for 20,000 rp are better value.

Further north, *Kambera Cottages* is out of the scene and costs 15,000/20,000 rp with mandi. *Periscopes* is around 1.5km north of the main beach towards the village and well off the main road. Its main attraction is the surf break of the same name, but the accommodation for 10,000 rp is basic and too far out to be appealing.

Getting There & Away

Huu is 44km south of Dompu and 90km from Bima. It is a god almighty effort to reach Huu by public transport. From Sumbawa Besar or Bima take a bus to Dompu's Ginte bus terminal on the northern outskirts of town, then a bemo (300 rp) to the *rumah sakit* (hospital). From here take a cidomo (250 rp per person) to the Lepardi bus terminal on the southern outskirts, from where four buses a day run to Rasabau (750 rp; 1½ hours), starting at 7.30 am. From Rasabau, 11km before Huu, you then have to take a bemo (500 rp) to the beach.

Try doing this with a surfboard and you'll soon see why everyone takes a taxi from Bima airport. The taxi price is fixed at a steep 67,500 rp.

When a bus arrives at the Dompu bus terminal, the sight of a 'turis' sends the transport guys into a frenzy. A chartered bemo or minibus taxi from Dompu to Huu costs 30,000 to 40,000 rp depending on your bargaining skills. It is an excellent paved road from Dompu to Huu.

East Sumbawa

DONGGO

From Rato/Sila, on the Dompu to Bima road, infrequent buses run to the villages of Donggo on the slopes of Gunung Lambuwu. It is 4km along a good road and then 10km on a rough road up the mountain. It may be possible to stay with the villagers. The villages have a few traditional houses and superb views. The Dou Donggo (Mountain People) living in these highlands speak an archaic form of the Bima language and may be descended from the original inhabitants of Sumbawa.

Numbering about 20,000, they've adopted Islam and Christianity over their traditional animism beliefs in the last few decades, with

varying degrees of enthusiasm; they're being absorbed into Bimanese culture and will probably disappear as a distinct group. The most traditional village is Mbawa where, at least until a few years ago, people still wore distinctive black clothes, and a few *uma leme* (traditional houses whose design was intimately connected with the traditional religion) were still standing. Nowadays the Donggo have been integrated into modern society and though they still remain a much studied group, traditional ways are not much in evidence.

WADU PAA

At the entrance to Teluk Bima (Bima Bay), Wadu Paa is an important archaeological site next to a freshwater spring on the shore of the bay. The low cliffs in the small inlet house carved rocks, in two locations, dating from the Hindu period. They are badly worn, but a carving of Ganesh, the elephant-headed Hindu god, can be made out.

Infrequent buses from Rato/Sila on the highway run past Wadu Paa, or it can also be reached by chartered boat from the other side of the bay at Kolo.

Another inscribed stone, the **Wadu Tunti**, is near the village of **Padende**, inland a few kilometres north of Rato/Sila. It's carved with human figures and the undeciphered inscriptions are said to date from the Javanese kingdom of Majapahit.

BIMA & RABA

Bima and Raba together form the major town in the eastern half of Sumbawa. Bima, Sumbawa's chief port, is the main centre and commercial hub. Raba, a few kilometres south-east, is the departure point for buses east to Sape, where you get the ferry to Komodo or Flores. Raba was established during the colonial period as the main administrative centre to escape the mosquito ridden plains of the coast.

The Bima region has been known since the 14th century for its sturdy horses, which even then were exported to Java, along with timber, particularly sappanwood, which is used for making dyes. Bima was an important

SUMBAWA

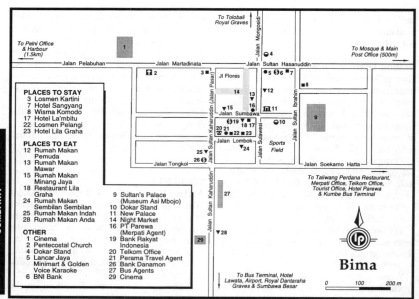

PLACES TO STAY
3 Losmen Kartini
7 Hotel Sangyang
8 Wisma Komodo
17 Hotel La'mbitu
22 Losmen Pelangi
23 Hotel Lila Graha

PLACES TO EAT
12 Rumah Makan Pemuda
13 Rumah Makan Mawar
15 Rumah Makan Minang Jaya
18 Restaurant Lila Graha
24 Rumah Makan Sembilan Sembilan
25 Rumah Makan Indah
28 Rumah Makan Anda

OTHER
1 Cinema
2 Pentecostal Church
4 Dokar Stand
5 Lancar Jaya Minimart & Golden Voice Karaoke
6 BNI Bank
9 Sultan's Palace (Museum Asi Mbojo)
10 Dokar Stand
11 New Palace
14 Night Market
16 PT Parewa (Merpati Agent)
19 Bank Rakyat Indonesia
20 Telkom Office
21 Perama Travel Agent
26 Bank Danamon
27 Bus Agents
29 Cinema

port on the trade route through the eastern islands from at least the early 16th century and had long contacts with Java. Local rulers claimed descent from Javanese royalty; before the arrival of Islam, Bima was a Hindu trading kingdom. The name Bima is derived from a hero of the Hindu epic, the *Mahabharata*.

Bima became a Muslim sultanate in 1621 under Sultan Abdul Kahir after being invaded by Makassar in 1619. It became a vassal state, and Bima expanded its influence despite the intervention of the Dutch. The VOC battled Makassar in the 1660s and blockaded the port of Bima to stop Bimanese intervention. After defeating Makassar with Bugis allies in 1669, the Dutch established their dominance of the spice trade and set up a fort at Bima.

However, Dutch control on Sumbawa was limited and Bima established links and laid claim to parts of western Sumba. In the 18th century it took over the rule of western Flores

from Makassar, and Bima became the pre-eminent kingdom on Sumbawa.

As the Dutch increased their stranglehold on trade, Bima's importance as a port declined, but the Dutch did not officially annexe Bima until 1905.

Today, the former sultan's palace apart, Bima is a rather practical place. Bima has a busy port that ships out buffaloes, cattle, onions and salt to other parts of Indonesia. Huge salt pans can be seen along the bay near the airport, and Bima's onions, though small, contain less water and are regarded as among the tastiest in Indonesia.

Bima is a relatively wealthy area and staunchly Islamic. Despite the high cost of the pilgrimage to Mecca (the equivalent of a dozen water buffaloes), Bima sends more than 2000 on the *haj* each year, one of the highest pilgrimage rates per head of population in Indonesia.

Bima is not really a tourist destination, but has a good range of services and shops, and the Jl Flores night market is worth a wander. Once a centre for the 'hello mister' cult, Bima is a bit more sophisticated these days, but the kids still insist on shouting out their only two words of English.

Information
Tourist Office The tourist information office (☎ 44331) is near the Telkom office on Jl Soekarno Hatta, about 2km from town past the Hotel Parewa. It is open Monday to Friday from 7 am to 3 pm, and on Saturday mornings until noon.

Money The Bank BNI on Jl Sultan Hasanuddin changes foreign currency and travellers cheques at reasonable rates, as does the Bank Rakyat Indonesia on Jl Sumbawa. If you're heading east, this is the last place to change money before Labuanbajo (Flores).

Post & Communications The main post office is on Jl Sultan Hasanuddin, about 500m east of the Hotel Sangyang. Opening hours are Monday to Saturday from 8 am to 2 pm. The Telkom office is on Jl Soekarno Hatta, about 2km from the town centre, and is open 24 hours. Wartels in the centre of town include the Telkom Warpostel Remaja on Jl Lombok and one in the Lancar Jaya Minimart on Jl Sultan Hasanuddin.

Travel Agencies Although Bima itself is not a major tourist destination, a number of travel agents cater to groups heading through to Komodo. They can also arrange trips and transport for individuals and small groups to attractions around Bima.

PT Parewa (☎ 43440), Jl Sumbawa 19, is good for air tickets and has a large boat for charter to Komodo. Perama (☎ 42888) on Jl Lombok sells tickets for its boat tours between Flores and Lombok, but offers little else.

Grand Komodo (☎ 42018), Jl Salahudin 11, is based in Bali and offers tours of Komodo and diving trips. Bintang Laut Express (☎ 43112), Jl Soekarno Hatta 26 in Raba, offers a variety of tours including Komodo tours for US$250 per person, and

more reasonably priced tours around Bima. Another agent is Fajar Bima (☎ 42197) at Jl Soekarno Hatta 30.

Sultan's Palace
The former home of Bima's rulers, until they were put out of a job after Indonesia's independence, is now the Museum Asi Mbojo. The building itself is less impressive than its counterpart in Sumbawa Besar, but the exhibits (chainmail shirts, sedan chairs, battle flags, weapons, sacred kris, jewellery, costumes and other heirlooms of the sultan) are interesting. You can see the royal bedchamber (with its four poster bed, and Koran on the dressing table). Built in 1927, the palace had fallen into complete disrepair by the late 1950s, but has been restored. The older wooden palace, the *asi bou*, lies in the grounds, but the newer palace follows the same traditional layout.

The museum is open daily from 8 am to 6 pm. The museum collection has recently been substantially upgraded with impressive artefacts donated by the royal family. The entry fee has also been substantially upgraded – a hefty 5000 rp for tourists.

Royal Graves
Various ancient graves are scattered around town. The royal tombs of Dantaraha, on a hill in the south of town, are the most important. From the centre of town, head south to the bus terminal and take the left fork, then the next main road on the left. It can also be reached from a side road next to the stadium near the Hotel Parewa.

The main bunker-style stone tomb is that of the first sultan, Abdul Kahir, and is topped by carved, Muslim tombstones. Good views of the town can be had from the hill and it's a pleasant 15 minute walk to get there.

Other royal graves are at Tolobali, just north of the river. Head north on Jl Mongosidi and turn right at the school. Further along Jl Mongosidi is the site of original Dutch fort, but nothing remains.

Horse Racing
Horse races are a popular pastime and are

SUMBAWA

held every Sunday in the dry season from May to October at the horse stadium at Desa Panda, 14km from town towards the airport. Practice sessions are held during the week. Boys on horses are cheered on by the crowds as they thunder around the dusty track, and the winner receives a small cow as prize money. There's a large grandstand and a gaggle of warungs. The height of the race carnival is 17 August.

Weaving

Bimanese weaving is of the Islamic tradition, and tends to avoid human or animal motifs. The *songket* technique is widely used, producing bright patterns from metallic thread. The *tembe* or sarong is most common and features plain checked patterns *(bali)* or a supplementary weave that looks like embroidery *(salungka)*. Bright *salampe* shawls use metallic thread and are more attractive souvenirs.

Much of the weaving is done in the suburb of Raba Dompu, on the outskirts of Raba, 5km east of Bima, and Ntobo, 10km from Bima. Muatmainah, at Jl Hasanuddin 46, sells a wide variety of cloth.

Places to Stay

Bima is compact, and most hotels are in the middle of town.

A good budget option is the *Wisma Komodo* (☎ 42070) on Jl Sultan Ibrahim. This government-run hostel hosts a lot of groups and can be full, but it's well run and the manager speaks excellent English. Double rooms are worn and cost 10,000 rp or 15,000 rp with mandi.

An old favourite is the *Hotel Lila Graha* (☎ 42740) at Jl Lombok 20. It has an excellent restaurant and is still popular, but while standards gradually slip the prices keep rising. Rooms without mandi for 9000/ 12,500 rp are dingy or singles/doubles with mandi for 15,000/17,500 rp are expensive, but better. Air-con double rooms with hot showers go for 42,500 rp. Add 10% tax to the rates, but breakfast is included.

The Lila Graha also has a new annexe next door. The mid-range rooms are well appointed

but dark and the building is poorly designed. Singles/doubles cost 55,000/66,000 rp.

Bima has a number of cheaper but seedy hotels. *Losmen Pelangi* (☎ 42878), next to the Lila Graha, has boxy doubles for 10,000 rp, or 15,000 rp with mandi. The cheapest in town is the crumbling *Losmen Kartini* (☎ 42072) at Jl Pasar 11. You can stay there for 4000 rp per person, but it is not recommended for women travelling alone.

The ramshackle *Hotel Sangyang* (☎ 42017) on Jl Sultan Hasanuddin was once the best in town, but now looks like a bomb hit it; however, the large, carpeted rooms out the back are quite good and have air-con and hot water (maybe) for 30,000/35,000 rp.

Hotel Parewa (☎ 42652), 1km from the town centre at Jl Soekarno Hatta 40, is a comfortable mid-range hotel and has a good upstairs restaurant, but the internal-facing rooms are dark and in need of maintenance. Economy rooms with fan cost 25,000 rp, or standard rooms with air-con and TV go for 35,000 rp and 40,000 rp. All have attached bathrooms, but the plumbing is hopeless.

The best hotel by far in the town centre is *Hotel La'mbitu* (☎ 42222), at Jl Sumbawa 4. Like most Bima hotels, rooms are internal facing, but this new hotel is well appointed and has a pleasant restaurant upstairs. Standard rooms with fan and hot water cost 27,500 rp, and air-con rooms are 44,000 rp or 55,000 rp with fridge.

The most luxurious hotel is the *Hotel Lawata* (☎ 43696), Jl Sultan Salahuddin, 10km from town on the way to the airport. It has a swimming pool, an excellent restaurant and attractive bungalows perched over the sea for 42,000/47,000 rp, or from 59,000/ 65,000 rp with air-con.

Places to Eat

Restaurant Lila Graha, attached to the hotel of the same name, has a long menu of good Chinese, Indonesian and seafood cuisine, with a few western dishes thrown in. The *Hotel Parewa* restaurant also has good Chinese food, as does the *Rumah Makan Pemuda* on Jl Sulawesi.

Rumah Makan Sembilan Sembilan on Jl

Lombok near the Hotel Lila Graha specialises in fried chicken and has other good Chinese and Indonesian dishes. The *Taliwang Perdana* on Jl Soekarno Hatta, 500m from the sultan's palace, is a pleasant, open restaurant and does excellent Taliwang chicken.

The *Rumah Makan Minang Jaya* on Jl Sumbawa is a good, clean Padang restaurant, while a couple of more basic restaurants, the *Rumah Makan Indah* and *Rumah Makan Anda*, are along Jl Sultan Kaharuddin. The *night market* has stalls selling interesting snacks and on the same street is the *Rumah Makan Mawar*, a very popular local haunt. The Mawar has unusual decor with tables in a ring facing each other. The bench seats are favoured by courting couples and the mostly Chinese food is good, although a little expensive.

Entertainment

Although Bima is a small, conservative city like most others in Indonesia, it has undeservedly acquired a reputation as some sort of outpost of Islamic fundamentalism. In fact, compared to the towns on Flores, it is almost a swinging city. Well, it has a couple of slightly seedy karaoke bars if you are desperate for something to do. The *Golden Voice Karaoke* is above the Lancar Jaya Minimart on Jl Sultan Hasanuddin, or the wilder *Ayoedia Karaoke* faces the bay on the airport road, next to the Sonco Tengge Hotel, 1km south of town.

Getting There & Away

Air Merpati (☎ 42697) has its office at Jl Soekarno Hatta 60, or PT Parewa is a better organised Merpati agent on the corner of Jl Sumbawa and Jl Monginsidi. Small planes fly between Bima and Denpasar (Bali), Mataram (Lombok), Labuanbajo (Flores), Ruteng (Timor), Ende (Flores) and Tambolaka (Sumba). Airport tax is 5500 rp.

Flights are subject to overbooking and cancellation. In the peak tourist months of July and August, the airport can fill up with stranded passengers, so it pays to allow a day or two extra for your schedule.

Bus Bima bus terminal, for most buses to and from the west, is a 10 minute walk from the centre of town. In addition to the daytime buses, there are night buses to Lombok, Bali or Java with ferry fares included. Several bus ticket offices are near the corner of Jl Sultan Kaharuddin and Jl Soekarno Hatta.

Most buses to Lombok leave around 6 or 7 am and 7 pm; try to book your ticket before departure. Fares to Mataram range from 14,000 rp for non air-con to 22,000 rp for the luxury, air-con buses that take about 11 hours. Surabaya Indah and Langsung Indah have the best buses. You can take these air-con buses to Sumbawa Besar for around 9000 rp. Many continue on to Denpasar (40,000 to 45,000 rp), arriving at 11 am the next morning, or you can even continue right through to Surabaya and Jakarta.

Sumbawa is also serviced by smaller, crowded, non air-con buses that are the local supply line, stopping anywhere and everywhere. They run between 6 am and 5 pm. Destinations from Bima include Dompu (1800 rp; two hours) and Sumbawa Besar (7200 rp; seven hours).

Buses east to Sape go from Kumbe bus terminal in Raba, a 20 minute (300 rp) bemo ride east of Bima. You should be able to pick up a bemo easily on Jl Sultan Kaharuddin or Jl Soekarno Hatta. Buses leave Kumbe terminal for Sape (2000 rp; two hours) from about 6 am until 5 pm. Don't rely on these local buses to get you to Sape in time for the morning ferry to Komodo or Flores. Alternatively, three big buses come through Bima from Surabaya at 5 am and continue on to Sape for 2500 rp. You can arrange this at the Bima bus terminal the evening before or turn up around 4.30 am at the terminal. The other alternative is a chartered bemo, which will do the run in 1½ hours and costs 20,000 to 25,000 rp with bargaining. A taxi will cost around 35,000 rp.

Boat The Pelni office is at Bima's port at Jl Pelabuhan 103. The *Pangrango* calls at Bima, sailing to and from Ujung Pandang (Sulawesi), Labuanbajo and Waingapu (Flores) and Kupang (Timor).

SUMBAWA

Getting Around

To/From the Airport Taxi prices are fixed at 12,500 rp for the 17km, 20 minute trip to town. To Huu it costs 67,500 rp, Dompu 35,000 rp and Sape 46,000 rp.

The airport is right on the highway, so you can walk out to the main road about 100m in front of the terminal and catch a bus there. Any local bus from Dompu or Sumbawa Besar can take you into town, but they can be very crowded and a taxi may be your best bet.

Local Transport Bemos around town cost 300 rp per person; cidomo are 200 rp.

Minibus taxis can be chartered at the airport and around town for trips outside Bima. For a day trip they generally want at least 100,000 rp, more if you venture off the sealed roads. Chartered bemos are cheaper.

SAMBORI

Sambori is one of the most traditional villages in Sumbawa. The village is Muslim, but it has an impressive collection of traditional houses in a pretty mountain setting.

The Sambori traditional house, or *uma lengge*, is an A-frame construction of three levels. Raised off the ground, the first platform is a sitting area with a ladder leading up through a trapdoor to the main house of one or two rooms where a family lives. Above this is an attic where rice is stored. The roof finials, known as *wange*, are usually buffalo horn symbols or winged symbols, said to represent Garuda. Uma lengge can be seen in other parts of Sumbawa, but Sambori is one of the few places where the houses are still inhabited and not merely used for grain storage.

The Sambori people are ethnically distinct from the Bimanese and speak their own language, Nggahi Sambori. The Sambori are more often referred to as the Donggo Bawah (Lower Donggo) by the Bimanese, as opposed to the Donggo Atas (Upper Donngo) or Dou Donggo to the west of Bima. Both groups are regarded as mountain hicks by the city-dwelling Bimanese.

The road to Sambori was built in the mid 90s and Sambori now gets a steady trickle of visitors. The villagers are unwilling to discuss or have lost their old traditions, but they are noted for their burial customs. Some of the thatch roofs have holes in them – this means that someone has recently died in the house. In respect for the dead, the body is not shunted down through the trapdoor, but carried out horizontally through a hole made in the roof. The body is placed on the platform beneath and cloth is strung around the base of the house, forming a temporary shrine where mourners wail.

Getting There & Away

Frequent bemos and buses run from Bima to Tente, just off the highway 24km south of Bima. From Tente only four buses per day go to Sambori (1000 rp) starting at 6 am.

From Tente the road continues 4km to Cenggu, just past Roka. The turn-off to Sambori from Cenggu leads up into the hills until it reaches the village of Kuta. Kuta is the first village of the Sambori people, full of kids screaming 'hello mister'. Past Kuta up through teak forest is the right turn leading to Sambori Baru, the new village built after independence. This stretch of road has spectacular views. It is then 5km along a very steep and rough road to Sambori – not for the faint hearted.

SOUTH COAST

The sparsely populated south coast has some wonderful beaches. **Wane** is a beautiful white-sand beach flanked by great outcrops of rock. It is promoted in Bima as the next Huu, but the sea is too rough for swimming, the surf is no good and there are no facilities. It can be reached by car via Tente on the highway and along the paved road to Parado.

Of more interest is the beach at **Rontu**, which has accommodation, but it is also difficult to reach. The turn-off is at Simpasari, halfway along the road to Parado. From Simpasari it is 5km along a terrible road to the large village of Sondo, from where the road inexplicably becomes sealed again (not quite inexplicably – Sondo votes for the opposition Muslim party, the PPP, and so it has missed out on a road upgrade). Buses run between Bima and Sondo (1500 rp), but for the last 9km to Rontu you'll have to hire a horse-drawn dokar for 1000 rp per person.

Rontu has a beautiful white-sand beach, partly sheltered by a reef. *Rontu Beach Bungalow* is a new place with a large, impressive restaurant, but the rooms are very simple for 25,000 rp. Apart from the constant southerlies blowing off the ocean, this is a fine place to get away from it all, if you can be bothered making the long journey. You'll probably be the only guests.

WAWO
On the main highway between Bima and Sape, the Wawo area is noted for its traditional houses, uma lengge. The most impressive are at Maria, just off the highway, and can be seen from the bus on the way to Sape. Maria is possibly the most visited 'traditional' village in Sumbawa because of its easy access, but the houses are no longer inhabited and serve as granaries. The Dou Wawo people are considered ethnically distinct from the Bimanese and speak a different language, but because of the proximity to the main road, Islam and modernisation have long penetrated these villages.

SAPE
Sape is a pleasant little town with amiable people and an immense number of dokars, which the locals call 'Ben Hur'. These jingling little buggies with their skinny, pompomed horses don't look much like Roman chariots, but the drivers obviously think they're Charlton Hestons as they race each other along the main street after dark.

There are two colourful daily markets in town; one right in the centre and the other behind the bus terminal. Sape has a handful of basic hotels and rumah makan, but it is a more convenient place to overnight than Bima if you want to catch the ferry to Komodo or Flores. The ferry leaves from Pelabuhan Sape, a Bugis fishing village, about 4km east of Sape. There's lots of boat building going on along the street running down to the port.

Information
The PHPA office is about 2.5km from the town centre along the road to Pelabuhan Sape. The office has some interesting brochures and maps, and is open daily.

Places to Stay
The most convenient place to stay if you arrive the night before the ferry leaves is *Losmen Mutiara*, nestled just outside the entrance to the port. The best rooms are upstairs, with access to a back balcony overlooking the harbour. All rooms have shared mandi and cost 7500/10,000 rp. There are a couple of small warungs and shops opposite the hotel, but if you're in Sape for more than a day or so, the 4km dokar ride into town could get tiresome.

In town, *Losmen Friendship* lives up to its name. Clean doubles with shared mandi cost 8000 rp (10,000 rp with private mandi). Two cheaper, more basic places are the *Losmen Ratna Sari* and the *Losmen Give* with rooms from 7000 rp.

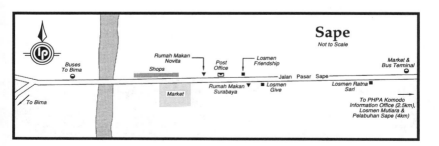

Getting There & Away

Bus Buses always meet ferries arriving at Pelabuhan Sape; they are usually express services direct to Lombok or Bali. Some sample fares for express air-con buses are Mataram (26,000 rp), Denpasar (40,000 rp), and Surabaya (50,000 rp).

For most destinations on Sumbawa, you will need to go to Bima for an onward bus. Buses leave from both Sape bus terminals every half hour for Raba (2000 rp; two hours) until around 5 pm. From Raba take a bemo to Bima (300 rp; 20 minutes). Taxi drivers may tell you buses have stopped running and you must charter a taxi to Bima – walk away and ask someone else. If you're coming from Mataram to Sape, make sure your bus continues right through to Sape and doesn't terminate in Bima.

Boat The ferries to Labuanbajo (Flores), stopping at Komodo Island on the way, leave at 8 am every day except Friday from Pelabuhan Sape. Tickets can be purchased at the pier about one hour before departure. In both directions, the ferries stop at Komodo, but can't dock at the island, so small fishing boats shuttle to Loh Liang for an extra 1500 rp. Sape to Komodo costs 10,000 rp, or to Labuanbajo 11,500 rp. You can take a bicycle from Sape across to Labuanbajo for 2000 rp, a motorcycle for 10,000 rp or a car for 97,550 rp.

The duration of the crossing varies with the tides and weather, but allow five to seven hours to Komodo and eight to 10 hours to Labuanbajo. Two companies operate on alternate days – the ferry leaving Sape on Monday, Wednesday and Saturday is the biggest and slightly faster. Ferries have been known to break down and be out of action for weeks, and a few years back passengers were stranded at Sape when a party of government officials commandeered a ferry for a jaunt to Komodo. Check the schedules in Bima.

You can also charter your own boat to Komodo – Bima travel agents have well equipped boats based at Pelabuan Sape – but this is more easily and cheaply done from Labuanbajo.

Getting Around

A dokar between Sape and the ferry pier costs 250 rp per person if you share, but charter rates are more like 1000 rp.

AROUND SAPE

Public bemos run along the north coast from Sape to Tawali. Some good beaches can be found on the coast near **Toronaro**. From Tawali, head to Sangeang Darat on the coast. The village is home to people resettled from **Pulau Sangeang**, a large island with an explosive volcano, Sangeang Api. When quiet, it is possible to rent boats across to the island and climb the 1950m volcano, but recent eruptions make this impossible. From Sangeang Darat, there are great views of the towering peak, which can be seen belching smoke from as far away as Labuanbajo.

Boats can be chartered from Sape to **Gili Banta**, near Komodo. It has good beaches and is noted as a nesting ground for green turtles, which unfortunately are still hunted. Most visitors are divers, attracted by the coral formations and the chance to see sharks.

Komodo & Rinca

Locator & Map Index

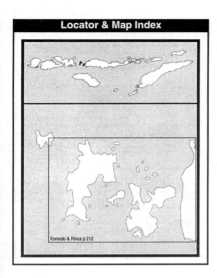

Komodo & Rinca p 212

Highlights

- **Komodo Dragons** – the most famed beasties in Indonesia can be seen on the islands of Komodo or Rinca.

- **Diving & Snorkelling** – Pantai Merah (Red Beach) has accessible snorkelling close to park headquarters on Komodo and good diving around the many islands of the national park.

- **Hiking** – see the dragons (maybe) in remote locations away from the main viewing area and climb Gunung Ara for views across the islands.

A hilly, desolate island sandwiched between Flores and Sumbawa, Komodo's big attraction is its monitor lizards – 3m-long, 100kg monsters known as *ora* by the locals and tagged 'Komodo dragons' by westerners. The island is surrounded by some of the most tempestuous waters in Indonesia, fraught with riptides and whirlpools. From the sea it looks a far more fitting habitat for monstrous lizards than for the few hundred people who live in the island's lone village.

Komodo gets a constant stream of visitors these days, but to understand how far off the beaten track it used to be, read *Zoo Quest for a Dragon* by naturalist-adventurer David Attenborough, who filmed the dragons in 1956. In 1997, the national park's tourism mushroomed to 32,000 visitors, mostly from the USA, Germany, UK and the Netherlands. Only 6% of visitors were Indonesian.

Dragons also inhabit the nearby islands of Rinca and Padar, and coastal western Flores. Some people now prefer to visit Rinca than Komodo, as it's closer to Flores, has fewer visitors and dragon-spotting is less organised.

ORIENTATION & INFORMATION
Komodo

The only village is Kampung Komodo, a Bajau/Bugis fishing village on the east coast. On the same bay and 30 minutes' walk north of the village is Loh Liang, the tourist accommodation camp run by the PHPA. The park entrance fee is 20,000 rp, payable on arrival at Loh Liang and valid for three days. If you are going on to Rinca, keep your park entrance ticket, as Rinca is part of the same national park.

The PHPA warns you not to walk outside the camp without one of its guides. Longer treks around the island can be organised, and the PHPA office has a list of guides' fees for them. Although the dragons are a docile bunch for the most part, a lot of emphasis is put on 'danger' – this includes encounters with Komodo dragons that can snap your leg as fast as they'll cut a goat's throat, or having a cobra spit poison at you. Several years ago an elderly European did wander off alone and was never found. Locals are attacked periodically, most commonly while sleeping out in the open.

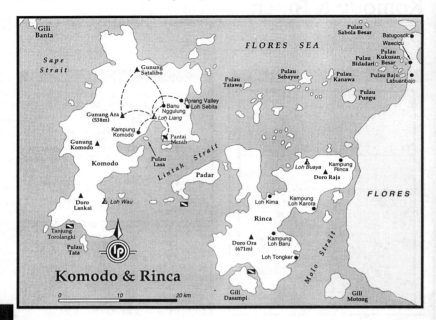

Komodo & Rinca

0   10   20 km

Rinca

The PHPA tourist camp is at Loh Buaya and it's possible to camp in some of the villages. The park entrance fee here is also 20,000 rp; PHPA guides are 1500 rp per person. Keep your ticket if you're going on to Komodo.

DRAGON SPOTTING
Komodo

You're likely to see dragons all year at Banu Nggulung, a dry river bed about a half hour walk from Loh Liang. The ritual feeding of dragons with goats is a thing of the past and dragons are now only fed when the PHPA wants to do a head count. The watering hole at Banu Nggulung still attracts dragons, but since the feeding has stopped numbers have declined. It is more than likely you will see a dragon, but in the future sightings may not be guaranteed as before.

A little 'grandstand' overlooks the river bed where the dragons gather. Spectators are fenced off from the dragons – don't expect to walk up to the dragons and have them say 'cheese'. A telephoto lens is handy, but not essential. A guide costs 3000 rp, or 1000 rp per person for groups of more than three. The PHPA prefers to organise fixed times and take large groups, although it's less zoo-like is you go in a smaller group.

You might spot dragons on some of the other walks (see Other Activities later in this chapter) and a few lazy examples can often be seen around the tourist camp looking for food.

Rinca

There are no established dragon feeding places on Rinca, so spotting monitors is more a matter of luck and your guide's knowledge, but high numbers of dragons are recorded around the PHPA post at Loh Buaya.

Other wildlife is abundant and includes several monkey colonies, wild water buffalos, deer, horses, pigs, bush turkeys and eagles.

Rinca is easily reached from Labuan-bajo by boat and is ideal for a dragon-spotting day trip.

DIVING & SNORKELLING

Good snorkelling can be found at **Pantai Merah** (Red Beach) and the small island of **Pulau Lasa** near Kampung Komodo. Dolphins are common in the seas between Komodo and Flores, and the area is also on a whale migration route from the Indian Ocean to the South China Sea.

Bomb fishing has destroyed up to 80% of the reefs in the national park. The southern tips of Komodo and Rinca have been less affected, with only 20% damage recorded.

The areas around Pulau Tata and Gili Dasampi offer some of the best diving in the park, but the currents can be ferocious. The southern tip of Padar also has reasonable diving.

The national park has a dive cooperative and diving and snorkelling can be arranged at Loh Liang. Mask and fins for snorkelling cost $US8 and boat rental is US$30 for four people. Dive packages start at US$150 for two divers. See Labuanbajo in the Flores chapter for dive sites and operators outside the national park.

To view coral without getting your feet wet, take the glass-bottom boat that cruises the bay around Loh Liang and Pantai Merah; it costs US$8 per person.

OTHER ACTIVITIES

Most visitors stay one night at Komodo and only visit Banu Nggulung, but Komodo has a number of other things to do and it is quite easy to spend two days or more on the island. Komodo is very hot most of the year, so take water on the walks.

Walks include the climb to **Gunung Ara** (538m). A guide costs 25,000 rp for up to five people and the trip takes 3½ hours return. The chances of seeing a dragon are slim, but from the mountain top there are expansive views right across the island.

Poreng Valley, 5.5km from Loh Liang, is another favourite dragon haunt and has a more out-in-the-wild feeling than Banu Nggulung. Guides cost 15,000 rp for five people and you can also continue on to Loh Sabita (35,000 rp for a guide). You may not spot dragons, but you will see other wildlife such as wild buffalos. You'll see plenty of other animals and birdlife on the island of Komodo, particularly deer and wild pigs, though not all are wild and a number of deer and pigs spend their days hanging out at park headquarters.

Kampung Komodo is a half hour walk from park headquarters along the beach. It's a friendly Muslim Bugis village of stilt houses full of goats, chickens and children. Many of Komodo's inhabitants are descendants of convicts who were exiled to there last century by a Sumbawanese sultan.

PLACES TO STAY & EAT

On Komodo, the PHPA camp at Loh Liang has a collection of large, spacious wooden cabins on stilts with balconies. Each cabin has four or five rooms, a sitting area and two mandis. Rooms are spartan with mattresses on the floor, but are comfortable and have plenty of rustic charm. Singles/doubles cost 10,000/15,000 rp, but single rooms are limited and you'll usually have to pay for a double. A few more luxurious rooms cost 25,000/35,000 rp.

During the peak tourist season – around July/August – the rooms may be full, but the PHPA will rustle up mattresses, even if you can't be guaranteed a room. Electricity, produced by a noisy generator, operates from 6 to 10 pm.

There's also a restaurant at the camp, with a limited menu of nasi/mie goreng meals for around 3000 rp, plus fish dishes and other simple meals, plus some drinks (including beer and drinking water). Bring any other food yourself, or pick up basic supplies at Kampung Komodo.

On Rinca, accommodation at the PHPA camp at Loh Buaya is similar to that on Komodo, with rooms for 10,000/15,000 rp, but there's no restaurant so bring your own food. The PHPA guides are very friendly; they don't get many people staying at the camp and are glad of the company.

KOMODO & RINCA

Komodo Dragons

There were rumours of these awesome creatures long before their existence was confirmed in the west. Fishers and pearl divers working in the area had brought back tales of ferocious lizards with enormous claws, fearsome teeth and fiery yellow tongues. One theory holds that the Chinese dragon is based on the Komodo lizard. The first Dutch expedition to the island was in 1910; two of the dragons were shot and their skins taken to Java, resulting in the first published description.

The Komodo dragon is actually a monitor lizard. Monitors range from tiny 20g things just 20cm long to the granddaddy of them all, the Komodo dragon (*Varanus komodoensis* in science-speak). All monitors have some physical features in common: the head is tapered; the ear openings are visible; the neck is long and slender; the eyes have eyelids and round pupils; and the jaws are powerful. But the dragons also have massive bodies, four powerful legs (each with five clawed toes) and long, thick tails (which function as rudders and can also be used for grasping or as a potent weapon). The body is covered in small, nonoverlapping scales; some may be spiny, others raised and bony.

The monitors' powerful legs allow them to sprint short distances, lifting their tails as they run. Many species stay in or near the water and can swim well, with an undulating movement of the trunk and tail. Dragons regularly swim across from Rinca to Padar, but don't stay there. When threatened they'll take refuge in their normal resting places – holes, trees (for the smaller monitors) or water.

Komodo dragons are dangerous if driven into a corner and will then attack a much larger opponent. They threaten by opening the mouth, inflating the neck and hissing. The ribs may spread or the body expand slightly, making the monitor look larger. It often rises up on its hind legs just before attacking, and the tail can deliver well aimed blows that will knock down a weaker adversary. Their best weapons are their sharp teeth and dagger-sharp claws which can inflict severe wounds.

All monitors feed on other animals: small ones on insects; larger ones on frogs and birds; and the ora on deer, wild pig and even water buffalo which inhabit the islands. The ora also eat their own dead. They can expand their mouth cavity considerably, enabling them to swallow large prey; the ora can push practically a whole goat into its throat.

Being such a large reptile, the ora rarely moves until warmed by the sun. They seem to be stone deaf, but have a very keen sense of smell. Of all the monitors, the ora lays the largest eggs – up to 12cm long and weighing around 200g. The female lays 20 or 30 eggs at a time and usually buries them in the wall of a dry river, where they hatch by themselves nine months later.

Monitors are not relics of the dinosaur age; they're remarkably versatile, hardy modern lizards, if not exactly sensitive and new age. Why they exist only on and around Pulau Komodo is a mystery, as is why males outnumber females by a ratio of 3.4 to one.

Populations of the ora vary, though there has been a decline on Komodo from 3336 dragons in 1990 down to an estimated 1600 in 1997. Rinca is estimated to have 500 dragons. Counts are done every year, but are only estimates and may be optimistic. At the last count, national park staff at 47 sites on Komodo counted 148 dragons in one day, while 29 sites on Rinca came up with 129 dragons. The most populous sites on Komodo were Sebita and Loh Wau in the south of the island. On Rinca, Loh Kima had the most dragons, followed by Loh Buaya, Loh Tongkor and Loh Ginggo.

The villagers never hunted the monitors, which weren't as good to eat as the numerous wild deer and pigs on the island, and for other reasons not too hard to imagine! It the said that the lizards are the animal cousins of the Komodo islanders and if a Komodo dragon is killed then its human counterpart will fall ill.

Today the ora is a protected species but poaching of deer – the ora's favourite food – has resulted in the decline of the population.

Below: The stuff of legend and fearsome predators, Komodo dragons are modern creatures well adapted to their environment. However, poaching of traditional prey such as deer and pigs has led to a decline in the dragon population.

KOMODO DRAGONS

GETTING THERE & AWAY
Komodo
From Sape (Sumbawa), a ferry departs at 8 am daily, except Friday, and costs 10,000 rp for the five to seven hour journey, depending on the sea conditions and the ferry (one ferry is faster than the other). Going the other way, the Labuanbajo-Komodo-Sape ferry departs from Labuan-bajo at 8 am daily, except Friday, and costs 4000 rp for the three hour journey. Tickets can be purchased from the harbours in Sape and Labuanbajo around one hour before departure.

The ferries cannot dock at Loh Liang so they stop about 1km out to sea, from where small boats transfer you to Komodo for an extra 1500 rp.

Leaving Komodo, the small boats depart at 10 am to meet the Labuanbajo-Sape ferry, and at noon to meet the Sape-Labuanbajo ferry.

Boats to Komodo can be chartered from Labuanbajo or Sape. It is easier and cheaper to arrange in Labuanbajo, although hotels and boat operators prefer to sell tours. Charter boats start at 75,000 rp for a day trip for up to six people. Labuanbajo to Komodo takes three to four hours in an ordinary boat. Komodo is often included on the boat tours between Lombok and Labuanbajo (see Organised Tours under Labuanbajo in the Flores chapter for more details).

Rinca
The Sinbad shuttle office in Labuan-bajo operates a shuttle to Rinca for 20,000 rp per person, leaving at 8 am and returning at 4 pm. It's only about two hours by motorboat from Labuanbajo to Rinca; a charter boat costs around 60,000 rp for up to six people. The boat tours between Lombok and Labuan-bajo sometimes also stop on Rinca.

Flores

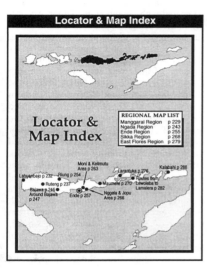

Locator &
Map Index

REGIONAL MAP LIST
Manggarai Region	p 229
Ngada Region	p 243
Ende Region	p 255
Sikka Region	p 268
East Flores Region	p 279

Moni & Kelimutu Area p 263
Labuanbajo p 232 • Riung p 254
Larantuka p 276
Kalabahi p 288
• Ruteng p 237
Bajawa p 245 •
Around Bajawa
p 247
• Maumere p 270
Routes from
Lewoleba to
Lamalera p 282
Nggela & Jopu
Area p 266
Ende p 257

Highlights

- **Kelimutu** – the famed Kelimutu volcano has three lakes that mysteriously change colour. The nearby village of Moni is a relaxing place to stay, with plenty of basic budget accommodation and weaving villages nearby to visit.

- **Bajawa** – a cool hill town surrounded by volcanoes and an ideal base to visit some of the region's most interesting and accessible traditional villages. Many villages can be visited, tourists are welcome and you can also climb Gunung Inerie volcano or relax in hot springs.

- **Labuanbajo** – a relaxed fishing village and gateway to Flores and the Komodo National Park. Good beaches lie around the town, or boats sail to beautiful atolls with even better beaches and excellent diving and snorkelling.

- **Maumere** – the other main gateway to Flores with relaxed beach resorts to the east of the town. Waiara has dive resorts, and Wairterang further east has budget accommodation and boat tours to excellent beaches on the nearby islands.

- **Ruteng** – a hill town and the centre for Manggarai culture. Visit the traditional village of Compang Ruteng just outside town or the more interesting, but difficult to reach, villages in Todo.

- **Riung** – just offshore from this village on the north coast is the Seventeen Islands Marine Park, which has excellent beaches and snorkelling.

- **Lembata** – take the spectacular ferry trip from Larantuka past dry islands studded with smoking volcanoes to the island of Lembata. In the village of Lamalera, whales are hunted with hand-held harpoons like something out of *Moby Dick*.

Flores is one of the biggest, most rugged and most beautiful islands in Nusa Tenggara. Dominated by a string of volcanoes, the long-impenetrable mountains have divided the island into many distinct ethnic groups. You'll find some interesting cultures here, with a layer of animism beneath the prevalent Christianity.

The island has attracted a steady flow of visitors in recent years, but has nothing like the tourist scene of Bali or even Lombok. Labuanbajo, a centre for trips to Komodo and Rinca, is a popular destination and developing beach spot, and the famed coloured lakes of Kelimutu are on everyone's itinerary. The other main tourist destination is Bajawa, from where traditional Ngada villages can easily be visited.

Many visitors don't get beyond these 'big three', but other good beaches and snorkelling can be found around Maumere in the east and at Riung on the north-central coast. Above all, Flores offers many opportunities for exploration into the interior, in search of ikat and traditional villages; the expanding road network now makes access easier.

FLORES

215

Facts About Flores

HISTORY
Early History

The first settlers on Flores were Neolithic cave dwellers, possibly dating back to *Homo erectus*, the early hominid predating modern man. Fossil evidence shows that these first settlers hunted pygmy stegadonts (early elephants) and giant turtles, possibly to extinction. Today's inhabitants date from much later migrations. Each ethnic group has its own migration legend, claiming their ancestors came from Sumatra, Java, Sulawesi or India, but little is known of Flores before the arrival of Europeans. The island's diverse cultures have enough similarities to suggest that they developed from a common type, differentiated by geographical isolation and the varying influence of outsiders.

The Javanese chronicle, the *Nagara-kertagama*, dating from the 14th century, places Flores (rather imaginatively) within the Majapahit realm. Lying just off the trade route to the spice islands of Maluku, Flores undoubtedly attracted visits from Javanese and Chinese traders, though it held little commercial interest. Hinduism and Buddhism, which flourished in Java, made little impact on Flores and trade was limited to sandalwood in East Flores, a secondary source compared with neighbouring Timor. According to the Portuguese chronicler Tome Pires, sulphur from Flores found its way to Melaka, the major Muslim trading port on the Malay Peninsula, but otherwise trade was limited.

Long before Europeans arrived in the 16th century, the north coast of Flores was visited by the Makassarese and Bugis from southern Sulawesi. These fierce warriors controlled the sea lanes to the north of Flores until the arrival of the Portuguese and their superior military might. The Bugis even established their own ports as part of a trading network throughout the archipelago. They brought gold, coarse porcelain, elephant tusks (used for money), a sort of machete known as a *parang*, linen and copperware, and left with rubber, sea cucumber (much of it fished from the bay of Maumere), shark fins, sandalwood, wild cinnamon, coconut oil, cotton and fabric from Ende.

The influence from Sulawesi increased from around 1530, when the Makassarese kingdom of Gowa rose to prominence and

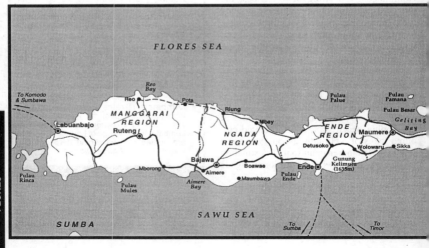

FLORES SEA

To Komodo & Sumbawa

Reo Bay

Reo   Pota

Riung

Labuanbajo

MANGGARAI REGION

Ruteng

Mbay

NGADA REGION

Pulau Palue

Pulau Pamana

Pulau Besar

Geliting Bay

ENDE REGION   Maumere

Detusoko   Wolowaru   Sikka

Bajawa

Mborong   Boawae

Aimere   Gunung Kelimutu (1635m)

Pulau Rinca

Pulau Mules

Aimere Bay

Maumbawa   Pulau Ende   Ende

SAWU SEA

SUMBA   To Sumba   To Timor

FLORES

began conquering its neighbours. The king of Gowa adopted Islam in 1605 and helped spread the religion, but Islam had already started to penetrate the coastal ports on Flores from the mid 16th century. Many of the coastal towns on Flores today are still Muslim and inhabited by settlers from Sulawesi (Makassarese, Bugis and the sea gypsy Bajau people).

Arrival of the Portuguese

In 1511, the Portuguese and their cannons arrived in South-East Asia to contest the lucrative Asia trade. They took Melaka, the region's major trading port, and then set sail for the eastern spice islands. As early as 1512, Flores was sighted by the Portuguese navigator Antonio de Abreu. Flores owes its name to the Portuguese, who called its easternmost cape Cabo das Flores, meaning 'Cape of Flowers'.

The Portuguese concentrated on controlling the spice islands of Maluku and largely ignored Flores until a Dominican priest, Antonio de Taviera, arrived on a conversion mission somewhere between 1556 and 1560. After converting thousands in Timor, he continued his efforts along the south coast of Flores as far as Ende.

In 1561, more Dominicans arrived on the island of Solor, which was to become Portugal's first colony in Flores. After Muslim attacks, a fort was built on Solor in 1556 providing a haven for Portuguese ships trading sandalwood in Timor and en route to the spice islands. From Solor, Portuguese missionary activity spread to Adonara and Larantuka.

In the late 16th century, the Portuguese also built a small fort on Pulau Ende, the island just off the coast from Ende. Pulau Ende was already a significant port, inhabited by Javanese Muslims, Chinese, Arabs and other traders. The Christian settlement at Pulau Ende was constantly under attack from Muslims. In 1602, a local chief, Amequira, sought help from a Muslim Makassarese prince to seize Ende. The Makassarese sent 40 ships and 3000 men, but the expedition was defeated. The Portuguese victory was short-lived, however, and in 1605 the fort at Ende was attacked and burnt by local Endenese and had to be abandoned. It was retaken by local Christians with Portuguese help in 1613, before being finally abandoned in the 1620s when the Christians settled on the mainland.

Portuguese missionary activity continued

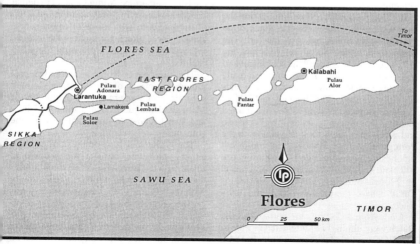

east of Ende, and in 1621 a Melakan born priest established himself on the south coast at Paga. While the north coast was effectively controlled by the Muslim kingdom of Gowa, the south coast became a bastion of Portuguese Catholicism.

However, very few Portuguese settled in Flores, and it was left to the mestizo Topasses to carry the Portuguese flag. The Topasses, originally from Melaka, were descended from intermarriage between the Portuguese and slaves from Melaka and India. They, in turn, integrated into the local community and became the main political force in eastern Flores. The raja of Sikka, the dominant kingdom around Maumere, was a Topasse and throughout eastern Flores today the descendants of the Topasses, with names such as da Silva and da Costa, are an influential group.

Dutch Era

The Dutch first arrived in the East Indies in 1595, but it wasn't until all the competing Dutch trading companies merged to form the Vereenigde Oost-Indische Compagnie (VOC) that the Dutch seriously threatened Portuguese dominance of trade. In 1605 they took Ambon (Maluku) from the Portuguese, and then set about harrying other Portuguese settlements.

In 1613, a Dutch expedition under the command of Apollonius Scotte attacked the Portuguese at Solor and took the fort. The Portuguese retook Solor in 1616, but the Dutch constantly attacked the settlement and laid claim to the fort. The Portuguese made Larantuka their main settlement, and successfully resisted a Dutch attack in 1618.

The Portuguese hold on Flores was limited to a few Dominican friars and the Topasses, and when the Dutch took Melaka from the Portuguese in 1641, Portugal's aspirations in Indonesia effectively ended. The Portuguese still claimed Larantuka and other settlements on Flores, but their attentions shifted to Timor where the sandalwood trade flourished.

Aside from dislodging the Portuguese, the Dutch were similarly uninterested in Flores. The VOC occupied the fort on Solor in 1646, but soon made Kupang their main base in the eastern islands. The VOC conducted a small amount of trade with Ende, and the company's ships regularly called in there on voyages between Kupang and Batavia (present-day Jakarta).

As soon as the Dutch eclipsed the Portuguese, they had to contend with the growing power of the Makassarese. The kingdom of Gowa continued to trade in spices, despite VOC attempts to establish a monopoly, and Makassarese ships plundered the shipping lanes. The Makassarese claimed sovereignty over western Flores, particularly the north coast and Ende. In 1664, the Makassarese again sent a fleet to Ende, ostensibly to evict the remnants of the Portuguese and defeat Christianity. This time they met little resistance and many Makassarese settled in Ende, which developed a reputation as a haven for pirates conducting slave raids on Sumba.

Much of the migration to Flores from Sulawesi dates from this time. Although the Makassarese kingdom of Gowa was preeminent, the Bugis launched a series of wars against it in southern Sulawesi. Many Makassarese and Buginese fled the bloody mayhem in Sulawesi, settling Sumbawa and Flores. The Dutch eventually combined with the Buginese prince Arung Palakka to defeat the Makassarese in 1669, and the break up of the kingdom sent bands of Makassarese and Buginese pirates throughout the islands, terrorising the seas well into the 18th century.

The kingdom of Bima on Sumbawa, previously a vassal of Gowa, then claimed suzerainty of western Flores. A number of Manggarai kingdoms sent tribute to Bima, and Reo became an important port for the Bimanese.

The VOC had little interest in western Flores, however, despite the occasional tussle with the Bimanese. VOC ships continued to call at Ende, which signed a treaty with the VOC in 1793, but the company was on the verge of bankruptcy and was abolished in 1799 by the Dutch government.

A new era of direct colonial government ensued, but it had little immediate impact on

Flores. The first notable intervention came in 1838 when a Dutch expedition from Kupang attacked Ende to stop the slave trade on Sumba, which the Endenese monopolised. Slavery was not officially abolished until 1860, and the Dutch had long engaged in the trade themselves, but Ende was trading slaves with French ships from Réunion and Mauritius, undermining Dutch authority in the region. The Dutch burnt Endenese ships, destroyed the town and forced the raja of Ende to sign allegiance to the Dutch, but the slave trade continued up until the 20th century.

Also in 1838, the Dutch attacked Larantuka in Eastern Flores, finally gaining control of the area in 1851. In Dili in 1859, the Portuguese signed an agreement relinquishing all of its claims on Flores on the condition that Flores remained Catholic. Dutch Jesuits then took over missionary work on Flores.

The Dutch administration comprised little more than observers appointed to the major kingdoms of Flores. At best, Dutch control was a weakened form of its divide-and-rule policy, with the occasional military intervention to maintain the status quo.

In 1890, an Endenese chieftain, Bara Nuri, tried to overthrow the Dutch-supported Raja of Ende. Bara Nuri escaped from a Dutch prison in Kupang and returned to Ende to raise a local army. The raja attacked Bara Nuri's stronghold to no avail and requested a Dutch warship to help, which he received. Further Dutch reinforcements arrived in 1891, but Bara Nuri was captured only after being treacherously lured to discuss a truce with the Dutch agent in Ende. Bara Nuri is today revered as the hero of Ende.

20th Century

The Dutch intervened in various skirmishes, particularly in eastern Flores which was most resistant to Dutch rule, but direct intervention on Flores did not begin until 1906. Ende became the Dutch capital with a *controleur* appointed to bring the kingdoms to heel. Rebellions against Dutch rule broke out across Flores in 1907 and Ende was razed after attacks from mountain chiefs. Rein-

forcements arrived from Kupang, and the Dutch mounted a 'pacification' campaign in the countryside until most of Flores was under direct Dutch authority by 1910.

The Dutch merged many of the small chiefdoms into larger kingdoms under the control of preferred rajas, who ruled with some autonomy under a Dutch hegemony. Minor skirmishes continued, and it was not until 1931, when the kingdoms of Larantuka and Sikka were reorganised, that the Dutch administration was firmly in control.

It was during this period that missionary activity peaked. Dutch Jesuits moved into the isolated western hills in the 1920s, and most of the population was converted before WWII. Catholicism flourished because it welded Christianity onto existing beliefs. Today, though Christianity prevails, animist practices and beliefs are still strong.

The Japanese occupied Flores in 1942 after the Dutch surrender. Ende became the Japanese military headquarters and major bases were built at Mbay on the north coast and on Solor at Hadakewa. After the Japanese military surrender in 1945, the Dutch returned to Flores and met little opposition. While Java was embroiled in the war for independence, life went on much as normal in Flores and it remained part of the Dutch-sponsored Negara Indonesia Timur (State of East Indonesia) until the Dutch finally quit Indonesia in 1949.

The Indonesian government abolished the power of the Florinese rajas in 1951. Although replaced by civil administrators, the royal families still command great respect in Flores.

After independence, schools and hospitals were built, and many villages were encouraged to move closer to the main roads and services such as electricity. Flores remained one of the poorest and least developed islands of Indonesia, however, and stretches of the main highway resembled a goat track right up until the late 80s. Increased spending from Jakarta, which targeted the eastern islands for development from 1988 onwards, has resulted in an improvement in living standards. New roads are being built and old

FLORES

ones sealed, and many traditional areas are now beginning to develop contacts with the modern world.

Development plans received a major setback in December 1992 when eastern Flores was rocked by an earthquake. One of the most severe in modern Indonesia's history, it registered 6.8 on the Richter scale with an epicentre just off the north coast near Maumere. The earthquake and subsequent tidal waves flattened Maumere, killing more than 2500 people, and eastern Flores from Ende to Larantuka suffered damage. Apart from a few buildings in Maumere that still haven't been rebuilt, you'll see no evidence of the earthquake today.

GEOGRAPHY

Geographically, the island's turbulent volcanic past has left a legacy of V-shaped valleys, knife-edged ridges, and a collection of active and extinct volcanoes. One of the finest volcanoes is the caldera of Kelimutu in central Flores, with its three coloured lakes. There are 14 active volcanoes on Flores – only Java and Sumatra have more. The central mountains slope gently to the north coast, but along the south coast the spurs of the volcanoes plunge steeply into the sea.

The island is part of one of the world's most geologically unstable zones, and earthquakes and tremors hit every year, although none in living memory match that of the December 1992 earthquake.

The rugged terrain makes road construction difficult; although Flores is only about 375km long, its end-to-end road winds, twists, ascends and descends for nearly 700km and heavy wet-season rains, as well as the frequent earthquakes and tremors, mean that it has to be repaired year-round.

CLIMATE

The rainy season (around November to March) is longer and more intense in western Flores, which receives the brunt of the northwest monsoon and also has the highest mountains. The town of Ruteng, near Flores' highest peak (the 2400m Ranaka), gets an average 3350mm of rain every year, but Ende has only 1140mm and Larantuka just 770mm. The north coast is also much drier than the south coast.

Average daytime temperature are around 30°C (86°F) in the coastal towns, and the north coast is hotter and very dry in the dry season. Mountain towns such as Ruteng and Bajawa are warm to hot during the day, but overnight temperatures drop dramatically to 17°C (62.6°F) or lower, and warm clothes are needed.

GOVERNMENT

Flores is part of Nusa Tenggara Timor province, whose capital is Kupang (Timor).

Flores is divided into five *kabupaten* (regencies), which reflect the major ethnographic boundaries on the island. In the west, the Manggarai regency has its capital at Ruteng and stretches west to Labuanbajo and includes Komodo. Ngada borders Manggarai with its capital at Bajawa, and stretches north to Riung and (in the east) includes Boawae and Mbay. The latter is slated to become the new capital of the regency.

Ende regency, with its capital at Ende, lies in the centre of Flores and includes Kelimutu. Further east is Sikka, named after the southern coastal kingdom that dominated the region up until the 20th century. Its capital is Maumere.

Flores Timur (East Flores) is the fifth regency and has it capital at Larantuka. It includes the islands of Solor, Adonara and Lembata.

ECONOMY

Flores has virtually no industry and the majority of the people survive through subsistence agriculture. Rice and corn are the staples, coffee is grown in the highlands and cotton in East Flores, as well as a host of small crops. The most fertile areas are in the western highlands, while the north coast and eastern Flores is arid for most of the year and the dry season can bring great hardship. The lontar palm flourishes in drier areas and coconuts are grown extensively on the south coast. Wet rice is grown in the fertile valleys around Ruteng, which is the main agricultural region of Flores. Horses, pigs and buffaloes, particularly in western Flores, are an important part of local economies and often form part of the bride price.

Tourism is a growing industry in Flores, but is still on a small scale.

POPULATION & PEOPLE
The island's 1.5 million people are divided into five main language and cultural groups: from west to east, these are the Manggarai (main town Ruteng); the Ngada (Bajawa); the closely related Ende and Lio peoples (Ende); the Sikkanese (Maumere); and the Lamaholot (Larantuka). Physically, the people of the western half of the island are more 'Malay', while the further east you head the inhabitants are a mixture of Melanesian and Malay.

Manggarai
The Manggarai people of western Flores are of Malay stock. Their language has many dialects, but there is a large degree of cultural and linguistic homogeneity through the regency. The eastern part of Manggarai is more diverse with pockets of different languages spoken. In many parts of Manggarai, the people claim descent from the Minangkabau of Sumatra, but apart from the ritual importance of the buffalo, only minor evidence supports this claim. The Manggarai claim common ancestry with neighbouring Bajawa, but many Bajawanese tribes believe otherwise, claiming decent from Java or even India.

The population is predominantly Catholic, apart from coastal settlements such as Labuanbajo and Reo, which have large Muslim populations. Manggarai came under the sway of the Makassarese kingdom of Gowa in the 17th century, and many people from Sulawesi settled the coastal areas, but influence of the kingdom of Bima in Sumbawa in the 18th century was more pronounced. In Reo, Bimanese is still spoken. Traditionally, Manggarai was composed of many small chiefdoms, headed by a *dalu*. The most powerful chiefdoms before Dutch intervention were Todo, Pongkor and Cibal

around Ruteng. When the Dutch took over they ruled through the local chiefs, combining smaller into larger kingdoms. The dalu of Todo became Raja of Manggarai, based in Ruteng.

Ngada
The Ngada people share many cultural similarities with the Manggarai, and the Ngada villages are among the most traditional on Flores. The term Ngada is sometimes used to refer to all the peoples of the Ngada regency, but strictly it refers to the people of the Bajawa region, also known as the Bajawanese (see the Bajawa section later in this chapter for more discussion of the Ngada).

Related groups in the regency are the peoples of Riung and Boawae, each speaking their own languages. The Boawae people are more closely related to the Ngada, and can further be divided into the Nage people who live on the northern slopes of Gunung Ebulobo, and the Keo who live to the south. The Soa region to the north of Bajawa is a transitional area between the Ngada and Boawae cultures.

The lightly populated area of Riung on the north coast is of mixed Islamic decent and they speak a very different language from the Ngada and Boawae peoples.

Endenese & Lio
The Endenese of south-central Flores are primarily Malay, but with mixed Papuan features. The city of Ende was the major port on Flores from the 16th century and hence has a very mixed population, with a large number of Muslims, originally from Sulawesi and Java. The rest of the countryside is predominantly Catholic. Ende has fewer traditional villages than the Ngada region, but traditional houses and animistic practices still exist in the mountains around Ende. Still, traditional religion is weaker here than in areas further west. The Lio people, who speak a related language, inhabit the region south of Ende – around Kelimutu and the south coast. Many Lio villages are still very traditional and the Lio share many common cultural attributes with the Endenese.

FLORES

The *musalaki* is the *adat* (traditional) leader of the village, acting as head of the clans and the keeper of ritual. Although the ancestors that settled the village play a prominent role, the most important graves in the village are usually of the musalaki, who often come from the one family. The musalaki acts as a spiritual chief and is usually separate from the *kepala kampong* (village head).

Sikkanese

The people of Sikka, the region around Maumere, are a mixture of Malay and Melanesian and have noticeably more Papuan features. The Sikkanese can be broken down into three main groups – the Sikka Natar of the south coast, based around the village of Sikka, the Krowe to the west and in the central hills around Nita, and the Tana Ai people to the east. The three groups speak very different dialects of Sikkanese.

· The dominant group is the Sikka Natar whose rajas controlled much of eastern Flores. Sikka village was settled by a line of kings from around 1600 and became a centre for Christianity and Portuguese influence. The first raja of Sikka took the Portuguese name of da Silva and was most likely a Topasse outsider of mestizo heritage from Solor. The other main kingdom was the lesser Krowe kingdom under control of the Raja of Nita.

The Sikkanese had complex social structures headed by the royal families, followed by a class of nobles, then commoners and finally slaves. Marriages were conducted to form alliances between clans and followed complex ritual. Ivory was an important part of the bride price, and is still given today in marriage.

Although animist ritual and belief in spirits persists, the long influence of Christianity has largely killed off traditional religion except in remote mountain areas.

Lamaholot

The Lamaholot live in the Larantuka region and the islands of the Solor Archipelago. They are related to the Sikkanese and similarly were classed as part of Portugal's realm

– Solor and Larantuka were the first Portuguese settlements on Flores. The Iberian influence is most notable in Larantuka, with its remnants of Portuguese church ritual and many descendants of the Topasses, who have Portuguese names.

Catholicism dominates the area, but Islam came to Solor before Christianity. The large village of Lamakera on Solor was Muslim when the Portuguese arrived. The islands were once known as the 'Islands of Murderers' because of a ritual war between two clans, the Demon and the Paji, that was waged for hundreds of years and continued well into the 20th century.

Despite a similar Portuguese Catholic background, traditional beliefs are more deeply entrenched than in Sikka. Planting and harvesting rituals are still very important in many villages and offerings are made to a variety of nature gods. Sacrifices, sometimes to volcanoes, are made to ensure fertility of the soil and the coming of the rain in this dry, harsh region. Many people have moved from their original villages to new settlements closer to the roads, but the ancestral villages are maintained and are the centres of ceremonial life.

The belief in spirits, particularly evil spirits, is widespread and the area is noted for its black magic. The *menaka* are practitioners of black magic that can call on the power of evil spirits called *eo*, while the *molang* are white magic practitioners that can counteract the menaka.

ARTS

Architecture

Flores has a wealth of traditional architecture, varying from region to region. The traditional house of the Manggarai is the *wunut*, a large conical house with a thatched roof extending to the ground. Entry is though a small semi-circular opening. The chief's house is typically the largest and the central column supporting the roof is the seat of the chief, where he sits in judgment on village matters. At the centre of the village is the *compang*, a fortress-like, circular meeting area ringed by stone walls. Traditional houses are becoming rare in Manggarai and are mostly found around Ruteng. The Todo area in the mountains to the south of Ruteng has the best examples of wunut.

Traditional villages thrive in Ngada, particularly in and around Bajawa. Bajawa houses are rectangular with high-peaked thatch roofs, often topped with small warrior (male) and house (female) statues. The central village compound contains *ngadhu* (male) and *bhaga* (female) totems representing the ancestors. Some villages also contain great shards of stone, graves of the ancestors and revered warriors, but most villages have relocated closer to the roads and the original graves often lie further away in the hills. The *peo* is a Y-shaped, wooden altar for sacrificial offerings found in the compound of some Bajawa villages, but is more common in the Boawae district.

Traditional houses in the Ende region are larger affairs with many partitioned rooms inside and they may house up to 20 families. The main meeting house usually has an open platform supported on carved and curved beams and the courtyard in front is centred around the *tubu musu*, a ceremonial stone where animals are slaughtered and prayers offered to the gods. Houses of the Lio people, south of Ende, are similar.

Houses in Sikka are traditionally arranged in rows with large offering stones in the centre of the village, but traditional houses are now rare and are mainly found in the mountains of west Sikka. Traditional houses of East Flores have high-peaked roofs topped by sharpened bamboo and are open-sided or have woven-bamboo walls. Many traditional villages have now been abandoned.

Ikat
In traditional society, women can only marry after they have learnt to weave, just as men can only marry after they have tilled their own plot and produced crops. Flores produces fine, intricate ikat weaving with designs mostly based on patola (a hexagon framing a star) motifs, and cloths are an important part of the bride price.

The Ende region produces some of the finest cloth, typically in browns, yellows, reds and blues. Patterns are often geometric or include small, stylised animal figures arranged in bands. Ikat is found in almost every village, but villages close to Ende and on the south coast of the Nggela area are noted weaving centres.

Further east around Maumere, Sikka village is a noted ikat centre, though fine cloth can be found in many centres. Larger motifs, a modern adaptation, are often employed. Around Larantuka and Pulau Solor, brighter reds are used (the Lamahalot were more adept at mastering the process to produce red dyes). Some of the most prized ikat on Flores comes from the islands of Lembata and Solor, largely because handspun thread and natural dyes are still common.

Manggarai weavings do not employ the ikat method, but use a supplementary-weft technique resembling embroidered cloth. The base is typically black, with motifs highlighted in gold and other colours.

Dance & Music
Dances accompany the ritual cycles and main village events – planting, the harvest, marriage, the building of a house etc – and are primarily performed by women. The 'circle dance', common in many parts of eastern Indonesia, where groups of dancers link arms, forms the basis for many dances. In Sikka, the *taja bobu* dance, introduced by the first Portuguese settlers, is still performed. War dances, reflecting a long history of intertribal warfare, are still performed in many areas, particularly East Flores.

The *caci* is the most well known ritual combat. These whip duels between two men or teams of men accompany many ceremonial events in western Flores. To the accompaniment of music, combatants try to draw blood with the stinging whips. In the Boawae district of Ngada, a form of boxing called *etu* or *sagi* accompanies harvest festivities. The boxers try to bash each other with lumps of wood or with gloves that may be studded with broken glass. Blood spilt on the ground ensures the fertility of the soil for next season's crop.

FLORES

Drums, gongs and singing accompany dances. Drums often have ritual significance, and ancient sets of drums representing the chief's authority and the harmony of the village have to be beaten in a particular order. Today, many events are also attended by government dignitaries and local officials, which means lots of speeches and a PA system, so amplified or even taped music may accompanying dances.

RELIGION

Around 85% of the people are Catholic (Muslims tend to congregate in the coastal towns), but Christianity is welded onto traditional beliefs, particularly in rural areas. Animist rituals are still important for a variety of occasions, ranging from birth, marriage and death to the building of new houses, or to mark important points in the agricultural cycle. Even educated, English-speaking Florinese still practise the odd chicken, pig or buffalo sacrifice to keep their ancestors happy when rice is planted or a new field opened up. In former times, it took more than animal blood to keep the gods and spirits friendly; there are persistent tales of children or virgin girls being sacrificed.

Flores is the stronghold of Catholicism in Indonesia, and all of the regencies have a bishop. The archbishop of Flores is based in Ende and the pope visited Flores in October 1989. Although the Portuguese brought Christianity to Flores, Dutch Jesuits are responsible for the overwhelming majority of conversions from the 1920s on. The main missionary group is the Society of the Divine Word, or Societas Verbi Divini (SVD), and their seminaries are prestigious centres of learning, responsible for educating most of Flores' elite. Missionaries were largely successful because they didn't set out to destroy existing practices and beliefs, but welded Christianity onto traditional ways. Priests have chronicled traditional societies and in many cases have supported the continuance of traditional arts, architecture and ceremonies. Not only tolerant, they are also one of the main providers of social services such as schools and hospitals. Although overseas priests were common up until only a decade ago, most missions and churches are now under the direction of Florinese.

Although a minority, the Muslim population is significant and mosques are found in all the major coastal centres. Most Muslims are descendants of migrants from Sulawesi, who established stilt-village settlements on the coast and lived from the sea. Many of these villages are still very traditional or 'backward' as the government on Flores tends to regard them, and Muslim communities are often the most disadvantaged. The regional government is largely controlled by mission-educated Christians, and Muslims are viewed with some suspicion. Christians and Muslims generally co-exist in harmony and with goodwill, but communal flare-ups are not unheard of. Often the problem is between Christians and recent Muslim settlers from Java and elsewhere, rather than established Muslim communities.

LANGUAGE

Just as Flores is an ethnologist's paradise, so too could it keep a team of linguists gainfully employed for a lifetime. Lack of detailed study makes it difficult to determine exactly how many languages exist on Flores, but there are believed to be at least 16 distinct languages and dozens of dialects and sub-dialects. All are Malayo-Polynesian and belong to the Austronesian family of languages which are spoken throughout most of Indonesia.

Major languages include Manggarai (west from Labuanbajo to the Ruteng region), Bajawa (central-west Flores, around Bajawa and in villages to the south), Ende (central Flores, around Ende and northwards), Lio (related to Ende and spoken in and around the Moni region), Sikka (central-east Flores, around Maumere) and Lamaholot (east from Larantuka through the Solor Archipelago). The number of dialects is mind-boggling. Sikka has three very different dialects, while Manggarai has five major dialects and as many as 43 sub-dialects.

Other minor languages in eastern Manggarai include Rajong, Rembong, Ronga and

Wairana. In Ngada regency, besides Bajawa, the main languages are Riung and Boawae (or Nage-Keo). Around Soa, a dialect of Bajawa is spoken which is different enough to arguably be classed as a language in its own right.

The tiny island of Pulau Palue off the north coast also has its own language, and Kedang is spoken only at the eastern tip of Solor. To this you can add migrant languages such as Makassarese and Bugis, spoken in various coastal ports, Sabu (spoken by Sabunese migrants particularly around Aimere) and Bimanese, spoken around Reo.

It's little wonder that Indonesian is the main language in the towns. A decade ago, Indonesian was still not spoken in many remote villages, but the teaching of Indonesian is now almost universal. All school children speak it, and even in the remotest villages most older people now understand at least the basics. English is spoken in the tourist areas, but elsewhere it pays to know a little Indonesian. A few words in some of the following local languages will endear you to your hosts and enhance your stay on the island.

Manggarai
Useful Phrases

Where are you going?	*Ngonia?*
I'm going to the market.	*Aku ngo le pasar.*
Which way is the market?	*Nia salang le pasar?*
How far is it from here to Ruteng?	*Pisa tadang no'o mai Ruteng?*
Where is Fran's house?	*Nia mbaru diha Frans?*
How are you?	*Co'o reba?*
Fine.	*Di'a.*

Useful Words

good	*di'a*
big	*mese*
small	*koe*
hot	*kolang*
cold	*ces*
day	*leso*
week	*minggu*

beach	*pante*
lake	*sano*
mountain	*golo*
river	*wae*
north	*utara*
south	*selatan*
east	*timur*
west	*barat*

People & Families

person	*ata*
woman	*inewai*
man	*atarona*
child	*atakoe*
mother	*ende*
father	*ema*
wife	*wina*
husband	*rona*

Numbers

1	*ca*	6	*enam*
2	*sua*	7	*pitu*
3	*telu*	8	*alo*
4	*pat*	9	*ciok*
5	*lima*	10	*cepulu*

11	*campuluca*
12	*campulasua*
13	*campulatelu*
20	*suampulu*
30	*telumpulu*
40	*patmpulu*
50	*limampulu*
100	*ceratus*
200	*suaratus*
1000	*cesebu*
one million	*cajuta*

Bajawa
Useful Phrases

Where are you going?	*Male de?*
I'm going to the market.	*Jao laa zeta pasa.*
Which way is the market?	*Wide zala male zeta pasa?*
How far is it from here to Bajawa?	*Dada de puu dia male zeta Bajawa?*
Where is Fran's house?	*Wide baru ko Frans?*

FLORES

| How are you? | *Moe de?* |
| Fine. | *Molo.* |

Useful Words

good	*modhe*
big	*mese*
small	*kedhi*
hot	*bana*
cold	*ja*
day	*leza*
week	*migu*
beach	*ma'u*
lake	*tiwu*
mountain	*wolo*
river	*leko*
village	*nua*
north	*zeta*
south	*lau*
east	*zili*
west	*mena*

People & Families

person	*ata*
woman	*anafai*
man	*anasaki*
child	*anakedhi*
mother	*ine*
father	*ema*
wife	*fai*
husband	*saki*

Numbers

1	*esa*	6	*limasa*
2	*zua*	7	*limazua*
3	*telu*	8	*ruabutu*
4	*wutu*	9	*taraesa*
5	*lima*	10	*sabulu*

11	*sabulu sawidha*
12	*sabulu widhazua*
13	*sabulu widhatelu*
20	*widhabulu zua*
21	*buluzua sawidha*
22	*buluzua widhazua*
23	*buluzua widhatelu*
30	*widhabulu telu*
31	*bulutelu sawidha*
32	*bulutelu widhazua*
33	*bulutelu widhatelu*
40	*widhabulu wutu*
50	*widhabulu lima*
100	*sangasu*
200	*ngasu zua*
1000	*saribu*

Lamaholot
Useful Phrases

Where are you going?	*Moe malaga?*
I'm going to the market.	*Goe kaik pasar kai.*
Which way is the market?	*Laran pasar tai tega?*
How far is it from here to Larantuka?	*Larantuka doan pira dari ti?*
Where is Fran's house?	*Frans langan tega?*
How do you do?	*Moe genai?*

Useful Words

good	*maen*
big	*belen*
small	*kene*
hot	*pelatin*
cold	*geleten*
day	*leron*
week	*minggu*
beach	*watan*
lake	*dano*
mountain	*ile*
river	*wai*
village	*lewo*
north	*prae*
south	*plau*
east	*pehete*
west	*pelali*

People & Families

person	*atadiken*
woman	*berkewain*
man	*belakin*
child	*anan*
mother	*ema*
father	*ama*
wife	*kewae*
husband	*lake*

Numbers

1	*tou*	6	*nemu*
2	*rua*	7	*pito*
3	*telo*	8	*buto*
4	*pat*	9	*hiwa*
5	*lema*	10	*pulo*

11	*pulok tou*
12	*pulok rua*
13	*pulok telo*
20	*pulu rua*
21	*pulu rua ne tou*
30	*pulu teo*
40	*pulu pat*
50	*pulu lema*
100	*teratu*
200	*ratu rua*
1000	*ribu*

Getting There & Around

AIR

The golden rules of air travel are: between Flores and other parts of Indonesia, fly to/from Maumere; within Flores, forget it and resign yourself to the buses.

All flights are with Merpati, except for Bouraq's Denpasar-Maumere-Kupang run. The main airport on Flores is at Maumere, which handles larger planes. Daily flights run between Maumere, Denpasar and Kupang, and from (but not to) Ujung Pan-dang in Sulawesi. The other main inter-island connection is from Labuanbajo to Bima in Sumbawa, which is useful if you're in a hurry, but seats are limited. Onward connections from Bima to Mataram and Denpasar are unreliable and often overbooked in the main tourist season. Flights also go from Ruteng to Bima and Kupang, but Ruteng is not a convenient arrival or departure point for most visitors, and the often fogged-in mountain airport is terrifying to fly into.

Flights within Flores are limited and it is often difficult to get seats. No intra-Flores flights go from Maumere, so the only options are the often full Ende-Labuanbajo run, or the limited Bajawa-Ende and Bajawa-Labuanbajo flights. Merpati claims to have a weekly Larantuka-Lewoleba-Kupang flight, but it hardly ever runs.

BUS

The road that one Indonesian tourist leaflet charitably calls the 'Trans-Flores Highway' loops and tumbles nearly 700 scenic kilometres from Labuanbajo to Larantuka. The road is now paved all the way, but bus trips across Flores still rate as some of the most uncomfortable in Indonesia. Small, cramped and overcrowded buses constantly stop to pick up or drop off passengers, and in the towns they will cruise the streets endlessly until they have a full complement of passengers. The road is narrow and forever winding. Floods or landslides in the rainy season are not uncommon, and the latest trouble spots are attended by scores of workers doing back-breaking work in difficult conditions – it must seem like patching a crumbling dyke.

The main highway runs take the southern route, but parts of the new northern highway are now open. The northern highway runs from Maumere to Mbay, with connections to Riung, and the Riung-Reo section is under construction. This road is much quicker because it runs along the mostly flat northern plains, but it doesn't pass any of the major tourist attractions.

In all the main towns, except for Ende, buses will do pick-ups and drop-offs at hotels, so there's generally no need to go to distant bus terminals. Most hotels can arrange tickets.

BOAT

Flores is well connected to neighbouring islands by ferry. All ferries take vehicles as well as passengers. For schedules and departure times, see the Getting There & Away sections of relevant destinations further on, but bear in mind that most schedules are subject to change. Pelni passenger boats also service Labuanbajo, Ende, Maumere and Larantuka.

In the west, ferries run between Labuanbajo and Sape, on Sumbawa, every day except Friday, stopping at Komodo on the way.

FLORES

In the east, two ferries a week connect Larantuka with Kupang on Timor. Other ferries run from Larantuka through the Solor and Alor archipelagos. From Alor a ferry runs to Atapupu in Timor, but you need plenty of time to travel from Larantuka through to Timor via this route.

Ende, in south-central Flores, also has a weekly ferry to Waingapu (Sumba), one of the main links to Sumba. A weekly ferry also sails between Ende and Kupang.

A new ferry service operates from Aimere, on the south coast near Bajawa, to Kupang and Waingapu, but this is not a popular route and may not last.

In addition to the ferries, Pelni passenger boats provide a variety of useful links including: Labuanbajo-Waingapu, Ende-Waingapu, Ende-Kupang, Maumere-Ujung Pandang (Sulawesi), Maumere-Dili, Larantuka-Dili, Larantuka-Kupang and Larantuka-Ujung Pandang.

A popular way to get between Lombok and Labuanbajo is on a budget boat tour, and tours also operate from Labuanbajo to Riung (see Organised Tours in the Labuanbajo section for details on both).

Small boats occasionally run between port towns on Flores, but now that many of the roads are sealed, and passable in the wet season, these services are rare – ask around at the docks.

CAR & MOTORCYCLE

Self-drive cars cannot be hired, but a car with driver can be found in the main towns. Options are much more limited and expensive than in Lombok. Car hire starts at around 100,000 rp per day, depending on where you want to go. For this price you can do a day trip to attractions around a town, or go from one major town to the next with a few stop-offs in between. Trips of a few days are more difficult to arrange and can be more expensive.

The best place to hire a car is Maumere. The town has a surplus of taxis – mostly small minibuses – and drivers are used to taking tourists right across Flores to Labuanbajo. You have to negotiate a daily rate and

an accommodation/food allowance for the driver (see the Maumere section for details). It is also reasonably easy to find a car and driver in Labuanbajo, but there's less competition and rates are higher. Car hire options are very limited and expensive in Bajawa, Ruteng and Larantuka. Ende, the largest city on the island, should be good for hiring a car, but it's a foreign concept because of the lack of tourists. Hotels and travel agents are the easiest places to arrange car hire, but are more expensive than negotiating directly with the driver.

Flores is not set up for motorcycle hire, but if you ask around you can always find someone willing to rent out their bike for a few extra rupiah. A motorcycle is ideal for day tripping to villages that are otherwise hard to reach. Traffic is light, but roads are often winding and not in good repair.

Western Flores

Comprising the regencies of Manggarai (capital Ruteng) and Ngada (capital Bajawa), western Flores has some good beaches in the west and north, rugged mountains and volcanoes in the south, and interesting traditional cultures.

Labuanbajo on the western tip is the gateway to Flores and Komodo. This relaxed little town has a good range of services, beaches, snorkelling and diving. The next main stop on the Trans-Flores highway is the mountain town of Ruteng or, further east, Bajawa is a major destination. Bajawa is ringed by volcanoes and well set up for visiting some of the most interesting villages on Flores. Riung, north of Bajawa on the coast, is the jumping off point for visits to the beaches and coral reefs of the Seventeen Islands Marine Park.

LABUANBAJO

A small Muslim/Christian fishing town at the extreme western end of Flores, Labuanbajo is a jumping-off point for the islands of Komodo and Rinca, and the most popular

swimming and sunning spot on Flores. If you have a few days to while away, Labuanbajo is a pleasant enough town in which to do it. There aren't any readily accessible walk-on-and-flop beaches, but many of the small islands nearby have white sand beaches and good snorkelling offshore. The harbour is littered with outrigger fishing boats and is sheltered by the islands, giving the impression that you're standing on the shores of a large lake.

Labuanbajo means 'Port of the Bajo', having been settled by the Bajo (or Bajau) from Sulawesi. They have been joined by many Bugis settlers from Sulawesi, as well as Bimanese and increasing numbers of Manggarai, some of whom have come as local transmigrants from poor rural areas of Flores. A large *translok* (inter-island migration) camp is just outside the town.

The town is about 50% Muslim and 50% Christian, although the mosque tends to dominate, partly because it is more audible

(somewhat to the chagrin of a good number of tourists). Labuanbajo was an isolated outpost until the road to Ruteng was built. Before that, access was by boat to Reo. Until the road was sealed in the early 90s, boat was the only access if the road was washed away in the wet season.

Information
Tourist Offices The tourist office (Dinas Pariwisata; ☎ 41170) for the Manggarai region is on the road to the airport. It has no brochures as yet, but staff are helpful in answering any queries. It is open weekdays from 7 am to 3 pm and Saturday mornings.

The PHPA administers Komodo National Park, which takes in Komodo and Rinca islands and other parts of western Flores, including the Riung area. The main PHPA office, a little out of town, is mostly an administrative office rather than an information service, but you may be able to find someone to answer your queries.

The Manggarai

The Manggarai hill people are shy, but friendly – you'll see them in their distinctive black sarongs, trailing droopy stomached black-haired pigs into market or herding beautiful miniature horses. The Manggarai language is unintelligible to the other people of Flores, but there is only slight linguistic variation throughout the Manggarai region. A few isolated language sub-groups are found in the east, such as Rembong and Rajong. Bimanese is still spoken in some of the north coast ports, such as Reo and Pota, and coastal settlers from Sulawesi also leaven the mix.

The Manggarai claim descent from the Minangkabau of Sumatra, but apart from the common buffalo horn motif and some similarities in weaving techniques, there is little hard evidence to support this claim. A common legend tells of the arrival of the first Minangkabau settlers, two brothers, one who settled in Warloka on the west coast and the other who went on to settle Nangaroro in Bajawa. However, the people of Bajawa have very different oral histories. It is claimed that Warloka is home to fossilised stone relics from the original Minangkabau houses.

Makassarese from Sulawesi have mixed with the coastal Manggarai for many centuries, and the Manggarai alternatively came under the control of the Makassarese and the Bimanese. After the fall of the Makassarese kingdom of Goa to the Dutch in 1669, Bima expanded its influence in Manggarai through marriage and military conquest, and it dominated the area from the 18th century until the early 20th century. Manggarai was ruled by numerous *dalu*, traditional chiefs or kings, who paid tribute to Bima. If no money was forthcoming, then buffaloes had to be sent, and if there were no buffaloes then people were offered as slaves.

Over 30 dalu ruled in Manggarai, though some were more powerful than others. Another legend tells of how the dalu agreed to pay tribute to Bima in return for independence and a battle ensued between the three main kingdoms of Todo, Cibal and Reo. To end the bloodshed a contest was devised among the kings and seeds were scattered in the sand. As related in Todo, only the Todo kings could find the seeds and, as further proof of their power, they shrunk a buffalo, allowing it to pass through the centre of a length of bamboo.

When the Dutch took over all of Flores in the first decade of the 20th century, the dalu from Todo became supreme, and in 1929 the Dutch appointed the first raja (king) of Manggarai from the Todo royal clan. Though Reo was the main port and centre of Bimanese influence, the Dutch established their headquarters in the fertile valley of Ruteng.

Catholic missionaries quickly followed the Dutch, and Christianity now predominates among the upland Manggarai; Ruteng has several large Christian schools and churches. Traditional animist practices still linger, but are dwindling – traditionally, the Manggarai would carry out a cycle of ceremonies, some involving buffalo or pig sacrifices, to ask favours from ancestor and nature spirits and the supreme being, Mori. In some villages you can still find the *compang*, a ring of flat stones on which offerings were placed, or you may be shown ritual paraphernalia used during sacrificial ceremonies. Whip fights of strength and courage known as *caci* still take place in Ruteng, especially during the national Independence Day celebrations (17 August).

The Manggarai traditionally practised slash-and-burn agriculture. They were introduced to rice cultivation around 1920 by the Dutch, but only in the past few decades has the area been devoted to permanent rice terraces. Maize (sweet corn) is the other main crop, though other crops (such as coffee and onions) are grown for export. The Manggarai also raise fine horses and large water buffalo, the latter primarily for export. ■

The PHPA information booth on the main road near the port has displays with some practical information about Komodo and Rinca islands, and is attended by members of the local guide association (☎ 41066) who are knowledgeable on the Labuanbajo area. Guides cost around 25,000 rp per day and some speak Dutch, German or French as well as English. Boat charters and overnight trips to Komodo and other islands can also be arranged there.

Money The Bank Rakyat Indonesia is open Monday to Friday from 7.30 am to 2 pm, and on Saturday from 9.30 to 11 am. Rates are low for US dollars and very poor for other currencies, and they can be choosy about which travellers cheques they will accept. Moneychangers around town, such as the Mega Buana Bahari, offer similar rates to the bank. If you're heading west, this is the last place to change money before Bima in Sumbawa.

Post & Communications The post office in the centre of the village is open Monday to Thursday from 7.30 to 3 pm, on Friday from 7.30 to 11 am, and on Saturday from 7.30 am to 1 pm. The Telkom office is a bit of a hike from town, near the PHPA office, or two wartels are on the main road in town.

Beaches, Snorkelling & Diving

The most easily reached beaches are south of the town. Head down the main street and take the road to the New Bajo Beach Hotel. The beaches around here and further south at Pantai Cendana are pleasant, but not spectacular.

To the north of Labuanbajo, **Waecicu** has a better beach and it is possible to swim to the tiny island of Kukusan Kecil just offshore and Kukusan Besar behind it, but beware of currents. Snorkelling is possible, but not exciting. Access is by the hotel boat – it leaves from the beach just north of the ferry terminal. Departures are at 9 am and 1 and 5 pm, and cost 3000 rp for non-guests. The boat leaves Waecicu at 6 and 10 am and 3 pm. From Waecicu you can walk south around the headland at low tide to **Wae Rana** where there is a reasonable beach and deserted bungalows. A road/track leads from the bungalows up the hill and eventually back to Labuanbajo, but it's a long, hot walk.

Further north around the coast, **Batugosok** has an excellent beach, but the water is very shallow at low tide. Access is by the resort's boat, but departures are infrequent and day trippers are not really encouraged.

The best beaches and snorkelling are on the islands. **Pulau Bidadari** has coral, clear water and the best snorkelling close to Labuanbajo. Further north, about 15km from Labuanbajo, **Sabola Besar** and **Sabola Kecil** have better snorkelling and good diving, noted for soft corals and abundant fishlife. There can be strong currents in the channel between the islands, but there's more sheltered diving around the islands. Boats can be chartered at reasonable rates, but the cheapest option is the shuttle boats operated through the Waecicu Beach/Sinbad shuttle office on the main street in Labuanbajo.

They depart at 8 am for Bidadari (5000 rp) and Sabola (7500 rp), returning at 4 pm. Contact dive operators in Labuanbajo for diving trips. There has been a shakeout in operators recently, but new ones are setting up. You can arrange diving through the Bajo Beach Hotel, or the Puri Bagus Komodo resort at Batugosok (see Places to Stay later in this section) has a well equipped operation and an office in town.

Other good dive sites closer to Komodo are the islands of **Sebayur** and especially **Tatawa**, which lies within the Komodo National Park boundaries. See the Komodo & Rinca chapter for other diving options.

Other beaches worth lounging on are at **Pulau Kanawa**, about one hour east by boat from Labuanbajo. Kanawa has bungalows and the shuttle boats to Rinca stops there.

Batu Cermin

Batu Cermin (Mirror Rock) is a limestone rock outcrop with caves about 4km from town. Take the road behind (east of) the airport, which ends at a car park and a guard post where you'll have to pay 500 rp if it is attended. Walk five minutes to the caves past a few octagonal bungalows; these were set up to provide rest areas and camping facilities, but they have been vandalised and there is no water.

The caves are impressive. The massive outcrop rises from the flat plain and is cloaked in forest. It is easy to spend an hour or two walking around the base and climbing into the canyons. The main cave is in the centre of the outcrop – take the ladder walkway up and around into the longest canyon. An unmarked cave lies in the centre. You will have to stoop to enter, but you can stand once inside. A torch (flashlight) is essential. You can walk for about five minutes through a series of rooms to where the cave emerges into a towering, narrow canyon with daylight visible above. This is the 'Mirror Rock' that gives the outcrop its name; around mid-morning, the sun shines directly into the canyon and reflects off the walls.

The caves were home to early Neolithic settlers on Flores. A Dutch archaeologist

FLORES

PLACES TO STAY
8 Homestay Gembira
12 Gardena Hotel
16 Mutiara Beach Hotel
19 Bajo Beach Hotel
21 Losmen Sinjai
23 Chez Felix
24 Sony Homestay
28 Mitra Hotel
30 Hotel Wisata
36 New Bajo Beach Hotel
37 Cendana Beach Hotel

PLACES TO EAT
14 Dewata Ayu Restaurant
15 Borobudur Restaurant
27 Sunset Restaurant
35 New Tenda Nikmat

OTHER
1 Batu Cermin Caves
2 Boats to Waecicu Beach & Batugosok
3 Ferry Office
4 Harbour Master's Office
5 Pelni Agent
6 Church
7 Mosque
9 PHPA Information Booth & Guide Association
10 Wartel
11 Suarmanik Kencana
13 Sinbad Shuttle & Waecicu Beach Office
17 Mega Buana Bahari
18 Viewpoint
20 Perama
22 Bank Rakyat Indonesia
25 Post Office
26 Puri Bagus Komodo Office
29 Wartel
31 PHPA Main Office
32 Tourist Office
33 Merpati
34 Telkom Office
38 Market

Labuanbajo

Not to Scale

found various Neolithic remains in the other cave complexes nearby. These caves are in a different direction from the guard post, but are less impressive and not set up for visitors. Take care if exploring them.

Organised Tours

Boat Tours A popular way to travel between Labuanbajo and Lombok is on boat tours. A typical itinerary takes in one of the offshore islands – Bidadari or Kanawa – then Rinca. You sleep overnight on the boat, usually at Pulau Kalong (Flying Fox Island; a mangrove island covered in bats), then head for Komodo to see the dragons and take in some snorkelling. The boats then head along the north coast of Sumbawa making several snorkelling stops off islands, including Pulau Moyo and Pulau Satonda off Sumbawa, before docking at Labuhan Lombok (Lombok).

The main companies are Mega Buana Bahari (☎ 41235), Suarmanik Kencana (☎ 41252) and Perama, which all have their own mid-sized boats. They all have offices on the main street in Labuanbajo. Fares are typically around US$95 (less during the frequent price wars) for a five or six day trip, though you may end up spending the last day at Labuhan Lombok, which has little of interest. Four day trips cost US$75. Bus transfers to Mataram, Lombok, may or may not be included. Shop around and find out exactly what is included – entrance fees, equipment, what sort of food is served, sleeping arrangements (always on the boat, but check the cabin) etc. Try to meet the guides who will take the tours, not just the ticket sellers. Travellers rate the trips from dismal to excellent – it often depends on the crew and your fellow travellers, who you are stuck with for almost a week. Don't expect a luxury cruise – conditions on the boats are very basic.

Mega Buana Bahari also has interesting boat tours along the north coast of Flores to Riung, taking in the iguana site at Torong Padang, the beach and water lily lake at Pota, and the islands off the coast of Riung. This trip can be combined with a through trip to Lombok.

If the ferry schedule to Komodo is not convenient, tours are available. A two day tour, sleeping overnight on the boat, to Komodo, Rinca and Kalong starts at around 50,000 rp per person on a fishing boat that takes eight people. Many hotels can arrange boats for day trips to Komodo or Pulau Sabolo, which has good snorkelling. Small boats for a day trip to Komodo start at around 75,000 rp for up to six people, which will give you about three hours to wander around the island. Boats to Rinca start at around 60,000 rp. Charter boats also can be taken to Bidadari and Sabolo – large boats will cost around 50,000 rp. To charter a boat, contact the main boat tour operators, the Guide Association or the Sinbad shuttle office. Hotels will also arrange boat charter.

The Sinbad shuttle office also operates a shuttle to Rinca for 20,000 rp per person, leaving at 8 am and returning at 4 pm, as well as a cheap shuttle to Bidadari and Sabola (see the earlier Beaches, Snorkelling & Diving section).

Other Tours Overland tours across Flores taking in Ruteng, Bajawa, Riung, Moni/Kelimutu and Maumere are offered by a few travel agents. Mega Buana Bahari, one of the

bigger budget agents, has a five day/six night trip for US$350 per person (minimum two) including meals and accommodation. The Mitra Hotel has a similarly priced trip and Limbunan, at the Bajo Beach Hotel, is a more professional travel agent with a large bus to cater for groups. If you want to hire a car to put together your own tour, it can be arranged, but options are limited and expensive – count on at least 100,000 rp per day for a car and driver.

Places to Stay
You can stay in Labuanbajo itself or at one of the beach hotels. Labuanbajo has a cutthroat tourist industry and price wars between the hotels can see rates drop to ridiculously low levels, especially in the off season. Rates are very variable, and those quoted here should be viewed as a guide to high season prices, but rates can change from week to week, even guest to guest. All hotel rates include breakfast.

Central Area The *Mutiara Beach Hotel* (☎ 41039) is one of Labuanbajo's original hotels and has a waterfront restaurant with a harbour view. Upstairs singles/doubles without mandi cost 5000/8000 rp. They are very basic, but overlook the harbour. Downstairs rooms are dark, but have mandis, and cost 6000/12,000 rp.

The well appointed *Bajo Beach Hotel* (☎ 41009) across the road is more upmarket. It has a range of clean rooms set around a central eating area. Basic economy single/double rooms with outside mandi go for 4000/7000 rp, rooms with mandi cost 7000/10,000 rp or better rooms with fan and shower cost from 10,000/15,000 to 12,500/17,500 rp.

The popular *Gardena Hotel* has a hilltop position above the main road and an attached restaurant serving good food. Simple bungalows around a garden, some with great harbour views, cost 7000/10,000 rp with shared mandi, or 9000/14,000 rp with shower and mosquito nets.

The *Mitra Hotel* (☎ 41003) is a switched-on budget place offering a variety of services, including tours. Simple but clean rooms cost 6000/8000 rp or 10,000/12,500 rp with mandi. It is well geared for travellers and also rents bicycles for 7500 rp per day and motorcycles for 25,000 rp per day.

The *Hotel Wisata* (☎ 41020) competes with the Bajo Beach to be the best hotel in town and has better service. Small rooms with shower and fan cost 10,000/12,500 rp; larger, double rooms facing the courtyard cost 15,000/20,000 rp. The restaurant here is good.

Labuanbajo also has a number of small homestays. The best of these is *Chez Felix*, run by a friendly family that speaks good English. Rooms are clean, with large windows, and there's a pleasant porch area for eating. Singles/doubles are 6000/8000 rp with shared bath, 8000/12,500 rp with mandi and 10,000/15,000 rp with fan and mandi.

Nearby is the quiet *Sony Homestay*, with a nice hilltop view. Basic but clean rooms with private bath are 5000/7500 rp.

Labuanbajo has plenty of other basic, anonymous losmen such as the *Losmen Sinjai* and *Homestay Gembira* next to the mosque. They all charge 5000/7000 rp for rooms without mandi.

The *Golo Hilltop Resort*, about 1km north of town on a hilltop with spectacular views, was one of the best hotels, but it has gone bankrupt. It may open again.

Beach Hotels You'll need to take a boat ride – free for guests – to get to most of these hotels from Labuanbajo.

The *Waecicu Beach Hotel* is a 20 minute boat ride north of Labuanbajo at Waecicu Beach. Boats leave at 9 am, 1 and 6 pm. The beach is dun coloured, but the calm waters are good for swimming and the small island opposite offers a white sand beach and good snorkelling. This has long been a popular budget option because of its price – 11,000 rp per person for a basic bamboo bungalow or 13,500 rp with attached mandi, including three meals.

Puri Bagus Komodo (☎ 41030) at Batugosok is set on a fine white beach on the mainland, a half hour boat ride from town. This is far and away the classiest accommo-

dation in Labuanbajo. Two storey bungalows and lodge rooms are very attractive, but expensive at US$75. The resort has a good restaurant and a dive shop. Boats supposedly leave Labuanbajo at 6, 9 and 11 am, and 7 pm, but enquire at the resort office in Labuanbajo.

The *New Bajo Beach Hotel* (☎ 41047) is 2.5km south of town and is the best hotel that can be reached by road. Air-con double rooms cost 60,000 rp. The beach is pleasant enough, but no world-beater.

The *Cendana Beach Hotel* (☎ 41125), 2km past the New Bajo Beach, is on a nondescript beach. This large hotel has become run down, but rooms are very spacious and reasonably priced at 10,000/20,000 rp with fan and shower; there's better rooms for 15,000/25,000 rp.

Kanawa Island Bungalows is on Pulau Kanawa, one hour by boat from Labuanbajo. The beach and snorkelling here are both very good, and simple bungalow accommodation costs 15,000 rp a double.

Pungu Hotel (☎ 41083) on Pulau Pungu is a new place with simple bungalows a half hour boat ride from Labuanbajo. Bungalows cost 7500/10,000 rp. The booking office is near the post office.

Places to Eat

Labuanbajo has a few good restaurants specialising in seafood at reasonable prices. The pick of the crop is the *Borobudur*, set above the road with lovely views. It has excellent fish, prawns, a few Thai dishes, steaks and even schnitzel. It's more expensive than most, but worth it. The Chinese owner worked as a cook in Australia, so western dishes are a speciality.

The *Dewata Ayu Restaurant* next door also does good seafood and cheaper Indonesian dishes. The *Sunset Restaurant* has a prime position on the harbour side of the road, overlooking the water, but the menu is limited. The *New Tenda Nikmat* has pleasant bamboo decor and does a mean ikan bakar (grilled fish). Otherwise, the restaurants in the *Gardena*, *Bajo Beach* and *Wisata* hotels all have long menus and reasonable prices.

Getting There & Away

Air Merpati has direct flights from Labuanbajo to Bima, Ruteng and Ende. There are also connections to Denpasar and Kupang. Departure tax is 5500 rp.

The Merpati office is between Labuanbajo and the airport, about 1.5km from the town. It is open Monday to Saturday from 7.30 am to 1 pm, and on Sunday from 4 to 5 pm.

Bus & Truck Buses to Ruteng (5000 rp; four hours) leave at 7, 9 and 10 am, noon and around 4 pm when the ferry arrives from Sape and Komodo. The midday buses are not always reliable and may not go if there are not enough passengers. Buses to Bajawa (10,000 rp; 10 hours) leave at 7 am and a bus also usually meets the ferry. The Damri bus to Ende (15,000 rp; 14 hours) also meets the ferry, if you are desperate to get to Kelimutu and are well stocked with painkillers. You can buy tickets from hotels, or from buses hanging around the pier. If you get an advance ticket, the bus will pick you up from your hotel.

Buses and passenger trucks also run to villages around Labuanbajo. Trucks are less comfortable, but cost the same. If you do find yourself on a truck, it's imperative to get a seat in front of the rear axle; positions behind it give good approximations of ejector seats.

Boat The ferry from Labuanbajo to Komodo (4000 rp; three hours) and Sape (11,500 rp; eight to 10 hours) leaves at 8 am every day, except Friday. If a ferry breaks down, the schedule may change, but this is usually a very reliable link. You can get tickets from the harbour master's office (in front of the pier) one hour before departure. Bicycles, motorcycles and cars can be taken on the ferry to Sape (see Sape in the Sumbawa chapter for more details). The ferry doesn't dock at Komodo, but small boats shuttle to the park headquarters for an extra 1500 rp.

The Pelni passenger ship *Pangrango* stops in at Labuanbajo and runs direct to/from Bima and Waingapu on its route through Nusa Tenggara and on to Sulawesi. The Pelni agent has the latest schedules and sells tickets.

Getting Around

To/From the Airport The airfield is 2.5km from the town and hotels can arrange a taxi (5000 rp).

AROUND LABUANBAJO

Around 15km south of Labuanbajo is a **petrified forest**, near the village of Kampung Benteng. It is best reached by motorcycle and with a guide. Also south of Labuanbajo are the **Dolat Lakes**, marshy lakes in a mangrove area that are home to prolific birdlife. They can be reached by taking a bemo to Marombok, on the Ruteng road just before Nggorang, then walking west to Nanganae village and on to the lakes; it's 3½ hours walking all up. Good views across the lake can be had from Gunung Muntung Kajang, 1km away. The lakes also can be reached on foot by the track past the New Bajo Beach Hotel. The full day trip is organised by Nasir Ridwan at the Sinbad shuttle office for 15,000 rp per person.

The Labuanbajo area has a number of **pearl farms**. Artificial pearls are cultivated and grown on the sea in outrigger huts, in the style of traditional *bagan* fishing platforms. Visitors aren't particularly encouraged, but you can visit the one at Kelumpang, about 3km past the Labuanbajo airport. Others are found at Loh Kima on Rinca and Pulau Sebayur.

The road from Labuanbajo to Ruteng climbs into the hills soon after leaving the town. Where they are not farmed, the hills are thickly forested in comparison with the barren, brown hills around Labuanbajo (much of which is due to burning off). About 20km from Labuanbajo, in the village of **Melo**, caci whip fights and traditional dances are staged in an open air venue perched on a hill just above the road with superb views across the coast. Performances are put on for groups and cost 200,000 rp, but plans are afoot to have regular set performances so you can just front up on the allotted days.

On the way to Melo is Nggorang and the turn-off to **Terang**, 32km away. In Terang, the *Hamzah Home Stay* offers basic accommodation for 2500 rp per person and meals

FLORES

are available. The homestay also arranges canoe trips out on the nearby mangrove lakes for 5000 rp per person, the main reason to make the long trip to Terang. Small crocodiles inhabit the lakes. One truck per day goes from Labuanbajo to Terang (2500 rp; 2½ hours) at 7 am along a rough road.

RUTENG

A market town and meeting point for the hill people of western Flores, Ruteng is the heart of Manggarai country – the region extending to the west coast from a line drawn north from Aimere. The town is surrounded by rice fields on gentle slopes beneath a line of volcanic hills. The crisp air gives Ruteng the feeling of a hill town, even though it's quite a sizeable place.

Although Ruteng had been settled long before the arrival of the Dutch, it only rose to prominence under the colonial administration in the 20th century. Although it had its own *dalu* (traditional chief), it only became a centre for the Manggarai when the dalu of Todo, the most important regional clan, moved to Ruteng and was appointed raja of all Manggarai by the Dutch in 1929. The raja's house was unfortunately burnt to the ground a few years ago, but its neglected and modernised reconstruction can be seen in the centre of town. Of more interest is the traditional village of Compang Ruteng, on the outskirts of town.

On a hill to the west of town is the huge mission of the Society of the Divine Word, or Societas Verbi Divini (SVD) as it is more commonly known. Founded in Holland by Arnold Janssen in 1875, this Catholic missionary organisation is active throughout the world. It's the main missionary force on Flores, and is responsible for the majority of conversions since its establishment in 1913. Its seminaries are prestigious centres of learning and, although once dominated by overseas missionaries, most priests are now Florinese. As well as providing modern education, SVD priests have been active in chronicling traditional customs on Flores, such as through the museum in Ladalero near Maumere and indirectly through films like the 1929 *Ria Rago*, a conversion feature film that is a unique history of life at that time.

Like Bajawa, Ruteng is a pleasantly cool town with few attractions in itself. Points of interest lie around the town, but most are difficult to reach. Unlike Bajawa, which has a well developed tourist industry, Ruteng only sees overnight visitors who stop to break the bone-shaking bus journey. Ruteng's market, at the southern edge of town near the cathedral, is a meeting place for people from the surrounding hills and Manggarai weaving can be found.

Information

The tourist office for Manggarai regency is in Labuanbajo, not Ruteng.

The Bank BNI on Jl Kartini and the Bank Rakyat Indonesia on Jl Yos Sudarso offer reasonable rates – better than in Labuanbajo. Banks are open Monday to Friday from 7.15 am to noon and 1 to 3 pm, and the Bank Rakyat Indonesia is also open on Saturday mornings.

The post office on Jl Baruk 6 is open Monday to Saturday from 7 am to 2 pm and for limited postal services on Sunday. The Telkom office on Jl Kartini is open 24 hours.

Places to Stay

The main backpackers choice is the new *Rima Hotel* (☎ 22196), at Jl A Yani 14. It's on the ball with information and arranges bus tickets and tours to surrounding attractions. Economy singles/doubles with shared mandi cost 10,000/15,000 rp, or a few lighter and more spacious rooms cost 15,000/25,000 rp and 25,000/35,000 rp. It has a reasonable restaurant, but make sure you order early.

The *Hotel Karya* on Jl Motang Rua is Ruteng's original hotel, and looks it. It's the cheapest in town at 6000/10,000 rp, but the rooms are dank.

The well run *Hotel Sindha* (☎ 21197) on Jl Yos Sudarso is central and a good option. Rooms with outside mandi for 7000/10,000 rp are bright, roomy and better value than those with mandi for 15,000/18,000 rp. Spacious rooms with western bath, TV and balcony are 20,000/24,000 rp. New VIP

PLACES TO STAY
1 Wisma Agung I
3 Hotel Sindha
5 Hotel Dahlia
7 Hotel Karya
11 Hotel Manggarai
12 Rima Hotel
15 Wisma Agung II

PLACES TO EAT
6 Restaurant Merlin
8 Bamboo Den
9 Rumah Makan
   Sari Bundo
10 Rumah Makan
   Pade Doang
13 Restaurant Dunia
   Baru

OTHER
2 Merpati Office
4 Bank Rakyat
   Indonesia

14 Mosque
16 Main Shops
17 Bus Terminal
18 Police
19 Telkom Office
20 BNI Bank
21 Rumah Adat
   (Raja's House)
22 Post Office
23 Cathedral

Ruteng

rooms with hot water showers cost 45,000 rp. The attached restaurant serves good Chinese food and has satellite TV if you're desperate for news.

Wisma Agung I (☎ 21080), at Jl Waeces 10, is one of the town's best hotels and good value, but is a 15 minute walk from the town centre. Pleasant economy rooms with shared mandi are 7000/10,000 rp, or good renovated rooms with bathroom are 15,000/20,000 rp. The new section next door, Agung III, has spacious, well appointed rooms for 25,000/30,000 rp.

Wisma Agung II (☎ 21835), behind Toko Agung on Jl Motang Rua, is basic but clean and right in the town centre. Economy rooms cost 7500/10,000 rp or rooms with mandi are 12,500/15,000 rp.

The *Hotel Manggarai* (☎ 21008) on Jl Adi Sucipto is close to the town centre and is reasonable value. Rooms with outside mandi go for 8000/10,000 rp, and rooms with mandi cost 10,000/15,000 rp.

The *Hotel Dahlia* (☎ 21377) on Jl Kartini is a fancy-looking hotel. Very ordinary rooms for 10,000 rp without mandi, or 20,000 rp with mandi, are overpriced, but the VIP rooms with hot water for 35,000 rp are among the most luxurious in Ruteng.

Places to Eat
On Jl Motang Rua, the cosy and friendly *Bamboo Den* next to the Hotel Karya has fried chicken, sate and other dishes. *Rumah Makan Sari Bundo* next door is a Padang restaurant serving big prawns and good rendang. Warungs around the market serve Padang food, buffalo soup and sate.

Ruteng has some good Chinese restaurants, such as the *Restaurant Dunia Baru*, at Jl Yos Sudarso 10, and the *Rumah Makan Pade Doang*, at Jl Motang Rua 34. The *Restaurant Merlin* on Jl Kartini near the Hotel Dahlia is also good. Many of the hotels have their own restaurants.

Getting There & Away
Air There are flights most days to/from Bima, Kupang, Denpasar and Mataram, and a couple a week to Labuanbajo, but the airport is ringed by mountains and often fogged in. Flying into Ruteng can be a frightening experience. The Merpati agent (☎ 21197) is out in the rice paddies, about a 10 minute walk north from the town centre.

Bus Buses will drop you at hotels on your arrival in Ruteng. Buses to Labuanbajo (5000 rp; four hours) leave at 8 and 11 am, noon, and 2 and 3 pm. Bajawa buses (5000 rp; five hours) leave around 8 am, 2 and 9 pm. Bajawa-bound buses also come through from Labuanbajo at around 11 am to noon, but can be crowded. To Ende (10,000 rp; nine hours), buses leave in the early morning around 7 am. The night bus, leaving at 5 pm, is quicker and will drop you at your hotel in Ende. The Surya Agung bus leaves at 6.30 am and goes right through to Maumere (17,000 rp), via Ende and Moni (14,000 rp). You can buy tickets for the long-distance buses at the bus terminal, or ticket agencies are scattered around town, but most hotels will get them for you and arrange for the bus to pick you up.

Regular buses run from 8 am to 3 pm to Reo (2500 rp; 2½ hours) along a paved road. Bemos, trucks and buses service other towns around Ruteng. You can catch these buses at the bus terminal or as they circle the streets.

Getting Around
To/From the Airport The airport is about 2km from the town centre, about a half hour walk. The Hotel Sindha offers guests free transport to the airport. Otherwise, you can charter a bemo.

Bemos run around town and to the surrounding villages for 400 rp.

AROUND RUTENG
Golo Curu
Golo Curu (Welcome mountain), 3km to the north of Ruteng, offers panoramic views of the hills, valleys, rice paddies, terraced slopes and distant mountain valleys. Go down the Reo road and, 15 minutes' walk past the Wisma Agung 1, turn right at the small bridge across a stream, just before the 2km post. From the turn-off continue for 500m past the Santo Fransiskus Asisi church to the base of the mountain.

Fourteen Stations of the Cross line the way to the shrine of the Virgin Mary in a small artificial cave on top of the hill. Each year around 31 May and 30 October, hundreds of chanting pilgrims make their way to the top.

Compang Ruteng
Three kilometres from Ruteng, Compang Ruteng is a traditional village centred on its *compang*, the traditional ancestor altar composed of a raised stone burial platform of rocks and ringed by a stone wall. Facing the altar are two *rumah adat* (traditional houses), renovated some 10 years ago. Although they still exhibit the traditional conical roof, in the modern adaptation the roof does not extend to the ground, but sits atop a more modern hexagonal construction.

Looking from the altar, the rumah adat on the right is the Mbaru Gendrang, once the chief's house and the more important of the two. It is used as a meeting house for the village elders and all ceremonies begin here. It is topped by a traditional buffalo head finial and takes its name from the *gendrang* drums that by tradition hang from the centre of the house. The gendrang is used for all important ceremonies and one end is open.

The less important rumah adat on the left is the Mbaru Tambur, so named for the two-ended *tambur* drums that it holds. Tambur drums lack ritual significance, and ceremonies often end at this more informal house.

The Mbaru Gendrang holds many sacred heirlooms, including a gold and silver *panggal*, the buffalo horn shaped headdress used in the caci. The *komak* robe, which can only be worn by a raja or other Manggarai dignitary, the gold *slepi* belt of the chiefs and sacred *kris* are also housed in the Mbaru Gendrang, but they are only brought out for important ceremonies.

The *penti* ceremony, held in August between the rice harvest and the next planting, is the most important Manggarai ceremony to honour the ancestors, and involves caci fights, dancing and the slaughter of buffalo and pigs. It is held every year, but because of the expense, scaled down versions are held most years and the villagers save up for a large penti held every four or five years which lasts for two or three days.

Other ceremonies are held at differing times to honour the ancestors or the recently dead. Small stones are ceremoniously placed on the altar from time to time to honour the ancestors; larger stones involve larger ceremonies. To be buried at the altar is the sole preserve of the rich, for it requires the slaughter of two buffalo, and the family must also pay for a caci and dances.

Caci

If you get the chance, don't miss the caci. These macho whip fights are a ritual contest performed at traditional ceremonies and weddings, and for numerous other events, including Independence Day celebrations. On one visit to Ruteng, a caci contest was held in front of the Catholic Cathedral in honour of the Bishop of Ruteng's 25th year in the priesthood.

Combatants wear protective *panggal* headcoverings like uptilted welder's masks with a buffalo horn motif on top. Dressed in traditional Manggarai sarongs and often adorned with bells and necklaces, they prance around with whips, one attacking while the other defends.

Experienced fighters wear the scars of previous contests, much admired by Manggarai women. Scars are usually on the arms and shoulders, but the prime areas for the attacker to score are on the face, neck and hands. Scars in these areas are not worn with pride for they are a sign that the contestant is not a skilled caci fighter. Make no mistake, when the whips connect they slash the skin and draw blood.

As they prepare for battle, the combatants prance around and sing the praises of manhood and courage to the beat of *gendrang* drums, gongs and singing. In hotly contested competitions between rival villages, the caci fighter sings out to his clansmen, who in turn sing back to encourage him on. As well as praising their own courage they throw jocular insults at their opponents, to the great amusement of the crowd. A good caci contestant is as much an entertainer as fighter. The caci is very much a festive occasion, as well as a blood sport.

The defender carries a rawhide oval shield and a 3m-long whip made from lengths of bound cane, designed to fend off blows. Extra head covering is often worn. The attacker, carrying a shorter 1m-long whip, approaches his opponent and cracks it to announce his intentions. They then engage in combat, feinting and parrying until the attacker lets loose with one fierce blow in the hope of connecting, while the defender does his best to avoid the sting of the whip.

They then swap places, and at more important ceremonies a group of caci fighters will pair off to engage in combat. ■

Dances (or *sae*) include the sae congkolap, performed for the building of a house, and the sae tambung watu, which accompanies a major ceremony when a large stone is place on the altar to honour the ancestors. The *danding* is a courting dance where unmarried men and women dance in a circle by way of introduction before marriage. The *mbata* is a water buffalo dance that involves singing and beating of drums, performed either inside the rumah adat or outside.

The village receives a steady trickle of tourists and the occasional tour group. You will be asked to sign the visitors book and make a sizeable donation. The village also puts on caci and dance performances for groups for 200,000 rp.

Gunung Ranaka

The 2140m Gunung Ranaka, an active volcano that erupted in 1987, can be reached by road – take an eastbound bus along the highway to the turn-off at the 8km mark. It is then a 9km walk along the old Telkom road to the abandoned transmitter station at the top. The road is flanked by two to 3m-high regrowth, so views are limited. It's a taxing walk. You can charter a bemo from Ruteng for around 10,000 rp, but drivers may not be willing to go right to the top. The paved road is in bad repair, especially the last 2km. There are good views from the top if you climb around the barbed wire fence surrounding the transmitter station (take care), but trees obstruct some of the view. You cannot reach the still-active crater, Anak Ranaka, further down the slopes.

Danau Ranamese

Known as 'little Kelimutu' to locals, this lake is 22km from Ruteng, right next to the main Bajawa road. This small lake is a pleasant picnic spot surrounded by jungle-covered hills. A new visitors' centre and accommodation has been built, but it is still not set up for guests and is rarely attended.

Ranamese is best avoided on weekends, when crowds of picnickers invade, but at other times it is a pleasant spot with some good short walks. Concrete trails surround

FLORES

the visitors' centre and lead to the lake, or more natural trails are on the other side of the highway and lead through the jungle at the base of the hills and are good short walks.

Spider Fields

The unique, round paddy fields of the Manggarai are called *lingko*, or 'spider fields' in tour parlance. They can be found all around the region, but one of the best vantage points is 16km west of Ruteng at Kampung Cara. Take the highway to Cancar and then turn off north. Follow the road for 1km past a quarry to the Gua Maria Dikandung Tanpa Noda (Cave of the Immaculate Mary) at Golo Tando. On the other side of the road a trail leads up the hill through the scruffy village of Cara, but great views can be had from the top of the hill across the plains and lingko fields.

The fields do indeed resemble a spider's web, and the pie-shaped segments are allocated to different families. The unusual shape is said to be derived from the cone-shaped *wunut* traditional houses of the Manggarai, the fields representing a flattened version of the houses.

Todo

While Compang Ruteng is an easily accessible taste of Manggarai culture, for a deeper insight it is worth heading into the hills south of Ruteng to Todo. Todo is the ancestral seat of the Manggarai kings and, though other kingdoms also held suzerainty in Manggarai, the Todo rajas were the most powerful.

They reached their peak under the Dutch when the Todo king, Raja Baruk, was appointed raja of Ruteng in 1929 under a plan to provide semi-autonomy and rule through traditional leaders. Raja Baruk's son, Raja Ngambut, was the supreme Manggarai king at the time of independence, when power was stripped from the traditional rulers. However, the first *bupati* (governor) in the new provincial government came from the royal family of neighbouring Pongkor. Descendants of the traditional rulers still command great respect and villagers will sit on the floor at their feet.

Todo village declined when the rajas moved to Ruteng. Todo's compang remains intact and is Manggarai's largest, but the raja's house, the Niang Woang Todo (Place of Judgement) fell into disrepair. With the backing of the government, but especially the church in Todo, a new house was built in the early 90s in traditional style and is Manggarai's largest. Much of the design and the carvings were reconstructed from photographs taken by a Dutch priest earlier this century.

From where the bus stops it is a five minute walk from the road to the traditional heart of the village. Old Dutch cannons, said to be a gift from the kingdom of Bima, guard the entrance to the compang and the main house lies beyond the central altar.

Unlike many villages in Indonesia where history and tradition are quickly forgotten in the headlong rush to the modern world, the villagers are keen to maintain adat, and the elders are repositories of a wealth of detail on Todo culture.

The raja's house is topped by the traditional *rangga kaba*, the buffalo horn finial that marks the house of a raja or chief. The roof, in old Manggarai style, extends down almost to the ground, and stone steps lead up to the doorway. The massive, high-peaked, thatched roof is supported on nine pillars. The central pillar, the *siri bongkok*, was traditionally the place of the raja where he could sit in conference and judgement with his people. The other eight pillars – representing the eight leading families that supply ministers to the king – are carved, but the siri bongkok is unadorned, representing the purity of the raja's judgement.

From the ceiling hang five sacred gendrang drums. Five (and only five) drums are allowed to hang there. The smallest is the 'king' drum and it sits above the others. When the drums are beaten for a ceremony, the king drum must be beaten first.

The towering ceiling of the room is impressive and some of the beams are carved, but the item of most interest lies on a beam directly above the doorway.

In a box tied with rope is the most bizarre drum of all. The drum's membrane is made from human skin, from the stomach of a woman named Welaloe. She was famed throughout Manggarai for her beauty and, as well as the raja of Todo, the rajas of Cibal, Reo and other kingdoms came from afar to seek her hand. She refused them all, and for her insolence she was killed and her blackened skin lies stretched across one end of the drum. The skin from her back was used to make another drum that ended up in Pongkor, but it was burnt in a fire. A huge donation is expected if you want to see the drum.

Getting There & Away Take the highway west towards Labuanbajo and near Bung is the turn-off to Ramut in the south. Todo is 25km from the highway. From Ruteng trucks run to Todo (or take one to Narang and get off in Todo). The road climbs up into the hills past rice paddies and is sealed most of the way, but the asphalt ends 5km before Todo and gives way to a medieval 'jalan batu' (stone road). Like many back roads in Flores, it is embedded with large stones that make for an incredibly bumpy ride, but allow vehicles to pass even in the wet season, which continues well into August in the hills of this region. It is a tough three hour journey by truck, or around two by chartered car or bemo from Ruteng.

Pongkor, a few kilometres before Todo, is another royal village that can be visited, but there is not much to see.

Wae Rero
A number of traditional houses can be found in the Todo area, but the biggest concentration is in Wae Rero, further along the road to Ramut. A dozen or so Manggarai houses have roofs that extend to the ground in traditional style. Although nowhere near as large as the meeting house in Todo, these are the oldest in Manggarai, and are said to be more than 250 years old.

Wae Rero can be reached by a Nangas-bound truck along the stony road past Todo, about 1½ hours from Todo. It's a very bumpy and uncomfortable journey, but the road climbs up into the hills through some superb jungle and over mountain streams.

Twelve kilometres south of Todo, on the way to Wae Rero, is an impressive stone bridge. It looks for all the world like something out of the Middle Ages, but it was built in the late 1980s under the direction of a Swiss priest. It took six months to build with up to 50 labourers per day working on it.

Liang Buah
This large cave is 11km north-west of Ruteng. The huge opening provided shelter for Neolithic settlers, and stegadont tusks were discovered here by a Dutch archaeologist in 1957. Later Indonesian research suggests that the cave was inhabited from at least 2000 BC. The journey to Liang Buah goes through pretty countryside, but it's a long trip just to see a cave. The cave is more like a huge rock overhang and, apart from a tiny cavern at the back, there are no opportunities for caving exploration.

A caretaker is in attendance – sign the visitors' book and make a donation. The caretaker tells the story of how the cave was discovered by hunters earlier this century. The hunters followed their dog, which had run off after quail. They found the dog scratching at the ground, from where ice miraculously appeared. The hunters then discovered that this was the entrance to an overgrown cave, which became known as Liang Buah (Ice Cave in Manggarai). Missionaries used the cave as a classroom in Dutch times.

Getting There & Away From Ruteng, head north along the Reo road and just past the 2km post at Karot is the left turn-off to Liang Buah. A sealed but rough road twists and winds its way through the hills to the friendly little village of **Rampasasa**. Bemos from Ruteng do the trip in just under an hour. The asphalt and the bemos stop at a warung, from where it is a 500m walk along the rough road to the caves.

Cibal
The Cibal district is centred on the village of **Pagal**, 21km north of Ruteng (1000 rp by bus) on the main road to Reo. The area is

noted for its weaving. Manggarai sarongs are black with colourful patterns that resemble embroidery, but are in fact woven using a supplementary weft technique. Manggarai is the only region of Flores that does not produce ikat weaving.

Weaving is produced in Pagal by a co-operative group, the Sinar Kencana. Ask around to see it being made. Women work their looms mainly from May to October. To buy it, ask for Cornelia Rindung who organises the group and collects weaving for sale in Ruteng. High quality sarongs *(lipa songke)* and scarves are produced. The Franciscan church in Pagal is also worth a look for its unusual architecture and multiple spires of corrugated iron.

The former royal village of **Cibal**, in the hills 5km west of Pagal, also produces some weaving, but it is difficult to reach and no public transport runs there. The original compang stone altar still stands in Cibal.

The **Lambaleda** district to the east of Cibal is recognised as the home of the best Manggarai weaving, although it is similar to that in Cibal. Buses run to Benteng Jaya, the main administrative town, but for weaving you'll have to head out to the more remote villages around Golomunga.

REO

Set on an estuary a little distance from the sea, Reo's focal point is the large Catholic compound in the middle of town. The port of Kedindi just outside town is the main port for Manggarai, an export centre since the days when it came under the sway of the sultanate of Bima. Bimanese is still spoken in the town. Not so long ago, when the now-sealed Flores highway was impassable in the wet season, the only way to get to Labuanbajo was by boat from Reo, and small passengers boats still occasionally ply the route.

The road from Reo to Ruteng is sealed and the road from Reo to Riung is under construction, so in the near future travellers can get to Riung via the north coast, which has some good beaches around Pota.

Places to Stay
The centrally located *Losmen Teluk Bayur*, at Jl Mesjid 8, has basic rooms for 10,000 rp and is near the mosque. The *Hotel Nisangnai* on Jl Pelabuhan, the road to Kedindi, is a notch better.

Getting There & Away
The 60km trip by bus from Ruteng takes 2½ hours and costs 2500 rp. Small passenger boats leave from the river dock in town to villages along the north coast; some occasionally go as far Labuanbajo.

RUTENG TO BAJAWA
From Ruteng the highway runs through the mountains and down to the south coast. **Borong** is a hot little settlement with one losmen on the main street. The town is 1km from a reasonable beach where it is possible to stay in villagers' homes. The road heads inland again to the shady village of **Wairana**, set in a fertile valley surrounded by jungle covered hills.

Just over the border between Manggarai and Ngada regencies, **Aimere** is the main town between Ruteng and Bajawa and has a large Sabunese population. There is no reason to pause in Aimere, except to catch ferries that leave from a concrete ramp that passes as a pier. Large car and passenger ferries run to Kupang (Timor) on Monday and Waingapu (Sumba) on Friday, but schedules are subject to change and cancellation.

From Aimere the road leaves the hot south coast and twists its way up to Bajawa. This is a scenic run with views of the coast and the volcano-studded landscape around Bajawa.

BAJAWA
The small hill town of Bajawa (population around 15,000) is the centre of the Ngada people, one of the most traditional groups on Flores. The town is sited at an altitude of 1100m and is surrounded by volcanic hills. It's dominated to the south by Gunung Inerie (2245m).

Bajawa is cool, low key and clean. It also has a good range of restaurants and accommodation, making it a popular place to spend

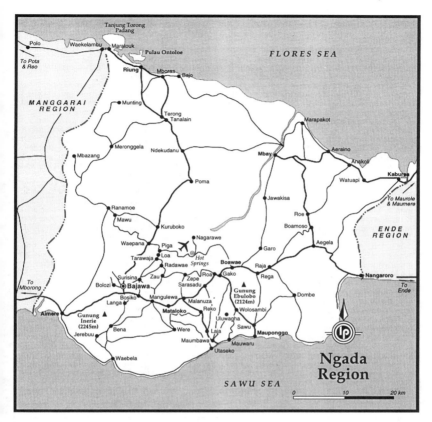

Ngada
Region

a few days exploring the countryside and making trips to the nearby Ngada villages. Along with Labuanbajo and Kelimutu, it is the main tourist destination in Flores.

Information

Bajawa's tourist office (☎ 21554), on Jl Soekarno Hatta, has a couple of brochures and is generally helpful.

The Bank BNI is the best place to change money, or you can try the Bank Rakyat Indonesia on Jl Soekarno Hatta. The post office is north of the latter and is open Monday to Saturday from 8 am to 2 pm.

Places to Stay

Bajawa has a surprising number of hotels for its size and new places are opening all the time. This still isn't enough in the high season around August when it can be hard to find a room. Rates rise when it is busy and are rarely fixed. Even in the off-season Bajawa hotels are expensive for the simple standards on offer, but all include breakfast in the price.

The long-running *Homestay Sunflower* (☎ 21236), on a small path off Jl Ahmad Yani, used to be *the* place to stay, but it is looking a little run down. It's good for

FLORES

The Ngada

The 60,000 Ngada people inhabit both the upland Bajawa plateau and the slopes around Gunung Inerie stretching down the south coast. They were subdued by the Dutch in 1907 and Christian missionaries arrived about 1920. Older animistic beliefs remain strong and the religion of many Ngada, to a greater extent than in most of Flores, is a fusion of animism and Christianity.

The most evident symbols of continuing Ngada tradition are the pairs of *ngadhu* and *bhaga*. The ngadhu is a parasol-like structure about 3m high consisting of a carved wooden pole and thatched 'roof', and the bhaga is like a miniature thatch-roof house. You'll see groups of them standing in most Ngada villages, though in the less-traditional ones some of the bhaga have disappeared.

The functions and meanings of ngadhu and bhaga are multiple, but basically they symbolise the continuing presence of ancestors. The ngadhu is 'male' and the bhaga 'female', and each pair is associated with a particular family group within a village. Though the carved trunks of ngadhu often feel like solid stone, their tops are often dilapidated. Some are said to have been built to commemorate people killed in long-past battles over land disputes and may be over 100 years old. Periodically, on instruction from ancestors in dreams, a pair of ngadhu and bhaga is remade according to a fixed pattern, accompanied by ceremonies which may involve buffalo sacrifices.

The main post of a ngadhu, known as *sebu*, should come from a tree which is dug up complete with its main root, then 'planted' in the appropriate place in the village. Each part of the post has specific designs carved on it on different days: an axe and a cassava on the top part; a dragon head in the form of a flower in the middle; and a geometric design around the base. The three parts are also said to represent the three classes of traditional Ngada society: from top to bottom, the *gae*, *gae kisa* and *hoo*. A crossbeam with two hands holding an arrow and a sword links the top of the pole to the roof. The walls of the bhaga must be cut from seven pieces of wood. Near the ngadhu there's usually a small stone post which is the 'gate keeper', while the bases of both ngadhu and bhaga are often surrounded by circles of stones, said to symbolise meeting places. The bhaga take on more ceremonial importance and food is placed inside as an offering for the ancestors. At some important ceremonies the food may actually be cooked inside the bhaga.

The traditional Ngada village layout – of which there are still a few examples left – is two rows of high-roofed houses on low stilts. These face each other across an open space which contains ngadhu and bhaga and groups of human-high stone slivers surrounding horizontal slabs. The latter, which appear to be graves of important ancestors, have led to some exotic theories about the Ngada's origins.

Traditionally, the Ngada believe themselves to have come from Java and they may have settled here three centuries ago. But stone structures which are in varying degrees similar to these 'graves' crop up in other remote parts of Indonesia – among them Pulau Nias, Sumatra's Batak Highlands, parts of Sulawesi, Sumba and Tanimbar – as well as in Malaysia and Laos. The common thread is thought to be the Dongson culture, which arose in southern China and northern Vietnam about 2700 years ago then migrated into Indonesia, bringing, among other things, the practice of erecting large monumental stones (megaliths). This practice, it's thought, survived only in isolated areas which were not in contact with later cultural changes.

Some writers also claim to have recognised Hindu, Semitic and even Caucasian elements in Ngada culture; one theory seeking to explain apparent similarities between Indonesian and Balkan culture suggests that the Dongson culture originated in south-east Europe!

What makes the Ngada unusual today is their preservation of animistic beliefs and practices. 'Straight' Christianity has made fewer inroads in the villages than in Bajawa itself. In addition to ngadhu and bhaga and the ancestor worship which goes with them, agricultural fertility rites continue (sometimes involving gory buffalo sacrifices) as well as ceremonies marking birth, marriage, death or house building. The major annual festival is the six day Reba ceremony at Bena, 21km from Bajawa, held on 15 December, which includes dancing, singing, buffalo sacrifices and the wearing of special black ikat costumes. The highest god in traditional Ngada belief is Gae Dewa who unites Dewa Zeta (the heavens) and Nitu Sale (the earth). ∎

seeking information and has a pleasant balcony overlooking the valley. Small and often dark singles/doubles cost 7000/9000 rp or 8000/10,000 rp with attached mandi. New rooms off to the side on the hill are much better and cost 15,000 rp.

Not far away, the *Hotel Korina* (☎ 21162) at Jl Ahmad Yani 81 is one of the better places, with friendly and efficient staff. Rooms with outside mandi cost 8000/12,000 rp, or new rooms at back with shower cost 15,000/20,000 rp.

PLACES TO STAY
1 Hotel Ariesta
3 Hotel Virgo
4 Hotel Anggrek
5 Hotel Kembang
6 Hotel Nusa Tera
7 Hotel Kambera
9 Hotel Johny
12 Hotel Kencana
19 Hotel Dam
21 Elizabeth Hotel
22 Stela Sasandy
24 Homestay
    Sunflower
25 Hotel Dagalos
27 Hotel Korina

PLACES TO EAT
8 Komodo Jaya
14 Rumah Makan
    Kasih Bahagia
15 Rumah Makan
    Wisata
26 Carmellya
    Restaurant
28 Borobudur

OTHER
2 Post Office
10 Bank Rakyat
    Indonesia
11 Telkom Office
13 Bemo Terminal
16 Merpati Office
17 Mosque
18 Church
20 Tourist Office
23 BNI Bank

Bajawa

The small *Hotel Ariesta* (☎ 21292) on Jl Diponegoro is bright, clean and a good choice. Rooms at the front or around the pleasant courtyard area at the back cost 15,000/20,000 rp with mandi or 10,000/ 15,000 rp with outside mandi, but are expensive when another 5000 rp is added in the high season.

The *Elizabeth Hotel* (☎ 21223) on Jl Inerie is a fair hike from the centre of town, but worth the effort. Spotless, bright rooms in this family-run establishment cost from 7000/10,000 rp with shared mandi, or very good rooms with shower cost 10,000/15,000 rp and 15,000/20,000 rp.

Nearby, the *Stela Sasandy* (☎ 21198), just off Jl Soekarno Hatta, is another friendly place, although the rooms for 7000/12,500 rp and 10,000/20,000 rp with mandi are not as good as those at the Elizabeth.

The *Hotel Dam* (☎ 21145) is a quiet little place near the church, run by a friendly family. Rooms with attached bath are 10,000/15,000 rp.

A group of hotels can be found close to the centre of town, just north of the market. *Hotel Anggrek* (☎ 21172) on Jl Letjen Haryono has reasonable rooms with mandi for 10,000/ 15,000 rp, and its restaurant serves excellent food.

FLORES

The largest hotel is the *Hotel Kembang* (☎ 21072) on Jl Marta Dinata, which has well appointed double rooms with private bath for 25,000 rp. The hotel is being extended and upgraded to include hot showers, a luxury in cold Bajawa.

Other less appealing options are the *Hotel Kambera* (☎ 21166), *Hotel Virgo* (☎ 21061); *Hotel Nusa Tera* (☎ 21357), *Hotel Johny* (☎ 21079) and *Hotel Dagalos*.

At the bottom of the barrel, the *Hotel Kencana* at Jl Palapa 7 is grungy but friendly and they don't come much cheaper at 4000/7000 rp with mandi.

Places to Eat

For a small town, Bajawa has a good range of restaurants.

The travellers' favourite is the small and friendly *Carmellya Restaurant* on Jl Ahmad Yani. It has good maps of the area and lots of other information. The food is primarily Chinese with a few western and Indonesian dishes. The hot competition is the new *Borobudur* further along the street. A branch of the Labuanbajo restaurant of the same name, it has a similar but more varied menu.

The *Rumah Makan Kasih Bahagia*, on Jl Gajah Mada, is a good Chinese restaurant with cold beer and decent food at reasonable prices. *Rumah Makan Wisata*, further along Jl Gajah Mada near the market, has passable Indonesian and Chinese fare, but slow service.

The *Komodo Jaya* has an extensive menu with a wide variety of good noodle dishes and seafood. Two smaller Padang restaurants right in the market are the *Rumah Makan Pondok Salero* and *Rumah Makan Roda Baru*.

The *Hotel Anggrek* and *Hotel Kambera* both have attached restaurants with long menus – the Hotel Anggrek, in particular, does excellent home-style cooking.

Things to Buy

Bajawa market is busy and colourful, with lots of women from the Ngada area and further afield wearing ikat cloth, some of which is for sale. The better local stuff is black with white motifs, often of horses. The fruit here is plentiful and of good quality.

Getting There & Away

Air Merpati flies from Bajawa to Bima and Ende, with onward connections. The Merpati booking office (☎ 21051) is opposite the Bajawa market.

Bus Most long-distance buses leave from Watujaji terminal, 3km south of town near the Ende-Ruteng road. Hotels can make bookings. Most buses do will pick-ups and drop-offs at hotels.

Buses to Labuanbajo (10,000 rp; 10 hours) leave around 7 am. The Gemini bus has the best reputation. More frequent buses go to Ruteng (5000 rp; five hours), most leaving at 7 am. Buses to Ende (5000 rp; five hours) leave at 7 and 11 am. Surya Agung and Sayang Indah have through buses to Maumere (12,000 rp) via Moni (7000 rp) at 7 am.

Buses go to Riung (4000 rp; 2½ hours) along the newly paved road at 8 am and noon. They leave from the Naru Terminal, 3km north of town, but also pick up in town and cruise the market area for passengers.

Bemo & Truck The town's bemo terminal is on Jl Basuki Rahmat. Regular bemos and some buses go from here to outlying villages such as Mangulewa, Mataloko (600 rp), Langa (500 rp), Boawae (1500 rp) and Aegela (2600 rp). Bemos to Jerebuu (1000 rp), passing Bena (700 rp, but expect to pay 1000 rp) and Malage (850 rp), run hourly from 7 am to 5 pm. There is only one morning and one afternoon bemo that goes direct to Nage. Bemos hang around the market and roam around town, so you can also pick them up on the street.

Getting Around

To/From the Airport The airport is 25km from Bajawa and 6km off the main road to Riung. Regular bemos and buses go to Waepana from the town's bemo terminal on Jl Basuki Rahmat. From here you may be able to get on another bemo to the airport, but don't count on it. Take the Merpati bus (5000 rp).

Bemo Yellow bemos cruise around town, but you can walk almost everywhere except to the bus terminals. Bemos cost 400 rp, or sometimes 500 rp for longer trips.

AROUND BAJAWA

The main attraction of Bajawa is the easily reached traditional villages around the town. You can visit villages by yourself or guides in Bajawa will offer their services. A guide is well worthwhile – instead of awkwardly fronting up yourself at a village, a good guide will provide an introduction, explain local customs and give an insight into village life. Members of the local guiding association have banded together to offer similar tours at 20,000 rp per person for a day trip to the villages, including lunch and public transport. You can also charter a bemo for around 60,000 rp per day or a car, such as a Kijang, for 100,000 rp. All guides are local and knowledgeable. The main difference is their ability to communicate with you, ie their proficiency in English (a few also know a little Dutch, German and French). Talk to your guide beforehand.

Villages in the area are now quite used to tourists and welcome tourism. Taking photos is usually not a problem, but ask and remember that entering a village is like entering someone's home. If visiting independently, sign the visitors' book and make a donation, currently 1000 rp. The rate is fixed by the local tourist office, which has instigated one of the more enlightened tourism programs in Indonesia. Villages are very keen to maintain their traditions, and the money provided by visitors contributes to the building of traditional houses and staging of ceremonies. Guides also liaise with the tourist office to receive training.

Bena and Wogo are the most traditional and impressive villages. Bena also has fine views and gets the most visitors by far. Guides can put together interesting tours and include plenty of other options not mentioned here.

Wolobobo

About 5km from Bajawa, the hill at Wolobobo has fine views across Bajawa and the

surrounding countryside. It is a good place to take in the sunset, but is not serviced by public transport. Head east of Bajawa to Boua and then south along the paved road a couple of kilometres to Wolobobo.

Bolozi

Bolozi has two impressive sets of ngadhu and bhaga totems and an old tomb. The village moved here in 1973, so the houses are mostly modern. The old village, Bolozi Lama, and its ancestor stones lie 1km away in the forest. Bolozi is noted for its dancing, particularly the *leonore*, *teke* and *ja'i* dances, many performed to flute accompaniment. Dances are put on for groups for 150,000 rp and performed frequently in the tourist season. Bemos (500 rp) run from the Bajawa market to Bolozi, or it is only a 30 to 45 minute walk. See the Bajawa town map for directions if walking; if in doubt, ask for Kampung Warusoba, which is on the way to Bolozi.

FLORES

Bomuzi & Langa

The road south from Bajawa passes Bomuzi, which has ngadhu and bhaga, but as its name suggests (Bo means village and muzi means new) it is not that interesting. Langa, 7km from Bajawa, is also a more modern village, but receives many visitors. Like many villages, it moved here after independence when the government encouraged people to move closer to the roads and amenities. The original village, Langa Gedha, is up the hill west of Langa.

Apart from the ngadhu and bhaga in Langa, of note is the graves of the two elders who made the decision to move the village in 1956. The *watu lengi* stone platform in the centre of the village is a central altar and the tall stones on it are used like high back chairs for the elders at ceremonial occasions. The Reba festival to honour the ancestors is celebrated on 15 January when many pigs are slaughtered (see Special Events in the Facts for the Visitor chapter for details of this festival).

Three kilometres from Langa is another traditional village, **Borado**.

Bela

This is the most interesting village in the Langa area. It is a five minute walk from the main road through the village of Dena. Bela is only a small village, but the houses are all traditional and well preserved.

Village lore has it that Bela was settled by two brothers, Bika and Legiwibu, from Borong in Manggarai. As in other Bajawa villages, each set of ngadhu and bhaga represents one clan in the village, but the ngadhu here, with arms projecting from the sides, are slightly different from those found in other villages. The main clan houses are topped with interesting ancestor symbols: the male house, known as the Sakalobo, has a small spear-wielding statue on top, and the female Sakapu'u house has a small statue of a house on the thatch roof.

If you are on foot and heading south, take the pretty side trail through the bamboo groves instead of returning through the village of Dena.

Gunung Inerie

Watumeze, a small settlement of just a few houses in the middle of nowhere between Langa and Bena, is the starting point for the climb to Gunung Inerie. At 2245m, Inerie is the highest peak around Bajawa. Inerie is a volcano, although it is quiet and the last major eruption was in 1882.

It is best to climb the mountain early in the morning because clouds often obscure the panoramic views later in the day. The return walk can be done in four or five hours. The start of the trail is not obvious – ask at one of the houses on the road. Once clear of the fields, the trail is easy to follow up the grassy slopes, then through stunted forest before the last stretch to the crater. The walk is a constant climb, but it's not too difficult, although the final climb up through loose scree to the crater is tedious. The actual peak, and the best views, are on the other side of the crater. Take care on the walk around the rim.

Bena

Underneath the Inerie volcano, 15km from Bajawa, Bena is one of the most traditional villages and its stone monuments are a protected site. High thatched houses are lined up in two rows on a ridge, and the space between them filled with ngadhu, bhaga and megalithic tombs. Built, like most villages, with war in mind, the hilltop position provides not just defence, but also spectacular views.

The village has nine sets of ngadhu and bhaga representing the nine clans, and the tall, jagged megalithic stones off to one side are the graves of the village heroes – warriors that died in battle. Offerings are placed in front of the stones on ceremonial occasions. It is rare to see these stones in villages today because most villages have relocated, leaving the megaliths behind in the original village. Bena is one of the oldest continually inhabited villages in the Bajawa area.

Each set of ngadhu and bhaga are given their own names, eg the first ones in the village are known as Atulolo. The name is decided using a divination ritual common in this region. A name is chosen and then a

Bena's Ancestors

As you enter the village, the first two sets of ngadhu and bhaga belong to the first of the Bena clans, descended from two sisters, Kengi and Kezo. The kepala desa relates the story of how the sisters, when young girls, went off all day to play out in the fields. When they returned, they found everyone in the village dead after eating contaminated buffalo meat. The grief stricken girls had no other relatives, so they lived on in the village alone. Many years passed and the girls grew to become young women, never meeting another soul.

Then one day, two men from Beiposo village were on a hunting expedition in the river valley below Bena. Near the hot springs, their dog sniffed out a pig and chased it, the men in pursuit, crashing through the undergrowth. The dog cornered the pig in a cave, where it was killed, and the men took shelter in the mouth of the cave. Weary and hungry, they wanted to eat the pig but had no fire for cooking, so one of the hunters, Leki, climbed a tree to survey the valley and saw smoke coming from the ridge.

Leki went to investigate, climbed up to Bena and the two beautiful sisters appeared before him like a vision. Leki explained his predicament and the sisters gave him fire. Descending down from the ridge, he threw the fire away and returned to ask for more. Again he took the fire and again dropped it so he would have an excuse to be with the sisters. Eventually the sisters asked what it was he really wanted, and so the two men brought the pig up to the village to share with the sisters. From pork chops sprang love and marriage, and thus the Bena clans were founded. ∎

piece of bamboo with a knot is placed on the fire. If the bamboo splits at the knot, then two more pieces are placed on the fire and if they all split at the knot then the chosen name is the true one. If not, then another name is chosen and the ritual repeated.

The houses of the village clans have a little model house on top of the roof and small warrior statues, representing the female and male clan houses respectively. A small Christian shrine sits on a mound at the top of the village, and behind it a recently built shelter offers a spectacular view of Gunung Inerie and the south coast.

Bena is far and away the most visited village, receiving an astonishing 6000 visitors per year. It is touristy – souvenirs and ikat for sale line the fronts of the houses, and it can be crowded when tour buses arrive – but traditional beliefs and customs are still strongly followed, and new houses are built in traditional style and ceremonially consecrated.

The main Reba ceremony is held in Bena on 15 December, when dozens of pigs and other animals are slaughtered as offerings to the ancestors. Reba was held on 27 December for many years, after the priests moved the day until after Christmas, but the ceremony has now moved back to the original date to conform with adat.

It may be possible to stay with the kepala desa, and you should make a donation to pay for accommodation. Plans are afoot to open a homestay.

Getting There & Away Bena is 12km from Langa. Occasionally, bemos go from Langa to Bena, but more often they finish in Langa and you'll have to charter one the rest of the way or walk. The easiest way to get to Bena is on the direct bemos from Bajawa, which go via Mangulewa. They run hourly from 7 am to 5 pm, cost 1000 rp and continue on to Jerebuu.

Malanage Hot Springs

The road south of Bena descends 2km to Bena's market, which comes alive on Tuesdays, and about 3km further along an increasingly rough road is Malanage, past the turn-off to Jerebuu. The hot springs here are a delight. Surrounded by forest, a boiling emerald-green river meets a cold water stream and you can bathe further down in the rock pools where the waters mingle to a comfortable temperature. This is also the mandi and laundry for the nearby village, so modest dress and behaviour are essential.

FLORES

Only one morning and one afternoon bemo pass Malanage, or more frequent bemos run to the Jerebuu turn-off and you can walk from there.

Nage

Nage is a unique traditional village on a plateau about 7km from Bena, also with great views of the countryside and Gunung Inerie. Several well maintained ngadhu and bhaga and some unusual tombs lie between the high-roofed houses. The ancestral tombs, *nabe tegu*, are topped with flat stone slabs, more like those of Sumba, and in front of the first ngadhu is the *peo*, the upright sacrificial stone where animals are tied for slaughter. The peo is common in many parts of central Flores, but unusual in the Bajawa area.

Reba is held on 1 January in Nage, but the most notable ceremony, Oluka, occurs two days later. During Oluka, elders stand on the stone slabs and utter profane abuse at anyone who enters the main compound.

The Nage houses are also slightly different from others in the area, and are a mixture of old and new. The four biggest traditional houses were built in 1997 and were accompanied by the slaughter of nine buffalo and more than 100 pigs in a huge and very expensive ceremony.

Getting There & Away One morning and one afternoon bemo runs between Nage and Bajawa, via Bena and Mangulewa. Nage is just a short walk uphill off the main road.

Wogo

Wogo is a large village with eight or nine sets of ngadhu and bhaga, ringed by traditional houses. This is one of the Bajawa area's largest and most impressive traditional villages, although a few signs of modernity can be seen. The original village, Wogo Lama, was abandoned many years ago when the villagers decided to move closer to the main road and the delights of modernity, such as electricity.

About 1km further on from Wogo, turn off through the bamboo grove at the Dadawea sign and follow the track off to the left to Wogo Lama, where vast, jagged groups of stones jut from the ground. These megalithic ancestor tombs are still important for use in ceremonies.

Similar megaliths can be seen at nearby Toda Lama. Continue about 500m east past the Mataloka seminary and the tombs are a further 500m from the road.

Getting There & Away Wogo is 1.5km from Mataloko, which is 18km from Bajawa on the Ende road and easily reached by bus or bemo. Mataloko is famous for its huge seminary on the highway.

SOA

Soa is about 20km north of Bajawa. It is often shown as a town on maps, though in fact there is no Soa town and the name refers to the region. The area is drier and less mountainous that the lush countryside around Bajawa in the south. The Soa people, though linguistically related to the Bajawanese, have a transitional culture related to the Boawae district bordering it to the east. The main attractions of Soa are the hot springs on the road past the airport, and the village of Loa.

Loa

Unless a special ceremony is happening, Loa has little to see, the houses are all modern and casual visitors might well as not bother. Yet despite the lack of traditional sights, Loa has rich and complex ceremonial traditions and its unique customs make it one of the most fascinating Ngada villages.

In June every year, after the harvest, villagers from miles around flock to Loa to witness traditional *sagi* fights, when two men fight holding a *woe*, two oblong lumps of wood wrapped in twine and joined by a length of string. Each holds one end of the woe and attempts to bash the other, while the free hand is used to fend off blows. Turban-like headgear and woven jackets are worn to provide some protection.

The object is to hit the forehead and draw blood, for it is believed that blood spilt on the earth will ensure fertility for the next

Loa's Ritual Cycle of Life

The main ceremonial cycle of Loa consists of seven main events, based on the rituals of puberty and marriage. Apart from the important social functions, the cycle serves to institute unique, traditional population controls. Many of the ceremonies are accompanied by feasting and dancing, but they are only held when felt necessary and may occur years apart.

As related by village elders, the cycle begins with the Sunat or circumcision ceremony for boys, unusual in this part of Indonesia. Sapu is next in the cycle and is the men's ceremony lasting three or four days. During this time, wives must go far enough away not to be able to see the fire of the village. Next is Dodho, the ear piercing ceremony for girls and women.

Then comes the most unusual ceremony of all, Feka. Practised by just one clan in Loa, men and women around 40 years of age declare that they will no longer have children. For 10 days they stay away from the village in a designated area, go naked from the waist up, and eat preserved meat and other prepared foods. Feka only occurs once every 10 or 15 years, but the young men and women of the village cannot marry unless it has been performed in their lifetime. A feast is held one year later on the day before sagi and then marriages can proceed. One year later, a large feast of 100 pigs follows, and marriage is again outlawed for one year.

Other ceremonies include Kiki, when women have their teeth filed, which must be performed before a woman can marry. Belis is held for arranging marriages, and the bride price is negotiated, fixed in the range from three to 11 buffaloes. But unless a woman or man has already experienced all the other ceremonies, they will have to wait to get married.

When the ceremonies from Sunat to Belis are complete, only then can the Para festival be held to complete the cycle. Para is a great feast of 30 or more buffaloes, when the square of Loa is fenced off and the men enter the ring to spear the buffalo, in much the same way as toreadors prepare to kill a bull. An elder sits in the fork of the peo altar, directing proceedings from above the mayhem. The buffaloes are finished off by having their throats cut with a *parang*. When all the buffaloes have been killed the feasting begins.

Para is very expensive and it may be decades before another one is held. After Para, the ceremonial cycle, beginning with the Sunat, starts again. ■

crop. Sagi honours the gods and the ancestors and is accompanied by dances and feasting. In Loa, the villagers dance all night on the day of dero, three nights before sagi. The sagi cycle actually begins in February, to accompany the young corn feast. Women have sagi fights then, but charcoal is used and it is enough just to mark the opponent.

Sagi, and most other ceremonies, are held in the main square of the village, facing smoking Gunung Ebulobo. At one end of the square is the *peo*, a large Y-shaped, wooden totem. The peo is intricately carved and brightly painted, and is the main altar where animals are sacrificed.

Rori lako (Running of the Dogs) is a hunting ceremony held in October, three days after the full moon. Wild pig and deer are hunted on horseback with spears, and a hunter claims a kill by shouting out the name of his horse. A hunting site is determined by throwing pieces of bamboo on a fire (the same divination ritual as in Bena), and two days of hunting are followed by a day of feasting and dancing.

Hot Springs

Mangeruda, past the airport on the back road to Boawae, has developed hot springs next to a river. Hot water bubbles up into a large clear pool. It's an excellent spot for a dip and you can cool off in the river. Entry costs 1000 rp, and new bungalows and a large restaurant have been built next to the springs. The bungalows are comfortable and cost 25,000 rp per person, but are usually empty and the complex is already starting to look run down.

The springs are far from anywhere and are not serviced by regular public transport. Most of the tours out of Bajawa visit the springs.

BOAWAE

Forty-one kilometres from Bajawa on the highway to Ende, Boawae is the centre of the Nage-Keo people, who speak a related but distinct language to the people of Bajawa.

FLORES

Boawae sits at the base of smoking **Gunung Ebulobo**. The 2124m-high volcano can be climbed with a guide hired in the village and usually involves an overnight stop on the mountain at the village of Mulakoli, then a two hour ascent early the next morning. It can be climbed in one day from Boawae by first taking a bus 3km east along the highway and then it is a one hour walk to Mulakoli. Because the surrounding area is relatively dry, the mountain is usually free of cloud throughout the day, but the later you start the hotter the walk.

Boawae is the source of most of the best Bajawa-area ikat. Gory buffalo-sacrifice rituals take place here, and an equally messy form of boxing called *etu*, virtually the same as sagi in Loa, is part of the March to July harvest festivities. The boxers wear garments made of tree bark painted with animal blood and their gloves may be studded with broken glass.

Places to Stay

Few visitors bother to stop at Boawae, but the *Wisma Nusa Bunga* on the highway has clean, simple rooms from 12,000 rp. A much better option is the *Hotel Sao Wisata* – take the road next to the Wisma Nusa Bunga and follow it for 1.5km down to the river and then around to the left near the church. In lush gardens by the river, this delightful guesthouse has doubles for 25,000 rp and meals are available. The owner, educated in Germany, is a cultured host and can arrange dance performances for groups.

RIUNG

This small Muslim/Christian fishing village is one of the few places on Flores with access to white sand beaches and excellent snorkelling over intact reefs. The village itself is nondescript – a Muslim Bugis stilt village sits on the harbour mudflats surrounded by a small sprawl of other houses. The people of Riung speak a very different language from that of the other Ngada people.

Like Labuanbajo, the real attraction is the offshore islands, now declared a marine park, and their fine white-sand beaches and

snorkelling. Getting to them requires a charter boat, which is easy to arrange.

Riung also has its own version of Komodo dragons, and these slightly smaller monitors can be seen further north along the mainland coast.

Watujapi Hill, about 3km from Riung, offers a magnificent view of the Seventeen Islands Marine Park offshore. If you count them, there are more like 24 islands, but the government authorities decided on the number as a neat tie-in with Independence Day!

Information

The PHPA office is near the Homestay Tamri Beach and is helpful with information about the Riung area. You must sign in and pay 750 rp before going to the islands. The office may have snorkelling equipment for rent, but don't count on it – the Nur Iklas and Pondok SVD are a better bet.

The tourist information office near the harbour is a local commercial cooperative and the place to arrange boats and guides. It is also good for general information.

Seventeen Islands Marine Park

The long-winded Taman Wisata Laut Tujuh Belas Pulau Riung, otherwise known as Seventeen Islands, is a marine reserve of 11,900ha administered by the PHPA. The islands are uninhabited and building is not permitted. Most islands are very small, but some have beautiful beaches and good snorkelling. The reefs are reasonably intact, and are noted for the prolific soft corals including sea roses. The reefs are mostly a snorkelling rather than a diving destination.

The nearest island, just a couple of hundred metres in front of Riung's harbour, is **Pulau Pata**. This tiny island once had a sizeable population until the people were resettled on the mainland. The kids used to swim to school and competent swimmers could do the same to reach the island. Pata itself is nothing special, but the reef on the north side of the island has some good snorkelling.

To reach all the other islands requires a

boat. To the north-west, the largest island by far is **Pulau Ontoloe**. The island has rolling grass-covered hills and is mostly ringed by mangroves. The north of the island has a couple of passable beaches and a mangrove bay where bats nest in their thousands. Ontoloe does have one inhabitant, a hermit Polish/Indonesian priest who has set up camp and conducts his own reafforestation project, planting trees all over the island.

Ontoloe is very close to the mainland in places and near the fishing village of Mbarungkali, about 4km from Riung, you can walk across to the island at low tide. At Tanjung Wingkoroe, the next headland north of Mbarungkali, good snorkelling can be found just offshore.

The islands of most interest are about 30 minutes by boat north-east of Riung. In a line are the islands of **Bakau**, **Rutong**, **Bampa** and **Tiga**. Pulau Bakau's reef has the best snorkelling while Pulau Bampa is home to small bats. Pulau Rutong and Pulau Tiga are the most visited islands because of their superb beaches – wide, pure white sands fronting clear turquoise waters. Day shelters have been built on these islands and there is good snorkelling on the reefs.

East of Pulau Tiga is another group of islands arcing back towards the mainland. They also have some good beaches and lie just a few hundred metres from the small port of Bajo, 10km east of Riung. Bajo handles the bigger boats that can't dock at Riung, but it is more difficult to charter a boat in Bajo to visit the islands.

Lying off by itself, the most easterly island is **Pulau Taor**. It also has coral reefs, but is better known as 'Sunrise Island' because this is where the boat tours come to see the sunrise and the view across all the islands.

Boat Trips The tourist information office in Riung runs a number of good day trips, leaving at 8 am and returning at 4 pm. The short trip goes to the north-east islands and takes in the best beaches and three snorkelling spots for 9000 rp per person (minimum of five) or 8000 rp per person for six to 10 people. The long trip also takes in Ontoloe,

the bat colony and another snorkelling spot and costs 12,500 rp or 10,000 rp for six to 10 people. All trips include the park entrance fee, snacks and a guide.

The sunrise trip starts at 4.30 am to see the sunrise from Pulau Taor and then takes in the long trip and more snorkelling options. It costs 20,000 rp per person or 17,500 rp for six to 10 people and includes lunch.

Boat tours operating out of Labuanbajo also run along the north coast of Flores to Riung (see the Labuanbajo section earlier in this chapter). There's no agent or schedule for the tours, but when a tour ends in Riung, the crew does the rounds of the homestays looking for return passengers. To charter a boat for a two day trip to Labuanbajo will cost around 300,000 rp.

Dragon Spotting
Known locally as *mbou*, the giant monitor lizards around Riung are related to, but more brightly coloured than, Komodo dragons, and have yellow markings. They are thinner and shorter, but can still grow to 3m or more in length. They can be seen at **Torong Padang**, a peninsula to the north-west of Riung past Damu and Pulau Ontoloe. However, chances of spotting the beasts are very slim and it requires a stakeout for hours, if not days, using a dead dog for bait.

If you are really interested you can arrange a trip in Riung. Much easier, and probably better for the mbou's habitat, is to see the one held by a PHPA ranger underneath a house opposite the PHPA office. The concrete cage is depressing, but the mbou is a large and healthy specimen.

Places to Stay & Eat
There are five *homestays* in Riung, all offering bed-and-meals deals for 10,000 rp per person or 6000 rp for room and breakfast only. They may add 10% tax to the rates. Given that the only other dining option is the *Rumah Makan Cilegon*, which serves fish, rice and more fish, you are better off eating in the homestays.

A good choice for information and originality is the *Nur Iklas*, right next to the

FLORES

Riung

To Seventeen
Islands Marine Park
Pulau
Pata

FLORES
SEA

0   125   250 m
Approximate Scale

Tourist Information
Nur Iklas

Homestay
Tamri
Beach

Mbou

PHPA
Office

Church

Homestay
Madona

Liberty
Homestay

Persona
Riung

Pondok
SVD

Rumah
Makan
Cilegon

Market

To Watujapi Hill,
Mbay & Ende

Homestay
Florida Inn

harbour. The wooden building, originally a traditional stilt house, features precarious stepladders and a large first floor balcony. The manager speaks excellent English.

Liberty Homestay has a nice balcony area and garden, and slightly more substantial rooms. Nearby, *Homestay Madona* is very similar and run by a friendly couple.

Homestay Tamri Beach is popular with travellers and has good maps and information. *Homestay Florida Inn*, on the road into town, is a bit far from the harbour.

Persona Riung are government-owned bungalows that cost 6000/10,000 rp for singles/doubles and 7500/15,000 with mandi. They are a notch up in quality and slightly more private than the homestays, but not as good value.

The most salubrious accommodation is the *Pondok SVD*, the church guesthouse. Spotless, comfortable rooms with bathroom face a courtyard garden, but are expensive at 25,000 rp per person. Lunch and dinner costs an extra 7500 rp.

Getting There & Away

The Bajawa-Riung road is an excellent 'hot mix' road, and buses do the trip in 2½ hours.

Buses leave Bajawa at 7 am and 1 pm. They cost 3500 rp to the terminal or 4000 rp to drop you at a hotel in Bajawa.

Buses to Ende (4500 rp; 4½ hours) leave at 7 am, but there are no direct buses on Sundays and Mondays, when you'll have to take a bemo to Mbay (1500 rp; 1½ hours) and then the noon bus to Ende. The road to Mbay is sealed but rough. Buses to Riung leave from Ende's Ndao terminal.

The Riung-Reo road is under construction and nearing completion. Until finished, trucks run only as far as Pota. Market boats still run along the north coast and there's one to Reo on Tuesday mornings.

MBAY

Mbay (previously known as Danga) is a town on the move, though it's hard to believe. This small, dusty market town is in the process of superseding Bajawa as the capital of the Ngada regency. Apart from a wartel behind the grotty market, it doesn't even have telephones.

The decision to move the capital is based on economic geography. The port of Marapakot is only 12km north of Mbay, and the old airstrip, which was a Japanese air base during WWII, is to be rehabilitated. Mbay is also on the new north coast highway, which, when complete, will be the main commercial artery on Flores. When the Dutch built a highway across Flores they chose the mountainous and wet southern route – slow, winding and subject to washouts. The north coast, however, is dry and mostly flat. The much quicker northern highway already runs from Maumere to Riung and will eventually run right through to Labuanbajo.

Apart from bus connections, Mbay has no attractions, unless you're interested in Japanese caves. The 'caves' are ammunition dumps carved out of the rocky hills during WWII and still have Nipponesque names such as Oki Sato, Sanga Toro and Oki Wajo. There's one about 3km from town. Take the highway east to the new government district – at present it's just a solitary building in a dust bowl where the governor sits in business two days a week until the rest of his administration eventually moves from Bajawa. Take the turn-off road to the office and continue to the far hill where there's a large cavernous bunker.

Mbay is about 50km east of Riung and 85km from Ende. The road to Ende is scenic and runs through mostly bare hills. The sea views are dominated by **Pulau Palue**, which hangs off the volcano of Rokatenda, which is also the name of a famous dance. This dry island, so dry that water has to be imported, once came under the sway of the rajas of Sikka in eastern Flores. It has its own unique culture and produces some fine ikat. The poor fishing communities on the island roam right along the north coast of Flores in search of catch.

Places to Stay
Hotel Stela Sesandy is the best option and has basic rooms with shared mandi for 6000 rp or a new block of 'VIP' rooms with mandi for 15,000 rp. It's a well run place, on the main highway a few hundred metres uphill from the market. Otherwise the grungy *Hotel Mandiri* is behind the market.

Getting There & Away
Buses stop at the market on the highway in the centre of town. Buses go to Ende (3000 rp; three hours) at 7 am and noon. Regular buses run to Maumere (5000 rp) in under four hours, which is twice as fast as using the Ende road. Buses also run to Riung (1500 rp; 1½ hours) and Bajawa in 2½ hours.

Central Flores

Comprising the regency of Ende (capital Ende), central Flores is home to the island's main natural attraction – the tri-coloured, volcanic lakes of Kelimutu. In their rush to get to Kelimutu, few visitors pause in Ende, the historic main city on Flores, but it is a

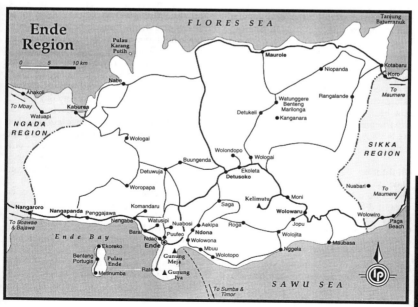

pleasant, easy-going city to wait for a boat to Sumba.

Moni, the gateway village to Kelimutu, gets the most visitors, and the surrounding region of the Lio people is still very traditional and noted for its fine ikat weaving.

ENDE

Like their neighbours, the people of south-central Flores in and around the port of Ende have a mix of Malay and Melanesian features. The aristocratic families of Ende link their ancestors, through mythical exploits and magical events, to the Hindu Majapahit kingdom of Java. Today, most of the 60,000 people living in Ende are Christians, but there is a large Muslim population, the descendants of immigrants from Java and particularly Sulawesi.

Ende is a pleasant enough city, the largest on Flores, and is surrounded by fine mountain scenery. The perfect cone of Gunung Meja rises almost beside the airport, with the larger Gunung Iya occupying a promontory south of Gunung Meja. Ende is primarily a stopover to eastern Flores, or a launching pad to Sumba, although trips to nearby villages are worthwhile if you are stuck for something to do, and there's interesting weaving from around Flores and Sumba to look at.

A December 1992 earthquake caused extensive damage in Ende, but things are now back to normal. Ende is very hot and dusty towards the end of the dry season, but the hills above the town are lush and very scenic.

Orientation

Ende is at the neck of a peninsula jutting south into the sea. The old port of Ende and most of the shops are on the western side of the neck; the main port, Pelabuhan Ipi, is on the eastern side. The predominantly Muslim market area is noisy and a bit grotty. Heading east up the hill from the old port are the greener suburbs, the churches, some colonial architecture and the houses of Ende's well-to-do residents.

Ende has two bus terminals: Wolowana,

about 5km east of town (for buses going east), and Ndao, along the waterfront 2km north of town (for buses going west).

Information

Money The Bank Rakyat Indonesia is in the same building as the Hotel Dwi Putri on Jl Yos Sudarso, and the Bank BNI is on Jl Gatot Subroto near the airport. The Bank Danamon on Jl Soekarno doesn't change foreign currency, but may be worth trying for credit card transactions. Hotel Ikhlas also changes money for after hours transactions.

Post & Communications The main post office is out in the north-eastern part of town on Jl Gajah Mada. If you need stamps, there's a sub-post office opposite the Bank Rakyat Indonesia. You'll find the Telkom office on Jl Kelimutu, about a 15 minute walk from the waterfront.

Things to See & Do

In 1933 the Dutch exiled Soekarno to Ende, and his house on Jl Perwira is now the **Muzium Bung Karno**. There's not a lot to see, apart from some photographs and household implements, but the caretaker can tell you a few stories if your Indonesian is good enough. It's open Monday to Saturday from 8 am to 1 pm.

On Jl Hatta, the new **Muzium Bahari** (Maritime Museum), open every day from 7 am to 8 pm, has a large collection of sea shells, but not much else. Entry is 500 rp. The **Muzium Rumah Adat** next door is a large traditional house and a stylised village compound in front with a *tubu musu* (sacrificial stone altar). It's worth a look and the museum holds a few unlabelled artefacts such as spears, drums and cooking utensils. It's open Monday to Saturday from 8 am to 2 pm. Entry is 500 rp.

Benteng Baranui is the remains of a traditional fort. Although often claimed to be a Portuguese fort, it is an ancestral Ende village with the stone ramparts and defensive walls typical of past warrior societies. Only a few stones remain in the jungle, but it is a pleasant walk with views of Ende from the

FLORES

FLORES

Ende

SAWU SEA

Runway

Pelabuhan Ipi

To Sumba & Kupang

Ende Bay

To Pulau Ende

To Ngao Terminal & Bajawa

To Hospital & Benteng Baranu

To Wolowona Bus Terminal/ Moni & Maumere

Gunung Meja (661m)

0   100   200 m

PLACES TO STAY
4 Hotel Nirwana
8 Hotel Dwi Putri; Bank Rakyat Indonesia
20 Hotel Hamansyur
22 Hotel Flores
26 Hotel Amica
30 Hotel Wisata
32 Losmen Makmur
33 Penginapan Rinjani
34 Hotel Safari
35 Hotel Ikhlas
37 Hotel Melati
40 Hotel Angrek
41 Bitta Beach Bungalows & Restaurant

PLACES TO EAT
13 Rumah Makan Minang Baru
19 Rumah Makan Bundo Kandang & Rumah Makan
23 Istana Bambu
29 Rumah Makan Tanur Merah
30 Rumah Makan Ampera Padang
38 Restoran Merlyn

OTHER
1 Main Post Office
2 Church
3 Gereja Salom (Protestant Church)
5 Muzium Bung Karno
6 Muzium Bahari;
   Muzium Rumah Adat
7 Bank Danamon
9 Sub-Post Office
10 Flores University
11 Bemo Stop
12 Soccer Field
14 Cathedral
15 Cendana Art Shop
16 Pelni Office
17 Ikat Market
18 Market;
   Bemo Terminal
21 Mosque
24 Telkom Office
25 Istana Photo
27 Pasar Potulando (Night Market)
28 Merpati Office
31 Mosque
36 Airport Terminal
39 BNI Bank
42 Harbour Master's Office

top. The trail starts in Kampung Nirananga on Jl Sam Ratulangi, directly behind the hospital. The trail is hard is hard to find, so ask one of the village boys to show you the way for a couple of thousand rupiah. If you draw a blank, ask for Pak Anton Riwu, who is helpful. After you negotiate the village and its bamboo and coconut groves, the trail is easy to follow and it's a 20 minute walk steeply uphill. At the top, among the low stone platforms (possibly old graves) are modern graves with bottles of tuak beside them. As on most of Flores, tuak is placed beside graves to slake the thirst of the spirits. Tobacco is also offered. Gunung Wongge can supposedly be climbed from here in two hours, but this looks like a very tough route through thick undergrowth – take a guide.

The waterfront **market** on Jl Pasar is a lively place to wander around, and there's an ikat market on the corner of Jl Pabean and Jl Pasar which sells a large variety of ikat from Flores and Sumba. The **Pasar Potulando** night market on Jl Kelimutu sells snacks, fruit and vegetables if you are desperate for something to do.

Places to Stay

Oversupply and stiff competition between the hotels keep prices down, so Ende hotels are good value. Accommodation is fairly spread out, but frequent bemos make it easy to get around.

Near the airport, *Hotel Ikhlas* (☎ 21695) on Jl Jenderal Ahmad Yani is in a 'klas' of its own – friendly, on the ball with travel information and exceptional value. There's a range of rooms starting with clean, basic singles/doubles for 3500/6000 rp with shared mandi, to small rooms with mandi and fan for 7000/10,000 rp and large new rooms for 10,000/15,000 rp. Good, cheap western and Indonesian food is available and it has satellite TV. Tours and transport can be arranged to Kelimutu and many attractions around Ende.

Next door, the spacious and airy *Hotel Safari* (☎ 21499) has friendly staff and a restaurant. Rooms are charged at 10,000/

15,000 rp with mandi, or 35,000/40,000 rp with air-con.

The small *Hotel Amica* (☎ 21683), at Jl Garuda 39, is a good budget hotel. Rooms go for 10,000/15,000 rp, all with attached bath. The young manager speaks excellent English and can fill you in on excursions around Ende.

If you want to be close to the centre of town near the market, the *Hotel Hamansyur* (☎ 21373), at Jl Loreng Aembonga 11, is cheap but dingy. Rooms in the old building cost 7000/10,000 rp, or newer, much better rooms with mandi cost 10,000/15,000 rp.

The *Hotel Flores* (☎ 21075) at Jl Sudirman 28 has a range of rooms starting with first floor economy rooms with shower for 10,000/15,000 rp, to clean rooms with fan and mandi for 16,500/22,500 rp and air-con doubles for 40,000 rp and 55,000 rp. There's a small restaurant as well.

The large and spotless *Hotel Dwi Putri* (☎ 21685) on Jl Yos Sudarso is the best in town and also has a good first floor restaurant. Rooms with fan, shower and flushing toilet are 20,000/25,000 rp, air-con rooms are well appointed and cost 40,000/50,000 rp, and VIP rooms are very large and have fridges, but are not worth 125,000 rp.

The quiet *Hotel Wisata* (☎ 21368) on Jl Kelimutu is another more upmarket hotel and is reasonably priced. Large, new rooms at the back cost 15,000/20,000 rp with mandi. Huge air-con rooms are 30,000/40,000 rp and VIP rooms are 45,000/60,000 rp. It also has a TV lounge and a restaurant.

The *Hotel Melati* (☎ 21311) is just around the corner from the airport on Jl Gatot Subroto, or the new *Hotel Anggrek* (☎ 22538) on Jl Gatot Subroto is better value and has rooms with shower for 15,000 rp.

The *Bitta Beach* (☎ 21965) could be a good nice spot away from the bustle of Ende, but the karaoke at the Bitta Beach Restaurant next door and the disreputable late night crowds on weekends are a deterrent. Bungalows with air-con cost 40,000 rp. They need maintenance, but the beach is decent and the sea views better. It's past the airport down a narrow road to the beach.

FLORES

The *Hotel Nirwana* (☎ 21199) at Jl Pahlawan 29 is a better class of hotel and is quiet, while the *Losmen Makmur* and *Penginapan Rinjani* are both cheap but seedy dives.

Places to Eat

The market area has the biggest concentration of rumah makan. These include the *Bundo Kandung* for Padang food and the *Istana Bambu* next door, one of Ende's best restaurants, with a long menu of Indonesian, Chinese and seafood dishes.

The *Rumah Makan Tanur Merah*, on Jl Kelimutu near the Telkom office, is an unpretentious but very clean place that does great nasi sate (soup, rice and sate) and other Madurese dishes. Most other restaurants serve Padang cuisine, such as the *Rumah Makan Minang Baru* on Jl Soekarno and the *Rumah Makan Ampera Padang* at Jl Kelimutu 31.

Restoran Merlyn, near the airport on Jl Gatot Subroto, is a fancy and slightly expensive Chinese restaurant. The remote *Bitta Beach Restaurant*, next door to Bitta Beach Bungalows, is a local favourite, as much for the karaoke as the food. The Chinese food is good, although expensive, and the tables outside overlooking the sea are very pleasant and away from the karaoke. It is open until midnight.

Things to Buy

The ikat market, near the waterfront on Jl Pabean, has a wide variety of central Flores ikat. Stiff bargaining is required. Ikat hawkers do the rounds of the hotels.

The Cendana Art Shop, at Jl Pabean 3, has ikat and a variety of souvenirs, including bags and a few carvings.

For photographic supplies, Istana Photo, around the corner from the Telkom office, has the best range on Flores and they sell slide film.

Getting There & Away

Air Merpati (☎ 21355) is on Jl Nangka, a 15 minute walk from the airstrip. This office isn't good for organising bookings on through flights originating in other cities. Staff will probably tell you to try your luck at the airport just before departure – seats are often available.

From Ende, direct flights go to Bajawa, Bima, Kupang and Labuanbajo. The airport has been extended and can now handle the larger F27s. More services to Bima and new flights to Waingapu are planned.

Bus Buses to the east leave from the Wolowana terminal, 4km from town. Buses to Moni (2000 rp; two hours) depart at 8 and 10 am and noon, or take a Wolowaru bus between 6 am and 2 pm. Buses to Maumere (6000 rp; five hours) leave around 8 and 10 am, noon and 5 pm. Maumere buses will drop you in Moni, but charge for the full fare through to Maumere. Through buses to Larantuka (11,000 rp) leave at 8 am. There's one service per day to Nggela (3500 rp; three hours); it leaves at 5.30 am.

Buses to the west leave from the Ndao terminal, 2km north of town on the beach road. Departures are: Bajawa (5000 rp; five hours) at 4, 7 and 11 am and 5 pm; Ruteng (10,000 rp; nine hours) at 7.30 am; Labuanbajo (15,000 rp; 14 hours) at 7 am; and Riung (4500 rp; 4½ hours) at 6 am.

Boat Ende is a popular place to get boats to Sumba, with a couple of connections per week, and there are direct boats to Kupang (West Timor). The following schedules are definitely subject to change.

Ships dock at Pelabuhan Ipi, the main port, 2.5km from the town. The ferry to Waingapu, on Sumba, (12,000 rp; 10 hours) leaves Ende on Monday at 7 pm. The ferry from Kupang to Ende (17,000 rp; 16 hours) departs on Friday at 7 pm, and returns the following day at 5 pm.

Pelni's KM *Pangrango* stops in Ende every two weeks and sails to Waingapu (23,000 rp ekonomi; eight hours) every two weeks and Sabu on alternate weeks. The KM *Awu* also sails between Ende and Waingapu and then on to Kupang (28,000 rp; 11 hours) every fortnight. The Pelni office (☎ 21043), on the corner of Jl Pabean and Jl Kemakmuran,

FLORES

is open Monday to Saturday from 8 am to noon and 2 to 4 pm.

Other boats sail irregularly to these and other destinations and ; ask at the harbour master's offices at Pelabuhan Ipi.

Getting Around

To/From the Airport You could walk to town, or just walk 100m to the roundabout on Jl Jenderal Ahmad Yani and catch a bemo (400 rp).

Bemo Bemos run frequently just about everywhere in town for a flat fare of 400 rp, even out to Pelabuhan Ipi. You can flag one down on the street; if not, pick one up at the bemo stop or on Jl Hatta (near the pier).

Car You can charter a car to Kelimutu for up to six people for 75,000 rp. Ask at your hotel. The Hotel Ikhlas arranges charter minibuses and does a Kelimutu, Nggela and return day tour for 125,000 rp. The charter/tour rate for a minibus to Labuanbajo with overnight stops and visits to places of interest is 350,000 rp, or to Maumere is 150,000 rp.

AROUND ENDE

Puufeo, Ndetukou & Nuabosi

The villages of Keluruhan Roworena, just north of Ende, can be visited in combination with a trip to Nuabosi to take in the scenic views of Ende and the surrounding volcanic landscape.

The Ende area has its own style of ikat weaving, mostly using abstract motifs. Weaving can be seen in almost every village, but one of the easiest to reach is **Puufeo**, 2km north of Ende. Take a Woloare or Nuabosi bemo from the market for 400 rp. This small village is a hive of activity and you can often see all the processes of ikat weaving from dyeing to the finished product. A good quality sarong will cost around 100,000 rp.

Just 150m uphill along the road is **Ndetukou**, a blacksmithing village. Using traditional forging methods, the iron is smelted on coconut-husk fires and beaten to fashion parangs and knives.

The road winds it's way up the hill for another couple of kilometres to **Woloare**, where the local industry is bamboo wall panels, woven by men.

For excellent views of Ende and the Meja Peninsula, head further uphill to **Nuabosi**, 12km from Ende. The road goes through more lush countryside with many vantage points over the town. The fertile hills are planted with many small plots growing everything from bananas to coffee. Tapioca is a favourite crop and the tapioca grown here is said to the best on Flores.

The village of Nuabosi lies in a valley, but a few kilometres before the village is the turn-off to the Telkom tower. Take this road for around 3km to the large, renovated **rumah adat**, sitting on the ridge at 600m with great views of Ende. The roof is of tin and the 1992 earthquake left it a little wobbly, but this is one of the best Ende-region traditional houses you'll see and the carved beams are unusual. About 50m past the rumah adat a trail just off the road leads to the site of the old Dutch resthouse, but it was destroyed in the earthquake and only a few building stones remain of this cool retreat for colonial officials. The road continues 1km further to the Telkom tower, but the views are no better than those from the rumah adat.

Take a Nuabosi bemo and ask the driver to make the detour to the rumah adat. The Telkom road is paved so they are usually willing to go the extra distance for around 500 rp on top of the 500 rp fare to Nuabosi. To return to Ende, you'll have to walk back to the main road and catch a bemo from there.

Gunung Meja & Gunung Iya

The mountains around Ende are quite spectacular when seen from a high vantage point. Flat-topped Gunung Meja is just south of the town and down the southern end of the bulbous peninsula is Gunung Iya, an active volcano. To the north of town is extinct Gunung Wongge.

Legend has it that handsome Gunung Meja and beautiful Gunung Iya were in love, but the coarse and ugly Gunung Wongge also sought Iya's affections. A fight broke out between Meja and Wongge. Wongge took a parang to Meja and lopped off his head, which fell into the sea and is now the small island of Pulau Koa (though another version has it that the head is the nearby hill of Teta Ndara). The parang fell into the sea and became Pulau Ende. Heart-broken Gunung Iya erupted and her tears of lava flowed down to the sea.

Gunung Meja can be climbed by a trail that leads off the road to the harbour. It's a constant but fairly easy climb and can be done in less than three hours return.

Gunung Iya, 637m, is more difficult. Iya last erupted in 1971, but it still quite active. The shortest route is from Rate, but it is a difficult and potentially dangerous route. The trail from the north-east is said to be easier.

Pulau Ende
Pulau Ende lies in the middle of the bay just a few kilometres from Ende. It is a heavily populated island of 10,000 people, almost all Muslim. Most live on the western side between the two main towns of Ekoreko and Metinumba. Tourists are very rare and you can expect crowds when you enter the mostly traditional fishing villages. There's not a lot to see on Pulau Ende except for some boat building and net repairing, and the men are still said to hunt *ikan pari* (stingray) with spears. Lobsters are farmed, but they are all exported to Bali.

Pulau Ende was a port of some consequence in the 16th century when it was visited by Muslim traders from Java, who later converted the local population. Portuguese missionaries arrived around 1560, but despite some success in conversion, the Christian settlement was constantly under threat of attack from Muslims. The Portuguese built a small fort (Benteng Portugis), like that on the island of Solor to the east, to resist attack.

Around 1595, the Christians were driven out to the mainland, but the mission was re-established under the direction of Pater Pacheco from Solor. The settlement was short-lived, and the Christians were driven out again in 1605, settling on the coast in a village called Numba. The fort was burned down and sometime between 1620 and 1630, the Dutch, who had already captured Solor, dismantled it. The site of the fort is on the western coast, halfway between Ekoreko and Metinumba. Apart from ancient banyan trees whose roots are wrapped around a few old stones, nothing remains.

An early morning boat goes from Ende's old harbour to Pulau Ende for 1000 rp. There is supposed to be a return afternoon boat, but it is not reliable and you may have to spend the night on the island. Otherwise you might be able to hitch a ride on the boats that go from Ekoreko to the coast near Penggajawa to collect drinking water.

Penggajawa
On the highway to Bajawa, 24km west of Ende, Penggajawa is otherwise known as Bluestone Beach. The coast along here is littered with bluish pebbles that the villagers sort into various grades and pack into 50kg boxes for shipment to Surabaya. The pebbles are ground down and used for ceramic colouring, much of it exported to Japan. They are also a popular decorative building material in and around Ende. Buses or bemos heading west can drop you at Penggajawa or the Hotel Ikhlas in Ende runs tours.

Wolotopo
One of the most interesting excursions is to the scenic traditional village of Wolotopo, 9km east of Ende. Until recently it could only be reached by a 4km trail from Mbuu, but now a paved road runs all the way. It is a scenic road along wide black-sand beaches and goes through a natural rock gorge about halfway.

The road ends at a dry river bed (in the wet season you have to use a suspension foot bridge to reach the village) and a large church greets you. Coloured glass windows in the church are supplemented by Sprite bottle friezes above the doorway.

The village lies beyond the church – to the left is the new section and to the right the old village nestles into the hill. This large village

FLORES

of 2000 people is a hive of activity – women weave and men attend to the paths and stone walls that terrace the old village. Take the pathway up the hill to the traditional houses on top. Two huge rumah adat look down on the village and each houses a dozen or more families.

Behind these two houses is the *keda kanga*, the ceremonial meeting house and sacrificial altar at front. Although few individual tourists visit, the village gets groups from the cruise ships and the villagers are used to, if not a little jaded by, tourists. They will ask for a donation of 3000 rp or so to see the keda kanga.

It's worth it. Right on the top of the hill, the ceremonial house has spectacular views across the ocean to Gunung Meja and Gunung Iya. Its high peaked, thatched roof lies above an open-sided platform with carved and curved sides like the bows of a ship. The *tubu musu* stone in front of the house is the focus for prayers to the gods and where animals are offered for slaughter. The villagers are not keen to talk about their traditional beliefs, however, and profess adherence to Christianity. Their main harvest festival, Mopo, is held only once every 10 years or so.

Around the courtyard are stone graves, like mini Sumbanese-style megaliths, and at one end is the *bhaku*, a small wooden burial house containing a carved coffin and the mummified body of a particularly revered musalaki, or adat priest. The graves here are only for the musalaki, such as the current musalaki, Pangge.

At least four bemos a day run to Wolotopo from the market in Ende.

Ndona

The road to Wolotopo branches off the road to Ndona, a noted ikat weaving centre 8km east of Ende. Ndona is also home to the Archbishop of Ende and the grounds of the mission are beautifully tended. The hills around Ndona are very scenic with small hamlets and vegetable plots hacked out of the dense jungle. Regular bemos run to Ndona from Ende.

DETUSOKO

At Detusoko, 35km north-east of Ende, *Wisma Santo Fransiskus*, attached to the church of the same name, is a quiet and peaceful guesthouse with beautiful gardens. Individuals are no longer encouraged because, incredibly, a number of visitors have sought to haggle with the sisters for a room. The sisters do expect a rather large donation as a contribution to the school fund, but this is not a hotel. Groups that make prior arrangements are welcome.

Detusoko has **hot springs** – take the road next to the market for 500m, cross a small bridge and next to the Kodim military post a trail leads down to the river and the springs. However, they are less than attractive. The springs are mounted by a concrete reservoir, which pipes the water to a pair of small concrete pools and a dilapidated mandi block.

Seekers of the grotesque should head for **Wolondopo**. From Ekoleta, on the highway 4km from Detusoko towards Moni, it is a 3km walk to this traditional village. The road is very steep and rough – no public transport goes there and only 4WD vehicles can make it. Near the top is Wolojita, which has a some interesting traditional houses, but continue a few hundred metres further to Wolondopo at the end of the road. The village is picturesque and contains a number of thatched houses, including a large communal house. Above the village is the ceremonial rumah adat, and in front of that is a stone burial platform and a small burial house on stilts containing three coffins. With apologies to the ancestors, the villagers will open it up to reveal a brightly painted coffin containing an inexplicably mummified body, over 50 years old. It can only be opened with a key held by the kepala desa who lives further down the valley.

Easier to reach, **Wologai** is 13km from Detusoko and then 2km down the paved road towards Watunggere. On the high ground of the village are a number of somewhat dilapidated rumah adat surrounding the stone burial altar overgrown with weeds. The village has received a number of visitors and will ask for money to take photographs.

KELIMUTU
Of all the sights in Nusa Tenggara, the coloured lakes of Kelimutu volcano are the most singularly spectacular. The three lakes, set in deep craters at an altitude of 1600m near the summit of the volcano *(keli* means mountain), have a habit of changing colour. Most recently, the largest was a light turquoise, the one next to it olive green and the third one black. A few years ago the colours were blue, maroon and black, while back in the 1960s the lakes were blue, red-brown and cafe-au-lait. Colours can also change in the rainy season, when they may be less spectacular.

No-one has managed to explain the cause of the colours, or why they change, except to suppose that different minerals are dissolved in each lake. The moonscape effect of the craters gives the whole summit area an ethereal atmosphere. There's a story among the locals that the souls of the dead go to these lakes: young people's souls go to the warmth of the green lake, old people's to the cold of the milky turquoise one, and those of thieves and murderers to the black lake.

Kelimutu has attracted sightseers since Dutch times and today there's a paved road up to the lakes from Moni, 13.5km away at the base of the mountain. You even get an occasional bus-load of tourists and a small helipad has been constructed for VIP guests. There's a staircase up to the highest lookout point, from where you can see all three lakes.

Fortunately, there's a wonderfully spacious feeling up there and you can scramble around the perimeters of two of the lake craters for a bit of solitude. Hope for a sunny day – sunrise is stunning at the top and the turquoise lake only reaches its full brilliance in the sunlight. If the weather is bad, come back the next day, because it really is worth seeing.

Getting There & Away
Moni, 52km north-east of Ende, is the usual base for visiting Kelimutu. From Moni you can assess the weather before going up to the lakes for sunrise, although even if it looks clear in Moni, there can be cloud cover at Kelimutu.

Most visitors make their way to the top at 4 am by truck or minibus arranged by the hotels for 3000 rp per person. The truck returns to Moni around 7 am, which can be a little hurried, so you may want to linger until the sun brings out the full brilliance of

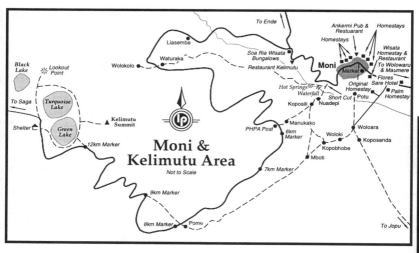

FLORES

the lakes, then walk down. The sun rises earlier at the top than in the valley below. Later in the day, clouds roll in and block out the view.

The walk down takes about 2½ hours and isn't too taxing. Some hardy souls also walk the 13.5km of winding (but not too steep) road from Moni. After about 6km there's a PHPA post, where you have to pay 1500 rp per person (more if you've hired a vehicle). Beware of false 'PHPA posts', which have been known to set up before the real post lower down the road. A short cut *(jalan potong)* leaves the Moni-Ende road about 750m from the centre of Moni and comes out on the Kelimutu road beside the PHPA post. This cuts about 6km off the journey, but is easier to follow in daylight, so most people only use it on the way down unless they've checked it out the day before.

Another path branches off the short cut at Koposili and goes via the villages of Mboti and Pome, reaching the Kelimutu road about 5.5km from the summit. It's no shorter, but it passes through villages where you can get drinks and breakfast.

MONI

Moni is a pretty village and the gateway to Flores' main tourist attraction, Kelimutu. It is cooler than the lowlands, scenic and a good place for walks.

The village is strung alongside the Ende-Maumere road and is the heart of the Lio region, which extends from just east of Ende to beyond Wolowaru. Lio people, who speak a dialect of the Ende language, are renowned for their ikat weaving, and a colourful market spreads over the playing field in front of Moni's church every Monday morning. The local ikat is attractive, with bands of blue and rusty-red. Cloth from the Nggela and Maumere regions also can be bought here.

Things to See & Do

In the kampung opposite the market, the high-thatched rumah adat serves as a cultural centre of sorts; traditional dance performances are held in front of it every evening and cost 3000 rp.

Apart from the trek to/from Kelimutu, there are several other walks from Moni. About 750m along the Ende road from the centre of Moni, paths lead down to a 10m **waterfall**, with a pool big enough for swimming, and a couple of **hot springs**. This is the village mandi and you can also bathe here – men to the left of the pool, women to the right. Another short walk is out past the church to **Potu** and **Woloara** (about 2.5km from Moni). From Woloara you could continue on through several villages to **Jopu** (about 5km). If you're energetic and well prepared, walk on to **Wolojita** and **Nggela**, or you can loop back to Wolowaru and catch a bus or truck back to Moni.

Places to Stay

Moni has a collection of homestays of a similar basic standard, charging similar prices. New, simple bungalows are sprouting everywhere. The bulk of places are within five minutes' walk of each other, so it's worth checking a few out. The correct price – fixed by the government for all homestays – is 5000 rp per person in a room with outside mandi or 7500 rp per person in a room with attached mandi, plus 10% tax. Breakfast is included. Competition outside the main June to August tourist season has seen prices drop to ridiculously low levels – as little as 3000 rp per person, or 10,000 rp or less for a double room with mandi.

Along the main road opposite the market are several cheap places where beds are rented mostly on a per person basis. *Homestay Daniel* is clean and tidy. *Homestay Amina Moe* is the most aggressive discounter and also has a few rooms with mandi. Next along, *Homestay Sao Lelegana* is a notch up in standards and has larger rooms with basin and attached mandi. *Homestay Friendly* is another more substantial place with a good aspect and better than average rooms, with and without mandi. *Homestay Maria* just behind is a tragic tale of tourism – a huge tree fell on the mandi, killing two tourists, and business. *Homestay Amina Moe II* just off the main road is the most basic of all, but is usually heavily discounted.

More homestays are clustered about five minutes' walk along the road to Ende. They tend to be quieter and less cramped. *Sylvester* has cheap, simple rooms, while *Lovely Rose* has better rooms with mandi and a decent restaurant. *Nusa Bunga*, *Regal Jaya* and *Lestari* are other reasonable places nearby, and *Hidayai* is further up the road. *Watugana Bungalow*, just off the main road, is one of the best options. New rooms and simple bungalows cost 8000 rp, 10,000 rp and 12,500 rp a double – breakfast is included, and the higher the price the more substantial the breakfast.

Another option is the *Wisata Homestay & Restaurant*, which has a large restaurant and rickety bamboo bungalows; it's about 500m back along the road to Maumere. Further along the road to Maumere, *Flores Sare Hotel* promises a little luxury among the basic accommodation options. Spacious rooms with mandi are way overpriced at 75,000 rp, but might be worth it when construction is completed.

On the Ende road 1.5km from Moni, *Sao Ria Wisata* has bungalows with attached mandis perched on the hillside. Once the best in Moni, they are run down and expensive at 20,000 rp and 25,000 rp, including breakfast.

Just outside Moni is the quiet *Palm Homestay*, on a side road to Woloara, a few hundred metres past Wisata Homestay. Further past the Palm, the *Original Homestay* is in a quiet rural setting. Typically basic rooms cost 10,000 rp, or 15,000 rp with mandi.

Places to Eat

Many of the homestays do simple but tasty buffet meals, usually vegetarian, for around 2500 to 3000 rp. Cheap restaurants abound and include the *Restaurant Moni Indah*, next to Homestay Daniel, and the *Sarty* and *Rona* rumah makans opposite the market.

The *Chenty*, above the main road between the two clusters of homestays, has the best aspect, but the food is no better than elsewhere. *Restaurant Kelimutu*, 200m down the road from Sao Ria Wisata, has reasonable food and slow service.

Getting There & Away

Moni is 52km north-east of Ende and 96km west of Maumere. For Ende (2500 rp; two hours), buses start around 5.30 am. Other buses come through from Maumere or Wolowaru to Ende until about noon. Late buses come through at around 9 pm. Many buses and trucks leave on Monday market day. Through buses from Maumere go all the way to Bajawa for 10,000 rp.

For Maumere (6000 rp; four hours) the first buses from Ende start coming though at around 9 or 10 am and then later in the evening around 7 am.

As most of the buses stop in Moni mid-route they can be crowded and it's first-come, first-served for a seat. Sometimes you'll be sitting in the aisle on a sack of rice, or a pig if you're lucky. A number of the homestays make 'bookings', which usually means they will just hail a bus down for you.

AROUND MONI
Wolowaru

The village of Wolowaru, straggling along the Maumere road just 13km south-east of Moni, can be used as a base for trips to the ikat-weaving villages of Jopu, Wolojita and Nggela. The road to these villages branches off from the main road in Wolowaru. The daily market winds down around 9 am, except on Saturday, the main market day.

Hotel Kelimutu (☎ 41020) is the most convenient place to stay and has simple rooms for 5,500 rp per person. It is right next to the *Rumah Makan Jawa Timur*, Wolowaru's premier dining establishment. The *Losmen Setia* near the market has basic rooms for the same price as the Hotel Kelimutu.

Getting There & Away All Maumere-Ende buses stop in Wolowaru, with fares and departure times much the same as from Moni. To Moni it costs 1000 rp. A few morning buses originate in Wolowaru. All the buses stop at the Rumah Makan Jawa Timur, usually for a meal break.

Nggela, Wolojita & Jopu

Beautiful ikat sarongs and shawls can be found here and in other villages between Wolowaru and the south coast. Impromptu stalls will spring up before your eyes as you approach the villages.

You can make a tour of the villages south of Moni by taking the road past the Palm and Original homestays. It's a long walk – and is better done by motorbike if you can find one to rent in Moni – but many visitors do it on foot. Most of the villages are modern Indonesian, but weaving is done everywhere and an interesting parade of daily life unfolds on the way. Kids let out a cry of 'turis' at your approach, and the 'hello misters' are best dealt with by a smile and a wave.

Nggela is worth a visit for its hilltop position above the coast, but the chief attraction is its weaving, usually done by hand and still using many natural dyes. All around the village, weaving is hung out to dry and women's hand are stained with dye. Al-

though the village has almost become a weaving factory, churning out ikat for the increasing tourist market, the weaving is still among the finest in Flores. You'll be able to watch women weaving and see at least part of the process that makes up the final product.

In former times the size, colour and pattern of the ikat shawls of this region indicated the status of the wearer. Nggela ikat typically has black or rich, dark-brown backgrounds, with patterns in earthy reds, browns or orange. Bargain hard, and cloth that uses chemical dyes should be cheaper.

So many tourists and tour groups visit, so if you're not interested in buying, it takes quite an effort to engage the villagers in conversation. Accommodation is available at the *Homestay Nggela Permai*, a very simple place that costs 5500 rp per person. Meals are available. The owner is very friendly, but speaks limited English.

Wolojita, about 7km inland from Nggela, has similar-quality weavings, but not Nggela's fine location.

Ranggase As you get closer to Jopu, a few traditional houses can be seen, but by far the most impressive village is Ranggase in Desa Jopu. Above the medieval stone walls is the finest rumah adat in the area with a high thatched roof and a base adorned with carvings. Believed to be over 400 years old (though no one really knows), this is the house of the musalaki, the chief of the clans and keeper of adat tradition. Ask around and you may be allowed inside, but a large donation may be expected. At least one person should wear traditional cloth when entering (you can borrow a salendang).

Entering through the low doorway, a passageway encircles the main room and this is used as a sleeping area. Entering the central room, it takes a while for the eyes to adjust to the darkness for there are no windows and the small door lets in little light. The roof towers above and cobwebs hang down. The house has been in the same family for six generations, and when we visited it was inhabited by the present musalaki, said to be

To Ende
Moni
Potu
To Kelimutu
Woloara
Koposenda
Nuanon
Tira
Neanga Wiwuwu
Nuamuri Mbuliloo
Ranggase Ona
Jopu
Wolowaru
To Maumere
Wolojita
Nggela
SAWU SEA

Nggela & Jopu Area

0   1.5   3 km

FLORES

108 years old. Nearing death, his rectangular stone altar and grave at the front of the house had already been prepared, but he managed to sit up and contribute to the conversation.

On a ledge in the main room are small statues of Sukalumba and his wife Mango, the original ancestors. A set of gongs used for ceremonial occasions lies to one side and from the centre of the roof hangs a ceremonial basket where food is first placed before being carried outside for ritual offerings at ceremonies. It symbolises the unity of the village and behind are sets of platforms where food is also placed for ceremonial offerings. When the first son of the musalaki is born, within two weeks he is placed on top of the platforms, some 4m off the ground. If he cries for five minutes then he will be the next musalaki. If not, then he is taken outside, placed under a banana tree and his head is tapped against the trunk. The process is repeated twice more over the following days. He is then returned to the platform and if he still doesn't cry for five minutes then a new musalaki must be found, usually the second son.

The villagers are Christian, but offerings are made to the sun goddess in April to ensure good crops, and the harvest festival is held in October. The main sacrificial altar lies further into the village, but can only be visited by those that don complete traditional clothing. The village and those around it produce a variety of ikat. The old ikat style is hard to find, but interesting; modern motifs are employed.

Getting There & Away A road branches off the Ende-Maumere road at Wolowaru to Jopu (6km), Wolojita (12km) and Nggela (19km). One bus per day leaves Ende at 5.30 am for Nggela, passing Moni at about 7.30 am and then Wolojita. Otherwise, it's a good half day's walk to Nggela from Wolowaru. It's only two or 3km further from Moni via Woloara, so you could just as easily start from there. The volcano-studded scenery is beautiful, particularly on the downhill stretch to Nggela.

From Wolojita to Nggela, you can either follow the road or take a short cut past the hot springs (ask for the *jalan potong ke Nggela*). You'd be pushing it to do the return walk the same day, but you might find a truck going back to Wolowaru.

Eastern Flores

Eastern Flores comprises the regencies of Sikka (capital Maumere) and East Flores (capital Larantuka) and is noticeably different from the rest of the island. The landscape is drier and the people are much more Melanesian in appearance. This region was a Portuguese stronghold, and although many people have Portuguese names, few reminders of Portugal can be seen.

Maumere is an important gateway to Flores, with good flight connections to Bali and Timor, and ferries to other parts of Nusa Tenggara. Good beaches are near the town and interesting day trips can be made to the south. Larantuka, on the eastern tip of Flores, sees few visitors and those who do come are mostly adventurers heading off to the remote islands of the Solor and Alor archipelagos. The Solor Archipelago is part of East Flores, but it is covered in the next section, along with the Alor Archipelago, for convenience.

PAGA
The road from Moni to Maumere winds down through the hills to the coast. The beach at Paga, 42km before Maumere, is a pleasant spot to break the journey. The *Paga Beach Hotel* (Hotel Pantai Paga) is right on the pandanus-palm beach and costs 5500 rp and 7500 rp per person in bungalows. The bungalows are very simple with mattresses on the floor, but the hotel is quite stylish and has an art shop and restaurant attached.

From Paga, you can head up into the hills and **Nuabari**, one of the most traditional villages in the Sikka region. Nuabari has stone slab graves built in Sumbanese style, but much smaller. The bones in the graves are taken out and cleaned periodically in a special ceremony. The village's rumah adat is also home to prized elephant tusks, and the views from the village and road are stunning. The turn-off to Nuabari is 6km west of Paga on the highway, and then it is a long drive along a bad road. You really need a 4WD, or tours are organised from the Paga Beach Hotel and from Maumere.

MAUMERE

This seaport is the main town of the Sikka district, which covers the neck of land between Central Flores and the Larantuka district (in the east). The Sikkanese language is closer to that of Larantuka than to Endenese. The name Sikka is taken from a village on the south coast controlled by Portuguese rulers and their descendants from the early 17th to 20th centuries.

This area has been one of the chief centres of Catholic activity on Flores since Portuguese Dominicans arrived some 400 years ago. Missionaries were one of the largest groups of foreigners to establish themselves on Flores, and many Dutch, German and Spanish priests spent decades surviving Japanese internment camps, as well as an often-hostile population during the independence wars.

Many of the priests made important studies of the island and its people. They also encouraged local arts and crafts and helped the Florinese with improved tools and seed for agriculture; as recently as two decades ago, many Florinese were still tilling the soil with sharpened sticks, and slash-and-burn farming is still common. Today the European priests have been replaced by Florinese.

In December 1992 Maumere was devastated by an earthquake, and the ensuing 20m-high tidal waves killed thousands. Maumere was only 30km from the epicentre of the quake, which almost flattened the entire town. Most of the town has now been rebuilt.

There's a strong ikat-weaving tradition in the Maumere region, and some interesting trips can be made out of town. Decent beaches are nearby, and although it has lost its status as a famed diving destination because of earthquake damage to the reefs, Maumere is still a tourism hub. It is the easiest city on Flores to reach by plane from the rest of Indonesia, has the best range of tour options and is the easiest place to hire a car.

Information
The tourist office (☎ 21652) on Jl Wairklau is well out of the way and has little in the way of literature, but tries hard.

Bank Rakyat Indonesia handles foreign exchange and is open from 7.30 am to 2.30 pm weekdays, and 7.30 am to 11.30 am Saturday. The Bank BNI on Jl Soekarno Hatta is also a good option for changing money, and is open 7 am to 3 pm weekdays. The Bank Danamon on Jl Pasar Baru Barat, open 8 am to 2 pm weekdays and 8 to 11.30 am Saturday, does not change cash or travellers cheques, but will give cash advances on Visa and MasterCard.

The post office, next to the soccer field on Jl Pos, is open every day until 5 pm for stamps, but for other services normal hours are 8 am to 2 pm weekdays and 8 to 11 am Saturdays. The Telkom office is further south from the town centre on Jl Soekarno Hatta.

Organised Tours
Maumere is the best place to arrange all-Flores tours. The city has a number of travel agents, though they primarily act as local agents for bigger tour companies out of Kupang and Jakarta. They include PT Citra Flores (☎ 22276) at Jl Nong Meak 35, Astura Tours (☎ 21778) at Jl Sudirman 1 and Ramayana Satrya (☎ 21161) at Jl Akasia 5.

A cheaper option is to find a guide and arrange your own tour. Dino Lopez is an experienced guide who hangs out at the Gardena Hotel. He arranges cheap backpackers tours to the sights around Maumere for 75,000 rp, including transport, for three people; tours to the islands off Wodong cost the same. Guides can also be found at the Hotel Wini Rai II and other hotels, who can arrange car hire for longer tours around

Flores. The Kota Pena Artshop (☎ 21032), Jl Gajah Mada 11, also runs day tours to Paga Beach (they own the hotel there), Nuabari and other interesting spots.

Places to Stay
Maumere has a number of hotels, most with a wide variety of rooms. Cheap rooms tend to be dismal, while better rooms with mandi are expensive compared with other towns on Flores.

The pick of the cheap hotels, the *Gardena Hotel* (☎ 21489), at Jl Patirangga 28, is on a quiet suburban street, but is close to the town centre. This friendly hotel is a good place to contact guides and get information on sights around Maumere. Well kept, if bare, rooms cost 10,000/15,000 rp with mandi and fan or 20,000/30,000 rp with air-con.

The *Hotel Senja Wair Bubuk* (☎ 21498) on Jl Komodor Yos Sudarso, near the waterfront, gets a steady stream of travellers, but the rooms need an upgrade, or at least a good clean. Singles/doubles with shared mandi cost 6600/11,000 rp or better rooms with mandi cost 11,000/16,000 rp. Other rooms with air-con range from 22,000/29,000 to 29,000/36,000 rp.

Nearby, the small and friendly *Hotel Jaya* (☎ 21292), Jl Hasanuddin 26, is good value and offers rooms with fan and mandi for 10,000/15,000 rp.

Hotel Beng Goan I (☎ 21041) on Jl Moa Toda is a popular local hotel and very central. Rooms start at 6000/10,000 rp, from 10,000/17,500 rp with mandi, or good new rooms with air-con are 25,000/30,000 and 35,000/50,000 rp. *Hotel Beng Goan III* is still undergoing post-earthquake restoration, which may make it one of the better hotels.

A little far from the town centre, but close to the Ende (west) bus terminal, the well run *Hotel Wini Rai* (☎ 21388), at Jl Gajah Mada 50, has a wide variety of rooms. Economy rooms with shared mandi are fairly basic for 7500/12,500 rp, while substantial rooms with private mandi and fan are a good mid-range choice for 20,000/25,500 rp or 32,500/37,500 rp to 42,500/47,500 rp with air-con. Add 10% to all rates.

FLORES

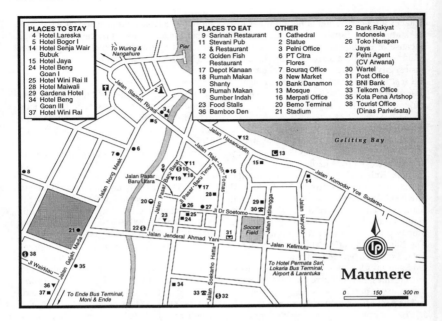

PLACES TO STAY
4 Hotel Lareska
5 Hotel Bogor I
14 Hotel Senja Wair Bubuk
15 Hotel Jaya
24 Hotel Beng Goan I
25 Hotel Wini Rai II
28 Hotel Maiwali
29 Gardena Hotel
34 Hotel Beng Goan III
37 Hotel Wini Rai

PLACES TO EAT
9 Sarinah Restaurant
11 Stevani Pub & Restaurant
12 Golden Fish Restaurant
17 Depot Kanaan
18 Rumah Makan Shanty
19 Rumah Makan Sumber Indah
23 Food Stalls
36 Bamboo Den

OTHER
1 Cathedral
2 Statue
3 Pelni Office
6 PT Citra Flores
7 Bouraq Office
8 New Market
10 Bank Danamon
13 Mosque
16 Merpati Office
20 Bemo Terminal
21 Stadium
22 Bank Rakyat Indonesia
26 Toko Harapan Jaya
27 Pelni Agent (CV Arwana)
30 Wartel
31 Post Office
32 BNI Bank
33 Telkom Office
35 Kota Pena Artshop
38 Tourist Office (Dinas Pariwisata)

Maumere

0   150   300 m

The new *Hotel Wini Rai II* (☎ 21362) on Jl Dr Soetomo is a smaller offshoot right in the centre of town. Rooms are spotlessly clean, if a little dark, and this is also a good hotel for information and to contact guides. Basic singles/doubles at the back cost 7500/12,500 rp with shared mandi or much better rooms at front are 20,000/25,000 rp with mandi or 32,500/37,500 rp with air-con.

The *Hotel Maiwali* (☎ 21220), at Jl Raja Don Tomas 40, is the best hotel close to the town centre and has a good restaurant. Budget rooms for 8000/14,000 rp are not great, but air-con rooms for 28,500/42,500 rp and 63,500/95,000 rp are very good, if expensive.

The fanciest place is the *Hotel Permata Sari* (☎ 21171) at Jl Jenderal Sudirman 49 on the waterfront about 2km from the town centre. Standard rooms and cottages with shower and fan go for 27,500/33,000 rp, while air-con rooms are 33,000/44,000 rp to 99,000/115,00 rp. The beach is decent, as is

the restaurant, but it's a long walk to town and a little dull. To get there, take a bemo heading east.

Other hotels include the Muslim-run *Hotel Lareska* (☎ 21137), at Jl Pranoto 3, a cheap option if you arrive at the port and can't be bothered walking further. It has presentable rooms with mandi for 11,000/16,500 rp, and upstairs rooms with shared mandi for 6600/11,000 rp. It is better than the seedy *Hotel Bogor I* opposite, but both hotels are hopelessly crowded just before and after a Pelni ship docks.

Places to Eat

The best place to hunt out a restaurant is Jl Pasar Baru Barat, the main street running down to the waterfront. The *Sarinah Restaurant* has Chinese food and does good squid. Most popular is the *Rumah Makan Sumber Indah* for good Javanese fare. The *Stevani Pub & Restaurant* has small huts dotted around in a garden setting. It's a pleasant

FLORES

place to sit with a drink, if you can endure the karaoke. Expensive western and Indonesian dishes are served.

Shinta Karaoke, 3km east of town on the beach and 1km past the Hotel Permata Sari, competes with the Stevani Pub in the noise stakes, but has good Chinese food.

Depot Kanaan on Jl Pasar Baru Timur is a spotless little restaurant serving mouthwatering kare ayam (chicken curry) and other excellent Javanese dishes at reasonable prices.

Maumere's old central market, burnt down after a Muslim/Christian flare up, has moved from Jl Pasar Baru Barat to the western outskirts and is being replaced with a shopping centre. A few *food stalls* can still be found at the southern side of the original site.

Rumah Makan Shanty is spacious and has a long menu of Chinese food and seafood. The air-con *Golden Fish* restaurant, on the waterfront, has good seafood. The *Bamboo Den* near the Hotel Wini Rai has slow service, but good, cheap Indonesian food, fish and cold beer.

Other restaurants include the *Bianca Cafe* in the Hotel Maiwali – a dark little corner, but one of the better restaurants with Chinese and other dishes.

Things to Buy
Toko Harapan Jaya on Jl Pasar Baru Timur has the most comprehensive collection of ikat (from Flores and other islands) that you'll find anywhere in Nusa Tenggara except Sumba. You can also buy carvings and other artefacts. Prices are fixed for most items.

Kota Pena Artshop on Jl Gajah Mada has a wide selection of Flores ikat, as well as carvings, souvenirs and more ikat from Sumba, Lombok, Sulawesi and other areas. Quoted prices are high, but not fixed.

Getting There & Away
Air Maumere handles bigger aircraft and is the easiest place on Flores to fly into from other islands, but there are no flights to anywhere else on Flores. Bouraq and Merpati fly to Kupang and Denpasar. Merpati flies via Bima (Sumbawa) en route to Bali and to Ujung Pandang in Sulawesi. Merpati (☎ 21342) is on Jl Raja Don Tomas 18 and is open 8 am to 1 pm and 6 to 8 pm, Monday to Saturday, and 10 am to noon Sunday. Bouraq's office (☎ 21467) is on Jl Nong Meak.

Bus There are two bus terminals in Maumere. Buses and bemos heading east to Larantuka (7000 rp; four hours), Wodong (1000 rp), Geliting, Waiara and Ipir leave from the Lokaria (or Wai Oti) terminal, about 3km east of town. Take a bemo (400 rp) there.

Buses west to Moni (5000 or 6000 rp; 3½ hours), Ende (6000 rp; five hours), Sikka and Ledalero leave from the Ende (or Barat) terminal, about 1.5km south-west of town. Most buses take the southern highway, but direct buses also run along the quicker but less scenic northern highway to Mbay (5000 rp; 3½ hours) from where buses run to Bajawa.

Buses often endlessly do the rounds of the town in their search for passengers. Hotels can arrange pick-up. Buses to Ende leave at 6, 7, 8 and 11.30 am and 2, 3 and 5 pm. For Moni, take an Ende bus. Buses to Larantuka leave throughout the day.

Boat Pelni's KM *Awu* sails between Maumere and Ujung Pandang on Sulawesi (23 hours) and Dili on Timor (18 hours). The Pelni office is on Jl Slamet Riyadi, next to Hotel Lareska, or CV Arwana is a Pelni agent on Jl Dr Soetomo.

Getting Around
To/From the Airport Maumere's Wai Oti airport is 3km from town, 800m off the Maumere-Larantuka road. A taxi to town is 6000 rp (5000 rp from town). Otherwise, it's about a 1km walk out of the airport to the Maumere-Larantuka road to pick up a bemo (500 rp) into town. Airport tax is 5500 rp.

Bemo Bemos run around town regularly and cost 400 rp anywhere within the city.

FLORES

Car & Motorcycle A car with driver will cost around 80,000 rp per day around town, including petrol, or 100,000 rp further afield. Hotels and travel agents can arrange them, but will charge around 20% commission. It is cheaper to negotiate directly with the drivers. They can be found around town, but the biggest selection is at the airport. For a tour of a few days around Flores, count on 100,000 rp a day for the car, and negotiate extra for the driver's hotel room and food (around 25,000 rp per day), and guides' fees if needed.

A few places around town hire out motorcycles for around 20,000 rp per day; ask at your hotel or the travel agencies.

AROUND MAUMERE
North-West Coast
Just 5km north-west of Maumere, **Wuring** is a large Bajo village dominated by its mosque. The stilt houses next to the sea are a hive of activity and interesting to wander around. A modern port is near the village. Considered unsafe, Wuring suffered damage from the 1992 earthquake, but government plans to move the population to new settlements are strongly resisted by the Bajo. Although branded 'backward' by the government, the Bajo are understandably reluctant to relocate further inland, away from the sea and their livelihood.

On the north coast highway, 15km north-west of Maumere, **Nangahure** is home to a couple of beach hotels. The grey sand beaches are not brilliant, and Wairtering to the east of Maumere is deservedly a more popular beach destination, but the area is quiet and relaxing for long walks along the shore; the sunsets and sea views are stunning. *Pang Bliran Ecolodge* (☎ 22225) is a very simple resort with bungalows for 7500/10,000 rp for singles/doubles. It has a variety of tours and an attractive restaurant. The 'eco' addition to the title is because the resort is built on mangroves – the beach here is nonexistent. A better option is the *Beach Hotel* a couple of kilometres further along the main road and down a sandy track to the beach. The beach is wide and sandy and

bungalows for 10,000/15,000 rp are scattered around the dry but well tended grounds. Better rooms with mandi cost 5000 rp extra, but are back from the beach. Nangahure is reached by bemo (500 rp) or a taxi from the airport is 10,000 rp.

Ledalero & Nita
Many Florinese priests studied at the Roman Catholic seminary in Ledalero, 19km from Maumere on the Ende road. The chief attraction here is the small **Bikon Blewut** museum run by Father Piet Petu, a sprightly 80-year-old, chain-smoking Florinese priest who is usually happy to chat about his unique collection. The museum houses historic stone implements and Florinese ikat – you'll see designs and natural dyes that are either rare or no longer produced, including softly textured, pastel-coloured old Jopu sarongs. Many of the finest gold and ivory items were sadly lost to thieves in 1992, but there is an assortment of other artefacts and wonderful old photographs detailing Florinese ethnic diversity. Labelling is almost nonexistent, but this is still a good place to try to piece together the jigsaw of Florinese culture. The museum is open 7.30 am to 12.30 pm and 3 to 7 pm every day. Admission is a steep 5000 rp for tourists.

Nita, 2km beyond Ledalero on the main road, has a Thursday market. Nita, together with Sikka and Kangai, was one of the three main kingdoms of the Maumere region. The descendants of the raja still live in Nita in a Dutch-colonial 'palace'. The royal heirlooms, including many elephant tusks, once the main form of wealth and an important part of the bride dowry in eastern Flores, can be viewed, but you'll need good contacts to get an invite. Bemos to Ledalero and Nita go from Maumere's Ende terminal.

Lela & Sikka
From Nita you can head to the south coast, home to the old kingdom of Sikka. The road hits the coast at Lela on a scenic bay with a long, rocky black-sand beach. Lela, 23km from Maumere, is home to the Rumah Sakit Elizabet, one of the largest and best hospitals

on Flores. Back from the beach on the inland road is a shrine to the Virgin Mary that attracts hundreds of pilgrims in May and October.

On the south coast, 4km from Lela and 27km from Maumere, Sikka was one of the first Portuguese settlements on Flores, dating from the early 17th century. The Portuguese dominated the Maumere region until the 20th century. Today it's famed for its distinctive ikat. A lot of Sikka weaving is in maroons, blues and browns, and design has been heavily influenced by the Dutch; you'll see the Dutch coat of arms and pairs of cherubs.

Sikka has received many visitors interested in ikat, and it shows. Dozens of women draped in ikat will flock to make a sale on your arrival. The local weaving cooperative is opposite the church and you can see the various processes from dyeing to weaving. For those not interested in weaving, the church is Sikka's most interesting attraction. Built in 1899, this beautiful colonial church with its stained glass and wood panelling is one of the finest on Flores. The priest will open the church for interested visitors.

On the beach in Sikka is the Lepo Geto (Big House) of the former raja. A sacrificial stone altar, the *watu mahe*, stands in front of the house. The house itself is anything but grand, but a huge, new house is being built next door as the focal point for the Sikkanese community.

The road continues along the coast a couple of kilometres past Sikka, but until the road is completed the only way to reach the neighbouring towns of Hokor and Bola is to return to Maumere. Regular bemos (1000 rp) run from Maumere to Lela and Sikka from 6 am to 6 pm.

Geliting

Geliting, about 10km east of Maumere on the Larantuka road, has a huge, colourful market on Friday mornings. There's lots of beautiful ikat around – more being worn than for sale – and thousands of villagers come to sell their produce. Get there by bemo from Maumere's Lokaria bus terminal.

Waiara

Thirteen kilometres east of Maumere, just off the Larantuka road, Waiara is the jumping-off point for the Maumere 'sea gardens'. Once regarded as one of Indonesia's best dive destinations, that all changed after the 1992 earthquake. The earthquake and the tidal wave destroyed many of the reefs, but some prolific fish populations can still be found, particularly on the offshore islands around Pulau Pemana and Pulau Besar.

Waiara has two dive resorts, though they are not exclusively for divers and they make a pleasant beach escape. Once the centre for tourism in eastern Flores, the resorts are slowly attracting customers again and arrange land trips as well as dives. The cheaper *Sea World Club* (Pondok Dunia Laut) (☎ 21570) is the more popular and better value. Simple cabin rooms start at US$10/15 for singles/doubles and range up to US$30/35 for very comfortable air-con rooms. Dive packages start at US$70 per day for cabin rooms, all meals and two dives. The resort is well equipped and the restaurant has buffet meals for around US$6. A tax and service charge of 15% is added to all rates.

The fancier *Flores Sao Resort* (☎ 21555) is group tour territory, with prices to match, but is looking tired and is often empty. Accommodation starts at US$25/30 for simple rooms. Air-con rooms for US$55/60 or US$65/70 with TV and fridge have their own sitting rooms and are among the best on Flores, but the hot water doesn't work and they are losing their shine. Two day/three night dive packages start at $240/$435 for one/two people. Add 15.5% to all prices.

To get there, catch a Talibura bus from Maumere to Waiara, or take a bemo to Geliting and walk 1.5km along the Larantuka road. You'll see the signs for the turn-off to Sea World Club first, and Flores Sao Resort is about 500m further along the road.

Watublapi

Watublapi, in the hills 20km south-east of Maumere, is a large Catholic mission. At 400m above sea level, it has fine views across the coast, and cacao, coffee, cloves

FLORES

and coconut are all grown in this cooler region. Watublapi produces some fine ikat employing modern motifs such as deer, flowers and trees. The Sanggar Budaya Bliran Sina is a local cultural group that stages dance performances (war, harvest and wedding dances) for groups and ikat demonstrations, from dyeing to the finished product. Tours out of Maumere and Waiara usually include Watublapi. Independent travellers may be lucky enough to strike a performance for tour groups. The village and surrounding area is very scenic, and bemos run from Maumere's Lokaria terminal to Watublapi (500 rp) between 6 am and 8 pm.

From Watublapi you can walk to **Ohe**, where you can see both coasts of Flores. **Bola** is a large village 6km from Watublapi on the south coast and 2km further on is the traditional coastal weaving village of **Ipir**. The coast here is thick with coconut groves framing black-sand beaches. This coast was the favourite staging ground for Christian missionaries, who no doubt chose the south because the north coast and the sea lanes were controlled by Muslims. Standing in the sea just off the beach is the large Watu Krus (Stone Cross), a poignant reminder of the missionary influence, but the original stone cross has long since been replaced by a wooden one. Market day in Ipir is Monday, and bemos go there from Maumere (1500 rp; 1½ hours). On other days, bemos usually finish at Bola. You should be able to stay with villagers or the kepala desa in Bola or Ipir.

Past Ipir, the road leads 12km to Habibola and then on to **Doreng**, where there is 4km of white-sand beach, but the road is very rough and there are no facilities.

Wodong/Wairterang

The beach of Wairterang, 28km east of Maumere just outside Wodong village, is developing into quite a beach scene. A number of budget homestays have sprung up, and they offer boat tours to the offshore islands. While not up with the great beaches of Asia, the beach at Wairterang is a pleasant and relaxing place to kick back for a few days.

The surrounding area has some interesting attractions, including the offshore islands to the north. The main island, **Pulau Besar**, has a small fishing population and good diving off the west coast. Pulau Besar is ringed by a number of smaller islands, the most visited of which is **Pulau Pangabatang**. Pangabatang has excellent white-sand beaches and good snorkelling on the reef. Boats can be chartered in Wodong village, but are easier to arrange with homestays in Wairterang. Boats cost 50,000 rp for a full-day trip or some of the homestays have guided trips for around 10,000 rp per person.

Nangahale, about 10km north-east of Wodong, is an interesting boat building village settled by survivors from Pulau Babi after the 1992 earthquake. It is easily reached by bemo or bus from Wairterang. On the way to Nangahale the road passes **Patiahu**, 33km from Maumere, which has a good white-sand beach, the best on this stretch of coast. Among the coconut trees is a hut owned by the missionaries which can be used by picnickers.

To the south-west of Wairterang, the landscape is dominated by smoking **Gunung Egon**. This active, 1703m-high volcano can be climbed from Blidit in around three hours, slightly less coming down. There is no shade on the way to top, so it pays to start early to avoid the heat of the day. It is a relatively easy climb apart from the final scramble to the top. Blidit is 6km from Wairterang – 15,000 rp by chartered bemo. You can take a public bemo to Waigete and then another to Blidit, but you could be in for a long wait. Guides to take you up Egon can be arranged in Wairterang for around 10,000 rp.

A detour from the trail up to Gunung Egon leads to **Sumber Air Panas Blidit**, the hot springs at the base of the mountain. It's about a 40 minute walk from Blidit across the plains where the hot water of the springs mixes with the cold water of the river.

Places to Stay & Eat *Flores Froggies*, near Wodong village, is the original homestay started by a French couple. Unfortunately they have left and, although Froggies is still popular, it is a now looking a little run down. Simple bungalows are 6000/8000 rp for singles/doubles and some have private mandi for 8000/10,000 rp. Although the French specialties are no longer on the menu, the beachside restaurant is still good.

On the eastern side of Froggies, *Pondok Praja* is the most substantial place and the friendly owner speaks good English. Large bungalows are Wairterang's best and cost 17,500 rp and 25,000 rp.

West along the beach from Froggies, *Wairterang Beach Cottage* is a well kept place with small bungalows going for 5000/10,000 rp. You can eat at its pleasant restaurant.

Further along is *Ankermi*, the pick of the places to stay. It has attractive grounds, a good restaurant and lots of information on nearby attractions. The switched-on owner used to run Moni's best restaurant and the story of his departure provides fascinating insights into the local tourism industry. Bungalows cost 7000/10,000 rp or 12,000/17,500 rp with mandi and there is also a dorm bungalow with two mattresses per room for 5000 rp per person.

Another good option is *Wodong Beach*

Homestay, off by itself further around the headland. Under Belgian management, it houses the funky little Coral Bar and runs good trips to the islands. Tiny bungalows are 6000 rp, and larger ones are 10,000 rp, or 15,000 rp with mandi.

Getting There & Away
Wodong is right on the Maumere-Larantuka road. Take any Talibura, Nangahale or Larantuka bemo or bus for 1000 rp from Maumere's Lokaria terminal. Through buses to Larantuka can be picked up in Wodong, but are often hopelessly crowded; to get a seat it is better to first go to Maumere. Heading west, a direct bus to Moni (7000 rp) passes Wodong around 10 am.

LARANTUKA
A busy little port at the eastern end of Flores, Larantuka (population 30,000) nestles around the base of the Ili Mandiri volcano, separated by a narrow strait from the islands of Solor and Adonara. Larantuka is the departure point for boats to the Solor Archipelago (east of Flores) and for a twice-weekly ferry to Kupang, Timor.

This corner of Indonesia, although always

The Lamaholot
The Larantuka area has long had closer links with the islands of the Solor Archipelago – Adonara, Solor and Lembata – than with the rest of Flores. It shares a language, Lamaholot, with the islands. The whole area, particularly outside the towns, fascinates anthropologists because of its complex social and ritual structure, which in some parts survives pretty well intact.

There's a web of myths about the origins of the Lamaholot people: one version has them descended from the offspring of Watowele (the extremely hairy goddess of Ili Mandiri) and a character called Patigolo, who was washed ashore, got Watowele drunk, cut her hair (thus removing her magic powers and discovering that she was female) and made her pregnant. Alternatively, locals believe their forbears came from Sina Jawa (China Java), Seram or India – take your pick.

At some stage, probably before the 16th century, the Lamaholot area became divided between two groups known as the Demon and the Paji. The Demon, associated with the 'Rajah' of Larantuka, were mainly grouped in eastern Flores and the western parts of Adonara, Solor and Lembata; the Paji, with their allegiance to the 'Rajah' of Adonara, were centred in the eastern parts of the three islands. Anthropologists tend to believe that the conflict between the two groups was mainly a ritual affair or, as one writer puts it, 'two groups representing the two halves of the universe engaged in regular combat to produce human sacrifices for the securing of fertility and health'. Such a pattern was not uncommon in eastern Indonesia. Today, people still know who is Paji and who is Demon, but ritual warfare has subsided. Other animist rites survive, including those for birth, name-giving, marriage, the building of a new house, the opening of new fields in *ladang* (slash-and-burn) agriculture, and the planting and harvesting of crops. ■

FLORES

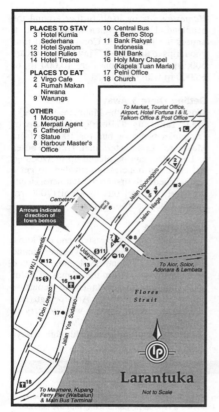

PLACES TO STAY
3 Hotel Kumia
   Sederhana
12 Hotel Syalom
13 Hotel Rulies
14 Hotel Tresna

PLACES TO EAT
2 Virgo Cafe
4 Rumah Makan
   Nirwana
9 Warungs

OTHER
1 Mosque
5 Merpati Agent
6 Cathedral
7 Statue
8 Harbour Master's
   Office
10 Central Bus
   & Bemo Stop
11 Bank Rakyat
   Indonesia
15 BNI Bank
16 Holy Mary Chapel
   (Kapela Tuan Maria)
17 Pelni Office
18 Church

To Market, Tourist Office,
Airport, Hotel Fortuna I & II,
Telkom Office & Post Office

Cemetery

Arrows indicate
direction of
town bemos

Jalan Diponegoro
Jalan Niaga
Jl Udayana
Jl W J Lalamentik
Jl Don Lorenzo
Jalan Yos Sudarso

To Alor, Solor,
Adonara & Lembata

Flores
Strait

Larantuka

Not to Scale

To Maumere, Kupang
Ferry Pier (Waibalun)
& Main Bus Terminal

Orientation & Information

Most hotels, the ferry pier, shipping offices and the main bus terminal are in the compact southern part of the town. The tourist office (☎ 21652) is on the main road a couple of kilometres north-east of town and has reasonable tourist maps and basic information. Further north-east are the post office, Telkom office and airport. The pier for boats to Kupang is around 4km from town.

The Bank BNI on Jalan Don Lorenzo and Bank Rakyat Indonesia on Jl Udayana both handle foreign exchange.

Things to See

Portuguese-style Catholicism flourishes in Larantuka. There's a large **cathedral**, while the smaller **Holy Mary Chapel** (Kapela Tuan Maria) contains Portuguese bronze and silver known as *ornamento*.

The main religious event and highlight of the tourist calendar is the **Good Friday procession** when an image of the Virgin Mary from the chapel is carried around the town. The ceremony begins on the Thursday when the statue of Mary in the Holy Mary Chapel is cleaned and draped in mourning dress. On the Friday evening, the procession begins with shrouded figures carrying the statue on a palanquin to chants and singing in Indonesian (which has replaced the politically incorrect Portuguese that was once used). A coffin, representing the body of Christ, is also carried in the procession that takes in eight churches around the town.

Larantuka's **market**, north-east of town, has some weaving – look for ikat from Lembata, Adonara and Solor.

Places to Stay

The family-run *Hotel Rulies* (☎ 21198) at Jl Yos Sudarso 44 has the best set-up for travellers. Clean singles/doubles/triples with shared bath cost 10,000/16,000/21,000 rp and food is available. The family speaks English and can answer most queries.

Next door, the *Hotel Tresna* (☎ 21072) is a reasonable place catering mainly for business travellers. It is slightly more upmarket than Rulies, but is not well run. Rooms with

isolated, was one of the first to attract European interest. Lying on sea routes used by the Portuguese seeking sandalwood from Timor, the Larantuka-Solor area was home to Portuguese forts and over 20 Dominican missions by 1575. Portugal even maintained a few enclaves until the mid-19th century, among them Larantuka, which was the centre of a community of Topasses (from *tupassi*, an Indian word for 'interpreter'), the mixed-blood descendants of Portuguese, slaves from Melaka and India and the local population. The Topasses are still a significant group in Larantuka today.

outside mandi are 8500/14,000 rp, while clean rooms with private mandi are 15,000/25,000 rp or 40,000/55,000 rp with air-con.

The *Hotel Kurnia Sederhana* (☎ 21066) is on Jl Niaga right in the middle of town. It looks very unpromising from the outside, but rooms at the back are relatively new and well kept, if a little noisy. Singles/doubles with outside mandi cost 10,000/15,000 rp.

Hotel Syalom (☎ 21464), at Jl WJ Lalamentik 35, is in a quiet residential street not far from the town centre, but it's a long grunt uphill when carrying a backpack. This friendly, family-run hotel has basic old rooms for 10,000 rp a double or bright new rooms with mandi at the back for 35,000 rp.

The *Hotel Fortuna I* (☎ 21140) is inconveniently located about 2km north-east of town at Jl Diponegoro 171 near the Telkom office. Rooms for 5000/10,000 rp with mandi are cramped and dreary, while much better rooms with fan cost 11,000/16,500 rp.

Its new offshoot, the *Hotel Fortuna II* (☎ 21383) is a small place directly across the road with the best rooms in town. Large, bright rooms with fan are 20,000/30,000 rp or quite plush rooms with air-con are 40,000/60,000 rp.

In Waibalun, near the ferry terminal, *Homestay Yonata* has basic rooms for 3500 rp and 5000 rp, but apart from the price there is little reason to stay this far out.

Places to Eat
Eating possibilities are limited, but a few warungs set up in the evening along Jl Niaga. *Rumah Makan Nirwana* is a decent Chinese restaurant and the best in town. Also good is the small *Virgo Cafe*, in a hairdressing salon of the same name, with fish and chips in addition to the usual nasi and mie meals. The owner speaks excellent English, with an Australian accent, and serves very cold beer.

Getting There & Away
Air The Merpati agent's house is at Jl Diponegoro 64, opposite the cathedral. One flight a week does a Kupang-Larantuka-Lewoleba (Lembata)-Kupang loop, but it's often cancelled.

Bus The main bus terminal is 5km southwest of the town, about 1km from Waibalun, but you can pick them up in the centre of town; hotels also may be able to arrange pick-up. Coming into town, buses can drop you at or near your hotel, depending on the one way street system, though the bemo drivers may insist that you get off and catch a bemo from the terminal (400 rp).

Buses to/from Maumere cost 7000 rp and take about four hours. If you arrive from the Solor Archipelago, enthusiastic bus jockeys will arm wrestle you into waiting buses. Too many buses do this run and if they are not full they will endlessly loop around town until they are, adding one or two hours to the journey time. It's best to book a front seat (500 rp to 1000 rp extra) through your hotel and get the bus to pick you up just before it leaves. Buses leave Larantuka for Maumere hourly throughout the day until around 5 pm.

Boat Ferries to Kupang (14,000 rp; 14 hours) depart Monday and Friday at noon from Waibalun, 4km south-west of Larantuka (400 rp by bemo). Going the other way, the ferries to Larantuka leave Kupang on Thursday and Sunday at 7 pm. Ferries can get crowded, so board early to get a seat. Take some food and water.

The Persero passenger/car ferry to Adonara, Lembata and Alor leaves from Waibalun on Tuesday, Thursday and Sunday at 7 am. More convenient, smaller boats to Adonara, Solor and Lembata leave from the pier in the centre of town. Two ferries run twice a day to Lewoleba (4000 rp; four hours) on Lembata leaving around 8 am, noon and 1.30 pm, stopping at Waiwerang (Adonara) on the way. Motorbikes can be taken on these boats. A boat goes once a week to Lamalera on Lembata's south-west coast (5000 rp; seven hours) on Friday at 9 am.

The Pelni passenger ship *Tatamailau* calls in at Larantuka on its route from Labuanbajo on to Dili and Irian Jaya, returning in the opposite direction two weeks later. The *Sirimau* runs from Larantuka to Kupang in Timor and Ujung Pandang in Sulawesi. The Pelni office on Jl Yos Sudarso has details on

FLORES

other Pelni boats and it's also worth asking around the pier and harbour master's office on Jl Niaga for other possibilities.

Getting Around

Bemos run up and down Jl Niaga and Jl Pasar, and to outlying villages. Bemos in town cost 400 rp. A chartered bemo to the airport, 12km east of town, will cost around 6000 rp.

AROUND LARANTUKA

Six kilometres north of Larantuka, **Weri** is the town's most popular beach. It's a reasonable stretch of white sand, but is denuded of vegetation, the water is very shallow and it's crowded on weekends. Nonetheless, it can make a pleasant excursion during the week. A bemo (400 rp) from the central bemo stop in Larantuka will drop you at the trail to the beach, a few hundred metres from the road. Walk back to town along the beach past secluded coves and much finer white sand beaches. Two kilometres from Weri, just before the lighthouse, is **Pantai Kota**, a picture postcard beach of dazzling white sand and coconut palms. This is the former playground of the raja, but be careful swimming here – the currents are ferocious just a few metres offshore. From the lighthouse you can continue walking back to town along the shore at low tide, but this stretch is less scenic. The lighthouse is just a few metres from a paved road – walk 50m along the road towards town and then turn right at the first dirt road, which leads to the main road and bemos back to town.

Of the traditional villages around Larantuka, one of the most interesting and easiest to reach is **Mokantarak**, 10km from Larantuka on the highway west to Maumere. The village's name is short for Mokanlewo-pulo Tarak Lonenribu (10 villages of many thousand people). From the main road it is a short walk uphill to the rumah adat of the central village. The circular meeting area in front of the house has eight stone 'chairs', one for each of the heads of the eight clans. Traditional dance performances for groups are staged in front of the rumah adat. The old

village of Mokantarak lies 5km inland by foot, but the rumah adat and *pusaka* (heirlooms) have long since moved. The heirlooms, which can only be viewed by men, comprise a quiver of rudimentary arrows used in the internecine wars that occupied this area until not so long ago. The arrows are little more than sticks, but we were sworn not to reveal their location for fear of thieves.

Lewoloba, near the village of Oka, also puts on traditional dancing occasionally for tour boats. **Danau Asmara** is a scenic lake two hours by bus north of Larantuka and is reputed to be home to freshwater crocodiles, but the crocs have long since disappeared. Buses leave from the market in Larantuka at 10 am and can drop you at Riang Kerokok. The lake is 500m from the road. The problem with a visit is that the bus returns at 1 pm.

Solor & Alor Archipelagos

A chain of small islands stretches out from the eastern end of Flores. These volcanic, mountainous specks separated by swift, narrow straits can be visited by a spectacular ferry ride from Larantuka. Adonara and Solor, where the Portuguese settled in the 16th century, are close to Larantuka. Further east, Lembata is the main island of interest because of the traditional whaling village of Lamalera. These islands form the Solor Archipelago, which has close cultural links with the Larantuka area on Flores. Together these people are known as the Lamaholot, and the Larantuka area on the mainland together with the Solor Archipelago, comprises the administrative district of East Flores.

Beyond Lembata are the main islands of the Alor Archipelago, Pantar and Alor, whose people were still head hunting in the 1950s.

The scenery is spectacular, all the islands (notably Lembata) produce distinctive ikat weaving, and there are some traditional, almost purely animist villages, despite the

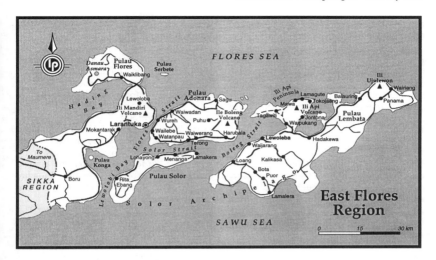

East Flores
Region

spread of Christianity and (to a lesser degree) Islam. In remote villages, people are poor and not used to westerners; children will follow you in excited bunches. Food is generally of bad quality. If you can't deal with all this, limit your stay to the urban centres of Kalabahi (Alor) and Lewoleba (Lembata) and make a few day trips into the surrounding countryside.

One thing you should bring is plenty of money. You can only change money in Kalabahi.

HISTORY

European contact was made as early as 1522, when the only remaining ship of Magellan's fleet sailed through the Lembata-Pantar strait. By the middle of the century, the Dominican Portuguese friar Antonio de Taviera had landed on Solor and set about spreading Catholicism. The Solor mission became the base for extending Christianity to mainland Flores and a fort was built to protect the converts from Muslim raids. The Portuguese were eventually kicked out of Solor by the Dutch, but until the mid-19th century, Portugal held on to Wurek (Adonara) and Pamakajo (Solor).

GETTING AROUND

The road systems on the islands are rapidly being upgraded, but are still poor compared to most parts of Flores. Bemos and trucks service most communities, but are infrequent and uncomfortable. Transport to more isolated areas is limited to a few trucks per week. Asking around the ports may prove more fruitful; on Alor and Lembata, the most reliable transport to their south coasts is by boat.

PULAU ADONARA

Adonara was known as the 'Island of Murderers' because of a feud between two clans. The feud ran for hundreds of years, with people in the hills being killed and houses burned year in, year out – very likely a case of ritual conflict between the Demon and Paji groups (see the earlier boxed text entitled The Lamaholot).

Although extremes of animism have died out, there are villages in the hinterland where Christianity has only the loosest of footholds. The Solor Archipelago is noted for its practitioners of black and white magic, but the most famous are those of Adonara. Be careful. One traveller reported placing her

FLORES

hands on a sacred rock above one village and being unable to remove them!

The chief settlements are Waiwerang (on the south coast) and Waiwadan and Wailebe (on the west coast). The island is dominated by Ile Boleng, the 1659m-high volcano that last erupted in 1974. Adonara has a few points of interest, but very few travellers stop and most head straight to more interesting Lembata.

Waiwerang

Market day is Monday and Thursday; follow the streets about 400m in the Lembata direction from the pier. Although it's not wildly exciting, the market attracts villagers from all over the island and from Solor. Waiwerang has a post office, a wartel and a bank, but money cannot be changed.

Places to Stay From the pier head to the main road and turn right. The very basic *Losmen Taufiq*, 50m around the corner, is run by a friendly Muslim woman and costs 5000/10,000 rp.

Continue past the Taufiq to the first cross-roads and the church with its bizarre statue of Christ as King. Turn left (north) at the crossroads and a few doors along is the *Hotel Asri*. Although still basic, it's a notch above the Taufiq and has a pleasant front porch. Singles/doubles with shared mandi cost 7500/13,000 rp.

It you turn right at the church, the road leads back to the waterfront and around to the *Hotel Ile Boleng* on Jl Pasar Baru. This is the pick of town's hotels. English is spoken and meals can be arranged. Singles/doubles/ triples cost 7500/14,000/18,000 rp or 10,000/ 19,000/27,000 rp with mandi. The rooms at back are built right above the water's edge and have great views.

Getting There & Away All the boats to Lewoleba on Lembata call in at Waiwerang on the way. The trip takes about two hours and costs 2000 rp. Passenger ferries dock at the main wharf in the centre of town, but at low tide they may dock at the port 1km west of town, where the car ferry docks. The boat to Lamalera (on Lembata) leaves on Friday evenings around 11 pm.

Small boats run between Waiwerang and the towns of eastern Solor (Lamakera, Menanga and Lohayong) on Mondays and Thursdays. Otherwise you can charter a boat to Solor for up to six people for around 100,000 rp.

Around Waiwerang

Using Waiwerang as a base, you can tour the island. A few bemos, buses and trucks link the main villages. Most depart Waiwerang soon after the ferry docks, but the biggest concentration is on Monday and Thursday market days. Roads around the island are mostly unsealed.

Adonara has a few decent beaches. The best is the white-sand **Pantai Eneburak**, 7km east of Waiwerang. It is possible to walk all the way to the beach at low tide, or take an eastbound bemo, which will drop you on the main road from where it is a 1.5km walk to the beach. Further along the coast is **Wera Botok**, a red-sand beach which has decent snorkelling offshore.

On the main eastern road is **Harubala**, 18km from Waiwerang, where Pak Simon Sabon Doni has built a cultural village, the Taman Wisata Budaya Tadon Boleng. This recreation of a traditional village, complete with rumah adat, was built to attract tourists who are conspicuously absent. Although the village is not overly exciting, Pak Simon is a congenial host and will put you up in his house for around 5000 rp. Excellent meals can be provided. English is not spoken, but if you understand some Indonesian, Pak Simon can outline points of interest in the area, including **Lamabayung**, a hill 20 minutes' walk from Harubala with great sunrise views of **Ile Boleng**. It is a further 1½ hour walk to the summit of the volcano and its deep crater, some 500m in diameter. Ile Boleng can also be climbed from the western side.

Five kilometres past Harubala is **Pantai Deri**, another beach touted as a tourist attraction, but it's nothing special. The road passes traditional rice barns.

The main road to the north coast skirts the western flank of Ile Boleng and reaches the coast at **Sagu**. This small port was settled by the Dutch and a broken marble pillar marks the grave of a Dutch plantation owner. The road west along the coast passes through the village of Adonara, where old ramparts and a few cannon are the only reminders of a Dutch fortress.

On the west coast, **Wureh** is noted for its old church and Good Friday procession like that in Larantuka. A statue of Christ is carried around the village on a palanquin by men in yellow togas. On Saturday morning the statue is carried back to the chapel and on Easter Sunday a statue of Mary is carried around the village to the accompaniment of songs in corrupted Portuguese.

The road continues south along the coast to **Wailebe**, on the strait directly opposite Larantuka. Small boats, to no fixed schedules, run to Larantuka. The road continues over the hill to the south coast, passing the village of **Watanpau**, noted for its black magic. This is the place to have a spell cast against an enemy or to find stolen objects. Black magic priests use chicken entrails or eggs to divine the identity of thieves.

A paved road runs along the south coast back to Wairwering, passing **Terong** where there is a huge old mosque.

PULAU SOLOR

Solor is a relatively low, dry and lightly populated island. Rita Ebang is the main town on the island and the main road runs along the north coast to Menanga, the main town in the east.

Solor became the centre for the Portuguese in Nusa Tenggara in the 16th century when they used it as a staging point for their ships en route to the spice islands of Maluku. In 1561, Dominican missionaries from Melaka, the Portuguese colony on the Malay Peninsula, established a Portuguese enclave at Port Hendriquez. After the settlement was attacked by Javanese Muslims, a fort was built in 1566.

The Portuguese were soon challenged by the Dutch. In 1613, a Dutch fleet under the command of Apollonius Scotte sailed for Kupang, attacking Solor on the way and

taking the fort. The settlers, mostly 'Black Portuguese' (slaves from Portuguese colonies in India and Melaka who intermarried with Solorese), fled to Larantuka.

For the next 30 years, the Dutch battled for control of Solor with the Portuguese, now based in Larantuka. The Portuguese retook Solor in 1616, but held it only until 1618, when the Dutch attacked Solor and Larantuka. The Portuguese again held the fort on Solor from 1629 until 1636, when they were driven out by the Dutch who increasingly assumed control of the sea lanes throughout Indonesia. The Dutch established a permanent settlement at the fort on Solor in 1646.

The site of the fort is at **Lohayong**, a few kilometres west of Menanga, but little remains after an earthquake in 1982. Lines of foundation stones can be seen in the village and one crumbling corner stands and gives some insight into the layout of the old fort, but apart from that and three small cannons, there is little to see.

The other main point of interest on Solor is **Lamakera** on the north-eastern tip of the island. Dominated by a onion-domed mosque, Lamakera is a whaling village, the Muslim equivalent of Lamalera on Lembata. The two villages have a symbiotic fishing relationship. At Lamalera, sperm whales are the main catch, while Lamakera hunts *ikan kelaru*, a type of whale shark. It is believed to bring misfortune if one village catches the wrong type of whale. The hunt by the Lamakerans is much more aggressive and a catch is accompanied by the ritual screaming of profanities. Compared to laid-back Lamalera, this village is less traditional and not set-up for visitors.

Rita Ebang, the main town and easiest to reach, is noted for its fine ikat and distinctive traditional dances.

Getting There & Away

From Larantuka there are boats to Rita Ebang every morning at about 7 am. From Waiwerang (Adonara), boats cross to Menanga, Lahoyang and Lamakera on Mondays and Thursdays. No regular bemos go right across the island from west to east.

FLORES

PULAU LEMBATA

Lembata is well known for the whaling village of Lamalera and for the smoking volcano, Ili Api, which towers over the main town of Lewoleba. As in the rest of the Lamaholot region, many Lembata villagers still use the slash-and-burn method to clear land. Corn, bananas, papayas and coconuts are grown; most rice is imported.

Lewoleba

Despite the ominous smoking of Ili Api volcano in the background, Lewoleba, the chief settlement on Lembata and the main town of the Solor Archipelago, is a relaxed little place. A couple of large government buildings, a Telkom office and a leprosy hospital are all that distinguishes it from any other scruffy village. The biggest event and the best time to be in Lewoleba is every Monday, when the market attracts villagers from all over Lembata and the other islands, and traders from Flores. Fish, rice, vegetables and modern plastic commodities are sold, though ikat can also be found.

Boats unload you at a pier about a 10 minute walk west of the town – take a *mikrolet* (small taxi) or *becak* (trishaw) for 500 rp.

Routes from Lewoleba to Lamalera

Below town, on the water, is a Bugis stilt village built out over the sea. Some of its people are pearl divers and you can arrange to go out with them on diving trips. Have a good look at the pearls you're offered in town as many are just shells. Locals will take you out by sampan to a sandbank (Pulau Siput) off Lewoleba – it's the closest place to town for a swim in beautifully clear water.

Orientation & Information The centre of Lewoleba is the market place, which comes alive every Monday with buyers and sellers from around the region.

The post office is off the main street near the south side of the market. The Bank Rakyat Indonesia is further along the same street, but it does not change money, so bring sufficient funds with you. The Flores Jaya shop opposite the post office will change US dollars at very poor rates if you are stuck. The Telkom office is 1km west of town along the main street and closes around 11 pm (you cannot make collect calls).

Places to Stay & Eat Halfway between the ferry wharf and the town, near the cemetery, the new *Lile Ile* is a switched-on homestay with plenty of information on Lembata. The main house has a large sitting area where simple meals are served for 2000 rp. Rooms off to the side have harbour views and cost 7500/13,000 rp for singles/doubles. The owner lived in Holland for many years and speaks Dutch and as well as English.

The *Hotel Rejeki* is right in the middle of town, opposite the market. Clean rooms with outside mandi cost 7500/13,500 rp downstairs and are better than the wooden rooms upstairs for the same price. New rooms with attached mandi are good, but expensive at 27,500/35,000 rp. Meals are generous and cheap, and there's always fresh seafood on the menu. Good information on Lembata is provided and transport can be hired.

Another good choice is the *Hotel Lewoleba* (☎ 41012), at Jl Awololong 15 – take the road opposite the Hotel Rejeki past the post office. It has a few rough rooms for 5000 rp per person, and much better rooms with mandi for 12,500 rp per person. The air-con rooms for 35,000/45,000 rp are luxurious in this part of world.

The Hotel Rejeki has far and away the best food in town or alternativelythere's a few dismal rumah makan near the market. *Rumah Makan Hosana* has Padang food or *Rumah Makan Bandung* has passable Javanese fare.

Getting There & Away Lewoleba is served by plane, bus and ferry.

Air Merpati flies Kupang-Larantuka-Lewoleba and return once a week on Thursday, but the flight is often cancelled due to lack of interest. The Merpati agent is in the Hotel Rejeki.

Bus The main road across the island is now sealed and a regular host of mikrolet and buses runs to destinations around Lewoleba, including Waipukang, Loang and Puor (for Lamalera). Buses to the east run to Hadakewa and direct to Balauring (5000 rp; two hours). Some of the rough back roads are plied by infrequent trucks. Buses terminate next to the ferry dock, or you can catch them in Lewoleba in front of the market.

Boat Small passenger ferries ply daily between Lewoleba and Larantuka (4000 rp; four hours). They leave around 8 am and 1 pm (noon on Mondays) from Lewoleba, at the same times from Larantuka, stopping at Waiwerang (on Adonara) on the way. They can be crowded, but there's usually no problem getting a seat. It is a spectacular journey through the islands past smoking volcanoes.

The large passenger/car ferries to Kalabahi (Alor) from Larantuka stop at Lewoleba on Tuesday, Thursday and Sunday (schedules are subject to change). They depart from Lewoleba at 11 am for Balauring (4500 rp; four hours) in north-eastern Lembata where they stop for the night. Balauring has a decent losmen or you can sleep on the deck of the boat. At 7 am the next morning the ferry continues on to Kalabahi (9000 rp; nine hours) via Baranusa (4000 rp; four hours) on Pantar. There are usually plenty of seats, though the ferry can fill up on Pantar. Bring

food and water. Coming from Kalabahi, these ferries depart from Lewoleba on Monday, Wednesday and Friday at 11 am for Waibalun harbour (4500 rp; four hours), 4km from Larantuka, but the smaller ferries are more convenient and dock in the centre of Larantuka.

Getting Around You can take mikrolet around town and to the ferry dock, or Lewoleba has a few becaks imported from Ujung Pandang and Java which cost 500 rp anywhere around town.

Ili Api Peninsula
Some interesting day trips can be made from Lewoleba to the Ili Api Peninsula, around 20km away. Ili Api itself can be climbed, ancestral villages can be visited and the area produces Lembata's best ikat, recognisable by its burgundy-coloured base and highly detailed patterning. Mostly natural dyes and hand-spun cotton are used. In the villages, men hand spin cotton onto spindles as they sit around and chat, though like everywhere else, women do the weaving.

Roads are mostly unsealed, but bemos and trucks run around the peninsula to Tokojaeng in the north-east and to Mawa in the north-west, but no bemos go in between to allow a loop. It pays to be able to speak some Indonesian if venturing further afield.

Jontona On the eastern side of peninsula, this straggling village full of shy and scruffy children is serviced by trucks and two bemos (1500 rp) a day from Lewoleba. The last bemo back to Lewoleba leaves around 2 pm, sometimes later, especially on Mondays when many more bemos shuttle to the Lewoleba market. You can stay at the decrepit *Homestay Seramgorang*, but there is little point – the main reason to visit is to walk up the hill to the old village. A scorching, sulphurous hot spring is near the beach, 1km from the village, but it is the haunt of ghosts and the villagers are reluctant to take you there. Like most villages, Jontona produces some fine ikat – ask to see it if you're interested in buying.

FLORES

Consult the kepala desa or village secretary before heading off to the old village (Lewohala, or Kampung Lama in Indonesian). You will be ushered into a house over the road from the church where a thoughtful sign on the wall states: 'Welcome mister and please sit down'. Here you can arrange a guide for a few thousand rupiah. A guide is essential. The old village is the sacred ancestral home of the villagers and contains their prized heirlooms – strangers heading off alone will be turned back.

It is a hot 1¼ hour walk uphill to the old village. Start as early as possible and bring plenty of water. Now deserted, the old village is occupied only for ceremonies such as the *kacang* (bean) festival in late September/early October. The villagers say they were forced to move down to the new village during WWII, when the Japanese rounded up labour to build a military base at Hadakewa.

Dozens of traditional thatched houses dot a small hill at the base of Ili Api. The largest house and the first you reach is the Laba Making (House of the Making clan). The large base platform sleeps 20 or more people when used, and the house contains bronze moko drums and a set of gamelan gongs. Other houses have sacred and prized objects, including elephant tusks, and many have bamboo tubes of rice and fish hanging from the ceiling – offerings for the ancestors. The main ceremonial house is the *koke* where the heads of the clans sit and preside over ceremonies. Dances are performed in the *namang* quadrangle in front of the koke, and animals are sacrificed on the Y-shaped stick altar. In the centre of the quadrangle is the *namang kepuhu* (naval of the namang), a flat stone where other offerings are made, in previous times possibly the heads of enemies taken in battle.

Ili Api Smouldering, 1450m-high Ili Api dominates central Lembata. Although its last major eruption was in the 19th century, it is still a very active volcano. If the wet season is late in coming, villagers climb to the top and make sacrificial offerings to bring the rains.

From old Jontona village it is possible to walk three hours more to the crater, but this is a tough route. It is the closest to the fumarole and near the top the wind often blows stinging clouds of sulphurous gas towards climbers. Ili Api can be climbed from many other villages, but trails on the mountain are hard to follow, so you'll need a guide. The problem is finding a guide willing to tackle the climb. It is an easier but longer climb from Tokojaeng in the north-east, which can be reached by trucks that pass through Jontong, but the usual starting point is Lamagute to the north.

As Lamagute gets the most climbers, chances of finding a guide are best here, but it is not serviced by regular public transport, except on Monday market days. The Hotel Rejeki has good information and may be able to put you in contact with a guide and arrange transport to Lamagute.

Ili Api is a seven hour return walk from Lamagute. Start as early as possible to avoid the heat of the day and bring plenty of water and food.

Other Villages The western side of the peninsula is the most populated. The road is sealed as far as the large village of Waipukang, with its school full of abnormally curious children. The road then turns to dirt and passes a number of villages noted for their weaving. **Mawa**, on the north coast, is one of the best places to see fine ikat. Further on, weaving can also be seen at **Lamagute**, a starting point for climbing Ili Api (see its previous entry). Inland from Lamagute on the flanks of the mountain is **Atawatu**, an ancestral village similar to Jontona.

Just past Petuntawa village, a road branches off to the west. You can take a mikrolet to **Tagawiti** and then it is a 2km walk to the beach where there is reasonable snorkelling out on the reef. Sunbathing is difficult – the crowds of kids block out the sunlight.

Lamalera
Like characters out of *Moby Dick*, the people who live in this village on the south coast of Lembata still use small boats to hunt whales.

The whaling season is limited to May through to October, when the seas aren't too rough and whales migrate south through the straits between Timor and the Solor Archipelago. The season officially begins when a ceremony is held around 1 May to call the whales at Watu Koteklemer (Whale Rock) on a hill above the village.

Most whales come through from mid-April to the end of May, but even then the whales are infrequent, with only about 15 to 25 caught each year. The villagers probably qualify as subsistence whalers and are therefore exempt from international bans on whaling.

The meat is shared according to traditional dictates. The heads go to two families of original landowners, a custom observed, it is said, since the 15th century. The blubber is melted to make fuel for lamps, and some is traded for fruit and vegetables in a barter-only market in the hills.

Most whales caught are sperm whales, although smaller pilot whales are occasionally taken. When whales are scarce, the villagers harpoon sharks, manta rays and dolphins, which are available year-round. Using nets is alien to these people and fishing rods are used only for sharks.

The whaling boats are made entirely of wood, with wooden dowel instead of nails. Each vessel carries a mast and a sail made of palm leaves, but these are lowered during the hunt, when the men (usually a crew of 12) row furiously to overtake the whale. As the gap between the boat and the whale narrows, the harpooner takes the 3m-long harpoon and leaps onto the back of the whale. An injured whale will try to dive, dragging the boat with it, but cannot escape, since it has to resurface.

Your chances of actually seeing a whale hunt, or the bloody business of butchering a whale, are quite small. Whale hunting aside, Lamalera is an interesting traditional village. A steady trickle of travellers make their way here and tourism is certainly welcome as an attractive economic alternative to uncertain whale hunting. For 15,000 rp you can even go out in the boats on a whale hunt, though it is unlikely you will see the bloody kill.

On Saturday, there's an interesting barter-only market at **Wulandoni**, about a 1½ hour walk along the coast from Lamalera. Another nice walk along the coast is to **Tapabali**, where you can see local weaving. In Lamalera, common ikat motifs are whales, manta rays and boats.

Places to Stay & Eat There are four small homestays in Lamalera, all costing around 10,000 rp per day, including meals. You may be served dolphin in season – if the idea of eating dolphin is repugnant, the dark, oily meat is even more repulsive. *Guru Ben's* is above the village, perched on a hill overlooking the shoreline. This is the most popular place to stay – Pak Ben speaks good English

---

Lamalera

The villagers of Lamalera are thought to have originated from Lapan Batan, a small island in the straits between Lembata and Pantar which was destroyed by a volcanic eruption. The ancestors arrived in boats that each clan has kept as the model for all future boats. While the original boats have been repaired and added to over the generations, the villagers consider them to be the same boats. To the villagers, each boat is a living being and a physical link to the ancestors and the ancestral home.

The loss of a boat from the village is more than an economic blow to the villagers – it means losing an important part of their heritage. Most recently, in March 1994, two small boats from Lamalera sank after being dragged almost to Timor by a wounded whale, a distance of around 80km. The crew of the two boats was later picked up by a third boat from the village and the 36 men then drifted for several days before being rescued by the P & O Spice Islands cruise ship.

The loss of the boats sent the village into a two month period of mourning in which no whaling was allowed. When the mourning period finished, a ceremony took place to 'let the boats go'. ■

and is a gracious host. The slightly more salubrious *Bapa Yosef's*, also known as the 'White House', is right on the point at the end of the beach. This small house sleeps four and someone will come in three times a day to cook meals. *Mama Maria's Homestay* is right in the heart of the village, behind the shady town square. *Abel Beding* is on the main path through the village, past the town square, and is on-the-ball with information.

Getting There & Away The easiest way to get to Lamalera is by boat from either Lewoleba or Larantuka. The boat from Lewoleba to Lamalera (3500 rp; six hours) leaves after the Monday night market (usually around midnight, but it may be as late as 5 am). From Larantuka, a boat leaves on Fridays, stopping in Waiwerang on the way.

Otherwise take a Surya Kasih or Taruna truck from Lewoleba to Puor, from where it's a 2½ hour walk, mostly downhill. Bring plenty of water for the walk. Trucks leave around 7 to 9 am. From Lewoleba, the bemos leave at 7 am and run only as far as Bota – a 45 minute walk before Puor. You may be able to hire a motorcycle in Lewoleba. This very tough ride is only for experienced riders with a trail bike; independent rentals are almost impossible. You can get someone to take you as a pillion passenger, but it is very expensive.

Leaving Lamalera the truck from Puor leaves around 10 am, so start the walk early. The market ferry from Lewoleba returns on Monday morning and the boat to Larantuka leaves on Wednesdays. Because of connections and Lamalera's isolation, you really need five days or more to visit Lamalera from Larantuka.

Hadakewa

This large village is the biggest before reaching Balauring in the east of the island. Hadakewa was the main administrative town during the Dutch occupation, when Lembata was called Lomblen. During WWII the Japanese built a military base at Hadakewa, but after the war Hadakewa was eclipsed in importance by Lewoleba.

A couple of kilometres east of Hadakewa, **Lerahinga** has good snorkelling on the reefs offshore. The village is an extension of Hadakewa and you are guaranteed a crowd of onlookers. A little further along, **Waienga** is a quieter beach shaded by pandanus palms. It is good for swimming and a pearl farm outrigger is just offshore. It is also a good place to try *tuak* (fermented palm sap alcohol) brewed from the pandanus you sit under. For a small tip, the local kids will bring you a metre length of bamboo filled with tuak, which is often freshly distilled and therefore sweeter. One length is enough to get two people rollickingly drunk, but at only a couple of thousand rupiah a length you don't have to drink it all.

Balauring

This small, predominantly Muslim town is on the peninsula jutting off the eastern end of Lembata. Ferries linking Alor and Lembata stop here for the night (on Tuesday, Thursday and Sunday), the only reason to visit. There are wonderful views of Ili Api as you come into Balauring.

The town has one place to stay, the welcoming *Losmen Telaga Sari*, though it's in a swampy area and mosquitos are a problem. Walk straight down the road leading off the end of the pier and the losmen is the second last building on the street. It costs 7500 rp per person in dilapidated rooms and meals are provided. Otherwise, you can sleep on the boat – the crew may be able to provide you with a mat to sleep on deck.

Mikrolet (4000 rp) and buses (5000 rp; two hours) run the 53km from Balauring over the paved road to Lewoleba.

Just east of Balauring, the landscape is dominated by **Ili Ujulewon**. The fertile slopes of this mountain are home to dozens of villages crammed between the mountain and the north coast, and more villages line the main road skirting the southern slopes of the mountain. Halfway between Balauring and Wairiang, **Panama** is a traditional village whose inhabitants claim to possess a human skull with horns. The skull is held in the ancestral village further up the mountain, but sceptics wishing to verify this astonishing claim may well be told by the villagers that they are too busy to take you there. **Wairiang** on the far eastern coast, is a 45 minute journey by bus from Balauring. A small ferry, the *Diana Ekspres* leaves for Kalabahi (Alor) on Wednesdays at 11 am, but takes nine hours.

PULAU ALOR

East of the Solor group are the islands of Alor and Pantar. Alor, in particular, is quite scenic and has a wide mix of cultures in a small area. Diving around the island is reputedly some of the best in South-East Asia. The island is so rugged, and travel there so difficult, that the roughly 140,000 inhabitants of Alor and Pantar are divided into some 50 tribes speaking numerous languages. Administratively, Alor is part of Timor, not Flores, but is included here for convenience as it is usually visited in conjunction with Lembata and other islands to the east.

The area has cultural ties with the Solor Archipelago, and Lamaholot is spoken in some coastal settlements, but these small islands have astonishingly rich linguistic diversity. Alor has eight languages and at least 25 dialects, while Pantar has four languages and a dozen or so dialects. The languages spoken by the inland tribes are of the Trans-New Guinea family, related to the languages of East Timor and Irian Jaya, and are completely different from the Malayo-Polynesian languages spoken further east. Alor lies just off the coast from East Timor and is clearly visible from Dili on a fine day.

Although the Dutch installed local rajas along the coastal regions after 1908, they had little influence over the interior, whose people were still head hunting in the 1950s. The mountain villages were hilltop fortresses above valleys so steep that horses were useless, and during the rainy season the trails became impassable. The different tribes had little contact with each other except during raids.

When the 20th century came, the warriors put western imports to good use by twisting wire from telegraph lines into multibarbed arrowheads, over the tip of which they pressed a sharpened, dried and hollowed chicken bone. When the arrow hit, the bone would splinter deep inside the wound.

The coastal populations are a mixture of Muslim and Christian. Christianity has made inroads, primarily through Dutch Protestant missionaries, but indigenous animist cultures

---

Moko Mania

Alor's chief fame lies in its mysterious *mokos* – bronze drums about half a metre high and a third of a metre in diameter, tapered in the middle like an hourglass and with four ear-shaped handles around the circumference. They're closed at the end with a sheet of bronze that sounds like a bongo when thumped with the hand. There are thousands of them on the island – the Alorese apparently found them buried in the ground and believed them to be gifts from the gods.

Most mokos have decorations similar to those on bronze utensils made on Java in the 13th and 14th century Majapahit era, but others resemble earlier South-East Asian designs and may be connected with the Dongson culture, which developed in Vietnam and China around 700 BC and then pushed its influence into Indonesia. Later mokos even have English or Dutch-influenced decorations.

Theories about the mokos' origins usually suggest they were brought to Alor from further west by Indian, Chinese or Makassarese traders, but this doesn't explain why they were buried in the ground. Maybe the Alorese buried them in some long-forgotten time, as an offering to spirits at a time of plague or to hide them during attacks.

Today mokos have acquired enormous value among the Alorese, and families devote great time and energy to amassing collections of them, along with pigs and land. Such wealth is the only avenue to obtaining a bride in traditional Alorese society. In former times, whole villages would sometimes go to war in an attempt to win possession of a prized moko. The export of mokos is restricted by the government. ■

still survive, mainly because travel around the island has been very difficult. New roads now cross the island, but boats are still a common form of transport.

Kalabahi

Kalabahi is the chief town on Alor, at the end of a long, narrow and spectacular palm-fringed bay on the west coast. It's a cliché tropical port – lazy and slow-moving, with wooden boats scattered around the harbour. The sea breezes make Kalabahi appreciably cooler than most other coastal towns in Nusa Tenggara.

Kalabahi is relatively prosperous, but outside the town living conditions are poor. There are a few interesting villages and nice beaches nearby. Some of the beaches have spectacular snorkelling and diving, but also dangerous currents.

It's worth strolling around the Pasar Inpres market in Kalabahi. It has a huge variety of fruit and you'll see women making bamboo mats.

Money Cash and travellers cheques can be exchanged at the Bank BNI and the Bank Rakyat Indonesia. The Ombay shop, one block back from the port, will also change US dollars outside banking hours at reasonable rates.

Places to Stay The central *Hotel Adi Dharma* (☎ 21049), at Jl Martadinata 12, is on the waterfront near the main pier. It has the best set-up for travel information and has great views across the harbour from the porch, especially at sunset. Singles/doubles/triples with outside bath are 6000/10,000/12,000 rp, while large, clean rooms with fan and bath are 12,500/20,000/24,000 rp.

The nearby *Hotel Melati* (☎ 21073) has a shady garden and old rooms for 6500/12,000 rp or 10,000/16,000 rp with mandi. A new block has better rooms for 15,000/20,000 rp or 25,000/30,000 rp with air-con.

Out near the bus terminal, *Hotel Pelangi Indah* (☎ 21251) at Jl Diponegoro 100 has the best rooms in town and the attached restaurant is a definite bonus. Spotless rooms with verandah, fan and mandi cost 15,000/20,000 rp, while those with air-con and shower are 35,000/40,000 rp. Any bemo going to the bus terminal can drop you there.

Nearby, the *Hotel Nusa Kenari* (☎ 21119), at Jl Diponegoro 11, has good rooms for

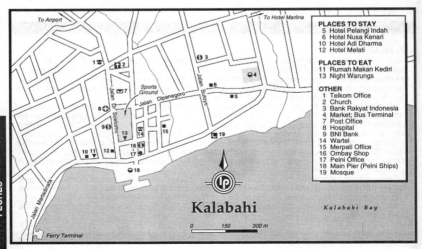

PLACES TO STAY
5 Hotel Pelangi Indah
6 Hotel Nusa Kenari
10 Hotel Adi Dharma
12 Hotel Melati

PLACES TO EAT
11 Rumah Makan Kediri
13 Night Warungs

OTHER
1 Telkom Office
2 Church
3 Bank Rakyat Indonesia
4 Market; Bus Terminal
7 Post Office
8 Hospital
9 BNI Bank
14 Wartel
15 Merpati Office
16 Ombay Shop
17 Pelni Office
18 Main Pier (Pelni Ships)
19 Mosque

Kalabahi

Kalabahi Bay

0   150   300 m

To Airport

To Hotel Marlina

Sports Ground

Jalan Dr Soetomo

Jalan Diponegoro

Jalan Suroyo

Jalan Martadinata

Ferry Terminal

FLORES

PETER TURNER

SARA-JANE CLELAND

SARA-JANE CLELAND

SARA-JANE CLELAND

Flores
Top: The coral atolls of the Seventeen Islands Marine Park have fine beaches and snorkelling.
Middle Left: Fisherman aboard his vessel in Labuanbajo.
Middle Right: Elderly woman from a village in Flores.
Bottom: A fishing vessel at low tide in Labuanbajo on Flores' north-western coast.

PETER TURNER

PETER TURNER

PETER TURNER

SARA-JANE CLELAND

Flores
Top: Ili Api dominates the Lewoleba harbour on Pulau Lembata in the Solor Archipelago.
Middle Left: Ferry boats – an essential element of travel between the islands.
Middle Right: An elder from Larantuka in warrior's garb prepares for a traditional dance performance.
Bottom: A villager fishes in the waters around Komodo Island.

15,000 rp with mandi, or 25,000 rp and 30,000 rp with air-con and shower.

The *Hotel Marlina* (☎ 21141) is inconveniently located 3km out of town on Jl El Tari, but you can get there by bemo. Room rates start at 6000 rp per person in three bed rooms with shared bath, or 15,000 rp with private bath.

Places to Eat Kalabahi has the best dining in the Solor and Alor archipelagos, which isn't saying much. The best option and Kalabahi's only restaurant is at the *Hotel Pelangi Indah*. Otherwise a few dreary rumah makan are scattered around town. They include the *Rumah Makan Kediri*, close to the pier, which serves reasonable Javanese food, and there is also a grungy *Padang restaurant* opposite the market on Jl Diponegoro.

At night, a few streetside warungs and kaki lima food stalls set up on the southern side of the sports ground. Sate, soto ayam and other Javanese fare are on offer. This meagre collection is about the closest thing to nightlife in Kalabahi, which otherwise closes down around 8 pm.

Getting There & Away Merpati flies to/from Kupang to Kalabahi daily, except Friday.

Kalabahi is linked by passenger/car ferries to Kupang and Atapupu on Timor, and Larantuka on Flores via Baranusa (Pantar), Balauring (Lembata), Lewoleba (Lembata), and Waiwerang (Adonara). Schedules are subject to change. These ferries leave from the ferry terminal 1km south-west of the town centre. It's a 10 minute walk or 400 rp bemo ride to the Hotel Adi Dharma.

The Perum ASDP ferry leaves Kupang's Bolok harbour for Kalabahi on Thursday and Saturday at 1 pm (16,500 rp; about 16 hours). From Kalabahi to Kupang departures are on Tuesday at 2 pm and Friday at 2 pm. On Sunday at 10 pm this ferry runs from Kalabahi to Atapupu (8000 rp; eight hours), from where buses run to Atambua with connections to Dili and Kupang. The ferry returns from Atapupu to Kalabahi on Monday at 9 am.

Ferries leave Kalabahi for Larantuka on Sunday, Tuesday and Thursday at 7 am. They stop at Baranusa (5000 rp; five hours) and then Balauring (9000 rp; nine hours) where they overnight. Balauring has a losmen. The next day at 7 am ferries continue from Balauring to Larantuka (9000 rp; nine hours) via Lewoleba and Waiwerang. Take food and water, as there's usually none on the boat.

Pelni boats leave from the main pier in the centre of town. The Pelni ship *Awu* calls in at Kalabahi twice every fortnight, sailing on to Dili (East Timor) and Kupang. Pelni cargo ships also regularly run from Kalabahi to Dili and Kupang and take passengers. Check at the Pelni office.

Cargo ships are slow (14 hours to Dili) and conditions are not the best. It pays to rent a cabin from one of the crew members for about 15,000 rp.

Other small boats from the central wharf chug their way to the other islands of the Alor Archipelago. A boat also travels once a week to Wairiang on the north-eastern tip of Lembata.

Getting Around Kalabahi airport is 28km from town. Merpati runs a minibus to meet flights. Transport around town is by bus and bemo (400 rp), which finish by 7 pm. It's also possible to rent a motorcycle through the Hotel Adi Dharma, or the Toko Kencana shop opposite the market on Jl Diponegoro, for 15,000 rp per day.

Around Kalabahi
Takpala is a traditional village about 13km east of Kalabahi. To get there, take a Mabu bus from the Kalabahi market. From where the bus drops you, walk about 1km uphill on a sealed road. There are several traditional high-roofed houses and the view over the Flores Sea from the village is stunning. The people warmly welcome visitors and occasionally put on dance performances for tour groups.

From Takpala it's possible to continue on to **Atimelang**, another traditional village which is rarely visited. You can take a bus to Mabu, but from there it's about a four hour

FLORES

walk; a guide is recommended. It's possible to stay with the kepala desa in Atimelang.

The villages of **Alor Kecil** and **Alor Besar** have good beaches nearby, with excellent snorkelling. The water is wonderfully cool, but the currents are very strong. The diving around the offshore islands is superb, but is best arranged in Kupang. Alor Kecil has some weaving and offers great views across to other islands. This area is being promoted as a potential diving resort. Buses to Alor Kecil and Alor Besar leave from the Kalabahi market or catch them outside the Hotel Melati.

Near the airport at the northernmost tip of the island is **Mali**, a lovely white-sand beach with good snorkelling. It's possible to rent a boat for a tour of the area and at high tide you can walk to **Pulau Suki**, off the beach at Mali. There's an old grave there, said to be that of a sultan from Sulawesi.

PULAU PANTAR

The second largest island of the Alor group, Pantar is about as far off the beaten track as you can get. The Perum ferries between Larantuka and Alor stop at **Baranusa**, the main town, a somnolent little place with a straggle of coconut palms and a couple of general stores. Baranusa's only accommodation is at the friendly *Homestay Burhan*, with just one room, costing 10,000 rp, including meals.

The main reason to visit Pantar is to climb **Gunung Sirung**, an active volcano with an impressive smouldering crater. From Baranusa take a truck to Kakamauta (2500 rp), from where it is a three hour walk to Sirung's crater.

The only other island of note is lightly populated **Pulau Pura**, sandwiched between Pantar and Alor. It is dominated by a towering, forested peak topped by a small crater lake.

Timor

Locator & Map Index

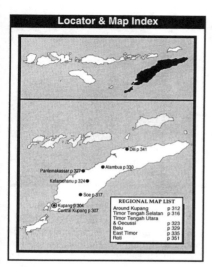

Dili p 341
Pantemakassar p 327 ● ● Atambua p 330
Kefamehanu p 324 ●
● Soe p 317
Kupang p 304
Central Kupang p 307

Highlights

- **Kupang** – the 'big city' of Nusa Tenggara Timur province, Kupang is primarily a transport hub, but some interesting day trips can made to beaches and offshore islands such as Pulau Semau and Pulau Kera.

- **Roti** – four hours by ferry from Kupang, Roti is an interesting, dry island, and has an excellent surf beach and accommodation at Nemberala.

- **Soe** – the best base from which to explore interesting Dawan villages and colourful traditional markets at Niki Niki and Oinlasi. Boti is the most visited traditional village, or head north into the hills for fine mountain scenery.

- **Traditional Villages** – as well as those around Soe, Timor has many fascinating traditional villages. Temkessi is in a spectacular setting, as is Lorodirman. Using Betun as a base, you can visit the matriarchal villages of the Belu people.

- **Pantemakassar** – there's not a lot to see, but it's a scenic trip to somewhere different over the hills and down to the coast. It's also the site of Portugal's first colony in Nusa Tenggara.

- **Dili** – a touch of Portugal in the tropics, Dili is one of the most attractive cities in the region. Trips can be made into the mountains to the hill town of Maubisse or to Baucau, which has some good Portuguese architecture and a fine beach.

If you arrive in Timor from Darwin, it will hit you with all the shock of Asia. Kupang, the main city, is very Indonesian, with its buzzing streets and honking horns and its Third World sights and smells. Away from Kupang, Timor hardly sees any tourists, although it's a scenic island with fascinating traditional cultures.

Timor's landscape is unique, with its spiky lontar palms, rocky soils and central mountains dotted with villages of beehive-shaped huts. The island has some fantastic coastline and rugged, scenic mountains. There are no tourist-type beach spots yet, although you can take trips from Kupang to nearby islands for swimming and snorkelling.

Christianity is widespread, though still fairly superficial in some rural areas; the old animistic cultures have not been completely eradicated. In the hills of the centre and the south, villagers still defer to their traditional chiefs. In the mountain areas, traditional ikat dress is common, and betel nut and *tuak*

(village liquor) are still preferred. It is well worthwhile venturing into the central mountains of West Timor, which receive relatively few tourists.

West Timor's lack of visitors can be attributed to that five-letter word – Timor. Despite popular misconception, West Timor was never embroiled in the war that gripped the eastern part of the island. It stood apart from the tragedy in East Timor; the two parts of the island are like separate countries, with distinct histories and development. Dutch-controlled

291

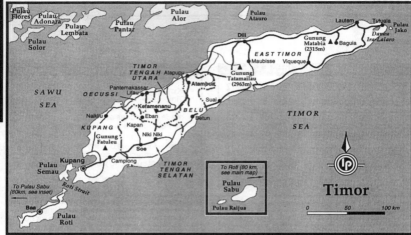

West Timor became part of independent Indonesia in 1949, while East Timor was controlled by Portugal until 1975, when Indonesia invaded.

East Timor is open for tourism and Dili is easily visited for a taste of Portugal in the tropics. Travel is possible throughout the rest of East Timor and can be very rewarding.

Thanks to Merpati's twice weekly flights between Kupang and Darwin, more travellers to or from Australia are passing through Timor, and there are interesting options for onward travel to East Timor and the Solor and Alor archipelagos, or from Kupang on to Roti, Sabu and Sumba.

Facts About Timor

HISTORY
Early History
The discovery of stone artefacts and evidence of pre-agricultural societies may mean that Timor was home to *Homo erectus*, early hominoids related to Java Man that settled the Indonesian archipelago up to one million years ago. Evidence of modern human set-

tlement on Timor dates back at least 13,000 years, when the Austronesian peoples of Asia migrated throughout the eastern islands. These hunter-gatherers were joined by later migrants from Asia, who introduced agriculture around 2000 BC.

Little is known of Timor before 1500 AD, though Chinese and Javanese traders visited the island from at least the 13th century, and possibly as early as the 7th century. Traders visited coastal settlements in search of the plentiful sandalwood (prized for its aroma and for the medicinal santalol made from the oil) and beeswax.

Timor was divided into a number of small kingdoms, which were little more than tribal groupings involved in frequent skirmishes, with head-hunting a popular activity. The Dawan (or Atoni) people, thought to be the earliest inhabitants of Timor, were the largest group in western Timor, but were divided into numerous small kingdoms.

The Tetum (or Belu) people, the other major ethnic group, migrated to Timor in the 14th century, settling the fertile central regions and pushing the Dawan westward. Their origins are uncertain, but they call their homeland Malaka, and they may well have migrated from the Malay peninsula. From their fertile base, that today straddles the West Timor/East Timor border, they expanded until four of their tribes had formed kingdoms and pushed further into East Timor.

Portuguese & Dutch

The first Europeans in Timor were the Portuguese, perhaps as early as 1509. Portuguese trading ships regularly visited the north coast in search of sandalwood. It wasn't until 1568 that Dutch traders first arrived in Timor. For the next 300 years the Dutch and Portuguese competed for control of Timor.

Portugal's era of influence really begins in 1556 at Lifau (in present-day Ambenu) when Dominican friars established a settlement and set about converting the Timorese to Catholicism. Official Portuguese efforts were minimal, and colonisation was left to a handful of Dominicans in the hope that conversion would spread Portuguese influence and keep out the Dutch.

A Dutch expedition, led by Apollonius Scotte, sailed to Kupang in 1613 and negotiated with the local ruler to build a fort in return for Dutch military help against competing tribes. Dutch claims to Timor dated from this time, but Scotte didn't act on the agreement and it was to be 40 years before the Dutch showed any interest in Timor. Although they occasionally harried the nearby Portuguese settlement on Solor, the Dutch were more concerned with the lucrative spice islands of Maluku to the north.

Away from the coast, a dozen or so Timorese kingdoms held sway over the island with no interference from the colonial powers until 1642. The most dominant kingdom in the west was the Dawan kingdom of Sonbai, while the central Tetum kingdom of Wehali, based around the present-day region of Belu, was the most powerful in central-east Timor.

In 1642, Francisco Fernandes landed in Naikliu and led a Portuguese military expedition to weaken the power of the Timor kings. With the assistance of Timorese allies, Fernandes marched across Sonbai territory, around present-day Kapan, and after suc-

cesses there went on to defeat Wehali. His small army of musketeers was comprised primarily of Topasses, the mestizo group from the Portuguese settlements at Larantuka (Flores) and Pulau Solor. The Christian, Portuguese-speaking Topasses, called 'Black Portuguese' by the Dutch, were descended from intermarriage between the Solorese, Portuguese and slaves from Portuguese colonies in India and Melaka.

After this show of strength, the Topasses settled in Timor, at Lifau on the coast and then further inland around present-day Kefamenanu and Niki Niki. These strangers representing a far-off, powerful kingdom were welcomed by local rulers and given land. Although acting on behalf of Portugal, through intermarriage they went on to form their own kingdoms and became a power unto themselves. Two clans of Topasses, the de Ornai and the da Costa clans, integrated into the local community and became the new rajas, controlling most of Timor, but not without skirmishes among themselves.

The Dutch, unsettled by growing Portuguese influence, arrived in Kupang in 1653 to stake their claim on Timor. First they fortified Kupang, and then they set about controlling the surrounding area. They forged alliances with local rulers around the Bay of Kupang, but a Dutch military expedition to the south was soundly defeated by Timorese and Topasse forces.

In the same year, 1656, a Portuguese was appointed to administer the settlement at Lifau, making it the first real Portuguese colony on Timor. When the Portuguese commander died, a Topasse *capitao* was appointed in 1663 and the Topasses went on to consolidate their power. In 1701, the Portuguese viceroy of Goa appointed a governor to control Lifau, but he lasted only until 1705 when he was driven out by the Topasses.

The Portuguese returned to Lifau, but their power was tenuous at best. By 1749, the Topasses controlled central Timor and marched on Kupang to confront the Dutch. Although outnumbered, the Dutch won and killed many Topasse leaders at the battle of Penfui, the site of Kupang airport today.

The Dutch in Kupang, comprising only a handful of Veerigde Oost-Indische Compagnie (VOC) officers, became the major force on Timor through alliances with inland chiefs and further military campaigns. The Portuguese, however, had to abandon Lifau in 1769 after more attacks from the Topasses, and the colony was moved east to Dili, the present-day capital of East Timor.

Although the VOC assumed the upper hand, their control was marginal and they relied on Timorese allies for power. Roti became the greatest ally of the Dutch. After the Dutch invaded Roti in 1681, it became a source of slaves. Roti provided soldiers for the Dutch army and, after the Rotinese ruler converted to Christianity in 1729, they petitioned the Dutch to provide schools. The Rotinese became an educated elite, and are still very prominent in West Timor today. The Dutch favoured the Rotinese's advancement and migration to Kupang to counter Timorese power.

Conflict continued throughout the 19th century – between Timorese kingdoms and against the Dutch. The Dutch were firmly ensconced in Kupang, but unable and unwilling to control the interior. The VOC went bankrupt in 1799, leaving the Dutch government to assume direct control, but they ignored far-flung Kupang which held little economic interest. Trade was largely conducted by Chinese merchants, and the Dutch colony was neglected.

It was a similar story in the east, where the Portuguese held on to power through strategic alliances against attacks from local chiefs. Portuguese settlement was minimal and the colony was ruled from Macau on the Chinese coast. Chinese outnumbered Europeans in Portuguese Timor, and the colony also had to cope with Chinese rebellions. The sandalwood trade began to die, and coffee, introduced as a cash crop in 1815, became the principle concern of the Portuguese.

Dutch-Portuguese conflict was mostly confined to Flores and the Dutch finally took Larantuka in 1851, forcing negotiations that resulted in the Treaty of Lisbon in 1859. The Portuguese relinquished all claims on Flores,

and Timor was divided in half, but the split was not formalised until a further treaty in 1904, with a slight rejigging of borders right up until 1916. Portugal claimed the east and the north coast pocket of Oecussi in the west, based around Lifau, while Holland received the rest of the west.

20th Century

The 20th century brought the greatest changes to Timor as the colonial powers increased their involvement. The new Dutch policy was to rule all of the East Indies possessions directly, establishing Dutch government throughout the archipelago. In 1905, Kupang was ordered to bring the local chiefs to heel. The various kingdoms were required to swear allegiance to Holland and submit to the authority of a Dutch Controller. In return, they were given autonomy to rule their principalities and collect taxes for the Dutch administration.

Rebellions broke out across West Timor from 1906 onwards and the Dutch reacted swiftly. In Niki Niki, Dutch forces surrounded the royal compound and the royal family self-immolated rather than yield to the Dutch. Rebellions continued right up until 1916, when the last kingdoms succumbed to Dutch rule.

It was a similar story in Portuguese Timor, which had become a separate colony from Macau in 1896. The crunch came in 1910 when the Portuguese raised taxes and introduced a forced labour policy to increase plantation productivity. Rebellions broke out and continued up until 1915.

In Dutch Timor, roads and schools were built, but most of the population outside the regional centres had little contact with the Dutch, except for aggressive, mostly Protestant, missionary activity. Control was limited and the traditional rajas held sway under a Dutch hegemony. Life in Portuguese Timor was even less changed. The Portuguese ruled through a similar traditional system of local chiefs *(liurai)*, who acted as Portuguese agents, but control outside Dili was very limited, despite early pacification campaigns in the interior.

WWII

The Japanese forces swept aside the colonial powers in their rapid march through Asia. Following air attacks which began in January 1942, the Japanese landed outside Kupang on 20 February and quickly took the city. Australian soldiers had earlier landed in Kupang, but were soon pushed backed to Camplong, and those not captured joined Australian forces stationed in Dili. Known as Sparrow Force, they continued a guerrilla war with the backing of Timorese in the villages, conducting hit and run raids on Japanese positions in East Timor. Less than 400 allied soldiers killed as many 1500 Japanese troops and tied up many more for nearly a year. Ultimately they were driven to the south coast by the Japanese juggernaut and had to evacuate.

As elsewhere in Asia, the Japanese promised independence and an end to the yolk of colonialism. Their promises were well received, but it soon became obvious that the Japanese were even harsher masters. Forced labour was used to build Japanese bases and as the war wore on, food was appropriated causing starvation in the countryside. When the war in the Pacific swung in favour of the Allies in 1944-45, Timor was isolated, causing even further hardship.

Independence

After the Japanese surrendered on 15 August 1945, Australian forces occupied Timor until the Dutch returned to claim their colony. Indonesia declared independence on 17 August 1945, but while Java was rocked by a bloody independence war, the eastern islands were largely calm. West Timor became part of the state of Negara Indonesia Timur, the Dutch answer to divide Indonesia under a Dutch government.

When the Dutch finally decided to quit Indonesia in 1949, West Timor became part of the independent Republic of Indonesia, but not without some disturbances and calls for independence.

In East Timor a nascent independence movement had arisen, but Portugal swiftly claimed its old colony and it remained Por-

tuguese up until the tragic events of 1975 (see the East Timor section of this chapter for more on these events).

Regional administration in West Timor remained largely in control of the local rajas until restructuring began in 1958. The abolition of the traditional rulers' power still rankles among the royal families today. For many years the rajas, not civil administrators, were considered by the people to be the rightful leaders, but most rajas from the time of independence are now dead. The royal families still command great respect, but their hold on traditional rule is finally waning.

Eastern Indonesia was largely forgotten for many years and on Timor, away from the main Kupang-Atambua highway, many communities remained isolated. Since 1988, Nusa Tenggara has been targeted for development by the central government. New roads have been pushed into the interior and old ones sealed. Despite rapidly increasing access to modernity and wholesale conversion to Christianity, traditional ways are very strong outside Kupang.

GEOGRAPHY

Timor is very different from the rest of Nusa Tenggara. The line of volcanoes that runs the length of the Indonesian archipelago from Sumatra to Flores, skirts Timor and continues north to the islands of Maluku. Timor has no volcanoes and is geologically related to Australia.

Timor was once part of the Australian continental shelf, and was a submerged island which drifted from the Australian land mass as it moved northwards and collided with the Eurasian plate. Parts of Timor emerged from the ocean up to 40 million years ago, but the island only fully emerged some four million years ago, and is therefore comprised mainly of marine sediment, principally limestone, and even Timor's highest peaks are home to marine fossils. Collision with the Banda Trench to the north resulted in a rapid uplift in the centre of the island, producing a significant mountain range that continues to grow.

Apart from the lowland hills in the south-west around Kupang, rugged mountains run the length of the island. Several peaks are over 2000m, the highest being Gunung Tatamailau (2963m) in East Timor, while the highest in West Timor is Gunung Mutis (2427m). Coastal plains are narrow, and there are no major highland valleys or significant rivers.

Rocky, limestone soils and low rainfall make agriculture difficult, resulting in food and water shortages in the dry season. The dry north coast is very barren in the dry season when the winds from Australia are blocked by the mountains. But Timor has many micro-systems, and the central mountains range from dry rocky hills to thickly forested peaks. As you cross over to the south coast, the countryside is generally lusher and coastal basins such as the Belu district are fertile.

CLIMATE

Timor has extreme wet and dry seasons. The dry season is very dry from May to November, when the north coast gets virtually no rain, the hills brown-off and agricultural activity all but ceases. The arid landscapes, particularly on the north coast of East Timor, are reminiscent of Australia, and temperatures soar around October/November. The cooler central mountains and the south coast get an occasional shower during this time, and are generally green. This is the season for sitting around the village, weaving, repairing houses and trading produce to survive the 'hungry season' until the rains come again and crops can be planted. To remedy the water problem, there is an intensive program of small earth-dam building.

When the rains come they often turn to floods and the wide stony rivers that are dust in the dry season become torrents. Roads are cut and landslides are common. Timor is transformed as gardens are planted and the land turns green. The forest areas and the lusher central south coast is steamy and almost tropical. The completion of the wet season, just after the harvest, is the time for festivities.

Kupang receives an annual rainfall of around 1500mm, half of it falling in the wettest months of January and February. Dili is drier, with an average rainfall of around 1000mm, most of it falling from December to March. In the west, the north-west monsoon starts earlier and finishes later, so the west of the island is slightly wetter than the east. The south coast is wetter than the north, and high rainfall occurs in the central south coast and in the southern mountains of East Timor. But weather patterns are erratic and the mountains create many microclimates.

Day temperatures are around 30 to 33°C (86 to 91.4°F) in the lowland areas, dropping to the low 20s overnight. In the mountain areas such as Soe, at 860m, day temperatures are still warm to hot, but night temperatures can drop down to a more chilly 15°C (59°F), or lower at greater altitudes. At the end of the dry season, parts of the north coast swelter with temperatures over 35°C (95°F), but humidity is low compared with the sticky heat in other parts of Indonesia.

ECONOMY

The majority of the population practices *ladang* (slash and burn) agriculture. Corn is the staple crop, but rice, cassava, millet and sweet potatoes are also important. Dry rice is important, and some irrigated rice is grown in the river valleys, but it is primarily for the wealthy; most villagers rely on corn.

Buffalo and cattle are extensively reared, and pigs and chickens play an important role in the village economy. The lontar palm is also important, as in most of Nusa Tenggara, and betel nut is grown everywhere because of its ritual importance.

The sandalwood trade trailed off into insignificance by 1925 as over-harvesting threatened it to extinction. Sandalwood is being replanted and is protected. It can only be harvested under government licence.

Timor has little industry, but the Timor Gap, lying between Australia and Timor, has rich offshore oil and natural gas deposits. The Timor Gap Treaty between the Australian and Indonesian governments, signed in 1989, splits the profits between the two countries, and many believe the deal explains the

Australian government's lack of pressure on the East Timor issue. Exploration began in 1993 and major installations to support drilling and processing are planned for Kupang. A support base is also slated for Suai in East Timor. However, most oil operations are based in Darwin.

The economy in East Timor has always languished and the war killed off what little enterprise existed. The Chinese merchant class fled East Timor when the Portuguese left and the Indonesian army confiscated Portuguese enterprises after the invasion, resulting in corruption and inefficiency. Once the main source of income, the coffee plantations declined, but under the direction of American aid groups the plantations are being rehabilitated and fine East Timorese coffee is exported. The Indonesian government is keen to highlight its development record in East Timor. It is true that, compared with the Portuguese, Indonesia has made a big investment in roads, hospitals and schools to win over the hearts (and the minds) of the Timorese and the international community, but East Timor is still very poor.

Exploration before 1975 revealed potential gold and oil deposits in East Timor, but until the political problems are resolved, the foreign investment needed for further exploration is unlikely to be forthcoming.

Tourism is a growing industry, but numbers are low. The Kupang area gets a steady trickle of tourists – Darwin residents who take the short flight over or backpackers overlanding it from South-East Asia to Australia – but most stay only a few days and few venture into the mountains, the most interesting part of Timor.

Before 1975, East Timor was the main tourist destination. Good beaches and a lazy Portuguese ambience made it popular, but the Indonesians burst that bubble in a big way. Even though East Timor can again be visited, you'll be hard pressed to meet any other tourists. While the provincial government in East Timor is keen to promote tourism, the army is less than enthusiastic at the prospect of foreigners roaming around and observing events.

POPULATION & PEOPLE

Timor has a population of more than two million people: around 840,000 in East Timor and 1.3 million in West Timor.

Timor has an extraordinary ethnic diversity. The two main groups are the Dawan (Atoni) of central West Timor, and the neighbouring Tetum (Belu) who extend into central East Timor, but Timor has up to 15 other ethno-linguistic groups, most of whom live in East Timor.

The Dawan and Tetum languages are related to other Austronesian languages in western Indonesia, from where these primarily Malay people migrated. However, the population of Timor is of very mixed decent, with a strong Papuan influence. This is particularly true in East Timor, where many people have more noticeably Melanesian features. Many of the East Timorese languages are of the Trans-New Guinea family, related to those of Maluku and Irian Jaya to the north-east.

In West Timor, the Dawan are the main ethnic group with a population of around 700,000 and the Tetum are the second largest with around 150,000 living in the Belu area. Smaller indigenous groups are the Helong (10,000), who live south-west of Kupang and on Pulau Semau, and the Bunak (20,000 in West Timor) who straddle the border with East Timor. The people of the nearby islands of Roti and Sabu are major immigrant groups in West Timor. The Rotinese in particular exert a great influence and many hold prominent positions in commerce and government. Kupang is very much the melting pot of the Nusa Tenggara Timur province, attracting migrants from Flores and Sumba, as well as Chinese, Buginese, Arab and other groups.

East Timor has an even greater ethnic mix, with at least a dozen indigenous groups. The Tetum are the largest group (around 250,000 people, possibly more), and live in western East Timor, along the south coast around Suai, as well as around Dili and Viqueque. The next largest group (around 90,000 people) are the Mambai in the mountains south of Dili around Maubisse, Ainaro and Same. The Kemak (60,000 people) live in the Ermera district and the Bobonaro district around Maliana. The Bunak (50,000 people in East Timor) also live in Bobonaro and their territory extends into the Suai area and West Timor. The Fataluku (35,000 people) are famous for their high-peaked houses in the Lautem district around Los Palos, and they are bordered to the west by the Makasai (80,000 people). The other major groups in East Timor are the Galoli (60,000 people) in the central north around Manatutu and Laeila, and the Tokodede (60,000 people) along the north coast around Maubara and Liquica. To these can be added small groups of mountain people such as the Idate, Kairui, Lakalei, Naueti and Habu.

Dawan (Atoni)

The main ethnic group of West Timor, the Dawan are also widely referred to as the Atoni or Atoni Pah Meto by anthropologists. However, the Dawan don't refer to themselves as Atoni, which means 'man' in Meto (the Dawan language).

The Dawan mostly inhabit the mountain regions, which includes all of West Timor apart from the Belu regency, the south-west tip in and around Kupang and a few coastal pockets. They are called the *orang gunung*, or mountain people, by Indonesian-speaking lowlanders. Although their language is of Malay origin, the Dawan exhibit mixed Papuan features and tend to be short, with dark skin and curly hair.

Tradition is still very strong in many areas. You'll know you have entered Dawan territory when you see the parasol-shaped *lopo* meeting houses and the *ume kebubu* beehive houses. Men wear distinctive red *selimut* (blankets), betel nut is chewed and corn is still the main staple.

Despite wholesale conversion to Christianity, animist traditions thrive. Traditional religion is based on a supreme god, Uis Neno, represented as a crocodile, and various spirits of nature and of the ancestors *(nitu)*. One's relationship within the extended family *(ume)* and the wider clan *(kanak)* are very important. The *kepala suku* or head of the clan is the keeper of tradition and oversees rituals.

Ceremonies accompany many social rites and may involve animal slaughter as an offering to the spirits. Most commonly, ceremonies follow the harvest, either the first harvest of the young corn or the main harvest. Corn may be presented to the raja or placed in the clan lopo for storage, and this cache can be called upon to feed the people over the severe dry season.

Legends point to the Sonbai kingdom as the ancestral kingdom for the Dawan, who from their base to the north of present-day Kapan, migrated and went on to control most of West Timor. In reality, the Dawan comprised many small chiefdoms headed by a raja (king) and warfare was endemic. Alliances formed larger kingdoms, but the boundaries of the most important kingdoms were only formalised by the Dutch in the 20th century.

Although the power of the rajas was officially abolished after independence, the royal families still command great respect and the kingdoms are not arbitrary lines on a map, but represent clan and dialect groups. A few small areas still have their own rajas, but these are not considered to be true kingdoms.

The main Dawan kingdoms in the west are the Amarasi kingdom around Baun, the Fatuleu around Gunung Fatuleu and the Amfaong extending north to Naikliu. In the south-central mountains around Soe, the main kingdoms are the Molo around Kapan, the Amanuban around Niki Niki and the Amanatun kingdom centred at Nunkolo to the south. In the north central region, the Insana kingdom around Oelolok, the Miamafo around Kefamenanu/Eban and the Biboki around Temkessi are the main kingdoms.

Tetum (Belu)

The second largest group on Timor, the Tetum are divided into two main groups, the Western Tetum (or Belu) of West Timor, and the Eastern Tetum in East Timor.

The Western Tetum live in the Belu regency of West Timor and across the border around Suai, and are often called the Belu (a Dawan word for friend). The Belu are noticeably lighter skinned and finer featured than the Dawan and migrated to Timor, possibly

TIMOR

from Melaka on the Malay peninsula, around the 14th century. According to Belu legend they sailed around Timor and landed on the southern coast near present-day Besikama and founded the Wehali kingdom. From this relatively fertile area they spread north and east.

The Belu are famous for their matrilineal society, one of only two in Indonesia – the other being the Minangkabau of Sumatra. Belu descent is determined through the mother's family and in Besikama a *ratu* (queen) still rules. Property inheritance and decision making is controlled by women. The men must approach the women's family to seek marriage (as opposed to the other way around in Dawan society), and a dowry is generally not paid. However, this social lineage is not universal or clear cut. In other parts of Belu and further east, the Tetum are often patrilineal.

The Eastern Tetum occupy a large area around Viqueque and the Luca river in central East Timor. Although they sometimes have more Papuan features, their society is very similar to the Western Tetum, and has both matrilineal and patrilineal groups.

Catholicism has made large inroads among the Tetum, but traditional ways continue. Indigenous religion revolved around an earth mother, from where all humans are born and return after death, and her male counterpart, the god of the sky or sun. These were accompanied by a complex world of ancestor, nature and evil spirits. The *matan do'ok* medicine man is the village mediator with the spirits, and can divine the future, cure illness and ward off evil spirits. The *macair lulik* is the chief priest attached to the royal courts – as well as bringing rain, in times past he officiated over war rituals which ensured the bravery of the warriors and the collection of many heads.

ARTS
Weaving
Timorese ikat is often overlooked and less coveted than ikat from Sumba, Flores and other islands. As in most of the eastern islands, synthetic dyes and factory-produced cotton thread are now used, but the Timorese love of bright colours makes them look less 'natural'. Timorese weaving, however, is just as intricate and the use of thinner, uniform thread makes for finer weaving and patterns. While ikat purists go to great lengths to seek out remote islands where traditional methods are still used, an increasing number of weaving enthusiasts are attracted to the rich cloth of Timor and many lay collectors find the colours more attractive.

Some natural dyes are still used, particularly indigo for blue, but most are chemical. Handspun cotton is rare and usually used by those than can't afford the store bought variety. The quality of handspun weavings is often poor, but some weaving groups are again encouraging traditional methods, largely to promote tourist interest.

Timorese weaving is still very traditional because it is made primarily to be worn not to be hung on a wall. Traditional dress is still the norm outside the Kupang region, and the styles, colours and motifs reflect the origin and identity of the wearer. At a country market, you can tell where everyone is from by the blankets they wear.

The ikat technique is widely, but not exclusively, used. Often weavings will have a central ikat panel and side panels of *sotis* weaving, which is a different technique, usually of stripes. A third type, *buna* weaving, is a supplementary weft weave producing a cloth that looks like embroidery.

Traditional Architecture
Distinctive Dawan houses can be found throughout the mountain areas of West Timor. The lopo, the meeting house, has four pillars representing the heads of the clans that assist a raja. It is open-sided and topped by a conical, thatched roof where sacred heirlooms or corn is stored.

Traditional Dawan houses (ume kebubu) are beehive shaped, with no windows and only a 1m-high doorway. The doors were often carved with crocodile, gecko or other motifs, but these doors are highly prized by collectors and most have now been sold and replaced by plain wooden doors. The ume kebubu are small and smoky and the authorities have instituted a program to replace them. The villagers, however, consider their new houses unhealthy, as they're cold, so they construct new ume kebubu behind the approved houses. Ume kebubu are also designed to store grain, particularly corn, which is kept in the roof, and the smoke from kitchen fires keeps the bugs away.

Many other styles of traditional house are found in Timor. Belu houses are of rectangular design, raised off the ground because of flooding, and an external wooden skeleton supports the thatch roof. Bunak houses (deuhoto) are conical, but much larger than Dawan houses. There are wide differences in the traditional houses of East Timor, but the Fataluku houses found on the eastern tip of Timor are unique. These tall, elongated houses have stilts supporting a main living room and are topped by a high, tapering thatch roof.

Dance & Music
Timor has a wide variety of dance and music styles, reflecting its ethnic mix. Around October/November each year an all-Timor cultural festival is held, in a different town every year, and it is an excellent event to see performances from all the cultures of Timor. Dances may also accompany the harvest, the building of a rumah adat (traditional house), weddings and other occasions.

The most popular dance is the Tebe-tebe, also known as the Tebedai, performed throughout West Timor and in parts of East Timor. This circle dance is accompanied by a drum, but in the Kupang area it is accompanied by singing only.

The Likurai is primarily a Tetum dance once performed to welcome the warriors returning from battle. Women danced with a small drum (babadok) tucked under the arm and would circle the village compound where heads taken in battle would be displayed. Today it is performed by unmarried women as a courtship dance.

The Bidu is danced by girls and is a common Dawan dance. It shows the weaving

process and is accompanied by a bijola, a lute-style of instrument, and the fiol, a Timorese violin. Both instruments reflect the Portuguese influence.

Bamboo flutes and gongs (butaki) are also common musical instruments. Sets of gongs, which are usually played by women, are often revered heirlooms hundreds of years old.

The most distinctive instrument is the sasando from Roti – it is often used as a symbol for Nusa Tenggara Timur province. This multi-stringed instrument has a resonating bowl made from lontar leaves and a neck of bamboo. It is played with two hands, something like a harp.

RELIGION
Timor is overwhelming Christian, although many animist beliefs and practices continue, and conversion is not complete. West Timor is 86% Protestant, mostly Lutheran, and 10% Catholic, mostly in the regency of Timor Tengah Utara (around Kefamenanu).

East Timor is more than 90% Catholic and the church is a rallying point for the East Timorese. The church in East Timor has resisted 'integration' into the Indonesia Church and reports directly to Rome. Masses are no longer conducted in Portuguese; Tetum is used instead.

LANGUAGE
Dawan (or Meto) is the main language of West Timor, and its 700,000 speakers are divided into at least seven main dialect groups. Geographically, Tetum is the most widely spoken language on Timor, with around 400,000 native speakers (in West and East Timor) in three main dialect groups. Dili Tetum, a fourth dialect with many appropriated Portuguese words, has relatively few native speakers, but many East Timorese speak it as a second language. It has long existed as an unofficial lingua franca in East Timor, where Portuguese was only ever spoken by an educated minority.

Other minor languages in West Timor are Helong and Bunak (which is also spoken in East Timor). Other East Timorese languages include Mambai, Kemak, Fataluku, Makasai, Galoli and Tokodede. There's even more minor languages in the east (some with only a few thousand speakers, some with only a few hundred), including Idate, Karui, Lakalei, Naueti, Habu and Waima'a. Maku'a, spoken at the eastern tip around Tutuala, is now almost extinct.

To these languages can be added Sabunese, from the island of Sabu, and Rotinese, from Roti. However, the people of Roti speak 18 dialects that are vastly different from each other. The tiny island of Ndao, just off the coast of Roti, has a different language again.

Not surprisingly, Indonesian is the main linking language and is widely, but not universally, spoken throughout Timor. You will still come across villages where Indonesian isn't understood by adults, although all school children speak it. Indonesian is the first language of many people in Kupang. Long before Indonesian became the national language, Malay was used in Kupang and as a result the city has developed a unique slang.

English is usually not spoken outside the cities. Some Indonesian is essential if travelling to the villages, and a guide who speaks the local dialect (not just the local language) may be needed. In East Timor, Portuguese was the language of instruction in schools up until 1975, and many educated people speak it well. It also tends to be the language of resistance, given that most Indonesians do not speak it.

Dawan
Useful Phrases

How are you?	*On me?*
Where are you going?	*Noe me?*
I'm going to ...	*Au nao no ...*
Which way is Soe?	*Lanan es me Soe?*
How far is it from here to Soe?	*Kilo fauk na ko i tia Soe?*
Where is Tomas' place?	*Tomas in ume es me?*

Useful Words

good	*leko*
big	*naek*
small	*an anna, ba baun*
hot	*maputu*
cold	*manikin*
day	*neno*
week	*klei*
beach	*tasipesen*
hill	*netu*
mountain	*tubu*
river	*noe*
north	*utara*
south	*selatan*
east	*neno saet*
west	*neno tes*

People & Families

person	*mansian*
woman	*bife, fetnai*
man	*atoni*
baby	*li ana k'tia*
child	*li ana*
mother	*enaf*
father	*amaf*
wife	*fe*
husband	*mone*

Numbers

1	*mese*		6	*ne*
2	*nua*		7	*hitu*
3	*tenu*		8	*fanu*
4	*ha*		9	*sio*
5	*nim*		10	*bo es*

11	*bo es sa mese*
12	*bo es sam nua*
13	*bo es sam tenu*
14	*bo es sam ha*
20	*bo nua*
21	*bo nua mese*
30	*bo tenu*
100	*naut nes*
200	*natu nua*
1000	*nifun mese*

Tetum
Useful Phrases

How are you?	*Diak kalai?*
Where are you going?	*Ita banebe?*
I'm going to ...	*Hau ba ...*

Which way is it to Dili?	*Dalam mak nebe Dili?*
How far is it from here to Dili?	*Ihane ba Dili iha distansia hira?*
Where is Pedro's place?	*Pedro nia uma ihane be?*

Useful Words

good	*diak*
big	*bot*
small	*kik*
hot	*manas*
cold	*malirin*
day	*loron*
week	*semana*
beach	*tasi ibung*
hill	*foho*
mountain	*foho*
river	*mota*
east	*loro sai*
west	*loro mono*

People & Families

person	*ema*
woman	*feto*
man	*mane*
child	*labarik*
father	*aman*
mother	*inang*
wife	*fen*
husband	*laen*

Numbers

1	*ida*	6	*neng*
2	*rua*	7	*hitu*
3	*tolo*	8	*walu*
4	*hat*	9	*sia*
5	*lima*	10	*sanulu*

11	*sanulu resi ida*
12	*sanulu resi rua*
20	*ruanulu*
30	*tolonulu*
100	*atus ida*
200	*atus rua*
1000	*rihung ida*

Getting There & Around

AIR

Australia

Merpati's international connection between Kupang and Darwin in Australia flies in both directions on Wednesday and Saturday. From Australia the published fare is $396 return or $244 one way rising to $536 return and $319 one way in the high season (December and January). Tickets can be bought from Merpati in Darwin (☎ (08) 8941 1606) or through travel agents, but there is very little discounting.

From Kupang to Darwin the price is US$180 one way, often slightly cheaper through a travel agent in Kupang. You won't be allowed on the plane without an Australian visa – obtainable in Denpasar or Jakarta, not Kupang.

Elsewhere in Indonesia

Kupang is an important travel hub. Merpati flies 737s directly to Denpasar and mid-sized planes to Maumere and then on to Bima and Denpasar. These are usually reliable flights and can be booked from overseas or from other parts of Indonesia. Merpati flies small planes from Kupang direct to Dili, Kalabahi, Roti, Waingapu, Ruteng and Ende. These are subject to cancellation and it can be hard to find a seat at short notice in peak travel times.

Sempati has direct flights to Dili and Surabaya in Java. Bouraq has unreliable flights to Waingapu and Maumere, with onward connections.

To/From the Airport

For details on getting to/from the airport in Kupang, see Getting Around in the following Kupang section.

BUS

The Kupang-Dili highway via Soe, Kefamenanu and Atambua is one of the best in the eastern islands and travel is relatively quick between the major towns. Regular buses run throughout the day to the main destinations and quicker night buses run between Kupang and Dili. Just like the buses on the other islands, the buses on Timor are small, non air-con, cramped and leave only when full. The long-distance buses don't stop everywhere and they are generally not as crowded as those that do shorter hops.

In Kupang and Dili you will have to go to terminals on the outskirts of town to catch a bus, but in most other towns buses will drop off and pick up at hotels. Most hotels can arrange bus tickets.

Off the main highway, crowded and uncomfortable buses, bemos and trucks run to the villages.

BOAT

Kupang is the hub for ferries and Pelni passenger boats to other parts of Nusa Tenggara Timur. See the Kupang section further on for full details, but note that routes and sailing times are subject to change – it is often difficult to find out the latest information until you arrive in Kupang.

Regular car and passenger ferries run from Kupang to Larantuka (Flores), Kalabahi (Alor), Roti, and Waingapu (Sumba) via Sabu. Pelni passenger ships run directly from Kupang to Dili, Ende, Larantuka and Roti with onward sailing to other ports in Nusa Tenggara, as well as other parts of Indonesia such as Sulawesi, Maluku, Irian Jaya and Java. From Atapupu, near Atambua in West Timor, a ferry runs once a week to/from Kalabahi.

Pelni boats connect Dili with Kupang, Kota Ambon (Maluku) and Larantuka.

CAR & MOTORCYCLE

A motorcycle or a car with driver can always be found, but Timor receives relatively few tourists and has no regular rental agencies. It is a case of asking around at your hotel or at travel agents. Kupang is by far the best place to arrange car or motorcycle rental and it is much more difficult and expensive elsewhere in Timor. Kupang has a number of private, unmetered taxis and if you can negotiate directly with the driver it will be

cheaper. Bemos can be chartered in the larger regional towns such as Soe, Kefamenanu and Atambua.

As many of Timor's attractions are remote villages, it is a good idea to take a guide. Guides can arrange transport. See the Organised Tours entry in the following Kupang section for more details.

Kupang

Kupang is the name of Timor's largest city and capital of Nusa Tenggara Timur (NTT) province, which covers West Timor, Roti, Sabu, the Solor and Alor archipelagos, Sumba, Flores and Komodo. Kupang is also the name of the *kabupaten* (regency) that includes the south-western tip of Timor and the islands of Roti and Sabu. Roti has fine beaches and is easily reached by ferry from Kupang, while Sabu is much more remote (see the Roti & Sabu section later in this chapter for details on these two islands).

Kupang city is a busy hub with international flights to Darwin. Some reasonable beaches can be found around town and a number of day trips can be made further afield.

KUPANG

Although only a small city, Kupang is a booming metropolis compared with the overgrown villages that pass for towns in other parts of Nusa Tenggara. Kupang attracts migrants from all over NTT province who come to seek work or study at Kupang's universities. As such, it comes equipped with footpaths, brightly coloured bemos with sophisticated sound systems and a nightlife of sorts.

The centre is busy, noisy and untidy; the wealthier residential areas are in the suburbs. The eastern outskirts are home to oversized government buildings, but even these monuments are not enough for the burgeoning bureaucracy and plans are afoot to move the regional administration to a new, planned city across the harbour at Sulamu.

TIMOR

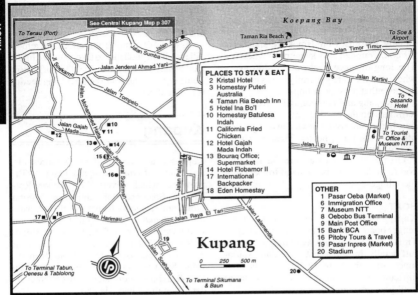

Kupang

PLACES TO STAY & EAT
2 Kristal Hotel
3 Homestay Puteri Australia
4 Taman Ria Beach Inn
5 Hotel Ina Bo'I
10 Homestay Batulesa Indah
11 California Fried Chicken
12 Hotel Gajah Mada Indah
13 Bouraq Office; Supermarket
14 Hotel Flobamor II
17 International Backpacker
18 Eden Homestay

OTHER
1 Pasar Oeba (Market)
6 Immigration Office
7 Museum NTT
8 Oebobo Bus Terminal
9 Main Post Office
15 Bank BCA
16 Pitoby Tours & Travel
19 Pasar Inpres (Market)
20 Stadium

Government is Kupang's biggest enterprise and, apart from a solitary cement factory, the city has no industry to speak of. Nevertheless, migrants continue to be attracted by the lights of the 'big city' and the promise of a better life. Some find comparatively high-paying jobs, but many others are forced to scrape a living on the streets selling cigarettes or *bakso* (meatball soup). In the villages of Flores, Sumba and elsewhere, you'll be told that Kupang is the crime centre of NTT, representing all the evils of the modern world. The local press reports any crime in great detail, but Kupang is a safe and easy-going city by most standards. Kupang's diverse ethnic mix means less social cohesion, but the citizens of Kupang have their own identity and their own local slang, much of it derived from Malay, the lingua franca of trade used in Dutch times.

Above all, Kupang is an optimistic city and many believe the inflated claims that it will one day become Indonesia's second most important trading port after the capital city of Jakarta. In spite of Indonesia's current economic woes, the exploitation of oil in the Timor Sea does point to a bright future for Kupang. Strong ties and growing trade with nearby Darwin in Australia are also a source of great optimism.

Merpati's twice weekly Darwin to Kupang flights have put Kupang well and truly on the South-East Asia travellers' route. Although not brimming with tourist attractions, Kupang is not a bad place to hang around for a few days – Captain Bligh did after his *Bounty* misadventures.

History
The VOC occupied Kupang in the middle of the 17th century, primarily to counter any Portuguese claims to eastern Indonesia. The Dutch campaign began with Apollonius Scotte, who set sail for the eastern islands in 1613, sacking the Portuguese fort in Solor before sailing on

to Kupang Bay. He reached agreement with the local Helong raja to establish a Dutch post on Timor, but after Scotte's departure the VOC promptly forgot all about Timor.

The Portuguese Dominicans continued their part missionary/part strategic expansion in the east and settled Kupang in the 1640s. They built a fort, but it was abandoned and only partly finished when the Dutch arrived in 1653 to finally claim their territory. The Dutch completed the fort with the backing of the local raja and named it Fort Concordia, but it was attacked by the Timorese under the command of the Topasses. Military reinforcements arrived in 1656 to drive out the Topasses, but after a disastrous military defeat in the interior, the Dutch almost abandoned Kupang in favour of Roti.

Kupang remained an isolated Dutch outpost and, apart from the lowlands around Kupang, the Topasses controlled Timor into the 18th century. Early reports of Kupang are mixed, but while the Dutch elite may have attempted to recreate the sumptuous lifestyle of home in Holland, by all accounts it was a bedraggled, insignificant little colony. Still, as the region's only European port of any significance, it attracted a number of seafarers. Early explorers such as William Dampier called in at Kupang in 1699, but Captain Cook, wary of its reputation for debauchery, sailed on by in 1770. Captain Bligh made a beeline for Kupang in 1789 after the mutiny on the HMS *Bounty* and had nothing but praise for the hospitality and comforts of the town after his mammoth six week, 5800km journey in an open longboat.

The Topasses, the new rajas of Timor, continued to expand their power and in 1749, with most of Timor under their control, they marched on Kupang. Although outnumbered, the Dutch and their Timorese allies in the south-west defeated the Topasses, and Dutch influence in the interior expanded.

Timor was, however, very much a sideshow for the Dutch. Supplies of sandalwood had dwindled, and by the late 18th century Kupang was little more than a symbol of the Dutch presence in Nusa Tenggara. Not until 1905, when it became Dutch policy to estab-lish direct control, did they pay much attention to the interior of the island.

The original inhabitants of the Kupang area were the Helong. Squeezed by the Dawan from the Sonbai kingdom to the west, the Helong had, by the 17th century, been limited to a small coastal strip at the western tip of the island. Later, partly because of the Dutch-supported migration to Kupang of people from the nearby island of Roti, most of the Helong migrated to the small island of Semau (off Kupang).

Orientation

Kupang is hilly and the central area hugs the waterfront. The central bemo terminal, Kota Kupang (or simply Terminal), almost doubles as a town square, although you're not likely to take a leisurely stroll across it with bemos coming at you from all directions. Many of the shops and restaurants are around this sprawling market area. Compared with other modern Indonesian cities, Kupang has no real department stores or shopping complexes, but Jl Jenderal Sudirman near the Hotel Flobamor II has a couple of small supermarkets – this is Kupang's most up-market shopping area.

Kupang's El Tari airport is 15km east of town; Tenau harbour is 10km west.

Information

Tourist Offices Kupang has three tourist offices – representing the central, provincial and regional governments – but all are a long way from the centre of town and hardly worth the effort. The most helpful is Diparda Kupang (☎ 21540), the regional government tourist office at Jl El Tari 338, grouped with other government offices east of Kupang. The office has only a few brochures and maps, but is keen to help. To get there, take bemo No 10 or 7. Get off at Jl Raya El Tari at the SMP5 secondary school and walk 200m east. The office is open Monday to Thursday from 7 am to 2 pm, Friday 7 to 11 am and Saturday 7 am to 12.30 pm.

Money Kupang is the best place to change money in Nusa Tenggara outside Lombok.

The Bank Dagang Negara, at Jl Urip Sumo-hardjo 16, is central and has excellent rates. It is open 8 am to 3.30 pm from Monday to Friday. Kupang has plenty of other banks with competitive rates. If you want a cash advance on Visa or MasterCard, get it in Kupang. The currency exchange office at Kupang airport is open when flights arrive from Darwin.

Post & Communications Poste restante mail goes to the central post office, Kantor Pos Besar at Jl Palapa 1 – take bemo No 5. In central Kupang, a branch post office is at Jl Soekarno 29. The Telkom office is at Jl Urip Sumohardjo 11. Home Country Direct phones are at the Telkom office and in the lobby of the Kristal Hotel.

Museum NTT
The Museum Nusa Tenggarah Timur, near the tourist office, is worth a look for a taste of what you're heading into, or to round out your Nusa Tenggara experience. It houses a good collection of arts, crafts and artefacts from all over the province. Aurora Arby, an anthropologist, will be happy to show you around. To get there, take a No 10 bemo from the Terminal. It's open daily from 8 am to 3 pm. Entry is free, but drop a donation in the box as you leave.

Colonial Kupang
Unfortunately, there's not much see here despite the long Dutch occupation. The only Dutch buildings are from the final colonial days. The Protestant church on Jl Soekarno dates from the 19th century and rings with hymns on Sunday evenings when half of Kupang turns out.

Fort Concordia has long since passed into oblivion and is now the Indonesian army garrison, just over the river from the church, on Jl Pahlawan. All that remains is an inscribed stone, and entry to see it requires a permit. Further along, you can visit the old Dutch cemetery where numerous gravestones survive.

The river used to be Kupang's main port and is where Bligh anchored after his epic journey. Dubbed 'Cholera Creek' because of its sludgy brown appearance, it turns into a real river in the wet season when boys in inner tubes white-water raft it, 5km upstream on the outskirts of Kupang.

Markets
The main market is the rambling Pasar Inpres off Jl Soeharto in the south of the city. To get there, take bemo No 1 or 2 and follow the crowd when you get off. It sells mostly fruit and vegetables, but some crafts and ikat can be found. A lesser market is on Jl Alor, 2km east of the town centre.

Pulau Kera (Monkey Island)
Pulau Kera is the blob of trees and sand visible from Kupang. This small, uninhab-ited island has sandy beaches and clear water. Taman Ria Beach Inn organises day trips, or you could talk to the people operat-ing the fishing boats.

Beaches
Kupang's beaches are grubby, but they get better the further you go from town. The beach at Taman Ria, 3km from the town centre, is the best place for a swim, or keep heading out to Pantai Lasiana, 12km east, or Tablolong, 15km south-west of Kupang (see the following Around Kupang section for details).

Organised Tours
Many fascinating traditional villages can be visited on Timor, but Indonesian (let alone English) may not be spoken so a local guide is often necessary. Although you can visit a number of villages alone, Timor is still a wild place in parts and a guide is essential if heading off into the unknown. Guides do the rounds of the hotels, particularly the back-packers places, and will ask around 20,000 rp per day. They can put together some excel-lent trips. You pay for public transport, accommodation and food, or the guide can arrange a motorcycle. One of the best guides is Aka Nahak, who speaks a number of Timorese languages, as well as excellent English.

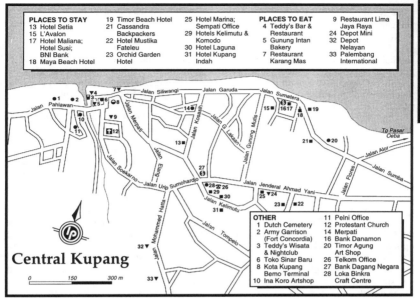

PLACES TO STAY
13 Hotel Setia
15 L'Avalon
17 Hotel Maliana;
    Hotel Susi;
    BNI Bank
18 Maya Beach Hotel
19 Timor Beach Hotel
21 Cassandra
    Backpackers
22 Hotel Mustika
    Fateleu
23 Orchid Garden
    Hotel
25 Hotel Marina;
    Sempati Office
29 Hotels Kelimutu &
    Komodo
30 Hotel Laguna
31 Hotel Kupang
    Indah

PLACES TO EAT
4 Teddy's Bar &
  Restaurant
5 Gunung Intan
  Bakery
7 Restaurant
  Karang Mas
9 Restaurant Lima
  Jaya Raya
24 Depot Mini
32 Depot
   Nelayan
33 Palembang
   International

OTHER
1 Dutch Cemetery
2 Army Garrison
  (Fort Concordia)
3 Teddy's Wisata
  & Nightclub
6 Toko Sinar Baru
8 Kota Kupang
  Bemo Terminal
10 Ina Koro Artshop
11 Pelni Office
12 Protestant Church
14 Merpati
16 Bank Danamon
20 Timor Agung
   Art Shop
26 Telkom Office
27 Bank Dagang Negara
28 Loka Binkra
   Craft Centre

Central Kupang

0   150   300 m

Many hotels also arrange trips around Kupang and across Timor. The Hotel Susi has overnight, all-inclusive tours to Soe, Niki Niki, Kapan and other destinations from 320,000 rp for one person or 110,000 rp per person for a group of six. Hotel Flobamor II has a variety of tours for a minimum of four, from four hour city tours (US$15) to Soe day trips (US$30). Teddy's Wisata (☎ 22422), at Jl Ikan Tongkal 1, is part of the burgeoning Teddy's tourist enterprise and has city tours (60,000 rp, minimum two people), and Semau (120,000 rp) and Soe (170,000 rp) tours.

Kupang's biggest travel agent, Pitoby Tours & Travel (☎ 32700) at Jl Jenderal Sudirman 118, arranges a variety of tours around Kupang and throughout Nusa Tenggara Timur. Other travel agents to check out include Floressa Wisata (☎ 32012), at Jl Mawar 15, and Astria (☎ 31991), at Jl Jenderal Sudirman 146.

Dive Trips Nusa Tenggara has some of Indonesia's best diving and Kupang is a good place to arrange diving trips. Graeme and Donavan Whitford (☎ 21154; fax 24833), two Australian dive masters based in Kupang, specialise in diving trips to Alor, and can also arrange dives around Timor and further afield.

Places to Stay – budget
Accommodation in Kupang is spread out, and many of the hotels have a range of prices, so the bottom, middle and top end overlap to some extent. There are also some good options a little further out if you want to escape the bustle of central Kupang. Kupang is a little more expensive than other cities in Nusa Tenggara, but the existence of dorm accommodation seems to be an extension of the Australian backpackers' network rather than a necessity through high prices.

Two popular budget options, despite their distance from town, are found in a quiet area on Jl Kencil. *Eden Homestay* (☎ 21931) at No 6 is opposite a shady freshwater pool, the local swimming spot known as Air Nona. Bungalows are about as basic as they get, but for 4000 rp per person it is hard to complain. This friendly place offers meals, cheap tours and has a shady garden. *International Backpacker* at No 37B is one street away behind the pool. Dormitories and small rooms are more substantial, and also cost 4000 rp per person. This is another friendly place that also has meals. To get there from the Terminal, catch a No 3 bemo.

Down an alleyway off Jl Mohammed Hatta, the *Homestay Batulesa Indah* (☎ 32863), at Jl Johar 1/5, used to be a popular backpackers, but under new management it is not as switched-on as it used to be. Singles, doubles and triples cost 10,000, 15,000 and 22,500 rp respectively.

Closer to town at Jl Sumatera 8, *L'Avalon* (☎ 32278) is another popular backpacker option. It's a laid-back place run by a local character, Edwin Lerrick, and is good for information on touring Timor. Well kept four and six-bed dorms cost 4000 rp per person, or the double room costs 10,000 rp.

Not far away, the *Cassandra Backpackers* (☎ 22392), at Jl Sumatera 13, is a new and very friendly homestay. Rooms are simple but spotless and cost 4000 rp in three-bed dorms. Alternatively, singles/doubles are 5000/10,000 rp. Good information and services are offered.

The *Taman Ria Beach Inn* (☎ 31320) at Jl Timor Timur 69 is on the beachfront about 3km from the Terminal – catch a No 10 bemo. The beach is pleasant and the restaurant is good. Singles/doubles with mandi and fan are 17,500/25,000 rp and they also rent beds in dorms for 7500 rp. The hotel is looking tired, but major renovations are planned.

The *Homestay Puteri Australia* (☎ 25532), down a small street opposite the Taman Ria Beach Inn, is a small, comfortable homestay run by an Australian woman and her Sumbanese husband. A share room costs 5000 rp a bed and a double with shared mandi is 12,000 rp; all include breakfast.

Hotel Mustika Fateleu (☎ 31374) at Jl Gunung Fateleu 1 is a friendly local hotel

close to the city centre. Basic rooms cost 9000/13,500 rp with fan and shared bath; rooms with private mandi are better, but expensive at 16,500/22,000 rp.

The central *Hotel Setia* (☎ 23291) at Jl Kosasih 13 used to be a popular place when it had good contacts with the Darwin hostels, but it has changed management and is now quiet. Nevertheless, it is clean and tidy with rooms for 8000/16,000 rp or 10,000/20,000 rp with mandi.

Places to Stay – middle

Kupang has no shortage of mid-range hotels, but they tend to be anonymous business hotels. Most have a variety of rooms, from budget to mid-range.

Along the waterfront on Jl Sumatera, a short bemo ride from the Terminal, are four hotels. The *Timor Beach Hotel* (☎ 31651) has a restaurant with panoramic sea views and rooms situated around an elongated courtyard. Rooms are a little dark, but good value at 12,500/17,000 rp with fan and bath. Air-con rooms go for 24,500/30,000 rp.

Also on Jl Sumatera, the large *Maya Beach Hotel* (☎ 32169) is next to the Bank BNI at No 31; this is a fancier hotel with air-con rooms ranging from 35,000 rp with bath to 60,000 rp with hot water. The others nearby are less inspiring. *Hotel Maliana* (☎ 21879) at No 35 has rooms with mandi for 22,000/25,000 rp, while air-con costs another 5000 rp. *Hotel Susi* (☎ 22172) at No 37 is deservedly the most popular hotel in this strip, with good service and fine sea views from the top floor. Rooms at the back cost 10,000 rp for a fan room and 15,000/20,000 rp with fan and bath. The most in demand are the 3rd floor rooms with great views, but they are often full. They cost 18,000/22,000 rp, or air-con rooms are 25,000/35,000 rp.

Another very good mid-range hotel is the *Hotel Ina Bo'i* (☎ 33619) at Jl Kartini 4. It has a bar, restaurant and spacious grounds. This former government guesthouse is relatively new, and comfortable rooms are good value at 15,000/25,000 rp or 35,000/42,000 rp with air-con. The only drawback is that it is 4km from town – take bemo No 10 or ring for free pick-up.

Clustered on Jl Kelimutu close to the city centre is a group of hotels: the *Hotel Kelimutu* (☎ 31179) at No 38, *Hotel Komodo* (☎ 21913) at No 40, and the *Hotel Laguna* at No 36. Standards are similar and competition keeps the prices down. The very clean and relatively new Kelimutu is a notch ahead of the pack and has good service. Rooms with bath and fan cost 20,000/25,000 rp and air-con rooms cost 27,500/31,500 rp.

Another decent option is the *Hotel Marina* (☎ 22566) at Jl Jenderal Ahmad Yani 79. Spacious rooms with fan and shared bath cost 17,500/20,000 rp, or air-con rooms start at 30,000/40,000 rp including private bath. The large, new *Hotel Gajah Mada Indah* (☎ 21930), at Jl Gajah Mada 70, has rooms from 17,500/25,500 rp to 50,000/65,000 rp. It is reasonable value, but a little soulless.

Hotel Flobamor II (☎ 33476), at Jl Jenderal Sudirman 21, is a declining hotel that was once one of Kupang's best. It has a tiny pool next to the restaurant. Large rooms are dog-eared but comfortable and cost from 80,000 rp to 150,000 rp (huge VIP rooms).

Places to Stay – top end

The *Orchid Garden Hotel* (☎ 33707; fax 33669), at Jl Gunung Fatuleu 2, is a small hotel with excellent bungalows built around a Balinese-style garden, and there is a swimming pool. Rooms with hot water, TV and minibar cost US$60/70 up to US$90/130, plus 21%, but discounts of up to 40% may apply.

The *Sasando Hotel* (☎ 33334; fax 33338), on Jl Kartini, is out in the middle of nowhere about 5km east of town. It is Kupang's biggest hotel, with a pool, restaurant and disco. It is built on a ridge with great views across the sea. Rooms with all the trimmings, including fridge, start at US$50/60. Add 21% to the rates, but similarly sized discounts may be available.

Kupang's newest and best hotel is the *Kristal Hotel* (☎ 25100; fax 25104), 2km east of the town centre on the beach at Jl Timor Timur 59. The beach is not great, but

this three star hotel has a pool, restaurant and disco. Well appointed rooms cost from US$70/80 to US$180, plus 21%. Big weekend discounts apply.

Places to Eat

Kupang has a greater variety of food than most places in Nusa Tenggara, so tuck in while you can.

Visiting Darwinites like to hang out at *Teddy's Bar & Restaurant*, at Jl Ikan Tongkol 1-3, for a meat pie and chips or sizzling steaks. The expensive food is compensated for by the cold beer and excellent waterside location, complete with fresh sea breezes. The *Restaurant Karang Mas*, at Jl Siliwangi 88, hangs over the water and is a favourite spot to take in the sunset over a beer. It has seen better days, but the food is OK and the beer is cheaper than at the similar *Pantai Laut Restaurant* nearby.

Around the Terminal, *Restaurant Lima Jaya Raya*, at Jl Soekarno 15, has Chinese and Indonesian food, and a loud and sweaty nightclub upstairs. When you can't eat another noodle or grain of rice, step into the *Gunung Intan Bakery* on Jl Pahlawan and sniff the air. It has a delicious selection of pastries, doughnuts and buns. *California Fried Chicken* on Jl Mohammed Hatta is a KFC clone and Kupang's only fast food restaurant, though the service is in fact slow.

The *Depot Mini* on Jl Jenderal Ahmad Yani is a spotless restaurant with good, cheap Chinese food. The *Depot Nelayan*, at Jl Mohammed Hatta 14, has Chinese seafood and great ikan bakar (grilled fish), but lots of road noise. Further along at No 54 on the same road, the *Palembang International* is packed every night and serves excellent Chinese and Indonesian food, including pigeon and giant prawns.

The *Timor Beach Hotel* has one of Kupang's better restaurants, with a varied menu and an elevated position overlooking the water. The only drawback is that it is often booked out with function and wedding groups, and the service is slow at the best of times.

You'll see night *warungs* around town, particularly around the Terminal. Try the bubur kacang (mung beans and black rice in coconut milk). Some of these warungs sell dog meat.

Entertainment

You'll have to travel a long way to find livelier nightlife, although Kupang is not exactly a swinging town and the nightclubs are usually very seedy. On weekends they tend to degenerate as the night wears on and it pays to keep your wits about you.

The round, thatched bar at *Teddy's* attracts tourists and expats and is open until the wee hours on weekends for a drink in quieter surrounds. Teddy's also has a loud and very dark nightclub attached to their travel agent across the road.

Other disreputable nightclubs include the *Surya Disco*, 6km east of town near the beach, and the *Kupang Pub*, 4km out on the same road and set back from the road on the right. The *Restaurant Lima Jaya Raya* on Jl Soekarno also has a loud and sweaty nightclub of sorts on weekends and attracts a local crowd.

More upmarket discos can be found at the *Sasando Hotel* and the *Kristal Hotel*.

Things to Buy

Timorese ikat is colourful, with a huge variety of designs, and there are also lots of other embroidered textiles. Purists will be disappointed that natural dyes are now rare in Timor, but interestingly, the tourist trade is starting to create a demand for them. You may see some at Kupang's market, Pasar Inpres, where villagers sometimes bring their weavings to sell.

Several shops in Kupang sell ikat, handcrafts, old silver jewellery, ornamental *sirih* (betel nut) containers and more. Bizarre hats *(ti'i langga)* from Roti make a fun purchase, but try fitting one in your backpack! These shops also have ikat from other parts of Nusa Tenggara Timur, including Roti and Sabu. Prices are quite high and bargaining won't bring them down dramatically, but Timorese crafts are hard to find elsewhere in Nusa Tenggara.

The Loka Binkra Craft Centre at the corner of Jl Kelimutu and Jl Jenderal Ahmad Yani is the best place to start looking. It sells ikat from Timor and further afield and a variety of other souvenirs at reasonable prices.

Toko Sinar Baru, at Jl Siliwangi 94 opposite the Terminal, has an interesting range of weaving, but it's hard to shift on prices. Ina Koro Artshop on Jl Pahlawan, near the Pelni office, also has a good selection of arts and crafts. The Timor Agung Art Shop on Jl Sumba has some fine pieces – everything from carved doors to silver jewellery – but prices are high.

For film and processing, Photo Prima, at Jl Jenderal Ahmad Yani 66 opposite the Hotel Marina, has a good range as does the Toko Roda Baru a few doors further east. They sell slide film and a few camera accessories, which are very hard to find anywhere else in the region – stock up in Kupang.

For everyday items, check out the market area on Jalan Siliwangi. Kupang's biggest supermarket is the Dutalia, 7km east of town on the Soe road, or small supermarkets can be found on Jl Jenderal Sudirman near the Bouraq office.

Getting There & Away

Kupang is the transport hub of Timor, with buses and flights to/from the rest of the island, plus planes and regular passenger boats to many destinations in Nusa Tenggara and beyond.

Air Merpati (☎ 33833) at Jl Kosasih 2 has direct flights to Dili, Roti, Denpasar (Bali), Waingapu (Sumba), Kalabahi (Alor), and Maumere, Ruteng and Ende (Flores).

Merpati also flies to/from Darwin (Australia) on Wednesday and Saturday. From Kupang the fare is around US$180 one way – shop around the travel agents for the best deal.

Bouraq (☎ 21421) at Jl Jenderal Sudirman 20 has direct flights to Waingapu and Maumere, with onward connections. Sempati (☎ 31612) at the Hotel Marina, Jl Jenderal Ahmad Yani 79, has direct flights to Dili and Surabaya.

Bus & Bemo Long-distance buses depart from the Oebobo terminal out near the museum – take a No 10 bemo. Destinations include: Soe (4250 rp; three hours) and Niki Niki (5250 rp; 3½ hours) every hour or two from 5 am to 6 pm; and Kefamenanu (7500 rp; 5½ hours) from 7 am to 3 pm. Many buses go to Atambua (10,500 rp; eight hours) and Dili (15,500 rp; 12 hours) around 7 am, noon and 7 pm; the night buses are quicker and Gemilan has the best buses.

Bemos and buses to the villages around Kupang go from four terminals. Oebobo handles buses to eastern destinations. For Tenau and Bolok, bemos go from the central terminal, Kota Kupang. Terminal Tabun is 8km south-west of the city and services south-west destination such as Tablolong. Bemos to Baun go from Terminal Sikumana, 5km south of the city centre on Jl Soeharto, but they also cruise for passengers at the Pasar Inpres market.

Boat Pelni passenger ships depart from Tenau, 10km south-west of Kupang (400 rp by bemo No 12). Ferries leave from Bolok, 13km south-west of Kupang (600 rp by bemo No 13).

Pelni (☎ 22646) is at Jl Pahlawan 3, near the waterfront. Pelni's KM *Dobonsolo* runs directly from Bali to Kupang, and on to Dili, Kota Ambon (Maluku) and Irian Jaya. The KM *Awu* sails from Kupang to Ende, Waingapu, Kalabahi and Dili. The KM *Sirimau* sails between Kupang and Larantuka and Ujung Pandang (Sulawesi). The KM *Pangrango* sails from Kupang to Ujung Pandang, via Roti, Sabu, Ende, Waingapu and Labuanbajo. It returns via the same ports.

Perum ASDP is Nusa Tenggara Timur's major ferry company, with passenger/car ferries operating throughout the province. Ferry schedules are subject to change, but unfortunately the Kupang office has closed and you'll have to go to Bolok harbour to get the latest sailing times. The better tourist hotels in Kupang have the latest schedules. Buy tickets at the harbour at least half an hour before departure – the ticket windows can get very crowded. Perum currently has

ferries from Bolok to: Larantuka (14,000 rp; 14 hours) on Thursday and Sunday at 7 pm; Kalabahi (16,500 rp; 16 hours) on Thursday and Saturday at 1 pm; and Ende (17,000 rp; 16 hours) on Monday at 7 pm. The Ende ferry continues on to Waingapu, and another ferry leaves Kupang on Wednesday at 7 pm to Sabu (14,000 rp; nine hours) and on to Waingapu.

Ferries to Roti (5700 rp; four hours) go every day except Friday from Bolok. Scheduled departure is at 8 am, but they invariably leave around 9 am. Ferries also go from Kupang and Pulau Sabu and Pulau Ndau off the Timor coast (see the Roti & Sabu section later in this chapter for details).

Getting Around

To/From the Airport Kupang's El Tari airport is 15km east of the town centre. Taxis cost a fixed 12,500 rp. To catch public transport, turn left out of the airport terminal and walk a full kilometre to the junction with the main highway, from where bemos to town cost 500 rp. From town, take bemo No 14 or 15 to the junction and then walk.

Bemo Around town, bemos cost a standard 400 rp and are fast, efficient, brightly painted and incredibly noisy – drivers like the bass turned up and a multi-speaker stereo system is *de rigueur*. They stop running by 9 pm.

Kupang is too spread out to do much walking. The hub of bemo routes is the Kota Kupang Terminal, usually just called 'Terminal' and the other main stop is on Jl Jenderal Amhad Yani opposite the Bank Dagang Negara. Bemos are numbered, with the main bemo routes as follows:

Nos 1 & 2 Kuanino-Oepura passing the following hotels: Maya; Maliana; Timor Beach; Fateleu; Orchid Garden; Marina; and Flobamor II

No 3 Aimona-Bakunase to Eden Homestay and Backpacker International

No 5 Oebob-Airnona-Bakunase passing the ferry office and the main post office

No 6 Oebobo-Oebufu to the stadium, but *not* to the Sikumana bus terminal

No 10 Kelapa Lima-Walikota from Terminal to the Taman Ria Beach Hotel, tourist information office and Oebobo bus terminal

No 12 Tenau

TIMOR

No 13 Bolok
Nos 14 & 15 Penfui (useful for getting to the airport)
No 17 Tarus to Pantai Lasiana

Car & Motorcycle It's possible to rent a car with driver for around 100,000 rp or a motorcycle for 25,000 rp per day. Ask at your hotel or travel agents.

AROUND KUPANG
Kupang to Bolok

The road west to Bolok harbour, the ferry harbour, runs along the coast past Tenau, the main port, and a few points of interest.

On the road to Tenau, 7km from Kupang, the PT Agung Flobamor **weaving factory** produces a wide variety of ikat cloth made by weavers from Timor and Sabu. Open Monday to Saturday, you can see the various processes of ikat and other weaving from dyeing to the finished product. Most of it is for sale in Kupang shops, but a few finished products can be bought here and tours are conducted for groups.

Just past the weaving factory is the enormous cement *(semen)* factory, the biggest industry in Kupang, and a little further on is **Tenau**, Kupang's main port. Cargo ships from all over the archipelago dock here and there is a shanty town red light district. Irregular, small boats ply across to Pulau Semau from Tenau.

Three kilometres past Tenau, **Bolok** is the main port for ferries to Roti, Sabu, Flores and Sumba. The Helong people are the largest group in the Bolok area, stretching to Tablolong, but most now live on Semau. If you continue 500m past the Bolok turn-off along the dirt road you reach **Gua Bolok**, a series of four limestone cave formations fed by freshwater springs. You can scramble 50m down into the well-like openings and swim in the pools. Bring a torch and take care.

Pulau Semau

Visible to the west of Kupang, Pulau Semau has some decent beaches where you can

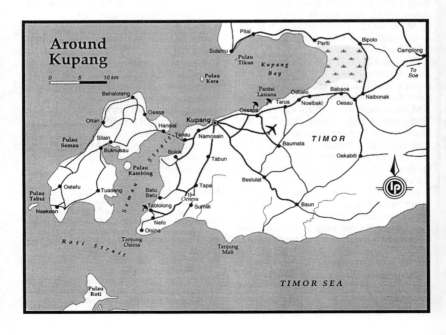

snorkel, and freshwater springs. Home to the Helong people, the main village is Hansisi, which faces Tenau. The Helong are possibly the oldest inhabitants of Timor and were the main ethnic group in the Kupang area when the Dutch arrived in 1653. Under threat from the expanding Dawan kingdoms, the Helong were keen to forge an alliance with the Dutch, but later migration of Rotinese and other groups to Kupang further squeezed the Helong and their last remaining stronghold is now Semau.

Villages are scattered all over the island. The road system is poor and consists of little more than walking tracks for the most part. The main point of interest is at Oeasa where two bungalow hotels have been built. The bungalows are mid-range, but becoming run down. Although not one of Asia's great island paradises, this relaxed island is a pleasant escape from Kupang and there is reasonable diving and snorkelling just off-shore. The pick of the accommodation, the *Flobamor Bungalows*, has substantial rooms for 125,000 rp per day including meals and should be booked through the Hotel Flo-bamor II in Kupang, which also arranges transport and diving. The more basic *Teddy's Bungalows* charges 50,000/80,000 rp for singles/doubles including meals and trans-port. Book at Teddy's Bar & Restaurant in Kupang. A natural spring is a 10 minute walk inland above the beach at Oeasa.

Semau is more often visited as a day trip from Kupang – the International Backpacker, Eden Homestay and Taman Ria Beach Inn all arrange trips (see the earlier Kupang Places to Stay entry), as do the bungalows on the island and local tour companies. A no-frills day trip organised by the backpackers hotels costs as little as 25,000 rp, including lunch. Teddy's will take you on their more luxurious boat direct from Kupang, departing at 10 am and returning at 4 pm, for 120,000 rp for two. The Hotel Flobomor II has day trips for US$35.

Irregular local boats go from Namosain village, 3km west of central Kupang, and from Tenau. Tenau is closest to Semau and small boats run to Hansisi. They go every one or two hours or when full, and cost 1000 rp per person or 10,000 rp to charter the whole boat. From Hansisi you'll have to walk to Oeasa or other villages – an interest-ing option for adventuring, but it is easier to charter a boat from Tenau straight to Oeasa for around 50,000 rp return.

Tablolong

The finest beaches close to Kupang can be found at the south-western tip of Timor near Tablolong, 27km from Kupang. Only a few bemos (750 rp) run daily to Tablolong from Kupang's Terminal Tabun through the dry, undulating hills of the south-west. Lontar palm is extensively grown in the region and used to thatch the houses. Fences are built of the pumice-looking limestone rock that is scattered throughout this relatively infertile and lightly populated area.

Tablolong is a small fishing village that comes alive in October when an interna-tional fishing tournament is held. Marlin is the prized catch. The white-sand beach is good, but a rocky reef fronts the beach and the water is shallow for swimming. A picnic pavilion has been built just along from the village. Better beaches lie south-west around the headland – you can walk for 20 minutes to over an hour to find your own deserted beach, such as **Air Cina**, a beautiful stretch of white sand. Air Cina can also be reached along a dirt track that turns off the main road 3km before Tablolong. The beaches look across to Semau and Roti, and make a good day trip, but bring plenty of food and water.

Oenesu

This waterfall lies off the Kupang-Tablolong road. The turn-off is 13km from Kupang near Tapa village, which is serviced by regular bemos from Tabun, but from the main road you'll have to walk 2.5km to the falls. Take the road to Sumlili and past the Imanuel Church is the right turn to the falls, 0.8km away along a rough road. The waterfall is a pleasant respite in this dry land and it is surrounded by greenery. It is a popular spot on weekends for families and guitar strum-mers from Kupang, but quiet during the week. A few kiosks sell drinks and you can walk down to the base of the falls and further along the river.

Baun

A small, quiet village 30km south-east of Kupang in the hilly Amarasi district, Baun is an ikat-weaving centre, with a few Dutch buildings. You can visit the *rumah raja*, the last raja's house, now occupied by his widow. She loves to chat to foreigners and will show you her weavings and rose garden. Market day in Baun is Saturday. From Baun to the south coast is a solid day's hike; there's a good surf beach down there.

To get to Baun, take a bemo from Kupang's Terminal Sikamuna or the Pasar Inpres market.

Oesapa

About 8km east of Kupang on the main east-west road is Oesapa Beach, a reasonable stretch of sand. Just back from the beach is the *Kupang Bay Bar*, a seedy hangout in the evenings. The *Nusa Timor Homestay* next door is even seedier.

Sandalwood Factory

One kilometre past Oesapa, take the turn-off to the airport (Jl Adisucipto) and just around the corner is the CV Horas sandalwood factory. Sandalwood can only be cut down under licence and strict quotas are applied by the government. This small factory processes the wood into pulp, which is then made into oil at the Tropical Oil factory in Batuplat, south-west of Kupang. The second factory is probably more interesting, but it cannot be visited. After you have sniffed a lump of sandalwood and seen the woodchip machine you can buy souvenirs at the office – sandalwood oil, pens, rosaries and small statues carved in Bali. The factory is open 8 am to 4 pm daily except Sunday.

The road to the airport continues on to **Baumata** where there is a cave that can be explored and a freshwater spring.

Pantai Lasiana

From Oesapa keep heading west on the main road to Kupang's most well known beach,

Lasiana, 12km from Kupang. At the 11km post you pass the *Rumah Makan RW*. Stop in for a bite of the local delicacy – dog meat.

Pantai Lasiana is a pleasant enough stretch of sand shaded by pandanus palms. Except for during the wet season, the water is clear. It's in a lovely setting, but is a busy picnic spot on weekends, when drink and snack stalls and litter are the order of the day. The local tourist office has built a swimming pool and bungalows, but they are empty and quickly becoming derelict. The beach is just not good enough to attract international tourists, and too far out to be convenient, but makes a pleasant enough day trip during the week. Take bemo No 17 from Kupang's Terminal.

Offshore are the giant *bagan* fishing platforms. At night, crews use lamps to attract the fish and winch up the haul in great nets.

Noelbaki

At the 17km mark on the Kupang-Soe road, take the lefthand turn-off and then turn left again over the ramshackle bridge. *Hotel Noelbaki* (☎ 23302), 300m along this road, is a little oasis in the dry landscape. Owned by Teddy's Bar in Kupang, it has a tiny swimming pool, bar and satellite TV showing the latest football or cricket matches from Australia. Simple rooms are A$18, deluxe rooms are A$26 with fan or A$32 with air-con, and a backpackers is planned. Tours can be arranged.

Oebelo

Oebelo, 22km from Kupang on the Soe road, is where Pak Pah and his family have set up a workshop (look for the Home Industri Sasando sign) producing the traditional 20 stringed Rotinese instrument, the *sasando* (featured on the 5000 rp note). They also make the Rotinese lontar-leaf hat, *ti'i langga*. If you're interested, Pak Pah will play the Rotinese version of *Waltzing Matilda* for you.

Oesau

Just before the market in Oesau, 28km from Kupang on the Soe road, a war memorial is dedicated to the 2/40th Australian Infantry Battalion. The memorial marks the battle of 20 February 1942 when many died as they tried to contain the advancing Japanese army. Those who escaped went on to join Australian troops in Dili and conducted a guerrilla war for almost a year in East Timor. The large market at Oesau is at its best on Fridays.

CAMPLONG

From Oesau the road to Soe winds up the hills to Camplong, a cool, quiet hill town, 46km from Kupang. One kilometre from town towards Soe on the highway, the **Taman Wisata Camplong** is a forest reserve that has some caves and a spring-fed swimming pool. It's a tough 7km walk to **Gunung Fatuleu**, which attracts botanists interested in the unique montane flora found on the slopes.

The Camplong convent at the reserve, *Wisma Oe Mat Honis* (☎ 50006), has excellent rooms for 7500 rp per person. See Sister Krista, who can also arrange all your meals for a donation (around 15,000 rp per day is appropriate).

Camplong is at the edge of the Dawan territory and 5km further towards Soe you'll see the first of many Dawan houses.

Regular buses run from Kupang's Oebobo terminal (1600 rp) to Camplong and on to Soe.

Timor Tengah Selatan

The regency of Timor Tengah Selatan (South Central Timor) straddles the central mountains of West Timor and extends to the south coast. The elevation makes the area slightly cooler and greener than the lowlands around Kupang and the mountain scenery is quite spectacular in places. The regency is home to the Dawan people, the main ethnic group in West Timor, and many traditional Dawan villages can be visited. Soe, the capital of Timor Tengah Selatan, makes a good base for trips into the countryside. The area is very traditional outside Soe – the people wear woven blankets, chew betel and tradition thrives despite the inroads of Protestantism.

Outside Soe, you'll see the Dawan beehive-shaped houses, ume kebubu, which give the region a distinctive character. Another type of Dawan house, the lopo, acts as a meeting place, has no walls and a toadstool-like roof.

SOE

The road from Kupang passes through rugged, scenic hill country, reminiscent of the Australian bush, to the regional centre of Soe (population 25,000). At an elevation of 800m, it's cool at night, but hot enough for shorts and T-shirts during the day. It makes an excellent base for side trips to traditional villages and colourful markets around the area. Soe itself is a dull sprawl of modern houses – the town has only existed since the 1920s when it was created by the Dutch – but has a large market, where you'll see people in their traditional garb.

Like most of rural Timor, the Soe district is poor. Australian aid projects in the area include health education and dam building to cope with the water shortages.

Information

The Tourist Information Centre (☎ 21149) on the main street, Jl Diponegoro, has good information on the surrounding area and can arrange guides. Pae Nope, a member of the Niki Niki royal family, is a very knowledgeable guide who can be contacted through the centre. Change money at the Bank BNI opposite.

Places to Stay

The travellers' favourite is the *Hotel Anda* (☎ 21323), at Jl Kartini 5. This would have to be the most eccentric losmen in Indonesia, with the gaudy statuary and dazzling paint job at the front, and replica of a warship at the back. Rooms with shared mandi are fairly basic, but the rooms in the ship are cute. The cost is 5500 rp and 6500 rp per person. Pak Yohannes is a wonderful host, speaks English, Dutch and German, and is a wealth of knowledge on the area's history and attractions.

If Hotel Anda is full, the *Hotel Cahaya*

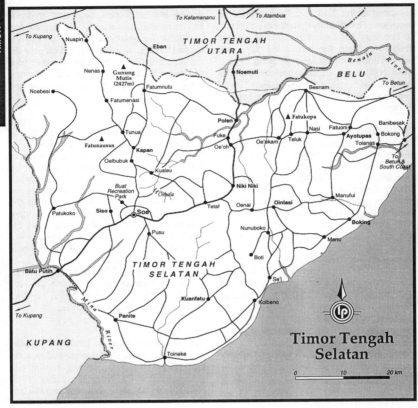

Timor Tengah Selatan

0   10   20 km

(☎ 21087) next door has clean rooms with mandi for 7500/15,000 rp.

Soe has a few mid-range hotels. The *Hotel Bahagia I* (☎ 21015), at Jl Diponegoro 72, is the best value and has rooms with outside mandi for 20,000 rp. Singles/doubles with mandi cost 22,000/25,000 rp and VIP rooms are 35,000 rp. Add 10% tax to all rates. *Hotel Bahagia II* (☎ 21095), on the way in to town from Kupang, is a long hike from the town centre, but it is Soe's best hotel. Air-con rooms range from 38,500 to 80,000 rp.

The *Hotel Makhota Plaza* (☎ 21068) at Jl Soeharto 11 is a passable mid-range option

with rooms for 22,000/27,500 rp. The *Hotel Sejati* (☎ 21101) at Jl Gajah Mada 18 is dowdy, but cheap enough at 15,000 rp a double; better rooms with mandi cost 20,000 rp.

Places to Eat

In the centre of town, the *Bundo Kanduang* has good Padang food and is the pick of the town's restaurants. On Jl Soeharto, the *Rumah Makan Harapan* serves tasty, good-value Chinese food (try the ikan tauco, fish with sweet sauce). The *Hotel Bahagia I* and the *Hotel Makhota Plaza* also have decent restaurants. Other recommended restaurants are

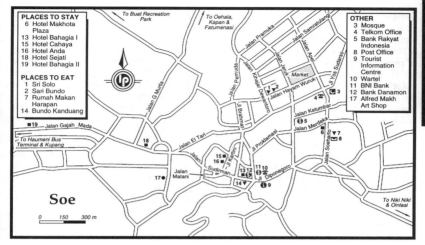

PLACES TO STAY
6 Hotel Makhota
   Plaza
13 Hotel Bahagia I
15 Hotel Cahaya
16 Hotel Anda
18 Hotel Sejati
19 Hotel Bahagia II

PLACES TO EAT
1 Sri Solo
2 Sari Bundo
7 Rumah Makan
   Harapan
14 Bundo Kanduang

OTHER
3 Mosque
4 Telkom Office
5 Bank Rakyat
   Indonesia
8 Post Office
9 Tourist
   Information
   Centre
10 Wartel
11 BNI Bank
12 Bank Danamon
17 Alfred Makh
   Art Shop

Soe

near the market on Jl Hayam Wuruk, including the *Sri Solo* for Javanese food and the *Sari Bundo* for Padang food. In the evening, roadside stalls sell delicious pisang molen (banana wrapped in pastry and deep fried).

Things to Buy
The souvenir shop attached to the Hotel Bahagia I has a good, but expensive, range of weaving and carvings. Bargaining is essential. If you are heading out to village markets, wait to see what's there and, if you don't find what you want, go back to the shop.

The Toko Timor Sakti, at Jl Diponegoro 70 next to Bank Danamon, has a much more impressive range of arts and crafts, from ikat to carved ume kebubu doors and East Timorese jewellery, but prices are very high. Serious collectors are better off seeking out the house of Alfred Makh, at Jl Cendana 11 in Kampung Sabu. His excellent collection is more reasonably priced.

Getting There & Away
The Haumeni bus terminal is 4km west of town (400 rp by bemo). Buses from the east can drop you off at a hotel, as can the evening buses from Kupang.

Regular buses run from Soe to Kupang (4250 rp; three hours), Kefamenanu (3000 rp; 2½ hours) and Atambua (6500 rp; 4½ hours). Buses and bemos run to Oinlasi (2500 rp; 1½ hours), Niki Niki (1000 rp), Kapan (1000 rp), Kolbano (4000 rp; via Batu Putih), Ayotupas (2000 rp) and other regional centres.

Soe has plenty of bemos and they can be chartered for trips into the countryside. It is difficult to rent a motorbike, but something may turn up if you ask around.

AROUND SOE
Buat Recreation Park
On the northern outskirts of Soe, a left turn leads 3km west to this wooded recreation park. It has a dirty swimming pool, playground, monkeys in a cage and a viewing tower (not that there is a lot to see). It is easily missed, but you can rent a self-contained, two bedroom bungalow here for US$20 a night. It is a peaceful place to stay if you have your own transport and do your own cooking. The two bungalows are managed by the tourist office in Soe – enquire there before heading out.

Oehala

Four kilometres north of Soe, a dirt road branches off the Kapan road and leads 3km to Oehala waterfalls. The name means 'waters of peace' *(oe* means water and *hala* peace, for this is where three warring clans gathered to forge a truce). More commonly known as the Seven Steps waterfall, a trail leads up from the road passing a series of cascades and some refreshing swimming holes. At the top, a lopo has been built for picnickers. The river emerges from a spring further up, and downstream it runs through a narrow gorge before going underground. Surrounded by greenery and stands of huge bamboo, it is very popular on Sunday, but is deserted during the week.

Take any Kapan bemo to the turn-off, but you'll have to walk from there.

Oelbubuk

On the road to Kapan, 16km from Soe, the Balai Beni Induk Hortikultura in Desa Oel-bubuk was once a Dutch botanic gardens and today continues agricultural research into new strains of fruit. Rows of oranges, mandarin, mango and wild roses are planted and disease resistant apples are being developed. The Kapan area was once known as the apple centre of Timor, but the orchards were wiped out by disease some 10 years ago. The area is now a prolific producer of mandarins.

Staff welcome visitors and are happy to show you around. Just before Oelbubuk, a turn-off near the 12km marker leads you 4km along a rough road to **Kualeu**, a noted weaving village producing fine buna work. Woven baskets are also produced by men.

Kapan

The cool hill town of Kapan, 21km north of Soe, has a lively market on Thursday, when the roads are blocked with stalls. The village is situated on steep slopes, and the main part of the town is downhill from the market where the buses stop.

Kapan is the centre of the Molo kingdom, once one of the three main Dawan kingdoms in Timor Tengah Selatan that ruled until independence. The other two are the Amanuban kingdom at Niki Niki and the Amanatun kingdom centred at Nunkolo, near Boking on the south coast.

Molo was once part of the Sonbai kingdom, which was invaded by Portuguese Topasses in 1642. The raja from the north of the kingdom fled and settled in Kupang. The Sonbai area was an alliance of small principalities ruled by numerous rajas until the Dutch merged them under the Raja of Molo in 1909.

The descendants of the Molo kings, the Oematan family, still live in Kapan and command great respect among the people. Some fine ikat is produced in the area, but you are unlikely to find it for sale – try the shops in Soe. Molo ikat usually has a white central panel, often with crocodile motifs, and predominantly red-striped side panels, typical of Dawan weaving.

Getting There & Away Regular bemos and buses run throughout the day to Soe. Less regular transport goes to surrounding villages, including Fatumenasi and Eban to the north. From Eban, nine mikrolet per day run to Kefamenanu.

Fatunausus

Past Kapan, the main road runs 8km to a huge windmill, an experimental electricity generator produced with Australian aid. From here you have fine views of the twin peaks of Fatunausus, a jutting rock outcrop that towers above the surrounding hills and dominates the landscape around Kapan.

The left turn at the windmill leads a couple of kilometres to the base of the rock. The rock can be climbed, but you should take a guide. This is a sacred site for the Molo rajas and home to an ancient fort and a rumah adat where harvest ceremonies are held around May/June.

Fatumenasi

The good road from Kapan winds its way 15km further into the hills and the town of Fatumenasi. This productive agricultural area, noted for its garlic, has fine mountain views and a pleasantly cool climate. Keep an eye out for the local raja's grave, a strange construction that look like the Flintstone's car.

At the northern edge of town is the start of the **Cagar Alam Gunung Mutis**, a 12,000 hectare forestry reserve managed by the World Wide Fund for Nature (WWF) and the Forestry Department. Rich montane forest is found on the slopes of Gunung Mutis and a number of short, forest walks can be made from Fatumenasi. At the top of the village, just past the forest reserve sign, take the trail past the first house on the left. This leads through eucalypt forest and meadow grass grazed by horses. After a couple of kilometres, the trail eventually leads back uphill to the Nenas road, from where you can walk back to Fatumenasi. A number of trails branch off the main trail – you can walk all the way to Nenas – but it is hard to get lost unless you head a long way downhill. Plenty of other walking opportunities exist and it is possible to climb Fatumenasi (Old Rock), the nearby outcrop that gives the town its name, but a guide is recommended if venturing further up the slopes of Gunung Mutis.

Places to Stay The tourist office in Soe has built bungalows in Fatumenasi. On the northern side of town a road forks back south from the main road – the bungalows are a little way down this road. The two bungalows are comfortable, have attached mandi and there is a kitchen for guest use. Bungalows cost 25,000 rp, but they are usually locked and the caretaker is often in Soe. Check in Soe with the tourist office before heading up here. Bring your own food. Fatumenasi has no warung for meals and the town's small kiosk sells basics only. The nights are very cold.

Getting There & Away Only a few bemos a day run to Kapan, but there's more frequent services on Thursday (market day).

Nenas

A very rough 8km road climbs from Fatumenasi further around the slopes of Gunung Mutis to another beautiful highland town, Nenas. Surrounded by green rice paddies and garlic fields, Nenas can also be used as base for climbing Gunung Mutis. The only problem is reaching Nenas. Transport only runs on Thursdays to Kapan for the market, otherwise you'll have to walk.

Nenas has a few shops, which is surprising for such a remote town, but no accommodation. Ask to stay with the kepala desa. From Nenas it is a three hour climb to **Gunung Mutis**, West Timor's highest peak at 2427m. The mountain is covered in dense montane forest and lichen hangs from the trees. The shortest route starts from the road a few kilometres before Nenas, but a number of trails cross the mountain and it is easy to get lost. You should be able to arrange a guide in Nenas.

Tetaf

East of Soe, before you reach Niki Niki, Tetaf has one of the largest and best maintained lopo in the area, some 12 generations old. The lopo lies about 1km from the main road through the village and you should seek permission from the kepala desa or kepala suku before visiting. It is the meeting house for the seven clans of the village – the Faot is the most prominent clan in the area. A number of traditional ceremonies are held here, including for the naming of a baby, and the planting, harvest and preparation of corn before it is placed in the roof of the lopo. If the wet season is late arriving then pigs, cows or water buffalo are sacrificed to the ancestors and the rain god, Poie Pah.

As in other parts of Timor, the village relies on hunting and if a forest area becomes depleted in animals, then it is designated as a *kio*, something like a traditional wildlife reserve, and the area is made off-limits for a couple of years.

NIKI NIKI

Niki Niki, 27km east of Soe along the Soe-Kefamenanu road, has a busy market on Wednesday. It is as large as the more celebrated Oinlasi market (see Oinlasi later in this chapter), but easier to reach, being on the main highway. Niki Niki has a couple of restaurants, but no accommodation. Regular buses and bemos run to Niki Niki from Soe (1000 rp).

A few hundred metres past the market, take the left turning to the royal compound of the Amanuban kings, who ruled over one of the largest kingdoms in south-central Timor. The kings, from the Nope royal family, are descended from Portuguese Topasses who were granted power by the local rulers and chose this site to establish their kingdom.

You first reach the new palace, a Dutch-styled house built in 1942 and occupied by members of the royal family. In front are four carved pillars, all that remains of the once large lopo. Continue around to the left to the high fortress walls. On top is the older house of the raja, built in 1912, also still inhabited by royals. Ask permission here to visit the graves, which lie further along the ridge with fine views across the countryside.

The most prominent grave is a large platform of stones, mounted by a cross, for this is a Christian graveyard (the pre-Christian kings are buried in another sacred graveyard that is off-limits to visitors). The grave marks the spot where the 9th raja, Bill Nope, faced the Dutch forces in 1912 from his bunker (you can see the remains of the bunker walls surrounding the grave). Rather than accept defeat, he self-immolated in a Balinese-style suicide along with 22 members of his family. Each family member is represented by openings in the small wall supporting the cross on top of the grave.

In a small house is one of the most important graves, that of the 10th raja, Pina Nope (1891-1959). Through strategic marriages – he had 24 wives – and later Dutch patronage he extended the influence and power of the Amanuban kingdom to its greatest heights.

The oldest grave is that of Noni Nope. The huge banyan tree that was planted on his grave has consumed most of the grave, but you can see the stones projecting out in the shape of a cross.

Up the hill between the graveyard and the house is an altar in a banyan tree where animals were sacrificed for the warrior class in preparation for battle. Over the hill is a large cave where the women hid during WWII to escape the attentions of Japanese soldiers. Take a powerful torch and venture through the narrow opening to a large cavern with stalactites. Other caverns adjoin it.

OINLASI

Regular buses from Soe make the 51km trip along a winding mountain road to Oinlasi in around 1½ hours. Oinlasi's Tuesday market, one of the biggest and best in West Timor, attracts villagers from the surrounding hill districts, many wearing their traditional ikat. Weavings, carvings, masks and elaborately carved betel nut containers can be found, but get there early. The market starts early in the morning and continues until 2 pm, but it is at its best before 10 am. A direct bus from Kupang makes the trip in about four hours.

BOTI

In an isolated mountain valley, 12km from Oinlasi along a rugged mountain road, the village of Boti is presided over by the sprightly 80-year-old Raja of Boti. The raja speaks only in the local dialect through a translator, and talks with all the flourish of a self-styled potentate, even though his 'kingdom' comprises only some 220 villagers.

Christianity never penetrated here and the raja maintains strict adherence to adat (tradition). Only clothes made from locally grown cotton may be worn, and the villagers wear home-spun shirts, ikat sarongs and shawls. Boti is one of the last remaining villages in Timor where men let their hair grow long, but only after they are married. Indonesian education is shunned, as is Christianity.

The adherence to tradition is a wise one it seems, for the village now attracts a steady stream of visitors, including the occasional tour group. The village openly welcomes visitors, which provide a welcome source of income.

On arrival you will be lead to the raja's house where, traditionally, betel nut should be placed in the tray on the table as a gift. It's possible to stay with the raja in his house, with all meals provided (around 15,000 rp

PETER TURNER

PETER TURNER

PETER TURNER

PETER TURNER

Timor
Top: Warming up in the morning sun in the cool mountain village of Afaloeki, East Timor.
Middle Left: The Portuguese, whose control of the interior of East Timor was always tenuous, built many defensive forts such as this one at Baguia.
Middle Right: The large, colourful markets of West Timor, such as this one at Niki Niki, are very traditional and attract villagers from the surrounding hill regions.
Bottom: A former Portuguese school at Haudere.

PETER TURNER

SARA-JANE CLELAND

SARA-JANE CLELAND

PETER TURNER

Sumba

Top Left: The massive stone tombs of Sumba are only for the rich and powerful, such as these tombs of the *rajas* (kings) at the royal village of Praiyawang in East Sumba.

Top Right: Boys from the village of Pero in West Sumba.

Bottom Left: A funeral ceremony in West Sumba.

Bottom Right: Sumbanese *hinggi* (blankets) are the most sought after of all ikat weaving. The best blankets have many small and varied motifs, such as this fine example from the village of Prailiu.

per person) and day trippers are also expected to contribute a sizeable donation. You can see the process of hand weaving ikat in the village's cooperative and, at night, there may be performances of traditional dance. Pay at the security post when you sign the visitors' book, or place it in the box provided for offerings at the raja's house, rather than handing it directly to the raja.

The raja will proudly show you his bizarre collection of name cards and photos. If you are asked to add to the collection, telephone cards, old credit cards, backpackers' discount cards etc would seem to suffice.

The village requests that you bring a guide conversant with Boti adat, though it is unlikely you will be turned away without one. However, a guide really is essential to get there and to converse with villagers. Only a few villagers speak any Bahasa Indonesia.

Getting There & Away

From Oinlasi you can take a bus south on the main road for 2km to the turn-off to Boti. It is then 9km on a hilly road. The road has been paved part of the way, making access much easier, but unless you have transport it is a three hour walk – take plenty of water. About 2km before the raja's house, the road crosses a wide, stony river bed that may be impassable in the wet season after heavy rain. Public transport runs as far as the river on Tuesdays for the Oinlasi market, or you can get a bus to Nunoboko from Oinlasi, which cuts a few kilometres off the walk.

The road passes through the seven gates of Bele village. The system of gates and fences is designed to keep the animals in, for in these parts if a farmer catches an animal eating his crops he has the right to kill it. The amount of crop damage is then assessed, and meat is distributed to the farmer as compensation and the owner of the animal keeps the rest.

It is also possible to catch a bus from Soe to Oenai, and then follow the tracks along the river for two hours. A guide is essential. Bring water from Soe. Alternatively, you can charter a bemo in Soe; count on about 80,000 rp for a full day trip to Boti.

NIKI NIKI TO BELU

Past Niki Niki, you can turn off the road to Kefamenanu at Oe'oh and head through scenic mountain countryside all the way to Belu regency and the south coast. The road is paved, but bumpy. The first town of any size that you reach is **Oe'ekam**, a straggling market town, distinguished only by a prominent row of TV satellite dishes attached to every second shop. Bus connections to/from Oinlasi can also be made here.

The road runs through scenic mountain countryside passing many traditional villages. Lopo and ume kebubu are numerous, villagers wear the typical red sarongs of the Dawan and their teeth are stained with betel. At the small village of Teluk, turn north towards Besnam and after about 1km you can see the impressive sight of **Fatukopa** – a huge tabletop mountain reminiscent of Australia's Uluru (Ayers Rock). The mountain is thickly forested and has stands of sandalwood on top. The name means 'rock ship' and one local legend has it that this is the resting place of Noah's Ark. Continue along the bad road to reach the base of the mountain, but climbing the steep rock slopes requires rock climbing experience.

From Teluk the road continues along to a number of picturesque villages, including **Oeuisneno**, 13km before Ayotupas. The sea can be glimpsed from here and this is a particularly scenic village, shaded by trees and areca palms (from which *pinang* nuts used in chewing betel come from). There is a distinct change in flora here on the southern side of the mountains. Palms, banana groves and coconuts are in abundance compared with the drier slopes of the mountains on the northern side. The lopo here are also larger, thatched with coconut palms and some are topped with ancestor carvings, while the ume kebubu houses have a larger verandah over the doorway compared with those around Soe.

Further on is **Nasi**, noted not for rice, but its fine weaving that employs a turtle motif. A couple of kilometres further brings you down the mountain to **Ayotupas**, the largest village in the area and site of a busy Thursday market that is a meeting ground for Dawan and Belu peoples. There is a particularly fine lopo next to government offices in Ayotupas, but the best example is in nearby **Fatuoni**. A few hundred metres uphill past the turn-off to the south coast, Fatuoni's large lopo is next to the kepala desa's office and has coconut palm thatch half a metre thick, and is topped with the usual grass thatch.

From Fatuoni, the road to Belu continues on to **Bokong**, the last Dawan village. The Belu influence is seen in the predominantly black sarongs worn by the Belu. From Bokong, the road continues on to Banibesak and eventually to Betun.

Getting There & Away
Regular buses run from Soe to Ayotupas (2000 rp; three hours), through Niki Niki and Oe'ekam. Many of these buses continue past Ayotupas to Banibesak and other towns on the south coast. There are also buses all the way from Kupang to Ayotupas.

Bemos and buses also run from Ayotupas to Weioe, in Belu regency, from where regular buses go throughout the day to Atambua via Betun and Besikama. Regular mikrolet also connect Oinlasi and Oe'ekam along a good road.

KOLBANO
The village of Kolbano, on the south coast 110km from Soe, has white-sand beaches and good surf between May and August. The easiest access is by bus via Batu Putih, just off the Kupang-Soe road (about six hours over a decent road). From Soe, there are regular buses to Se'i along a twisting, dipping road that passes through some isolated communities. Se'i buses sometimes continue on to Kolbano. A joint Australian-US-Indonesian oil project has begun in the area.

Timor Tengah Utara

The regency of Timor Tenggah Utara (North Central Timor), is also Dawan country and was home to the Sonbai kingdom, the main

kingdom in West Timor until it became fragmented after European intervention. Sonbai is the ancestral homeland of the Dawan, who spread south and west and now inhabit most of West Timor. Catholicism is more prevalent than Protestantism, but the villages in this lightly populated region are still very traditional.

Kefamenanu is the capital of TTU (as it is abbreviated) and from this base you can visit villages or head through to the former Portuguese enclave of Oecussi.

KEFAMENANU
Kefamenanu, 217km from Kupang, is cool and quiet, with some pleasant walks to the surrounding hills. The town is very Catholic and has a few impressive churches and colonial buildings. 'Kefa', as it's known to locals, is a quiet town with no attractions in itself, but it is one of the most attractive Timorese towns. Kefa is the traditional home of the Miomafo kings, who broke away from the Sonbai kingdom.

Orientation & Information
Kefa is fairly spread out; the Pasar Lama (Old Market), a few kilometres north of the bus terminal, is in the town centre. The tourist office, Dinas Pariwisata (☎ 31520), is on Jl Sudirman opposite the playing field and has a brochure. The post office is on Jl Imam Bonjol, opposite the market. The Telkom office is nearby on Jl Sudirman.

Kefa's two banks do not as yet handle foreign exchange – change money in Soe or Atambua.

Maslete
On the outskirts of town, about 1.5km south of the bus terminal, Maslete is an interesting village. Headed by a Miomafo raja, you can see his traditional palace *(sonaf)*, where the roof of the entrance is lined with 14 wooden ancestor statues representing the main clans. An impressive lopo lies off to the side and is lined with similar statues of the extended clans. In the main courtyard stands the *hautolo*, the Y-shaped sacrificial altar. The main festival, the *tama maus*, is held in January when

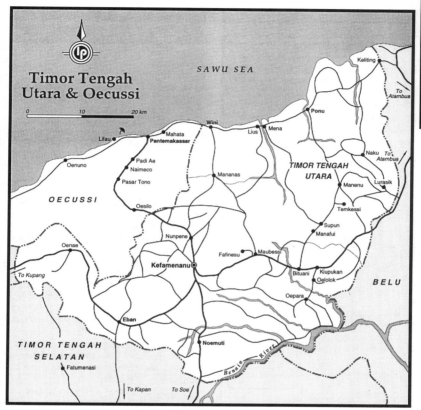

sacrifices are made to the ancestors and the people present the raja with corn, which is stored in the sonaf. The young corn festival is held in March.

Places to Stay

The primary budget option is the *Hotel Soko Windu* (☎ 31122) on Jl Kartini. This airy, friendly place is a short bemo ride from the bus terminal, but close to the centre of town. Large, clean rooms with shared bath cost 7500 rp per person. Breakfast is included.

Losmen Setangkai (☎ 31217) on Jl Sonday is basic and cramped, but central and cheap

at 7000 rp per person in rooms without mandi. The friendly *Losmen Sederhana* (☎ 31069) on Jl Pattimura at the northern edge of town is better, but it's a long way out and overpriced with dusty rooms at 15,000 rp or 17,500 rp with mandi. The *Losmen Bahtera* near the hospital is a last resort.

The *Hotel Ariesta* (☎ 31002) on Jl Basuki Rahmat is a spacious, mid-range hotel with a good restaurant. Clean doubles with shared mandi are 16,500 rp or with bathroom and air-con they are 33,000 rp and 55,000 rp.

The cool, quiet *Hotel Cendana* (☎ 31168) on Jl Sonbay competes with the Ariesta to be

TIMOR

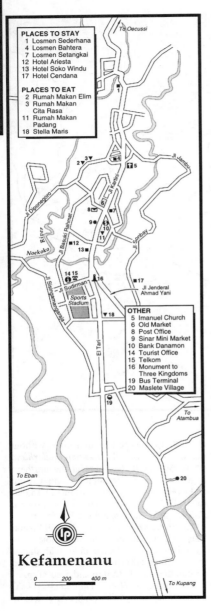

Kefamenanu

0   200   400 m

PLACES TO STAY
1 Losmen Sederhana
4 Losmen Bahtera
7 Losmen Setangkai
12 Hotel Ariesta
13 Hotel Soko Windu
17 Hotel Cendana

PLACES TO EAT
2 Rumah Makan Elim
3 Rumah Makan
   Cita Rasa
11 Rumah Makan
   Padang
18 Stella Maris

OTHER
5 Imanuel Church
6 Old Market
8 Post Office
9 Sinar Mini Market
10 Bank Danamon
14 Tourist Office
15 Telkom
16 Monument to
   Three Kingdoms
19 Bus Terminal
20 Maslete Village

the town's best hotel. Rooms with mandi and fan are 22,000 rp, or air-con rooms are 33,000 to 44,000 rp. The staff can help you charter bemos and rent motorcycles.

Places to Eat

Kefa has a collection of rumah makan serving mostly Javanese food. The pick of the town's eateries are the *Stella Maris*, on the corner of Jl El Tari and Jl Sudirman, and *Rumah Makan Padang* in the centre of town for Padang food. The *Hotel Ariesta* has a good restaurant and the *Hotel Cendana* also serves meals.

The *Sinar Mini Market* has a wide range of foodstuffs at good prices. Shops sell the delicious local snack, Kueh Solo, vaguely related to the famous srabi cakes of Solo in Java, but the Kefa version is with grated coconut and deep fried. Buy them hot if you can.

Getting There & Away

The main bus and bemo terminal is south of the town centre. Buses go roughly every hour throughout the day to Soe (3000 rp; 2½ hours), Kupang (7500 rp; 5½ hours) and Atambua (3000 rp; two hours). Morning buses to Kupang originate in Kefa, but others are through buses from the east and can be crowded. Night buses also pass through Kefa on their way to Kupang.

Five buses a buses a day go to Oecussi (3000 rp; three hours) between 8 am and 4 pm. Smaller, more uncomfortable mikrolet also do the run. Mikrolet services also run to Manafui (1500 rp), Oelolok (1000 rp) and Eban (1500 rp).

Getting Around

Within Kefa there are no regular bemo routes; just tell the driver where you are going. Bemos cost 400 rp around town.

FAFINESU

The turn-off to this large village is on the highway 19km east of Kefa, just before Maubessi. A rough road runs along the river and then crosses the river bed – 1.5km from the turn-off to the centre of Fafinesu. Fafinesu is in fact three desas – A, B and C – and Fafinesu A is the most interesting.

In the centre of Fafinesu A is a rumat adat built in Dutch colonial style in 1984. It contains sacred drums and nearby is a very fine lopo with thick thatch and an unusual woven top. Many of the houses are modern, but lopo are numerous because the TTU government has a program to build a lopo for every house. This is a very friendly village and it is possible to stay with the kepala desa.

OELOLOK

This weaving village, 30km east of Kefa and a further 3km from the village of Kiupukan on the main road, was the capital of the former Insana kingdom. The Istana Raja Taolin is a Dutch bungalow built in 1942 that served as the palace of the raja, who died in 1991, the last of Timor's rajas from the early independence days. The queen now lives alone in the fine old Dutch house, and the sitting room is lined with woodcarvings. Next to the house is a modern lopo with eight pillars. The raja sat in audience here to solve village disputes and the people often preferred his traditional authority to that of the police. A rumah adat stands on the other side of the house and has carved doors done by the raja himself. It was to be a cultural museum and house many artefacts, but the raja died before it was completed. Oelolok is also a noted weaving centre and has an active Tuesday market.

Near Oelolok at Bituani is the **Gua Santa Maria**. It is 28km from Kefa on the highway before the turn-off to Oelolok. This large cave is on the side of a hill terraced with massive stone walls. A long flight of steps leads up to the cave where a statue of the Virgin Mary attracts many pilgrims.

TEMKESSI

Temkessi is a spectacular traditional village around 50km north-east of Kefa, but sees few travellers because of its isolation. Sitting high on a hilltop, its only entrance is a small passage between two jutting peaks, which are the spiritual symbols for the surrounding Biboki kingdom. The village has been inhab-ited for some 23 generations. Only 13 families now live in Temkessi and many have moved away, including the present raja who lives in Manafui. The village is Catholic, but traditional customs are still observed. Traditional dress is worn and woven in the village, and high-ranking women are draped in curious necklaces of Dutch and Portuguese coins.

The sheer pinnacle on your right as you enter the village has a small shrine on top where white goats and chickens are sacrificed for ceremonies that accompany planting (mid-November) and the harvest (late April/early May). At these times, the animals are strapped to the back of a climber, usually one of the raja's sons, who climbs the rock face to make the sacrifices.

Introduce yourself when entering the village and you will probably be taken to meet the raja's brother. Steps lead up past the very traditional houses to the *tainlassi* (meaning 'solve the problem'), the open-sided meeting house where the raja sits in judgement. Just beyond the tainlassi is the *paunleo*, the raja's house, but this is usually off-limits to visitors. If you ask, it may be possible to climb the highest rock through a cleft around the side for expansive views across the coast.

This is a wild, isolated part of Timor and strangers are eyed with suspicion. It is wise to take a Dawan-speaking guide, though some Indonesian is spoken. Most importantly, the guide should be known to the village. If not, you are probably better off going alone. Curious foreigners are viewed as oddities, but Indonesian strangers are regarded with greater suspicion. It may be possible to stay the night, but don't expect overwhelming hospitality. Make a donation if visiting or staying overnight.

Getting There & Away

Regular buses run from Kefa to Manafui, 12km from Bituani on the main highway. Three kilometres from Manafui keep an eye out for yet another Gua Maria on the side of the road with gaudy statuary portraying the serpent's temptation of Eve. From Manafui, occasional buses run north through Supun to Manenu and other villages, some continuing as far as Ponu on the coast. Buses can drop you at the turn-off to Temkessi, 8km from Manafui, from where it is a 2km walk along a dirt track traversing a bare ridge in the middle of nowhere.

On market day in Manafui (Saturday), trucks or buses should run through to Temkessi. Otherwise, it may be possible to charter a bemo in Manafui (around 30,000 rp).

Oecussi (Ambenu)

This former Portuguese coastal enclave north-west of Kefamenanu is part of East Timor, but geographically and culturally it is a part of West Timor.

This isolated and undeveloped area is rarely visited. The main town of Pantemakassar is a sleepy little settlement, and the rest of the population (50,000 people) is scattered throughout the province in traditional hamlets. The people are primarily Dawan and the hills are dotted with traditional lopo and ume kebubu houses, while the coastal settlements have mixed populations.

Oecussi (now referred to as Ambenu by the Indonesian administration) was the first Portuguese colony on Timor. Dominican missionaries first settled in 1556 at Lifau, on the coast 5km west of Pantemakassar, but it was not until 1656 that it became a colony with a Portuguese administrator. In 1701, a governor was appointed, but was driven out by the Topasses who controlled Lifau. The Portuguese returned, but finally abandoned the colony in favour of Dili in 1769.

Although the Portuguese always laid claim to the area, it served little purpose and was not formally part of Portuguese Timor until the treaty of 1904 with the Dutch. Apart from a fort and a small port in Pantemakassar, it was the forgotten part of East Timor. In 1911 a rebellion broke out against Portuguese forced labour policies and the brutal Portuguese response sent many Dawan refugees fleeing to West Timor.

Oecussi did have an airport in Portuguese times, but a plane crashed into the fort and partly destroyed it. Come independence, the colony escaped the horrors of the war. Fretilin was not active here and the province was integrated into Indonesia without resistance in 1976. Oecussi remained isolated from the turmoil in the rest of East Timor, but the people are keenly aware of events further east – politically Oecussi is very much a part of East Timor. Portugal neglected Oecussi, and so has Indonesia. While the eastern part of East Timor has good roads to transport the army, Oecussi has only one neglected road from Kefamenanu to Pantemakassar and one partly sealed coastal road.

When East Timor was reopened to tourists in 1989, travellers were only allowed to pass through Oecussi, but this restriction has long since been lifted. Oecussi has a minimal army presence and travel is much easier than in the rest of East Timor.

KEFAMENANU TO PANTEMAKASSAR

Regular buses run from Kefa to Pantemakassar on a very scenic route. From Kefa buses head north up into the dry mountains and cross the border, marked by a solitary and usually unattended boom gate. Further on is the first town, **Oesilo**, and the Portuguese influence is immediately noticeable. Perched above the road, the town's hospital is a classic example of white-washed Portuguese architecture and the roof is rimmed with terracotta tiles. Oesilo is otherwise just a small town, but the Saturday market is lively.

Oesilo is perched on a mountainous escarpment that rings the entire enclave, with peaks rising to over 1200m. From Oesilo the road descends 28km to the coast with spectacular views down the main river valley and across the sea. A couple of kilometres past Oesilo the road passes the first of the Dawan villages. The arid hills are dotted with traditional Dawan houses, and the people somehow eke a living in this inhospitable land, waiting for the short wet season to bring rain.

The road is sealed, or at least once was sealed, and it is a rough, twisting journey to the bottom of the mountains where the road meets the Sungai Tono. This wide river carries flash floods in the wet season, but is otherwise just a trickle of water. Vehicles bump across the riverbed, an often impossible task in the wet season, but a new bridge further inland is nearing completion.

On the other side of the river is **Pasar Tono**, one of Timor's most interesting markets in a scenic spot shaded by huge banyan trees. On Tuesday, the main market day, people flock from all over Oecussi and from as far away as Belu district in West Timor. Although many are dressed in traditional garb, ikat and other handicrafts are hard to find, for this is a traditional produce market complemented by traders from the towns. Serious buyers come early in the morning, but the crowds linger on for hours to socialise. On other days this is just a small market with scrappy vegetables and rows of *sopi* bottles for sale. Sopi, distilled from pandanus juice, fuels the men who gather under the trees to play cards and *kupu kupu*, a dice game. The East Timorese are big gamblers, and unlike other provinces of Indonesia, gambling is legal and cock fights are regularly held.

From Pasar Tono the roads runs 12km to Pantemakassar through the most fertile valley in the enclave. Just past Naimeco village are extensive wet-rice paddy fields, a glorious carpet of green in the dry season when everything else has died off. Further on is **Padi Ae**, a large village that sprawls along the road. Life is very traditional and the village is noted for its sopi – ask around and you may see it being made.

PANTEMAKASSAR

Pantemakassar, the capital of Oecussi, was the first permanent Portuguese settlement on Timor in the 17th century. It was settled by mestizo Topasses, who never accepted Portuguese domination, rebelling and forcing the Portuguese to flee to Dili in 1769. It was later retaken by the Portuguese, and a fort, garrison and mission were built.

Today Pantemakassar is a sleepy coastal town of around 8000 people, sandwiched between rugged hills and the coast. Evidence of Portuguese settlement is minimal. Apart from the fort outside town, an old fountain

and the hospital on Jl Ir Soekarno, the only Portuguese building of note is the light blue Kantor Kabupaten, formerly the *concelho* administrative offices, opposite the children's playground on the waterfront. A few Indonesian flags flutter outside government offices, but apart from the town's tacky integration monument, a clone of the one in Dili, even the Indonesian influence is limited.

The town is set on a wide, grey beach, good for swimming. There is little to do in Pantemakassar, but it's a pleasant place to wind down for a few days.

Information

The post office is on the corner of Jl Integrasi and Jl Jose Osorio. The Telkom office is further east, past the fountain, on Jl Santa Rosa. The town has a bank, but it does not change money. It is not necessary to register with the police, and it is unlikely you'll be questioned, unless you happen to bump into some officious bureaucrat who has just been posted from Dili.

Places to Stay & Eat

The town has one hotel, the friendly and clean *Hotel Aneka Jaya* (π 2128) on Jl Ir Soekarno. Singles/doubles with mandi are 11,000/16,000 rp. The hotel is also an agent for the Dili-Atambua-Oecussi bus. The hotel has a handy restaurant next door or the small, basic *Rumah Makan Sami Jaya* is just around the corner, one block east of the hotel, on Jl Merdeka. The only other place to eat is the *Rumah Makan Arema*, west of town on Jl Integrasi.

TIMOR

Getting There & Away
Five buses leave every morning at 7 am for Dili (10,000 rp; six hours), via Kefa (3000 rp; three hours) and Atambua. The Hotel Aneka Jaya can arrange pick-up.

Bemos also run east along the coast to Wini, just over the border. From Wini you might be able to get a bemo south to Mananas on to Maubessi, but don't count on it. The coastal road from Wini to Atambua is in shocking condition and is not serviced by regular public transport, but a new road is being built and is due to be completed by 1999.

AROUND PANTEMAKASSAR
The main points of interest lie just outside the town.

Fort Fatusuba
The old Portuguese garrison of Fatusuba is south of town on the hill. Take the road up the hill next to the Bank Rakyat Indonesia for 1.5km to a huge white cross at the entrance to the fort.

The fort is in poor condition, but the old walls are mostly intact. The original sandstone pokes through a crumbling covering of concrete, a later addition. The gun turret on the front west corner was once the local prison, and miscreants were pushed down into the dank, black hole from above.

Inside the fort are two ramshackle buildings. The first is the old kitchen, where you can still see the ovens, and the next block housed Portuguese soldiers. In front of the fountain in the courtyard is a little coral grotto housing a statue of the Virgin Mary – the only reason locals visit the fort these days. Behind the fort are ransacked graves.

Lifau
On a deserted stretch of beach 5km west of Pantemakassar, Lifau is the original Portuguese settlement. A memorial marks the spot where the Portuguese supposedly first landed on 18 August 1540 and a couple of cannons point out to sea. This is a popular local picnic spot with plenty of shade and the black-sand beach is pleasant. The road to

Lifau is mostly sealed and passes the old airport, now just a paddock.

The swimming is good, but if you are just after a swim, **Pantai Mahata**, 2km east of the town past the port, is a better beach and easier to reach.

Belu

Belu regency (capital Atambua) borders East Timor. Belu has some beautiful scenery and traditional villages. The district is mainly dry farming, using traditional time-consuming methods, although there are some wet paddy lands on the south coast. Belu is one of Timor's more productive agricultural areas and gave rise to the Wehali kingdom that extended its influence further east.

The Belu people speak Tetum and are racially very different from the Dawan people to the west. The related Bunak people live in the Lamaknen district, north-east of Atambua around Weluli. The Bunak straddle the West/East Timor border, and speak their own language.

Few travellers visit the region, except to catch a bus in Atambua, but there is plenty of scope for the more adventurous. Betun in the south has hotels and can be used as a base to visit interesting matrilineal villages. From Betun buses run to Suai on the south coast of East Timor. The scenic mountains in the Bunak area east of Atambua also have points of interest and opportunities for exploration.

ATAMBUA
Atambua is the major town at the eastern end of West Timor, the largest outside Kupang. It's quite a cosmopolitan place; the shops have a wide range of goods and the streets are lively at night. Since the bus route to Dili changed to the coast road, it's only a three hour journey between the two cities.

Information
The tourist office, at Jl Basuki Rahmat 2, has a map on the wall of tourist attractions and will try to answer queries. Money can now

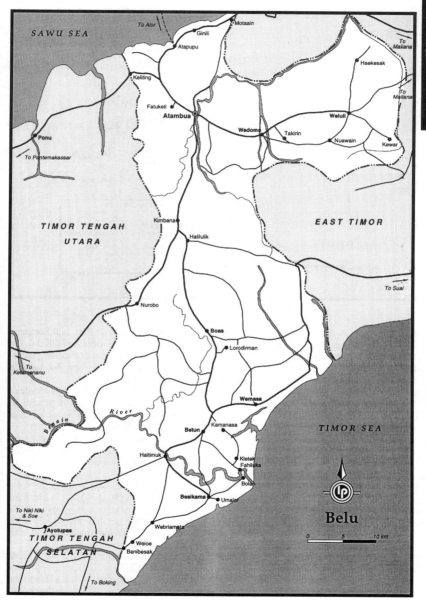

Belu

TIMOR

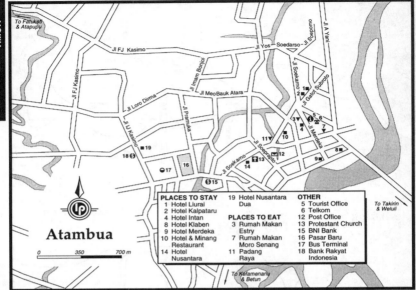

PLACES TO STAY
1 Hotel Liurai
2 Hotel Kalpataru
4 Hotel Intan
8 Hotel Klaben
9 Hotel Merdeka
10 Hotel & Minang Restaurant
14 Hotel Nusantara
19 Hotel Nusantara Dua

PLACES TO EAT
3 Rumah Makan Estry
7 Rumah Makan Moro Senang
11 Padang Raya

OTHER
5 Tourist Office
6 Telkom
12 Post Office
13 Protestant Church
15 BNI Bank
16 Pasar Baru
17 Bus Terminal
18 Bank Rakyat Indonesia

Atambua

0   350   700 m

be changed in Atambua at the Bank BNI. Most major currencies can be exchanged, but US dollars, Australian dollars and Netherlands guilders attract the best rates. The bank is open 7.30 am to 4.45 pm weekdays and 7 to 11 am on Saturdays. The Bank Rakyat Indonesia does not as yet change money.

Places to Stay

All hotels offer a free breakfast. You can ask the bus to drop you at a hotel.

The best budget choice is the central *Hotel Kalpataru* (☎ 21351), at Jl Gatot Subroto 3. Pak Manik speaks English and Dutch and his colonial-style house is an oasis of hospitality. Simple but clean, well kept rooms with outside mandi cost 8500 rp per person.

Next door, the *Hotel Liurai* (☎ 21084), at Jl Gatot Subroto 4, doesn't have the same atmosphere, but is a good hotel. Singles/doubles with attached mandi cost 11,000/16,500 rp; newer rooms for 12,500/20,000 rp are much better.

Hotel Nusantara (☎ 21377), at Jl Soekarno 42, is also central. The rooms are OK, but the walls are covered in years of grubby handmarks and need a coat of paint. Rooms with mandi cost 12,500/20,000 rp.

Hotel Merdeka (☎ 21197), at Jl Merdeka 37, has reasonable rooms with mandi at 12,500/20,000 rp in a big jailhouse block at the back. The dull *Hotel Klaben* (☎ 21079), at Jl Dubesi Nanaet 4, costs the same, or the *Hotel Minang* (☎ 21379), at Jl Soekarno 129, has large, bare rooms for 10,000 rp per person.

The best of the central hotels is the sparkling *Hotel Intan* (☎ 21343), at Jl Merdeka 12. Good, but expensive, rooms cost 15,000/23,000 rp with outside mandi, 23,000/31,000 rp with attached mandi and 42,000/49,500 rp with air-con.

The town's best hotel is the *Hotel Nusantara Dua* (☎ 21773) on Jl IJ Kasimo opposite the Bank Rakyat Indonesia. It is close to the bus terminal, but a fair walk from the centre.

Rooms with bathroom cost 17,500/27,500 rp, or 35,000/45,000 rp with air-con. Meals can be ordered.

Places to Eat
The *Rumah Makan Moro Senang* has excellent Chinese and Indonesian food and does a great udang goreng (fried prawns). *Rumah Makan Estry*, at Jl Merdeka 11, also has reasonable Chinese food. Atambua has two good Padang restaurants: the *Padang Raya* on Jl Soekarno and the *Minang*, on the opposite side of the street in the hotel of the same name.

Getting There & Away
Bus The bus terminal is 1.5km west of the town centre (400 rp by mikrolet No 3 or 4). Long-distance buses run to: Kupang (10,500 rp; eight hours), Kefa (3000 rp; two hours), Soe (6500 rp; 4½ hours) and Dili (5000 rp; three hours). Buses to Dili leave regularly until about 11 am and you can easily arrange for the bus to pick you up at your hotel in the morning. The trip to Dili is quite scenic, hugging the coast most of the way (sometimes closer than you'd like!).

Seven buses a day run to Belu's port, Atapupu (1500 rp; 40 minutes), or you can also take a Dili bus there. Regular buses also run to Weluli (1000 rp), Betun (2500 rp) and Besikama (3000 rp).

Boat The ferry from the port of Atapupu, 25km from Atambua, to Kalabahi (Alor) sails Monday morning at 9 am and costs 8000 rp for the eight hour crossing.

AROUND ATAMBUA
Atapupu
This long sprawl of a village, 25km north of Atambua, has a port at the western end, but no hotels. Originally a Portuguese settlement, no reminders of those days remain and Atapupu is just a sleepy port to catch a ferry to Kalabahi on Alor (see under Atambua earlier in this section). Pelni cargo boats also call in here and you might find boats to other islands.

A couple of half-decent beaches are east

of town. **Ginili**, 4km from Atapupu, has a grey-sand beach and a fenced off picnic area. Two kilometres further, **Pasir Putih** is a better beach, but still not really 'white sand' (as the name translates) and the water is shallow. The government has built a few concrete huts for day trippers. Of more interest, a couple of kilometres further along, is the first of the salt villages. On the low, swampy flats back from the beach, the villagers dig up the sand slurry and boil it up to produce salt. A number of villages along the coast rely on this hot, heavy work to make a living.

Motaain, 11km from Atapupu, is the last town in West Timor, right on the border with East Timor. Four kilometres along you reach Batugede, the first town in East Timor (see the East Timor section later in this chapter).

Fatuketi
This is the closest traditional Belu village to Atambua, but it still takes quite an effort to reach. If you're heading south, the villages near Betun are easier to reach and more impressive.

Take any bus or bemo heading towards Atapupu and get off around the 4km mark, where there is a roadside warung. Pak Wido Atok, the kepala desa, lives nearby and can arrange a guide for a few thousand rupiah. A rough road (no transport) leads 2.5km south of the main road to the village.

Fatuketi is the royal village for the Tukuneno kingdom and it is still headed by a raja, but the villagers now live closer to the main road. When entering the village you pass a clump of stones, the graves of the *pahlawan* (heroes), and nearby are two large, refurbished rumah adat used for ceremonial occasions. The holiest house is the *uma kakaluk*, the warriors' house draped in strings of sacrificed animal skulls. Warriors would gather inside the house before battle and women were not allowed to enter. Here the warriors would summon the spirits to give them power and strength, and they could not drink water, even though it was placed before them, as they should not feel thirst until after they had returned from battle.

TIMOR

Takirin

The ancestral village of Takirin is also difficult to reach, but is an impressive example of a fortified Belu village. Head east on the road to Weluli, and 16km from Atambua is a wide river spanned by a bridge. Just past the bridge, take the unsealed road to the right for 2.5km to the kepala desa's office. Only one or two buses a day run to Takirin, otherwise take a Weluli bus, get off at the turn-off and walk.

Desa Takirin encompasses a large area, but the main interest is the ancient fortress, 1.5km along a trail opposite the kepala desa's office. This sacred site, the centre of the Bauho kingdom, can only be visited with a guide and the kepala desa can arrange one. The trail goes uphill through cattle-grazing scrub with views of the surrounding countryside.

The fort is ringed by a high, impressive stone wall and inside are two ringed areas and a slightly dilapidated rumah adat. As you enter the compound, the first circle is for dances and minor ceremonies while the main circle lies behind. This raised stone circle is inset with seats – the most prominent for the raja and the rest for the heads of the clans – and here the war council would meet. The small flat stone in the centre of the circle (don't step on it!) is the sacrificial altar where the heads of enemies taken in war were placed. Although head-hunting has died out, animal sacrifices are still made on the stone during young corn and harvest festivals.

Behind the main circle is another stone, dish-shaped altar and two more sacrificial stones representing the male and female forces.

Weluli

Regular buses run from Atambua to Weluli, the main town of the Lamaknen district, home to the Bunak people. Weluli has no hotels, but the *camat* might be able to arrange accommodation. Weluli is nothing special and the points of interest are outside the town.

Kewar, 8km south-east of Weluli, is in a scenic setting and has a massive Bunak raja's house. South of Weluli is **Nuawain** from where you can walk to the Benteng Makes,

a Bunak fortress in the hills. A rough road runs from Takirin to Nuawain, but access is easier via Weluli.

Lorodirman

South of Atambua, a good road branches off the highway and heads through Halilulik to Betun. Halilulik is primarily a bus junction, with frequent connections to Betun, Atambua and Kefa.

Continue on through the large village of Boas, and a couple of kilometres further, in Desa Sanleo, is a bamboo archway that marks the turn-off to Lorodirman, 2km from the main road. About 20 to 30 people live in this very traditional complex, and the spiritual centre of the village is uphill through impressive stone terraces. This spectacular village has fine views, megalithic structures and excellent examples of Belu architecture.

Before you can enter, an adat priest offers prayers to the ancestors at the *sadan*, the 'reception area' in front of the main meeting house, then picks up a handful of soil. A pinch is placed in the right hand of all newcomers and it must be kept in your hand while visiting the sacred area.

Behind the main house is a grave of one of the kings. Further up the hill is the Uma Maromak, the holiest and most spiritual rumah adat. Ask before taking a picture.

Lorodirman is used to visitors – Mick Jagger and Jerry Hall even visited on a group tour some years back – but the village requests that you take a guide. While happy to receive tourists and the income they can bring, they don't want uncontrolled tourism and people tramping all over their sacred village. Respect their culture and traditions and don't just walk in and start snapping photos – always ask first, seek permission to wander off and make a donation to the village coffers.

BETUN

Betun, the service town for southern Belu, sprawls along the main road, 60km south of Atambua. It makes a good base for visiting Belu villages. This small but prosperous town has a few Chinese shops, hotels, rumah makan and a new wartel – the first telephone in town, but it doesn't always work. Shops sell plant and shellfish fossils. The first asking price is a crazy six million rp, which indicates how few travellers make it to Betun.

The most interesting traditional villages are to the south, but eastern villages close to town hold some interest. **Kamanasa** is a traditional Belu village, as is **Kletek**, which is noted for its corn fights. Further south on a mangrove river is **Fahiluka** where boats can be chartered to visit bat colonies, or this can also be done at **Bolan** on the south side of the river. This area is easiest seen by chartered bemo from Betun.

Places to Stay & Eat

A few hundred metres north of the shops on the main road, the new *Hotel Sesawi* has the best standards of the town's simple hotels, but is a little expensive. Spick-and-span rooms cost 10,000 rp.

In the centre of town, the *Hotel Cinta Damai* is a good choice and has rooms for 7500 rp per person, but bargaining may be required and check your bill. Across the road, the *Losmen Adi Indah* is very basic, but the cheapest of the lot at 5000 rp per person.

Wisma Ramayana, 200m along the road opposite the market, is peaceful and has a pleasant garden with a sludgy pool. This could be a lovely hotel, but maintenance is nonexistent. Rooms are 7500 rp per person and a couple of them have attached mandis.

The town has two rumah makan, the unnamed rumah makan next to the Losmen Adi Indah and the *Asia Bagus*, 100m south past the market on the way to the wartel.

Getting There & Away

Betun is connected by an excellent hot mix road to Atambua and to Besikama. Frequent buses shuttle between Atambua and Betun and many continue further south to Weioe via Besikama. Three buses per day run between Kupang and Betun via Kefa, or you can take a bus from Betun to Halilulik, from where more frequent buses go to Kefa.

A few buses a day also run to Suai in East Timor. These buses do a Dili-Atambua-Betun-Suai run, the main route and the quickest way between Dili and Suai.

AROUND BETUN

Interesting Belu villages lie south of Betun. They can be visited on day trips from Betun or it is possible to continue west along the south coast right through to Niki Niki and Soe. This very scenic route takes in a number of points of interest and allows you to observe the transition between Belu and Dawan cultures. Public transport services the whole route, but must be done in stages – this trip is more ideally done with your own wheels. By car, motorcycle or chartered bemo (to Ayotupas or beyond) you can make it right through to Soe in one long day, stopping off at points of interest on the way.

The traditional village of **Haitimuk** is easily reached, lying on the main highway just 6km south-west of Betun. It has many fine rumah adat, which are completely different from Dawan houses. No lopo are found here, and the houses are of rectangular design, raised off the ground because of flooding, and an external wooden skeleton supports the thatch roof. Once headed by a queen, Haitimuk is now headed by a raja, for the matrilineal lines are somewhat indistinct and men also occupy positions of

---

The Belu

The Belu, more widely known as the Tetum in East Timor, are lighter skinned and finer featured than the Dawan. The south coast *kecematan* (districts) are called Malaka (East, Central and West Malaka) – as the Belu legends tell of their ancestors' migration to southern Timor from Melaka on the Malay peninsula around the 14th century.

The southern Belu are matrilineal, making them one of only two such societies in Indonesia – the other is the Minangkabau of Sumatra. The southern Belu may in fact be related to the Minangkabau, if they did indeed come from the Melaka region as the legends tell it. In this region ratus (queens) rather than rajas rule, and property inheritance and decision making is controlled by women. ■

power in Belu society, especially further north in the district.

The good hot mix road runs 11km more to **Besikama**, a sprawling village to the left off the main road. Besikama is the best known matrilineal society, home to Queen Ina Mako Neno Meta. Besikama in fact comprises of a number of adjoining villages that seem to spread out for ever. Ask for Desa Umalor, which is a few kilometres to the south-east. Here you'll find the royal compound, the kaberanrai, where the queen's palace (Umalor), is located. The queen receives guests in her house opposite the compound, and you may be able to visit the palace (or you may be told to come back next week).

Past Besikama the road turns to gravel and reaches **Webriamata**, noted for its pottery. Various pottery groups have been set up with the help of New Zealand aid workers. The fine grey soil of the area makes for good clay and some attractive pots and pottery ornaments with a 'primitive' look are produced. The work is similar to Lombok pottery (the villagers are very much aware of the international success of Lombok pottery, and some have trained there), but designs and motifs are local. A common motif, taken from ikat designs, is of the *akidiran* (gecko). There is a fine beach 2km from Webriamata which, like most of the southern coast, has white sand and crashing waves.

Further on from Webriamata is **Weioe**, another large traditional village and a crossroads for public transport. Regular buses run throughout the day to Betun and Atambua, and west to Ayotupas, from where buses run right through to Soe via Niki Niki.

Past Weioe is **Banibesak**, the last of the Belu villages. Banibesak is a large village, overrun with young children – the government's family planning programs seem to have no place here. From Banibesak the road crosses the border into Timor Tengah Selatan and reaches the first Dawan village of Bokong. The change is instantly obvious, and Dawan traditional houses are very different from the Belu. See Niki Niki to Belu in the Timor Tengah Selatan section for details of onward travel along this route.

East Timor

East Timor (Timor Timur or simply Tim Tim), a former Portuguese colony, has been open for travel since 1989, when foreign tourists were allowed to visit for the first time since Indonesia invaded and took it over in 1975.

Very few visitors experience East Timor's charms because of its troubled reputation, but East Timor is not a war zone. Occasional guerrilla raids are still directed against the army in remote areas, but Dili, the capital, is easily visited and travel is possible throughout East Timor.

This is a beautiful land and the Portuguese influence, though fading, gives East Timor a unique character. Dili is a graceful city with many reminders of Portugal. Most visitors only make it to Dili, but it is well worth venturing into the countryside. The north coast, the driest part of Timor and almost a desert in the dry season, has some fine beaches and colonial towns such as Baucau. In contrast, rugged mountains run the length of East Timor and the interior is lush. Old Portuguese forts dot the countryside and former colonial hill stations provide a cooling break from the heat of the coast.

One is left pondering what might have been. East Timor could be the biggest travel destination in the region, but while you'll see little evidence of political unrest, it is impossible to forget its tragedy. Travel in East Timor can be very rewarding, but it is not always comfortable.

HISTORY
Until the end of the 19th century, Portuguese authority over their half of the island was never very strong. Their control was often effectively opposed by the *liurai*, the native Timorese rulers, and the Topasses, the influential descendants of local women, and Portuguese men and slaves from Melaka and India. The Dominican missionaries were also involved in revolts or opposition to the government. Eventually a series of rebellions

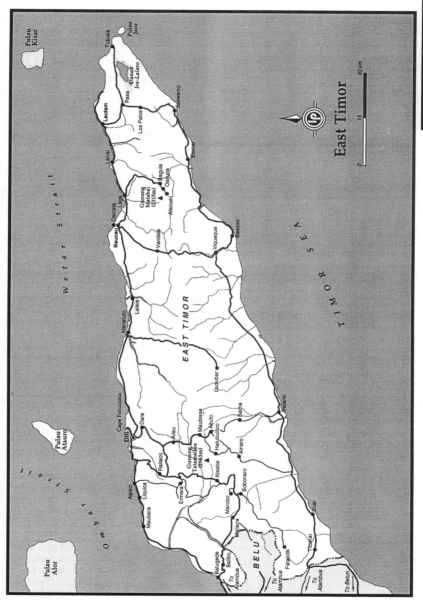

East Timor

between 1893 and 1912 led to bloody and conclusive 'pacification' by the colonisers.

The colony had been on the decline much earlier, as the sandalwood trade fizzled out, and when Portugal fell into a depression after WWI, East Timor drifted into an economic torpor. Neglected by Portugal, it was notable only for its modest production of high-quality coffee and as a distant place of exile for opponents of the Portuguese regime. The ordinary Timorese were subsistence farmers using the destructive ladang (slash-and-burn) system, with maize the main crop.

In WWII, although Portugal and its overseas territories were neutral, the Allies assumed that the Japanese would use Timor as a base from which to attack Australia. Several hundred Australian troops were sent to East Timor and, until their evacuation (in January 1943), they carried out a guerrilla war which tied down 20,000 Japanese troops, of which 1500 were killed. The Australian success was largely due to the support they received from the East Timorese, for whom the cost was phenomenal. Japanese soldiers razed whole villages, seized food supplies and killed Timorese in areas where the Australians were operating. In other areas the Japanese had incited rebellion against the Portuguese, which resulted in horrific repression when the Japanese left. By the end of the war, between 40,000 and 60,000 East Timorese had died.

After WWII, the Portuguese resumed full control. They remained until 1974, when a military coup in Portugal overthrew the Salazar dictatorship and the new government sought to discard the remnants of the empire as quickly as possible. With the real possibility of East Timor becoming an independent state, two major political groups – the Timorese Social Democrats (later known as Fretilin) and the Timorese Democratic Union (UDT) – quickly formed in the colony. A third group, known as Apodeti, was a minor player, but its stated preference for integration with Indonesia eventually turned it into little more than a front for Indonesia's goals.

Although both major political groups advocated independence for East Timor,

Fretilin gained the edge over the UDT, partly because of its more radical social policies. Indonesian leaders had had their eyes on East Timor since the 1940s and, as Fretilin was regarded by them as communist, they were itching for a reason to step into East Timor.

Their opportunity came on 11 August 1975, when the UDT staged a coup in Dili which led to a brief civil war between it and Fretilin. Military superiority lay from the outset with Fretilin; by the end of August, the bulk of the fighting was over and the UDT withdrew to Indonesian West Timor.

Fretilin proved surprisingly effective in getting things back to normal, but by the end of September that year Indonesia was gearing up for a takeover. East Timor and Fretilin now faced Indonesia alone; the Portuguese were certainly not coming back. On 7 December the Indonesians launched their attack on Dili.

From the start the invasion met strong resistance from Fretilin troops, who quickly proved their worth as guerrilla fighters. Although East Timor was officially declared Indonesia's 27th province on 16 July 1976, Fretilin kept up regular attacks on the Indonesians, even on targets very close to Dili, until at least 1977. But gradually, Indonesia's military strength and Fretilin's lack of outside support took their toll.

The cost of the takeover to the East Timorese was huge. International humanitarian organisations estimate that in the hostilities, and the disease and famine that followed, at least 100,000 people died. Large sections of the population were relocated for 'security reasons' and lost contact with their ancestral sites.

By 1989 Fretilin had been pushed back to just a few hideouts in the far east of the island and Indonesia was confident enough to open up East Timor to foreign tourists. Then on 12 November 1991, about 1000 Timorese staged a rally at the Santa Cruz cemetery in Dili where they had gathered to commemorate the death of an independence activist two weeks earlier. Indonesian troops opened fire on the crowd and East Timor was once again in the world headlines. The severely embarrassed Indonesian government admitted to 19 deaths, but other reports claimed many more.

East Timor remains a political thorn for Indonesia that will not go away. Although guerrilla activity is now isolated, the people continue to demonstrate and dissent is accompanied by arrests and torture by the security forces. Student rallies may be quickly crushed, but wider riots also occur. When an Indonesian officer reportedly attended a Christian mass and desecrated the host in September 1995, rioting spread across East Timor as the people vented their anger against Indonesian settlement. A similar incident occurred in Baguia in June 1996 and spread to Baucau. The 1997 Indonesian general elections prompted widespread protests and guerrilla activity, including the bombing of an army truck.

In 1996 Bishop Carlos Belo of Dili and Jose Ramos-Horta, Fretilin's UN representative, were awarded the Nobel Peace Prize for their work in highlighting East Timor's struggle. The Indonesian government responded by reiterating its stance that it will never consider independence for East Timor.

Jakarta will not even contemplate the relatively minor concession to make East Timor a *daerah istimewa* (special district), as is the case in Aceh and Yogyakarta, giving it limited self-rule within the Indonesian republic. The army has invested heavily in East Timor. Apart from its economic interests, it lost thousands of men in the war, and is stubbornly intent on controlling East Timor despite talk of troop withdrawals and moves towards a truly civilian administration. While the army remains in East Timor in large numbers, and the army remains a major political force in Indonesia, East Timor will never be granted independence.

TRAVELLING IN EAST TIMOR

East Timor is crying out for tourists to help its economic development, and visitors are slowly making their way to Dili. Outside Dili, bus travel can be gruelling and facilities are still limited, but the government has opened resthouses in some of the towns.

There are no official restrictions on travel anywhere in East Timor.

Very few tourists visit East Timor, but those who do rarely experience any problems. Despite East Timor's reputation as one of the world's hot spots, the army controls East Timor. East Timor has experienced long periods of quiet, but it can change, such as in 1997 when a number of incidents accompanied the Indonesian general elections. East Timor is not in the grips of a war, but it is subject to 'disturbances', mostly demonstrations. While Fretilin still has an armed wing, called Falintil, it is estimated to be only around 200 strong. During the 90s, the number of guerrilla attacks have been low and mostly directed towards the military.

Foreigners are in no way targeted (though it may be wise to avoid hitching a lift on an army truck), and unless you foolishly join in a demonstration, the chance of coming across any incident is remote.

The problem for travellers is not so much the guerrillas but the army. Don't worry, soldiers are not going to shoot tourists, and for the most part you will find the police and the army very friendly. Many are keen to chat with foreigners and practise their English, but there are some overzealous officials who assume all foreigners are journalists or spies, and you may have to answer a few questions as to your intentions. Smile and explain that you are a tourist there to see the sights.

Be aware that in sensitive areas after an incident, the army will be out in force and they don't want any foreign observers around. Travel may still be possible, but if you arrive in the wrong place at the wrong time, you can expect a grilling. Stick to the quiet areas.

It pays to know exactly what is happening before travelling outside Dili. On three visits to Timor, we have never experienced any problems or met any other tourists who have (not that we have ever met many tourists), but some periods are definitely better than others. Our first visit was on the anniversary of the Santa Cruz massacre, when the army was putting on a show of strength – the land border was closed and you could only fly into Dili. Around 12 November is not a good time to visit East Timor. The second visit was after a long period of quiet, and travel was easy. The third was a few months after a guerrilla attack, and while Dili and the west were quiet, travelling around the east was possible, but the sight of a foreigner aroused suspicion and the atmosphere was strained.

Some areas are better than others. Los Palos, Tutuala and Viqueque are regarded as problem areas. When it is quiet, travel is usually no problem, but road blocks quickly appear in the east after any incident. Baucau is usually OK, but student demonstrations are not unheard of, and also occur in Dili. Maubisse is not a problem, and west of Dili to the border is also usually quiet. Suai is easily visited from Betun in West Timor.

Travelling to Dili is usually very straightforward and easy. When crossing the border from Atambua to Dili on the bus, Indonesians are required to show their identity cards, but the authorities usually don't bother with tourists. Staying in Dili is as easy as in any Indonesian city, but if you're staying overnight outside Dili, you should register with the town's police on arrival. This is just a formality. Every town also has an army post, but it is not necessary to report to the army.

On the roads, army checkpoints tend to come and go. You may not strike any, but if you do you will have to show your passport. There is often a checkpoint on the main road just before Dili, but this is just a formality. If you strike a lot of army checkpoints and a lot of questions, then you are probably heading into a sensitive area. If questioned, try to get a Surat Laporan (Letter of Report), which will save time if stopped at other posts.

For the East Timorese life now goes on much as normal – as much as it can under the watchful eye of the security forces. Indonesian education and culture may have permeated East Timor, but most Timorese don't consider themselves to be Indonesian. Many are resigned to Indonesian rule, but hopes for independence are still high. Although young East Timorese have spent most or all of their lives under Indonesian rule, Timorese youth are at the forefront of anti-Indonesian demonstrations.

Indonesians have migrated to East Timor under transmigrasi schemes, but apart from army personnel and government officials, settlement outside the main towns is limited. Although the two communities co-exist, the Timorese are suspicious of Indonesians, and vice versa. Indonesian settlement is resented and many Indonesians are afraid to travel outside Dili.

Some travellers to East Timor have an activist bent and are intent on delving into politics. If you want to help the East Timorese, enjoy the attractions but avoid politics. Amateur journalists are not appreciated. You only risk getting your hosts into trouble.

The authorities tend to be suspicious if you make contact with the East Timorese people. As such, you may find people reserved and unwilling to chat to you, especially in public. In private, they may be more open, but use common sense if discussing politics and always let them make the first move.

Tourists are very rare and you may attract crowds of inquisitive kids in the villages. English is not widely spoken, though you will find the occasional student who knows more than 'hello mister'. You really need a working knowledge of Indonesian or Portuguese to travel outside Dili. Almost everyone speaks at least some Indonesian. Educated older people speak Portuguese, and appreciate it. They may open up more to you in Portuguese, knowing that Indonesians don't speak it. *Obrigãodo* ('thank you' in Portuguese) will often bring a smile, but use *terima kasih* with the army.

Of the few hotels outside Dili, most are government run. You will be directed to these hotels, though they are often quite sterile and you'll usually only meet Indonesian officials, not Timorese. There are a few simple Timorese-run hotels, and these are often the best places to stay because the staff are very keen to promote tourism and their country. These hotels, because they take foreigners, sometimes run into problems with the authorities and may not have signs out the front, but it pays to seek them out, even though you may be told they no longer exist.

Some privately owned Indonesian hotels in Dili refuse to take foreigners.

Spellings of placenames is variable. Indonesian spellings may be used, but old Portuguese spellings are still common. The Portuguese 'qu' and 'c' often become 'k', while a soft 'c' becomes 's'.

NORTH COAST TO DILI

The first town in East Timor, 4km over the border from West Timor, is **Batugede**, 111km from Dili. The Portuguese fort has massive walls and a couple of old cannons. Although not occupied by the army, it is locked. There's a police checkpoint where you may have to show your passport, but they don't usually bother with foreigners. The highway to Dili branches off to the left around the corner from the fort, or continue straight ahead to Maliana.

From Batugede the twisting, dipping road hugs the cliffs around the coast and eventually drops to the Lois river, 75km from Dili, where a Portuguese-style villa hangs off a rock outcrop overlooking the river. The long bridge that spans the river was only finished in the early 90s, allowing year round access to Dili by this main route.

Maubara, on the coast 49km west of Dili, has a 17th century Portuguese fort and an impressive church. This was the centre of one of the most important old kingdoms in Portuguese Timor, and it was here, in 1893, that a series of revolts took place, eventually leading to the bloody pacification of the island by the Portuguese.

Liquica, 35km west of Dili, is a large, shaded town with some reasonable beaches, mostly with black sand. The town has some fine Portuguese buildings, including the governor's office and the hospital. The eastern edge of town has a lively market. There are regular Dili-Liquica-Maubara return buses for day trips from Dili.

At Aipelo, 29km from Dili, the **Bekas Penjara Aipelo** is a 19th century Portuguese jail that has been fenced and attempts have been made to turn it into a tourist attraction. Once an impressive building, the walls still stand, but it is in ruins.

INLAND ROAD TO DILI

Until the coast road was completed, the main road to Dili used to go from Batugede inland through the mountains.

From Batugede the road heads up into the hills and **Balibo**, which has a Portuguese fort. In 1976, five Australian journalists reporting the war were executed by Indonesian soldiers in Balibo, but Indonesia has never admitted responsibility.

Buses from Batugede run 40km right through to **Maliana** at the edge of the Nunura Plains, a fertile flood plain and rice-growing district. The town has a busy market and Portuguese church. Maliana is the capital of the Bobonaro district, home to the Kemak people and their rectangular stilt houses dot the countryside. The war and resettlement has resulted in a loss of tradition in much of East Timor, but this region still produces some fine ikat, mostly with a black background. Buses run to Atambua in West Timor, usually via the coast, though there is a backroad across the border to Atambua via Weluli.

Leaving Maliana, buses wind their way through the mountains. **Bobonaro**, 20km east of Maliana, is a hill town with a straggling market where you might find some ikat.

Just east of town is the turn-off to **Marobo**, 3km along a rough road. Marobo was once a Portuguese hot spring resort and mountain retreat. Although the hotel has gone, there is a large swimming pool fed by the spring in a beautiful setting.

Further east in the hills is the market town of **Atsabe**, and a high waterfall is just outside town. This region also produces ikat. From Atsabe a very rough road runs over the hills to Ermera.

Ermera, 62km south-west of Dili, was the main coffee plantation of Portuguese Timor and is still a major coffee producing area. Coffee brought wealth to the town and good examples of Portuguese architecture can be seen, including the beautiful church. The old part of town is a delight to wander around and Ermera is easily reached by bus from Dili. It makes a good day trip.

DILI

Dili was once the capital of Portuguese Timor. Although it had been a popular stop on the Asian trail, it was off-limits from 1975 to 1989 and only now are visitors starting to trickle in again. Dili is a pleasant, lazy city – the most attractive in Nusa Tenggara. Centred around a sweeping harbour, with parkland edging the waterfront on either side, it still has the feel of a tropical Portuguese outpost. A number of Portuguese buildings survive, you can sample Portuguese food and wine, and everything closes down for the afternoon siesta from noon until 4.30 pm.

The dry season is *really* dry in this part of Timor, but it makes for some spectacular scenery, with rocky, brown hills dropping right into a turquoise sea lined with exotic tropical plants. To top it off, Dili has some beautiful sunsets over the harbour.

Information

Tourist Office The tourist office, Dinas Pariwisata (☎ 21350), is on Jl Kaikoli. Mr Da Silva speaks good English, and the office has some good brochures and maps.

Money The Bank Danamon on Jl Avenida Sada Bandeira is the best place to change money, but accepts only US and Australian dollar travellers cheques. It will change cash in other currencies. The Bank Dagang Negara, next to the New Resende Inn, also changes money, with the same restrictions.

Portuguese Dili

Dili was never a jewel in the crown of the Portuguese colonial empire, and it lacks lavish public buildings. When the English scientist Alfred Russel Wallace spent several months here in 1861, he noted Dili as:

... a most miserable place compared with even the poorest of Dutch towns ... After three hundred years of occupation there has not been a mile of road made beyond the town, and there is not a solitary European resident anywhere in the interior. All the government officials oppress and rob the natives as much as they can, and yet there is no care taken to render the town defensible should the Timorese attempt to attack it.

Despite Wallaces' unflattering assessment, Dili has plenty of reminders of colonial rule, most of it dating from the 20th century. Many Portuguese buildings remain, especially along the waterfront, which was once the preserve of colonial officials and the well-to-do. Most of the buildings are now inhabited by the armed forces, which commandeered them after the takeover. As such, entry is prohibited and photography is generally a no-no.

You can take a pleasant stroll which includes most of the sights, preferably in the morning or late afternoon to avoid the heat of the day.

Starting at the east of the harbour, the old **Chinese Chamber of Commerce** is a delightful Portuguese villa. Dili once had a large Chinese population, and Chinese merchants conducted much of the city's trade, although many fled in 1975. The building has high arches and pillars, decorated in hues of pink and crimson. The scalloped roof tiles around the eaves are typical of Dili's Portuguese architecture. The building served as the Taiwanese consulate before the Indonesian takeover and is now the naval headquarters. Underneath the Indonesian crest the original Portuguese lettering has been painted over, but is still visible.

Further along is the old **Garrison**, dating from 1627, with massive, thick walls and heavy, wooden-shuttered windows. Portuguese cannons grace the front of the building on Jl Dr Antonio de Corvalho. It now serves as the garrison for the Indonesian army.

The most imposing building in Dili is the **Governor's Office**. It dates from 1960 and, although the modern lines are plain, it is built in early colonial style with wide, arched verandahs. In front is the **Monument of Henry the Navigator**, also erected in 1960 to commemorate the Portuguese presence in Asia and Henrique's role in opening up the sea lanes some 500 years earlier. It is one of the few memorials to the Portuguese presence still standing in Dili.

On Jl Formosa, a block across from the Governor's Office, is the solid, neoclassical **Liceu Dr Francisco Machado**, a former school and now government offices. On the

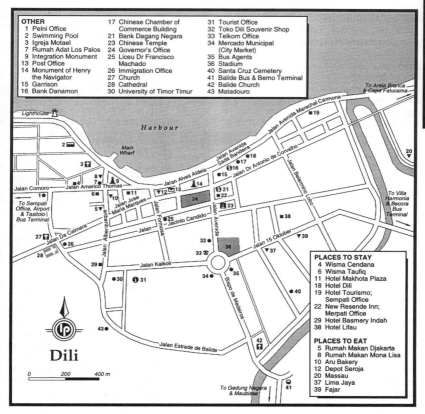

OTHER
1 Pelni Office
2 Swimming Pool
3 Igreja Motael
7 Rumah Adat Los Palos
9 Integration Monument
13 Post Office
14 Monument of Henry
   the Navigator
15 Garrison
16 Bank Danamon
17 Chinese Chamber of
   Commerce Building
21 Bank Dagang Negara
23 Chinese Temple
24 Governor's Office
25 Liceu Dr Francisco
   Machado
26 Immigration Office
27 Church
28 Cathedral
30 University of Timor Timur
31 Tourist Office
32 Toko Dili Souvenir Shop
33 Telkom Office
34 Mercado Municipal
   (City Market)
35 Bus Agents
36 Stadium
40 Santa Cruz Cemetery
41 Balide Bus & Bemo Terminal
42 Balide Church
43 Matadouro

PLACES TO STAY
4 Wisma Cendana
6 Wisma Taufiq
11 Hotel Makhota Plaza
18 Hotel Dili
19 Hotel Tourismo;
   Sempati Office
22 New Resende Inn;
   Merpati Office
29 Hotel Basmery Indah
38 Hotel Lifau

PLACES TO EAT
5 Rumah Makan Djakarta
8 Rumah Makan Mona Lisa
10 Aru Bakery
12 Depot Seroja
20 Massau
37 Lima Jaya
39 Fajar

Dili

0   200   400 m

opposite corner are the old godowns (warehouses) and offices of the former Sociedade Agricola Patria e Trabacho (SAPT). Similar godowns can be seen around town.

Back on the waterfront is the **Integration Monument**, a memorial to Indonesian rule. A Timorese in traditional costume breaks the chains of colonialism, in much the same tacky style as the Free Irian monument (the 'Howzat' man) in Jakarta. Across from the monument is the **Rumah Adat Los Palos**, a traditional house from the Los Palos region that has been taken as the symbol of East Timorese architecture.

The waterfront boulevard leads further west past the **Igreja Motael** church, rebuilt in 1955, but retaining its old Portuguese style. The road runs along the beachside park and is lined with shady banyan trees. You pass more whitewashed old villas, some of Dili's prime real estate, to the still-functioning old **lighthouse**.

Back in town towards the stadium, one of Dili's major attractions is the **Mercado Municipal** (City Market). From the outside it looks for all the world like a piece of Portugal or South America, though renovations to the interior are modern Indonesian and not *simpático*. The market is a lively focal point and well worth a browse. It has only the usual offerings – vegetables, plastic buckets, clothes etc – but a few peddlers will sidle up to you offering Portuguese (sometimes Mexican) coins.

Other Portuguese buildings include the simply styled **Matadouro**, the still-functioning city abattoir with tomorrow's *bifstek* tethered alongside. One of Dili's finest colonial edifices is the **Gedung Negara** to the south of town not far past the Balide bus and bemo terminal. This former Portuguese governor's residence features jutting bay windows, solid walls and ancient fan palms in the gardens. Now the government guesthouse, the Pope stayed here on his visit to Timor in 1989.

Pasir Putih

About 4km east of town, this beach has white sand *(pasir putih* in Indonesian), clear water, and sweeping views of the harbour and the hills to the south. It has the feel of an abandoned resort, with small thatched shelters. It is a pleasant escape from the city, but the new motocross circuit nearby is noisy when the budding motorcycle grand prix champions let rip. One kilometre further just before Cape Fatucama is a similar beach, Areia Branca (which means white sand in Portuguese). A taxi from the town centre costs around 3000 rp.

Cape Fatucama

At the eastern end of the bay, about 1km past Areia Branca, Cape Fatucama is Dili's newest attraction. A massive statue of Christ occupies the hilltop headland and can be seen from all around the harbour. Styled after Rio de Janiero's Christ the Redeemer, 14 Stations of the Cross line the road to the top, from where there are magnificent views across Dili and to nearby islands. This extravagance is a contentious project. At 27m, its height symbolises the 27 provinces of Indonesia (including East Timor).

There's a very good beach around the headland.

Atauro

This dry island is only about 30km north of Dili. The main town on Atauro (meaning goat) is Villa Maumeta and occasional boats run there from Dili (ask at the main wharf). The island has some good beaches and the Beloi Beach Hotel is under construction. This may be a tourism dream that comes to nought, but once it's open it could be an interesting side trip from Dili. Enquire at the tourist office or the Villa Harmonia.

Places to Stay

The only backpackers' hotel is the *Villa Harmonia* (☎ 23595), 3km from town on the road to the Becora bus terminal. This friendly, well run establishment is the best place for travel information and the manager speaks excellent English. Singles/doubles with outside mandi cost 14,000/18,000 rp. Food and drinks are available. Mikrolet I (300 rp) or bus D (200 rp) run to the Becora terminal past the Villa Harmonia.

The other vaguely cheap options are usually 'full' and won't take foreigners. The *Wisma Taufiq* (☎ 21934) on Jl Americo Thomas has reasonable rooms for 13,500/20,000 rp or 16,000/22,000 rp with mandi. *Hotel Basmery Indah* (☎ 22151) on Jl Estrade de Balide, opposite the University of Timor Timur, has large but run down rooms with mandi from 24,000 rp for a double. The more expensive *Wisma Cendana* (☎ 21141) on Jl Americo Thomas is a large hotel with a garden and faded rooms from 40,000 rp.

Everyone will direct you to *Hotel Tourismo* (☎ 22029) on the waterfront, on Jl Avenida Marechal Carmona. Apart from the Villa Harmonia, almost all foreigners stay here, with good reason. It has a good restaurant with Portuguese, Chinese and Indonesian food, satellite TV and a delightful garden eating area. The cheapest rooms need maintenance, but the others are good. Singles/doubles with fan and shower go for 30,000/38,000 rp or 42,000/50,000 rp with a sea view; air-con bumps the price up to 53,000/64,000 rp, and more expensive rooms and suites are available.

Hotel Dili (☎ 21871) is nearby on the

waterfront at Jl Avenida Sada Bandeira 25. It is deserted most of the time, but the rooms are clean and have their own sitting areas, as well as balconies. Large rooms with fan and bath cost 30,000 rp, or 35,000 rp overlooking the waterfront. Rooms with air-con cost 45,000 rp.

Hotel Lifau (☎ 24880), at Jl Belarmino Lobo 10, also takes foreigners. Although it is nothing special, it is relatively new and has large rooms with exterior mandi for 30,000 rp.

New Resende Inn (☎ 22094) is centrally located on Jl Avenida Bispo de Medeiros 5. Well appointed rooms are large and it has a restaurant, but the Tourismo has more appeal. Singles/doubles with air-con and bath range from 70,000/55,000 rp to 80,000/85,000 rp.

Hotel Makhota Plaza (☎ 21662), right in the town centre on Jl Alves Aldeia, is a big soulless hotel favoured by government officials. Air-con doubles with shower, TV, phone and minibar start at 80,000 rp, plus 15% tax.

Places to Eat

Dili has a good range of restaurants and some of the best dining in Nusa Tenggara. One legacy of the army is that East Timor imports cheap Portuguese, French and US wines and Tiger beer directly from Singapore. Wine *(tintu)* can be bought in Dili's Chinese shops.

Budget eats are confined to Javanese, Padang and other introduced fare. Kaki lima pushcarts offer the cheapest food – soto, bakso, mie etc – and can be found on the waterfront near the Hotel Dili or around the Integration Monument.

The *Rumah Makan Mona Lisa* on Jl Alberqueque has cheap and tasty Javanese food – the kering tempe is good. The *Depot Seroja* on Jl Alves Aldeia, next to the cinema, has reasonable nasi/mie dishes and cold drinks in clean surroundings. In the town centre, the more upmarket *Rumah Makan Djakarta*, just off Jl Alberqueque, has Indonesian food and a cool interior. For cakes and pastries, try the *Aru Bakery* on Jl Alberqueque.

Timorese Portuguese food is a real treat in Dili, and you can get good steaks, stews and salads with olive oil dressing. Dili's best Portuguese restaurant is the *Massau*, a fair hike from the town centre, or take a taxi. The pleasant bamboo decor and excellent food is best appreciated with a bottle of Portuguese wine brought with you. It is moderately priced.

The *Hotel Tourismo* has one of the best restaurants in town with a lovely garden setting. As well as Chinese and Indonesian food, Portuguese dishes are featured. The *New Resende Inn* also has a decent restaurant with a similar menu.

There's a few good Chinese restaurants on Jl 15 Oktober, including the *Lima Jaya* or the fancier *Fajar*, at No 10, which has an extensive menu and dark interior.

On the waterfront, about 3km east of town on Jl Pasir Putih, Sulawesi restaurants such as *Rumah Makan Bonto Matene* serve delicious ikan bakar (grilled fish). They are great places to sit with a drink and enjoy cool sea breezes in the evening.

Getting There & Away

Air Merpati (☎ 21088) in the New Resende Inn has daily direct flights to Bali and a Wednesday flight to Kupang. Sempati (☎ 22029) is on Jl Comoro Delta Permai, west of town on the way to the airport. Sempati has three flights a week to Kupang and on to Surabaya.

Bus Coming into East Timor on the bus from West Timor, Indonesians are required to show their identity cards at police checkpoints along the way, but they don't seem to bother with foreigners. There is usually one army checkpoint before Dili where the bus jockey will take your passport to be inspected.

Terminal Tasitolo, 7km west of town past the airport, has buses to towns in West Timor, such as Atambua (5000 rp; 3½ hours) and Kupang (15,500 rp; 12 hours), as well as to western East Timor, including Suai (8000 rp; eight hours via Atambua), Ermera (2500 rp) and Maliana. Day and night buses run to Kupang. Tickets for long-distance buses can be bought in advance from agents opposite the Mercado Municipal.

Buses east to Baucau (4000 rp; three hours), Los Palos (7000 rp; seven hours) and Viqueque (7000 rp; seven hours) leave from Terminal Becora, 4km east of town.

Buses and bemos to Maubisse (3000 rp; three hours) and other southern destinations such as Ainaro and Same leave from the Balide Terminal, 1km south of town. Most buses leave before 8 am.

Boat The Pelni office (☎ 21415) at Jl Sebastian de Costa 1 is on the road to the airport near the town centre. The KM *Awu* travels from Kupang to Kalabahi, Dili, Maumere and Ujung Pandang and in the reverse direction. The *KM Dobonsolo* sails from Kupang to Dili and then Ambon (Maluku) before continuing on to Irian Java. It travels in the reverse direction two weeks later. The *KM Tatamailau* comes from Labuanbajo via Larantuka to Dili and continues on to southern Maluku and Irian Jaya, and then reverses its route. Pelni's Perintis cargo ships also have some interesting routes.

Getting Around

Dili's Comoro airport is 5km west of town; the standard taxi fare is 7500 rp. Buses A or B (200 rp) stop on the main road outside the airport and also go Terminal Tasitolo. From Terminal Tasitolo, Mikrolet I (300 rp) or bus D (200 rp) run to the Villa Harmonia and Becora bus terminal, through the town centre.

Dili's beat-up taxis cost a flat 1500 rp around town. To Terminal Tasitolo they will ask 7500 rp, but may take less with a little bargaining. A few new taxis run around town and are more expensive.

DILI TO THE SOUTH COAST

An easy day or overnight trip can be made south to Maubisse. The road is paved all the way and it is a spectacular journey through the mountains.

From the southern outskirts of Dili the road immediately begins to climb. About 8km from Dili at Dare in the Fatunaba hills is an **Australian War Memorial** built by the

2/2 Independent Company, the Australian guerrilla unit otherwise known as Sparrow Force that held out against the Japanese in 1942-43. There is a small shelter with great views across Dili and a plaque commemorating the guerrillas and the assistance they received from the Timorese and Portuguese.

The road continues to climb and goes through dense eucalyptus forest shrouded in fog at higher altitudes. A few small villages are spaced out along the road and 14km before Aileu is a very traditional high-peaked house perched above the road.

The road drops down into a fertile highland valley and the town of **Aileu**, surrounded by rice paddies and garden plots. There is an army checkpoint here, but this is a quiet area and it is not usually attended. This reasonably large town is the capital of the regency of the same name, but has few points of interest. After Aileu the road climbs again and runs through the mountains 45km to Maubisse.

Maubisse

About 70km south of Dili, the small town of Maubisse sits high in rugged mountains, surrounded by spectacular scenery. The large market is at its most active on Sunday when villagers come from miles around. A few market traders sell ikat, but most of it is from Bobonaro and the prices are outrageous.

This old hill town makes a delightful break from the heat of the coast, and you can stay at the fine old Portuguese guesthouse, once the governor's residence, just east of town on the hill. Take the road next to the market from where it is a 500m grunt to the top. The views are stunning and ruins of the old fort walls terrace the side of the hill.

About 1km south past the market is the police station, where you should register if staying overnight. The road heads downhill a few kilometres to some traditional Mambai villages. Apart from long walks, Maubisse has no attractions, but it is a peaceful, cool spot to relax.

Places to Stay & Eat The guesthouse is usually locked, but the caretaker lives nearby.

Big rooms in the guesthouse, or more modern rooms in the renovated servants quarters, cost 20,000 rp and 30,000 rp. Don't expect much in the way of service. Eat in the rumah makan around the market: the *Sumber Rejeki*, *Jawa Timur* and *Sehati Solo* all serve reasonable Javanese food.

Getting There & Away Direct buses leave Balide Terminal in Dili for Maubisse (3000 rp; three hours) between 6 and 9 am. Later buses may finish in Aileu, where you should be able to find a bemo going through to Maubisse. Return buses finish around noon (perhaps later on Sunday and Friday market days), or take a bemo to Aileu and then another to Dili. Buses and bemos also go to Ainaro, Same and Suai.

Hatubuilico

The road south from Maubisse has spectacular scenery and heads to the village of **Aitutu**, where the road forks left to Same and right to Ainaro. Just before Aitutu is the turn-off to Hatubuilico village, the base for climbing **Gunung Tatamailau**, Timor's highest peak at 2963m. Hatubuilico can also be reached from Ainaro along an equally bad road, but it is easier to charter a bemo in Maubisse for around 40,000 rp. Getting back is a problem as there is no regular public transport and you may have to walk the 15km back to the main road.

Hatubuilico has a government *losmen* where mostly soldiers stay, but they are usually very friendly. Standards are good and it costs 15,000 rp per person. It gets very cold at night. The town has no rumah makan, but shops sell basic supplies.

The hike to Tatamailau is a steady, long haul to the top rather than a steep climb and takes around three hours. It's around two hours coming down.

Ainaro

Ainaro, 45km south of Maubisse, is the capital of the regency of the same name. The trip here is stunning and roadside stalls sell edelweiss along the way. Ainaro has a large church and a few other Portuguese buildings.

You can stay at the *Semar Inn* for 15,000 rp per night and the town also has a few small restaurants.

Direct buses run to/from Dili and south to Suai.

Same

Same is also 45km from Maubisse along a scenic route. During the late 19th and early 20th century, this was a centre of revolts led by Boaventura, the *liurai* (native ruler) of Same. There's one *losmen* in town.

Betano, a coastal village about 20km from Same, has a long, black-sand beach. Regular bemos do the 40 minute trip from Same, but there is little to see along the south coast heading east from here to Viqueque and the army may dissuade you from taking this route.

Suai

Capital of the Covalima regency, Suai on the south coast can be reached by direct bus from Ainaro, and is also easily reached from Dili by a direct bus that goes via Atambua and Betun in West Timor (the quickest route from Dili). See Getting There & Away under both Dili and Betun for details. Coming from West Timor, two or three checkpoints are passed on the way, but these are usually just formalities. After passing through the small market town of Salele, look out for the as yet unfinished Suai Cathedral, a grandiose extravagance.

Suai is a sprawling town on the move, due to imminent offshore oil drilling. Everything is spread out and the town is really a collection of mostly Tetum villages. It also has a transmigrasi area out along Jl Kamanasa, including a Balinese village and temple. Continue further along the road to the dry, pretty little village of Zumelai which has a few eccentric houses.

Four kilometres from town, **Suai Loro** (South Suai) has a spectacular black-sand beach and expansive vistas. At low tide rock pools can be explored and at high tide there's good swimming, but currents can be treacherous in places. Nearby are the remains of a Portuguese fort, but this is a restricted area controlled by the Indonesian navy. On the way to Suai Loro the road passes mudflats where women crouch in tiny lean-tos, stoking fires under large tin trays of water from which salt is extracted.

Mikrolet run from Suai's *mercado* (market) to villages in the district. An interesting trip can be made north to the mountains and **Tilomar**, which has an old residence of the Portuguese governor and superb views over Suai and the coast. Further on is **Fatalulik**, which has a large, three level traditional house with hand-carved posts and beams bound together in a stylish rope pattern. A fertility goddess is carved into one panel of the wall.

Places to Stay Debos, the centre of Suai, has three hotels. *Losmen Sabor* has four basic rooms at 15,000 rp. *Hotel Cendana* has doubles with mandi from 16,500 rp and a family unit with sitting rooms and TV for 45,000 rp. The very clean and comfortable *Wisma Covalima* has four rooms with fan or air-con from 25,000 rp.

Down by the beach in Suai Loro, you can stay at the *Wisma Suaidah*. It is comfortable enough at around 15,000 rp with mandi, and there is a shop, but no cooking facilities. Fairly regular mikrolet run into town or you can put out your thumb for a lift on the back of a motorbike.

Places to Eat Just down from Wisma Covalima, before the post office and opposite Telkom, *Wadang Surya* offers good Javanese food. The little shack next door, *Warung Surabaya*, is just as tasty and cheaper. Further on towards the cathedral, the market on the corner of Jl Tabaco is a good place to mingle with the friendly but wary locals. Opposite the market, *Warung Bali* is a good place for a feed of pork with crackling. Next door, *Warung Sinar* has sate and fresh iced juices of avocado, coconut and tomato. Next along, the *Muli* store sells hot *pao* (Portuguese bread rolls), a nice treat for breakfast.

At the crossroads on the way to Kamanasa and Suai Loro, marked by yet another tacky Indonesian monument, is the *Rumah Makan Priangan*. This is the town's best restaurant, featuring a changing menu and good chicken and eggplant dishes. The former Australian prime minister, Gough Whitlam, ate here during his barnstorming, three day, fact-finding mission in 1989.

DILI TO BAUCAU

An excellent road runs east of Dili along the coast to Baucau and beyond. Some twisting stretches of road climb high above the sea, but for the most part it is flat and fast. Occasional army trucks hurtle along at great speed and are known by the local people as the *tidak apa apa* (no problem) because of the army attitude if a pedestrian is hit. The trucks don't stop for fear of an ambush.

The north coast has some good beaches. **Manleo**, 34km east of Dili and 400m off the main road, has a pleasant stretch of sand and bungalows built by the government. The bungalows, however, are empty and there is not a lot of reason to stop.

At the 65km mark a huge bridge spans the Laclo river at **Manatuto**, a large regional town with a big Sunday market. Not much happens the rest of the week – just a few vegetable stalls and an inevitable group of men gambling on cards, dice or sometimes cockfights.

Twenty kilometres further is **Laleia**. Keep an eye out for the town's Portuguese church, overlooking the river and back from the road towards the sea. Although not particularly old or large, the design and pastel colours make it one of the most beautiful in East Timor. From Laleia the road runs to Baucau, inland from the coast through mostly flat, dry and lightly populated countryside.

BAUCAU

The second largest town of East Timor, the charmingly raffish colonial town of Baucau has many Portuguese buildings. Like most Portuguese settlements it was sited with defence in mind, sitting above the sea to repel attack from the water and backed by steep cliffs, a natural barrier to incursions from the interior. The altitude of 400m and the sea breezes makes Baucau slightly cooler than the coast.

The town has a split personality. The streets of the Kota Lama (Old Town) are lined with Portuguese buildings, centred on the impressive Mercado Municipal. This market has been renovated in a fashion, but lies empty. The new market and all the activity is now inland above the cliffs in the characterless Kota Baru (New Town), the modern Indonesian administrative town that sprang up after the war.

Baucau once had an international airport, 8km west of the town centre, but it's now used by the Indonesian military. Tourists used to flock here on flights from Darwin before 1975, but few visitors now experience Baucau's charms. Under the Portuguese, the fine old Hotel Flamboyan (now the Hotel Bacau) flourished, but is now run down and usually empty.

Osolata

The white-sand beach at Osolata, 5km sharply downhill from Baucau township, is breathtakingly beautiful. Next to a fishing village and lined with coconut palms, this used to be Baucau's port. The abandoned Portuguese customs house, the *alfandega*, fronts the beach. Infrequent bemos run from Baucau to Osolata, but you might have to charter. Otherwise take the road downhill from the Hotel Bacau past the public swimming pool. At the 1km post, turn left, then left again after a few hundred metres. It's a pleasant walk downhill all the way to the beach, shaded in parts through small villages, but the walk back is a long slog.

Places to Stay & Eat

In Kota Baru, opposite the Kantor Bupati on Jl Kota Baru, *Hotel Los Amigos* (☎ 21252) is a basic Timorese-run losmen (no sign). It is closed for renovation, but ask for Jose Antonio Suares, who speaks English and Portuguese. Even if the place isn't open by the time you read this, Jose will put you up in his house in Kota Lama for 7500 rp per person. Jose and his sons are fine hosts and their experience in catering for backpackers dates back to the 60s.

About 1.5km past the Los Amigos, the road drops to the Kota Lama and the *Hotel Antika* (☎ 21193), above the Padang restaurant of the same name on Jalan Kota Lama. This new hotel has well kept rooms with shared mandi for 20,000 rp.

Behind the hospital on Jl Tirilolo, *Hotel Bella Vista* lives up to its name. Perched above the cliff, it has magnificent views down to the Kota Lama and across the ocean. Rooms with outside mandi cost 15,000 rp. Portuguese and Indonesian are both spoken here and the elderly Timorese couple that runs this homestay are very welcoming. It is 100m down the road opposite the Telkom office, set back from the street.

The central *Hotel Baucau* has plenty of colonial style, but most rooms are in the more modern wings, built in the 60s. It may have been special once, but now nothing seems to work, the restaurant is closed, it often has no water and service is nonexistent. Rooms with mandi (make sure the mandi's full of water first) cost 20,000 rp. Large and more gracious rooms in the original building cost 30,000 rp with shared mandi.

Except for the Hotel Baucau, all hotels provide food. The Padang restaurant in the Hotel Antika is the pick of the very limited dining options in Kota Lama. Kota Baru has a few basic rumah makan, a long way from anywhere.

Getting There & Around

Dili to Baucau is a three hour bus trip (4000 rp) along the coast. The bus stops briefly at Manatuto on the way. Buses and bemos run from Baucau to Los Palos for 8000 rp. Bemos around town cost 200 rp. You should check in at the police station when you arrive, otherwise they may come looking for you to give them an English lesson.

AROUND BAUCAU

A good road heads south over the mountains from Baucau to Viqueque, which is near the south coast. **Venilale**, about 25km from Baucau, has Portuguese architecture, a large school and Catholic orphanage. It is possible to stay at the orphanage with the nuns, who come from Timor, Italy and the USA.

Around 70km from Baucau, **Viqueque** is a largish regional town with a notable army presence. The very average *Wisma Wisata* costs 20,000 rp per night. You can usually reach Viqueque, which is serviced by direct buses from Dili (7000 rp; seven hours), but the army is unlikely to let you venture further along the south coast.

Laga

On the main highway about 20km east of Baucau is Laga, which has an old, crumbling Portuguese fort. It was near Laga, during the Indonesian general elections in 1997, that guerrillas lobbed grenades at an army truck and killed all but one of the 18 soldiers in it. Despite the attack, Laga is a peaceful little town with a small market. The fort is on a low hill just south of the main road, but is occupied by the army. Another road leads from the market down to a pleasant pebbly beach about 1km away.

Just east of Laga is the turn-off to the town of Baguia.

Baguia

An interesting side trip can be made south of Laga to the small town of Baguia, 25km away. The mountains are very scenic and it is a peaceful rural area with minimal army presence. Obscure and unique languages are spoken in this area, and can vary from one slope of a mountain to another. Indonesian and Tetum are widely spoken, but very little English.

A sealed but rough road leads up through the dry northern hills scattered with the occasional traditional village. Small cemeteries with white crosses also dot the hills, not an uncommon sight in East Timor.

About halfway along, the road crosses the northern mountain range and the countryside becomes much greener and lusher as you approach Gunung Matabai, which towers over the area.

Two kilometres before Baguia in **Haudere** are the ruins of the Escola do Reino de Haudere. Only the walls remain of this impressive Portuguese school that fell into disrepair and disuse after WWII.

Baguia is a small, relaxed hill town with a small Portuguese fort built in 1915. The walls are reasonably intact and inside is an old villa, now the house of the camat. Ask permission before wandering around – it shouldn't be a problem. You can walk along the walls, and the corner turrets that were once used as a prison. The name Baguia is derived from the Portuguese for 'under the cave' and the large rock outcrop overlooking the town is said to contain caves. Baguia hasn't always been peaceful – the burnt out mosque opposite the fort is a reminder of a 1996 incident.

Report to the police station in the centre of the town if staying the night. The small army post is a couple of doors along, but it is not necessary to report there as well. Baguia has no hotels, but you can stay with villagers. Baguia was once headed by a raja and his family puts up travellers. Their house is the last in the village on the right, about 500m uphill from the police station.

The main attraction of the area is the climb to 2315m-high **Gunung Matabai**, one of the highest peaks in East Timor. The mountain is considered holy and on top is a statue of Christ (Cristo Raja) that attracts thousands of pilgrims every October. The road past Baguia leads 5km to the village of **Ossuna** at the base of a jutting rock outcrop. From Ossuna it is about a 30 minute walk from the road around the outcrop to the village of Oeiburu where the trail begins. It is a steep climb for the first half an hour, then a more gradual one hour climb around the flank of the mountain to the barren ridge. It is then a fairly strenuous one hour climb along the ridge to the top. The views are stunning, right across the south and north coasts.

It may be possible to stay in Ossuna or you can definitely stay in Afaloeki, 3km further along the road. Afaloeki has a superb aspect, in the shadow of the mountain and with views down the valleys to the south coast. Sunrise is stunning there. The kepala desa will put you up in his office, which has beds but no mattresses, and he can arrange meals. Count on 15,000 rp per person or more depending on the food served.

There are plenty of opportunities for further exploration in the area. Benteng Daralari is another old fort three hours walk to the south. Buibela and Lena are said to be the two most traditional villages in the area, three hours on foot to the west and over the mountain behind Afaloeki.

Getting There & Away Four or five buses a day run between Baguia and Baucau (3000 rp; 2½ hours) via Laga. It is a gruelling trip, even though the road is sealed. The asphalt continues for 4km past Baguia and then the condition of the road deteriorates rapidly. Buses may continue on a little way past Baguia to drop off passengers, but don't count on it.

LAUTEM

Lautem has a large Portuguese fort in various states of disrepair, but many of the huge walls are still standing, giving the town the look of a medieval walled city. The fort is impressive, but it's used by the army so cannot be visited.

Buses between Baucau and Lautem often stop halfway for a break by the beach at **Laivai**. Roadside stalls under the shade trees sell small grilled fish – a local delicacy – and palm wine to ease the long bus journey.

From Lautem it is 27km south to Los Palos, the administrative town of the Lautem regency. The road leads into the hills past a small, barren machine-gun post before hitting the plateau around Los Palos.

Los Palos

Los Palos, home of the Fataluku people, is in the middle of a gently rising plain that stretches off to the southern hills on the horizon. Although quite a fertile area, it is dusty in the dry season and the region supports mostly livestock grazing.

Los Palos has a big army base on the northern edge of town. After checking into your hotel you should report to the police post in the centre of town, 100m west of the main road. They may ask a few questions. A steady trickle of travellers make it here and, while it is no problem travelling to Los Palos,

onward travel is difficult. Tutuala, on the eastern tip of East Timor, is usually OK, but the south is often off-limits.

The market and bus station are 3km east of the centre, but buses also do drop-offs in town. A large Catholic college with fine Portuguese buildings is just off the road about 5km north of Los Palos. You can wander around and the priests are friendly.

Los Palos itself is a rather practical town of modern buildings. A replica high-pitched Fataluku house is on Jl Sentral near the hospital and the Losmen Verissimo. These impressive houses on stilts support a main living room and are topped by a high, tapering thatch roof – almost a skyscraper in traditional architecture terms. These houses are a symbol for all East Timor and grace every tourist brochure. Much better, original examples can be seen in the village of **Rasa**, 11km north of Los Palos. Rasa is passed on the bus to Los Palos or is easily reached by bemo (500 rp). The two large houses right next to the road are fine examples, although one of them leans precariously.

Places to Stay Opposite the police station, the government-run *Wisma Wisata* costs 20,000 rp for rooms with mandi. It is well kept and quite good value, but lacking in atmosphere.

Everyone will direct you to the Wisma Wisata, but there is a cheaper option. Take the road east from the police station, cross over the main road and then turn left at the next street, then right at the next corner. About 50m down this street, opposite the hospital, is the *Losmen Verrisimo*, at Jl Sentral 3. There is no sign – it is a large house with shady banyan trees along the side. This Timorese-run losmen has a few rooms at the back for 8000 rp per person and, although basic, it is a friendly place.

Getting There & Away Buses leave in the morning to Baucau (8000 rp) around 7 am, but bemos run until the early afternoon. It is a good paved road all the way to Baucau. The bemo to Tutuala leaves ridiculously early – 5 am or even earlier.

TIMOR

TUTUALA
From Los Palos, an early morning bemo goes along a bad road to Tutuala (2500 rp; two hours) on the eastern tip of the island. The government resthouse there is perched on cliffs high above the sea and has breath-taking views along the coast, but often has no water, which has to be pumped up from the well below. It costs 20,000 rp and expensive meals can be prepared. A steep and difficult trail leads down the cliffs to a pretty beach – 45 minutes down and much longer back up.

Roti & Sabu

The small islands of Roti (or Rote) and Sabu (also spelled Sawu or Savu), between Timor and Sumba, are little visited, however, their successful economies based on the lontar palm, have played a significant role in Nusa Tenggara's history and development, and now preserve some interesting cultures. Roti, in particular, has a few beautiful coastal villages and some of the best surf in Nusa Tenggara.

ROTI (ROTE)
Off the west end of Timor, Roti is the southernmost island in Indonesia. Traditionally, Roti was divided into 18 domains, each headed by a raja and each with its own distinct dialect. The lightly built Rotinese have migrated to many parts of West Timor. Bahasa Indonesia is almost universally understood on the island.

In 1681 a bloody Dutch invasion placed their local Timorese allies in control of the island, and Roti became the source of slaves and supplies for the Dutch base at Kupang. In the 18th century, the Rotinese began taking advantage of the Dutch presence, gradually adopting Christianity and, with Dutch support, establishing a school system which eventually turned them into the region's elite.

The Rotinese openness to change is the main reason their old culture is no longer as strong as Sabu's, although there are still pockets of animism. In the villages, a layer of old beliefs lingers behind Protestantism. At some festivals, families still cut chunks from a live buffalo and take them away to eat.

Ikat weaving on Roti today uses mainly red, black and yellow chemical dyes, but the designs can still be complex: floral and *patola* (traditional geometric ikat design) motifs are typical. One tradition that hasn't disappeared is the wearing of the wide-brimmed lontar hat, ti'i langga, which has a curious spike sticking up near the front like a unicorn's horn (perhaps representing a lontar palm or a Portuguese helmet or mast).

The Lontar Economy
For centuries, the traditional Rotinese and Sabunese economies have centred on the lontar palm. The wood from this multipurpose tree can be used to make houses, furniture, musical instruments, mats, baskets and even cigarette papers. Its juice can be tapped and drunk fresh, or boiled into a syrup and diluted with water – this syrup formed the staple traditional diet. The juice can be further boiled into palm sugar and the froth fed to pigs and goats. Meanwhile, vegetables were grown in dry fields, fertilised by animal manure and lontar leaves. Basically, it's your archetypal useful tree and, with coconuts in abundance as well, the annual period of hunger on Roti or Sabu was not as severe as on other islands in Nusa Tenggara.

Because the lontar palm required only two or three months of work each year, the women had time for weaving and other handcrafts and the men became the entrepreneurs of Nusa Tenggara. In fact, many Rotinese and Sabunese migrated to Sumba and Timor with Dutch encouragement and, by the 20th century, dominated both the civil service and the local anti-colonial movements on those islands. ■

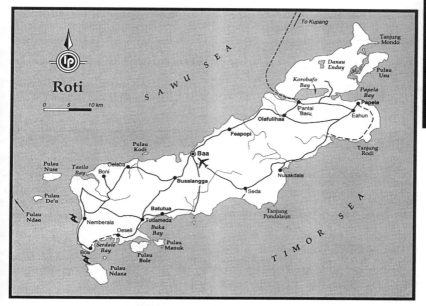

Rotinese also love music and dancing; the traditional Rotinese 20 stringed instrument, the *sasando*, features on the 5000 rp note.

Pantai Baru

Pantai Baru is a large ferry terminal out in the middle of nowhere. Apart from a string of warungs that sell snacks for departing passengers, there is nothing at Pantai Baru. Buses meet the ferry to whisk you around the island. After 15 minutes the place is deserted, so don't linger. See the Getting There & Away and Getting Around sections further on for details on ferries to Kupang and transport to/from Pantai Baru.

Baa

Roti's main town is Baa, on the north coast. The main street, Jl Pabean, is close to the ocean and some houses have boat-shaped thatched roofs with carvings (connected with traditional ancestor cults) at various points. The coast from Pantai Baru to Baa is very

lightly populated and has some superb coral beaches. There is an excellent, deserted beach just 3km from Baa.

Baa's market day is Saturday, when stalls line the area around the central town square. Otherwise Baa has little to offer and most travellers pass straight through on their way to Nemberala.

The Bank Rakyat Indonesia in Baa does not change money.

Places to Stay & Eat The *Pondok Wisata Karya* (☎ 71290), at Jl Kartini 1 just off Jl Pabean, has clean rooms with outside mandi for 7500 rp per person. The manager speaks good English and will change money at a reduced rate if you're desperate.

A few doors along Jl Pabean is the *Hotel Ricky* (☎ 71045), although the main entrance is around the corner on Jl Gereja. This is Baa's best hotel – it has a variety of rooms, all with mandi, around a central courtyard. Economy rooms are 7500/10,000 rp, fan

TIMOR

rooms are 10,000/15,000 rp and air-con rooms are 25,000/30,000 rp. It has a good restaurant and can arrange car hire at high rates.

Further along Jl Pabean is the *Hotel Kezia* (☎ 71038). It is dark but cool and has reasonable rooms with mandi for 10,000/15,000 rp or 25,000/30,000 rp with air-con.

Rumah Makan Karya and *Warung Makan Lumayah*, both on Jl Pabean near the town centre, serve basic meals, or the *Hotel Ricky* has the fanciest restaurant. Shops sell the local delicacy, susu goreng, made from buffalo milk that's cooked until it becomes a brown powder. It doesn't look much, but it is sweet and very tasty.

Papela

This Muslim Bugis fishing village in the far east of Roti is set on a beautiful harbour. Every Saturday, it hosts the biggest market on the island. There is one hotel, the *Wisma Karya* on Jl Lorong Asem, which costs 25,000 rp per person. Buses go to Papela from Baa and Pantai Baru over the best road on the island.

Nemberala

A surfers' secret for a few years, Nemberala is a relaxed little coastal village with white-sand beaches, and good surf between April and July, earning it the title of T-land. A long coral reef runs right along the main beach, with snorkelling possibilities. Nemberala has some good accommodation and is the only real tourist centre on the whole island. Nemberala can be used as a base to explore other points of interest on Roti, but you need to charter transport or hire a motorbike.

Places to Stay & Eat Nemberala has a small selection of simple homestays, which all charge about 10,000 to 15,000 rp per person, including meals. The price is variable and depends on the season. As you come into Nemberala, the road swings around to the left and near the corner is *Mr Tomas Homestay*, one of the most popular places. Small and family-run, it has old rooms in the original house and a new block of good rooms with shared mandi.

If you turn right at the corner and head north along the dirt road for 500m, you reach *Tirosa*, right near the beach. Run by the kepala desa and his family, who speak good English, this simple losmen also operates the town's bus.

A few hundred metres south of Mr Tomas, *Losmen Anugurah* is set back from the beach, but is close to the main surf break. This surfers' favourite has cold beer and rooms with and without mandi.

A little further south and right on the beach is *Nemberala Beach Resort* (☎ Kupang 23073), a very pleasant but expensive midrange option. Run by an Australian and his Indonesian wife, it gets a mixed clientele – surfers, Australian families on packages and walk-ins. Bungalows are 65,000/105,000 rp plus tax for singles/doubles, including meals served in the restaurant-bar. Family quads are 210,000 rp. It also operates yacht and surfing tours to Roti from Australia (book through Indah Travel in Darwin) and organises trips around Roti.

Around Nemberala

About 8km from Nemberala, **Boa** has a spectacular white-sand beach and good surf. You should be able to charter a motorcycle to Boa in Nemberala. Further east, **Oesili** also has a superb beach, but is more easily approached from Tudameda to the east.

Pulau Ndana is an island which can be reached by boat from Nemberala – the Nemberala Beach Resort runs tours for 65,000 rp per person. Local legend has it that the island is uninhabited because the entire population was murdered in a revenge act in the 17th century, and the small lake on the island turned red with the victims' blood. The island is populated by wild deer, a wide variety of birds and (reportedly) turtles, which come to lay their eggs on the beaches.

Boni, about 15km from Nemberala near the north coast, is one of the last villages on Roti where traditional religion is still followed. Market day is Thursday. To get there, you can charter or perhaps rent a motorcycle in Nemberala. Boni lies off the main road along a very rough road.

Ndana Legends

The small island of Ndana is uninhabited, but descendants of the island's original inhabitants now live on Roti and so the oral history of the island lives on.

They claim to have invented the sasando, Roti's famous stringed instrument, whose name comes from the words *sari* (to strum) and *sando* (to pick). Nale Sanggu, of the Nunuhitu clan, was visited in a series of dreams by a spirit who told him to fashion lontar leaves into a bowl, then to take bamboo and the roots of the banyan tree to complete the sasando. Not knowing what to do with this strange instrument, the spirit then told him to watch the movements of a spider to learn how to play it.

Nale Sanggu's life was shortlived, and he was killed after he made the raja's daughter pregnant. She fled to Roti where she brought up their son, Sangguana. It was not until he reached manhood that Sangguana learnt of the fate that had befallen his father. Sangguana then spent many weeks fashioning a sword and practising with it until he could slice through bone with one blow. Then he sailed to Ndana with a water buffalo.

Ndana was already populated with deer, a previous dowry gift from the raja of Termanu, but the islanders had never laid eyes on this strange creature. When they came running from the village to see it, Sangguana killed them all, one by one, yielding his sword with mighty blows. He then went to the village to burn all the remaining evidence of the Ndana people, but discovered that five inhabitants had not come to see the water buffalo. He spared them on the condition that they leave Ndana and never return. This inland has been uninhabited ever since. ∎

The tiny island of **Ndao** is another ikat-weaving and lontar-tapping (see The Lontar Economy boxed text) island, 10km west of Nemberala. Although administratively part of Roti, the people are very different and speak a language related to Sabunese. Ndao is famous for its gold and silversmiths and also produces some fine ikat. You can see weavings and jewellery in Ndao's one large village. Baa also has a Ndao community that sells jewellery and silver boxes around the town.

A small ferry leaves Namosain near Kupang on Wednesday and stops in at Nemberala on Thursday before continuing on to Ndao. It runs in the reverse direction on Mondays. It's possible to charter a boat to Ndao in Nemberala.

Getting There & Away

Air Merpati flies the Kupang-Roti-Sabu-Roti-Kupang route on Monday (maybe). The Merpati agent is on Jl Pabean. The airport is 8km from Baa. A Merpati minibus will meet the flight and drop you in Baa (2500 rp).

Boat Ferries run to Kupang every day except Friday, leaving at 1 pm (in reality 2 pm). The four hour trip costs 5700 rp or 7100 rp in 1st class, which has more comfortable seats. Ferries are fairly reliable, but a cancellation is not unheard of. A motorbike is 5000 rp to transport, while cars are 51,000 rp.

Getting Around

A pack of buses and bemos greet the ferry and run to Baa (2000 rp; 1½ hours), Nemberala (5000 rp; 3½ hours), Papela (2000 rp; one hour), as well as other towns in the south. Most bus transport around the island relies on the ferry timetable. Buses leave Baa for Pantai Baru around 11 am to meet the ferry. In the other direction, buses to Nemberala from the ferry pass through Baa, otherwise connections around the island are limited.

Regular bemos do run from Baa to Busalangga and at least one bemo runs to Papela in the morning, while trucks service more remote locations. Baa also has a few ojek, who mainly shuttle between Baa and the ferry for around 10,000 rp, but will take you anywhere, including Nemberala, for around 15,000 rp.

The Hotel Ricky in Baa and the Nemberala Beach Resort in Nemberala can arrange a car and driver, but it will cost at least 150,000 rp a day. It is cheaper to charter a bemo for the day, but that will probably set you back 100,000 rp. Nemberala has no bemos to charter – the nearest are in Busalangga.

In Nemberala, you can hire a motorbike for around 20,000 rp a day or the Nemberala Beach Resort rents bicycles for 12,000 rp a day.

SABU (SAWU)

Midway between Roti and Sumba, but with closer linguistic links to Sumba, the low, bare island of Sabu (also spelled Sawu) is still a stronghold of animistic beliefs collectively known as *jingitui*. These persist, even though Portuguese missionaries first arrived before 1600 and their work was continued by the Dutch.

Sabu's population (about 60,000 people) is divided into five traditional domains; the main settlement, **Seba** (on the north-west coast), was the centre of the leading domain in Dutch times. Sabunese society is divided into clans, named after their male founders, but it is also divided in half – into the 'noble' and 'common' halves, which are determined by the mother's lineage. The halves are called *hubi ae* (greater flower stalk) and *hubi iki* (lesser flower stalk). Sabunese women have a thriving ikat-weaving tradition. Their cloth typically has stripes of black or dark blue interspersed with stripes decorated with floral motifs, clan or hubi emblems.

A group of stones near **Namata** is a ritual site: animal sacrifices, followed by the whole community sharing the meat, take place around August to October. Another festival in the second quarter of the year sees a boat pushed out to sea as an offering.

There are three places to stay on Sabu: *Ongka Da'i Homestay*, *Makarim Homestay* and *Petykuswan Homestay*, each costing around 12,000 rp, including meals. Seba has a market, and a handful of trucks provides the island's transport, although you can hire a motorcycle for 15,000 rp per day.

Getting There & Away

Boat Ferries leave Kupang's Bolok harbour for Sabu on Tuesday and Wednesday (14,000 rp; nine hours), and continue on to Waingapu on Sumba. From Sabu, ferries to Kupang leave on Tuesday and Wednesday. Ferries from Waingapu to Sabu leave on Monday and Saturday, and in the reverse direction on Sunday and Thursday.

Pelni passenger ships also call in at Sabu. The *Pangrango* sails Kupang-Roti-Sabu-Ende and back every two weeks.

Sumba

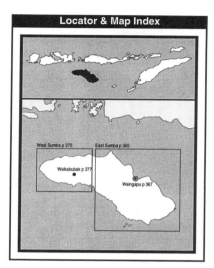

Highlights

- **Waikabubak** – the best place to base yourself on Sumba, Waikabubak is on a green agricultural plateau and has some interesting traditional villages right within the town.

- **Traditional Villages** – Sumba's villages of high peaked houses and massive stone tombs are the most traditional and fascinating examples in Nusa Tenggara. Pero has a losmen and many villages nearby, but traditional villages are everywhere. In West Sumba visit Kampung Tarung in Waikabubak, Lai Tarung in Anakalang, Kadenga in Lamboya and Ratenggaro in Kodi. Prainatang is East Sumba's most traditional village.

- **Weaving Villages** – Sumba's fabulous ikat is produced in the royal villages of East Sumba. Praiyawang, Umabara, Pau and Kaliuda are all noted weaving centres.

- **Waingapu** – Sumba's main town, with a lazy port and nearby weaving villages.

- **Beaches** – Sumba's many stunning but isolated beaches have pure white sands, good waves for surfers, and swimming for the board-challenged. Tarimbang (East Sumba) is the loveliest, closely followed by Pantai Morosi (West Sumba), but the latter has no accommodation. Pantai Rua (West Sumba), Ngihiwatu (West Sumba) and Kallala (East Sumba) are also fine beaches.

SUMBA

A great ladder once connected heaven and earth. The first people used it to come down to earth on Sumba and settle at Cape Sasar, on the northern tip of the island – or so the myth goes. Another Sumbanese tale recounts how Umbu Walu Sasar, one of their two ancestors, was driven away from Java by the wars. Transported to Sumba by the powers of heaven, he came to live at Cape Sasar. The other ancestor, Umbu Walu Mandoko, arrived by boat, travelled to the east and lived at the mouth of the Sungai Kambaniru.

Such myths may come as near to the truth as any version of the origins of a people who are physically of Malay stock with a tinge of Melanesian; whose language falls into the same bag that holds the Bimanese of eastern Sumbawa, the Manggarai and Ngada of western Flores and the Sabunese of Sabu; whose death and burial ceremonies are so strongly reminiscent of Torajaland in Sulawesi; and whose brilliant ikat textiles, fine carved stone tombs and high, thatched clan houses suggest common origins with similar traditions scattered from Sumatra to Maluku.

Wherever they came from, the island on which the Sumbanese have ended up making their home – south of Flores and midway between Sumbawa and Timor – lies far from Indonesia's main cultural currents. Sumba's isolation has helped preserve one of Indonesia's most remarkable cultures, particularly in the wetter, more fertile and more remote western half.

Right up until this century, Sumbanese life was punctuated by periodic warfare between a huge number of rival princedoms. Although Christianity and (to a much lesser extent)

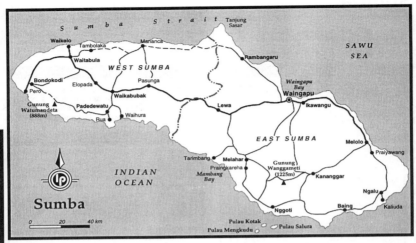

Islam have now made inroads, around half the people in the west and a significant minority of people in the east still adhere to the animist *marapu* religion.

Old conflicts are recalled every year at western Sumba's often-violent Pasola festivals, which involve mock battles between teams of mounted horse riders. The 'mock' battles sometimes become real, as in August 1992 when two villages went to war: several people were killed and more than 80 homes were burned down.

The last 20 years have seen an increasing flow of visitors to Sumba, many attracted by the ikat cloth of East Sumba. Other Sumbanese traditions are much stronger in the west, where you'll see exotic houses, ceremonies and tombs. The tombs are a constant reminder that, for a Sumbanese, death is the most important event in life. Against this background, the most recent attraction of Sumba – surfing – hardly seems to fit.

Despite their warlike past, the Sumbanese are friendly, but more reserved than many other peoples in Nusa Tenggara. Foreigners should consider hiring a guide when going to villages, at least until they learn some visitor behaviour.

Facts About Sumba

HISTORY
Early History
Fourteenth century Javanese chronicles place Sumba under the control of the Majapahits, although apart from a number of exploratory expeditions, it is doubtful that the Javanese had any real influence on Sumba. Lying well outside the main trade routes and with little of economic interest, Sumbanese history is mostly a saga of internal wars, mainly over land and trading rights, between a great number of petty kingdoms. The most powerful clans claimed direct descent from the legendary original settlers, Sasar and Mandoko.

Despite their mutual hostility, princedoms often depended on each other economically. The inland regions produced horses, timber, betel nuts, rice, fruit and dyewoods, while the much-valued ikat cloth was made on the coast, where the drier climate was suitable for cotton growing. The coastal people also controlled trade with other islands.

Sumba only really began to attract outside

attention in the 17th century. While the Portuguese and Dutch battled for control of the spice trade (well away from Sumba), local trading empires began to emerge just to the north of the island. The sultanate of Bima in Sumbawa rose to prominence. Although in 1633 it became a vassal of the Makassarese kingdom of Gowa in southern Sulawesi, Bima expanded its influence. By 1662, the Sultan of Bima claimed control of Sumba. Bimanese ships, just a short sail away from western Sumba, undoubtedly called in at Sumba, but exactly how much control Bima exerted is unknown.

The trading enclave of Ende, just to the north on Flores, was already well established at this time. Originally settled by Javanese, Arabs and other merchants, Ende also forged links with the warlike Makassarese, who settled at Ende. Ende acquired a reputation as a haven for Makassarese pirates, and looked south to Sumba for trading possibilities. It found it in slaves.

Slave Trade

In the late 17th century, Portuguese from Timor visited East Sumba for sandalwood, but Portuguese fortunes were already on the wane. By the 18th century the Dutch laid claim to the eastern islands and in 1750 the Veerigde Oost-Indische Compagnie (VOC) sent an expedition to Sumba to forge agreements with the local rajas. In 1751, the VOC sought to monopolise the slave trade on Sumba and stipulated that the island's rulers were not to trade with the Makassarese (meaning the Endenese).

By 1757, Sumba had become a significant source of slaves for the VOC. Slaves were sent to work plantations in Java, inducted into native armies or sold on the open market. The VOC also exported slaves, mostly through Batavia (Jakarta), to Cape Town, Mauritius and other colonies. The slave trade was already well established in Bali and Sulawesi, where the Makassarese were major players. The Sumbanese rulers for their part were happy to trade in slaves and themselves maintained a large slave class.

Meanwhile, bands of Makassarese (Enden-

ese) pirates plundered the seas, and their flotillas of *prahu* were a formidable force. In 1758, they raided Sumba, carrying off anyone they could find for sale in the slave markets. Apart from these raids, they also acted as mercenaries in local wars, receiving slaves for payment. In 1759, the Raja of Lewa asked for the assistance of Endenese ships to help defeat the Raja of Melolo, who in turn called on the VOC for help.

Although keen to rid the seas of piracy, the Dutch were reluctant to get involved in Sumba and had little hope of controlling the warring interior. Endenese slave raids increased, though the 'legitimate' trade also continued. The coastal villages were terrorised and many moved inland to protected mountain locations. One anthropologist reported that during the 1950s, in one West Sumba village the villagers would panic at the sight of a ship offshore, with mothers grabbing their children and fleeing. The low population density of the island, especially in East Sumba, is thought to be due to extensive slaving.

When the VOC went bankrupt in 1799 and the Dutch government assumed direct control, Dutch slave trading stopped on Sumba. Endenese raids continued, however, and other traders joined the plunder. By the middle of the 19th century the whole of the north coast was all but depopulated. Around this time, the Endenese, rather than simply raiding Sumba, began to settle on the island. From their bases, such as Pero in the Kodi region, they made raids deep into the interior. The Endenese also acted as mercenaries and traded in guns, increasing warfare between the kingdoms.

The Dutch attacked Ende in 1838 to force the Endenese to stop the trade, but even though the Endenese raja signed a treaty promising just that, the trade continued.

In 1843, an Arab trader, Sharif Abdulrahman, founded Waingapu to trade horses, with backing from the Dutch Resident of Kupang. The export of horses from East Sumba flourished and continues to this day.

Slavery was officially abolished in 1860, and the Dutch stepped up their activities to stop the trade. When the Raja of Kapunduk

SUMBA

enlisted the help of the Endenese to conquer the tribes of the interior in return for slaves, the Dutch sent a warship to Sumba and sank Endenese ships.

Slavery unofficially continued up until the 20th century. The export of slaves slowed, especially with increased Dutch naval patrols in the shipping lanes, but the Endenese continued slave raids and sold them to the Sumbanese rajas.

Wars between the kingdoms continued with assistance from the Endenese, and Sharif Abdulrahman joined in and sacked Lewa with Endenese backing. In 1866, the Dutch installed an administrator in Waingapu, but Dutch control was limited to supervising the horse trade and was almost nonexistent against the warring kingdoms.

20th Century

With a change of colonial policy, the Dutch set about establishing direct control on Sumba in 1906. It took years of 'pacification' campaigns before an effective colonial administration was established, but even then large parts of the island were too remote for the Dutch to establish contact, let alone control.

They established rule through the local rajas, but Sumba was not considered safe until 1933 when police finally replaced the army, making Sumba one of the last islands in Indonesia to be effectively controlled by the Dutch.

Dutch rule was short-lived, and in 1942 the Japanese took over the island and proved to be brutal masters. The Dutch returned to Sumba in 1946, but were forced to finally quit and grant independence to Indonesia in 1949.

The system of rule through kings continued in Sumba right up until 1962 when a *bupati* (governor) was appointed. The bupati also came from a royal family and Sumbanese social structure remained largely intact. Although the slave system was abolished, many slaves remained in the service of the rajas as 'servants'.

Development throughout the eastern islands was slow in coming, and nowhere more so than on Sumba. The lack of roads meant that much of the island had no contact with the Indonesian administration, just as it had no contact with the Dutch. Only in the 1990s has Indonesian education penetrated in many areas, and even now it is not complete. Sumba, particularly West Sumba, remains very traditional and although good roads now make access easy, age-old customs remain intact.

GEOGRAPHY

Sumba lies outside the volcanic belt that runs through most of Indonesia and is more closely related to Timor. Soils are less fertile and limestone is prevalent. Theories on Sumba's geological origins are divided; some claim that, like Timor, it is a fragment of the Australian continent that moved northwards, though it seems more likely to be a fragment of the Asian plate. Although Sumba has no volcanoes, it is subject to earthquakes.

The dry northern plains are reminiscent of Australia, while the low mountains of West Sumba are wetter and more fertile. The island's most prominent mountains lie in the south-east and contain Sumba's highest peak Gunung Wanggameti (1255m). This relatively lush area is in strong contrast to the arid lowlands in the rest of East Sumba. Coastal reefs are dotted all around the islands and are responsible for Sumba's many beautiful white sand beaches.

CLIMATE

The wet season is from around December to March, although it's longer in the west and along the south coast. The east and northern half of the island are much drier than the west and south.

The driest areas of Sumba are the coastal plains in the east, extending from the Waingapu region to the Baing region. Rainfall is less than 500mm per year and the wet season is very short, lasting only around three or four months. In the wet, the area turns green with a covering of grass, but it soon dies around May.

The highland areas, extending from the west coast inland to central Sumba, have a more pronounced wet season and receive at least some rain throughout the year. This is the most prolific crop-growing area and at Waikabubak, where the average rainfall is around 1800mm, wet rice is grown well into the dry season.

Maximum temperatures are uniformly in the low 30s throughout Sumba, and are slightly cooler in the highland regions. The only area where overnight temperatures can be classed as cold is in the higher south-east mountains.

ECONOMY
Sumba's extensive grasslands made it one of Indonesia's leading horse-breeding islands. The trade boomed in the 19th century; horses are still a symbol of wealth and status, and traditionally have been used as part of the bride-price. Horses have been interbred with stock imported from Australia, and Sumbanese horses are the largest in Indonesia.

Brahmin bulls, first brought to Sumba in the 1920s, are also bred and exported in East Sumba. Buffalo are more common in West Sumba.

Agriculture is primarily subsistence, with corn and rice the staples.

POPULATION & PEOPLE
Sumba's population of around 400,000 people makes it the least densely populated of the major islands in Nusa Tenggara. Two-thirds live in West Sumba.

Although the people are divided into seven linguistic groups – six of them in West Sumba – all share a largely homogenous culture. The Sumbanese are of Malay descent with some Melanesian features and tend to be much taller than other Indonesians. Some of the royal families claim their ancestors came from India (others from Java or Bima), but while the dashing, tall and turbaned Sumbanese men do bear a resemblance to Indian princes from a Hindi pop movie, there is little evidence to suggest direct migration from India.

Muslim Endenese settlements are found on the coast and Sumba also has a significant Sabunese population. Chinese inhabit the main towns and control almost all commerce, while Waingapu also has a small number of Arab settlers.

ARTS
Ikat
The ikat woven by the women of the eastern coastal regions of Sumba is the most dramatic in Indonesia. The colours are mostly bright: earthy oranges, browns, yellows and reds that come from the *kombu* root and blue from *nila* (indigo). Sumba motifs are a pictorial history, reminders of tribal wars and an age which ended with the coming of the Dutch – the skulls of vanquished enemies dangle off trees and mounted riders wield spears. A huge variety of animals and mythical creatures is also depicted on Sumba ikat, including *nagas* (crowned snake-dragons with large teeth, wings and legs), deer, dogs, turtles, crocodile, apes and eagles.

Traditionally, ikat cloth was used only on special occasions: at rituals accompanying harvests; as offerings to the sponsors of a festival; or as clothing for rajas, their relatives and their attendants. Less than 90 years ago, only members of Sumba's highest clans, and their personal attendants, could make or wear it. Slaves could only wear black sarongs. The most impressive use of the cloth was at important funerals where dancers and the guards of the corpse were dressed in richly decorated costumes and glittering headdresses. The corpse itself was dressed in the finest textiles, then bound with so many more that it resembled a huge mound. The first missionary on Sumba, DK Wielenga, described a funeral in 1925:

The brilliant examples of decorated cloths were carefully kept till the day of the burial. The prominent chief took 40 or 50 to the grave with him and the raja was put to rest with no less than 100 or 200. When they appeared in the hereafter among their ancestors, then they must appear in full splendour. And so the most attractive cloths went into the earth.

The Dutch conquest broke the Sumbanese nobility's monopoly on the production of ikat and opened up a large external market which, in turn, increased production. Collected by

SUMBA

Dutch ethnographers and museums since the late 19th century (the Rotterdam and Basel museums have fine collections), the large cloths became popular in Java and Holland. By the 1920s, visitors were already noting the introduction of nontraditional designs, such as rampant lions from the Dutch coat of arms.

A Sumbanese woman's ikat sarong is known as a *lau*, while the large rectangular blankets or *hinggi* are the most sought after form of ikat and are used by men as a sarong or shawl. The hinggi comes in two forms, based on the colours used: the *kombu*, employing brown, red, yellow and blue is used for a variety of occasions including funerals, while the *kawaru* is blue and white and used for festive occasions.

A third type of weaving from the Melolo area of East Sumba is the *pahikung* where a supplementary weft technique is used, producing an effect that looks like embroidery. Pahikung pieces are much narrower and smaller.

A fine ikat hinggi would traditionally take up to 18 months to produce, from the time the cotton was harvested and hand-spun until the weaving was finished. The length of time was determined primarily by the dyeing process. Kombu, which grows wild and was gathered by hand, is only available in the dry season from April to September, while indigo could only be harvested in the wet season.

The introduction of chemical dyes and machine-spun cotton thread has greatly reduced the time needed to produce a blanket. Traditional dyes are still widely used, but hand-spun thread is rare and even when used it may not be of a high quality.

The actual weaving time varies enormously, depending on the skill of the weaver and the complexity of the design. A fast weaver can churn out a simple cloth in a couple of days, while a very intricate piece will take a month or more of weaving. The weaving is only done by women.

The bulk of the ikat trade is now controlled by Chinese merchants who place large orders and sell the cloth in Waingapu, Bali and further afield. Traditional designs are still employed, but modern motifs such as butterflies are common. Large human figures are a modern invention, quicker to weave and said to appeal to the Japanese market. Superb, intricate pieces are still produced, but the best ikat usually has to be ordered and may take six months to produce.

When shopping for ikat, the clarity and size of the motifs are all important. The very best blankets with many small and varied motifs and distinct edges on the motifs may set you back a million rupiah or more, though high-quality blankets can be purchased for a third that amount. A blanket with just a few large figures, hazy edges and loose weave probably isn't worth 50,000 rp, but you'll be hard pressed to find a large blanket under 100,000 rp and the first asking price may be much higher. Know your stuff before you invest a large amount of money, be prepared to bargain and be very wary of 'antiques'. The art shops in Waingapu are a good first stop to get an overall idea of designs, quality and price before buying in the villages.

Ikat is still largely the preserve of the royal villages of East Sumba.

TRADITIONAL CULTURE

Old beliefs fade, customs die and rituals change: the Sumbanese still make textiles, but no longer hunt heads; 25 years ago the bride-price may have been coloured beads and buffalos, while today it might include a bicycle. Certainly though, the bride dowry can be very high and some Sumbanese men migrate to areas where the bride price is more reasonable.

Churches are now a fairly common sight, and in some areas traditions are dying, but elsewhere, particularly in the west, they thrive.

Villages

A traditional village usually consists of two more or less parallel rows of houses facing each other, with a square in between. In the middle of the square is a stone with another flat stone on top of it, on which offerings are made to the village's protective marapu.

These structures, spirit stones or *kateda*, can also be found in the fields around the village, and are used for offerings to the agricultural marapu when planting or harvesting.

The village square also contains the stone-slab tombs of important ancestors, usually finely carved, but nowadays often made of cement. In former times the heads of slain enemies would be hung on a dead tree in the village square while ceremonies and feasts took place. These skull-trees, called *andung*, have all but disappeared from villages today, but are still a popular motif on Sumbanese ikat.

A traditional Sumbanese dwelling is a large rectangular structure raised on piles; it houses an extended family. The thatched (or nowadays often corrugated-iron) roof slopes gently upwards from all four sides and in the loft are placed *marapu maluri* objects (see Religion later in this section for further details).

Rituals accompanying the building of a house include an offering, at the time of planting the first pillar, to find out if the marapu agree with the location; one method is to cut open a chicken and examine its liver. Many houses are decked with buffalo horns or pigs' jaws from past sacrifices.

Dress

Many Sumbanese men still carry long-bladed knives in wooden sheaths tucked into their waistbands. Traditionally a *sirih* (betel nut) pouch and *tongal* would also be carried. The tongal is a wooden or horn pouch with magic powers to protect the owner, and contains mamuli or other magical objects. Men wear *tiara patang*, scarves wrapped as turbans with a peak at the front pointing to marapu. The *kelambu herang* is a brightly coloured sarong tied around the waist with ends trailing in front to expose the lower two-thirds of their legs, with a long piece of cloth hanging down in front and pointing to the earth, symbolising the mother.

A woman may have her legs tattooed after the birth of her first child as a recognition of status; often it will be the same motifs that are on her sarong. Another custom, teeth filing, has all but died out, but you'll still see older people with short, brown teeth from the time when white teeth were considered ugly.

Social Structure

Traditional Sumbanese society has four levels; although there is little evidence of Hindu religious influence in Sumba, these levels have distinct resemblances to the Hindu caste system.

The top level belongs to the *ratu*, the spiritual chief or priest. In West Sumba, the term *rato* is used. The ratu are the keepers of the spiritual wellbeing of the clan or village and are responsible for maintaining marapu tradition, divining ceremonial dates and consulting the ancestors on other important decisions. The ratu are said to have magical powers.

The next level belongs to the *maramba*, the royal or ruling classes. This level is further divided into three strata. The first is that of the *tamu umbu* (kings) and *tamu rambu* (queens). Although a clan or village grouping may be headed by a king, descent is not necessarily of direct blood line. Through strategic alliances or to appease factions, a new king or even a queen may be chosen from a royal family other than that of the present ruler. The second level of maramba belongs to the *umbu* and *rambu*, which are royal rankings below that of the kings and queens. The third level belongs to the *umbu nai* and *rambu nai*, wealthy individuals that are allowed to own slaves. In fact, they take the name of their slaves, eg if the slave is called Ndilu then his master is Umbu Nai Ndilu.

Below the maramba are the *kabisu* or ordinary people, and then come the *ata* or slaves. Slaves have always played an important part in Sumbanese society and were taken in war, but they also exist as a hereditary caste serving the maramba. They performed duties more like servants than slaves and even when the practice of slavery was abolished after independence, many ata willingly remained in the households of their owners. When a slave owner died, the ata also would be killed, although many gladly threw themselves into their masters or mistresses graves to appease marapu tradition. A few ata still exist, particularly in the royal villages of East Sumba, and it is said that though they are no longer killed when their owner dies, soon after the ata will often pass away in a car accident or through some other divine intervention. Ata are divided into two categories: *ata umung*, hereditary slaves belonging to the household, and the *ata nganding*, slaves taken in war or slaves owned by a woman and brought into the household by marriage.

Visiting Villages

Many Sumbanese villages these days are accustomed to tourists, but even those that get a steady stream sometimes have difficulty understanding the strange custom of westerners who simply want to observe 'exotic' cultures. If you're interested in their weavings or other artefacts, the villagers can put you down as a potential trader. If all you want to do is chat and look around, they may be puzzled about why you've come, and if you simply turn up with a camera and start putting it in their faces, they're likely to be offended.

On Sumba, giving betel nut *(sirih pinang)* is the traditional way of greeting guests or hosts, and it's a great idea to take some with you – it's cheap and you can get it at most markets in Sumba. Offer it to the *kepala desa* (village head) or to the other most 'senior'-looking person around.

Some villages have grown used to foreigners arriving without sirih. In these places, appointed representatives keep a visitors' book, which they'll produce for you to sign and you should donate 1000 rp or so. In off-the-beaten-track kampungs, offering money or cigarettes is also OK, especially if you make it clear that you're offering it because you don't have any sirih. This way you still conform to the give-and-take principle.

Whatever the circumstances, taking a guide, at least to isolated villages, is a big help. A guide smooths over any language difficulties and through them you should learn enough about the behaviour expected of guests to feel confident visiting villages alone. No matter where you go, taking the time to chat with the villagers helps them to treat you more as a guest than a customer or alien. Remember that when you enter a village, you are in effect walking into a home.

RELIGION

Catholic missionaries came to Sumba in the 1890s, but because of the island's isolation and lack of colonial control, Christianity did not penetrate until relatively recently. In 1903, Sumba had only 3000 Christians and many were Sabunese migrants. Dutch Calvinist missionaries, with their main base at Lewa, were the main proselytising force from the 1930s and continued after WWII, but while Christianity has penetrated many villages, animism is still strong and many villages have not converted. Islam has made few inroads, and Muslims are mostly Endenese or other migrants.

The basis of traditional Sumbanese religion is marapu, the first ancestors of a clan, or more generally a collective term for the ancestral spirits that look after the village and mediate with the other gods and spirits. The most important event in a person's life is death, when they join the invisible world of the marapu, from where they can influence the world of the living. *Marapu mameti* is the collective name for all dead people. The living can appeal to them for help, especially to their own relatives, though the dead can be harmful if irritated. The *marapu maluri* are the original people placed on earth by god; their power is concentrated in certain places or objects, much like the Javanese idea of *semangat*.

Death Ceremonies

On the day of burial, horses or buffalos are killed to provide the deceased with food for their journey to the land of marapu. Ornaments and a sirih bag are also buried with the body. The living must bury their dead as richly as possible to avoid being reprimanded by the marapu mameti. Without a complete and honourable ceremony, the dead cannot enter the invisible world and roam about menacing the living. It was said the dead travel to Cape Sasar to climb the ladder to the invisible world above.

One Sumbanese custom which parallels the Torajan customs of central Sulawesi is the deliberate destruction of wealth to gain prestige, often by sponsoring festivals where many buffalos would be slaughtered. Funerals may be delayed for several years, until enough wealth has been accumulated for a second burial accompanied by the erection of a massive stone-slab tomb. In some cases the dragging of the tombstone from outside the village is an important part of the procedure. Sometimes hundreds are needed to move the block of stone and the family of the deceased feeds them all. A *ratu*, or priest, sings for the pullers, which is answered in chorus by the group. The song functions as an invocation to the stone.

When the Indonesian republic was founded, the government introduced a slaughter tax in an attempt to stop the destruction of livestock and lessen the economic burden imposed by large ritual slaughters. This reduced the number of animals killed, but didn't alter basic attitudes. The Sumbanese believe you *can* take it with you. More recently, laws have been passed restricting the number of animals that can be killed, but this applies mostly in West Sumba, where the slaughter of more than four or five large animals will attract the attention of the police. In East Sumba, the ritual slaughter of dozens of large animals still takes place.

LANGUAGE

Sumba has seven main languages. Sumbanese (also referred to as East Sumbanese or, locally, as Hilu Humba) is spoken throughout East Sumba. The six languages of West Sumba are: Anakalang, Wejewa, Mamboru, Wanokaka, Lamboya and Kodi. These are all closely related, but mutually unintelligible.

Bahasa Indonesia is spoken almost everywhere, but you'll come across a number of isolated villages where it isn't spoken, particularly in the west around Kodi. English isn't widely spoken outside the main towns of Waingapu and Waikabubak.

Sumbanese (Hilu Humba)
Useful Phrases

How are you?	*Mala hiana?*
Where are you going?	*Nggi lua mu?*
I'm going to the market.	*Lua nggu la pahang.*
Which way is (Rindi)?	*Langgiya na anda laku la (Rindi)?*
How far is it from here to (Rindi)?	*Pira marauna weli yohung laku la (Rindi)?*
Where is Riatang's house?	*Langgiya na umanai Riatang?*

Useful Words

good	*hamu*
big	*bokul*
small	*kudu*
hot	*mbana*
cold	*maringu*
beach	*tehik*
hill	*ana palindi*
mountain	*palindi*
river	*luku*
village	*kuatak*
day	*lodu*
week	*minggu*
east	*pahunga lodu* (lit: sunrise)
west	*patama lodu* (lit: sunset)

People & Families

person	*tau*
woman	*tau kawini*
man	*tau mini*
baby	*ana rara*
child	*ana keda*
father	*ama*
mother	*ina*
wife	*papaha*
husband	*lei*

Numbers

1	*diha*	6	*nomu*
2	*dua*	7	*pihu*
3	*tailu*	8	*walu*
4	*patu*	9	*hiwa*
5	*lima*	10	*hakambulu*

SUMBA

11	*hakambulu hau*
12	*hakambulu dambu*
13	*hakambulu tailu*
14	*hakambulu patu*
20	*dua kambulu*
21	*dua kambulu hau*
22	*dua kambulu dambu*
30	*tailu kambulu*
100	*hangahu*
101	*hangahu hau*
200	*dua ngahu*
300	*tailu ngahu*
1000	*hariu* (Rende)
	harata (Waingapu)

Getting There & Around

AIR

Waingapu is the main entry point into Sumba. Merpati has flights to/from Kupang and Denpasar, but planes are small, seats limited and flights are subject to cancellation. Book as far ahead as possible when you arrive in Waingapu if you intend to fly out of Sumba, and make sure your booking is confirmed. This is most important in the main tourist season around August. Bouraq also has services between Waingapu, Kupang and Denpasar. Its beat-up plane is larger and seats are slightly easier to get, but again it is subject to cancellation and should be booked as far in advance as possible.

Merpati also flies from Tambolaka, 42km north-west of Waingapu, to Bima. Very small planes fly on this route and are subject to cancellation. Onward bookings from Bima are difficult to confirm and flights may be overbooked.

Although in theory you can book flights out of Sumba from Merpati offices in the rest of Indonesia, in practice they simply can't be bothered. Even if you do have a booking, it won't be confirmed until you front up at the airline office in Waingapu or Waikabubak. Don't rely on a flight out of Sumba – have a few days up your sleeve in case something goes wrong.

BUS

As in most of East Nusa Tenggara, buses are small, crowded and stop everywhere. Many of the roads, however, are good and travel between the main towns is relatively quick once the bus finally departs after endlessly doing the rounds for passengers. Bus stations are central, but in any case buses will pick up and drop off at hotels.

The main highway from Waingapu to Waikabubak and on to Waikelo is one of the best in the region – relatively flat, straight and well made. From Waingapu an excellent road runs to Melolo; from Melolo to Baing the road is sealed, but rougher. Many other roads are now sealed, the main exceptions are those along the south coast and most of the north coast road west of Napu.

A reasonable network of buses and bemos runs to the villages, while trucks do the runs on the bad roads. Travel is much slower and harder on the back roads. Market days are the best days to travel into the backblocks when many more services are available.

BOAT

Waingapu is well serviced by ferries from Ende on Flores, the main departure point for getting to Sumba. Ferries also run to/from Kupang (Timor) via Sabu or Ende. Pelni has useful services between Ende and Waingapu, and Labuanbajo and Waingapu, and long-distance hops from Lombok and to Denpasar. See under Waingapu and other departure towns for details.

The main port in West Sumba is Waikelo. Rumours persist of a connection to Bima starting up, but don't hold your breath.

CAR & MOTORCYCLE

Sumba is relatively compact and with your own vehicle it's easy to get out into the countryside and explore many sights. Cars can be hired through hotels in Waingapu and Waikabubak, but they are not cheap. Hire is more easily arranged in Waingapu, which also has a few private taxis. Waikabubak has few cars – private or for hire. For days trips around these towns it is usually cheaper to charter a bemo.

Motorcycling is an ideal way to see the

SUMBA

countryside. Traffic is light and many of the roads are in good condition, but make sure you know the state of the roads before heading down them. Motorcycle hire can easily be arranged in Waikabubak, and though Waingapu has no regular rental agencies, if you ask around you can always find something.

East Sumba

Centred on Waingapu, East Sumba is the usual first stop on a visit to Sumba. Waingapu is by far the largest town on Sumba and the main commercial centre, but outside Waingapu, East Sumba is very lightly populated compared with the more fertile west and has the lowest population density in all Nusa Tenggara. Most villages are on the barren, dry and inhospitable northern plains that primarily support husbandry. Further inland, the countryside rises to steep mountains that form a barrier to the much lusher south coast, but this long-isolated area is also lightly populated and difficult to access.

East Sumba has some fine beaches, but the main points of interest are the royal villages

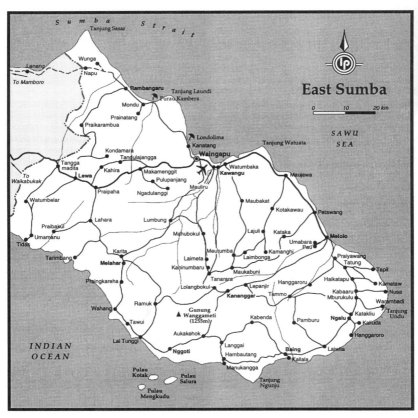

around Waingapu, which are the production centres for Sumba's famed ikat. With a longer trading contact with the outside world, these villages generally developed more sophisticated societies than the villages of West Sumba, but modern influences are also more noticeable.

Saturday is the main market day throughout East Sumba.

WAINGAPU

The largest town on Sumba, Waingapu (population 30,000) became the administrative centre after the Dutch took over the island in 1906. It had long been the centre of the trade controlled by the coastal princedoms, with textiles and metal goods brought in by traders from Makassar, Bima and Ende, and the much-prized Sumba horses, dyewoods and timber being exported.

Waingapu is the main entry point to Sumba, but the island's attractions lie elsewhere, in the west and south-east. The town does have a large group of ikat traders who run shops or hang around outside hotels (see Things to Buy later in this section).

Orientation & Information

Waingapu has two centres: the older, northern one focuses on the harbour; the southern one is around the main market and bus terminal, about 1km inland.

The Bank BNI on Jl Ampera near the market is open Monday to Friday from 7.45 am to 3.45 pm (closed for lunch from 1 to 2 pm) and Saturday from 7.30 am to noon. The Bank Rakyat Indonesia on Jl Ahmad Yani is open weekdays from 7 am to 4.45 pm and Saturday from 7 to 11 am.

The post office is on Jl Hasanuddin and the Telkom office on Jl Tjut Nya Dien is open 24 hours. In the new part of town, a wartel is attached to the Hotel Surabaya.

Places to Stay

Hotel Permata Sari, otherwise known as Ali's, is near the harbour and is handy if arriving by ferry. Ali, the owner, speaks excellent English and is a mine of information on things to do in Sumba. Well kept rooms are 5000 rp per person and face a half-finished new block that had its permit withdrawn because of Ali's involvement with the PDI, the opposition political party.

If the Permata Sari is full, as it sometimes is when the ferries dock, the *Hotel Lima Saudara* (☎ 61083) at Jl Wanggameti 2 is the nearest hotel, but apart from the pleasant front porch, it's an overpriced dive. Singles/doubles with mandi and midget-sized beds are 9000/17,500 rp.

The other hotels are in the new part of town. The next best budget choice after Ali's is the quiet and friendly *Hotel Kaliuda* (☎ 61264) at Jl WJ Lalaimentik 3. This well run hotel has rooms with shared mandi for 12,100 rp and pleasant rooms with mandi at the back facing the garden for 16,500 rp.

Hotel Surabaya (☎ 61125), at Jl El Tari 2, has nondescript rooms upstairs above its nondescript restaurant for 8500/15,000 rp, or 10,000/18,000 rp for rooms with attached mandi.

The *Hotel Sandle Wood* (☎ 61887), at Jl Panjaitan 23, is an attractive mid-range hotel close to the bus terminal. It has a landscaped garden, an art shop and a wide variety of rooms. Small, run-down rooms with outside mandi cost 11,000/16,500 rp, but much better rooms with attached mandi are good value for 16,500/22,000 rp. Air-con rooms are 27,500/38,500 rp. It has a restaurant, but don't bother. Service is sometimes a bit lacking.

The *Hotel Elvin* (☎ 62097) at Jl Ahmad Yani 73 is well run and has a good restaurant and large rooms. Renovated rooms with bathroom and air-con cost 15,000/20,000 rp and 25,000/35,000 rp. Older rooms are empty awaiting a renovation that will turn this into one of Waingapu's bigger hotels.

The *Hotel Merlin* (☎ 61300) on Jl Panjaitan 25 has good service and is the top hotel in town. Rooms start at 16,500/22,000 rp with shower, intercom and comfy beds. Air-con rooms with TV are 27,500/38,500 rp, while the VIP rooms at 44,000/55,000 rp have hot water. The 4th floor restaurant has great views, and the hotel has an art shop attached.

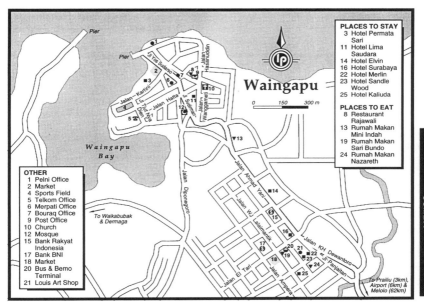

PLACES TO STAY
3 Hotel Permata Sari
11 Hotel Lima Saudara
14 Hotel Elvin
16 Hotel Surabaya
22 Hotel Merlin
23 Hotel Sandle Wood
25 Hotel Kaliuda

PLACES TO EAT
8 Restaurant Rajawali
13 Rumah Makan Mini Indah
19 Rumah Makan Sari Bundo
24 Rumah Makan Nazareth

OTHER
1 Pelni Office
2 Market
4 Sports Field
5 Telkom Office
6 Merpati Office
7 Bouraq Office
9 Post Office
10 Church
12 Mosque
15 Bank Rakyat Indonesia
17 Bank BNI
18 Market
20 Bus & Bemo Terminal
21 Louis Art Shop

SUMBA

Places to Eat

Waingapu is not overly endowed with good eateries.

The *Rumah Makan Mini Indah* at Jl Ahmad Yani 27 is a simple place, but has very tasty food – choose from the selection in the showcase. *Restaurant Rajawali* on Jl Sutomo is a reasonable choice in the old part of town. The *Rumah Makan Sari Bundo*, near the market, serves Padang food.

The new *Rumah Makan Nazareth* opposite the hotel Kaliuda is the pick of the town's restaurants and serves good Chinese and Indonesian food.

Otherwise, try your luck at the hotels. The *Hotel Merlin* has a large 4th floor restaurant with Indonesian and western food, and great views. The *Hotel Elvin* has a spick-and-span restaurant with a wide variety of good Indo-nesian and Chinese dishes. The slightly grotty *Hotel Surabaya* has cold beer and cheap but quite small servings of Chinese food.

Things to Buy

Waingapu has several 'art shops' selling ikat from the villages of south-eastern Sumba and artefacts from the west of the island. Traders will also set up impromptu stalls in front of your hotel – some will squat there patiently all day. You can get an idea of the range of quality, design and price before heading out into the villages. Prices in town are higher, though not necessarily by that much, and the range is good.

The Louis Art Shop, at Jl W J Lalaimantik 15 near the Hotel Sandle Wood, is one of the better shops to browse in and has some good ikat pieces and a variety of carvings and other souvenirs. The Hotel Sandle Wood has a huge collection of ikat tucked away in a musty back room; the Hotel Merlin also has a decent range and the owner of the Hotel Elvin has a large collection at his house. Amin Art Shop, at Jl Panjaitan 45 behind the Hotel Merlin, has a good general range and better prices for ikat than most.

Getting There & Away

Air Merpati (☎ 61329) on Jl Soekarno has flights to Denpasar on Monday, Wednesday, Friday and Sunday at 7 am and to Kupang on Monday, Tuesday, Saturday and Sunday at 1 pm. Planes are small, so book as far in advance as possible. Flights are subject to sudden cancellation. Airport tax is 5500 rp.

Bouraq (☎ 61363), at Jl Yos Sudarso 57, also has flights to Denpasar on Tuesday, Thursday, Saturday and Sunday at 7 am and on the same days to Kupang at 1 pm. It has slightly larger planes, but they're also subject to cancellation.

Bus The bus terminal is in the southern part of town, close to the market. Buses to Waika-bubak (5000 rp; five hours) depart at 8 and 8.30 am, noon and 3 pm, but can spend up to an hour cruising town for passengers. Buses pick up from hotels and will drop you at your hotel in Waikabubak. Hotels will book tickets; otherwise go to one of the bus agents opposite the bus terminal. The road to Waika-bubak goes through the Lewa district and Anakalang. It's an excellent paved road. At least seven buses a day go to Lewa (2500 rp) between 8 am and 2 pm, passing Anakalang.

Buses also go via Waikabubak to Waita-bula (6500 rp) at 8.30 am and noon if you are desperate to get to the very west of Sumba in a hurry. There is even a Damri bus all the way to Waikelo at 8 am.

Buses also head south-east to Melolo, Rende and Baing. Several travel through the morning and afternoon to Melolo, with a few continuing on to Rende, Ngalu and Baing. Most return to Waingapu the same day.

Car & Motorcycle Hotels rent cars with driver for out-of-town trips, but may require bargaining. Count on at least 100,000 rp for a full day's touring around eastern Sumba, or 80,000 rp to Waikabubak. There are no motorcycle hire shops, but if you ask around someone will always rent you a bike for around 20,000 rp per day.

Boat Waingapu is well serviced by Perum ASDP ferries sailing to/from Ende and Aimere

on Flores, and to/from Sabu and on to Kupang (Timor). All ferries depart from the old pier in the centre of town. Schedules are subject to change – check them at the harbour.

The KMP *Ile Ape* departs Ende for Waingapu (12,000 rp; 10 hours) on Sunday at 7 pm and continues to Sabu (13,500 rp; nine hours) on Monday at 2 pm. From Sabu it continues on to Kupang on Tuesday at 2 pm. It returns from Sabu on Thursday and sails from Waingapu to Ende on Saturday at 2 pm.

KMP *Rokatenda* sails from Kupang to Ende, and then departs Ende for Waingapu on Tuesday at 7 pm. It returns to Ende on Wednesday at 7 pm.

KMP *Ile Mandiri* does a Sabu-Waingapu-Aimere run, leaving Sabu on Sunday and returning from Aimere on Thursday, but this new run is lightly patronised and may well change.

Pelni ships leave from the Dermaga dock to the west of town – a bemo to this pier is 400 rp per person. The KM *Pangrango* calls in every two weeks at Waingapu on its way to/from Ende or Labuanbajo. The KM *Awu* runs from Lembar on Lombok to Waingapu and on to Ende and in the reverse direction comes from Ende and goes to Bali.

Getting Around

To/From the Airport The airport is 6km south of town on the Melolo road. A taxi into town costs 3000 rp, or minibuses from the Elvin, Sandle Wood and Merlin hotels usually meet incoming flights and offer a free ride to intending guests.

Bemo A bemo to any destination around town costs 400 rp.

AROUND WAINGAPU

Just 3km south of central Waingapu, a few hundred metres west of the main road to the airport, **Prailiu** is the central village of the old Lewa Kambero kingdom and a busy ikat-weaving centre. This mostly modern village, now a suburb of Waingapu, has a few traditional houses and stone tombs worth a look, but the weaving is the main reason to visit. You can see at least some aspects of production going on, and the open-sided central meeting house acts as a showroom for the weavers. Much of the weaving is done to fill large orders, and the quality may not be that high, but some fine pieces can be bought. Bemos to Prailiu run from Waingapu's main bus and bemo terminal (400 rp).

Kawangu, 11km from Waingapu and just off the main road south to Melolo, has some stone-slab tombs and also produces weaving, but it is less interesting than Prailiu.

North-West Coast

The road north-west along the coast from Waingapu makes an interesting day trip from that town. The road leads towards Tanjung (Cape) Sasar, which features in many ancestral stories as the landing site of the first people on Sumba, and is where the oldest villages on Sumba can be visited. The coast also has fine beaches, which are deserted during the week and easily accessed from Waingapu. The road is paved and flat most of the way and traffic is light. Several buses a day run to Mondu, mostly in the morning.

Londalima Ten kilometres out of Waingapu, an old Merpati DC3 is perched above the highway and marks the beach at Londalima. Much like the plane, the planned resort here never got off the ground, but this is a popular weekend beach haunt for Waingapu residents. The derelict plane is in a condition disconcertingly similar to some of Merpati's current fleet.

Purau Kambera A much better beach can be found at Purau Kambera, around 28km from Waingapu, before Mondu. The superb white sand beach here gets few visitors despite the easy access from Waingapu. A fenced compound and a lone bungalow back from the beach marks a planned resort, but don't hold your breath.

Prainatang The only village of note on this lonely stretch of coast is the settlement of **Mondu**, 32km from Waingapu, just before a large bridge spanning the river. This is where

you turn off to Prainatang (also known by the newer name of Prailiang), one of East Sumba's most impressive traditional villages. Villagers have received enough visitors not to be startled by the arrival of tourists, although you should call in and sign the visitors' book at the kepala desa's house in Mondu before heading off. You can ask directions here although you really need a guide to find the village. The road to Prainatang is little more than a goat track, though buses are supposed to go most of the way on market days. Otherwise it is a 3.5km walk up into the barren hills.

The road leads 3km to a paddock on a ridge – a 4WD could make it here – then it is 500m along a walking track. Around a hill, the hidden village of Prainatang emerges. The hilltop village is surrounded by defensive stone walls and has expansive views over a dry, highland plateau where rivers have carved out wide, craggy gorges. The coconut palms and vegetable plots in the valleys below are tended by the villagers.

The village's isolation hid it from the attention of slave traders in past times, but now many of the villagers have moved closer to the highway. The houses of Prainatang are all in traditional design and this is the main marapu village for the area. Traditions and dances are strongly preserved. The elders may tell you that this is the original settlement in Sumba, even though Wunga further down the road is widely held throughout Sumba to take that claim. Whichever was first, this is certainly one of the oldest in Sumba. The houses here are similar, but distinct from others in Sumba, while the squat, weather-beaten stone tombs attest to the village's antiquity and are less adorned than later Sumbanese tombs.

Wunga It is also possible to visit Wunga on the Cape Sasar headland, some 20km beyond Mondu. Similarly hidden in the hills outside Napu, many legends point to Wunga as the first settlement on Sumba. This is a much larger village than Prainatang, and though it has traditional houses, it is less attractive. Crowds of children herald your arrival – this very dry village has to cart water from far away in the dry season and little of this precious commodity can be spared for washing.

Of the many legends about how the first humans arrived at Cape Sasar, one of the most consistent and most interesting is that the first settlers came via a stone bridge from Flores (others say Bima), mirroring scientific explanations of ancient settlement throughout the Indonesian archipelago when the sea level was much lower than today. Another legend tells of how two brothers landed at Cape Sasar and one left to settle Sawu before returning to the eastern tip of Sumba and founding settlement there. It is claimed in Wunga that a fossilised boat can be seen in the cliffs, a few kilometres away on the coast.

From **Napu**, further west, the road continues along the north coast through to West Sumba, but the gravel road is very rough.

SOUTH-EASTERN SUMBA

A number of the traditional villages in the south-east can be visited from Waingapu. The stone ancestor tombs are impressive and the area produces some of Sumba's best ikat. The villagers are quite used to tourists. Almost every village has a visitors' book, and a donation of 1000 rp or so is expected. Ikat for sale will appear.

Melolo

If you don't want to visit the south-east on a day trip from Waingapu, the small town of Melolo, 62km from Waingapu and close to some interesting villages, has one losmen, the friendly and security-conscious *Losmen Hermindo*. Clean rooms with mandi cost 5000 rp per person. If no-one is around, enquire at the Toko Purnamakasih shop on the main street. Basic meals are available on request. Alternatively, the *Warung Pojok* has beef and goat concoctions and the *Warung Ujung* has good sate. A 10 minute walk through the mangroves from Losmen Hermindo brings you to a long, sandy beach, although the water's a bit murky.

The market is about 3km out of town, in the middle of nowhere on a dusty hill. The main market day is Friday, when you may see good blankets and *pahikung* cloth. Bemos run regularly from town to the market (400 rp).

An interesting stop on the way to Melolo is the small *penaraci* factory at Wanga, out in the middle of nowhere on the highway, 47km from Waingapu. Penaraci is the Sumbanese variety of arak, and is distilled from the lontar palm. Although the factory is little more than a shed, friendly Pak Riwu speaks a little English and is proud to show visitors the distillation process. His penaraci is particularly potent, but very smooth.

Getting There & Away Buses and bemos to Melolo from Waingapu (2000 rp; 1½ hours) run hourly until around 4 pm. It's an excellent, paved road and crosses mainly flat grasslands. From Melolo the road continues on to Baing. Another road from Melolo crosses the mountains to Nggongi; trucks run along this road, at least in the dry season.

Praiyawang

Praiyawang, about 7km towards Baing from Melolo, is one of the most important royal villages in East Sumba. It is the central village of Desa Rende (also spelt Rindi) and has an imposing line-up of big stone-slab tombs. A massive, newly built traditional Sumbanese house with concrete pillars faces the tombs, along with a number of older *rumah adat* (traditional houses). Praiyawang provided the main research for Gregory Forth's classic study of Sumbanese society, *Rindi: An Ethnographic Study of a Traditional Domain in Eastern Sumba* in the 70s.

The village is still marapu and the most important ancestral spirit is that of the first ancestor, Umbu Lutung Etindamung. Although the kingdom has been in existence for 18 generations, Praiyawang has only been inhabited for six generations – the village having moved many times because of war. The last raja died in 1961 and the village is now headed by a queen.

The tombs are all of former rajas. As you enter the village, on the left is a group of four old tombs. The one on the far left belongs to the first raja, dating from when Praiyawang was first settled. The raja is represented by a strange half human/half animal figure mounted on top. To the right of this tomb group is a small, oddly shaped rock that marks the place where the andung, or skull tree, once stood. Heads taken in war would be hung from the tree, which has now been removed (as has happened in most villages on Sumba).

Further to the right are two more tombs, including the huge tomb of the third raja. It consists of four stone pillars 2m high, supporting a monstrous slab of stone about 5m long, 2.5m wide and 1m thick. Two stone tablets stand atop the main slab, carved with human, buffalo, deer, lobster, fish, crocodile and turtle figures.

Some fine-quality ikat is produced in Praiyawang. You'll be shown some magnificent ikat, but prices are high. It's possible to stay in the village, but remember that these are members of a royal family, not hotel staff. Act accordingly. Ceremonies can be elaborate, and the main regular ceremonies accompany the harvest around August and the summoning of the rain in November.

Getting There & Away A few buses go from Waingapu to Praiyawang, or Waijelu buses pass right by the village. Otherwise take a bus to Melolo, from where bemos run throughout the day.

Umabara & Pau

Like Praiyawang, these two villages about 4km south-west of Melolo have traditional Sumbanese houses, stone tombs, weavings and are headed by a raja. Umabara, the royal village, is of more interest and the largest tombs are for relatives of the present raja, who speaks some English. The tombs and traditional houses here are very impressive, but the villagers may not be overly interested in you unless you want to buy ikat. Ikat sellers come running at your arrival and sell mostly pahikung cloth. The is the main centre for pahikung, and most of the weavers work in Pau, just a few hundred metres from Umabara.

Getting There & Away From Melolo, bemos can drop you at the turn-off to the villages on the main Waingapu-Melolo road. After about a 20 minute walk there is a horse statue, where you fork right for Umabara or left for Pau, both just a few minutes' further on. A trail also links the two villages. From Waingapu, ask the bus driver to drop you at the turn-off.

Mangili

The Mangili district, centred on Ngalu on the highway, 38km from Melolo, is famed for its ikat. Many villages in the area produce fine weaving, but the most famous weaving centre is **Kaliuda**, reputed to produce the best ikat in all of Indonesia. Kaliuda ikat is noted for its rich natural colours and the fine lines of its motives. However, you might have trouble finding what you want – much of the best stuff gets bought up in large quantities and shipped off to Bali. Still, the villagers are happy to chat and you may see some of the work being produced, even if the prices make you weep. Kaliuda also has some stone-slab tombs.

Getting There & Away About six buses a day leave from Waingapu and Melolo and pass through Ngalu, the first leaving Waingapu at about 7 am and passing through Melolo at about 8.30 am.

From Melolo, the trip takes about one hour and costs 1000 rp. Kaliuda is a 3km walk from Ngalu towards the coast.

Baing

Baing is the main village of the Waijelu district, 124km from Waingapu. This spread out, sleepy settlement has little of interest, but **Kallala**, 2km away on the coast, has a wide, white sand beach and good surf between May and August. An Australian, the renowned Mr David (as he is referred to throughout East Sumba), has lived in Sumba for 20 years, is a mine of information and has set up bungalow accommodation at Kallala (also known as Watulibung). It mostly attracts surfers, but the seas are also renowned for game fishing and the resort has a boat. Accommodation costs 35,000 rp per person in relatively simple bungalows, but the price includes all meals.

Getting There & Away Five or six Waijelu buses per day go to Baing, leaving Waingapu between 7 and 8 am and then noon and 1 pm. They cost 5000 rp, or slightly more for a seat up front, and take about 3½ hours. The road is paved all the way, but is bumpy past Melolo.

A dirt track runs from Baing to Kallala, with many branches, but buses will drop you off at the beach if you ask. To charter a bemo from Waingapu to Kallala will cost around 60,000 to 75,000 rp or a car from the hotels will cost 100,000 rp.

SOUTH COAST

While the north coast is flat and very dry in the dry season, the south coast is more lush and houses Sumba's finest forest areas. Like most of East Sumba it is lightly populated. Cultural attractions are limited, but the scenery is spectacular in parts, with dense forest, beautiful beaches and high mountains. This part of the island is little explored and difficult to access.

Public transport runs to the main villages in the south, but services are infrequent and connections all the way across are very difficult – you really need a jeep. Most roads are sealed, or at least were sealed at some stage, but steep sections and river crossings make a loop along the south coast too tough a trip to contemplate doing by motorcycle.

Lewa

On the main highway west of Waingapu, Lewa is the second largest town in East Sumba. Long the centre of horse breeding, it also has a large Dutch mission and a school. Outside town is a spring with cool, clear water. Lewa has a large market, but is otherwise just a place for bus connections or to get to Tarimbang from the west.

Tarimbang

Tarimbang is a beautiful horseshoe bay, with imposing cliffs on its flanks and reefs on either side of the entry to the bay. It is ringed with superb white sand beaches, backed by forest and the reefs provide right and left-hand breaks for surfers. Tarimbang has good barrels when it is working and the waves are all but deserted, but the surf is fickle.

Although this is primarily a surfing destination, the reefs shelter the bay so the water close to shore is good for swimming and there is decent snorkelling on the sheltered side of the reef. You'll go a long way to find a more beautiful beach, but you'll also have to go a long way to reach Tarimbang.

Tarimbang village, 1km from the beach, has simple homestay accommodation. You'll have to walk to the beach, but the last stretch is through shaded forest. Although surf is the main attraction, you can also visit **Taimandino**, a small marapu village about a 1km walk from Tarimbang.

Places to Stay The friendly *Bogenvil* is the best place to stay and costs 12,500 rp per person including meals. Rooms are of very simple bamboo construction with a mattress on the floor, but English is spoken and the food is good.

The kepala desa also has a six room homestay with a high-peaked Sumbanese roof behind his house. It is also very simple but attractive and costs the same. The main drawback is that there are no mattresses as yet and English is not spoken.

Getting There & Away Two buses per day run to Tarimbang from Waingapu leaving at 7.30 am (maybe 8 or 9 am by the time they find a full complement of passengers). Buses are marked 'Tabundung', the name of the district. The cost is 3500 rp and the trip takes about four hours all up.

Buses take the main highway and then turn off just before Lewa. You could do it in two hours with a car, although it's slightly longer by motorbike. The road is sealed all the way, but very narrow and winding. It crosses the bare mountains south of the highway, and runs along a ridge for much of the way, with drop-offs on either side of the road. You strike forest as you descend to the coast.

Malahar

The road from Tarimbang to Malahar climbs into the mountains, which are higher and more fertile as you approach Malahar. Just before Malahar, the road crosses permanent rivers with bridges.

Malahar is set in a fertile valley and is the administrative centre for the area. This sprawling village is modern and of no particular interest, but five buses per day run to Waingapu (3000 rp). There are no regular buses to Tarimbang. It may be possible to stay with the district administrator, located opposite the football field in the lower part of town.

Praingkareha

This pretty highland village is nestled at the foot of a mountain range that contains the most extensive forests in Sumba. Praingkareha, 118km from Waingapu, is green almost all year round and is surrounded by paddy fields. A small kampung in the village has some interesting high-peaked rumah adat and stone slab tombs, though some of the slabs are broken and the rumah adat need repair. A few minibuses per day run from Waingapu through Malahar and continue on as far as Lai Tunggi.

Air Terjun Laputi (Laputi means 'turning water') is a pretty waterfall that can be seen from the village on the flanks of the mountain, dropping 100m down a rock face. Not much water flows in the dry season, but there's a beautiful pool at the base of the falls. By tradition, women are forbidden to look into it, but an exception is made for foreigners. The falls are about 3km from the village. You can walk through the valley, but it is difficult to find the way – a boy may take you for a few thousand rupiah. By car, head out of town to where the road forks – take the old road to the left which is only a short detour from the main road and rejoins it later. You can walk down to the falls from here, a steep descent and long hike back up.

The source of the falls is a small lake (more of a large pond) a couple of hundred metres further along the road. The lake is fed by a spring, which in turn feeds the waterfall,

and in the lake are tame eels. Feed the eels or splash the water and they will come to you.

Praingkareha to Nggoti

The road from Praingkareha to Wahang is only partly sealed, very rough and fords a number of small rivers. Just past the Air Terjun Laputi it goes through brilliant dense forest on the edge of Sumba's largest forest area.

You pass a few small settlements with thatch houses before reaching **Wahang** on the coast. Wahang has a couple of modern tombs and is on a dark sand beach. Caves in the headland are home to swiftlets and a thriving bird's nest industry. The small opening to the cave opens up into a large, high cavern. A guard is in attendance and may let you in.

From Wahang the road follows the coast to **Lai Tunggi**, a nondescript little settlement. There is a fairly deep river that has to be forded here. Buses run only as far as the river from Waingapu via Praingkareha.

Beyong Lai Tunggi the road follows a surf-pounded stretch of coast and beaches of large pebbles before turning inland to Nggoti. Offshore is the low island of **Pulau Mengkudu** with beautiful wide stretches of beach. Further east is the large island of **Pulau Salura**, which is inhabited, and small **Pulau Kotak** lies in between. No regular boats run to these islands – you might be able to arrange a boat in Kallala.

Nggoti

Nggoti is another royal village with a few tombs, but it is mostly modern and little weaving is produced. The main tomb is that of Umbu Nai Ngguli, the last raja who was buried in 1984, but this is a large concrete tomb. Some more impressive older tombs lie further away into the village. The main adat house opposite the new tomb is interesting for the two buffalo heads adorning the roof, an unusual addition symbolising the power of the kingdom.

The son of the raja, a wealthy man with seven wives, now lives in Waingapu. He has already built his own tomb, an extravagant pavilion bearing little resemblance to traditional Sumbanese tombs, 5km from Nggoti on the way to Kananggar.

Lumbung
As at Praingkareha, the main attraction here is the spectacular 25m-high **waterfall**. Although the falls are not extremely high, the volume of water is huge and it's crystal clear. The road south of Waingapu runs to Lumbung from where it is a 3km walk to the falls unless you have a 4WD.

West Sumba

The traditional village culture of western Sumba is one of the most intact in Indonesia. Kampungs of high-roofed houses are still clustered on their hilltops (a place of defence in times past) surrounding the large stone tombs of their important ancestors.

Away from the towns, old women with filed teeth still go bare breasted and men in the traditional 'turban' and short sarong can be seen on horseback. The agricultural cycle turns up rituals, often involving animal sacrifices, almost year-round, and ceremonies for events like house building and marriage can take place at any time. Some kampungs are unaccustomed to foreigners; take betel nut and contact the kepala desa or other senior villagers before you go wandering around.

West Sumba is much more visited than East Sumba. West Sumba is not necessarily more traditional in its beliefs than East Sumba, but the countryside is more heavily populated and many traditional kampungs are scattered around. Although the north coast is mostly flat and dry, the west coast and the highlands of the interior are more lush, fertile and cooler. Apart from the more attractive scenery and accessible traditional culture, West Sumba is also home to one of Indonesia's most spectacular events – the Pasola.

You should give yourself at least a few days around West Sumba; once you have learned some basic manners as a guest arriving in a village, hopefully armed with some Indonesian, it's possible to do without a guide.

Public transport runs all over West Sumba, but some of the more interesting villages are difficult to reach. Motorbikes can be readily hired in Waikabubak, but cars for hire are rare and expensive. Market days throughout West Sumba are Wednesday and Saturday; on these days public transport connections are much more frequent and service many small villages.

Pasola Festival
During this most famous of Nusa Tenggara's festivals, large teams of colourfully clad horse riders engage in mock battles. Its pattern is similar to that of other ritual warfare that used to take place in Indonesia – the cause not so much a quarrel between opposing forces, as a need for human blood to be spilled to keep the spirits happy and bring a good harvest. Despite the blunt spears that the combatants now use and the efforts of Indonesian authorities to supervise the events, few holds are barred; injuries and sometimes deaths still occur.

The Pasola is part of a series of rituals connected with the beginning of the planting season. It takes place in four different areas in February or March each year, its exact timing determined by the arrival on nearby coasts of a certain type of seaworm called *nyale*. Priests examine the nyale at dawn and from their behaviour predict how good the year's harvest will be. Then the Pasola can begin: it's usually fought first on the beach and then, later the same day, further inland. The opposing 'armies' are drawn from coastal and inland dwellers.

The nyale are usually found on the eighth or ninth day after a full moon. In February Pasola is celebrated in the Kodi area (centred on Kampung Tosi) and the Lamboya area (Kampung Sodan); in March it's in the Wanokaka area (Kampung Waigalli) and the remote Gaura area west of Lamboya (Kampung Ubu Olehka).

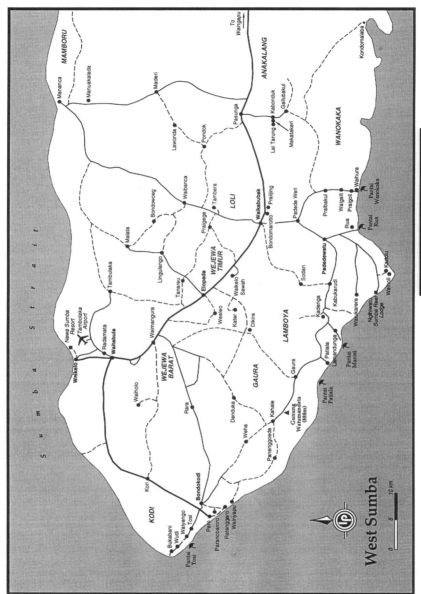

SUMBA

WAIKABUBAK

The neat little town of Waikabubak is at the greener, western end of Sumba, where the tropical trees and rice paddies contrast with the dry grasslands around Waingapu. While the main shopping street and market are modern Indonesian, and the commercial life of town is almost completely Chinese run, dotted in and around the town are traditional clan houses and small graveyards of old stone-slab tombs carved with buffalo horn motifs.

About 600m above sea level, and cooler than the east, Waikabubak is a good base for exploring the villages of West Sumba. In fact there's no need to leave the town at all to experience traditional villages, as some important marapu centres are found right in the town.

Information

The tourist office (☎ 21240), at Jl Teratai 1, is a fair walk to the outskirts of town, but it has a couple of good publications.

The BNI bank on Jl A Yani changes most major currencies and has the best rates. It's open Monday to Friday from 7 am to 4.45 pm (closed for lunch between 12.30 and 1.30 pm) and on Saturday from 7 to 11 am.

The Telkom office is open 24 hours.

Tombs & Traditional Kampungs

From the main street, Waikabubak looks like any other unprepossessing Indonesian town of shops, houses and concrete, but right within the town are very traditional kampungs with stone-slab tombs and thatch houses. Some of these kampungs are more traditional and visiting them is less formalised than many further out – perhaps because most can only be reached on foot along narrow paths, while others further out of town are accessible by vehicle. At most of the kampungs around Waikabubak, locals are accustomed to tourists, so you can see some traditional culture without offending anybody. Many have a visitors book and it is customary to give 1000 rp or so. You may be invited to chew betel nut.

There are at least a dozen kampungs within walking distance of the town centre. Some are architecturally more traditional than others. Ask around to see if anything is happening. Various ceremonies take place throughout the year – stone dragging, and offerings for the harvest season, ancestors, for the building of a rumah adat, weddings etc. Most kampungs are very friendly and they can tell you about any special events in the area.

Kampung Tambelar has very impressive

Betel Nut – The Peacekeeper

One traditional custom that still thrives in parts of Nusa Tenggara, particularly Sumba and Timor, is the chewing of betel nut, or *sirih pinang*. Apart from the obvious reason for chewing it – it gives you a little pep up to help you through the day – there are more complex social and cultural reasons.

Chewing betel is a statement of adulthood, and the three parts that make up the 'mix' that are chewed together have symbolic meaning. The green stalk of the sirih represents the male, the nut or pinang the female ovaries and the lime *(kapor)* is symbolic of sperm. The lime reacts with the betel to cause the characteristic flood of red saliva in the mouth, and when the saliva is spat out, it is believed to be returning the blood of childbirth back to the earth.

Betel nut traditionally played an important role in negotiation and discussion between different clans. Betel nut would always be offered to visitors to a village as a gesture of welcome. If a male entering a village did not accept the betel offered, it was tantamount to a declaration of war.

Even today, if you're offered betel nut never refuse it! Some foreigners have really caused offence by saying, 'No, I don't want to buy it'. If you don't want to chew it, just put it in your pocket or bag. Most foreigners find betel nut pretty disgusting – it tastes a bit like bark. It gives you a mild buzz and a bright red mouth. Fresh betel is much stronger and will give the uninitiated hot flushes. It also creates an amazing amount of saliva, so if you're going to be embarrassed about spitting constantly, you'd better not have any. Whatever you do, don't swallow it – or you're likely to really embarrass yourself! ■

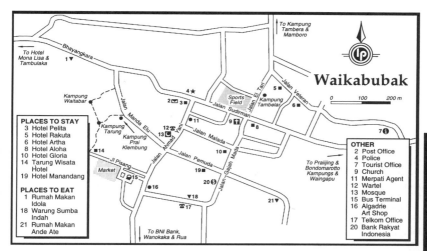

SUMBA

tombs – you could spend days travelling to a remote village and not see better – but the most interesting kampungs are on the western edge of town. It's only a short stroll from most hotels to **Prai Klembung** and then up the ridge to Tarung and **Waitabar**.

Kampung Tarung, reached by a path next to the Hotel Tarung Wisata or off Jl Manda Elu, is one of the most important ritual villages for the whole valley. It is the scene of an important month-long ritual sequence, the Wula Podu, each November. This is an austere period when even weeping for the dead is prohibited. Rites consist mainly of offerings to the spirits the day before it ends, when hundreds of chickens are sacrificed. People sing and dance for the entire final day. Tarung's monuments are under official protection. You might also be shown the human skin drum held in the village.

Plenty of other kampungs are dotted around Waikabubak, such as those on the road to the Hotel Mona Lisa and just off the road at Puunaga, but these are more modern kampungs with concrete tombs.

Other notable kampungs occupying ridge or hilltop positions outside town include **Bondomarotto** and **Praijing**. Kampung

Praijing is especially scenic, perched on a hilltop about 4km from town. There are five neat rows of traditional houses and large stone tombs. **Kampung Prairami** and **Kampung Primkateti** are also beautifully located on adjacent hilltops. You can take a bemo to the turn-off to Praijing.

Another major kampung worth visiting is **Tambera**, 10km north on the road to Mamboru.

Horse Races
Sumba's fine horses are large beasts crossbred with introduced Australian horses, and horse racing is a local obsession. The horse race stadium is about 1.5km west of town, to the left off Jl Bhayangkara heading towards the Hotel Mona Lisa. Races are held sporadically and you may see them practising at any time of the year, but the main races are held for one week around Independence Day in August.

Places to Stay
The friendly *Hotel Aloha* (☎ 21245), at Jl Sudirman 26, is a popular budget choice. It has good information on West Sumba and is housed in spacious new premises. Clean

singles/doubles with shared bath cost 7500/
11,000 rp or 10,000/15,000 rp; with private
bath it's 15,000/20,000 rp.

Another new backpackers' hotel is the
Tarung Wisata Hotel (☎ 21332), at Jl Pisang
26. It is right near the bus station and has a
variety of rooms from 5000/9000 rp up to
12,500/20,000 rp, all including breakfast.
Staff are on the ball with travel information.
It also has a restaurant and a great rooftop
sitting area looking up at Tarung village.

The small *Gloria Hotel* (☎ 21024), at Jl
Gajah Mada 14, is also good value and has
rooms for 7000/9000 rp, or 12,000/15,500 rp
with mandi. It has a good restaurant serving
Chinese food.

The cheapest rooms in town are found at
the *Hotel Pelita* (☎ 21392) on Jl Ahmad Yani.
Dingy rooms are 6000/10,000 rp with shared
mandi, while much better rooms with shower
in the newer block at the back are a reasonable choice and cost 15,000/20,000 rp.

Just around the corner from the Gloria
Hotel at Jl Pemuda 4, the *Hotel Manandang*
(☎ 21197) is the best hotel in town and is
favoured by tour groups. It has a variety of
rooms around the pleasant garden and a good
restaurant. Large, spotless rooms with wash-
basin and comfy beds are good value at
11,000/16,000 rp. Rooms with private bath
range from 20,000/ 25,000 to 40,000/45,000
rp. Prices exclude 10% tax.

Hotel Artha (☎ 21112), at Jl Veteran 11, is
quiet, well run and the next best in town. The
rooms around the courtyard garden start at
17,500 rp with private mandi. VIP rooms
with fan, shower and fridge go for 32,500 rp
and 47,500 rp.

Hotel Rakuta (☎ 21075) on Jl Veteran is
little more than a deserted shell, but will rent
huge rooms for 25,000 rp, if you can find
someone.

The *Hotel Mona Lisa* (☎ 21364) on Jl
Adhyaksa has some of the best rooms, but it
is 2.5km from town and looking tired. Bungalows overlooking the rice paddies cost
25,000/35,000 to 40,000/55,000 rp with TV
and fridge, or a few spotless rooms with
shower cost 15,000/25,000 rp. Add 10% tax
to all prices.

Places to Eat

The *Hotel Manandang* has the best restaurant in town, even if it is a little expensive.
Most of the other hotels serve food, which is
just as well because dining options elsewhere are limited. The *Warung Sumba Indah*
near the Telkom office is a small, Balinese-
run place with a wide variety of tourist services and tasty Balinese food.

There are a few grotty warungs on the
main road opposite the mosque, but the sate
is good and you can see it cooked before your
eyes. Otherwise Waikabubak has some
decent rumah makan. *Rumah Makan Ande
Ate* is cheap, and popular with locals. The
small *Rumah Makan Idola*, at Jl Bhayangkara 55, is a long walk from the centre of
town, but has good Chinese and Indonesian
dishes.

Things to Buy

Traders hang around hotels with ikat cloth,
nearly all of it from East Sumba, and you're
better off buying it there. West Sumba is
noted for elaborate bone, wood, horn and
stone carvings, metal symbols and jewellery.
There are wooden betel nut and *kapor* (lime)
containers with stoppers carved into animal
and human heads; knives with Pasola horse-
men or fertility symbols carved into their
wooden handles; tobacco and money containers made of wood and coconut shell;
stone figures representing marapu ancestors;
and metal omega-shaped symbols called
mamuli, which are worn as earrings and pen-
dants. The one art shop in Waikabubak,
Algadrie on Jl Ahmad Yani, is worth checking before you go out to the villages. Mostly
poor quality souvenirs at high prices are on
display, but a few better pieces can be found
and some interesting stone carvings litter the
garden at back.

Getting There & Away

Air The Merpati agent (☎ 21051) is upstairs
at Jl Ahmad Yani 11. Flights from Tambolaka
go to Bima at 7 am on Monday, Wednesday,
Thursday and Saturday, but only small
planes fly this route and are subject to cancellation. This flight supposedly connects

with flights to Denpasar and Surabaya from Bima, but it is difficult to get confirmation of onward bookings from Bima and if the Tambolaka-Bima flight is late then you are in trouble. Airport tax is 5500 rp.

Bus The bus terminal is central. Buses run to Waingapu (5500 rp; five hours) from 8 am to 1 pm, and every hour throughout the day to Anakalang (1500 rp; 40 minutes), Wanokaka (1000 rp), Lamboya (1500 rp), Waitabula (2000 rp; one hour) and Waikelo. Less frequent and less certain minibuses and trucks run to other villages.

To Waingapu, it's best to book your ticket the day before leaving – your hotel can help, or visit the bus ticket agencies along Jl Ahmad Yani. Buses pick up and drop off at hotels.

Getting Around
To/From the Airport The airport is at Tambolaka, 42km north-west of Waikabubak. Minibuses meet planes and run from the airport to Waikabubak for 4000 rp, but are not reliable running to the airport to meet the flights at 7 am. Ask at Merpati, which is supposed to have a minibus, or a taxi or charter bemo will cost a nasty 45,000 rp. It's not a bad idea to check the flight list at Merpati the day before; if you find out who is going and where they are staying, you can arrange to split the cost.

Bus Bemos run around town and to nearby villages for 400 rp.

Car & Motorcycle Waikabubak is an excellent place to rent a motorbike for exploring West Sumba. Experienced guides are hard to find, though you can probably get someone to go with you for around 10,000 rp per day.

The very friendly Warung Sumba Indah (☎ 21633), at Jl Patimura 7, has a variety of motorcycles for rent for 20,000 rp and 25,000 rp. They are in most demand on weekends. A car and driver can also be hired for 65,000 rp, or 100,000 rp for a better vehicle.

Most hotels can also find a motorcycle for rent, and the Mona Lisa and Manandang

hotels rent vehicles with driver at high rates. They have lists of rates, depending on the destination, but it may be cheaper to ask around elsewhere.

ANAKALANG DISTRICT
Right beside the main road to Waingapu in Anakalang district, **Kampung Pasunga**, 22km east of Waikabubak, boasts one of Sumba's most impressive tomb line-ups. The grave of particular interest consists of a horizontal stone slab with a vertical slab in front of it. The vertical slab took six months to carve with the figures of a man and a woman. The tomb was constructed in 1926; five people are buried here and 150 buffalo were sacrificed during its construction. You can see it from the road.

The more interesting villages are south of town. Walk 10 minutes along the road past the market to **Kabonduk**, home to Sumba's heaviest tomb weighing in at 70 tonnes. The construction is said to have taken 2000 workers three years to chisel the tomb out of a hillside and drag it to the site.

From Kabonduk, it is a very pleasant 15 minute walk across the fields and up the hill to **Makatakeri**, where you may be offered some 'antik' woodcarvings. Makatakeri has interesting traditional houses, though most people now live further down the hill. Five minutes further on from Makatakeri is **Lai Tarung**, the original ancestral village for the area and the most important marapu centre in Anakalang. This ancestral village of 12 local clans is now mostly deserted except for a few families that act as marapu caretakers. There are impressive views over the surrounding countryside to the coast, and there are traditional houses and several tombs scattered around. One traditional house, rebuilt with government assistance, acts as a meeting house and heirloom storehouse for the surrounding villages. A large and unique ancestral stone lies in its own small house. Lai Tarung comes alive for the Purungu Takadonga Ratu – a festival honouring the ancestors – held every year around June. Festivals here are celebrated with extra pomp and the local dancers are renowned for their artistry – you will be proudly told how a group was selected to dance overseas some years back. From Lai Tarung it is possible to walk further north and down the hill back to the highway.

At **Gallubakul**, 2.5km down the road from Kabonduk, the Umba Sawola tomb is a single piece of carved stone about 5m long, 4m wide and nearly 1m thick. You'll be asked to sign in and pay 1000 rp to take photos.

Getting There & Away

Regular bus services run throughout the day between Waikabubak and Anakalang (1500 rp; 40 minutes) or buses to Waingapu can drop you on the highway.

SOUTH OF WAIKABUBAK

The road south of Waikabubak runs over the hills and down to the superb beaches of the coast. The south, comprising the Wanokaka and Lamboya districts, is also home to some interesting traditional villages and hosts the Pasola in February and March. The area makes a good day trip, although basic accommodation is available.

Heading south of Waikabubak the sealed road climbs to the first main crossroad at Padede Weri which is little more than a barren ridge. The road forks left and heads down the hills past many villages to Wanokaka district, centred around Waigalli about 15km south of Waikabubak. The area has numerous traditional kampungs and is the scene of one of the March Pasolas. The Watu Kajiwa tomb in **Praigoli** is said to be one of the oldest in the area. **Waihura** is close to a fine beach on an impressive bay, but the road to the beach is very rough.

Continuing straight on from Padede Weri, the road leads to the large market at Padedewatu. Just beyond the market stalls is the small village and the turn off to Gaura. Continue straight on and after 1km the road forks again – left to Rua and right to Ngihiwatu.

The Rua road leads downhill about 3km to **Pantai Rua**, passing Rua village en route. Pantai Rua is a superb beach, partly sheltered by a reef. The only blight on the landscape is

the new concrete wharf jutting out into the middle of the bay, a misguided development scheme that attracts few ships because of the continual swells. Pantai Rua has a couple of kiosks selling biscuits, drinks and not much else. Directly opposite the kiosks is the *Homestay Ahong*. Right on the beach, this is a simple but comfortable holiday house belonging to a Waikabubak shop owner, but when not in use it can be rented for around 10,000 rp per person. Ask around for the *penjaga* (caretaker). It is best to bring your own food.

Ngihiwatu is 6km from Padede Watu, south along a sealed road past the turnoff to Rua. On the headland overlooking another beautiful beach is the *Sumba Reef Lodge*, a long-standing luxury resort that never really got off the ground because of lack of funds. However, reconstruction has started and it may be open again in the near future. Until then you will be turned back at the gate.

The beaches at Ngihiwatu and west along the coast to Pantai Morosi have some excellent breaks for surfers, and you can stay at **Watukarere** with Pak Mete Bulu, the kepala desa. Watukarere is 5km from Padede Watu, back from the beach on a hill, the next headland west from Ngihiwatu. Take the road south from Padede Watu, and about 1km past the Rua turnoff is the school. Just beyond the school is a rough, dirt track leading 2km to Watukarere.

Watukarere is an interesting traditional village of high-roofed houses and stone tombs. The kepala desa's *Homestay Mete Bulu* is the largest traditional house and the only one with an iron roof. It costs 15,000 rp per person including meals, but conditions are very basic. You get a mattress on the floor and the mandi is the local spring, 100m away. However, it's an interesting place to stay and, although primarily a bunkhouse for surfers, it is also a convenient base in the Pasola season. The village podhu festival is held in October. Buses run only as far as Padede Watu or charter a bemo from Waikabubak for 25,000 to 30,000 rp.

The main road through the Lamboya district runs west from Padede Watu. The first village of any importance is **Kabukarudi**, a large village – almost a town – but modern and of little interest. **Sodan** lies further inland in the hills along a bad road. This important marapu village is the centre for the Lamboya Pasola (further west), but a fire destroyed many of the traditional houses some years ago.

Further along the main road is **Kadenga** one of the most impressive traditional villages in Lamboya with many high-peaked houses clustered together on a small hill next to the road. Just before Kadenga is **Liling**, noted for the tomb of Rato Dere, a powerful priest who it is said could kill with the point of a finger.

Just past Kadenga the road descends to a flat plain. A turnoff to the right leads to Gaura or continue straight ahead through the modern village of **Lamandunga** to **Pantai Marosi**, one of the finest beaches on the coast. Pantai Marosi has good surf, sheltered areas for swimming and a walk in either direction will take you to more deserted white sand beaches. Pantai Marosi is supposed to have homestay accommodation – perhaps you will have more success finding it than we did. Pantai Marosi is not serviced by public transport.

The road to Gaura is paved and scenic, passing the turnoff to **Patiala**, another good beach, before winding its way into the hills. **Gaura** itself is just a large village with a mission school on the outskirts. This is more or less the end of the road unless you have a jeep. From Gaura a road runs all the way to the Kodi district through isolated and lightly populated countryside, but it is only partly paved with steep, gravelly sections leading down to river beds that are impassable in the wet season. Halfway along, it turns into little more than a dirt track. Experienced motocross riders with a trail bike could negotiate this torture trail, but it is quicker and safer to return to Waikabubak and then take the main road to Kodi.

Getting There & Away
Wanokaka district buses run south-east to Waigalli from where it is a 5km walk to

Praigoli. Lamboya district buses cover the towns of the south-west and run through Padede Watu to Kadenga, Kabukarudi and Walakaka, but they don't usually run to the beaches. Buses leave roughly ever hour throughout the day from Waikabubak.

By far the best way to visit the area is by car or motorcycle. Most roads are sealed and traffic is light. The hills south of Waikabubak are a very taxing ride for cyclists.

KODI DISTRICT
Kodi is the westernmost region of Sumba, and the small town of Bondokodi, 3km from the coast, is the centre of this district. The Kodi area offers plenty of attractions: villages with incredible, high-peaked houses and unusual megalithic tombs; long, white sand beaches with waves pounding off coral reefs; and the opportunity to see or buy some fascinating local wood, bone and horn carvings. If you're on foot, you won't see much of the region unless you stay at least a couple of days.

The biggest **market** in the region is at Kori, held every Wednesday; to get there, people from around the region hang off any vehicle they can get hold of, so it must be good. A couple of buses run from Bondokodi in the morning, before 8 am.

Visiting Villages
Kodi is one of the most traditional areas of Sumba. Modernity has hardly penetrated in some villages, the roads are rough, electricity and contacts with the outside world limited, some women still go bare breasted in the villages, education is limited and many villagers don't speak Indonesian. The local language is very different from the others in West Sumba and is considered very *kasar* (crude or coarse) compared with the more refined Wanokaka dialect. Christianity has made few inroads.

The people are also regarded as very kasar by the others on West Sumba, and it is true that they can be very direct, if not downright aggressive. Some villages get a steady trickle of visitors, which perhaps explains the negative reaction that you may encounter. There

SUMBA

are persistent (but unconfirmed) rumours of tourists who have wandered into villages, behaved inappropriately and have been chased out by rock-throwing villagers. The reaction you receive may well depend upon the behaviour of the tourists that have preceded you. You can visit one village and receive a warm welcome and then head just 1km along the road to another village to a completely different reception.

The kids in particular can be a real pain. Tourists are rare, but kids have seen enough to know that they are a source of cigarettes, pens and money, and may not just ask but demand them. Some travellers have reported being mobbed by kids, jostled, cigarette packets snatched from their hands and even being spat on, while the elders look on. This is certainly the exception rather than the rule, and many villages are friendly if you take the time and behave appropriately. If your reception is unwelcoming, make a polite exit and don't hang around.

Tourism is not organised and villages generally cannot see the reason, let alone the benefit, of tourists visiting. A guest book/ donation system generally doesn't exist – perhaps if it did, tourism would be more welcome. You should bring betel nut and follow usual protocol when visiting a village – ask permission to enter a village, try to meet the kepala desa first and make an effort to chat and introduce yourself to the villagers. Male visitors should be cautious about approaching women (first approach a senior looking man). Don't start snapping photos and always ask permission first. Don't strip off and start bathing on a beach near a village.

The best answer is to take someone with you who speaks Kodi and is preferably known to the village, but guides are virtually nonexistent. Even if you speak Indonesian, many villagers don't, though you can always find someone who does.

Asking directions can be a problem. Establish that the person you ask can speak Indonesian before you take their advice. A wave of the arm or a nod in answer to your queries for directions may mean that they don't understand a word of what you have said.

Pero

Pero is a friendly coastal village situated on spectacular coastline just a couple of kilometres from Bondokodi. Settled by descendants of Endenese slave traders, this Muslim village makes a very relaxed and easy-going base for visiting the surrounding area.

Bone, horn, wood and stone carvings are unique to the area; many inexpensive and attractive souvenirs can be purchased. Pero has a fine beach, and the break in the reef allows entry for boats to this small harbour. Although not much good for swimming, Pero has good left and right breaks for surfers out on the channel.

Places to Stay *Homestay Stori* in the centre of Pero is clean and cosy. The cost is 13,000 rp per person, including three meals, and the food is excellent. The only drawback is the proximity to the mosque. It can be full in the main August tourist season and at Pasola time, but the friendly Muslim family will always find you a bed with relatives down the road. At night, an impromptu art shop sets up on the front porch.

Getting There & Away From Kodi a direct bus leaves for Waikabubak (3000 rp; four hours) at around 6 am, returning to Kodi around noon. Otherwise, from Waikabubak take one of the frequent buses to Waitabula (1500 rp) and then a bus or bemo to Bondokodi. Most of the Bondokodi buses will drop you in Kodi on request. From Waikabubak to Bondokodi, the main road goes via Waitabula. The road via Rara is scenic, but much rougher and hillier.

Transport to surrounding villages is more frequent on Wednesday and Saturday market days.

Around Pero

To visit traditional kampungs on foot, go either north or south along the coast.

To get to **Ratenggaro**, first cross the freshwater pool that runs to the coast below Pero. At low tide you could wade across; otherwise small boys will get you across in canoes. From the other side, follow the dirt track for about 3km along Pantai Radukapal, a long stretch of white sand beach, until you come to the fenced kampung of Ratenggaro. Numerous tombs are scattered outside the wall in the front of the village; most are concrete, but some are impressive. The villagers, particularly the women, are very shy, but this is usually a friendly village. The kepala desa speaks Indonesian and it may be possible to stay with him.

The view from Ratenggaro along the coastline is breathtaking – coconut palms fringe the shoreline and the high roofs of **Wainyapu** peep out above the trees across the river. On the near side of the river mouth, unusual stone tombs occupy a small headland, and you'll find some impressive megaliths. To get to Wainyapu, you'll have to wade across the river at low tide or take a canoe, or it can be approached by a rough road from the south. Wainyapu also gets the occasional surfer, attracted by the good right-hand break.

On the way to Ratenggaro you can see the roofs of **Kampung Paranobaroro** through the trees about 1km inland. Here are houses with even higher roofs, stone statues, and an elaborate house with pig jaws and numerous buffalo horns hanging from its verandah. During the day, women weave and the men may be out tending the crops.

Another way to reach Ratenggaro and Paranobaroro is to head south from Bondokodi market for about 1km and take the road to the right past the school. It is paved half of the way and runs past a few houses. After about 3km you reach a fence where the road turns to a dirt track – follow the track around to the left towards to coast to reach Ratenggaro, 2km away. About a kilometre before Ratenggaro you pass another fenced traditional village with a few tombs. For Paranobaroro, keep heading straight ahead from the fence, but many tracks criss-cross the plain around here – ask directions, if you can find someone who speaks Indonesian. This way is a long hot walk on foot, but is easily negotiable by motorbike in the dry season.

Wainyapu can also be reached by a rough

road off the main road south. The main road is sealed much of the way to **Weha** where an impressive bridge crosses a deep gorge and swift river. Weha has a lively Wednesday market, but is more noted throughout Kodi for the fact that its kepala desa has 12 wives. The road beyond Weha becomes increasing bad.

To reach **Tosi**, about 6km west of Bondokodi and the scene of the Kodi Pasola in February, head north from Bondokodi market along the paved road. If you are coming from Pero, it's simply left at the T-intersection. About 1km along the road you'll see a track on your left. Follow it for 5km, past a series of tombs. You'll soon see Tosi's roofs on your right, but Tosi has obviously received too many tourists. Many people report problems here and we found it to be decidedly aggressive. Avoid entering the village. From Tosi it is a 10 minute walk to the beach, and a track runs all the way back to Pero. Back on the paved road, from the turnoff to Tosi you can continue right along to the cape for fine coastal views. The road is negotiable by motorbike, but becomes progressively rougher. Other villages just off the road can be visited, and the reception is better than at Tosi.

WEJEWA TIMUR
This region less than 20km west of Waikabubak sees relatively few tourists because of the lack of transport. You will probably need a jeep to explore the area. The people here have maintained their traditional culture and are very friendly. The villages of **Weeleo** and **Kater**, both near Elopada, make interesting day trips.

WAITABULA
This market town, on the main highway between Tambolaka airport and Waikabubak, is West Sumba's second largest town. It almost adjoins nearby Radamata, but even combined this conurbation is sleepy by any standards. Waitabula's market, on the outskirts of town to the north, comes alive on Wednesday and is one of the biggest in West Sumba.

SUMBA

Waitabula is mostly a transit point, with frequent buses to Bondokodi/Pero, Waikelo and Waikabubak. Direct buses run all the way to Waingapu. The town also has a good losmen, which can be used as a base to explore the surrounding area.

Places to Stay & Eat

Losmen Anggrek is on the main road opposite the Catholic church as you come into Waitabula from the south. There is no sign – ask for Ibu Imanudu if you draw a blank. Well kept rooms at the back cost 8000 rp per person or 10,000 rp with attached mandi. Meals are not provided, but Waitabula has a couple of basic *warungs* in the centre of town.

WAIKELO

This small, predominantly Muslim town north of Waitabula is the main port for West Sumba. Although there are rumours of a planned Pelni service to Bima starting operation, as yet only cargo ships go to other ports in Nusa Tenggara.

The town has a superb beach and you can find relative solitude if you walk west around the bay. Regular buses and bemos run between Waikelo and Waitabula and a few continue on to Waikabubak.

Places to Stay

Newa Sumba Resort is a mid-range resort 3km east of Waikelo down a rough road, or it is slightly closer to the airport along an equally rough road. Bungalows are very comfortable and attractive, but overpriced at US$45/60 to US$75/90 – expect discounts. The resort is on a fine stretch of beach and has a restaurant, but because of its isolation and lack of a telephone it rarely gets any guests. The only contact number is in Jakarta (☎ 525 1685).

Glossary

ABRI – Angkatan Bersenjata Republik Indonesia, the Indonesian armed forces

adat – traditional laws and regulations; custom

air – water

air panas – hot springs

air terjun – waterfall

anak – child

anjing – dog

arak – colourless distilled palm wine; the local firewater

asfal – asphalt, as in the road surface. Asphalt roads are laid manually from drums of tar and are much rougher than 'hot mix' roads.

ayam – chicken

babi – pork

Bahasa Indonesia – Indonesia's national language

bakar – barbecued, roasted

bakmi – rice-flour noodles

bakso – meatball soup

banjar – local area of a Balinese village in which community activities are organised

banyan – see *waringin*

bapak – father; also a polite form of address to any older man

barat – west

barong tengkok – Lombok name for portable form of gamelan used for wedding processions and circumcision ceremonies

batik – cloth made by coating part of the cloth with wax, then dyeing it and melting the wax out. The waxed part is not coloured and repeated waxing and dyeing builds up a pattern.

becak – trishaw (bicycle-rickshaw)

bemo – popular local transport. Traditionally a small pick-up truck with a bench seat down each side in the back, they have mostly disappeared in favour of small minibuses. Bemo (a contraction of *becak* and *motor)* is a dated term, but still commonly used in Bali and much of Nusa Tenggara.

bensin – petrol

berempah – traditional Sumbawan bare-fisted boxing

bhaga – a miniature, thatched house dedicated to the ancestors of the Ngada people of Flores

bis – bus

bouraq – winged horse-like creature with the head of a woman; also the name of the domestic airline which mostly services the outer islands

brem – Balinese fermented rice wine

bubur ayam – Indonesian porridge of rice or beans with chicken

bukit – hill

buna – the Timorese name for a supplementary weft weaving technique, looking something like embroidery

bupati – government official in charge of a kabupaten (regency)

camat – government official in charge of a kecamatan (district)

candi – shrine, or temple, of originally Javanese design, also known as a *prasada*

candi bentar – split gateway entrance to a Balinese temple

cap cai – fried vegetables, sometimes with meat

cidomo – horse-drawn cart found throughout Lombok and Sumbawa

cumi cumi – squid

danau – lake

desa – village or village administrative area; a desa is larger than a *kampung* and can include a number of *kampung* in a small area

Dewi Sri – Balinese rice goddess

dinas pariwisata – tourist office

DIPARDA – contraction of Departmen Pariwisata Daerah, the regional tourist offices found in most major cities in Nusa Tenggara

durian – fruit that 'smells like hell and tastes like heaven'

fu yung hai – sweet and sour omelette

gado-gado – traditional Indonesian dish of steamed bean sprouts, vegetables and a spicy peanut sauce

Gajah Mada – famous Majapahit prime minister

Galungan – Bali's major feast event, when all the gods come down to earth for the festivities. Also celebrated in West Lombok.

gamelan – traditional Javanese and Balinese orchestra, usually almost solely percussion, with large xylophones and gongs

Ganesh – Shiva's elephant-headed son

gang – alley or footpath

Garuda – mythical man-bird, the vehicle of Vishnu and the modern symbol of Indonesia; also the name of Indonesia's international airline

gereja – church

gili – islet or atoll

gua – cave

gunung – mountain

haji, haja – Muslim who has made the pilgrimage *(hajj)* to Mecca. Many Indonesians save all their lives to make the pilgrimage, and a haji (man) or haja (woman) commands great respect in the village.

harga biasa – usual price

harga touris – tourist price

homestay – small family-run losmen

hot mix – the term given to a road surface where the tar is laid by machine. Unlike 'asfal' roads, a hot mix road is smooth and is best to travel on.

hutan – forest

ibu – mother; also polite form of address to any older woman

ikan – fish

ikat – cloth in which the pattern is produced by dyeing the individual threads before weaving

jalan – street or road

jalan jalan – to walk, to wander around

jalan potong – short cut

jam karet – 'rubber time'

jamu – herbal medicine; most tonics go under this name and are reputed to cure everything from menstrual problems to baldness

jembatan – bridge

jeruk – citrus fruit

jidur – large cylindrical drums played widely throughout Lombok

jukung – see *prahu*

kabupaten – regency or district; the next regional division below a province

kacang – peanuts

kain – cloth

kamar kecil – toilet, usually the traditional hole in the ground with footrests either side

kampung – village, hamlet, or a residential quarter in a town

kantor – office, as in *kantor imigrasi* (immigration office) or *kantor pos* (post office)

kebaya – Chinese long-sleeved blouse with plunging front and embroidered edges

kebun – garden

kecamatan – district; the next regional division below a *kabupaten*

kelapa – coconut

keliling – driving around (buses and bemos) to pick up passengers

kelod – towards the sea

kelurahan – administrative district comprising a group of villages. Headed by a *lurah*, the kelurahan is not as important in lightly populated Nusa Tenggara, where the *desa* is the main village administrative unit.

kepala desa – head of a village

kepiting – crab

Kijang – a cross between a family sedan and an off-road vehicle, these very popular cars are used as taxis or hire vehicles throughout Indonesia. The kijang is also a type of deer.

kina – quinine

kopi – coffee

KORPRI – Korp Pegawai Republik Indonesia; the Indonesian bureaucracy

kretek – Indonesian clove cigarette

kueh – cake

Kuningan – a holy day celebrated throughout Bali and West Lombok 10 days after Galungan

ladang – non-irrigated field, often using slash-and-burn agriculture, for dry-land crops

lesahan – traditional style of dining on straw mats

lontar – type of palm tree, common throughout Nusa Tenggara, particularly in the east. Fermented palm wine and sugar are made from it and the leaves are used for thatch.

lopo – parasol-shaped meeting house of the Dawan people on Timor

losmen – basic accommodation, usually cheaper than hotels and often family-run

lumbung – traditional barn for storing rice or other produce. Used primarily to refer to the distinctive barns of Lombok, the term is also used in other parts of eastern Indonesia.

lumpia – spring rolls

Majapahit – last great Hindu dynasty in Java, pushed out of Java into Bali by the rise of Islamic power

mandi – usual Indonesian form of bath, consisting of a large water tank from which you ladle water to pour over yourself like a shower

marapu – Sumbanese term for all spiritual forces, including gods, spirits and ancestors

martabak – pancake found at foodstalls; can be savoury, but is usually very sweet

Merpati – the main domestic airline; the name means dove

meru – multi-roofed shrines in Balinese temples; they take their name from the Hindu holy mountain, Mahameru

mesjid – mosque

mie goreng – fried noodles, usually with vegetables, and sometimes meat

mikrolet – minibus or bemo

moko – bronze drum from Alor

muezzin – those who call the faithful to the mosque

naga – mythical snake-like creature; serpent

nanas – pineapple

nasi – cooked rice. Nasi goreng is the ubiquitous fried rice. Nasi campur is rice 'with the lot' – vegetables, meat or fish, peanuts, krupuk. Nasi rames is rice with egg, vegetables, fish or meat. Nasi rawon is rice with a spicy hot beef soup.

ngadhu – parasol-like thatched roof; ancestor totem of the Ngada people of Flores

nusa – island, as in Nusa Tenggara (South East Islands)

Nusa Tenggara Barat – West Nusa Tenggara province, comprising Lombok and Sumbawa

Nusa Tenggara Timur – East Nusa Tenggara province, comprising Komodo, Flores, Sumba, West Timor and the small islands in between

ojek – motorbike rider that takes a passenger on the back for a bargainable price

opor ayam – chicken cooked in coconut milk

orang – person

Padang – city and region of Sumatra which has exported its cuisine to all corners of Indonesia. Padang food consists of spicy curries and rice, and is traditionally eaten with the fingers of the right hand. In a Padang restaurant a number of dishes are laid out on the table, and only those that are eaten are paid for.

pak – shortened form of *bapak*

Pancasila – the 'Five Principles' devised by Soekarno to represent the philosophical backbone of the Indonesian state: faith in god, the unbroken unity of humankind, ethnic nationalism, representative government, and social justice

pantai – beach

Pantun – ancient Malay poetical verse in rhyming couplets or quatrains

pasar – market

pasar malam – night market

patola – *ikat* motif of a hexagon framing a type of four pronged star

peci – black Muslim felt cap

pelan pelan – slowly

Pelni – Pelayaran Nasional Indonesia, the national shipping line with major passenger ships operating throughout the archipelago

pencak silat – form of martial arts originally from Sumatra, but now popular throughout Indonesia

penginapan – a simple lodging house; *losmen*

perbekel – government official in charge of a Balinese village *(desa)*

peresehan – popular form of one-to-one physical combat peculiar to Lombok, in which two men fight armed with a small hide shield for protection and a long rattan stave as a weapon

Pertamina – huge state-owned oil company

pinang – betel nut from the areca palm; the oblong fruit is yellowish-red when ripe and contains an acorn-sized seed which is mottled like nutmeg inside. The nut is cut up and chewed with sirih. Fresh pinang is picked green and is stronger.

pisang goreng – fried banana

pompa bensin – petrol station

pondok – hut, bungalow, guesthouse or lodge

propinsi – province

prahu – traditional Indonesian outrigger boat

pulau – island

pura – temple

pura dalem – Balinese temple of the dead

puri – palace

pusaka – sacred heirlooms

raja – king or chief

Ramadan – Muslim month of fasting, when devout Muslims refrain from eating, drinking and smoking during daylight hours

rebab – two stringed bowed lute

rijsttafel – Dutch for 'rice table'; a banquet of Dutch-style Indonesian food

rotan – rattan; a hardy, pliable vine used for handicrafts, furniture and weapons (such as the staves in the spectacular trial of strength ceremony, *peresehan*, in Lombok)

roti – bread; usually white and sweet

rudat – traditional Sasak dance overlaid with Islamic influence

rumah adat – traditional house. A rumah adat can be any house built in traditional style, but often refers to the main meeting house of a village.

rumah makan – restaurant or *warung* (eating house)

rumah sakit – hospital

RW – spicy dog meat, a delicacy in some areas, particularly Timor. The initials come from *rintek wuuk*, Minahasan (Sulawesi) for 'fine hair'.

sambal – chilli sauce

Sanghyang – trance dance in which the dancers impersonate a local village god

Sanghyang Widi – Balinese supreme being, although never actually worshipped as such; represented by an empty throne

santri – orthodox, devout Muslim

saron – xylophone-like gamelan instrument, with bronze bars struck with a wooden mallet

sarong – or sarung; all-purpose cloth, often sewed into a tube, and worn by women, men and children

Sasak – native of Lombok

sate (satay) – classic Indonesian dish; small pieces of charcoal-grilled meat on a skewer served with spicy peanut sauce

sawah – an individual rice field, or the wet-rice method of cultivation

sayur – vegetable

selat – strait

selatan – south

selendang – shawl

selimut – blanket

sirih – betel vine, chewed as a mild narcotic. Although the sirih leaves are chewed in some areas, in Nusa Tenggara it is more common to chew the green, elongated seed of the vine with *pinang* (areca or betel nut) and lime, and the whole mixture is known as *sirih pinang*.

songket – silver or gold-threaded cloth, hand woven using floating weft technique

sop, soto – soup

setengah mati – 'half dead'; an oft-heard phrase in these parts, usually from bus travellers suffering from hours of torturous travel. It can also mean difficult or confusing.

sudra – lowest or common caste to which most Balinese belong

sungai – river

syahbandar – harbour master

tahu – soybean curd (tofu)

taman – ornamental garden, park

telur – egg

tempe – fermented soybean cake

Tim-Tim – the shortened form of Timor Timur (East Timor)

timur – east

transmigrasi – a program to resettle people from Indonesia's heavily populated provinces (particularly Java) to more remote areas. It's been criticised for its dilution of traditional cultures.

tuak – alcoholic drink fermented from palm sap or rice

uang – money
udang – prawn
ume kebube – traditional, conical house of the Dawan people of West Timor
utara – north

VOC – Veerigde Oost-Indische Compagnie (United East India Company), the Dutch trading monopoly formed to contest trade in Indonesia. Through a policy of divide and rule became a quasi-colonial master. It was dissolved in 1799 when the Dutch government assumed direct control.

Wallace Line – the line named after Alfred Wallace that runs between Bali and Lombok and Kalimantan and Sulawesi, marking the end of Asian and the beginning of Australasian flora and fauna

waringin – banyan tree; a large and shady tree with drooping branches which root and can produce new trees. It was under a banyan *(bo)* tree that the Buddha achieved enlightenment, and waringin are found at many temples in Bali.

wartel – private telephone office
warpostel or warpapostel – *wartel* that also handles postage

warung – food stall; a kind of Indonesian equivalent to a combination corner shop and snack bar

Wektu Telu – religion, peculiar to Lombok, which originated in Bayan and combines many tenets of Islam and aspects of other faiths

wisma – guesthouse or lodge

Index

TEXT

396 Index

398 Index

BOXED TEXT

LONELY PLANET PHRASEBOOKS

Building bridges,
Breaking barriers,
Beyond babble-on

Listen for the gems

Speak your own words

Ask your own questions

Master of your own image

- handy pocket-sized books
- easy to understand Pronunciation chapter
- clear and comprehensive Grammar chapter
- romanisation alongside script to allow ease of pronunciation
- script throughout so users can point to phrases
- extensive vocabulary sections, words and phrases for every situation
- full of cultural information and tips for the traveller

'...vital for a real DIY spirit and attitude in language learning' – Backpacker

'the phrasebooks have good cultural backgrounders and offer solid advice for challenging situations in remote locations' – San Francisco Examiner

'...they are unbeatable for their coverage of the world's more obscure languages' – The Geographical Magazine

---

Arabic (Egyptian)
Arabic (Moroccan)
Australia
  Australian English, Aboriginal and
  Torres Strait languages
Baltic States
  Estonian, Latvian, Lithuanian
Bengali
Brazilian
Burmese
Cantonese
Central Asia
Central Europe
  Czech, French, German, Hungarian,
  Italian and Slovak
Eastern Europe
  Bulgarian, Czech, Hungarian, Polish,
  Romanian and Slovak
Ethiopian (Amharic)
Fijian
French
German
Greek

Hindi/Urdu
Indonesian
Italian
Japanese
Korean
Lao
Latin American Spanish
Malay
Mandarin
Mediterranean Europe
  Albanian, Croatian, Greek,
  Italian, Macedonian, Maltese,
  Serbian and Slovene
Mongolian
Nepali
Papua New Guinea
Pilipino (Tagalog)
Quechua
Russian
Scandinavian Europe
  Danish, Finnish, Icelandic, Norwegian
  and Swedish

South-East Asia
  Burmese, Indonesian, Khmer, Lao,
  Malay, Tagalog (Pilipino), Thai and
  Vietnamese
Spanish (Castilian)
  Basque, Catalan and Galician
Sri Lanka
Swahili
Thai
Thai Hill Tribes
Tibetan
Turkish
Ukrainian
USA
  US English, Vernacular,
  Native American languages and
  Hawaiian
Vietnamese
Western Europe
  Basque, Catalan, Dutch, French,
  German, Irish, Italian, Portuguese,
  Scottish Gaelic, Spanish (Castilian)
  and Welsh

LONELY PLANET JOURNEYS

JOURNEYS is a unique collection of travel writing – published by the company that understands travel better than anyone else. It is a series for anyone who has ever experienced – or dreamed of – the magical moment when they encountered a strange culture or saw a place for the first time. They are tales to read while you're planning a trip, while you're on the road or while you're in an armchair, in front of a fire.

JOURNEYS books catch the spirit of a place, illuminate a culture, recount a crazy adventure, or introduce a fascinating way of life. They always entertain, and always enrich the experience of travel.

ISLANDS IN THE CLOUDS
Travels in the Highlands of New Guinea
Isabella Tree

Isabella Tree's remarkable journey takes us to the heart of the remote and beautiful Highlands of Papua New Guinea and Irian Jaya – one of the most extraordinary and dangerous regions on earth. Funny and tragic by turns, *Islands in the Clouds* is her moving story of the Highland people and the changes transforming their world.

Isabella Tree, who lives in England, has worked as a freelance journalist on a variety of newspapers and magazines, including a stint as senior travel correspondent for the *Evening Standard*. A fellow of the Royal Geographical Society, she has also written a biography of the Victorian ornithologist John Gould.

'One of the most accomplished travel writers to appear on the horizon for many years . . . the dialogue is brilliant' – Eric Newby

SEAN & DAVID'S LONG DRIVE
Sean Condon

Sean Condon is young, urban and a connoisseur of hair wax. He can't drive, and he doesn't really travel well. So when Sean and his friend David set out to explore Australia in a 1966 Ford Falcon, the result is a decidedly offbeat look at life on the road. Over 14,000 death-defying kilometres, our heroes check out the re-runs on tv, get fabulously drunk, listen to Neil Young cassettes and wonder why they ever left home.

Sean Condon lives in Melbourne. He played drums in several mediocre bands until he found his way into advertising and an above-average band called Boilersuit. *Sean & David's Long Drive* is his first book.

'Funny, pithy, kitsch and surreal . . . This book will do for Australia what Chernobyl did for Kiev, but hey you'll laugh as the stereotypes go boom'
– Time Out

LONELY PLANET TRAVEL ATLASES

Lonely Planet has long been famous for the number and quality of its guidebook maps. Now we've gone one step further and produced a handy companion series: Lonely Planet travel atlases – maps of a country produced in book form.

Unlike other maps, which look good but lead travellers astray, our travel atlases have been researched on the road by Lonely Planet's experienced team of writers. All details are carefully checked to ensure the atlas corresponds with the equivalent Lonely Planet guidebook.

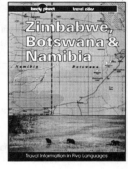

The handy atlas format means no holes, wrinkles, torn sections or constant folding and unfolding. These atlases can survive long periods on the road, unlike cumbersome fold-out maps. The comprehensive index ensures easy reference.

- full-colour throughout
- maps researched and checked by Lonely Planet authors
- place names correspond with Lonely Planet guidebooks
  – no confusing spelling differences
- legend and travelling information in English, French, German, Japanese and Spanish
- size: 230 x 160 mm

Available now:

Chile & Easter Island • Egypt • India & Bangladesh • Israel & the Palestinian Territories •Jordan, Syria & Lebanon • Kenya • Laos • Portugal • South Africa, Lesotho & Swaziland • Thailand • Turkey • Vietnam • Zimbabwe, Botswana & Namibia

---

LONELY PLANET TV SERIES & VIDEOS

Lonely Planet travel guides have been brought to life on television screens around the world. Like our guides, the programmes are based on the joy of independent travel, and look honestly at some of the most exciting, picturesque and frustrating places in the world. Each show is presented by one of three travellers from Australia, England or the USA and combines an innovative mixture of video, Super-8 film, atmospheric soundscapes and original music.

Videos of each episode – containing additional footage not shown on television – are available from good book and video shops, but the availability of individual videos varies with regional screening schedules.

Video destinations include: Alaska • American Rockies • Australia – The South-East • Baja California & the Copper Canyon • Brazil • Central Asia • Chile & Easter Island • Corsica, Sicily & Sardinia – The Mediterranean Islands • East Africa (Tanzania & Zanzibar) • Ecuador & the Galapagos Islands • Greenland & Iceland • Indonesia • Israel & the Sinai Desert • Jamaica • Japan • La Ruta Maya • Morocco • New York • North India • Pacific Islands (Fiji, Solomon Islands & Vanuatu) • South India • South West China • Turkey • Vietnam • West Africa • Zimbabwe, Botswana & Namibia

The Lonely Planet TV series is produced by:
Pilot Productions
The Old Studio
18 Middle Row
London W10 5AT UK

For video availability and ordering information contact your nearest Lonely Planet office.

Music from the TV series is available on CD & cassette.

PLANET TALK

Lonely Planet's FREE quarterly newsletter

We love hearing from you and think you'd like to hear from us.

When...is the right time to see reindeer in Finland?
Where...can you hear the best palm-wine music in Ghana?
How...do you get from Asunción to Areguá by steam train?
What...is the best way to see India?

For the answer to these and many other questions read PLANET TALK.

Every issue is packed with up-to-date travel news and advice including:

- a letter from Lonely Planet co-founders Tony and Maureen Wheeler
- go behind the scenes on the road with a Lonely Planet author
- feature article on an important and topical travel issue
- a selection of recent letters from travellers
- details on forthcoming Lonely Planet promotions
- complete list of Lonely Planet products

To join our mailing list contact any Lonely Planet office.

Also available: Lonely Planet T-shirts. 100% heavyweight cotton.

LONELY PLANET ONLINE

Get the latest travel information before you leave or while you're on the road

Whether you've just begun planning your next trip, or you're chasing down specific info on currency regulations or visa requirements, check out Lonely Planet Online for up-to-the minute travel information.

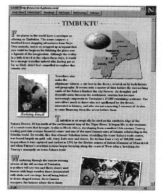

As well as travel profiles of your favourite destinations (including maps and photos), you'll find current reports from our researchers and other travellers, updates on health and visas, travel advisories, and discussion of the ecological and political issues you need to be aware of as you travel.

There's also an online travellers' forum where you can share your experience of life on the road, meet travel companions and ask other travellers for their recommendations and advice. We also have plenty of links to other online sites useful to independent travellers.

And of course we have a complete and up-to-date list of all Lonely Planet travel products including guides, phrasebooks, atlases, Journeys and videos and a simple online ordering facility if you can't find the book you want elsewhere.

www.lonelyplanet.com
or
AOL keyword: lp

LONELY PLANET PRODUCTS

Lonely Planet is known worldwide for publishing practical, reliable and no-nonsense travel information in our guides and on our web site. The Lonely Planet list covers just about every accessible part of the world. Currently there are nine series: *travel guides, shoestring guides, walking guides, city guides, phrasebooks, audio packs, travel atlases, Journeys – a unique collection of travel writing and Pisces Books - diving and snorkeling guides.*

EUROPE

Amsterdam • Austria • Baltic States phrasebook • Berlin • Britain • Canary Islands• Central Europe on a shoestring • Central Europe phrasebook • Czech & Slovak Republics • Denmark • Dublin • Eastern Europe on a shoestring • Eastern Europe phrasebook • Estonia, Latvia & Lithuania • Finland • France • French phrasebook • Germany • German phrasebook • Greece • Greek phrasebook • Hungary • Iceland, Greenland & the Faroe Islands • Ireland • Italian phrasebook • Italy • Lisbon • London • Mediterranean Europe on a shoestring • Mediterranean Europe phrasebook • Paris • Poland • Portugal • Portugal travel atlas • Prague • Romania & Moldova • Russia, Ukraine & Belarus • Russian phrasebook • Scandinavian & Baltic Europe on a shoestring • Scandinavian Europe phrasebook • Slovenia • Spain • Spanish phrasebook • St Petersburg • Switzerland • Trekking in Spain • Ukrainian phrasebook • Vienna • Walking in Britain • Walking in Italy • Walking in Switzerland • Western Europe on a shoestring • Western Europe phrasebook

Travel Literature: The Olive Grove: Travels in Greece

NORTH AMERICA

Alaska • Backpacking in Alaska • Baja California • California & Nevada • Canada • Chicago • Deep South• Florida • Hawaii • Honolulu • Los Angeles • Mexico • Mexico City • Miami • New England • New Orleans • New York City • New York, New Jersey & Pennsylvania • Pacific Northwest USA • Rocky Mountain States • San Francisco • Southwest USA • USA phrasebook • Washington, DC & the Capital Region

Travel Literature: Drive thru America

CENTRAL AMERICA & THE CARIBBEAN

•Bahamas and Turks & Caicos •Bermuda •Central America on a shoestring • Costa Rica • Cuba •Eastern Caribbean •Guatemala, Belize & Yucatán: La Ruta Maya • Jamaica

SOUTH AMERICA

Argentina, Uruguay & Paraguay • Bolivia • Brazil • Brazilian phrasebook • Buenos Aires • Chile & Easter Island • Chile & Easter Island travel atlas • Colombia Ecuador & the Galápagos Islands • Latin American Spanish phrasebook • Peru • Quechua phrasebook • Rio de Janeiro • South America on a shoestring • Trekking in the Patagonian Andes • Venezuela

Travel Literature: Full Circle: A South American Journey

ISLANDS OF THE INDIAN OCEAN

Madagascar & Comoros • Maldives• Mauritius, Réunion & Seychelles

AFRICA

Africa - the South • Africa on a shoestring • Arabic (Moroccan) phrasebook • Cairo • Cape Town • Central Africa • East Africa • Egypt • Egypt travel atlas• Ethiopian (Amharic) phrasebook • Kenya • Kenya travel atlas • Malawi, Mozambique & Zambia • Morocco • North Africa • South Africa, Lesotho & Swaziland • South Africa, Lesotho & Swaziland travel atlas • Swahili phrasebook • Tunisia • Trekking in East Africa • West Africa • Zimbabwe, Botswana & Namibia • Zimbabwe, Botswana & Namibia travel atlas

Travel Literature: The Rainbird: A Central African Journey • Songs to an African Sunset: A Zimbabwean Story

MAIL ORDER

Lonely Planet products are distributed worldwide. They are also available by mail order from Lonely Planet, so if you have difficulty finding a title please write to us. North American and South American residents should write to 150 Linden St, Oakland CA 94607, USA; European and African residents should write to 10a Spring Place, London NW5 3BH; and residents of other countries to PO Box 617, Hawthorn, Victoria 3122, Australia.

NORTH-EAST ASIA

Beijing • Cantonese phrasebook • China • Hong Kong • Hong Kong, Macau & Guangzhou • Japan • Japanese phrasebook • Japanese audio pack • Korea • Korean phrasebook • Mandarin phrasebook • Mongolia • Mongolian phrasebook • North-East Asia on a shoestring • Seoul • Taiwan • Tibet • Tibet phrasebook • Tokyo

Travel Literature: Lost Japan

MIDDLE EAST & CENTRAL ASIA

Arab Gulf States • Arabic (Egyptian) phrasebook • Central Asia • Central Asia phrasebook • Iran • Israel & the Palestinian Territories • Israel & the Palestinian Territories travel atlas • Istanbul • Jerusalem • Jordan & Syria • Jordan, Syria & Lebanon travel atlas • Lebanon • Middle East • Turkey • Turkish phrasebook • Turkey travel atlas • Yemen

Travel Literature: The Gates of Damascus • Kingdom of the Film Stars: Journey into Jordan

ALSO AVAILABLE:

Brief Encounters • Travel with Children • Traveller's Tales

INDIAN SUBCONTINENT

Bangladesh • Bengali phrasebook • Delhi • Goa • Hindi/Urdu phrasebook • India • India & Bangladesh travel atlas • Indian Himalaya • Karakoram Highway • Nepal • Nepali phrasebook • Pakistan • Rajasthan • Sri Lanka • Sri Lanka phrasebook • Trekking in the Indian Himalaya • Trekking in the Karakoram & Hindukush • Trekking in the Nepal Himalaya

Travel Literature: In Rajasthan • Shopping for Buddhas

SOUTH-EAST ASIA

Bali & Lombok • Bangkok • Burmese phrasebook • Cambodia • Ho Chi Minh City • Indonesia • Indonesian phrasebook • Indonesian audio pack • Jakarta • Java • Laos • Lao phrasebook • Laos travel atlas • Malay phrasebook • Malaysia, Singapore & Brunei • Myanmar (Burma) • Philippines • Pilipino phrasebook • Singapore • South-East Asia on a shoestring • South-East Asia phrasebook • Thailand • Thailand's Islands & Beaches • Thailand travel atlas • Thai phrasebook • Thai audio pack • Thai Hill Tribes phrasebook • Vietnam • Vietnamese phrasebook • Vietnam travel atlas

AUSTRALIA & THE PACIFIC

Australia • Australian phrasebook • Bushwalking in Australia • Bushwalking in Papua New Guinea • Fiji • Fijian phrasebook • Islands of Australia's Great Barrier Reef • Melbourne • Micronesia • New Caledonia • New South Wales • New Zealand • Northern Territory • Outback Australia • Papua New Guinea • Papua New Guinea phrasebook • Queensland • Rarotonga & the Cook Islands • Samoa • Solomon Islands • South Australia • Sydney • Tahiti & French Polynesia • Tasmania • Tonga • Tramping in New Zealand • Vanuatu • Victoria • Western Australia

Travel Literature: Islands in the Clouds • Sean & David's Long Drive

ANTARCTICA

Antarctica

THE LONELY PLANET STORY

Lonely Planet published its first book in 1973 in response to the numerous 'How did you do it?' questions Maureen and Tony Wheeler were asked after driving, busing, hitching, sailing and railing their way from England to Australia.

Written at a kitchen table and hand collated, trimmed and stapled, *Across Asia on the Cheap* became an instant local bestseller, inspiring thoughts of another book.

Eighteen months in South-East Asia resulted in their second guide, *South-East Asia on a shoestring*, which they put together in a backstreet Chinese hotel in Singapore in 1975. The 'yellow bible', as it quickly became known to backpackers around the world, soon became *the* guide to the region. It has sold well over half a million copies and is now in its 9th edition, still retaining its familiar yellow cover.

Today there are over 350 titles, including travel guides, walking guides, language kits & phrasebooks, travel atlases and travel literature. The company is the largest independent travel publisher in the world. Although Lonely Planet initially specialised in guides to Asia, today there are few corners of the globe that have not been covered.

The emphasis continues to be on travel for independent travellers. Tony and Maureen still travel for several months of each year and play an active part in the writing, updating and quality control of Lonely Planet's guides.

They have been joined by over 80 authors and 200 staff at our offices in Melbourne (Australia), Oakland (USA), London (UK) and Paris (France). Travellers themselves also make a valuable contribution to the guides through the feedback we receive in thousands of letters each year and on our web site.

The people at Lonely Planet strongly believe that travellers can make a positive contribution to the countries they visit, both through their appreciation of the countries' culture, wildlife and natural features, and through the money they spend. In addition, the company makes a direct contribution to the countries and regions it covers. Since 1986 a percentage of the income from each book has been donated to ventures such as famine relief in Africa; aid projects in India; agricultural projects in Central America; Greenpeace's efforts to halt French nuclear testing in the Pacific; and Amnesty International.

'I hope we send people out with the right attitude about travel. You realise when you travel that there are so many different perspectives about the world, so we hope these books will make people more interested in what they see. Guidebooks can't really guide people. All you can do is point them in the right direction.'

– Tony Wheeler

LONELY PLANET PUBLICATIONS

Australia
PO Box 617, Hawthorn 3122, Victoria
tel: (03) 9819 1877 fax: (03) 9819 6459
e-mail: talk2us@lonelyplanet.com.au

USA
150 Linden St
Oakland, CA 94607
tel: (510) 893 8555 TOLL FREE: 800 275-8555
fax: (510) 893 8572
e-mail: info@lonelyplanet.com

UK
10a Spring Place,
London NW5 3BH
tel: (0171) 428 4800 fax: (0171) 428 4828
e-mail: go@lonelyplanet.co.uk

France:
71 bis rue du Cardinal Lemoine, 75005 Paris
tel: 01 44 32 06 20 fax: 01 46 34 72 55
e-mail: bip@lonelyplanet.fr

World Wide Web: http://www.lonelyplanet.com
or *AOL keyword: lp*